W9-DHM-352

American Literary Scholarship

1977

American Literary Scholarship

An Annual / 1977

Edited by James Woodress

Essays by Wendell Glick, J. Donald Crowley, Donald B. Stauffer, Hershel Parker, Willis J. Buckingham, Louis J. Budd, Robert L. Gale, George Bornstein, Panthea Reid Broughton, Jackson R. Bryer, Robert D. Arner, Thomas Wortham, David Stouck, Margaret Anne O'Connor, James H. Justus, Richard Crowder, James E. Breslin, Winifred Frazer, Charles Nilon, Michael J. Hoffman, F. Lyra, Maurice Couturier, Hans Galinsky, Rolando Anzilotti, Keiko Beppu, Rolf Lundén

Duke University Press, Durham, North Carolina, 1979

 Library of Congress Catalogue Card number 65–19450. I.S.B.N. 0–8223–0423–6. Printed in the United States of America by Heritage Printers, Inc.

Foreword

This is the 15th volume of *American Literary Scholarship* to appear since the series began in 1965. As the foreword announced last year, the editorial chores now have been divided between J. Albert Robbins of Indiana University and the undersigned. *ALS 1978* will be edited by Professor Robbins. Two years ago when I edited the volume covering the scholarship for 1975 it looked as though this work would grow into a convenient size for a doorstop as well as a reference work. But by urging our contributors to be more selective, succinct, and to ignore trivial or redundant scholarship, Professor Robbins and I have managed to keep the volumes for 1976 and 1977 to approximately the length of our *ALS 1975*. We will continue our policy of omitting (usually) dissertation literature and inferior scholarship, and of noticing significant new books at usually briefer lengths than the book sections of the scholarly journals.

There are two innovations in this year's volume. We have begun a "Bibliographical Addendum" that follows Chapter 21 in an effort to keep our readers abreast of the continuing stream of useful reference works. This new section reports on general reference works only and does not attempt to be exhaustive. Reference works that are of special interest to individual chapters will continue to be dealt with in their respective places. The other innovation this year is the addition of an "East Europe" section to the coverage of foreign scholarship. We still lack coverage of Spain and Latin America, but for some reason American literature attracts less attention there than in other parts of the world.

There are several new contributors this year and one change from joint to single authorship. Robert Gale succeeds William Stafford, our veteran Jamesian contributor; George Bornstein has succeeded Stuart McDougal on Eliot and Pound; on 19th-century literature Thomas Wortham replaces Warren French, who has contributed to eleven of the fifteen volumes in this series. James Breslin has taken over the contemporary poetry chapter that Linda Wagner did for half a decade, and Willis Buckingham has written the entire Whitman-Dickinson chapter that he previously shared with Marvin Fisher. Finally, the contributor of the new chapter on Eastern Europe is Professor F. Lyra of the University of Warsaw.

Next year the contributors to *ALS 1978* will be mostly the same scholars as this year with a few exceptions: the chapter on black writers will be written by Darwin T. Turner of the University of Iowa; fiction from the 1930s to 1950s will be taken over by Jack Salzman of Hofstra University (Hempstead, N.Y.); colonial literature will be covered by William Scheick of the University of Texas at Austin. As usual, we urge scholars to send books and offprints directly to the authors of the appropriate chapters.

As this series rounds out its first decade and a half, it becomes clear that American literary scholarship is alive and flourishing everywhere. This is not surprising among domestic scholars, but it seems that the decline of the dollar on the international money markets has not been matched by any decline of interest in American literature abroad. As the yen and the mark increase in value, the attention paid in Japan and Germany to American literature seems to increase. Japanese scholarship, which a few years ago was largely derivative and aimed mostly at introducing Japanese readers to the critical points of view of American scholars, now is moving into original research, and there is so much of it that our Japanese correspondent, Keiko Beppu, can only report the most significant work. The same situation exists in Germany in regard to quantity of scholarship, although there the quality always has been high. Hans Galinsky, who has been covering German scholarship since the foreign section was started with *ALS 1973*, notes that in Germany now there are approximately 40 American studies departments or divisions, each staffed with an average of 18 persons. Thus with 720 full-time German scholars hard at work producing articles and monographs on American literature it is no wonder that there has been a knowledge explosion. It seems to me that in the future we will have to require our graduate students to learn German. The Japanese and German interest in American literature, however, has been apparent ever since our coverage began, although the impact is just now beginning to be felt; but the quantity of scholarship in Eastern Europe comes as a shock. Professor Lyra, who is trying to cover Russia, Poland, Czechslovakia, Hungary, and Rumania, finds it impossible to deal with anything smaller than a book-length work, and he reports that an entire chapter could easily be written on Russian scholarship alone.

James Woodress
January, 1979

University of California, Davis

Table of Contents

Key to Abbreviations xi

Part I

1. **Emerson, Thoreau, and Transcendentalism** 3 *Wendell Glick*
2. **Hawthorne** 17 *J. Donald Crowley*
3. **Poe** 35 *Donald B. Stauffer*
4. **Melville** 49 *Hershel Parker*
5. **Whitman and Dickinson** 65 *Willis J. Buckingham*
6. **Mark Twain** 87 *Louis J. Budd*
7. **Henry James** 99 *Robert L. Gale*
8. **Pound and Eliot** 119 *George Bornstein*
9. **Faulkner** 135 *Panthea Reid Broughton*
10. **Fitzgerald and Hemingway** 163 *Jackson R. Bryer*

Part II

11. **Literature to 1800** 189 *Robert D. Arner*
12. **19th-Century Literature** 207 *Thomas Wortham*
13. **Fiction: 1900 to the 1930s** 245 *David Stouck*
14. **Fiction: The 1930s to the 1950s** 273 *Margaret Anne O'Connor*

15. Fiction: The 1950s to the Present	303	*James H. Justus*
16. Poetry: 1900 to the 1930s	343	*Richard Crowder*
17. Poetry: The 1930s to the Present	365	*James E. Breslin*
18. Drama	389	*Winifred Frazer*
19. Black Literature	405	*Charles Nilon*
20. Themes, Topics, Criticism	433	*Michael J. Hoffman*
21. Foreign Scholarship	463	*F. Lyra, Maurice Couturier, Hans Galinsky, Rolando Anzilotti, Keiko Beppu, Rolf Lundén*
Bibliographical Addendum	511	*James Woodress*
Author Index	517	
Subject Index	536	

Key to Abbreviations

Festschrifts, Essay Collections, and Books Discussed in More than One Chapter

The Adventurous Muse / William C. Spengeman, *The Adventurous Muse: The Poetics of American Fiction, 1789–1900* (New Haven: Yale Univ. Press)

The American Idea / *Everett Carter, The American Idea: The Literary Response to American Optimism* (Chapel Hill: Univ. of N.C. Press)

The American Short Story / *The American Short Story*, ed. Calvin Skaggs (New York: Dell)

The Art of Life / *Mutln Konuk Blasing, The Art of Life: Studies in American Autobiography* (Austin: Univ. of Tex Press)

The Classic American Novel and the Movies / *The Classic American Novel and the Movies*, ed. Gerald Peary and Roger Shatzkin (New York: Ungar)

Conversations with Writers I, II / *Conversations with Writers I, II*, ed. Matthew Bruccoli et al. (Detroit: Gale Research Co.)

Educated Lives / Thomas Cooley, *Educated Lives: The Rise of Modern Autobiography in America* (Columbus: Ohio State Univ. Press)

Gay American History / Jonathan Katz, *Gay American History: Lesbians and Gay Men in the U.S.A.: A Documentary* (New York: Crowell, 1976)

Gerber Festschrift / *American Humor: Essays Presented to John C. Gerber*, ed. O. M. Brack, Jr. (Scottsdale, Ariz.: Arete Publications)

Harriet Monroe and the Poetry Renaissance / Ellen Williams, *Harriet Monroe and the Poetry Renaissance* (Urbana: Univ. of. Ill. Press)

Hillway Festschrift / *Essays in Honor of Professor Tyrus Hillway*, ed. Erwin A. Stürz (Salzburg: Salzburg Universtität)

In Time and Place / Floyd C. Watkins, *In Time and Place: Some Origins of American Fiction* (Athens: Univ. of Ga. Press)

Literature and the Occult / *Literature and the Occult: Essays in Comparative Literature*, ed. Luanne Frank (Arlington: Univ. of Tex. at Arlington)

Makers of the Twentieth-Century Novel / *Makers of the Twentieth-Century Novel*, ed. Harry R. Garvin (Lewisburg, Pa.: Bucknell Univ. Press)

The Middle Way / Michael T. Gilmore, *The Middle Way: Puritanism and Ideology in American Romantic Fiction* (New Brunswick: Rutgers Univ. Press)

The Poetry of American Women / Emily Stipes Watts, *The Poetry of American Women from 1632 to 1945* (Austin: Univ. of Tex. Press)

Prospects / *Prospects: An Annual of American Cultural Studies*, Vol. 3, ed. Jack Salzman (New York: Burt Franklin)

Romantic and Modern / *Romantic and Modern: Revaluations of Literary Traditions*, ed. George

Bornstein (Pittsburgh: Univ. of Pittsburgh Press)
Studies in Interpretation II / *Studies in Interpretation, Vol. II*, ed. E. M. Doyle and Virginia Hastings (Amsterdam: Rodopi)
Westering Experience / *The Westering Experience in American Literature: Bicentennial Essays*, ed. Merrill Lewis and L. L. Lee (Bellingham, Wash.: Bureau for Faculty Research)

Periodicals, Annuals, Series

AAAm / *Arbeiten aus Anglistik und Amerikanistik*
ABR / *American Benedictine Review*
AI / *American Imago*
AL / *American Literature*
ALR / *American Literary Realism*
ALS / *American Literary Scholarship*
AmerS / *American Studies*
AmS / *Amerikastudien*
AN / *Acta Neophilologica* (Ljubljana)
Annales (Univ. of Bordeaux)
AN&Q / *American Notes and Queries*
AppalJ / *Appalachian Journal*
APR / *American Poetry Review*
AQ / *American Quarterly*
AR / *Antioch Review*
ArielE / *Ariel: A Review of International English Literature*
ArmD / *Armchair Detective* (White Bear Lake, Minn.)
ArQ / *Arizona Quarterly*
ASch / *American Scholar*
ASI / *Archivo Storico Italiano*
AtM / *Atlantic Monthly*
ATQ / *American Transcendental Quarterly*
AWR / *Anglo-Welsh Review* (Pembroke Dock, Wales)
BALF / *Black American Literature Forum*
BB / *Bulletin of Bibliography*
BBr / *Books at Brown*
BlackI / *Black Images: A Critical Quarterly on Black Arts and Culture*
BlackW / *Black World*
Boundary2 / *Boundary 2: A Journal of Postmodern Literature*
BRMMLA / *Bulletin of the Rocky Mountain Modern Language Association*
BSUF / *Ball State University Forum*
BuR / *Bucknell Review*
CanL / *Canadian Literature*
CE / *College English*
CEA / *C.E.A. Critic*
CEAA / Center for Editions of American Authors
CentR / *The Centennial Review*
Centrum / *Working Papers of the Minnesota Center for Advanced Studies in Language, Style, and Literary Theory*
ChiR / *Chicago Review*
CimR / *Cimarron Review*
CL / *Comparative Literature*
CLAJ / *College Language Association Journal*
ClioW / *Clio: An Interdisciplinary Journal of Literature, History, and the Philosophy of History* (Univ. of Wisc.)
CLQ / *Colby Library Quarterly*
CLS / *Comparative Literature Studies*
CollL / *College Literature* (Westchester State College)
ColQ / *Colorado Quarterly*
ConL / *Contemporary Literature*
CP / *Concerning Poetry*
CQ / *The Cambridge Quarterly*
CR / *Critical Review* (Australia)
CRCL / *Canadian Review of Comparative Literature*
CRevAS / *Canadian Review of American Studies*
Crit / *Critique: Studies in Modern Fiction*
CritI / *Critical Inquiry*
Criticism / *Criticism* (Wayne State)
CritQ / *Critical Quarterly*
CS / *Concord Saunterer*
DAI / *Dissertation Abstracts International*
Delta (Montpellier)

Descant / *The Texas Christian Univ. Library Journal*
DHLR / *D. H. Lawrence Review*
DN / *Dreiser Newsletter*
DQR / *Dutch Quarterly Review of American Letters*
DR / *Dalhousie Review*
DVLG / *Deutsche Vierteljahrsschrift für Literaturwissenschaft und Geistesgeschichte*
EA / *Etudes Anglaises*
EAL / *Early American Literature*
E&S / *Essays and Studies by Members of the English Association*
EDB / *Emily Dickinson Bulletin*
EIC / *Essays in Criticism*
EigoS / *Eigo Seinen* [*The Rising Generation*] (Tokyo)
EJ / *English Journal*
ELH / *English Literary History*
ELN / *English Language Notes*
ELS / English Literary Studies (Univ. of Victoria)
ELWIU / *Essays in Literature* (Western Ill. Univ.)
EM / *English Miscellany*, ed. B. S. Lee (London: Oxford Univ. Press)
EngR / *English Record*
ES / *English Studies*
ESC / *English Studies in Canada* (Toronto)
ESColl / *English Studies Collections*
ESQ / *Emerson Society Quarterly*
ETJ / *Educational Theatre Journal*
Expl / *Explicator*
Extracts / *Extracts* (Newsletter of the Melville Society)
FAR / *French-American Review*
FemS / *Feminist Studies*
FHA / *Fitzgerald-Hemingway Annual*
FOB / *Flannery O'Connor Bulletin*
ForumH / *Forum* (Houston)
FrF / *French Forum*
GaR / *Georgia Review*
GHQ / *Georgia Historical Quarterly*
Glyph / Ed. Samuel Weber and Henry Sussman (Baltimore: Johns Hopkins Univ. Press)
GrLR / *Great Lakes Review: A Journal of Midwest Culture*
GRM / *Germanische Romanische Monatschrift*, Neue Folge
GSlav / *Germano-Slavica: A Canadian Journal of Germanic and Slavic Comparative Studies*
GyS / *Gypsy Scholar*
HAB / *Humanities Association Bulletin* (Canada)
Hispam / *Hispamerica: Revista de Literatura*
Hispano / *Hispanófilia* (Univ. of N.C.)
HJP / *Higginson Journal of Poetry*
HK / *Heritage of Kansas* (Emporia)
HLB / *Harvard Library Bulletin*
HNH / *Historical New Hampshire*
HSE / *Hungarian Studies in English*
HSL / *Hartford Studies in Literature*
HudR / *Hudson Review*
IEY / *Iowa English Bulletin: Yearbook*
IFR / *International Fiction Review*
IJAS / *Indian Journal of American Studies*
IJES / *Indian Journal of English Studies*
IllQ / *Illinois Quarterly*
IndLing / *Indian Linguistics: Journal of the Linguistics Society of India*
Inquiry / *Inquiry: An Interdisciplinary Journal of Philosophy and the Social Sciences* (Trondheim, Norway)
IowaR / *Iowa Review*
Ironwood / (Tucson, Ariz.)
ItalAm / *Italian Americana*
JAAR / *Journal of the American Academy of Religion*
JAF / *Journal of American Folklore*
JAmS / *Journal of American Studies*
JBlS / *Journal of Black Studies*
JBS / *John Berryman Studies*
JEGP / *Journal of English & Germanic Philology*
JEthS / *Journal of Ethnic Studies* Western Wash. State Univ.
JGE / *Journal of General Education*
JHI / *Journal of the History of Ideas*
JLN / *Jack London Newsletter*
JMiH / *Journal of Mississippi History*
JML / *Journal of Modern Literature*
JNT / *Journal of Narrative Technique*
JPC / *Journal of Popular Culture*
JPH / *Journal of Presbyterian History*
KAL / *Kyushu American Literature*

Kalki / *Studies in James Branch Cabell*
KanQ / *Kansas Quarterly*
L&P / *Literature and Psychology*
Lang&S / *Language and Style*
LC / *Library Chronicle* (Univ. of Penn.)
LFQ / *Literature/Film Quarterly*
LGJ / *Lost Generation Journal*
LH / *Literature and History*
LitR / *Literary Review* (Fairleigh Dickinson Univ.)
LNL / *Linguistics in Literature*
LWU / *Literatur in Wissenschraft und Unterricht* (Kiel)
MAQR / *Michigan Alumnus Quarterly Review*
MarkhamR / *Markham Review*
MD / *Modern Drama*
Meanjin / *Meanjin Quarterly* (Univ. of Melbourne)
MFS / *Modern Fiction Studies*
MHSB / *Missouri Historical Society Bulletin*
MichA / *Michigan Academician* (replaces PMASAL)
MidAmerica (East Lansing, Mich.)
MidSF / *Mid-South Folklore*
MinnH / *Minnesota History*
MinnR / *Minnesota Review*
MissQ / *Mississippi Quarterly*
ML / *Modern Languages* (London)
MLN / *Modern Language Notes*
MLQ / *Modern Language Quarterly*
MLS / *Modern Language Studies*
MMN / *Marianne Moore Newsletter*
Mosaic / *Mosaic: A Journal for the Comparative Study of Literature and Ideas*
MPS / *Modern Poetry Studies*
MQ / *Midwest Quarterly*
MQR / *Michigan Quarterly Review*
MR / *Massachusetts Review*
MSE / *Massachusetts Studies in English*
MTJ / *Mark Twain Journal*
NALF / *Negro American Literature Forum*
N&Q / *Notes and Queries*
NCF / *Nineteenth-Century Fiction*
NConL / *Notes on Contemporary Literature*
NDQ / *North Dakota Quarterly*
NEG / *New England Galaxy*
NEQ / .*New England Quarterly*
NewRep / *New Republic*
NH / *Natural History*
NHJ / *Nathaniel Hawthorne Journal*
NMAL / *Notes on Modern American Literature*
NMW / *Notes on Mississippi Writers*
Novel / *A Forum on Fiction*
NsM / *Neusprachliche Milleilungen aus Wissenschaft und Praxis*
NUQ / *New Universities Quarterly* (Blackwell: London)
NYFQ / *New York Folklore Quarterly*
NYH / *New York History*
NYTM / *New York Times Magazine*
OhR / *Ohio Review*
ON / *Old Northwest* (Oxford, Ohio)
OQ / *Ohioana Quarterly*
PAAS / *Papers of the American Antiquarian Society*
Paideuma / *Paideuma: A Journal Devoted to Ezra Pound Scholarship*
PanA / *Pan African Journal*
ParisR / *Paris Review*
Parnassus / *Poetry in Review*
PBSA / *Papers of the Bibliographical Society of America*
PCL / *Perspectives in Contemporary Literature*
PLL / *Papers on Language and Literature*
Ploughshares (Cambridge, Mass.)
PMLA / *Publications of the Modern Language Association*
PoeS / *Poe Studies*
PR / *Partisan Review*
Prologue (Milwaukee Repertory Theatre Company)
PrS / *Prairie Schooner*
QJS / *Quarterly Journal of Speech*
QQ / *Queen's Quarterly*
RALS / *Resources for American Literary Study*
RANAM / *Recherches Anglaises et Américaines* (Strasbourg)
REH / *Revista de Estudios Hispánicos*
ReL / *Religion in Life*
Rendezvous / *Rendezvous: A Journal of Arts and Letters* (Idaho State)
Renditions (Hong Kong)

RFEA / *Revue Francaise d'Etudes Americaines* (Paris)
RFI / *Regionalism and the Female Imagination* (formerly the *Kate Chopin Newletter*)
RJN / *Robinson Jeffers Newsletter*
RLV / *Revue des Langues Vivantes*
RMR / *Rocky Mountain Review of Language and Literature*
RMS / *Renaissance and Modern Studies*
RS / *Research Studies* (Wash. State Univ.)
SAB / *South Atlantic Bulletin*
SAF / *Studies in American Fiction*
SALit / *Studies in American Literature* (Kyoto)
SalSEL / *Salzburg Studies in English Literature*
SAQ / *South Atlantic Quarterly*
SAR / *Studies in the American Renaissance*
SatR / *Saturday Review*
SB / *Studies in Bibliography*
SBL / *Studies in Black Literature*
ScanR / *Scandinavian Review* (formerly *The American-Scandinavian Review*)
SCN / *Seventeenth-Century News*
SCR / *South Carolina Review*
SDR / *South Dakota Review*
SEEJ / *Slavic and Eastern European Journal*
SELit / *Studies in English Literature* (Japan)
SFS / *Science-Fiction Studies*
SHR / *Southern Humanities Review*
SIH / *Studies in the Humanities*
SJS / *San Jose Studies*
SLJ / *Southern Literary Journal*
SLN / *Sinclair Lewis Newsletter*
SN / *Studio Neophilologica*
SNNTS / *Studies in the Novel* (North Tex. State Univ.)
SoQ / *The Southern Quarterly*
SoR / *Southern Review*
SoSt / *Southern Studies: An Interdisciplinary Journal of the South* (formerly *LaS*)
SoT / *Southern Theatre*
Sprachkunst: Beiträge zur Literaturwissenschaft
SR / *Sewanee Review*
SSF / *Studies in Short Fiction*
SSML Misc. / *Society for the Study of Midwestern Literature* (*Midwestern Miscellany*)
SSMLN / *Society for the Study of Midwestern Literature Newsletter*
StQ / *Steinbeck Quarterly*
SwAL / *Southwest American Literature*
SWR / *Southwest Review*
TCL / *Twentieth-Century Literature*
TDR : *Drama Review* (formerly *Tulane Drama Review*)
TJQ / *Thoreau Journal Quarterly*
TLOP / *The Language of Poems* (Univ. of S. Car.)
TLS / *Times Literary Supplement*
Topic / *A Journal of the Liberal Arts* (Washington and Jefferson College)
TQ / *Texas Quarterly*
TR / *Transatlantic Review*
TREMA (Univ. of Paris III)
TSB / *Thoreau Society Bulletin*
TSER / *T. S. Eliot Review*
TSL / *Tennessee Studies in Literature*
TSLL / *Texas Studies in Literature and Language*
TUSAS / Twayne United States Authors Series
UDQ / *Univ. of Denver Quarterly*
UWR / *University of Windsor Review*
VC / *Virginia Cavalcade*
VQR / *Virginia Quarterly Review*
VWQ / *Virginia Woolf Quarterly*
WAL / *Western American Literature*
W&L / *Women and Literature*
WCWN / *William Carlos Williams Newsletter* (Middletown, Pa.)
WF / *Western Folklore*
WHR / *Western Humanities Review*
WLT / *World Literature Today* (formerly *Books Abroad*)
WS / *Women's Studies*
WStJ / *Wallace Stevens Journal*
WVUPP / *West Virginia University Philological Papers*
WWR / *Walt Whitman Review*
WWS / Western Writers Series
YFS / *Yale French Studies*
YR / *Yale Review*
YULG / *Yale University Library Gazette*

Part I

1. Emerson, Thoreau, and Transcendentalism

Wendell Glick

This is the year of Thoreau. I can remember no other like it for scholarly creativity, either qualitative or quantitative. Issues that have been picked at and pushed around desultorily for years reached book-length synthesis. Emerson fared less well; I have examined no long studies, and with a half-dozen or so significant exceptions, I have found the periodical literature to be soft and impressionistic, building on nothing that has been done before. As for the minor Transcendentalists, only Fuller and Elizabeth Peabody received even passing notice. To save space, I have omitted any mention of dissertations and reprints.

i. General Studies, Textual Studies, Bibliography

Little on the Transcendentalist movement per se appeared in 1977. An exception is "Unitarian Historiography and the American Renaissance" (*ESQ* 23:130–37) by David Robinson, whose review-critique of four recent books that deal with the theological and aesthetic interests of the period makes it clear that Emerson's facile dubbing of Unitarianism as a religion of "pale negations" has perhaps diverted us from a proper concern for the subtleties of the relation between Transcendentalism and Unitarian theology. What this essay argues to me is the need for less parochialism in American literary and religious historians of the period and a more active dialog. Joel Myerson's "A History of the Transcendental Club" (*ESQ* 23:27–35) is also a key article: based on primary materials, it relieves us of the need to rely on the untrustworthy testimony of Frank Sanborn, a hanger-

Author's Note: I owe gratitude to my colleague, Roger Lips, for aiding me in critiquing the year's Emerson scholarship. His good judgment was most helpful.

on of the great, and dramatizes with good effect the early tensions between Boston Unitarians and the Transcendentalists. Myerson is very modest, it seems to me, in drawing his conclusions; his new material has broader implications than he claims for it. Lawrence Buell's "Identification of Contributors to the *Monthly Anthology and Boston Review*: 1804–1811" (*ESQ* 23:99–105) also is basic in that it settles, apparently definitively, a number of moot questions as to authorship of articles in that important journal. Eugene Green's "Reading Local History: Shattuck's *History*, Emerson's *Discourse*, and Thoreau's *Walden* (*NEQ* 50:303–14)—which I include here because it fits nowhere else—takes an interesting tack by viewing Emerson and Thoreau (along with Shattuck) in the role of Concord historians: "All [Green suggests] shared a common vision of a larger whole to which Concord and its past belonged. Shattuck regarded his account of Concord as one segment of a general history; Emerson saw Concord as a manifestation of a universal mind. For Thoreau, however, Concord history was but one act in a natural and human drama."

Bits and pieces of primary source material surfaced in print during the year. Thomas Blanding of the Princeton Edition published additional new Thoreau items unearthed in New England collections, one of the most important being a late Thoreau letter of 31 March 1861 to a Maine cousin, George Thatcher (*CS* 12:21–22). Francis Dedmond discovered a typescript of what apparently was a letter from Emerson to Christopher Cranch in the Cranch papers ("'Croaking at book-sellers': An Unpublished Emerson Letter" [*AL* 49:415–17]). Madeline Stern alleges in "Mrs. Alcott of Concord to Mrs. Adams of Dubuque" (*NEQ* 50:331–40) that these new, chatty letters from Bronson Alcott's wife "provide an arresting analysis of the character and temperament of the Concord seer." Richard Fleck published in *TJQ* (9:5–23) what he calls "The Text of the Hitherto Unpublished Fragmentary Essay on Primitive Cultures," less an essay than a succession of fragments, from the Indian notebooks at the Morgan Library. *The Letters and Journals of Waldo Emerson Forbes*, edited by Amelia Forbes Thomas (Philadelphia: Dorrance), lacks any literary value and should never have been published if its raison d'être was to contribute to what we know of Emerson. A like caveat applies to "New Letters from the Grimm-Emerson Correspondence" by Luther S. Luedtke and Winfried Schleiner (*HLB* 25:399–465). What justifies devoting 66 pages to letters from the Grimms to Emerson (Emerson's twelve letters to them having been previously published by Holls and Rusk) I fail to see. Moreover, the authors of this interminable paper extract the last ounce of significance from the Emerson-Grimm "friendship," though Roger Lips and I have been able to discover no significance in German belles lettres for the Grimms. If we have reached the point where everyone who knew Emerson or wrote to Emerson has to have his/her letters published, we should gird our loins.

In the area of textual studies and bibliography an important event is the addition of volume 13 to *The Journals and Miscellaneous Notebooks of Ralph Waldo Emerson* (Cambridge, Mass.: The Belknap Press). Editors were Ralph H. Orth and the late Alfred R. Ferguson. The editorial group for this edition has now lost by death its Chief Editor, William H. Gilman, and its Senior Editor, Ferguson; and Orth has assumed the duties of Chief Editor. Volume 13 includes the journals from 1852 to 1855, a period when Emerson published little, lectured frequently, and ruminated *English Traits*, to be published in 1856. Though the period is not the most interesting of Emerson's life, the journal for these years shows him trying to relate to the events of the pre-Civil War period, demonstrates the breadth of his continuing interests, and proves that he can still turn the pithy phrase (e.g. p. 444): "A man is not to aim at innocence, any more than he is to aim at hair; but he is to keep it." Emerson omits any mention of the publication of *Walden*. Volume 13 bears the CEAA seal. Also important is Joel Myerson's *Margaret Fuller: An Annotated Secondary Bibliography* (New York: Burt Franklin), which will no doubt become a standard tool. The work contains 1,245 items about Fuller published from 1834 to 1975 and taken as a whole they reflect Fuller's reputation for well over a century.

Two articles deal with the textual editing of the Thoreau Edition. Elizabeth Witherell of the Princeton editorial group comments cryptically on problems encountered in editing the poetry ("An Editor's Nightmare: 'It is no Dream of Mine' in the Princeton Edition of Thoreau's Poetry" [*CS* 12:5–9]). Though there were no new volumes in the Princeton Edition of Thoreau's works in 1977, one review of previously published volumes appeared, John Seelye's "Frightfully Thoreau" (*AQ* 29:222–29). Not much about the CEAA editions pleases Seelye. *The Illustrated Walden* and *Reform Papers* Seelye sees as typifying "the religiosity which characterizes the academic study of American literature," and he likens the CEAA editors to the "patristic commentators [who] once filled libraries with laborious explications of murky passages in the Revealed Word of God." Having thus established his own personal threshold of objectivity, he moves on to censure the Thoreau Edition for its alleged "fear of leaving out anything Thoreau wrote" [apparently unaware that the Houghton Library holds reams of Thoreau manuscript never before published and deemed unpublishable by modern textual criteria]; to object to the length of the apparatus and notes in *Reform Papers* [though he uses them, as they are intended to be used, to call attention to errors and to question editorial judgments]; to regret in *Reform Papers* the act of "errant pedantry" by which I substituted Thoreau's title of "Resistance to Civil Government" for what was almost surely (we now know) the title supplied by Ellery Channing. He objects to adding to the text of "Herald of Freedom" several paragraphs of new and revised material that Thoreau prepared after the first publication, arguing that the revised material "was once intended but was then rejected by the author for inclusion in *A Week*." He does not offer his proof for this alleged intention of Thoreau's, and I'd certainly like to have it. I have looked for it for six years, with the help of other textual scholars.

Under this heading, finally, I call attention to the year's publications at Hartford by Transcendental Books. Kenneth Cameron's *Transcendentalism and American Renaissance Bibliography* lists, with a brief synopsis of each, the 66 collections of primary materials and criticism that have been issued from Hartford through the years. *ATQ* 36: *Parts One and Two and a Supplement* continues the tradition, publishing a broad assortment of information on Emerson, Thoreau, the minor transcendentalists, and the Concord area. Cameron's "Current Bibliography on Ralph Waldo Emerson" (*ATQ* 36 [Part 2]: 86–90) is a useful supplement to other bibliographies.

ii. Emerson

***a.* Life and Thought.** My nominee for the most illuminating essay on Emerson during the year is Leonard Neufeldt's "The Science of Power: Emerson's Views on Science and Technology in America" (*JHI* 38:329–44). The issue is complex, and Neufeldt's treatment of it therefore is subtle. His analysis of the grounds for Emerson's optimism in a period of rapidly expanding technology is anchored firmly upon primary evidence. Whitman's view of science, I discover, is not as far removed from Emerson's as I had always assumed. Patently for Emerson, "In its use of nature, technology explains the mind's natural and necessary use of the world." Yet Emerson was not blind to the dangers of technology, as Neufeldt shows. "We are coaxed, flattered and duped from morn to eve [Emerson observed], from birth to death, and where is the old eye that ever saw through the deception?" The pattern Neufeldt's essay reveals leaves me both with admiration for Emerson's grasp of this problem and for Neufeldt's precision in revealing it. Scarcely less important is Lewis Leary's "The Maneuverings of a Transcendental Mind: Emerson's *Essays* of 1841" in *Prospects*, pp. 499–520, an engrossing challenge to the cliché that Emerson was an aphoristic sentence maker whose works lacked symmetry and form. Leary argues that *Essays* of 1841 is a self-contained volume with "a form of its own" and not a miscellany of essays as I (for one) had always assumed. Emerson's method Leary sees as one of "undulant accumulation"—the method evolving organically from the argument—in "an unfolding, a massive accumulative enlarging and progressive exegesis." Thus for Leary the volume is "an intricately cohesive work, with a beginning, a middle, and an end that circles back to the beginning," the form being fully consonant with Emerson's belief that "Nature is a mutable cloud which is always and ever the same." Emerson emerges from this essay as "an artist, expert in his craft," rather than "a mystic, placing random thoughts in attractive disarray." Students of Emerson should not miss this antidote to the commonly held perception of Emerson's formlessness. "Emerson's Aesthetics of Fiction" is an intriguing topic, and J. A. Magat (*ESQ* 23:139–55) raises a broader issue in suggesting that "Emerson's aesthetics was concerned more with a psychological than a religious or social morality." But Magat's conclusions are suspect. The impression left by the paper that Emerson had a developed theory of the novel is belied by the desultory nature of Emerson's comments through the years. Moreover, Magat is slipshod in his handling quoted matter from Emerson and repeatedly inaccurate in his citing his sources. This essay should be read warily. John Stephen Martin's "Finding a Usable Past: Emerson's Response to the Predicament of Early American Letters" (from *Hillway Festschrift*, pp. 159–90) also promises more than it delivers. Much of this monograph has nothing to do with Emerson; and much of the generalizing about the American search for cultural identity is unsupported by evidence and moves unconscionably fast. The paper is long, and pretends to a synthesis that Martin never achieves. What is one supposed to make, for instance, of such an unsupported observation as this: "Neither tied to the past nor sure of the future, Americans suffered from a funk of the spirit, an unnerving anxiety" (p. 173)? Walter Scott, according to Martin, happened to be the panacea for the "funk." Martin hasn't been reading Mark Twain lately. Herwig Friedl in "Des Dichters Dilemma: Ralph Waldo Emerson and der mexikanisch-amerikanische Krieg" (*AmS* 22:261–68) raises once more the tantalizing question of Emerson's reluctance to participate actively in the political and social life of his day, and sees Emerson's "dilemma" to be one of "responsible action as a citizen [as opposed to] adherence to the visionary ideal of ultimate historical truth." The essay is a somewhat more metaphysical examination of the same problem treated by Merton Sealts, Jr., in "The American Scholar and Public Issues: The Case of Emerson" (*Ariel* 7:109–21). Barbara Packer's thesis in "Uriel's Cloud: Emerson's Rhetoric" (*GaR* 31:322–42) is that Emerson "deliberately made his own texts hard to understand," and she vows to understand him anyway by leading us through a swirl of her own rhetoric that (for me) makes Emerson seem lucid. She has her fun with the question of Emerson's seriousness in the "eyeball" passage (citing Cranch, Kenner, and Jonathan Bishop), but suggests with a straight face (I think) that "perhaps it is always risky to introduce an Eyeball into sublime discourse." I find little new on "literary ethics" in Richard Lee Francis's "Granite Reflections: Emerson's 'Literary Ethics' " (*HNH* 32:116–28), which is for the most part an explication of "The American Scholar."

Less than usual was written during the year on Emerson's influence—a perennial magnet to Emerson's scholars. One very useful article by David Robinson clarifies the effect of Emerson upon the art of Charles Ives ("Children of the Fire: Charles Ives on Emerson and Art" [*AL* 48:564–76]). Robinson explains how Ives accepted without change Emerson's equation of the aesthetic with the moral, along with Emerson's advice for the use of the commonplace as a source for the symbols of art. Mario L. D'Avanzo in "Emerson and Shakespeare in Stevens' 'Bantams in Pine-woods' " (*AL* 49: 103–7) makes a good case for Stevens having appropriated Emerson's symbol of the pine-woods as an "earthly setting in which the poet finds universal truth." Martha M. Park in "How Far from Emerson's Man of One Idea to Anderson's Grotesques?" (*CLAJ* 20: 364–79) sees enough similarities in concept and phrasing in *Winesburg, Ohio* to conclude that Anderson *may* have known Emerson "quite well." Proof of Anderson's having read *Essays, First Series* would improve her case considerably. A firmer case for influence is Patricia Deery's "Emerson, Haydon and the Elgin Marbles" (*N&Q* 24:353–54), the influence being Haydon's *Life* (owned by Emerson) upon *English Traits.*

iii. Thoreau

***a.* Life and Thought.** For books on Thoreau, this year was *annus mirabilis.* The year produced the most penetrating study of the Thoreau imagination since Sherman Paul (Garber); the most comprehensive analysis of Thoreau's interest in the Indian (Sayre); by all odds the most complete and well-written survey of Thoreau's political reputation in America (Meyer); and the first solidly developed Thoreau psychobiography to be printed (Lebeaux). In addition George Hendrick issued two volumes that contain impressions of Thoreau by persons who knew him.

For the book of the year on Thoreau, and perhaps of the decade, I nominate Frederick Garber's *Thoreau's Redemptive Imagination* (New York: New York University Press). This may be the most original, the most discriminating delineation of the relationship of Thoreau's sensibility to external nature that we shall have in a long time, and perhaps that we shall need. Building on Anderson, Broderick, Marx, and Paul, and holding Thoreau firmly against the backdrop of English and American Romanticism, Garber, with the restraint and modulation of a critic and scholar in total mastery of his material, traces the record of Thoreau's attempts to use his imagination to assimilate nature, explains the resistance he encountered on Ktaadn, and clarifies his final recognition of the inadequacies of both nature and consciousness to his purposes. Reading this record of the odyssey of Thoreau's imagination recalls the like odyssey of Wallace Stevens. Garber's book is criticism on the level where genius is made understandable, and by a scholar in comparative literature rather than one of the critics we associate with Thoreau.

Thoreau and the American Indians by Robert F. Sayre (Princeton: Princeton Univ. Press) may be read as a subset of Garber's more subtle study; Garber is able to put Thoreau's concern for the Indian into a context that lends it a significance that the Sayre study with its more limited aim cannot achieve. Sayre speculates intelligently on Thoreau's possible intention of writing a book on Indians; he labors somewhat in employing Thoreau's stereotype of "savagism" to interpret *A Week* and *Walden*; but he provides useful information on Thoreau's twelve "Indian Books" in the Morgan Library. It is now much clearer the extent to which Thoreau accepted current stereotypes. But the reader of Sayre will find additional illumination by reading Garber's thoughtful analysis of "wildness" as Thoreau's perceived center of the "self." With these two fine books Thoreau's attempts to understand the Indian has now (and finally) had the treatment it deserves.

Richard Lebeaux's *Young Man Thoreau* (Amherst: Univ. of Mass. Press [paper, Harper Colophon Books]) will probably be the most widely read of the year's books on Thoreau. For Lebeaux's study taps a deep concern of Thoreau scholars and readers that has remained largely submerged—his sexuality, his relation to father, mother, and brother John—and his ambivalences when judged by the norms of the Concord of his day. This is a work of psychobiography, which builds upon the earlier unpublished but widely influential study of Raymond Gozzi, with the difference that Gozzi's lens is Freudian while Lebeaux's is that of Erik Erickson. Much of the early Journal Lebeaux reads as veiled autobiography—as a record of Thoreau's prolonged adolescence as he struggled through an "identity crisis" protracted by a tangle of guilt induced by competition with a weak father for the affection of a strong mother and with his brother John for the affection of Ellen Sewall. Lebeaux is most convincing when he is least encumbered by his procrustean Ericksonian apparatus, as, for example, when he reconstructs the relationship between Henry and John. To me, it seems risky to so completely subordinate ideology to alleged psychological stress. And how reliable are conclusions drawn from skeins of hypotheses? I don't know what to do, for example (p. 202), with this: "It will be remembered that Thoreau had once imagined that the crows sullenly disapproved of his pursuit of Ellen; in effect, the crows had been the imagined accusation of John incarnate. Thus it is indicative that Henry should allude to the presence of so many blackbirds in *Cape Cod*." But interest in Thoreau's alleged hangups will probably grow.

Michael Meyer's *Several More Lives to Live: Thoreau's Political Reputation in America* (Westport, Conn.: Greenwood) is a survey of commentary on Thoreau's political thought and writings, by decades, from the twenties into the early seventies. Its scope is impressive, and also the exuberance of its style. For a survey of largely academic scholarship to escape almost completely lapses into the stale rhetoric of the profession is a signal achievement. I sense some conflicts among Meyer's stated intentions for his book and feel some uneasiness with his very pat decade-by-decade summaries. But the book fills a critical lacuna, and I am not surprised that it won the second annual Ralph Henry Gabriel Prize in American Studies. It is intelligently reviewed (along with Lebeaux's *Young Man Thoreau*) in *NEQ* (50:684–88) by Lawrence Buell.

Two additional books add to the anecdotal material that has accumulated around Thoreau, supplied by friends and neighbors. *Remembrances of Concord and the Thoreaus: Letters of Horace Hosmer to Dr. S. A. Jones* (Urbana: Univ. of Ill. Press), edited by George Hendrick, is a compilation of letters sent to Dr. Jones, the Ann Arbor physician, between 25 February 1891 and 30 December 1893. They are of interest for their reflections on the school conducted by John and Henry Thoreau, attended by Hosmer in 1840, and for their droll comments upon Concord life in the last decade of the century. But they are the reflections of a man looking back some fifty years. More intriguing than the letters themselves is the serendipitous circumstance of Hendrick's discovery of the cache in Urbana, and his tantalizing observation in his preface that the trunk contained also "letters by Thoreau, Dr. Oliver Wendell Holmes, Harriet Beecher Stowe, Henry Wadsworth Longfellow, and others," along with a Holmes and an Emerson MS. Hendrick's *Henry Salt: Humanitarian Reformer and Man of Letters* (Urbana: Univ. of Ill. Press) is of interest for its story of the circumstances of Salt's becoming interested in Thoreau and his writing of the first noteworthy biography in 1890 (pp. 99–112). It was through Salt that Gandhi became aware of *Walden* and "Resistance to Civil Government."

Some of the periodical articles on Thoreau can profitably be read in tandem with the longer book studies. Philip F. Gura's "Thoreau's

Maine Woods Indians: More Representative Men" (*AL* 49:366–84), which focuses on Joe Polis, covers much of the same material examined by Sayre. Gura's article shows that Emerson's attempts to identify the "complete" representative genius paralleled the attempt of Thoreau to understand the integrity of the Indian's relationship with nature. The article shared the Norman Foerster prize for the year for the best article published in *American Literature*. George Hendrick's "Henry S. Salt, the Late Victorian Socialists, and Thoreau" (*NEQ* 50:409–22), a spin-off of his biography of Salt, corrects the view of Harding and others that rather than to the Fabians and the early Labour party members, the credit for popularizing Thoreau in England should go principally to Salt, Robert Blatchford, and Edward Carpenter. Building his case with care, Robert Glenn Deamer in "Thoreau: Walking Toward England" (*The Westering Experience*, pp. 85–92) notes that for Thoreau the American West was not fact, but a metaphor. Deamer goes on to argue that Emerson's English traits (and Santayana's) add up to "a portrait of Thoreau himself." "If his quest for wildness, for a truly westering experience, took him to the woods," Deamer concludes, "it also took him, unknowingly, to England." Two articles appeared on Thoreau's aesthetics. Ulrick Horstmann, in "Die Transzendenz des Konkreten: Anmerkungen zur Kunsttheorie Henry David Thoreaus" (*AmS* 22:247–60) argues that Thoreau's aesthetics moved away from Emersonian doctrine into what Horstmann terms an "anti-transcendentalist 'concretism,' which foreshadowed a positivistic methodology," and "involuntarily ended in a secularized mysticism." That is a very long distance. An article by Sister Regina Hansen, O.S.B., in *ABR* (28:188–200), "The Conditions For Poetry: A Study of Thoreau's Challenge to Transcendence," fails to make clear the nature of Thoreau's "challenge." For the most part, it adumbrates the obvious.

M. Claire Kolbenschlag, in "Thoreau and Crusoe: The Construction of an American Myth and Style" (*AmS* 22:229–46), views Thoreau as a central figure in the American search for identity. Her contention is that if "the Crusoe-Franklin myth" represents the dominant mode of the American consciousness, "a downward conversion of transcendental aspiration into materialistic pragmatism—then, Thoreau's *Walden* parodies, contradicts and disputes this consciousness by inverting the religious-commercial idiom." I don't feel easy with the premise of this essay. I feel some strain, moreover, in the parallels drawn between Crusoe on his island and Thoreau at Walden. That Thoreau inverts the "religious-commercial idiom" is clear enough, but Kolbenschlag extracts a significance from Thoreau's use of his tropes that is probably extreme. "Economic Metaphor Redefined: The Transcendental Capitalist at Walden" by Judith P. Saunders (*ATQ* 36 [Part 1]:4–7) argues more modestly that Thoreau's use of commercial idioms was a device "to undermine our commitment to commerce." Herbert F. Smith, in "Thoreau Among the Classical Economists" (*ESQ* 23:114–22), views "Economy," the "most important chapter of *Walden*," as Thoreau's attempt "to enter the materialist camp of Smith, Malthus, and Ricardo, to destroy it from within." To say this about *Walden* is to see Thoreau's anti-materialism too narrowly. Charles Anderson has suggested that Thoreau might have had Mill and Marx in mind. Frederick Busch in "Thoreau and Melville as Cellmates" (*MFS* 23:239–42) strains to discover parallels between Melville and Bartleby, and between Bartleby and Thoreau, coming up with such insights as "Bartleby at the jail wall and Thoreau in his cell make a prison of the world." Mary Elkins Moller has diligently combed Thoreau's works for passages on death (" 'You Must First Have Lived': Thoreau and the Problem of Death" [*ESQ* 23:226–39]) but fails to bring into a focus what she has found. In "The Search for Walden" Richard Ruland (*ESQ* 23:188–200) develops a critique-review around my *The Recognition of Henry David Thoreau: Selected Criticism Since 1848* (Ann Arbor: The Univ. of Mich. Press, 1969), and Stanley Cavell's *The Senses of Walden* (New York: Viking, 1972, 1974). He corrects—I believe justly—my strong disparagement of Lowell's judgment of Thoreau. But a greater service is to express concern for our neglect of Cavell, a concern which I share. Whether, as Ruland believes, Cavell's is "the most profound and provocative reading we have of Thoreau's masterpiece" may be debatable, but it offers insights that Thoreau scholars have neglected. The interest in Thoreau and John Brown is perennial: Wesley T. Mott harrows the old soil once more in "John Brown in Concord" (*NEG* 19:25–31) but unearths nothing new. "Nature as Spiritual Frontier: Melville, Thoreau, Whitman" (*IEY* 26:14–17) by Stephen Tanner develops in four pages the symbolic significance of "Melville's sea, Thoreau's river, and Whitman's night." Brevity is not always a virtue.

Testimonials to the influence of Thoreau upon particular lives continue to be written in the long tradition going back to Daniel

Ricketson and Dr. Samuel Arthur Jones. Loren Eiseley has been through the years one of the most lucid of this group, a group that includes E. B. White, N. C. Wyeth, and Charles Ives. "Thoreau's Unfinished Business" (*NH* 87:6–19) will be Eiseley's last tribute. He died in July 1977.

***b.* Criticism of Individual Works.** One significant article appeared on *A Week*; the remainder were concerned with *Walden*. Paul David Johnson in "Thoreau's Redemptive *Week*" (*AL* 49:22–23) takes up once again the problem of *A Week*'s alleged discursiveness. Building upon William Drake and Sherman Paul, who saw the journey on the Concord and Merrimack as an analogue of inner exploration, Johnson develops the thesis that "*A Week*, like *Walden*, is carefully structured around the quest for self-liberation." This interpretation is consistent with Lebeaux's view in *Young Man Thoreau* that much of Thoreau's early writing related to his search for identity; and it is a not unexpected reading given the predilection this year to view Thoreau as a lifelong seeker for personal "redemption."

Searching for the thematic center of *Walden* is still a seductive enterprise, and this year there were new entries. Walter Benn Michaels takes the interesting position in "*Walden*'s False Bottoms" (*Glyph*, 1:132–49) that the readings of Anderson, Cavell, and Buell show that critics have given up finding a "solid bottom" in *Walden*, i.e., a thematic center: "The unity which was once claimed for the object itself is now claimed for the reader's experience of it." Thoreau built in "the principle of uncertainty": "*Walden* insists upon the necessity for such a search [for a solid bottom] at the same time that it dramatizes the theoretical impossibility of succeeding in it." The search, I predict, will nonetheless continue. Earl Fendelman in "Toward Walden Pond: The American Voice in Autobiography" (*CRevAS* 8:11–25) reads *Walden* as the culmination of the "Puritan genre of spiritual autobiography," a linear development from Shepard and Increase Mather through Franklin and P. T. Barnum. Biographical ontogeny, Fendelman argues, recapitulates phylogeny: "*Walden* repeats within itself the steps toward autobiographical form from Mather to Emerson." Fendelman claims too much for his angle of vision: "his [Thoreau's] personal narrative derives its importance entirely from the way it portrays a soul triumphing over its own doubts." John O. Rees in "Et in Arcadia Thoreau" calls attention to Thoreau's use in *Walden* of the "once-familiar elegiac phrase *Et in Arcadia ego*" (*ESQ* 23:240–43). "Elements of Anatomy in *Walden*" by Paul McCarthy (*BSUF* 18, ii:67–78) attempts to place *Walden* in the "Genre of Anatomy" as defined by Northrop Frye and Philip Stevick. Wayne Warncke in "*Walden* Reenvisoned" (*SHR* 2:331–36) comes up with the imaginative notion that *Walden* is "an invitation to dream," perhaps because he feels that "much of *Walden* is tedious reading." Mario L. D'Avanzo's "Thoreau's Brick Pillow" (*NEQ* 50:664–66) is a worthwhile note that relates Thoreau's use of a chimney brick for a pillow with Jacob's vision of the heavenly ladder dreamed while Jacob slept with a rock for a pillow. After lamenting that "the trouble with Transcendentalism is transcendence," Larry R. Bowden in "Transcendence in 'Walden'" (*ReL* 46:166–71) demonstrates that his trouble is his failure to read the minutes of past meetings. The problem is widespread; a good deal being "discovered" is already in print. We would accomplish more if we would read each other.

Many short articles are published each year in *The Thoreau Society Bulletin* (*TSB*), *The Concord Saunterer* (*CS*) and *The Thoreau Journal Quarterly* (*TJQ*). I have called attention to only the most significant. Scholars should remember that "Additions to the Thoreau Bibliography" published quarterly in *TSB* by Walter Harding is the most complete of Thoreau bibliographies. *CS*, ably edited by Anne McGrath of the Thoreau Lyceum, publishes in almost every issue new material supplied chiefly by the Thoreau Edition editors at Princeton. The emphasis of *TJQ* is more popular than scholarly.

iv. Minor Transcendentalists

Two essays of scope appeared during the year, both on Elizabeth Peabody. Bruce A. Ronda's "Elizabeth Palmer Peabody's Views of the Child" (*ESQ* 23:106–13) moves too fast, perhaps—one has the feeling Ronda is digesting a book length study—yet his case that Peabody as an educational theorist was able paradoxically to view the child both from the viewpoint of Locke and the Scottish Common Sense philosophers is plausible. "While her synthesis was not logically coherent," Ronda argues, "it gave her a flexible and balanced view of the child which avoided both extremes of Lockean sensationalism and Alcottian child-worship and maintained that the child was both body to be trained and spirit possessing divine insight." Philip F. Gura in

"Elizabeth Palmer Peabody and the Philosophy of Language" (*ESQ* 23:154–63) shows that Peabody's interest in Herder, Hazard and Kraitsir stemmed from her attempt to develop a theory of language compatible with Idealistic philosophy; and that she used language theory in a practical way in Alcott's Temple School. Gura demonstrates why language was a necessary concern of the Transcendentalists; his study thus has an importance beyond Peabody.

University of Minnesota, Duluth

2. Hawthorne

J. Donald Crowley

Three books devoted wholly or in part to Hawthorne appeared in 1977. One (reviewed in Chapter 20) is Michael T. Gilmore's *The Middle Way*, which makes what many readers will find an egregiously anachronistic claim that "*The House of the Seven Gables* is nothing less than Hawthorne's defense of 'the great Christian doctrine of original sin.'" The two others want obviously to enjoy a much more original relation to the universe of Hawthorne criticism. Kenneth Dauber "would like to think" that *Rediscovering Hawthorne* (Princeton: Princeton Univ. Press) "is the poetics that Hawthorne might have written"; and Edgar A. Dryden, in *Nathaniel Hawthorne: The Poetics of Enchantment* (Ithaca: Cornell Univ. Press), can at this late date still ask, as if for the first time, "Who is Nathaniel Hawthorne?" Gilmore's methods are those of the historicist, and his view of Hawthorne's fiction has it grounded in history and unabashedly referential. Dauber's critical foundations are mostly structuralist, topped off here and there with a Freudian gable. For him, the possibilities of historical criticism have long since been exhausted, and the New Criticism's insistence on the discrete integrity of the literary text was from the start wrong-headed. Hawthorne's works are to be understood now as "structures that contain no vision" and Hawthorne himself as "properly no psyche, but a disposition towards works of literature." Here tenor—to be supplied by the reader—displaces vehicle, which is present only as "a necessary condition of literature as a tool of action." Dryden's approach is phenomenological, "an inside narrative" attempting to resolve the biographical problem by putting together the "real and fictive selves" of Hawthorne into a "thematic self" which is "the organizing principle or conceptual center of his work." Dryden draws on Georges Poulet to explain his presuppositions: "Criticism is the mimetic duplication of a conceptual action. . . . To experience anew in one's own mind the *cogito* of a writer or a philosopher means to rediscover the manner of thinking and feeling, means to see how this thinking and feeling originate and assume form and what obstacles they encounter. It means also to rediscover the purpose of a life which takes shape out of the experience of the individual consciousness."

Both books give the appearance of being radical departures in Hawthorne criticism, their sophisticated methods aimed at revealing the enigmatic patterns, not in individual fictions, but behind them and between them, between Hawthorne and them and Hawthorne and his readers. They are often perceptive and stimulating on the "intentional" and "affective" dimensions of literary meaning. And they have the power to offend. Dauber's study is a deconstruction of much of the "codified" Hawthorne of earlier criticism; both are ahistorical and too deliberately uncontextual. But when one takes in Dauber's elaboration of the fiction as "never an end in itself but a vehicle to effect intimacy" and Dryden's exploration of the life and art as mutually shaped by the themes of "enchantment and disenchantment—enchantment as the condition generated by the lure of others and disenchantment as the discovery that the lure is deceptive and dangerous, that the experience of the other is at best fugitive and tenuous, at worst alienating and threatening," one can easily arrive at the sense that Dauber and Dryden do nothing, finally, so much as that they give new names to and provide new frameworks for the metaphorical content of Gilmore's naively stated claim. By some critical imp of the perverse, all the novelty of method dominates their novel "texts" to yield up, at least among other things, old "original" ideas. Read sympathetically, Dauber and Dryden at their best bring the reader full circle, back round again to a fresh realization of the Hawthorne Melville saw. Their critical intentions aside, the studies are rich glosses on Melville's perception that Hawthorne, in his weighing of the world, saw "the uneven balance" and threw in "something, somehow like Original Sin to strike" it. No other metaphor, it seems to me, comprehends so fully and succinctly the complexities, tacit and otherwise, of the Hawthorne whom Dauber describes as forever inventing structures which would at once invite intimacy and resist exposure or of the Hawthorne whom Dryden sees oscillating ambivalently between desire for enchantment with, and fear of bewitchment by, "Distance," "Other," "Love," "Reading," and "Origins."

There are other problems as well. With Dauber the first difficulty lies in the discrepancy between theoretical desire and critical act: his theory locates "real" meanings in the interstices between printed texts, but his practice insists that Hawthorne's "purposive" archetypes are trackable only within single texts. Dryden, with his thematic arrangement of chapters and his citation of multiple texts to "unravel the form of their interconnection," is truer to Dauber's theory than Dauber is. If both studies are welcome correctives to the pretensions of earlier criticism to scientific objectivity, they tend to pay the price of overcorrection. Both risk an exaggerated arbitrariness. Dauber would have us think that we can touch any part and make the whole vibrate; but his selection of tales and sketches and his omission of fragments, notebooks, and juvenile collections make his principles suspicious at best. Dryden's hybridization of references to letters, tales, romances, and notebooks, on the other hand, arouses the Jamesian question of the possible other case: what would become of the tissue, one wonders, if this, that, or another quote were inserted?

Dryden's risks seem more worth the taking, for his critical sensibility remains focused on Hawthorne. Dauber, however, does something else, suggested perhaps by his protestations that his study is not unduly influenced by "recent developments in Continental thinking" but is in "the American tradition of empiricism and practicality." He goes on to say: "I share with structuralism a loss of belief in centers; hence my willingness to construct a system around a figure not often seen as central. I share a general sense that we are cut off from origins, that to follow the objects of our investigation back to their beginnings is impossible; hence my decision to make do with six or seven volumes of literature as complete in themselves and build a total system around them." All this has too much the nonchalance of boys who are sure of a good dinner to get at the ineluctably historical nature of Hawthorne's vision. Such suppositions end up putting the fiction in the service of the criticism.

i. Manuscripts, Texts, Hawthorniana, Bibliography

The American Claimant Manuscripts and *The Elixir of Life Manuscripts,* Volumes 12 and 13 of the Centenary Edition, appeared this year, both edited by Claude M. Simpson, Edward H. Davidson, and

L. Neal Smith. In contrast to the relatively straightforward textual history of the finished romances, these volumes, each containing three sets of unfinished manuscript materials and ancillary working papers, make available for the first time the compositional sequences of aborted works posthumously published in fragmentary form. A complete text of "Septimius Felton" is printed for the first time. Using manuscript copy-texts wherever possible, the editors have recovered numerous previously undecipherable readings, corrected other misreadings in the earlier printed forms, and listed, along with their emendations, all of Hawthorne's own manuscript alterations. The historical commentaries trace Hawthorne's developing intentions and failures, give an account of the editing done by family members after his death, and survey the history of publication and the critical reception given these fragments. The scholarship is thorough and exacting. What remains to be seen now is whether these reconstructions will advance our understanding of Hawthorne's dwindling powers after 1860.

In "Serendipity—Perhaps" (*NHJ* 6:129–32) Claude M. Simpson writes a footnote to the Septimius Felton/Norton drafts which investigates the question of Hawthorne's changing of characters' names between and within manuscripts. Wayne Allen Jones, in "A New Love Letter: Hawthorne's Proposal? Discovery of a Sophia Hawthorne Transcript" (*NHJ* 6:10–13), prints an undated transcript of a letter dated 28 April 1840 from Hawthorne to Sophia. That this letter, however, any more than several others, amounts to a proposal is questionable. C. E. Frazer Clark, Jr., prints just what his title specifies in "Hawthorne to John Appleton: An Unpublished Letter" (*NHJ* 6:14–16), a brief pro forma note of welcome to an American whom Hawthorne as United States consul plainly had no wish to know better.

Several pieces might best be listed as Hawthorniana. In "A Lost Miniature of Hawthorne" (*NHJ* 6:80–85) C. E. Frazer Clark, Jr., reproduces a photograph of what is, according to Julian Hawthorne, an 1836 miniature, the only one made of his father, and traces the history of the original to 1925. Clark tells a lively tale involving Julian's invention of the theft of the painting. Raymona E. Hull's "Una Hawthorne: A Biographical Sketch" (*NHJ* 6:86–119) puts together a well-documented, gracefully written account of the life of the Hawthornes' eldest child, especially her troubled adult years and her precarious health following the deaths of her parents. The essay is a model of balance and proportion for biographical studies of peripheral interest. Hull keeps the agitated reality of the life before us even when the evidence is scanty. More peripheral and less impressive is Maurice Bassan's "Bay Area Hawthorniana" (*NHJ* 6:69–79), which adds little to the same writer's biography of Julian beyond offering up several more details about the routines of his late California years. The essay's one intriguing suggestion—that a drawing of Hawthorne in an 1858 sketchbook kept by Julian and Sophia might have inspired several lines in Robert Lowell's poem—is more pleasant than persuasive.

The "families" of great writers grow by leaps and unknown distant cousins and, oftentimes, strained critical connections. James H. Matlack's "Hawthorne and Elizabeth Barstow Stoddard" (*NEQ* 50: 278–302) seems at first artificially inseminated, the Hawthorne relationship merely the occasion to get into print a concern about a largely forgotten novel, *The Morgesons*, which most of the essay is devoted to explicating. Though the connection turns out to be real—there are two Hawthorne letters mentioning the novel, there is Mrs. Stoddard's husband, an early Hawthorne biographer whom the writer helped in office-seeking in 1853—Matlack doesn't use the occasion to comment freshly on Hawthorne's attitudes about fiction in the declining years of 1862–63. Something might have been said, for example, about his response to the regionalism of the novel. John L. Idol, Jr.'s "Nathaniel Hawthorne and Harriet Hosmer" (*NHJ* 6:120–28) fleshes out some details of biography and comments aptly on Hawthorne's interest in the life and admiration of the art of the sculptor, whose "Zenobia" fascinated him in Rome and perhaps led him to have Hosmer in mind as a partial prototype for Hilda in *The Marble Faun*.

The year's work includes half a dozen bibliographical items. Wayne Allen Jones's "Hawthorne's First Published Review" (*AL* 48: 492–500) identifies and reprints Hawthorne's *Boston Daily Atlas* notice (Feb. 23, 1836) of Samuel G. Goodrich's *The Outcast and Other Poems*. Jones's observation that the distinction Hawthorne draws between Imagination and Fancy "explains" his "radical shift to the highly abstract mode of allegory" in the 1840s, however, seems illogical. In "Origins of the American Renaissance: A Front-Page Story" (*SAR*, pp. 155–64) C. E. Frazer Clark, Jr., compiles information about newspaper reprints of "A Rill from the Town-Pump" and

"The Great Stone Face" and concludes that in spite of their freebooting, newspapers contributed to the formation of a popular public literary awareness. In the same annual volume (pp. 261–312) John J. McDonald's "A Guide to Primary Source Materials for the Study of Hawthorne's Old Manse Period" contains checklists of published materials, miscellaneous manuscripts, an index, and—most important—a comprehensive calendar of correspondence, from July 9, 1842, to October 2, 1845, written by or to Nathaniel and Sophia, with brief descriptions of the contents. An invaluable aid for the study of the Manse years, the work invites a scholarly assessment of the relevance of Sophia's many letters, "a rarely tapped reservoir of information about Hawthorne as man and artist." Two compilations of recent Hawthorne criticism are Buford Jones's "Current Hawthorne Bibliography" (*Nathaniel Hawthorne Society Newsletter* 3: 6–10) and Wayne Allen Jones's "A Checklist of Recent Hawthorne Scholarship, 1974–1975" (*NHJ* 6:313–20), which has sections on recent editions, critical books, articles and essays, and dissertations.

ii. General Studies

Studies here present Hawthorne as allegorical moralist, ironist, rhetorical con-artist. Some have vigorous insight, others seem tired, oft-played recordings. In "Unreliable Artist-Narrators in Hawthorne's Short Stories" (*SSF* 14:145–50) Nancy L. Bunge gives us a steadfastly didactic Hawthorne who declares that art's "ethical corollary [is] that the artist must possess a strong sense of brotherhood." And she siphons off narrators in ten of the tales and sketches who don't measure up ("Wakefield" and "Chippings with a Chisel" are named, along with others such as "A Virtuoso's Collection") without ever telling us how the other, presumably reliable narrators—say, of "My Kinsman, Major Molineux"—exude "a highly developed sense of brotherly love." It is, unfortunately, an uninformed, simplistic reading. The Hawthorne of most interest to James G. Janssen in "Impaled Butterflies and the Misleading Moral in Hawthorne's Short Works" (*NHJ* 6:269–75), on the other hand, is the ironist who toys with the conventions of the explicitly pronounced moral, inserting it at times as "an afterthought or a hastily discharged duty," at others—his example is "The Prophetic Pictures"—stating it in a playfully misleading manner. Janssen's Hawthorne is familiar: ironic, humorous, he is still the moralist who would mean his meanings on a little lower layer.

As Terence Martin aptly put it several years ago, Hawthorne's task was not only to write fiction but to "create the conditions of fiction," and now we have him as trickster in that pursuit. Timothy Dow Adams's "To Prepare a Preface to Meet the Faces that You Meet: Autobiographical Rhetoric in Hawthorne's Prefaces" (*ESQ* 23:89–98) claims that Hawthorne anticipates the "labyrinthian, solipsistic, meta-fiction" of contemporary writers by constantly keeping his readers off guard about his "semiautobiographical" fiction. In early tales such as "The Gray Champion" and "The Gentle Boy" Hawthorne writes trustworthy prefaces; in later ones such as "Wakefield" and "Main-street" he deliberately breaks down the "illusion of truth." Adams's terms—the distinctions he draws, for example, between "formal" and "fictional" prefaces and between the "false letter" and the "*real* letter to Bridge" in *The Snow-Image*—are slippery or confused more often than not. Several points are mystifying: "The narrator [of "Tanglewood Porch"] also claims that the stories to follow will be told by Eustace Bright, the storyteller's real name." Adams seems uncertain about what parts self-revelation and self-concealment the prefaces exhibit, and one misses a clear analysis of Hawthorne's purposes in the literary gamesmanship. More perceptive and provocative is Kent Bales's "Hawthorne's Prefaces and Romantic Perspectivism" (*ESQ* 23:69–88), which argues that the major prefaces are not so much restatements of the romance theories of Scott and Cooper as they are strategies of "perspectivism" shared by earlier German writers and the later English romantic poets. Bales focuses on "The Custom-House," "The Old Manse," and the prefatory remarks in "Rappaccini's Daughter" and "Roger Malvin's Burial" as "essential parts of the works they precede." Multiple perspectives and the irreducible ambiguities they generate tend to be old wine in new bottles for Hawthorne students, however; and Bales's conclusion—that shifting perspectives lead to the subversion of "common sense and morals" and simultaneously to the creation of "sympathy"—seems to make Hawthorne over into today's "caring person." Bales is best along the way and has penetrating things to say about how "spatial relations . . . symbolize other relations, placement and distance, for example, suggesting psychological and moral relations or categories."

Several essays investigate the processes of Hawthorne's imagination as these are registered in his letters and notebooks. Rita K. Gollin's "Hawthorne: The Writer as Dreamer" (*SAR*, pp. 313–25) is essentially a catalogue of Hawthorne's wide-ranging references to, and attitudes towards, dreams and his efforts to convert them into the stuff of fiction. Although useful, it is too long of quotation, too brief of commentary; Dryden's book, alluding to many of the same materials, invests them with much more compelling meaning. In a second essay, "Hawthorne on Perception, Lucubration, and Reverie" (*NHJ* 6:227–39), Gollin examines more perspicaciously the extent to which, in his notebooks and "The Custom-House," Hawthorne deliberately initiates creative reverie "to make possible a fusion" of Actual and Imaginary. Hawthorne, she contends, did not need so much the moral significance of observable fact as he did the time to assimilate the "characteristic" and the "remarkable" features of phenomena. Whereas she implies Hawthorne's fundamental success in creating fictions in which a controlled condition of daydream unites ideal and real, artist and reader, Samuel Coale, in "Hawthorne's *American Notebooks*: Contours of a Haunted Mind" (*NHJ* 6:257–68), has Hawthorne creating unreal "neutral territory" in his fiction precisely because he could not fuse Actual and Imaginary. For Coale, what Hawthorne had to fuse—and could not—are the actual world that fed the "undecipherable 'darksome shade' " of his imagination and those light, colorful scenes of the moral picturesque that nurtured his own simplistic instinct for clear-cut moral categories. Failing that, Hawthorne, says Coale (citing another critic), lacks "the talisman of the modern novelist—namely, development. He could not conceive of sin as the means by which evil may be worked out of a nature and its good forces allowed to come into play." If Gollin offers insufficient evidence for Hawthorne's continuous "fusions" of his materials, Coale would seem to say more about us and our faddish ideal of "open confession" than he would about Hawthorne, a writer who plainly refused to let himself or us have our *felix culpas* so effortlessly.

Bales's "romantic perspectivism" is one answer to Coale's charge that Hawthorne's bifurcated imagination led to static allegorical conceptions; James F. Walter's "The Metaphysical Vision of History in Hawthorne's Fiction" (*NHJ* 6:276–85) constitutes another. Walter locates the "metaphysical" quality of Hawthorne's work in an existential "realism" of "multi-layered drama" which acts as a persistent counterpoise to the "unrooted idealism" of his gnostic characters. "At the heart of Hawthorne's special narrative form," Walter suggests, "is a dramatic statement of the possibility of hope" and, behind that, the tacit necessity of love. It was a falsifying "spirit of abstraction" that Hawthorne saw characterizing his own time. But Walter's discussion is too general to be more than suggestive.

Other essays address Hawthorne's transformation of historical materials into fictional form. In "Hawthorne and the American Revolution: An Exploration" (*NHJ* 6:17–61) Blair Rouse surveys the corpus for what turn out to be vagrant remarks on the Revolution in order, Rouse says, to gauge the impact of "all History" on Hawthorne's mind. There is little by way of conclusion other than the complaint that Hawthorne saw the Revolution provincially, New-Englandly. The superb studies of John P. McWilliams, Jr., and Lewis P. Simpson (see *ALS 1976*, pp. 20–22) demonstrate conclusively the depth of Hawthorne's symbolic treatment of the subject, however, and suggest that Rouse is much too literalistic and directionless. So too do two other essays: Peter Shaw's "Hawthorne's Ritual Typology of the American Revolution" (*Prospects*, pp. 483–98) and John P. McWilliams, Jr.'s "Fictions of Merry Mount" (*AQ* 29:3–30). Shaw's thesis is a penetrating clarification of Hawthorne's discovery and mastery of a usable national past: five tales—"The May-Pole of Merry Mount," "Endicott and the Red Cross," "The Gray Champion," "My Kinsman, Major Molineux," and "Howe's Masquerade"—make up "a ritual history of protorevolutionary events in New England extending from the beginning of the settlement of Massachusetts Bay to the eve of the American Revolution." Too intricate to summarize adequately here, Shaw's argument defines and illustrates deftly the ways in which Hawthorne's typological (rather than allegorical) vision embraces ritual origins, folk sources, and prophetic intimations of the future. Thus, for example, the American Revolution is seen as a "*realization*," not a mere parallel, of Endicott's rebellious act. Shaw's analysis is sufficiently detailed that he gives fresh life to Hawthorne's ambivalence toward the Puritan patriarchs. One wonders, however, whether other historical tales need to be included here. McWilliams's essay places Hawthorne's tale in the context of the biased accounts of the antagonists Morton and Bradford, the fictional versions of Lydia Child and Catherine Sedgwick, the later historical account of Charles Francis Adams, Jr., Motley's romance, and the 20th-century views of William Carlos Williams and Robert Lowell. His careful reconstruction of the obscured and incomplete facts surrounding the controversy provides an illuminating background for Hawthorne's tale and authenticates his achievement in transforming these materials into cultural mythology. Whereas McWilliams finds Hawthorne abandoning the historical issues implied in his materials because he makes no attempt to define a future for Edith and Edgar, Shaw asserts a hope based on the typological analysis of history as pointing to destinies still concealed.

A companion piece to McWilliams's is Michael Zuckerman's "Pilgrims in the Wilderness: Community, Modernity, and the Maypole at Merry Mount" (*NEQ* 50:255–77), a study whose vigorous advocacy of Morton's values and equally strong criticism of the Pilgrim and Puritan insistence on moral and social conformity would seem to lead to a too neatly schematic analysis of the conflict. Zuckerman's assessment is at points based on evidence that McWilliams describes as incomplete or unreliable, but his central conclusions are by no means vitiated. In defeating Morton the rebel, Pilgrims and Puritans severed themselves from the traditional community-conserving values he embodied: thus, their own paradoxically greater rebellion. "The inner tendency of Puritanism was fissive. Its outward history was accordingly a chronicle of efforts to arrest that tendency." Interesting too in the light of these studies is Gene Bluestein's "The Brotherhood of Sinners: Literary Calvinism" (*NEQ* 50:195–213), which draws a distinction between the religious dogma and the literary ideology and traces the ironic history in which universal depravity and radical democracy converge: "the God who is the author of such a system in which all men and women are absolutely equal in sin, inescapably joined in the brotherhood and sisterhood which devolves from this depravity—that deity is indeed a democratic God." The acceptance, then, of the fact of the conservative philosophy issues in literary as well as political stances which are equalitarian—as Melville's comments, in "Hawthorne and His Mosses," on both literary nationalism and Hawthorne's power of blackness would seem to have it.

Benjamin Lease's "Hawthorne and the Archeology of the Cinema" (*NHJ* 6:133–71) is a fact-filled survey of the widespread popularity of visual entertainments that frequently make their way into Hawthorne's thought and fiction—diorama, panorama, phantasmagoric displays, shadow plays, the camera obscura, *trompe l'oeil* painting, the daguerreotype, the stagecraft of mesmerism. It is a useful addition in the sociology behind Hawthorne's art and suggests that the writer's contemporary world is the source of what are oftentimes taken to be merely Gothic or sentimental paraphernalia in his work. Hawthorne quite obviously assimilated for his art what he could from every corner of his experience—from his direct observation of nature, his contemporary scene, from his study of his personal past, New England history, English history, from his wider reading. Richard Harter Fogle, in "The Great English Romantics in Hawthorne's Major Romances" (*NHJ* 6:62–68), mentions various, admittedly approximate, parallels in the poetry of these writers. Implicit in Fogle's comments is the view that nothing like a measurable "influence" is manifest; and some of the "analogies" seem indeterminate enough to invite other explanations.

iii. Long Romances

No work appeared on *Fanshawe* in 1977, and there was precious little on *The Scarlet Letter*. It's a bad beginning here: Diane Mae Sims claims, in "Chillingworth's Clue in *The Scarlet Letter*" (*NHJ* 6:292–93), that Chillingworth puts the finger on Dimmesdale immediately "upon arrival in Boston" and tells Hester, in Chapter IV, that "he detects her partner in infamy because he 'read it on his heart.'" Neither the fact that Hawthorne happens to have had Chillingworth say "shall read" here nor the fact that the chapter has a race horse's impulsion of future tenses has made any difference to Sims. In "Chillingworth and His 'Dark Necessity'" (*CollL* 4:136–43) Edward Stone seems to beat a dead horse—Martin Green's 1965 reading that Hawthorne fails to dramatize Chillingworth's change into a "fiend"—in order to resurrect Austin Warren's description of the romance as "a *literary* exercise in moral theology." Stone does away with Green easily enough and has several close readings that deserve attention; but his secondary purpose loses sight of itself even though he invokes Augustine, Aquinas, and Francis Bacon. In a second study, "Of Lambence and Hawthorne's Hell Fire" (*NHJ* 6:196–204), Stone adduces evidence to suggest that Hawthorne's characterization of *The Scarlet Letter* as "a positively hell-fired story" is exaggerated and misleading. A genial wit, a warm and whimsical tone often cut across the somber gravity of situation, character, and motive, Stone contends.

His is a minor point but a wholesome reminder that even here Hawthorne has his own mark of native American humor. More energetic and sustained is Frederick Newberry's "Tradition and Disinheritance in *The Scarlet Letter*" (*ESQ* 23:1–26), which reasserts boldly and carefully that the romance is "about history," more specifically about both New and Old World history as residing in the conflicting strains—"dominant" and "recessive"—of both American and English Puritanism from 1642 to 1649. A rich historicist reading, Newberry's analysis has Hawthorne seeing as analogues his 17th-century oppressively righteous forebears and his smugly materialistic contemporaries. Both are antipathetic to the values of art, continuity, and culture, the severity of the one and the iconoclasm of the other, rejecting as well "sympathy, charity, gaiety." Newberry's vision of Hawthorne's association of Hester with the aristocratic and ecclesiastical art of inherited culture, his reading of the importance of Dimmesdale's Oxford/Anglican education, his assessment of the irony in the Pentacostal imagery surrounding the Election Day sermon at once complicate and clarify. The essay deserves a place among the required readings.

Not so, unfortunately, Judith A. Gustafson's "Parody in *The House of the Seven Gables*" (*NHJ* 6:294–302), a relentlessly tough-toned effort to lay a foundation for *The House*, not in "the actual soil of the County of Essex," which Hawthorne himself denied, but somewhere in the ticky-tacky of late 20th-century suburbia sexuality. In creating character, situation, and resolution, Hawthorne is merely mocking the stock contrivances of popular-sentimental fiction. There's an incipient Lolita in his black-comedy Phoebe: for why, we're left to ponder, did she show up in the first place unless her new step-father, like Uncle Venner later, took "a more than parental interest in her?"

Fiction as self-reflexive, fiction striving after the condition of metafiction seems to be deep in the saddle these days, if one can judge on the basis of the fascination shown for *The Blithedale Romance*. The case against Miles Coverdale has been made, now, many times and more thoroughly and thoughtfully than it is in Deborah Ayer Sitter's "The Case Against Miles Coverdale" (*MSE* 3:6–12). The risks of the Emersonian ideal of Self-Culture translated into literary criticism become painfully apparent here: private rediscoveries of now threadbare ideas are published for a frayed critical public. Not a whole lot more can be said for Terence J. Matheson's "Feminism and Femininity in *The Blithedale Romance*" (*NHJ* 6:215–26), which tries, rather half-heartedly, to demonstrate that we need only look at the romance as a statement on the status of women in Hawthorne's society to discover that it is "a unified and coherent work of art." Zenobia—strong-willed, self-possessed ideologue—and Priscilla—submissive, vegetating—are uncompromising opposites, both of whom Hawthorne and Coverdale together reject. Coverdale is an ideal narrator, critical and sympathetic, and Zenobia's suicide epitomizes what Matheson defines as Hawthorne's "moral": "true fulfilment can only occur when both the heart and the mind develop together." James Walter's "A Farewell to Blithedale: Coverdale's Aborted Pastoral" (*SAQ* 76:73–92) is more substantial and sheds some light on the problematic nature of the narrator and his story. Walter has Hawthorne taking the measure of the Transcendental idealism of Brook Farm and its commitment to Arcadian myth by way of an essentially "tragic myth" of human destiny. The combination of "abstract idealism and simple-minded pragmatism" causes Coverdale to participate in a gnostic contempt for circumstantial actuality. This flaw he can never wholly overcome: although he is gradually less aloof and more sensitive to the solid pressures of earth, he remains at the end the prisoner of his mocking self-consciousness, pathetically incapable of love and art alike. Whatever the critical method applied, Coverdale's problems tend never to vary. William E. Grant's "Hawthorne's *Hamlet*: The Archetypal Structure of *The Blithedale Romance*" (*RMR* 31:1–15) employs Freudian/Jungian terms. Coverdale's archetype, like Hamlet's, is the Oedipus legend and its attending paralysis of will and emotion, its urge, too, towards spying. Claudius "is roughly analogous to Hollingsworth," and other schematic "parallels" and "counterparts" follow: Polonius and Moodie, Zenobia–Priscilla and Gertrude–Ophelia, the tale of the Veiled Lady and the play-within-the play, and so on. Grant's comments on Westervelt as the Jungian shadow of Coverdale rather than the alter ego of Hollingsworth are illuminating, but his essay, like so much archetypal criticism, ignores or distorts the individual particularities of a text in tailoring it to the larger pattern. In addition, Grant leaves us with problems. He wishes to show only that the romance does not falter at the level of structure, that, if it in fact fails, it does so at those levels Kenneth Burke calls "poem as prayer" and "poem as chart." Structure in this view becomes, as Grant says, "neutral"; and he leaves hanging the question of structure's functional value at these other levels. In "New Light on Hawthorne's Miles Coverdale" (*JNT* 7:189–99) Joan D. Winslow defines the romance's problem not as Coverdale's paralysis but as Hawthorne's inability to negotiate all the curves of unreliable narration. This assessment has been made before, but Winslow's discussions of Myles Coverdale, a 16th-century Bible translator, as a possible prototype and of the import of Hawthorne's 11th-hour addition of the last chapter in the manuscript and of another addition in page proofs point to pertinent facts too often overlooked in recent interpretations.

iv. Short Works

In "Imagined Redemption in 'Roger Malvin's Burial'" (*SAF* 5:257–62) Burton J. Fisher argues succinctly that the Biblical source for Reuben's tears "gush[ing] out like water from a rock" is not, as Ely Stock has proposed, the restorative passage in Isaiah 48:21 but Numbers 20:7–12, where Moses' disobedience and impiety in striking the rock denied him the Promised Land. Reuben Bourne's absolution, then, is as illusory at the tale's conclusion as his tormenting guilt has been delusive from the beginning. What is insufficiently considered here is the possibility that Hawthorne heightened the tale's ambiguity and inscrutability by alluding to both passages.

The extent to which he drew on multiple literary and historical materials for his early tales is suggested by two essays on "The Gentle Boy." In "Hawthorne's Debt to Edmund Spenser and Charles Chauncy in 'The Gentle Boy'" (*NHJ* 6:189–95) James Duban examines the question of why Hawthorne found "gentleness" to be that special moral virtue most appropriate to the Quaker boy Ilbrahim. He finds his answer in Book VI of the *Faerie Queene*, where Spenser introduces Tristram, a boy forced to flee his home after his father's death and armed only with courtesy in his struggles against the Blatant Beast; and in Chauncy's *Seasonable Thoughts on the State of Religion in New England*, where gentleness epitomizes the ideal of religious toleration destroyed by the excesses of enthusiasm. The thesis is convincingly developed, and it gives historical substance to what many readers probably misperceive as a merely sentimental quality. Peter White's "The Monstrous Birth and 'The Gentle Boy': Hawthorne's Use of the Past" (*NHJ* 6:172–88) argues that the tale draws heavily on the accounts of the trial of Anne Hutchinson and her fellow-Quaker Mary Dyre for themes, characters, images and that Ilbrahim and the sickly Puritan child he befriends are ironic adaptations of the "monstrous births" which, as rumor and tradition came to have it, were cruelly visited upon the two women as God's punishment for their heresy. White's survey of 17th- and 18th-century commentary on the Antinomian controversy is full and to the point.

In "Young Goody Brown" (*EA* 30:407–19) M. M. Shriver attempts to pinpoint Hawthorne's ambiguity but instead uncovers an unambiguous and "highly sensuous [sensual?]" Faith, who is no "inhibited, decorous, sombre-souled Puritan maid or mistress" but "an ardent fully responsive woman" of "unbridled eagerness," who, as both Goodman Brown and the reader know "perfectly well . . . has already signed her pact with the Black Man." When we read that the "haunting rhythmic pulse-beat" of the forest ritual is a "sound-track of a night of frenzied young love," we need hardly perk up our ears to hear the electric guitars. What gets lost sight of altogether is Faith's ambiguous dual role as person and as symbol and the integral force on her character of Brown's obsessive projection of his own sexual desires. Another of Hawthorne's errant husbands, Wakefield, is the subject of two other essays, one of them Jungian, the other quasi-sociological. Roberta F. Weldon, in "Wakefield's Second Journey" (*SSF* 14:69–74), explores the tale as the mythic journey of the late middle years, an effort to rediscover and be reconciled with identity before death. Far from successful, the upshot of Wakefield's experiment, in Weldon's view, is that he has imposed his conventional image of himself on his wife, who in her "phallic angularity" has become a solipsistic extension of his own identity. In " 'Busy and Selfish London': The Urban Figure in Hawthorne's 'Wakefield' " (*ESQ* 23:164–72) John Gatta, Jr., proposes that the story is a dramatization of what Hawthorne perceived as "the anomic terrors and threats to interior selfhood posed by an age of rapid urban expansion." Gatta marshalls evidence to show that Hawthorne had a cultural analyst's interest in contemporary urbanization and its attenuation of traditional social bonds and domestic, marital ties. The motives underlying Wakefield's behavior arise out of the psychopathology induced by London's immensity, which creates a condition of anonymity and, in Wakefield, a perverse but accurate realization that the only possibility of being "noticed" lies in being "missed." Although Wakefield's alienation and return are without redemptive value, "the story's final import is corrective," Gatta claims, "rather than antagonistic" in that it warns of "the psychic readjustments—and the need for neighborhood ties—demanded by the burgeoning metropolis." To be sure, Hawthorne escaped, as Gatta says, the stereotypically romantic condemnation of the city; but one doubts that he would construe "neighborhood ties" as a lasting solution.

William T. Blair's " 'Dr. Heidegger's Experiment': An Allegory of Sin" (*NHJ* 6:286–91) seems a misguided, weakly argued attempt to define this slight tale as a weighty, well-wrought allegory of the Devil and the Seven Deadly Sins. Almost as overstated and unpersuasive is Paul Lewis's "Victor Frankenstein and Owen Warland: The Artist as Satan and as God" (*SSF* 14:279–82), which asserts that "The Artist of the Beautiful" is Hawthorne's "reaction to," indeed, his ironic "retelling of" Mary Shelley's Gothic tale. Harry C. West's "The Evolution of Hawthorne's 'The Birth-mark' " (*NHJ* 6:240–56), on the other hand, merits attention because its claim that Hawthorne found in Isaac D'Israeli's *Curiosities of Literature* elements of incident, action, theme, and even a suggestion of central symbol is credibly, sensitively pursued. The essay is admirable in the balanced view it gives of the fullness of the sources Hawthorne worked with and the artistry by which he "force[s] the material to circulate about a symbolic center of his own invention."

In "The Demonic in 'Endicott and the Red Cross' " (*PLL* 13:251 59) Frederick Newberry attempts to refute the recent critical consensus that Hawthorne's attitude toward Puritanism and the founding fathers is deeply and steadily ambivalent. Newberry's Endicott is roundly condemned for a "demonic cruelty" which issues in political oppression and is patently anti-Christian. His reading of the tale is acute and detailed, but the assertion that its events do not qualify even "as an archetypal dress rehearsal for the American Revolution" ignores several recent studies about the implications of Hawthorne's typological vision. Newberry has Hawthorne employing rich ironies in the service of a neodidacticism that oversimplifies his major historical themes. Perhaps not out of place here is Donald G. Darnell's " 'Visions of Hereditary Rank': The Loyalist in the Fiction of Hawthorne, Cooper, and Frederic" (*SAB* 42,ii:45–54), which, insofar as it treats Hawthorne, errs on the same score if in the opposite direction. To say that Hawthorne "measures his Loyalists against democratic and Puritan values and finds them wanting" is to leap to at least two questionable conclusions. Darnell fails to discuss his conjunction of democratic and Puritan values and implies that they are easy companions; and in his account of Hawthorne's Loyalists he has nothing to say about Robin's kinsman, an omission which, if corrected, would have had to qualify Darnell's analysis.

v. Hawthorne and Others

There were no Hawthorne-Melville items this year, and just two essays take up the matter of Hawthorne's influence on other writers. Walter Hesford's "Literary Contexts of 'Life in the Iron-Mills'" (*AL* 49:70–85) demonstrates the idea, perhaps more charming than substantial, that Rebecca Harding Davis's 1861 tale—"the first notable work of fiction to concern itself with the life of the factory worker in an industrial American town"—owes something of the genesis of its vision to her childhood reading of "A Rill from the Town-Pump," "Little Annie's Ramble," and "Sunday at Home." Charming because one hardly gets the chance to think of these sketches as influencing anyone, and substantial as well because Hesford demonstrates rather amply how Davis employed Hawthornian qualities of observation to extend for herself the province of romance. In " 'The Impressions of a Cousin': Henry James' Transformation of *The Marble Faun*" (*NHJ* 6:205–14) Adeline R. Tintner shows beyond any doubt that James patterned the characters and the structure of this 1883 story after elements in Hawthorne's romance. Read without *The Marble Faun* as literary tourist guidebook, in fact, the story is in itself "ambiguous or even absurd." Even with Hawthorne as a "key" James did not think well enough of the tale to include it in his New York Edition. One surmises from Tintner's account that in 1883 James, in one of the lighter exercises of his imagination, could toy self-consciously with Hawthorne's moonshiny romance with something of the condescension of his 1879 *Hawthorne*.

University of Missouri, Columbia

3. Poe

Donald B. Stauffer

The quantity of writing about Poe fell off sharply this year; following the new *ALS* policy to skip over minor notes and marginal items, I ended up with a total of only 35 books and articles, down from the last three or four years when there were over 50. But questions of quantity aside, what about quality? I cannot be as sanguine as some of my *ALS* colleagues who discern a kind of renascence in literary scholarship. I think Poe scholarship has momentarily reached a saturation point after those exciting years of rediscovery and possession of a major American writer that occurred in the late sixties and was spurred on by the founding of *Poe Studies* and the Poe Society. The redirection of Poe scholarship and criticism that took place after the seminal work of Davidson, Wilbur, Patrick Quinn, and others gave rise to some solid and necessary reexamination of all of Poe's work, but this activity has slowed down, and what are being published now are refinements of some of these well-charted areas, or reworkings of them (one exception is the growing influence of the French structuralists). I too often have the uneasy feeling that we Poe scholars are writing mainly for each other, in a highly specialized context of themes, archetypes, and earlier criticism, and not for the wider world of scholarship (if there is such a thing). But, these objections aside, there were good things, including a number of essays on various aspects of "Usher" and Robert D. Jacobs's reexamination of Poe's early poems, which I would say conforms to Hershel Parker's definition of "the New Scholarship."

i. Sources, Influence, Reputation, Biography

No one had much to add to existing information about Poe texts or sources. But one possible addition to the canon is a two-paragraph sketch accompanying a caricature of Margaret Fuller in the *Broadway Journal*, for which Burton R. Pollin finds evidence of Poe's authorship ("Poe on Margaret Fuller in 1845: An Unknown Caricature and Lampoon," *W&L* 5:47–51). The only source study of note is Barton L. St. Armand, "Some Poe Debts to Irving's *Alhambra*," (*PoeS* 10:42). He finds two sources: a raven which bears resemblances to the one in Poe's poem in the story, "Legend of Prince Ahmed Al Kamel, or the Pilgrim of Love"; and, in Irving's original 1832 Dedication, a reference to the "Arabesque" which Poe may have noticed.

Two of the four influence studies show it is still possible to find new things to say about Poe and French writers, even someone as thoroughly studied as Paul Valéry. Lois Vines, in "Dupin-Teste: Poe's Direct Influence on Valéry" (*FrF* 2:147–59), shows that Valéry had a strong interest in Poe's prose works, especially "The Murders in the Rue Morgue" and "The Domain of Arnheim." "Early in his literary career," she writes, "Valéry discovered in Poe's detective character Dupin the model he needed to help him transform his obsession with pure intellectual power into the fictional character Monsieur Teste." Her excellent comparative study of Baudelaire's translation of the tale and Valéry's "La Soirée Avec Monsieur Teste" supports her point. She also points out that Poe's description of how his mind operated during the creation of "The Raven" fascinated Valéry to the point of obsession.

A more general treatment of the subject of influence is Georges Zayed's long appreciative essay on the importance of Poe in France, "Le Génie d'Edgar Poe et le Goût Français" (*Aquila* 3 [1976]:201–47). This is a well-written survey of the forces in America, particularly Griswold and his followers, that have worked against a proper appreciation of Poe, and of the forces in France, particularly Baudelaire, Mallarmé, and Valéry, that have elevated him to comparisons with Shakespeare and Plato as writers of genius. The sections on the French writers' reactions to Poe's work are thoroughly documented with passages from letters and journals.

Poe has also been a considerable influence on Japanese writers, as Noriko M. Lippitt shows in two comparative studies. In "Tanizaki and Poe: The Grotesque and the Quest for Supernal Beauty" (*CL* 29:221–40), she traces Poe's influence on the writers of the aesthetic school and looks more closely at the similarity of themes and subject matter of Poe and the major novelist Tanizaki Junichiro. In another interesting article she looks at the role the novelist Natsume Sohseki played in stimulating an interest in Poe among Japanese readers and writers. She points out that Sosēki was probably the first critic to notice the affinity between Swift and Poe, both of whose imaginative worlds are created by the surprising juxtaposition of the fantastic and the realistic ("Natsume Sosēki on Poe," *CLS* 14:30–37).

Vulgarity and puerility are still words that frequently crop up in discussions of Poe, and in a charming, provocative, and meditative essay Elizabeth Sewell sets out to discover why. Among her many speculations and personal reflections is the suggestion that Poe shares his childishness with both Edward Lear and Lewis Carroll, and that the works of all three are marked by an interest in method ("Poe for the Sixth Time," *Parnassus* 5 [1976]:9–19).

A total of three books on Poe appeared this year, all having something to do with biography. They vary considerably both in focus and quality, and I shall discuss them in descending order of quality.

First, then, is John Carl Miller's *Building Poe Biography* (Baton Rouge: La. State Univ. Press), the beginning of a large-scale effort to get into print a sizable quantity of the materials gathered by Poe's 19th-century English biographer, John Henry Ingram, which are now housed at the University of Virginia. Ingram's indefatigable efforts to accumulate letters, newspaper clippings, photographs, and other memorabilia of Poe resulted in an extraordinary collection of over a thousand items. For many years, they were virtually inaccessible to scholars, but since 1967 they have been available on microfilm, with a catalog and "calendar" prepared by Professor Miller. He can hope to publish only a fragment of the total, and we are therefore dependent upon his own selections unless we go to the microfilm source. Still, this book makes us see, as we have long suspected, the extent of the debt we owe to Ingram's efforts to vindicate Poe from the accusations of Rufus Griswold. It also makes us see the extent of Ingram's own achievements as well as his decided peculiarities.

This is the first of a projected four-volume series which reproduces many of the letters for the first time, along with a running commentary on the letter writers and their roles in the lives of both Poe and Ingram. There are 86 letters from six correspondents Ingram used: Maria Clemm, Rosalie Poe, Marie Louise Shew, Annie Richmond,

William Hand Browne, and George Eveleth. The second and third will contain Ingram's unpublished correspondence between Ingram and Sarah Helen Whitman, while the fourth will deal with Ingram's struggles and achievements from 1880 to 1916.

Miller's account of Ingram's career and his relationships with the eccentric people he dealt with is not always as clear as it might be, nor does it go as far as it might. The book is an interesting record of Ingram's efforts to collect this material, but it does not contain enough insights into his own, not wholly pleasant, personality, nor does it show us fully how he "built" his biography out of his materials. But to have even these few letters published for the first time is helpful, even though much research in the entire collection remains for future scholars. Miller has also written a brief summary sketch of Ingram and his contributions, which appears as "John Henry Ingram: English Architect of Poe Biography" (*Topic* 17:20–28).

Vincent Buranelli's revision of his 1961 Twayne study, *Edgar Allan Poe*, reissued in a second edition (Boston: G. K. Hall), retains the original format with slightly revised chapters and an enlarged bibliography which to a limited extent takes account of a new generation of Poe scholars and critics. The book is essentially the same, with the exception of a few revisions, including a section which tones down his denial of morality in Poe's fiction, a section defending the poetry against charges of vulgarity, and a passage on Poe and Mesmerism. This is a respectable scholarly job by a nonspecialist, which is reliable even though it breaks no new ground.

I cannot say the same for an attempt at a popular biography by a British journalist, David Sinclair, *Edgar Allan Poe* (London/Totowa, N.J.: Dent/Rowan and Littlefield). His book is intended, he says, not as a literary or critical biography but as a sympathetic picture of Poe the man which will correct the average reader's distorted view of Poe as a drug-crazed pervert or drunken waster. This much he might possibly achieve (as would have other biographers if that much-maligned average reader had read them), but the book falls far short of being the updating of A. H. Quinn that we very much need. Between passages of pseudoanalysis à la Bonaparte and long circumstantial accounts of Poe's comings and goings, Average Reader will very likely become either confused or bored.

Sinclair's most original idea (to me at least) is that Poe was a victim of diabetes; this is the condition that possibly led him to behave so erratically whenever he used alcohol. The evidence, slim as it is, is at least plausible, even though, as he says, we are not able to take a urine sample. But the book is for neither the layman nor the scholar: its pedantic recitation of facts and reprinting of letters invite skipping; and its folksy tone and lack of sound critical judgments upon the works make it of little value to the serious student.

ii. Fiction

***a.* General.** The idea of Poe as a thinker continues to be attractive to those who believe he is more than a mere teller of tales. James W. Gargano, for instance, in "The Masquerade Vision in Poe's Short Stories," a lecture published by The Edgar Allan Poe Society of Baltimore, adeptly shows how Poe, of all American writers, makes the most consistent use of masquerade devices to convey in various ways his complex view of life, involving deception, appearance and reality, and questions of man's identity in a mysterious universe. Max L. Autrey goes out on a limb to speculate about Poe's attitudes toward early theories of evolution. Basing his rather muddled argument on the recurring appearance of various animals in Poe's tales, particularly the frog and the ape, he notes that Poe supported the views of Baron Cuvier and others who believed that new species were produced not by natural selection or transmutation but out of a creative life force. Poe, Autrey says, looks at lower and higher forms of life principally for the purpose of satire and to show man's tendency to retrogress to animal traits. The presence of these animals in various tales is certainly striking, but the idea is not well developed ("Edgar Allan Poe's Satiric View of Evolution," *Extrapolation* 18:186–99).

The Dostoyevskian qualities of Poe's tales have been noted by many readers, including Dostoyevsky himself, but no one has done as thorough a job of comparing them as Louis Harap, in "Poe and Dostoyevsky: A Case of Affinity," *Weapons of Criticism: Marxism in America and the Literary Tradition*, edited by Norman Rudich (Palo Alto, Calif.: Ramparts Press), pp. 271–85. This Marxist approach bears some interesting fruit. Harap emphasizes the idea that both writers were alienated from their society; in Poe the prevailing mood is one of intense suffering, while Dostoyevsky was also alienated, fighting throughout his life for the integrity and freedom of the individual. Both, Harap finds, were against the social and political movements of the 19th century, and both also recoiled from learning the truth about the self. Specifically, he notes similarities between *Notes from the Underground* and "The Black Cat" and "The Imp of the Perverse," and between "William Wilson" and "The Double." Harap is writing not about influence, but about the philosophy and attitudes the two writers had in common. Still, it is curious that he nowhere mentions the fact that Dostoyevsky wrote an appreciative preface to translations of three Poe tales that appeared in his magazine *Wremia* in 1861.

***b.* Comic Tales.** Not much on the comic tales this year, but the two articles that did appear both sustain the growing conviction that Poe was writing for more than one audience in his burlesques. In the case of "Doctor Tarr and Professor Fether," Benjamin Franklin Fisher IV believes that one of his audiences consisted of those who had read his Gothic tales. In "Poe's 'Tarr and Fether': Hoaxing in the Blackwood Mode" (*Topic* 17:29–40), Fisher points out that the parallels between the opening of this tale and the opening of "Usher" is just one of several examples of self-parody, in which Poe deliberately plays with references to his own earlier Gothic tales. He concludes that Poe poked fun at methods of how to write a Blackwood "article" early and late in his career.

David H. Hirsch's complicated close reading of "The Duc de l'Omelette" makes stronger claims for the intellectual sophistication of Poe's readers by placing the tale in the context of English Romanticism. Although he recognizes that it is slight in substance and contains the parodic elements that already have been pointed out by others, Hirsch says that in this tale Poe examines the motif of the soul through the metaphor of the bird-in-cage as soul-in-body. In fact, he says, all five of the early tales which were first published in the Philadelphia *Saturday Courier* take up different traditional ways of talking about the soul. Hirsch finds arcane allusions to Keats, to Neo-Platonic theories of beauty, to metempsychosis, and to other favorite Poe subjects, and he succeeds in showing how it is possible to see the tale as one of Poe's clever efforts to work on two levels at once; burlesque and parody of his contemporaries, along with satiric treatment of some philosophical ideas current at the time ("'The Duc de l'Omelette' as Anti-Visionary Tale," *PoeS* 10:36–39).

c. Gothic Tales and Tales of Ratiocination. One might think it would be difficult to come up with something new to say about "The Fall of the House of Usher," yet four of this year's five articles about it either present new information or offer new possibilities for interpretation. The narrator is of particular interest in two important and challenging essays on Poe's narrators which range widely over his work but focus on "Usher."

In a cogently argued, sensitive reading of the tales of terror Robert Crossley sees the narrators as "story-writers" rather than "story-tellers"; they are tongue-tied, unable to speak, therefore taking up pen and ink in their efforts to explain themselves to their best audience—themselves. His paradigm is "MS. Found in a Bottle," in which an anonymous narrator writes in total isolation from his audience. Crossley follows Halliburton's phenomenological discussions of narrative technique (see *ALS 1973*, pp. 41–42) to arrive at his conclusion that the tales are not confessions or intimate revelations, but "sealed texts, self-sustaining monologues . . . penned talk rather than conversation." His readings of "The Cask of Amontillado," "Berenice," and "The Tell-Tale Heart" are especially good, while that of "The Fall of the House of Usher" is bound to be most controversial in its view of the narrator as a vapid, uncomprehending indecisive madman, a "shabby version of Hamlet," who is incapable of using words to convey thought" ("Poe's Closet Monologues," *Genre* 10:215–32). In the second essay, "The Fall of the House: A Reappraisal of Poe's Attitudes Toward Life and Death" (*SLJ* 9, ii:30–50), E. Miller Budick presents a formidable argument against two conflicting views of Poe's philosophy: (1) that his fiction is a burlesque of a suicidal cosmic insanity, or (2) that it embodies a philosophy of cosmic and personal self-destructiveness. Budick sees the self-destructive pattern in "MS. Found in a Bottle" as one which Poe rejects elsewhere. The narrator of that tale fatally embraces a destructive idealism which fails to take account of reason and the material world. In "A Descent Into the Maelström," on the other hand, the narrator rejects the abyss and returns to the creation which he has viewed with awe and wonder. In "The Oval Portrait" the narrator comes to see that life is preferable to art, as does the narrator of "The Fall of the House of Usher." Budick sees the latter as the hero of the tale, who escapes the physical and spiritual destruction of that worshipper of art and abstractions, Roderick Usher. This is a lucidly argued and challenging essay which takes a position opposite to that of Crossley and calls into question the views of G. R. Thompson on the one hand and Davidson, Wilbur, and Moldenhauer on the other.

Still another view of the narrator is taken by Barton St. Armand, who places the tale in the context of the history of ideas. For him the narrator is a follower of Archibald Alison's associationist theories who cannot understand why the landscape has such an oppressive effect upon him. Associationist theory maintains that the emotions conjured up by the landscape have their origin in the mind itself; but in this tale the landscape itself is sad, and produces a corresponding sadness in the mind of the narrator. The common-sense narrator resists the idea that the landscape has a soul, and he resists its power to terrorize his psyche. The tale may be seen, therefore, as a dramatic struggle between 18th-century Scottish Common-Sense theory and 19th century, Romantic, visionary speculation ("Poe's Landscape of the Soul: Association Theory and 'The Fall of the House of Usher,'" *MLS* 7:32–41).

Still another rewarding approach to "Usher" is that of Renata R. M. Wasserman, who comes at it through modern anthropologists' theories concerning the incest taboo and sees the actions of Roderick as a turning away of the self from the Other. In her view, the final catastrophe is a result of the disorder the Ushers brought about by their severing of ties with other human beings; only the narrator turns back to the world, away from the self ("The Self, the Mirror, the Other: 'The Fall of the House of Usher,'" *PoeS* 10:33–35). In a more conventional study of the tale, Walter Evans, in "'The Fall of the House of Usher' and Poe's Theory of the Tale" (*SSF* 14:137–44), finds that Poe's tale does not conform to his own theories of the short story in respect to the idea of combining incidents to establish a preconceived effect. "Usher" contains virtually no incidents, Evans points out; instead, it is a "lyric" story built on thematically patterned images. George B. von der Lippe in an interesting source study makes a convincing case that Poe modeled Usher on a conception of the character of E. T. A. Hoffmann he derived from three popular biographical sketches: Scott's "On the Supernatural in Fictitious Composition . . . ,"

Carlyle's description in *German Romance*, and Longfellow's in *Hyperion: A Romance*. A number of characteristics of Usher are paralleled in these accounts ("The Figure of E. T. A. Hoffmann as *Doppelgänger* to Poe's Roderick Usher," *MLN* 92:525–34).

The handful of other articles on the Gothic tales includes James Twitchell's "Poe's 'The Oval Portrait' and the Vampire Motif" (*SSF* 14:387–93), an attempt to see this tale as Poe's "most sophisticated variation on the vampire theme," a subgenre which includes "Berenice," "Morella," and "Ligeia." He sees the treatment of the motif in "The Oval Portrait" as more subtle, since the vampire-lover is transformed into the vampire-artist, whose art becomes life-consuming, a point similar to that made by Budick (above). Although others have attempted to make thematic sense out of the Roman Catholic elements in "The Cask of Amontillado" (see *ALS 1975*, pp. 48–49), John Clendenning goes too far in his dubious claim that Montresor is acting out the events leading up to the murder by making a grotesque mockery of the Holy Mass ("Anything Goes: Comic Aspects in 'The Cask of Amontillado,'" *Gerber Festschrift*, pp. 13–26). Clendenning is on surer ground when he looks at the tale operating on several ironic levels, including that involving the use of wines: he discovers much deliberate oenological misinformation and pretense which he says expose Fortunato and Montresor as comical impostors, thus making the tale both a tale of terror and a burlesque. *Poe Studies* continued its policy of printing translations of European Poe criticism with Donald G. Marshall's excellent translation and introduction to Roland Barthes' 1973 article, "Textual Analysis of a Tale by Edgar Poe," in which he applies his analytic methods to the first three paragraphs of "The Facts in the Case of M. Valdemar" (*PoeS* 10:1–12).

There were only two items on Dupin. LeRoy L. Panek ingeniously applies Huizinga's definition of play to the character of Dupin to help explain his character and behavior ("Play and Games: An Approach to Poe's Detective Tales," *PoeS* 10:39–41). Barbara Johnson, in "The Frame of Reference: Poe, Lacan, Derrida," (*YFS* 55/56: 457–505), is an am-*pli*-fication of Derrida's study of Lacan's seminar on Poe's "The Purloined Letter" (see *ALS 1976*, p. 42). As she points out, Derrida's reading is an "*act of analysis of the act of analysis.*" My efforts to "read" *her* article would thus raise this game to the fourth power, an opportunity I will resist, instead referring interested readers to the essay itself, which is included in a special double issue of *YFS* on literature and psychoanalysis called "The Question of Reading: Otherwise."

d. **The Narrative of Arthur Gordon Pym.** Recent French structuralist criticism of *Pym* by Ricardou, Lévy, Mourier, and Richard is beginning to make itself felt on this side of the Atlantic, while some are still working to unlock its mysteries in other ways. The first major American essay on *Pym* to follow the French models is John Carlos Rowe's "Writing and Truth in Poe's *The Narrative of Arthur Gordon Pym*" (*Glyph* 2:102–21). Investigating what he calls the metaliterary character of *Pym*, Rowe sees it as a work which questions the nature and possibility of literary form, and a work concerned explicitly with the problem of how one writes. His strategy is that of Derridean deconstruction, dismantling in order to reconstitute what is already inscribed. To achieve this he posits a "Mr. Poe," a character different from the historical Poe, who is intended to be the main writer of the text interpreting Pym's psychic experience in ways Pym himself cannot. Rowe's conception of the work as essentially about the text itself follows Lévy, who has seen it as a "voyage to the end of the page." For him the major theme of the work is the doubleness of writing itself, leading to ultimate uncertainty about the nature of truth. His most interesting metaphor is that of the text of the novel as a "psychic palimpsest, . . . the illusory 'depth' of which involves an inevitable encounter with the 'surface' of writing itself. His thought-provoking conclusion is that in this novel, as in *Eureka*, Poe's usual monism is denied by irreconcilable ambiguities and internal differences.

Daniel Wells, in "Engraved Within the Hills: Further Perspectives on the Ending of *Pym*" (*PoeS* 10:13–15), also makes use of the insights of Ricardou, Lévy, et al., especially their thoughts about the cryptic ending. Wells sees in the reproductions of those mysterious chasms "Poe" spelled backwards. Although he does not, as he claims, provide "the first strong proof that the elements of involution in the text are intentional," he does cite some interesting examples of the theme of reversal in the story. He also offers plausible evidence for considering the white-shrouded figure as a symbol of the author's creative imagination.

William C. Spengemann uses more conventional literary and historical methods to arrive at conclusions similar to those of Rowe. In a chapter of his book, *The Adventurous Muse*, a study of the relation between travel writing and American fiction, he discusses what he considers the central place of *Pym* in the development of the American novel ("The Adventurous Muse: 'The Algerine Captive' and 'Arthur Gordon Pym,'" pp. 119–50). Spengemann believes that by going against the conventions of the domestic romance and exploiting the possibilities of such popular literary materials as the gothic, travel-writing, and the hoax, Poe upset the normal expectations of his readers and carried them into unknown territory. Since *Pym* points to no world of meaning beyond itself, the reader is carried into a different order of being—toward a wholly imagined destination with no moral order which reflects only the disordered psyche of the narrator. This kind of symbolic psychological journey is best rendered through a voyage narrative, and Spengemann sees *Pym* therefore as an important precursor of other major American voyage narratives, *Moby-Dick*, *Huckleberry Finn*, and *The Ambassadors*, in each of which the central character is heading toward the unknown.

Still another approach is the "mythic," which Evelyn J. Hinz and John J. Teunissen use boldly. They see Pym as the secular representative of a failed scientific and materialistic culture who cannot understand and accept the symbols and values of a primitive culture. In "Poe, Pym, and Primitivism" (*SSF* 14: 13–20), they put together a well-argued, though far-out, case to show that primitivism is Poe's major concern. Using James Baird's 1956 study of primitivism in *Moby-Dick* as a guide, they attempt to show how Pym's failure to respond to such "obvious" religious symbolism as the "Eucharistic banquet" of cannibalism renders him, in Poe's view, incapable of appreciating the values of another culture, i.e., that of the Tsalalians. The tale is therefore about an imaginative journey "into the 'south' of the *soul* where the pure archetypes exist and manifest themselves in a new and commanding symbolism." I was put off by the idea that AGP suggests AGAPE; nevertheless, I found this a fascinating article well worth reading.

iii. Poetry and Criticism

One of the best articles of the year is Robert D. Jacobs's close study of the early poems and Poe's revisions of them, a chronicle of the development of Poe's poetic technique through the first three books of verse, and an examination of the revisions, variants, and borrowings which T. O. Mabbott recorded in his edition ("The Self and the World: Poe's Early Poems," *GaR* 31:638–68). Jacobs sees Poe moving away from raw and youthful Byronic self-expression toward a refinement of technique which allowed him to handle his feelings and ideas with greater artistic control and objectivity. He studies the development of a "strategy of indirection," which eventually allowed Poe to avoid too-explicit self-revelation and raw statement of feeling of the kind that occurs in "Song," "Dreams," and other early poems. He assumes that if Poe left an 1827 poem unprinted in a subsequent edition he was dissatisfied with it (five of the ten were not reprinted); he also assumes that continuing revisions and reprintings suggest both a continuing interest in the themes of the poem and a growing ability to deal with them in a more "objective" way. By 1831, Jacobs says, Poe had developed a mature idiom, "which uses rhetorical strategies to create a distance between the self that suffers and the self that tells," or what we would call aesthetic distance. Jacobs uses close readings of individual poems, a very profitable study of revisions and reprintings, and graciously acknowledged insights of David Halliburton to give us some new ways of thinking about what Poe was trying to accomplish in his early poetry.

In another of his Jungian analyses of Poe's work (see *ALS 1975*, p. 46) Martin Bickman sees parallels between the illuminist traditions of the Neoplatonists and the paradigm of individuation in Jungian psychology, in which consciousness moves from primordial unity to duality and ultimately toward reintegration of the self and the ego. In analyzing Poe's "To Helen" and Whitman's "Chanting the Square Deific" he sees the former as a poem in which Helen becomes the focal symbol for the meeting of the conscious and the unconscious ("Occult Traditions and American Romanticism: A Jungian Perspective," *Literature and the Occult*, pp. 1–11).

Burton Pollin studies in detail what he concludes to be a Poe coinage, the word "autorial," which Poe used in eight separate instances between 1841 and 1848. Noting that it appeared neither in other writers' works nor in dictionaries of Poe's (or virtually any other) time, Pollin suggests that Poe critics should use the word anyway, since Poe found it useful ("The Word 'Autorial' in Poe's Criticism: History and Implications," *PoeS* 10:15–18).

Kent Ljungquist, in "Poe's 'The Island of the Fay': The Passing of Fairyland" (*SSF* 14:265–71), makes some telling points about Poe's attitude toward the use of fairies and fairyland in both poetry and prose. He takes the interesting approach of looking at the poem "Fairy-Land," the sketch "The Island of the Fay," and the review of Joseph Rodman Drake's *The Culprit Fay and Other Poems* and finds that Poe shows an awareness in all three works of the hazards of the unbridled imagination. Poe's attack on Drake's methods in *The Culprit Fay* suggests that "The Island of Fay" contains elements of parody and ironic treatment of literary conventions found in romantic nature poetry. Ljungquist's argument is based on sound scholarship and is largely convincing; however, he is less plausible when dealing in too short a space with the connection between this sketch and "Sonnet–To Science." His reading of this poem slights the connections Poe made between it and "Al Aaraaf."

In "Poe's Criticism: The Circular Pursuit" (*CentR* 21:140–49), John A. Hodgson wrestles with the contradictions between Poe's theories of beauty as they are expressed in his essays and criticism. In the criticism the pursuit of beauty is the path to pure poetry, while the characters in the poems who pursue beauty are perverse or mentally deranged. Hodgson attempts to explain this contradiction by showing how Poe shifts his various abstractions, passion, duty, truth, and beauty, and how passion in this world is bad taste, since it is desire of worldly, rather than supernal, beauty. An interesting point is that Poe's lectures and essays are really perverse versions of the poetics of his own gothic protagonists.

State University of New York at Albany

4. Melville

Hershel Parker

In 1973 Jay Leyda protested against the dreariness of most recent criticism and the neglect of biographical research: "With so much left to be known, how can we allow the present state of our knowledge to freeze and become permanently acceptable? Perhaps we have become too content with the biographical materials already at our disposal." Leyda was right: his own *Melville Log* had come to seem so monumental that a belated New Critical generation could not search behind it. Now, only a few years later, all hell is breaking loose in Melville biography again. Last year we had the Kring-Carey discoveries on the marital crisis of 1867, painful validation of some of the rumors Henry A. Murray had picked up as early as the 1920s. Now there are new riches, not the quantitative garnering of the 1940s, which will hardly be repeated, but a series of newly found documents which will allow us to make greater sense of Melville's life and writings. The year's criticism was pretty dreary, still, and no one managed to combine scholarship and criticism meaningfully, but the late 1970s are turning out to be a great time to be a Melvillean.

i. Biographical Studies

After Amy Puett Emmers's "Melville's Closet Skeleton: A New Letter about the Illegitimacy Incident in *Pierre*" (*SAR* 1977, pp. 339–43), we can be less skeptical toward autobiographical interpretations of *Pierre*. The only thing wrong with the article is the title, for what Emmers has found is a letter from Melville's Uncle Thomas to Lemuel Shaw about two women who turned up in Boston between January and September 1832, with claims against Allan Melvill's share of old Thomas Melvill's estate. Emmers's best guess is that "Mrs. B." was once Allan's mistress and that "Mrs. A. M. A." was his daughter, and it's hard to think of a plausible, mundane explanation. Even allowing full measure to Melville's Uncle Thomas's habitual histrionics, this is a remarkably incriminating letter. But if Emmers's conclusion is right, we have a worse problem than ever. Assuming that Herman Melville learned such a dark secret somehow, why would he have worked it into the plot of *Pierre*, in which all kinds of instantly recognizable family paraphernalia figured? What would he have wanted his family to think, assuming that he supposed anyone else who knew was still alive? As Melville's Uncle Peter said, "Oh Herman, Herman, Herman, truly thou art an 'Ambiguity.'"

The "Two New Melville Letters" (*AL* 49:418–21) which Patricia Barber has found are anguishingly unambiguous proof that Melville's financial plight between 1851 and 1856 was desperate. The "T. D. S." long known to have loaned Melville $2,050 in 1851 is named as T. D. Stewart; in May 1856, he was pressing for full payment plus interest. (Frederick J. and Joyce Deveau Kennedy in a 1978 article show that Stewart was an old friend from Lansingburgh.) The new letters (both addressed to Lemuel Shaw) have profound significance for biography, and for criticism of Melville's writings of 1851–56, most obviously "The Story of China Aster," which contains far more than the mere "oblique allusion" to the T. D. S. loan I speculated about in the Norton *Confidence-Man* (1971). Now we know for sure what some scholars like Harrison Hayford have suspected all along, that the nest egg Melville supposedly had in the bank was a face-saving fiction.

Other biographical studies are not so astonishing, but at this stage every new fact is of potential value to someone, if not always to the discoverer. The first third of T. Walter Herbert, Jr.'s *"Moby-Dick" and Calvinism: A World Dismantled* (New Brunswick: Rutgers Univ. Press) is a much-needed supplement and occasional corrective to one important aspect of the more comprehensive account of Melville's childhood in William H. Gilman's *Melville's Early Life and "Redburn."* Herbert is about the first since Alice P. Kenney to work with the Gansevoort-Lansing Collection, and he also records the actual words used in Dutch Reform ceremonies that Melville's parents participated in and actual words used in sermons or other talks by ministers they knew in New York and Albany or Melville's Unitarian grandparents knew in Boston. Carmella M. Vessella in "Melville on Christmas Day, 1840" (*AL* 49:107–8) shows that Melville's Shipping Paper for his voyage as a "Green Hand" on the *Acushnet* was signed in Fairhaven on 25 December 1840; by the next day Melville was in

New Bedford, where he signed the Seaman's Protection Papers. The same week is studied in Curtis Dahl's "Of Foul Weather and Bulkingtons" (*Extracts* 30:10–11), new evidence that the New Bedford weather on 27 December was as blustery as the weather when Ishmael arrives in New Bedford and that the *Grampus* of *Moby-Dick* may have been suggested by the *Charles*, which sent her crew ashore in New Bedford on 26 December after a three-years' voyage.

Frederick J. Kennedy and Joyce Deveau Kennedy have rummaged to good effect through the Boston Public Library and the Massachusetts Historical Society, and now offer "Additions to *The Melville Log*" (*Extracts* 31:4–8). This notable collection of new documents runs from 1847 through 1853. Frederick J. Kennedy also published two other extremely interesting articles, "Herman Melville's Lecture in Montreal" (*NEQ* 50:125–37), a valuable supplement to Merton M. Sealts, Jr.'s account of the 1857–58 season in *Melville as Lecturer* (1957), and "Dr. Samuel Arthur Jones and Herman Melville" (*Extracts* 32:3–7), which presents a letter that Dr. Jones (best remembered as an early Thoreauvean) wrote to Archibald MacMechan on 7 January 1900, after receiving a copy of MacMechan's 1899 article on *Moby-Dick*. Jones describes Melville's outward appearance in his last years and wryly boasts about his collection of Melville first editions once owned by Melville himself. (Jones's claim was based on the bookseller's description. G. Thomas Tanselle is investigating the matter, but now it is known that some of the books, at least, had belonged to Allan Melville, and that preserved in the *Moby-Dick* is the only known early form of the American title-page, with *The Whale* as the title.)

Edwin S. Shneidman's "Some Psychological Reflections on the Death of Malcolm Melville" (*Suicide and Life-Threatening Behavior* 6 [1976]:231–42) was read to the Melville Society in San Francisco on 28 December 1975. Shneidman includes an account of the psychological autopsy performed on Malcolm at a meeting of the Los Angeles Suicide Prevention Center in which, with Henry A. Murray in attendance, Leon Howard assumed the role of the boy's uncle.

This is a good place to correct an old oversight by mentioning Henry A. Murray's "Dead to the World: The Passions of Herman Melville" in *Essays in Self-Destruction*, ed. Edwin S. Shneidman (New York: Science House, 1967), pp. 7–29. There is nothing outdated in what Murray calls his "crude macro survey of Melville's whole works and a few micro analyses," restricted to "the four negative affects and the one action which the SPC [Suicide Prevention Center] had found to be correlated with suicide in neuropsychiatric subjects." Recent biographical discoveries are enriching the way we read all of Murray's and Shneidman's essays on Melville.

ii. Melville's Reading

In "Melville and Wordsworth" (*AL* 49:338–51) Thomas F. Heffernan reports a major discovery, Melville's copy of *The Complete Poetical Works of William Wordsworth* (1839), and declares that from "Melville's markings and annotations, it is possible not only to judge his response to Wordsworth but to reach some conclusions about his critical thinking in general, his private feelings, and his knowledge of several other authors." Possible, indeed, for Heffernan has achieved those diverse feats in this fine, mature study. In a smaller but excellent bit of detective work, "The Translation of Pierre Bayle's *An Historical and Critical Dictionary* Owned by Melville" (*PBSA* 71:347–51), James Duban shows that Melville almost surely used the 1710 edition. Stanton Garner in "Melville and Thomas Campbell: The 'Deadly Space Between'" (*ELN* 14:289–90) identifies Campbell's "Battle of the Baltic" as the source of an elusive reference in *Billy Budd.* Margaret Wiley Marshall has a wonderful story to tell in "A Footnote to *Billy Budd*" (*Extracts* 30:1–3). She thinks her late husband, Roderick Marshall, ordered a copy of an Indian drama, *Arichandra, The Martyr of Truth* in an English translation (London, 1863) because he had the idea that Melville had used it in *Billy Budd.* At any rate, the copy Marshall received was the one Melville himself had purchased in 1871. The drama may or may not be a source for *Billy Budd,* but one more book has been added to those known to have been in Melville's library. Julian Markels's "Melville's Markings in Shakespeare's Plays" (*AL* 49:34–48) attempts to exhibit the range and variety of those markings "more fully than has yet been done," to show that Melville was not "inspired chiefly by Shakespeare's intimations of a godless or demonic universe," and to describe "the whole set of markings taken as an aggregate." This is a handy selection of Melville's markings, but anyone seriously working on the topic will want to go to Walker Cowen's 1965 Harvard dissertation on *Melville's Marginalia* (which

Markels does not mention), then to the actual volumes in the Houghton.

iii. Reputation

Daniel A. Wells's "A Checklist of Melville Allusions in Duyckinck's *Literary World*: A Supplement to the Mailloux-Parker *Checklist*" (*Extracts* 29:14–17) is extremely welcome, although the subtitle may suggest that Wells is offering reviews, not other allusions. The 3 January 1852 item, which was news to me, is of considerable biographical interest, since at its writing Melville's friendship with Evert A. Duyckinck was plainly unimpaired. (Wells does not point out that the reference to the thermometer is a private joke: Melville had received one from Duyckinck the previous August as a bread-and-butter gift.) Wells also performed the same useful service with two other magazines, as reported in "Melville Allusions in *The Southern Literary Messenger*" (*Extracts* 31:13) and "Melville Allusions in *The American Whig Review*" (*Extracts* 32:9–10).

Supplements to the Mailloux-Parker *Checklist of Melville Reviews* are abundant. George Monteiro (predictably) has squinted at more microfilm and inhaled more dust from crumbling newspapers than anyone else, as is proved by his "*Clarel* in the *Catholic World*" (*Extracts* 30:11); "More on Herman Melville in the 1890s" (*Extracts* 30:12–14); "An Unnoticed Contemporary Review of *Battle-Pieces*" (*Extracts* 31:11–12); and "'Not a Novel . . . a Most Astounding Epic': *Moby-Dick* in 1900" (*Extracts* 32:9). Pursuing a hunch of Steven J. Mailloux's, Johannes D. Bergmann brings new information to a much-discussed topic, "The New York *Morning News* and *Typee*" (*Extracts* 31:1–4). Since the *Checklist* has been noted in *American Litterature,* referees for that journal should consult it for articles such as Robert J. Scholnick's "Politics and Poetics: The Reception of Melville's *Battle-Pieces and Aspects of the War*" (*AL* 49:422–30), a presentation of two reviews, one of which is listed in the *Checklist.* Barton Levi St. Armand offers a small discovery: "Curtis's 'Bartleby': An Unrecorded Melville Reference" (*PBSA* 71:219–20), "Curtis" being G. W. Curtis.

While not advancing strong claims for Melville's influence, Joyce Sparer Adler explores affinities between him and Wilson Harris (the novelist born in British Guiana and now living in England) in her wide-ranging "Melville and Harris: Poetic Imaginations Related in their Response to the Modern World," in *Commonwealth Literature and the Modern World*, edited by Hena Maes-Jelinek (Brussels: Didier, 1975), pp. 33–41. A helpful guide to a book not previously mentioned in *ALS* is A. Rodríguez-Seda's review (*CRCL* 4:112–14) of José de Onís's *Melville y el mundo hispánico* (Río Piedras: Editorial Universitaria, 1974).

iv. General

Jonathan Katz's *Gay American History* contains sections on various American writers, including Melville. Katz's reliance on others leads him into factual blunders, and he ignores larger literary contexts. Now we need to move beyond the Old MacDonald school of homosexual inquiry (here a passage, there a passage) and take a broad view of Melville's knowledge of human sexuality—at least as broad as that taken by Walter E. Bezanson in his edition of *Clarel* and more recently by Nina Baym (*TSLL* 16:315–28). But Katz's book, Melville aside, is a fascinating, enlightening compilation.

Robert Waite's "Melville's *Memento Mori*" (*SAF* 5:187–97) is a pleasantly written although unenergetic survey of some (not all) of Melville's emblematic reminders of mortality. Paul McCarthy takes on an unusual topic in "Melville's Families: Facts, Figures, and Fates" (*SDR* 15:79–93). The niceties of Melville's characterizations sometimes become blurred in this survey, but it is good to have a pragmatic look at families in Melville's works (excluding the poems) focused on the financial situations, the number and nature of parents (is one parent absent? is one parent dominant?), relations within the family, and external circumstances. Hyland Packard's "*Mardi*: The Role of Hyperbole in Melville's Search for Expression" (*AL* 49:241–53) strikes me as a lumping of disparate kinds of evidence in an attempt to prove the obvious, that Melville's third book was "the product of an age of hyperbolic expression." In chapter 20 of this volume Michael J. Hoffman is reviewing Michael T. Gilmore's *The Middle Way*, so I will merely say that I found the discussions of "Puritanism and Ideology" in *Moby-Dick*, *Israel Potter*, "Benito Cereno," and *Billy Budd* dully written and unenlightening; by contrast, the intellectual density of Herbert's book on a related topic (see sections i and v) is much greater. Hoffman is also reviewing William C. Spengemann's *The Adventurous Muse*, one chapter of which deals with *Typee, Moby-Dick*, and *Pierre* in self-indulgent fashion, worrying about the contradictory stances of hero and narrator in *Typee* without considering what is known about the process of composition, making a rigid distinction between the "narrator" of *Moby-Dick* and Ishmael as if there were not already a sometimes brilliant body of writing on the topic, and repeating commonplaces about *Pierre*.

The most important review of the year, Kenneth Dauber's "Criticism of American Literature" (*Diacritics* 8:55–66) places Harry B. Henderson, III's *Versions of the Past* (1974), Warwick Wadlington's *The Confidence Game in American Literature* (1975), and Richard H. Brodhead's *Hawthorne, Melville, and the Novel* (1976) in the context of post-phenomenological criticism in the United States. I recommend Dauber as a corrective to my sometimes skeptical comments about these critics. Two pre-1977 essays need to be mentioned. Nathalia Wright's "Herman Melville and the Muse of Italy" (*ItalAm* 1[1975]:169–84) is valuable especially as an introduction to Melville's late preoccupation with aesthetics. *Weapons of Criticism: Marxism in America and the Literary Tradition*, edited by Norman Rudich (Palo Alto: Ramparts Press, 1976), pp. 287–309, contains H. Bruce Franklin's "Herman Melville: Artist of the Worker's World," a rapid survey of Melville (in his prose writings) as "an artist whose creative imagination was forged in the furnace of proletarian experience, an artist who saw the world of nineteenth-century U.S. society and its commercial empire through the eyes of a class-conscious worker." Franklin passionately insists that "the Melville that is taught is a Melville redesigned in the image of the professors." I doubt that it's Melville's economic views that prevent most academicians from dealing adequately with him, but Franklin is near a truth: think how long it's been since you read a piece of academic writing which reminded you of the grandeur that drew you to Melville in the first place.

v. Moby-Dick

This year there was little criticism of any value but some excellent scholarship. Willard Thorp long ago began exploring Melville's use of the *Penny Cyclopaedia*, and more recently Harrison Hayford found that Melville had made use of the article on "Whales" in writing *Moby-Dick*. Now Kendra H. Gaines pursues that discovery in "A Consideration of an Additional Source for Melville's *Moby-Dick*" (*Extracts* 29:6–12), important for the evidence that from the outset of his work on the whaling book Melville may have had access to quotations from or digests of Thomas Beale and other cetological writers even before he gained (or regained) access to actual books by Beale and the others. The implications for theories about two or three or four *Moby-Dicks* are obvious. Robert Milder's "The Composition of *Moby-Dick*: A Review and a Prospect" (*ESQ* 23:203–16), a rebuttal to James Barbour's Foerster Prize article (*AL* 47:343–60), is a refreshingly cautious, undoctrinaire study of what will continue to be a much-debated topic. I still feel that no one has read the 1 May 1850 letter to Dana with full sense of the edginess in the friendship and with full attention to the rhetorical aim (what about the "poetry" and the "fancy" Melville has to warn against?), and I don't think Milder or anyone else has proved that there ever was a "pre-philosophical" form of *Moby-Dick*, but Milder's essay deserves careful pondering.

Like other reviewers (compare what Nathalia Wright says in *Extracts* 32:8 and what Edgar Dryden says in *NEQ* 51:134–36), I think T. Walter Herbert, Jr.'s *"Moby-Dick" and Calvinism* (see section i) is much more valuable for its biographical opening than its application of Calvinistic ideas to Melville's book. There's tunnel-vision in Herbert's concentration on Calvinistic tenets to the exclusion of literature, aesthetics, philosophy, and, in fact, everything else. There's no fun left in the *Moby-Dick* that Herbert reads, and no literary masterpiece. But I'm glad someone who thoroughly knows the historical development of American Calvinism has written this book so that we can weigh it against more comprehensive readings. For a good sense of Herbert's limited but real value, compare his reading of "The Chart" (pp. 145–46) with Paul Brodtkorb, Jr.'s in *Ishmael's White World* (1965) or Thomas Woodson's (*ELH* 33[1966]:351–69), both of which are in *"Moby-Dick" as Doubloon*. (One serious misreading: in Evert A. Duyckinck's letter to his brother [*The Melville Log*, p. 273] the reference to Melville's being a representative of the old Arminius is, I'd say, just a pun on the name of a ship, the *Hermann*, which was to carry the letter, not an indication that Melville held theologically to Arminianism.)

Carole Fabricant's "*Tristram Shandy* and *Moby-Dick*: A Cock and Bull Story and a Tale of a Tub" (*JNT* 7:57–69) is a very sensible treatment of an old topic, a model for how to make suggestive comparisons without being reductive. Fabricant attempts "to suggest the more general significance of Sterne's subtle, often intangible yet pervasive presence in *Moby-Dick*" rather than making a case for specific borrowings. She concludes that the two books "embody similar visions, in each case through an 'omniscient' narrator who dramatizes the limits of all men's knowledge including his own, and who employs consummate artistry in order to deny the possibility of art as a finished and perfected creation."

Other pieces are slighter. Stephen A. Black's "On Reading Psychoanalytically" (*CE* 39:267–74) has a less than original hypothesis, "that we regard literary meaning as inhering in the relationship which occurs between a reader and a literary work," but the comments on teaching *Moby-Dick* are interesting. Carey H. Kirk in "*Moby-Dick*: The Challenge of Response" (*PLL* 13:383–90) is likewise unoriginal in noting that Ishmael's attempt to comprehend the painting at the Spouter Inn "forecasts the kind of experience Melville's audience will have trying to hit upon the novel's meaning," but he is the first to relate Ishmael's response to the painting to "the progressive interaction between literature and reader described by Stanley Fish"! Dr. Jerome M. Schneck's "Hypnagogic Hallucinations: Herman Melville's *Moby Dick*" (*N.Y. State Jour. of Med.* 77:2145–47) is too cursory a look at Ishmael's dream in the Spouter Inn as an "illustration of a psychiatric theme playing an important role in classic literature." John Harmon McElroy's "The Dating of the Action in *Moby Dick*" (*PLL* 13:420–23) reminds us that Ishmael's voyage on the *Pequod* most likely took place between the election of 1840 and the Kabul Massacre of 1842, but I confess to being more comfortable with Ishmael's injunction: "Some years ago—never mind how long precisely."

A treat for Rockwell Kent buffs is Dan Burne Jones's "*Moby-Dick*: The Un-used Kent Illustrations" (*Extracts* 30:4–9), which reviews the history of Kent's illustrations for the Lakeside Press edition and reproduces nine illustrations which got as far as engraver's proofs but not into the published volumes. Michael T. Gilmore's *Twentieth Century Interpretations of "Moby-Dick"* (Englewood Cliffs: Prentice-Hall) has 115 pages of selections, most of them brief excerpts. Like any such compendium, it will be useful in directing some readers to the full essays.

vi. Pierre

Two articles deal with influences on *Pierre* and one with the possible influence *of Pierre.* In "The Spenserian Maze of Melville's *Pierre*" (*ESQ* 23:217–25) James Duban musters some uncompelling comparisons but does not come close to showing that *Pierre* "features deliberate and meaningful variations on Book One of *The Faerie Queene.*" Helen A. Hauser's "Spinozan Philosophy in *Pierre*" (*AL* 49:49–56) evades the basic research her topic calls for. Undoubtedly, Melville was interested in Spinoza, but precisely what information about the philosopher was available to Melville in encyclopaedias, other books, magazines, and newspapers? In "*Pierre's* Progeny: O'Neill and the Melville Revival" (*ESC* 3:103–17) Joyce Deveau Kennedy assembles what can be proven about Eugene O'Neill's knowledge of Melville and speculates inconclusively about the possible influence of *Pierre* on *Mourning Becomes Electra.* Kennedy shows that O'Neill was in spirit so close to some aspects of Melville that he *ought* to have read *Pierre* and might well have found it fascinating if he had. My own fantasy is that William Faulkner would have loved the book if he had read it; dammit, he probably didn't.

Hershel Parker's "Contract: *Pierre*, by Herman Melville" (*Proof* 5:27–44) supplements his 1976 study (*SNNTS* 8:7–23) with photographic reproductions (Allan Melville's surviving notes for the contract, his 21 January 1852 letter to the Harpers about the increased size of the manuscript, and Herman Melville's copy of the contract) and with detailed comparison of the *Pierre* contract to the earlier Harper contracts. Parker's judgment is that Melville must have felt the contract was insultingly punitive and that the humiliation of having to accept its terms directly and adversely affected the completion of the manuscript.

vii. The Stories

There are two books, Marvin Fisher's *Going Under: Melville's Short Fiction and the American 1850s* (Baton Rouge: La. State Univ. Press) and William B. Dillingham's *Melville's Short Fiction, 1853–1856*

(Athens: Univ. of Ga. Press). Fisher's book has appeared piecemeal over the last decade and more, and holds no surprises. Dillingham's book, which appeared later in the year than Fisher's, takes Fisher into account all along by referring to his earlier articles; none of Dillingham's own book had appeared previously, so Fisher's index has no mention of Dillingham. Fisher pursues several themes which now appear obvious partly because of his own long-sustained public discussion of them: "(1) innocence and experience; (2) contrasts between America and Europe; (3) freedom and servitude, and class and caste in American society; (4) the condition of Christianity; (5) the interrelatedness of political community, spiritual communion, and artistic communication; (6) the dilemma of the artist in America; and (7) irreconcilable differences and irrepressible conflicts in American attitudes and values." Dillingham describes the chapters of his much longer book as "directed chiefly at uncovering submerged characterizations," since the short stories "are a gallery of people, and it is through their characterization that Melville's two motives—concealment and artistic experimentation—fuse into his greatest achievement." The book's ruling premise (that it "has not been generally recognized" that in his short stories Melville carried the "fine art of concealment" even further than in *Moby-Dick* and *Pierre* and earlier works) strikes me as simply untrue. Precisely that notion is the cornerstone of modern scholarship and criticism, from Sealts, Leyda, and Elizabeth S. Foster on down to its repetition as a truism in Parker's foreword to the Norton *Confidence-Man* (1971). I suspect that this claim for novelty in Dillingham's premise is a clue to the pervasive weakness in both books—the need to find at least a slightly new twist in writing about over-analyzed (if sometimes poorly analyzed) stories.

These two books will prove to be as unneeded as R. Bruce Bickley, Jr.'s *The Method of Melville's Short Fiction* (1975), although Dillingham's has the value of containing a near-comprehensive listing of earlier critical opinion in his footnotes. Both books are either too late or too early. A decade ago an alternative to Richard Harter Fogle's *Melville's Shorter Tales* (1960) would have been welcome. Now, too much is known to go on writing books like Fogle's. A genuine contribution can still be made by strenuously exploring what Fisher promises in his subtitle: the relation of the stories to "the American 1850s"—and the European 1850s. A genuine contribution can still be made by painstakingly dating—and redating—the composition and submission of the stories. Evidence for such a study has been available for years, but no one has made wise use of it. (I write with the advantage of having read in manuscript Merton M. Sealts, Jr.'s remarkable account of the chronology of the composition, submission, and publication of the tales in the Historical Note to his Northwestern-Newberry volume, *The Piazza Tales and Other Prose Pieces, 1839–1860.*) And new documentary evidence, profoundly relevant to Melville's activities and states of mind in the 1850s, has appeared just too late for Fisher and Dillingham to take it into account. After Sealts's volume appears and after we have learned more about the relationships between Melville's life and the historical contexts, somebody can surprise us with a blockbuster of a book on the stories, and on their relationship to the longer works of the early 1850s and Melville's other writings.

There were a few shorter pieces. To *The Authority of Experience: Essays in Feminist Criticism*, edited by Arlyn Diamond and Lee R. Edwards (Amherst: Univ. of Mass. Press), pp. 212–23, 298–300, Patricia Barber contributed the consciousness-raising "What if Bartleby Were a Woman?" She concludes that by "imagining the story of Miss Bartleby, we realize that the story of the lawyer and Bartleby—for all its oddity, dry humor, and stuffy rhetoric—is essentially a love story, a story about a man who is confined in an office setting that forbids intimacy and who comes to love a person he cannot save." John Franzosa's "Darwin and Melville: Why a Tortoise?" (*AI* 33[1976]:361–79) is a disquisition upon the Englishness of Charles Darwin *vs.* the Americanness of Melville as supposedly revealed by a paragraph by each man on the Galapagos tortoises. I found the article exhilarating, partly because it sometimes reads like a parody of psychoanalytical criticism. In "The Homer of the Pacific: Melville's Art and the Ambiguities of Judging Evil" (*Michigan Law Review* 75:823–44) Lee C. Bollinger uses "Benito Cereno" as lead-in to a discussion of three recent books on judicial injustice and consequent judicial posing. (See section x. for one of the three, Robert Cover's *Justice Accused.*) Helmbrecht Breinig's "Symbol, Satire, and the Will to Communicate in Melville's 'The Apple-Tree Table'" (*AmS* 22:269–85) is an attempt, probably overzealous, to read the story as a retort to the "Conclusion" of *Walden.* Nancy Roundy's "Fancies, Reflections, and Things: The Imagination as Perception in 'The Piazza'" (*CLAJ* 20:

539–46) sensibly treats the piece as "a literary manifesto, exploring both epistemology and art."

viii. The Confidence-Man

Two collaborative essays are excellent. Hans-Joachim Lang and Benjamin Lease in "Melville's Cosmopolitan: Bayard Taylor in *The Confidence-Man*" (*AmS* 22:286–89) show that Melville's description of the last avatar of the Confidence Man may well owe much to contemporary writings by Bayard Taylor and engravings of him in costume. Lang and Lease quote Evert A. Duyckinck's record of what Melville said about Taylor a few months after the manuscript of *The Confidence-Man* was completed, and I would add in support that without exception the topics of Melville's conversation which Duyckinck recorded on that occasion have close relationship to topics in *The Confidence-Man.* The second collaboration is Robert Sattelmeyer and James Barbour's "A Possible Source and Model for 'The Story of China Aster' in Melville's *The Confidence-Man*" (*AL* 48: 577–83). The authors do not claim to have found an undeniable source, but they richly add to our sense of how the book works. Like Johannes D. Bergmann's recent discovery of a possible source for "Bartleby" (*AL* 47:432–36), this piece is presented with a sure sense of just how far evidence should be pushed. But unlike most writing on Melville this year, the Sattelmeyer and Barbour essay is written in genuine English prose which reminds me of how much good academic prose has been devoted to Melville over the years—Leon Howard's, for instance, or Elizabeth S. Foster's, or Walter E. Bezanson's, or Harrison Hayford's.

Alexander C. Kern's "Melville's *The Confidence-Man*: A Structure of Satire" in *Gerber Festschrift*, pp. 27–41, advances a commonplace. Elizabeth S. Foster understood quite well that the book was satiric, and even understood what was being satirized. Back to her introduction and explanatory notes to *The Confidence-Man*, everybody!

ix. Poetry

There is a book left over from last year, Ferdinand Schunck's *Das lyrische Werk Herman Melvilles* (Bonn: Bouvier, 1976), a paperback printing of a recent dissertation. It is not based on original research among the manuscripts at the Houghton, and my best guess is that readers of English will not profit from it, although it should be helpful in introducing Melville's poetry to readers of German (at least those with enough English to follow the quotations from the poems, which Schunck does not translate).

x. *Billy Budd, Sailor*

Two routine essays were probably written before the three important essays appeared last year (see *ALS 1976*, pp. 57–59): Walter L. Reed's "The Measured Forms of Captain Vere" (*MFS* 23:227–35), a look at the "pervasive parallelism in *Billy Budd* between the forms of art and the forms of military law," and Marlene Longenecker's "Captain Vere and the Form of Truth" (*SSF* 14:337–43), a look at the pervasive parallelism in *Billy Budd* between the forms of art and the forms of "moral and political" law. A third essay, Nathaniel M. Floyd's "*Billy Budd*: A Psychological Autopsy" (*AI* 34:28–49) really should not have italics in the title, for it is a psychological autopsy of the title character, using "a single respectable if not unimpeachable source—Herman Melville—who has provided us with 'An inside narrative,' the closest thing to an eyewitness account as we have." Like Murray's and Shneidman's similar work (see Section i) this is a sensitive, perturbing study, untinged by the glib flippancy that pervades some of the writing in *American Imago* by literary critics with only amateur standing in psychiatry and only a commercial interest in writing on Melville.

Finally, there were two pieces of impassioned advocacy. Marvin Mandell's "Martyrs or Murderers? A Defense of Innocence" (*MQ* 18:131–43) is a vehement rebuttal to Rollo May's treatment of Billy Budd and Allison Krause in *Power and Innocence* (*ALS 1972*, p. 55). Robert M. Cover's *Justice Accused: Antislavery and the Judicial Process* (New Haven: Yale Univ. Press, 1975), to which I was led by the Bollinger article discussed in section vii, in the "Prelude: Of Creon and Captain Vere" (pp. 1–7) and elsewhere argues that Lemuel Shaw was the real-life source for Vere's "choice between the demands of role and the voice of conscience." The dispassionate truth is that no one has yet come close to identifying what Shaw meant to Melville over many decades. We would learn a great deal about that relationship if a researcher as competent as T. Walter Herbert, Jr., would give us an economic history of the Melvilles, Gansevoorts, and Shaws.

University of Southern California

5. Whitman and Dickinson

Willis J. Buckingham

Though it produced no full-length critical studies of either poet, and no books at all on Dickinson, the year reflects little real dimunition of scholarly interest in the two writers. In both cases 1977 might better be understood as a period of reassessment. On the whole, readers of Whitman seem to be quietly searching for firmer ground: the gathering of documents has replaced psychobiography, and intuitive, holistic responses to the poetry have given way to more exacting discussions of structure, form, and historical context. Dickinson specialists, on the other hand, are somewhat cautiously probing for new positions from which to estimate their famously elusive subject. Particularly notable this year are two groups, those who wish to better understand ways in which the poet expresses 19th-century preoccupations, and those who prefer more subjective, conceptualist approaches to the poetry. Among the latter, phenomenologists and Jungians have almost entirely gained the field.

i. Whitman

***a.* Bibliography, Editing.** In the decade since Edwin Haviland Miller completed his admirable five-volume edition of Whitman's correspondence, enough new letters and notes have surfaced to warrant an additional volume, *Walt Whitman: The Correspondence*, Volume 6: A Supplement with a Composite Index (New York: N.Y. Univ. Press). Among the 90-odd items gathered here is the earliest extant letter (1841) and others from the 1880s which add to our knowledge of Whitman's publishing activities. Of special interest is one letter in which Whitman remarks that the first edition of *Leaves of Grass* had a press run of only 800 copies, rather than the figure of a thousand he is supposed to have given on other occasions. Though most of these letters are brief and rather mundane, Miller himself provides valuable new material in his "Introduction" (pp. xi–xxii), a detailed study of the poet's income, 1876–92. Drawing resourcefully on a variety of published and unpublished documents, Miller shows that Whitman's average earnings during those years was about twelve hundred dollars. "This was not a large sum," Miller says, "but in an era when one could buy a two-story house for $1,750.00, it was not small." As in previous volumes of the letters, Volume 6 provides inventories of manuscript sources, lost letters, and letters addressed to Whitman. Unique to this work, however, is a list of corrections and additions to the earlier volumes and a composite name and title index to the entire *Correspondence*. Volume 6 includes one Whitman letter published elsewhere this year by Robert Del Greco ("A New Whitman Letter to Talcott Williams," *WWR* 23:52–53) but does not contain a postcard reprinted by William White ("A New Whitman Letter to Deborah Browning," *WWR* 23:143–44).

Mattie: The Letters of Martha Mitchell Whitman, edited by Randall H. Waldron (New York: N.Y. Univ. Press), the correspondence of Walt's brother Jeff's wife, gives us a little more information about relationships within the poet's large family. Though most of the 26 newly discovered letters published here were written to Whitman's mother, the half dozen addressed to Walt suggest that his affectionate feelings for Mattie, and hers for him, were stronger than has before been realized. As for the poet's now worldwide family of readers, two new studies clarify Whitman's considerable reception in Russia and Yugoslavia. In the final chapter of his Whitman biography (see below), Maurice Mendelson surveys Russian translations and studies of the American bard from their inception in 1861 to the 150th anniversary celebrations of Whitman's birth held in the Soviet Union in 1969. As thoroughgoing and helpful on Whitman's reception as a socialist writer is Ljiljana Babić's "What Whitman in Yugoslavia" (*AN* 9[1976]:9–58).

***b.* Biography.** In his essay on Whitman's finances, just noted, Miller devotes several pages to examining a newspaper piece Whitman wrote and had published anonymously, charging that persecution by the American literary establishment had limited his audience and kept him from earning a decent income. Robert Scholnick argues that this article constituted the opening shot of a war between the critics in which volleys were exchanged on both sides of the Atlantic ("The

Selling of the 'Author's Edition': Whitman, O'Connor, and the West Jersey Press Affair," *WWR* 23:3–23). Though Whitman's intent had been primarily to advertise a new edition of his work, the ensuing debate raised much larger questions having to do with America's cultural identity and her ability to support the arts.

By this time in his career, of course, Whitman enjoyed the support of a number of quite vocal defenders, among them Maurice Bucke and William O'Connor. The relationships of each of these men to the poet have, this year, received separate, book-length treatments. For access to Bucke's lengthy correspondence with Whitman, Artem Lozynsky has simultaneously published two works, the first an annotated edition of his collected letters to the poet, with a bibliography of Bucke's writings, available on demand through University Microfilms: *The Letters of Dr. Richard Maurice Bucke to Walt Whitman* (Detroit: Wayne State Univ. Press). The second is a selection of about forty of Bucke's more important letters to Whitman, and sixty others to Bucke's friends, the correspondence generously interspersed with explanatory commentary by the editor: *Richard Maurice Bucke, Medical Mystic: Letters of Dr. Bucke to Walt Whitman and His Friends* (Detroit: Wayne State Univ. Press). These letters show that far from encouraging Bucke, as has commonly been thought, Whitman actually had to restrain his friend's enthusiasm, particularly when they were collaborating on Bucke's 1883 biography of the poet. As Lozynsky shows, in his *Medical Mystic* volume and in "Dr. Richard Maurice Bucke: A Religious Disciple of Whitman" (*SAR*, pp. 387–403), Bucke found in Whitman the messianic exemplar of a new religion, "Cosmic Consciousness." His interest in the poet as artist was comparatively slight.

Whitman's friendship with another disciple and publicist is the subject of Jerome Loving's study, *Walt Whitman's Champion: William Douglas O'Connor* (College Station: Tex. A. and M. Univ. Press). The first half of this book is a "literary biography" in which Loving examines O'Connor's own writings to reveal that the figure of "the good grey poet" was only the extension of a heroic personality O'Connor had projected in his fiction before he had even met Whitman. The second half of the volume furnishes annotated texts of O'Connor's major essays in behalf of Whitman, including *The Good Grey Poet*. Loving persuasively argues that O'Connor boosted and maintained Whitman's morale at a crucial point in the early 1860s and that thereafter Whitman in fact altered his own self-concept to conform more closely to O'Connor's image of him as a socio-religious reformer and poet of democracy. In a companion article, "Genesis of *The Good Grey Poet*" (*TSLL* 19:227–33), Loving stresses that not only were O'Connor's ideas well defined before he began his pamphlet, but he also was temperamentally too independent to be greatly influenced by Whitman in its composition.

The subject on which O'Connor and Whitman most sharply disagreed, as Loving makes clear, was race. Whitman was more ambivalent than his abolitionist friend about the place of the black in American society, fearing that white backlash to enfranchisement might threaten the moral growth of the nation. William J. Scheick makes a similar point in "Whitman's Grotesque Half-Breed" (*WWR* 23:133–36), arguing that in his short story "The Half-Breed," written while still in his twenties, Whitman reveals an early distaste for miscegenation. Even more complex, perhaps, are Whitman's feelings about homosexuality. Jonathan Katz judiciously threads together a number of documents, some of them never before published, all having a bearing on this issue, in *Gay American History* (pp. 337–65, 449–508). Katz reports the correspondence of several homosexual men (among them John Addington Symonds, Edward Carpenter, and Charles Warren Stoddard) with Whitman and about him, and prints for the first time a manuscript diary of 1862–63 in which the poet names some of the men he "slept with" in New York, Brooklyn, and Washington, D.C. Katz believes that even if "slept with" was not a euphemism for sexual relations in the 19th century, these entries, when placed alongside other evidence of the poet's homoerotic impulses, reveal that sharing a bed with another man had more than casual significance for him. Another contemporary perspective is taken by Muriel Kolinsky in " 'Me Tarzan You Jane?': Whitman's Attitudes Toward Women from a Women's Liberation Point of View" (*WWR* 23:155–65). She tries to refute charges that Whitman's ideas about women were regressive by arguing that if they were, one could trace out, in Whitman's own language, tell-tale clues of masculine superiority. On the contrary, Kolinsky finds, after examining the evidence, that "If Whitman did have a fault, from a women's liberationist point of view, it would be that he often said, especially in his prose, that women were *superior*."

One comes away from these assessments of Whitman's feelings

in regard to race and sexuality with a renewed sense that some of the old problems in Whitman biography are still to be settled. If one is inclined to find a place for contradictions in Whitman, however, it will be hard not to feel disappointed with Maurice Mendelson's *Life and Work of Walt Whitman: A Soviet View* (Moscow: Progress Publishers, 1976). This study, published in both the original and an enlarged edition in the sixties, but only made available in English translation last year, draws a portrait of Whitman which might almost be titled, "The Good Grey Poet-Revolutionary." Mendelson finds the principle of collectivism everywhere in Whitman, even in the "Calamus" poems in the image of "the new city of friends." He stoutly denies those "bourgeois" critics who perceive Whitman as a celebrant of individualism or who find "decadent" (e.g., homosexual) motifs in his work. The merit of Mendelson's study is that it explores in some detail certain socialist-utopian influences on Whitman and his parents—books they had read, lectures they had heard. Mendelson also offers new evidence of Whitman's popularity with leaders of the American Communist party, Ella Reeve Bloor, Elizabeth Gurley Flynn (who once took *Leaves of Grass* to prison with her), and Gus Hall. Mendelson is weak, however, as a literary critic, for he is unable to go beyond a simple equation of ideological purity with artistic logic.

Finally, in "Whitmaniana from the *Boston Journal*" (*WWR* 23: 90–92), Willard E. Martin, Jr., locates some unrecorded newspaper references to Whitman. Collected here is the report of an 1881 lecture Whitman gave to a Boston audience on his recollections of Lincoln as well as scattered references to Whitman by the Washington correspondent for the Boston paper. The only other item is the reprinting, a week later, of a well-known Washington *Star* interview in which Whitman confesses to having overcome his earlier distaste for the writings of Edgar Allan Poe.

c. Criticism: General. Whitman's revaluation of Poe confirms V. K. Chari's belief that later editions of *Leaves of Grass* show a movement toward qualities Whitman had earlier sought to avoid, "the artificial rhetoric of the Romantic sublime" and "the decorative, melodious lyricism of Poe, Tennyson, and Longfellow" ("Whitman and the Language of the Romantics," *EA* 30:314–28). Chari argues that Whitman's use of such 18th-century poetic devices as apostrophe and personification and his use of epithets in 1855 gradually declined as he moved away from objectivity toward Romantic subjectivity and idealization. On the other hand, while there may have been a development in this direction, Quentin Anderson is probably closer to the truth in pointing out that from first to last in Whitman there is a tension between objective and subjective experience, between being, as Whitman put it, "in and out of the game" ("Practical and Visionary Americans," *ASch* 45[1976]:405–18). In an especially thoughtful essay, connecting Whitman with Emerson, Thoreau, and Henry James, Anderson suggests that Whitman centrally embodies a duality inherent in the American character in which the need to define and possess the world according to one's own higher laws is countered by the spirit of fearful accommodation to the everyday (i.e. commercial) world and its life-defeating values.

It is also the visionary side of Whitman, particularly his conception of a cohesive, robust, "good-natured" society, which interests Guy Davenport in "Walt Whitman an American" (*Parnassus* 5,i[1976]:35–48). In charged and evocative language of his own, Davenport notes the Adamic, preindustrial insouciance of Whitman's voice and finds intriguing similarities between the poet's utopian social ideals and those espoused a generation earlier by Charles Fourier. Equating the spirit of rapacity with 19th-century industrial culture, Davenport argues that Whitman's social optimism, "for all its acceptance of the city crowds and the bustle of commerce . . . is in essence pastoral, following natural rhythm, with sympathies that depend on the broad and easy freedom of country people." On the other hand, Whitman's attitude toward metropolitan life is studied by J. Thomas Chaffin, Jr., in "'Give Me Faces and Streets': Walt Whitman and the City" (*WWR* 23:109–20). He points out that not only did Whitman perceive urbanization as coincident with American destiny but also he sought to celebrate the city as a metaphor for the moral viability of democratic institutions. Nevertheless, Chaffin acknowledges that Whitman's portrait of the city is an ideal one, emphasizing its fluid, "procreative" qualities.

The egalitarian values Whitman associates with an urban setting can be discovered as well in his poetic theory, according to Donald D. Kummings in "Walt Whitman's Vernacular Poetics" (*CRevAS* 7[1976]:119–31). Kummings sees this aesthetic as originating in the poet's distaste for art which stresses order and uniformity and which pictures life as it was or as it should be according to values limited to a specific, "aristocratic" class. Whitman's indirections are means by which readers can be brought instead to imaginative empathy with things as they are, becoming themselves "vernacular Heroes" capable of making their own poems. A similar conclusion is reached by Eric Reed Birdsall's dissertation, "Translating the Hints: Walt Whitman's Poetry of Indirection" (*DAI* 37:6482–83A). In two related articles, Richard P. Adams suggests that Whitman's use of sound and rhythm are his principal means for eliciting reader involvement with the external world ("Whitman and the Rhythms of Life," *Calamus* 14:17–24), while V. K. Chari believes that Whitman uses a combination of direct and indirect techniques to accomplish the same purpose ("Whitman and His Reader," *Calamus* 15:23–33). Examples of the former are "elliptical or euphemistic modes of expression" and descriptive catalogues; direct devices include oratorical and prophetical exhortation and direct address to a character within the poem.

An even closer look at Whitman's poetic technique is achieved by Mark Kinkead-Weekes in "Walt Whitman Passes the Full-Stop By . . ." (*EM*, pp. 163–78). He calls attention to Whitman's syntactical manipulation of the present tense so that it indicates the "continuous present" in which time is made to extend beyond any apparent "end." To display the poet's artistry in this respect, Kinkead-Weekes furnishes discerning readings of "Lilacs," "Out of the Cradle," and "Crossing Brooklyn Ferry." In "The Organic Metaphor and the Unity of the First Edition of *Leaves of Grass*" (*Calamus* 15:34–50), Martin F. Chesin argues once more that the poems of the 1855 edition are a unified whole. He sees them as arranged in interrelated pairs of opposites. The ending of "Song of Myself" with the poem's emphasis on the "I," for example, is transitional to "A Song for Occupations" where "the poet places primary emphasis on assuring the reader that what he has learned of himself is just as surely true for others."

***d.* Criticism: Individual Works.** Although some (like Kinkead-Weekes, above) still feel that Whitman's catalogues are too "formless," the weight of critical opinion has for some time been shifting in favor of his inventories. Counting more than 150 catalogues in the 1855 "Preface," Donez Xiques reminds us that Whitman does not limit this device to the poetry ("Whitman's Catalogues and the Preface to *Leaves of Grass*, 1855," *WWR* 23:68–76). In "Song of Myself," according to Michael D. Reed, these lists are designed to proclaim —and embody—unity in diversity, a paradoxical experience Whitman believed was inherent in democratic life ("First Person Persona and the Catalogue in 'Song of Myself,'" *WWR* 23:147–55). Whitman's stylistically imposed unities within the catalogues allowed him to "create an actual whole from the diversity of America." The use of catalogues as a vehicle for realizing a world and a self interacting with it is studied by Suzanne Beth Schneider in her thesis, "Porches of the Sun: The Problem of Form in Whitman's *Song of Myself*" (*DAI* 38:268–69A). Since the poem *is* about the bringing into being of a self, rather than, as in traditional autobiography, about a self, Schneider classifies it as an "anti-autobiography." Roger Ramsey, on the other hand, following Northrop Frye, prefers to call the poem a "rhapsody" because it is a recitable medley of songs ("Whitman Rhapsade," *RS* 45:243–48). As Ramsey defines it, a rhapsody is an "oral-episodic-audience-oriented part-encyclopedia with near-oracular themes."

Though his title might suggest another generic discussion, George Y. Trail, in "Whitman's Spear of Summer Grass: Epic Invocations in 'Song of Myself'" (*WWR* 23:120–25), is quick to point out that the poem begins by diverging from, rather than satisfying, epic conventions. Limiting his focus to sections i and v, Trail deftly explores metaphorical contexts and connections within these two passages, particularly as they relate to the image of the leaf of grass as a "tongue" and "spear." Taking a broader approach to "Song of Myself," Donald Kummings, in a companion piece to his essay on Whitman's "vernacular poetics" (see above), insists that the poem's speaker is not the introspective solipsist some critics have pictured ("The Vernacular Hero in Whitman's 'Song of Myself,'" *WWR* 23:23–34). Kummings brings forward evidence to show that as "vernacular hero" Whitman makes extraordinary efforts to connect with an audience and to develop in each reader an ability "to be his own heroic poet."

Questions of structure and voice are also considered in two shorter Whitman poems. Harsharan Singh Ahluwalia studies psychological integration of the two selves in "Lilacs" wherein the private, mourning self evolves into the public consoling self ("The Private Self and the Public Self in Whitman's 'Lilacs,'" *WWR* 23:166–74). In an especially clear-headed explication, attention to image, syntax, and rhythm allows Roberts W. French to discover an opening-out movement in "Cavalry Crossing a Ford" ("Reading Whitman: 'Cavalry Crossing a Ford,'" *EngR* 27,iii–iv[1976]:16–19).

However, most discussions of individual poems this year step outside the immediate text to investigate sources and contexts. For example, Joel R. Kehler invokes traditional Christian typology to explore literal, historical, mythic, and spiritual levels of discourse in "Passage to India" ("A Typological Reading of 'Passage to India,'" *ESQ* 23:123–29). According to Kehler, typology serves as an enriching structural metaphor through which the contemporary events Whitman celebrates serve as a type pointing the way to divine ends. Erna Emmighausen Kelly's "Whitman and Wordsworth: Childhood Experiences and the Future Poet" (*WWR* 23:59–68) is also at least partly historical in its approach to "Out of the Cradle." Kelly observes that both poets rejected 18th- and early 19th-century attitudes toward children and that in "Out of the Cradle" and *The Prelude* perceptions of universal unity occasion the child's rebirth and poetic calling.

Reading "By Blue Ontario's Shore" in the light of its many revisions, Gary A. Culbert concludes that changes Whitman made in the poem after the Civil War are far more significant than those he made earlier ("Whitman's Revisions of 'By Blue Ontario's Shore,'" *WWR* 23:35–45). Culbert believes that the poet's war experiences caused him to place greater stress on the poet-bard's role in fostering democratic institutions and free individuals. (Jerome Loving attributes this new emphasis to William O'Connor's influence on Whitman, see above). Other poems comprising "Whispers of Heavenly Death" provide Fred D. White with a reinforcing context for understanding man's soul as the deific unifier of the universe in "A Noiseless Patient Spider" ("Whitman's Cosmic Spider," *WWR* 23:85–88). Myrth Jimmie Killingsworth helpfully suggests that in "I Sing the Body Electric" Whitman drew on the idea of "sexual electricity" from medical authorities contemporary with him who linked electrical qualities to sexuality ("Another Source for Whitman's Use of 'Electric,'" *WWR* 23:129–32). She might also have taken into account animal magnetism, a pseudomedical science Whitman was much inteersted in, which often rendered the magnetic connection in sexual imagery. A neglected fact of Civil War medicine can enhance our sense of the dramatic situation in "A March in the Ranks Hard-Prest," according to Dominick A. Labiance and William J. Reeves. They point out that since ether is highly volatile, its use in conjunction with torches for lighting after-battle surgery means that the place of healing, as described in the poem, is ironically also a site of potential explosion ("'A March in the Ranks Hard-Prest, and the Road Unknown': A Chemical Analysis," *AN&Q* 15:110–11).

In "The 'Confession' in 'Crossing Brooklyn Ferry' and the Jewish Day of Atonement Prayers" (*WWR* 23:125–29), Barbara Kroll focuses on the catalogue of sins in section vi of Whitman's poem, noting similarities and differences with Yom Kippur prayers of confession. The opening lines of the poem, according to Wilson F. Engel, III, recall passages from Proverbs and I Corinthians ("Two Biblical Echoes in 'Crossing Brooklyn Ferry,'" *WWR* 23:88–90). Finally, C. Scott Pugh provides a plausible solution to the mystery posed in a later poem: "The End as Means in "A Riddle Song,'" (*WWR* 23:82–85). He believes that creation, a world without apparent end, is God's riddle to mankind and that Whitman implies that the only answer to the "end" of existence is an intuition of ultimate purpose achieved through mystical dialogue with the divine.

***e.* Affinities and Influences.** Since even sympathetic readers tend to pass over, with half a smile, Whitman's use of foreign languages, a particularly instructive source study this year is Michael R. Dressman's "Whitman, Chaucer, and French Words" (*WWR* 23:77–82). Dressman suggests that because the poet saw Chaucer's writings "as the literary vehicle whereby certain words 'much needed' in English came to be 'crystalized,'" Whitman, in his turn, drew on French expressions as a way of enriching the American language. Without coming to new conclusions, Augustine G. Pallikunnen sorts again through the evidence of Whitman's indebtedness to Eastern thought and concludes that most of the poet's familiarity with Hindu philosophy came indirectly through other Western writers: "Eastern Influence on Whitman's Mysticism" in *Eastern Influence on Whitman's Mysticism and Other Essays in Literature* (Alwaye, India: Pontifical Institute Publications [1975]), pp. 1–21.

On 19th-century reactions to Whitman, Rayburn S. Moore reports that the distinguished southern poet Paul Hamilton Hayne scorned Whitman in print, wrote parodies of his poems, and declined to change his opinion over a period of 25 years ("The Literary World

Gone Mad: Hayne on Whitman," *SLJ* 10,i:75–83). Valden Madsen compares William Dean Howells's reaction to Whitman and Dickinson, concluding that Victorian adherence to metrical regularity kept Howells from appreciating the former's "unmeasured" lines, though he was willing to suspend some of his critical dicta in his admiration for Dickinson's distinctive manner of expression ("W. D. Howells's Formal Poetics and His Appraisals of Whitman and Emily Dickinson," *WWR* 23:103–9). Howells's admirer, Hamlin Garland, took a different view. Nancy Bunge argues that Garland esteemed the poet sufficiently to adopt his beliefs as the guiding ideology behind his own work ("Walt Whitman's Influence on Hamlin Garland," *WWR* 23:45–50). Like Whitman, Bunge thinks, Garland believed the artist should record experiences and states of consciousness honestly, without offering conclusions, in order to involve and expand his readers' point of view. Maybe, but Garland could be polemical and didactic even before he retreated into writing *Saturday Evening Post* romance.

The outstanding study of Whitman's relation to other writers this year is Betsy Jacqueline Erkkila's exhaustive thesis, "Walt Whitman and the French Tradition" (*DAI* 38:774A). She shows that he was drawn to French writers whose views strengthened his resolve to "liberate American sensibility" from its Puritan past. Whitman's affinity with French thought in turn prepared the way for his reciprocal and decisive influence on French literature during and immediately after the Symbolist period, 1885–90. By World War I Whitman's techniques had been thoroughly absorbed into the mainstream of French writing. During the early part of the century, when other American artists were beginning to discover Whitman via the French literary sources he had nourished, Whitman had already made a profound impression on Frank Lloyd Wright, as Peter J. Abernethy observes in "Frank Lloyd Wright, Walt Whitman: The Expatriate's Dream of Home" (*AmerS* 18:45–53). He argues that Whitman is responsible for some of Wright's notions about the common man and speculates that Wright may have gone to Europe in 1909 partially because "Whitman's vision of the free, creative individual in an open, expanding frontier America was fading for him."

Among recent studies which suggest parallels with other writers, without claiming influence, the most provocative is Kenneth Burke's discussion of Whitman and Henry Adams ("Towards Looking Back," *JGE* 28[1976], 167–89). Burke's main point, that the American future that Whitman spiritualized and celebrated began to disintegrate before Adams's eyes into "pandemonious" multiplicity, admittedly, is almost a commonplace. In the course of his essay, however, Burke furnishes sidelong, invigorating insights into the poet's gospelizing, his catalogues, and his wily, personally cathartic, attachment of manly love to nationally sanctioned ideals of brotherhood. Also useful is Paul Ferlazzo's "Dylan Thomas and Walt Whitman: Birth, Death, and Time" (*WWR* 23:136–41). In regard to all three subjects, Ferlazzo finds more differences than similarities between the two writers. Thomas, for example, has little of Whitman's cheerfulness about death.

ii. Dickinson

***a.* Bibliography, Editing.** On the cover of an issue of *Prairie Schooner*, George Monteiro and Barton Levi St. Armand publish for the first time the facsimile text of a Dickinson letter addressed to the poet's niece, Martha Dickinson ("A New Emily Dickinson Letter: A Manuscript Facsimile," *PrS* 51:324). Written in the 1870s, when Martha was still a child, it is an affectionate, half-playful note of condolence for some unhappiness that had befallen the young girl. Muriel Safferson reviews the circumstances which led Millicent Todd Bingham inadvertently to publish, as the poet's own, two stanzas from a George Herbert poem Dickinson had copied and left among her manuscripts ("Some Textual Problems in *Bolts of Melody*," *EDB* 31:4–14). She notes that the full Herbert poem expresses faith in God, but the stanzas Dickinson copied, when they are taken out of context, call God's motives into question. Safferson believes that Dickinson's transcription of only these two stanzas reveals she is unable to share Herbert's piety. In "Emily Dickinson's Dictionary," Willis Buckingham shows that the Webster's *American Dictionary* used in the Dickinson home was not the 1847 edition commonly cited but a different and much scarcer two-volume work first published in 1841 (*HLB* 25:489–92).

There was little secondary bibliographical work on Dickinson this year. William White discusses books by and about the poet published in England and notes an unrecorded German volume in which 129 Dickinson poems are translated ("Four Dickinson Notes," *HJP* 16: 12–14,16). Five other Dickinson items, four from the 1890s, are cited by James Stronks in "Addenda to the Bibliographies of Emily Dickinson and Edgar Allan Poe" (*PBSA* 71:360–62), though one of the five citations duplicates an entry in the 1970 Buckingham bibliography.

b. **Biography.** One of the most intense and problematic friendships of Dickinson's life was with her girlhood friend, sister-in-law, and next-door neighbor, Susan Gilbert Dickinson. Unfortunately, some (we don't know how many) letters between the two have been deliberately destroyed, passages in others have been cut out, and taken altogether, the pieces of evidence that remain do not fit together well. The subject, then, of Lillian Faderman's article, "Emily Dickinson's Letters to Sue Gilbert" (*MR* 18:197–225) is a welcome one. In execution, though, the essay is a little disappointing, for it does not seem to take us beyond John Cody's conclusion, reached some years ago, that Dickinson loved Susan Gilbert deeply, even obsessively, during her early twenties, and that she became stunned and angry when Sue formed an intimacy in marriage which excluded her. While the Cody-Faderman interpretation helps to account for the complexity in tone of some of Dickinson's letters to her sister-in-law, both critics tend to subject the correspondence to over-solemn and programatic readings.

If Faderman implicitly criticizes Richard B. Sewall's Dickinson biography (*ALS 1974*, pp. 70–71) for overcautiousness in generalizing about the Emily Dickinson–Susan Gilbert relationship, Barton St. Armand clearly intends to make the charge apply to the entire two-volume work in his prickly and vigorous essay-review, "Emily Dickinson at Yale: Recent Biography and Criticism" (*MQR* 16:83–93). He argues that Sewall and those Dickinson specialists he may have influenced, especially Inder Nath Kher (*ALS 1974*, p. 72) and Jean McClure Mudge (*ALS 1975*, pp. 97–98) seek "to appropriate Dickinson from the romanticists, the psychologists, the Americanists, in order to place her on a pedestal for all the world to see, and worship." In faulting Sewall for his "bland" objectivity, St. Armand takes a minority view among Dickinson scholars, but in calling for more vivid, intuitive portraits of the poet, he may in fact be accurately forecasting the direction Dickinson biographical studies are likely to take, now that Sewall has gathered together virtually all the known facts. Prof. St. Armand himself, along with his colleague at Brown University, George Monteiro, furnish one new piece of biographical information, a chapter from an unpublished autobiography by Martha Dickinson Bianchi, the poet's niece ("My Surviving Aunt: Lavinia Dickinson," *PrS* 51:325–44). Written in 1934, the chapter is an appreciative recollection of the poet's sister, Lavinia, particularly during the years shortly before Lavinia's death in 1899. Sometimes called the "uncomplicated" Dickinson, Vinnie emerges from this sketch much as she does from Sewall's *Life*, a determined, capable, fiercely loyal family partisan, sharing some of her father's and sister's qualities of alert, intelligent independence of mind and pithiness of expression.

c. Criticism: General. Dickinson's poetry has generally yielded itself more easily to formalist than to biographical or philosophical analysis. Now the new generation of phenomenological and structuralist critics are surveying, with good results, the "landscape" of an interior world the poems project and inhabit. For example, by examining Dickinson's manipulation of syntax in those of her poems which begin with the words "There is a . . . ," as in "There's a certain Slant of light," Elizabeth F. Perlmutter skillfully shows how Dickinson is able to intensify states of feeling by "disembodying" them from some understood speaker or occasion ("Hide and Seek: Emily Dickinson's Use of the Existential Sentence," *Lang&S* 10:109–19). Thus subjective phenomena like fears, hopes, and intimations are transformed into animate, self-existent entities. "They become certainties in a world composed of bits and pieces, violent changes, and unstable selves." In another grammatical analysis, Suzanne Juhasz notes that in Dickinson's case subjunctive verb forms are used not to express wish fulfillment but to articulate a conceptual framework in which intense, "extravagantly" emotional activities can take place ("'I Dwell in Possibility,' Emily Dickinson in the Subjunctive Mood," *EDB* 32:105–9).

Describing her poetic world more specifically in spatial terms, two other critics examine Dickinson's way of delineating the limits of consciousness. So much has been said about her use of the word "circumference," it almost makes sense to write about it as if it had never been discussed before, as Audrey T. Rodgers virtually does in "'Circumference' in the Poetry of Emily Dickinson" (*EDB* 31:15–32). Defining Dickinson's poetic quest as a transcendental search for meaning, Rodgers argues that "circumference" is used both to define the limits of human understanding, and to describe the ecstatic, though quite earthbound, triumph over those boundaries. In a related article, J. Brooks Bouson looks at enclosure imagery in the poems, finding in them a system of boxes within boxes, and concluding that the poet "wants to domesticate the haunted houses of spirit, death, and mind and finally to enter them as she would enter a friend's house" ("Emily Dickinson and the Riddle of Containment," *EDB* 31:33–49). In "Zones of the Soul: Emily Dickinson's Geographical Imagery," (*CLAJ* 21:62–73), Patrick O'Donnell surveys the poet's use of places and directions as metaphors for inner experience. Limiting herself to only a few poems, R. Betsy Tenenbaum likewise observes several in which Dickinson forcefully vivifies dislocation within the self through pictorial means ("Varieties of 'Extremity' in Emily Dickinson's Poetry," *EDB* 32:119–21).

As productive as domestic and geographical images were for Dickinson, it might still be said that her most powerful metaphors were drawn from the Bible and Christian doctrine. But was religion more than a book of tropes for her, did she in fact take any part of it seriously? The most sustained answer in the affirmative has been, for the past decade, William R. Sherwood's *Circumference and Circumstance* (*ALS 1968*, pp. 62–63), which argues that Dickinson groped for, and eventually reached, something like orthodox Christian faith. In "Empress of Calvary: Mystical Marriage in the Poems of Emily Dickinson" (*SAB* 42,i:39–43), Michael R. Dressman reads a group of matrimonial poems and concludes that Dickinson must have at least experimented with the idea of becoming the Bride of God. The bulk of recent investigations have stressed the poet's heretical side, however, though seldom with more freshness and clarity than Barton St. Armand brings to his cross-disciplinary article, "Emily Dickinson's American Grotesque: The Poet as Folk Artist" (*Topic* 31:3–19). In demonstrating that features of American primitivist painting ("qualities of the vernacular, the grotesque, and the comic") occur also in Dickinson's poems, St. Armand examines a cluster of poems in which God is imagined as a capricious, predatory cat. He goes on to suggest that Harriet Prescott Spofford's sensational tale about a woman captured by an American panther provided a source for some of this feline imagery. Another uncommon approach to a group of related poems is that taken by Hastings Moore in discussing

Dickinson's attitudes toward death ("Emily Dickinson and Orthothanasia," *EDB* 32:110–18). To those who feel that the poet's interest in the subject was exaggerated, even morbid, Moore replies that her ways of looking at life's final experience were healthy and life-enhancing. She saw the value of bringing death into full consciousness, while living, and she understood the dying person's need to be accompanied, "companioned," during this ultimate event.

More disciplined and analytical is Martin Bickman's Jungian treatment of those Dickinson poems which imagine death as a suitor ("Kora in Heaven: Love and Death in the Poetry of Emily Dickinson," *EDB* 32:79–104). Drawing material from his earlier dissertation (*ALS 1975*, p. 97), Bickman finds a psychic "equivalence" in these poems linking eroticism with dissolution. He shows how archetypal myth (e.g., the abduction of Persephone to Hades) and empirical studies of women's death fantasies tally with Dickinson's poetic enactments of death, sacred marriage, and rebirth. Conceptually quite similar and equally astute is Albert Gelpi's analysis of several poems which chart the speaker's passage from girlhood to "wife" and "Woman," accomplished through mystical union with the masculine component of her being ("Emily Dickinson and the Deerslayer: The Dilemma of the Woman Poet in America," *SJS* 3:80–95). Gelpi has discussed these matters in a chapter of his *The Tenth Muse* (*ALS 1975*, p. 97), but here he takes as his focus a poem not treated there, the haunting and difficult "My Life had stood—a Loaded Gun." He finds in the poem interesting analogues between its psychosexual situation and Cooper's version, in the *Leatherstocking Tales*, of the myth of the American pioneer hero and his struggle with the wilderness.

***d.* Criticism: Individual Works.** As rewarding as Gelpi's reading of "My Life had stood—a Loaded Gun" (see above) is Barton St. Armand's masterful study of Dickinson's use of ballad tradition in her overlooked early poem, "Through lane it lay—thro' bramble" ("Emily Dickinson's 'Babes in the Wood': A Ballad Reborn," *JAF* 90: 430–41). He demonstrates that the ancestry of the ill-fated children in the poem can be traced back to an English ballad which achieved wide currency in the United States, "The Children in the Wood." He also examines Gothic iconography, derived from various sources in American popular culture, which Dickinson skillfully uses to heighten the melodramatic situation of the poem. St. Armand concludes that though Dickinson seems to tag the poem with a sentimental conclusion, the horrifying enchantments the children must endure before they reach heaven contain her characteristically tough-minded protest against all the indecipherable casualties and woe of the experienced world. This article has the added advantage of reminding us that Dickinson's creative use of folk motifs and sources from popular culture is still a comparatively—and undeservedly—neglected subject.

Two other source studies valuably consider implications, for individual poems, of the poet's reading. Agreeing with those who feel that the reference to "mail from Tunis" in "A Route of Evanescence" derives from Shakespeare's *The Tempest*, Linda J. Taylor goes on to explain how the poem embodies larger themes from the play as well ("Shakespeare and Circumference: Dickinson's Hummingbird and *The Tempest*," *ESQ* 23:252–61). Both Prospero in the play and the speaker in Dickinson's poem, she says, are engaged in acts of magic which reveal the wonderful in the commonplace: "Wild, chaotic nature alone is not sufficient, but transformed by human perception, art, and effort, it becomes, if only temporarily as in both the play and the poem, a harmonious paradise." Citing parallels and verbal echoes, Janet E. DeRosa argues that a possible source for "Bereaved of all, I went abroad" is Emerson's thoughts on traveling in his essay "Self-Reliance" (" 'Bereaved of All, I went Abroad,' " *EDB* 31:70–76). By the end of the poem, however, as DeRosa points out, the Amherst pilgrim is much more darkly stoic than her Concord predecessor.

Another connection between the two New England writers, though the evidence for it seems more adventitious, is observed by Mario L. D'Avanzo, who believes that Dickinson wrote "I like to see it lap the Miles" in direct response to Emerson's call (in "The Poet") for visionary reattachment of things to nature and personification of inanimate objects (" 'I like to see it lap the Miles,' " *EDB* 31:59–61). Certainly there are times when Dickinson finds it difficult to maintain Emersonian spiritual expansiveness, as F. K. Bartsch notes in brief remarks on a seldom studied "circumference" poem (" 'I saw no Way—the Heavens were stitched,' " *EDB* 31:62–64). Aida A. Farrag looks at another poem expressing cosmic alienation, arguing with some justification that its second version is superior to its first (" 'The

Wind begun to rock the Grass,'" *EDB* 31:65–69). Dickinson's need to achieve perfection in her art, as well as her struggle for an ideal love, Barton St. Armand believes, are the subjects of a poem in which she questions both cherished aspirations ("Dickinson's 'For every Bird a Nest,'" *Expl* 35,iii:34–35).

Forgetting that Dickinson was capable of writing poems of faith, Dennis Grunes strains unconvincingly to prove that her very early "On this wondrous sea" contains all of the metaphysical dubieties she later entertained ("Child and Stranger," *EDB* 32:135–40). Relying for his text on Johnson's single-volume trade edition of the poems, rather than the three-volume variorum, this critic is unable to consider the poem's original appearance in a playful letter to Susan Gilbert or a second version written about five years later. By contrast, George Fortenberry supplies a sensible, if almost dismayingly down-to-earth reading for "This was a Poet" (*Expl* 35,iii:26–27), suggesting that the poem was one of Dickinson's characteristic verse riddles attached to a gift of flowers.

e. **Affinities and Influences.** As much a motif study as it is an examination of sources, George H. Soule, Jr.'s "Emily Dickinson and Jacob: 'Pugilist and Poet' Wrestling to the Dawn" (*EDB* 31:50–58) contends that Dickinson used Jacob's sparring with the angel as a metaphor for her own disputes with God and for her struggle to be a poet. Among the poems briefly treated here is "Two swimmers wrestled on the spar," a poem two other critics this year believe originated in an Emersonian, rather than a biblical, parable. In his essay "Fate," Emerson uses the situation of men thrown overboard in a storm as an example of human helplessness before the blind, torrential force of prevailing circumstance. The similarity between Dickinson's poem and Emerson's exemplum, along with other evidence, leads David H. Watters to conclude that Emerson's thought in his later essays must have been congenial to Dickinson ("Emerson, Dickinson, and the Atomic Self," *EDB* 32:122–34). The most suggestive section of Watters's essay, however, deals not with Emerson but with the Amherst College scientist Edward Hitchcock, whose lectures Dickinson must have heard as a schoolgirl. It was Hitchcock's theory that human identity is a force residing in the "ether," which, because it is only transiently attached to atoms, is undestroyed at death. This "chemical" theory for immortality casts revealing new light on more poems than Watters takes up, and should be pursued further.

Joanne Feit Diehl acknowledges some of the similarities between Emerson and Dickinson that occur to Watters, but she also insists on important differences between the two writers in "Emerson, Dickinson, and the Abyss" (*ELH* 44:683–700). Reaching conclusions like those enunciated in her thesis (*ALS 1975*, p. 102), Diehl claims that in contrast to Emerson's concept of multiple selves, Dickinson polarizes human identity into two components, the self and the masculine "other," the latter an "awful internal stranger she must repeatedly confront." The poet's redaction of Emerson, in her poem on the two drowning swimmers, illustrates how she subverts his compensatory vision by rendering experience as a series of precarious encounters with nothingness.

In addition to his paper on the ballad tradition (see above), Barton St. Armand offers two other essays demonstrating how features of 19th-century popular culture find expression in Dickinson poems. In "Emily Dickinson and the Occult: The Rosicrucian Connection" (*PrS* 51:345–57), he points out that the oracular speaker of the poems in effect dons the veil of a medium and that the poet, dressing in white, was apparently drawn to the figure of the Vestal guarding the sacred flame of the divine Logos as expressed through the poet's Word. That another set of sentimental, heterodox, middle-of-the-century ideas inform Dickinson's poems on spiritual marriage is St. Armand's adroitly argued thesis in "Paradise Deferred: The Image of Heaven in the Work of Emily Dickinson and Elizabeth Stuart Phelps" (*AQ* 29:55–78). Phelps's potboiler, *The Gates Ajar*, and Dickinson's speculations about ideal love consummated after death, he suggests, are both indebted to conceptions of the life beyond as a personal home, even a "honeymoon cottage," where lovers separated in this world can be reunited. St. Armand's belief that the poet took quite seriously these preposterous Emmeline Grangerford notions about heaven helps us understand why he is impatient with critics who seem to tone down the poet's passionate personal myth-making (see above his "Emily Dickinson at Yale").

As for the poet's earliest public interpreter, Thomas Wentworth Higginson, his criticism of her verse as "spasmodic" and "uncontrolled" is examined by Jonathan Morse in "Emily Dickinson and the Spasmodic School: A Note on Thomas Wentworth Higginson's Esthetics" (*NEQ* 50:505–10). Since the Spasmodists indulged in "loud, loose bombast," he thinks Higginson must have used the term to refer not to the form of Dickinson's poetry but to its content—or rather to its lack of it—its insufficient high seriousness, its "art-for-art's-sake" amoralism. Though it is useful, for purposes of critical contrast, to place Dickinson within the context of 19th-century spasmodism, to argue that Higginson was dissatisfied with her ideas rather than her expression of them does not accord well with what Dickinson evidently thought he meant when she replied "you think my *gait* 'spasmodic' " (italics mine), nor does it tally with his first published description of her poems as being strong in thought "but without the proper control and chastening of literary expression."

Discussions of Dickinson's influence on other artists, though they are few in number this year, all have the advantage of breaking new ground. In "Emily Dickinson and Robert Frost" (*PrS* 51:369–86), George Monteiro ably reviews the young Frost's discovery of the Amherst poet as a "kindred New England soul" shortly after her poems were first issued in the 1890s. Monteiro goes on to suggest that a number of Frost's earliest verses, those published between 1894 and 1901, may be read as responses to certain Dickinson poems, and that in other cases her themes, images, and personal voice helped Frost discover his own poetic resources during the first decade of his career. Drawing parallels that lead one to wonder why they have not been noticed before, Joyce DeVeau Kennedy persuasively demonstrates that Eugene O'Neill's heroine, Lavinia Mannon, in *Mourning Becomes Electra*, is a composite portrait of Emily and Lavinia Dickinson as they were popularly understood in 1930 when O'Neill was working on the play ("O'Neill's Lavinia Mannon and the Dickinson Legend," *AL* 49:108–13).

Finally, two studies rather extensively describe Aaron Copland's song cycle, "Twelve Poems of Emily Dickinson," though in both cases focus is held on the composer rather than the poet. Nancy Cluck's "Aaron Copland/Emily Dickinson" (*EDB* 32:141–53) describes the twelve songs, indicating that in each case Copland's reading of the original Dickinson poem was sensitive and informed. Sharon Cody Mabry similarly discusses the relationship between text and musical setting in her thesis, the first half of which is devoted to

Copland's Dickinson songs ("Monograph I: *Twelve Poems of Emily Dickinson* by Aaron Copland: A Stylistic Analysis," *DAI* 38:2403–04A).

Arizona State University[1]

1. Preparation of this chapter was greatly facilitated by the research assistance of Norman J. Gehrlein, Jr.

6. Mark Twain

Louis J. Budd

Though the flow of specialized articles may have dropped in 1977, interest in Mark Twain is as lively as ever, as anybody can gauge in Hannibal while bumping elbows with the tourists, many of whom also get over to the birthplace in out-of-the-way Florida, Missouri. Even the French, who—according to Roger Asselineau in "The Impact of American Literature on French Writers" (*CLS* 14:119–34)—find his jokes "below their dignity," have come to treasure his boyhood books as "charming idylls." Such fame keeps generating broad essays that scholars often find repetitious. More useful are the essays that make him a point of comparison with which any educated reader will be familiar. Likewise, Huck Finn has become almost a real-life human to some who introduce him into places that bibliographers of American literature do not check regularly.

i. Bibliography and Editing

However, Thomas A. Tenney is determined to find all such places, and his *Mark Twain: A Reference Guide* (Boston: G. K. Hall) leaps into position as the keystone of future bibliography. Reaching out even for book reviews, it holds 4,900 entries which are meticulously indexed down to such details as photographs and drawings of Clemens or citations from unpublished letters. Tenney, having made a heroic effort to examine each item, has screened out some carryovers with misleading titles. But his chief aim was inclusion; he has driven so near to completeness that if anybody who stumbles across an omission will report it, Twainians can soon feel confident about having an inventory of whatever is in print. Tenney himself has already published his "First Annual Supplement" (*ALR* 10:327–412) that adds many items from as far back as 1875, marches up into 1977, and closes in further on a "genuinely thorough list of everything significant."

Through his expert annotations scholars can judge significances for themselves; indeed, a particular entry may often give all they need or want to know about it. But, again, the main thrust of the *Reference Guide* is exploratory, encouraged by an index that, for example, breaks down the heading of Clemens's "Interests and Attitudes" into a gamut from "Baseball," "Bicycles," "Billiards," and "Cats" through "Telephone," "Theater," and "Women and Girls." With such help a scholar can even locate articles he or she recalls vaguely but would like to consult again. A much less ambitious search[1] has produced *A Listing of and Selection from Newspaper and Magazine Interviews with Samuel L. Clemens* (*ALR* 10:1–100; also published in book form by *ALR*), edited by Louis J. Budd with an introduction, a note on the contents of each of the 278 items, and a reprinting of some of the more revealing or else less accessible ones. This compiler also will be grateful to hear of omissions, which surely exist.

Another kind of bibliography goes on as patiently as ever. Philip B. Eppard's "Mark Twain Dissects an Overrated Book" (*AL* 49:430–40) establishes the authorship of an unsigned essay in the *Atlantic Monthly* which again ridicules, this time with more restraint and therefore finesse, some "literary hogwash"—a book of verse by a revivalist living near Hartford, Connecticut. In a note that does credit to both Hamlin Hill and George Monteiro, the latter changes his mind (*PBSA* 71:512–14) about which brief item in the "Contributors' Club" of the January 1903 *Atlantic* is by Clemens; the content and other signs now point to "A Song Composed in a Dream." Twainians may hope for a bigger find in the recently unveiled manuscripts described in the booklet by Alan Simpson, *Mark Twain Goes Back to Vassar* (Poughkeepsie, N.Y: Vassar College). However, though these papers come down through the only living descendants of Clemens's parents, it is Mark Twain as "publisher and promoter who are most fully represented"; moreover, the 405 pages of "writings" had already been available to Albert Bigelow Paine and Dixon Wecter. They can hardly prove as important as the two painstakingly edited volumes of notebooks and journals which, produced in 1975, sparked discussions well into 1977 after many an editor commissioned an essay on them.

1. Professor Budd is much too modest in describing this extensive bibliography of Twain interviews that span 35 years. Twain was probably the most-interviewed man of his time, and there is an abundance of material here for the study of Twain as a public figure—Ed.

Since many of these essays, by seasoned critics, try to smoke out the quintessential Mark Twain, they are more engrossing than some supposedly original explications. For instance, Harold Kolb's wittily perceptive "The Literary Remains of Mark Twain" (*VQR* 53:353–62) argues that in themselves the notebooks "reveal the habits of a journalist rather than an artist." More provocatively, James M. Cox (*NCF* 31:475–80), declaring we have been hoaxed by the notion that the Mark Twain Papers hid startling treasures, belittles the "remarkably external" notebooks as the "executive shorthand of a totally professional writer whose every instinct is to make capital of his observations." Goaded by Cox's complaint that annotating "everything" in the notebooks "isn't much" while "more is less," Alan Gribben (*ALR* 10:413–19), for four years an assistant on the project, sets down a historically valuable account of how the editors grew into the conviction that any cutting of corners would lead sooner or later to a consensus that their job was done wrongheadedly. As for grumblings about its elaborateness, this edition should be reasonably profitable for its university press publisher.

ii. Biography

With "'I Detest Novels, Poetry & Theology': Origin of a Fiction Concerning Mark Twain's Reading" (*TSL* 22:154–61), Gribben continues the sifting of hard fact that he did so well last year (see *ALS 1976*, p. 81), revealing now that Paine distorted the "totality" while going so far as to truncate and then misdate by 35 years Clemens's famous comment about his taste in books. More positively we are informed that contrary to Paine's portrait of a novelty seeker who seldom picked up a mainline book, the "diversity and magnitude" of his reading rounded out to an "astonishing knowledge of literature." In a less surprising vein, in "Mark Twain: Clubman in South Africa" (*NEQ* 50:234–54) Coleman O. Parsons continues his sleuthing of the world lecture tour of 1895–1896 (see *ALS 1976*, p. 89). He now documents Clemens's hearty appetite for stag banquets crammed with drink, smoking, and yarns while his private letters complained of ennui. Casting down a bucket in his own backyard, Norton D. Kinghorn, in "Mark Twain in the Red River Valley of the North" (*MinnH* 45:321–28), amasses the particulars on an early stop during that tour in a town whose rawness is made vivid by photographs. Kinghorn fosters a better sense of how reverently such towns greeted a famous Mark Twain and how gallantly he tried to please, such as by stepping off the platform to shake hands. The Red River Valley, however, is much less important for Mark Twain biography than Elmira, New York, from which has come a rich gathering of materials with the promise of more to come. This gathering is the work of the Mark Twain Society of Elmira, which began in 1978 to issue its *Bulletin.* While mostly a reprinting of articles from journals of varying reach, *Mark Twain in Elmira,* edited by Robert D. Jerome and Herbert A. Wisbey, Jr. (Elmira, N.Y.: Mark Twain Society), amplifies the basis for testing theories about the community in which Clemens spent his summers during the 1870s and 1880s; more specifically, in supplying a more intimate and problematic picture of the Langdon family than we have had, it reopens the question of whether his marriage need have been or indeed was repressive imaginatively. The volume also holds worthwhile curiosa, anecdotes of mixed reliability, and some arresting photographs. (The Chamber of Commerce can count on a rise in tourists.) In "Mark Twain and the Southern Evangelical Mind" (*MHSB* 33:246–64) Lloyd A. Hunter carries the formative patterns back again to Hannibal's varieties of Protestantism. Despite a careful survey of the scholarship, including Ph.D. dissertations, his essay is not so incisive as John Q. Hays's in 1973 (see *ALS 1976*, p. 83).

In the realm of more speculative biography two challenging chapters in Alan Henry Rose, *Demonic Vision: Racial Fantasy and Southern Fiction* (Hamden, Conn.: Archon Books, 1976) set up a Freudian model, too complex to sketch here, for confronting the problem of how whites can vacillate between seeing the black man as a devil to be exorcised and a dehumanized, tractable Sambo; naturally Rose spends most of his space for Clemens on the subsurfaces of *Huck Finn* and *Pudd'nhead Wilson.* Guy A. Cardwell's "The Metaphoric Hero as Battleground" (*ESQ* 23:52–66) also defies summary because it moves leisurely yet searchingly through the Brooks-DeVoto debate. Showing that they both started from a "naive cultural determinism," Cardwell is most original when identifying Brooks's mentors and most impressive when questioning the cliché that the adversaries eventually adopted much of each other's argument. Another essay by Cardwell, keyed on "indubitable verbal bowdlerizing" of *Life on the Mississippi* done in 1908 without urging from either the deceased Olivia Clemens or William Dean Howells, "Mark Twain: A Self-

Emasculated Hero" (*ESQ* 23:173–87), contends persuasively that Brooks was much closer than DeVoto to the truth about self-censorship, which became more instinctive as Clemens evolved into a "generally prudent, only fitfully unruly middle-class Eastern gentleman, a hero who clung to his status." In passing, Cardwell undermines the myth fostered by Clemens that he was a careful proofreader.

The storm center for 1977 is John Seelye's *Mark Twain in the Movies: A Meditation with Pictures* (New York: Viking), or ought to be, though it looks like just another coffee-table book. Seelye himself is unique: a sophisticated critic who delights in chasing ideas yet can tune in to mass culture; a fearless punster with a wit so flashing that it can rival Mark Twain and upstage some captivating snapshots included in the book. His judgments, piled on at a pace that will leave skeptics spluttering, and compounded with "asperity" in etching a "counterimage" to the public faces Mark Twain projected, become increasingly speculative. Also, he stares so quizzically at the snapshots (recovered from the Isabel V. Lyon papers) that they dissolve for him into optical illusions, paper masks, or enigmas that cannot or will not speak candidly. Still, after many disagreements verging on outrage my mind grants that Seelye pushes nearer than anybody else to the true (but maybe not the most enduring) S. L. Clemens, that kaleidoscope of earthiness, vanity, extreme moods, warmth, staginess, ebullience, pathos, and—Seelye never forgets—humor.

Although a few formalists still deny that biography entwines with theory about an *oeuvre*, several good essays this year focus clearly on a thematic overview of Mark Twain's works. Indeed, the man and his writings seem welded in Arthur G. Pettit's smoothly written "Mark Twain and His Times: A Bicentennial Appreciation" (*SAQ* 76:133–46), which presents him as embodying his era with an inconsistency and ambiguity that made him an Everyman and finally a "common cultural property . . . who was expected to act out certain national mannerisms." Focusing on the theme perhaps dearest to the 19th century, Everett Carter's *The American Idea* warns (pp. 212–42) that the desire to recruit Mark Twain for modernism inverts the patent thrust of his work before *A Connecticut Yankee in King Arthur's Court*, particularly his commitment to the ideal of a "decent, homely middle-class" society with its religion of material along with social progress. On a currently fashionable subject William C. Panagakos's "The Violence of Mark Twain" emerges with a tripartite pattern: (1)

a stress up through 1885 on man's cruelty toward his fellows; (2) the expansion—sharpest in *A Connecticut Yankee*—from the individual to the "organized" social act; (3) ever-rising resentment of "God's violence toward the human race He created." Panagakos is obviously right to center on the violence in Mark Twain; on the other hand, 32 pages cannot allow enough room for sophisticated treatment of so tangled a problem. (His essay was sold for $2.95 by *ESColl*, whose obituary is in *ALS 1976*, p. vi.) Working carefully within a perspective that Seelye and others have lately felt to be fundamental, Sargent Bush, Jr., in "The Showman as Hero in Mark Twain's Fiction" (*Gerber Festschrift*, pp. 79–98), elicits the covert pattern beneath the posturings of five main characters, a pattern that climaxes with the Satan of the *Mysterious Stranger* manuscripts as a consciously theatrical performer before a gaping humanity—a figure who cannot keep clear the line between fantasy and reality. William C. Spengemann's wide-arching *The Adventurous Muse* is reviewed elsewhere, but I cannot help remarking that he goes beyond blurring the line between imagination and experience by proposing that literature dominates over life, that—in one of his more subdued dicta—"Twain's determinism derives as much from what happens to Huck as from what happened to Susy or the Paige typesetter" (pp. 213–40). It remains to be seen whether Spengemann heralds a renewed estheticism whose credo will get firmer exegesis.

iii. On Individual Writings

Two happy trends in Mark Twain scholarship call for attention this year: "A Note on 'The Notorious Jumping Frog of Calavaras County' " (*KAL* 18:52–56) by Masanori Tokunaga rates mention primarily as a mark of the increasingly specialized study of our literature in Japan, and the level of the *Mark Twain Journal* keeps rising. Tokunaga, after deciding that the famous yarn shows frontier "goodness" being poisoned by civilization, sorts out the elements that infuse an anecdote with "literary essence." Although my chapter passes over many of the articles in *MTJ*, an example of its rising quality is the veteran Mark Twain scholar Walter Blair's "The Petrified Man and His French Ancestor" (19, i:1–3). Blair soundly offers *The Second Book of Rabelais* as a source for one of the hoaxes set in Nevada. The same number (pp. 14–15) also carries the reasonable if unexciting

"Mark Twain's Pistol Characteristics in *Roughing It*," in which James R. Saucerman points out that three characters are given handguns typical of their status.

The weightiest article on the early journalism is Tom Reigstad's "From Buffalo *Express* to *Sketches New and Old*" (*EngR* 28, iv:19–22), which studies the revision of those pieces selected for book form in 1875. Reigstad demonstrates that the changes could be careless, erratic in their redirection toward a national audience, and sometimes just bad. The year's most provocative article bears down too hard on its thesis that the tourist-narrator of *The Innocents Abroad* comes across as devoted to "pure play," as a persona who so "vigorously and consistently tries to entertain *himself*" that he absorbs the other "apparently incongruous impersonations." Most of those critics who have pinned down some persona or other in the earlier writings will respond to Bruce Michelson's "Mark Twain the Tourist: The Form of *The Innocents Abroad*" (*AL* 49:385–98), with the argument that the wiles of humor helped Mark Twain to cover up his reckless touches and to have it not merely both but several ways in his scattergun efforts to write a first book. As a handy example of these reckless touches, "Mark Twain in the Middle East" (*TQ* 20, ii:35–41) by Steven G. Kellman remarks on the inconsistencies of the narrative voice in *The Innocents Abroad.* He is mainly interested, however, in the rise in negative tones as the book reaches the Middle East.

Curiously, no other essayists worried much about any of the books before *Huck Finn,* which in turn elicited little explication. There were two attempts, however (*MTJ* 18, iv), to find *Huck Finn's* key in the first chapter, and it was approached by Claude Simpson, Jr., from the supposedly fallacious angle of the author's intention. In his lucid and sane "Huck Finn after *Huck Finn*" (*Gerber Festschrift*, pp. 59–72) Simpson concludes that Mark Twain was fuzzy about his purposes and their resulting achievement, because his later tries at matching his masterpiece depended on Huck's "narrative voice rather than the full range" of his personality and its opportunities for irony. Joseph M. Griska, Jr., in "Two New Joel Chandler Harris Reviews of Mark Twain" (*AL* 48:584–89), reveals that a conservative southerner could praise *Huck Finn* as an "almost artistically perfect picture of life and character"; Harris also thought he perceived distinctly that its "moral . . . teaches the necessity of manliness and self-sacrifice." Cooly ignoring his own *Mark Twain and Southwestern Humor* (1959),

Kenneth S. Lynn's "Welcome Back from the Raft, Huck Honey!" (*ASch* 46:338–47) protests that since the 1950s *Huck Finn* has been mistaught as a rejection of family and the enveloping society, that such a "Dropoutsville" gospel fitted the mood of American academics rather than the author's plans, which included restoring Huck to the St. Petersburg where he had been reasonably content in *The Adventures of Tom Sawyer.* Moreover, continues Lynn, *Tom Sawyer Abroad* proved that Huck can go home again.

With *Mark Twain's "Huckleberry Finn": Race, Class and Society* (London: Chatto and Windus; distrib. in U.S.A. by Humanities Press, Atlantic Highlands, N.J.), which was written for a series emphasizing how past masterpieces can "throw light" on current "matters of moral, social, and political concern," Michael Egan expounds a low-pitched Marxist interpretation. Having determined that he is dealing with "one of the darkest novels in American fiction" whose hero ranks as virtually the "loneliest figure in all fiction," he deduces that the novel meant to portray a "profoundly corrupting and violent milieu in which few human virtues" can survive so long as the system of slavery deforms whites as much as blacks; for a 20th-century public, *Huck Finn,* through a fidelity surpassed only by its vividness, carries a still-needed indictment of the "cash-nexus" society, cruelty toward human beings, and a "religionism" that perpetuates rather than combats such evils. Egan keeps his analysis both more responsive to the text and less melioristic than Philip S. Foner's similar approach in *Mark Twain: Social Critic* (1958). His most intriguing angle may be his distinction between Clemens's "subjective public"—his "own social class" typified by rural southern whites—and his "objective public" very palpable in the Nook Farm circle, on whose taste Egan blames the faults of the Evasion or the fake-rescue episode at the Phelps farm. Critics who deplore it may like having a fresh culprit, though Van Wyck Brooks would claim he had pointed the finger much earlier.

Among the essayists who invoke *Huck Finn* for a broader argument Gary Stephens, in "Haunted Americana: The Endurance of American Realism" (*PR* 44:71–84), marches toward the position that since every realistic novel erects a "dialectic between public assertion and hidden yearning," Clemens's "most moral impulses are embodied in Huck but thwarted by the mad energy embodied in Tom." The stickiest patch comes when Stephens classes *Huck Finn* with the Howells-Dreiser mode of mimesis; for another pattern Jackson J. Benson, in "John Steinbeck's *Cannery Row*: A Reconsideration" (*WAL* 12:11–40), puts it at the head of a "folk tradition" in our fiction. To propound a dichotomy between kinds of the comic spirit, Edward L. Galligan in "True Comedians and False: *Don Quixote* and *Huckleberry Finn*" (*SR* 86, i:66–83), ends up maintaining that, better than he knew, Mark Twain exposed Tom Sawyer's cruel, egocentric, applause-seeking "false" humor by contrasting it with a "spontaneous and free-flowing" fun radiated not only by Huck but also by Jim. Most arresting may be the hypothesis that after *Huck Finn* Tom's creator was torn between dislike for his then most popular character and delight in his marketability. Though Frank Scafella, in "Models of the Soul: Authorship as Moral Action in Four American Novels" (*JAAR* 44[1976]:459–75) sets out mainly to praise an Emersonian-Christian mysticism, he achieves freshness through his precision of proposing that during the much-cited sunrise scene of chapter 19 Huck breaks through to an "original relation of love with the river." Scafella also stirs thought by observing that Huck thus becomes "author of his life, and it is this fact with its self-transcendent possibilities that so fascinated Hemingway," and not simply his vernacular. With John Harris, in "Principles, Sympathy and Doing What's Right" (*Philosophy* 52:96–99), we pass to a specialist in ethics refuting a colleague who had utilized Huck to exemplify the potential tug between precepts and instinctive kindness. It is worth pondering the conclusion that if Huck had "some minimum level of consciousness about his moral principles" he might feel he owes less to Miss Watson than to Jim, for whom more is at stake besides.

Hank Morgan has receded from the limelight, perhaps because the critics emphasizing his violences have carried the day. With "The Conflict of Dialects in *A Connecticut Yankee*" (*BSUF* 18, iii:51–58) Dennis Berthold adds to their consensus the twist that Hank's "gradual, unconscious acceptance of the Arthurian 'dialect' . . . underscores the failure of vernacular values in the face of ingrained, conventional, genteel values." In fleshing out this contention Berthold does sensitize us to lapses in Hank's idiom which bulk large if we ignore irony even more than parody. But to proclaim that Hank crystalizes the author's "doubt as to the ultimate worth" of vernacular values is to ignore many pages written after 1889—including facets of *Pudd'nhead Wilson*, which continues to get more respect than it may deserve. For example, David L. Vanderwerken, in "The Triumph of Medievalism in *Pudd'nhead Wilson*" (*MTJ* 18, iv:7–10), believes that Wilson's fortunes reflect the benighted "feudalism" of an antebellum town because he is a rounded character who can eventually shoulder the burden of one of Mark Twain's "darkest moral and political statements." Joseph B. McCullough, however, in "*Pudd'nhead Wilson*: A Search for Identity" (*MTJ* 18, iv:1–6), judges Wilson to be "relatively unrealized" in a "mechanistic function." He nevertheless admires the novel as a firmly conceived inquiry into the process "whereby man may ascertain his identity . . . if, indeed, an identity could be established at all" when the disorienting gap between the apparent and the actual is acknowledged. Evidently those critics who cannot soar to anagogic heights from what they see as the pedestrian workmanship of the novel have no impact on the thinking of Vanderwerken and McCullough.

The scholarship for 1977 might seem to imply that *Pudd'nhead Wilson* was Mark Twain's last book of consequence. For what came after there were only articles on the shorter pieces. Ricki Morgan, in "Mark Twain's Money Imagery in 'The £1,000,000 Bank Note' and 'The $30,000 Bequest' " (*MTJ* 19, i:6–10), compares two stories that are seldom discussed. If one of them is fairly transparent, Morgan helpfully proposes that the hero of "The £1,000,000 Bank Note" merits his prosperity because his scale of values climbs above the prevalent worship of money. In "Moralism and Determinism in 'The Man That Corrupted Hadleyburg' " (*SSF* 14:49–54) Mary E. Rucker decides that while the Richardses' environment makes them susceptible to the stranger's plot the author gives them an active conscience they are free to obey, that the story contains firm ethical standards. Revisiting a well-trodden grave William L. Andrews, in "The Politics of Publishing: A Note on the Bowdlerization of Mark Twain" (*MarkhamR* 7:17–20), adds to the list of A. B. Paine's sins his cutting of 145 words from "To the Person Sitting in Darkness" for its reprinting in *Europe and Elsewhere*, presumably to accommodate it to the isolationist mood of the 1920s. Almost too succinctly, Gay S. Herzberg, in "*A Dog's Tale*: An Expanded View" (*MTJ* 19, i:20), elevates a pathetic story into an attack on the "misuse of language, the cold-bloodedness of science and the evils of slavery." Finally, linking the ends of a long career, Daryl E. Jones, in "The Source of 'Everlasting Sunday': A Note on Twain's 'Enchanted Sea-Wilderness' "

(*MTJ* 19, i:18–19), believably traces a fragment of late writing back to an incident of 1866.

"Scholarship" is firmer than most abstractions, and a contributor seldom agonizes over what is relevant for *ALS*. But the renewed emphasis on teaching encourages interest in materials that can help out with an undergraduate class; furthermore, outside perspectives can sharpen the vision of a literary critic. So I find it worthwhile to mention Herman Jay's "Hollywood and American Literature: The American Novel on the Screen" (*EJ* 66, i:82–6) for its terse comments on the 1939 filming of *Huck Finn*. Two essays in *The Classic American Novel and the Movies* are more enlivening. In "Tom Sawyer: Saturday Matinee" (pp. 73–82) Dan Fuller enhances sensitivity to the visual and dramatic aspects of *Tom Sawyer* by comparing it with the Paramount film of 1930 but also underlines its wavering between adult and juvenile readerships. Peter Brunette's "Faces in the Mirror: Twain's Pauper, Warner's Prince" (pp. 105–13) offends elitism by maintaining that the 1937 film made better sense than the original *Prince and the Pauper*, thus bringing Mark Twain back into pop culture with a vengeance.

Duke University

7. Henry James

Robert L. Gale

As I take over for a lustrum (or less) from William T. Stafford the happy task of surveying the scholarship on James, I should like to make four points. First, Professor Stafford should be commended for a superb job; he always selected the best and commented temperately. Second, I will not second-guess him by touching on anything published in 1976 (or earlier) which he omitted. Third, the James factory is so productive that I apologize here and now for my omissions and askances. And fourth, when you (or your friends) publish on James, it would help greatly if you could send me a citation or—better—a copy.

Five books and about a hundred articles, chapters, and essays concerning James appeared in 1977. A surprising number are excellent. Charles R. Anderson's *Person, Place, and Thing in Henry James's Novels* and Elsa Nettels's *James & Conrad* are excellent, and Strother B. Purdy's *The Hole in the Fabric* (while generating some weird reviews) is full of value. Essays by Bert Bender, Mildred Hartsock, Michael Routh, David Seed, Carl S. Smith, William Bysshe Stein, and Adeline R. Tintner seem especially noteworthy. Works by James receiving most critical attention are *The Portrait of a Lady*, *The Princess Casamassima*, "The Turn of the Screw," *The Wings of the Dove*, *The Ambassadors*, and the autobiographical volumes.

i. Sources, Parallels, Influences

Andrea Roberts Beauchamp, in "'Isabel Archer': A Possible Source for *The Portrait of a Lady*" (*AL* 49:267–71), identifies "Isabel Archer" by Professor Alden, D.D., in *The Ladies' Wreath*, 1848–49 volume, as a possible "germinal motive" for James's novel, since Alden's heroine, like James's, is bright, beautiful, and then blighted by marriage to a cold hypocrite. Further, both fictions contrast simplicity and smooth corruption, and both Isabels let appearance mask reality too long.

The indefatigable Adeline R. Tintner is blessedly still at it. In her "James and Balzac: *The Bostonians* and 'La Fille aux yeux d'or'" (*CL* 29:241–54), she masses relevant details with her customary clarity to note similarities between James's novel and Honoré de Balzac's decadent story. In the latter, Henri De Marsay vies with the Marquise de San-Réal for total possession of gifted Paquita Valdèz, all of which sounds like Basil Ransom struggling with Olive Chancellor over Verena Tarrant. An interesting point in this absorbing essay is Tintner's tracing of the word *curious* in James "to connote strange or unusual sexual behavior."

It is well known that Robert Browning is the model of Clare Vawdrey in James's fantastic story "The Private Life." James said so in the pertinent Preface; further, his *Notebooks* reinforce the critical truism. Rehearsing this evidence well, Earl F. Bargainnier has as his main purpose, in "Browning, James, and 'The Private Life'" (*SSF* 14:151–58), the dismantling of an earlier theory that "The Private Life" is in reality disguised autobiography. Bargainnier exposes the faults of such reasoning, presents definitive "evidence of James's knowledge of Browning's work and personality," and concludes that James's own statements on his story are totally credible. A related essay is George Monteiro's "Henry James and the Lessons of Sordello" (*WHR* 31: 69–78), which presents parallels between the "plot" of Browning's poem entitled "A Light Woman," and those of James's short stories "A Light Man" and "The Lesson of the Master." In each work, we have "three individuals, two of whom compete for the favor of the third"; further, James borrows certain key words and imagery. Such parallels may seem obvious, but only when they are pointed out, as Monteiro neatly does. He also details James's relationship to Browning, briefly discusses the American writer's story "The Private Life," and closes with the fascinating implication that James may have regretted his self-sacrificial dedication to the literary muse, since Browning was so obviously able to combine devotion to art and a life of gregariousness.

The latest in a list of superb Plutarchian studies of James and other authors of comparable stature is Elsa Nettels's *James & Conrad* (Athens: Univ. of Ga. Press). In earlier book-length works, James has been compared to Mark Twain, Edith Wharton, John Hay, Henry

Adams, Balzac, and Ivan Turgenev. *James & Conrad* is as fine as any of its predecessors. Nettels begins by tracing the personal and professional relationship between the two authors; then she compares and contrasts their narrative methods, their handling of romance elements, satire, the grotesque, and tragedy.

James and Conrad met at a time of crisis in the life of each, became neighbors for a while, had several mutual friends, and criticized each other's work; Conrad saw James as an example of inexhaustible artistic power. Their aesthetic aims were slightly different: James sought to represent life and be a watcher from a window, and relished the lonely joys of creation, whereas Conrad was self-expressive, and imaged himself as a spinning spider and a coal miner whose creative isolation was an agony. James's protagonists move from comfortable ignorance into a strange world, where they learn; Conrad's characters jump in time, see their worlds harrowed, are baffled, and grow less certain. In separate chapters, Nettels steadily contrasts her authors with respect to romance: James has some romantic characters and other characters who are thrown into a romanticized world. On the other hand, as the critic says, Conrad plays Coleridge to James's Wordsworth. The chapter on satire is perhaps the best in the whole book: James satirizes to ameliorate, caricatures, and uses a variety of rhetorical tricks but little sneering; Conrad exposes squalor, the rot of civilization, and political and financial dishonesty. James's grotesques may be ugly, sordid, and licentious, but they usually play relatively minor roles, whereas Conrad's are often of major importance as they move in vain across inhuman, even hellish scenes. The chapter on tragedy is also superb: Nettels efficiently regards James as more Hegelian, Conrad more Schopenhauerian. That is, the former sees life in uneasy balance, a strange alloy, while the latter sees life as a conflict of opposites. James's heroes are aware, while Conrad's are aware that they are nature's victims.

Parallels between James's *The American* and William Makepeace Thackeray's *The Newcomes* are identified and exhaustively discussed by Michael C. Kotzin in "*The American* and *The Newcomes*" (*EA* 30:420–29). Kotzin notes similarities in locale of composition, fictive scenes, onomastic techniques, fairy-tale plot elements, a common target of satire, and the protagonists' victory-in-defeat behavior.

Mary M. Lay, in "Parallels: Henry James's *The Portrait of a Lady* and Nella Larson's *Quicksand*" (*CLAJ* 20:475–86), identifies parallels between James's novel and Larsen's 1928 one (heroine isolation and longings, patterns of dark and light, and subordinate characters —including hypocritical female friends and children in need). Lay also notes vital differences (Isabel Archer makes a conscious choice at the end and has hope, whereas Helga Crane stays only through default and is pretty hopeless). Interesting, but did Nella Larsen ever read James?

With brevity, charm, and persuasiveness, Raymond J. Wilson in "Henry James and F. Scott Fitzgerald: Americans Abroad" (*RS* 45: 82–91) reveals similarities in setting and character descriptions, in character challenges and decisions, and in criteria for reader judgment with respect to James and F. Scott Fitzgerald. Evidence comes from *The American*, "Daisy Miller," and *Tender Is the Night*. Wilson ponders the likelihood of conscious or unconscious imitation of James by Fitzgerald, but then daringly hopes that "the expatriate experience" for each author was so "powerful" that "the parallels do not result from any form of imitation."

Cynthia Griffin Wolff in *A Feast of Words: The Triumph of Edith Wharton* (New York: Oxford Univ. Press) says that Edith Wharton rarely tried to imitate James and was inferior to him when she did—as in *Madame de Treymes*. Wolff abundantly proves that "Wharton never intended to perpetuate the Jamesian sensibility: she openly disavowed a debt to 'le maître' and found herself genuinely hard put to admire much that James wrote after 1889." All the same, Adeline R. Tintner, in "A Source from *Roderick Hudson* for the Title *The Custom of the Country*" (*NMAL* 1: item 34), finds minor word and action parallels in James's *Roderick Hudson*, and Wharton's *The Custom of the Country* and *The Age of Innocence*. All three novels feature heroines indifferent to rigid social customs in their respective countries.

Tintner also discusses the possible influence of James's autobiographical volumes on Marcel Proust and James Joyce, in her "Autobiography as Fiction: 'The Usurping Consciousness' as Hero of James's Memoirs" (*TCL* 23:239–60). But since the main value of this splendid essay lies in the light it sheds on James's autobiographical techniques, I shall discuss it below.

Several essays discuss film adaptations of James's fiction. Jerry W. Carlson in "*Washington Square* and *The Heiress*: Comparing Artistic Forms" (in *The Classic American Novel and the Movies*, pp. 95–104), after "weigh[ing] the inevitable alterations and transformations in terms of their appropriateness to the individual artistic wholes," prefers James, whose heroine Catherine Sloper, unlike her filmic counterpart, "never stoops to conquer." This volume also has an essay by Jeanne Thomas Allen (pp. 132–42) entitled "*Turn of the Screw* and *The Innocents*: Two Types of Ambiguity," in which James's fiction and Jack Clayton's film adaptation of it are contrasted. Topics discussed include narrative aspects, the governess's sensitivity, the ordering of events, point of view, sound effects, reader-viewer sympathy, and the ending. Allen says that the movie requires "the viewer's sympathies [to] vacillat[e]" as it "produces tension," whereas James gives us "the supreme tension of ambiguity." (See also James W. Palmer's "Cinematic Ambiguity: James's *The Turn of the Screw* and Clayton's *The Innocents*" [*LFQ* 5:198–215].) Henry Nash Smith greatly admires Arthur Barron's film script of "The Jolly Corner," for being better than standard critical interpretations of James's tale. After exposing the limitations of representative critical approaches, Smith praises Barron for identifying "the buried part of Brydon's psyche as his male sexuality." Smith's comments appear in a misnamed anthology called *The American Short Story*, edited by Calvin Skaggs (New York: Dell), which includes James's story and scenes from the film script.

ii. Criticism: General

The most ambitious book this year dealing with James, and the one which is the most complimentary to him, is Strother B. Purdy's *The Hole in the Fabric: Science, Contemporary Literature, and Henry James* (Pittsburgh: Univ. of Pittsburgh Press). It is rich and ranging, and places James in the thrilling, sometimes depressing context of modern science and the writings of such "postmodern" figures as John Barth, Samuel Beckett, Friedrich Dürrenmatt, Günter Grass, Thomas McMahon, Vladimir Nabokov, Alain Robbe-Grillet, and Kurt Vonnegut.

Purdy considers James to be "a portentous event for the contemporary novel," and discusses him in relation to many later authors aware of and using modern scientific research on terror and horror, disorientation in time, the implications of space travel, sexuality and the erotic and the feminine psyche, and the concept of nothingness. Purdy finds "notable precedents of several kinds in James," who, he adds, "is one of those writers who got there ahead of us, for the eerie *absences* in his work . . . express what we can only now better see." The texts by James on which Purdy focuses include "The Turn of the Screw" for murder, "The Jolly Corner" for terror, *The Sense of the Past* for time's looping and forking relativities, *The Awkward Age* for eroticism, and "The Beast in the Jungle" for *nada*. He relates "The Turn of the Screw" to Vonnegut's *Cat's Cradle*, "The Jolly Corner" to James Blish's *Spock Must Die!*, *The Sense of the Past* to Miles Breuer's *The Gostak and the Doshes* and Nabokov's *Ada*, *The Awkward Age* to Nabokov's *Lolita*, and "The Beast in the Jungle" to Beckett's *Waiting for Godot*.

The Hole in the Fabric is captivating but imperfect. I wish that it were either twice as long or a little shorter. It meanders with what is either occasional rambling or steady subtlety beyond most readers. James disappears too much of the time, and perhaps too much is made of his current relevance on insufficient evidence. Specialists in Dürrenmatt's *The Pledge*, J. W. Dunne's time theory, tachyon travel, the Gödelian loop, positrons and antiprotons, chess symbolism, Noam Chomsky's linguistic theories, nonverbal communication, Marcel Proust, sexual dysfunction, and unreliable narrators—all of which are flirted with by Purdy—may wish to offer correctives to and refinements of his insights.

The purpose of Charles R. Anderson's *Person, Place, and Thing in Henry James's Novels* (Durham: Duke Univ. Press) is to show that James is the world's first modern novelist in technique, because, perfecting a lead from Balzac, he renders character in terms of place and thing, and in the process makes into symbols of characters such "places" as landscapes, cities, gardens, hotels, museums, theaters, streets, *palazzi*, mansions and estates, *châteaux*, apartments, studios, and dining places, and such "things" as walls and façades, statues, paintings, furniture, clothing, paper documents, sewing, dishes and silver, books, objets d'art, and jewelry. Anderson shows that James became more interested in letting place and thing "clarify . . . the relations among characters" and less in having them "releas[e] emotions and advanc[e] the plot." Anderson confines himself almost exclusively to two novels from each of James's three phases; they are *Roderick Hudson*, *The American*, *The Portrait of a Lady*, *The Princess Casamassima*, *The Wings of the Dove*, and *The Ambassadors*. To show that James's artistic evolution was unified and seamless, Anderson adduces evidence not only from some of James's other fiction but also from his nonfictional prose (including his *Autobiography*, letters, reviews, travel essays, and criticism). Anderson brilliantly analyzes the subtle relationships of fictive scene and picture, drama scene, and painting.

In my view, Anderson is at his best when he treats *The American* (especially the ball scene), *The Portrait of a Lady* (especially its owner-symbolizing habitats), *The Wings of the Dove* (mostly for discussing the Bronzino at Matcham, Milly Theale's sickness, and the teetering of "appreciators" and "exploiters"), and *The Ambassadors* (in part for the spellbinding discussion of Renoir, Lambinet, and Monet). Anderson keeps his lucid thesis in mind admirably; but his criticism is so ranging and erudite, so explicatory and analogical, that the reader may still be dazzled at times. For this reason, it is imperative, in my view, to consult the extensive index frequently: reviewing it will remind the reader of the thesis, especially the numerous entries under "Painting as symbol," "Person-place-thing," "Place-as-symbol," "Technique," and "Thing-as-symbol."

The Concept of Ambiguity—the Example of James (Chicago: Univ. of Chicago Press) by Shlomith Rimmon is a tough book which seems more likely to be the work of a logician or a mathematician than that of a lover of literature. In the first part, Rimmon "attempt[s] a definition of the 'concrete' microstructural units which constitute . . . ambiguity, and of the linkages among them." She "redefine[s] narrative ambiguity as the coexistence of mutually exclusive *fabulas* in one *sjužet*, or—at a more concrete level—the coexistence of two (or more) mutually exclusive systems of gap-filling clues." She also "describe[s] verbal ambiguity as a combination of inherent (potential) ambiguity arising from various phonological, lexical, and grammatical factors, and the contextual permission given to discordant isotopies to unfold concurrently." Having narrowed her definition of ambiguity, she can rule out such "cognate phenomena" as "double and multiple meaning, openness, ambivalence, vagueness, irony, and symbolism."

In the second part, which is somewhat less abstruse, Rimmon analyzes four ambiguous fictional works by James; they are "The Lesson of the Master," "The Figure in the Carpet," "The Turn of the Screw," and that prolix lemon *The Sacred Fount.* As for "The Lesson of the Master," Rimmon weighs all evidence tending to support either of these statements: "St. George tricks Paul" and "St. George saves Paul." She considers the reversal scene, retrospective ambiguity, singly directed clues, and doubly directed clues. "The Figure in the Carpet" is ambiguous because "There is a figure in Vereker's carpet" and "There is no figure in Vereker's carpet." Discussion centers on the permanent central gap (together with mutually exclusive systems of gap-filling clues, both singly and doubly directed), and on the awakening of suspicion. Rimmon especially delights in "The Turn of the Screw" and *The Sacred Fount.*

S. Gorley Putt, in his gracefully written "Henry James, Radical Gentleman" (*MR* 18:179–86), contends that James has been "praised for the wrong reasons." He was not squeamish. Instead, especially in several later works, he lashed out at well-heeled American "moral and aesthetic" vulgarity. He also criticized "The ignorant callousness of the luckier inhabitants of Victorian London" in "downright soap-box denunciation," especially in *The Princess Casamassima.* Throughout his fiction he excoriated greed, especially emotional and sexual. Putt comments comprehensively that "By instinct James was a radical; by temperament he was a gentleman; by profession he was an artist." Putt also discusses James's profound respect for innate British decency and his loathing of cheap journalism.

In Mildred Hartsock's essay "The Most Valuable Thing: James on Death" (*MFS* 22:507–24) we have a beautiful treatment of James's attitude toward death and also a splendid model of academic scholarship. Hartsock gracefully but tough-mindedly reviews earlier critical pronouncements on the subject, summarizes James's public and private comments on it, and generalizes from his treatment of it in his fiction. She gently chides earlier critics for conclusions with which she cannot agree, and for good and sufficiently presented reasons. She labels James's essay "Is There a Life After Death?" "a rejection of absolutism and a hesitant commitment to openness and futurity. It is pragmatic. . . ." But in Hartsock's mind its "major thrust is an affirmation of life and an impatience with all who are 'dead' before they die." This "thrust" is also that of James's fiction, in which death frequently figures. Hartsock concludes that in it James dramatizes the following: the burdens of the past must not keep us from living in the present, zombies must be shaken back to life, and "conventionality or fear of life" should never be allowed to "repress fulfillment of the individual."

Citing Hartsock mainly to disagree, Joan S. Korenman, in "Henry

James and the Murderous Mind" (*ELWIU* 4:198–211), suggests that to James heightened consciousness is a great good and yet hypersensitivity can kill. "From James's early works to those of the celebrated major phase, the mind figures as the primary—indeed, almost the *only*—instrument of death." Surveying the pertinent fiction, Korenman shows that death in James is often self-willed or at least quickly follows when a sensitive creature, sometimes already sick, finds himself—or more often herself—misused by another (often of the opposite sex) who is inadequately conscious of subtle psychic ramifications. James paradoxically advises others to live all they can while depicting the fatal consequences of their doing so; for example, he dramatizes sexuality as "one of the most threatening aspects of life." A somber, disturbing essay. Yet I think that it often goes astray down its one dark path. For example, it suggests that John Marcher induced May Bartram's blood disorder in "The Beast in the Jungle" and that the governess's conduct in "The Turn of the Screw" is simply "destructive."

In a moving essay called "Henry James's Lyric Meditations upon the Mysteries of Fate and Self-Sacrifice" (*Genre* 9:247–62), Bert Bender praises James's most troublesome fictive form, the long short story. Bender suggests that "the best way to see through their seeming 'lack of interest in [story] as story' and into the dense flowerings of his unconventional narrative language and, further, into the organic wholeness of a particular piece—is to see them as lyric meditations." James's very ideas for stories fell into his mind from "mystic origins," we are told, and have a fated aesthetic organicism of their own, which James watches and meditates on in the ensuing fictions themselves. The process has a kind of secular religiosity, involving such Christian elements as "predestination, self-sacrifice, and love," as well as sainthood and martyrdom. Bender pays detailed but not exclusive attention to "The Bench of Desolation," which is, he contends, "not an ordinary story. Its wholeness [he adds] . . . is contained neither in its plot nor in its germ alone. Rather, it is contained in the tale's display—its stylistic recording—of the author's 'prime sensibility' as, through meditation and wonder, he sees his germ develop."

Ronald L. Lycette, in "Perceptual Touchstones for the Jamesian Artist-Hero" (*SSF* 14:55–62), moralizes to the effect that, for James, the typical artist—whether he is a painter like the narrator of "The Real Thing" or a writer like Dencombe in "The Middle Years"—is incomplete until he learns to transcend what is seen in order to share the felt life. Like Hawthorne, James clearly saw the personal danger in viewing life as a well-posed picture and other people's play.

iii. Criticism: Individual Novels

Critical attention this year to individual novels by James has been extensive, with *The Portrait of a Lady*, *The Princess Casamassima*, and *The Ambassadors* winning top honors.

In *Henry James: "The Portrait of a Lady": An Assessment* (Delhi: Oxford Univ. Press), Darsham Singh Maini offers a pleasant essay on James's first masterpiece. Maini combines routine derivative material from previous critics with sound insights of his own. He discusses James's life, career, and techniques; Isabel Archer's attributes, including her "ravaging ego"; her return to Rome, which is partly "irrational"; the centrality of Ralph Touchett; international aspects of the novel; the evil of Gilbert Osmond and Madame Merle (Maini's best chapter); and James's preoccupation with form and technique. Maini's work is essentially a study guide, intelligent and earnest, but also a trifle stilted.

More natural is Michael Routh's solid essay entitled "Isabel Archer's 'Inconsequence': A Motif Analysis of *The Portrait of a Lady*" (*JNT* 7:128–41), in which it is "argue[d] that Isabel's return to Rome is the inevitable and tragic result of a fatal character flaw: inconsequence. . . . Isabel Archer is a divided self, a 'two-sided' person whose intellect and spirit are irreconcilably at odds with each other." She is inconsistent, contradictory, and inconsequent regarding life and death, courtship and marriage, and travel; she confuses appearances and realities, imagines and theorizes inconsequently, is unnatural, likes surfaces but fears depths, and is wrenched by distinctions between head and heart. "The final act, then [running from Caspar Goodwood] of Isabel's self-contradictory type of inconsequence is to render her life inconsequent in the sense that it lacks ultimate significance." A bitter reading, surely, but with the virtue of consistency.

Eugene L. Stelzig, in "Henry James and the 'Immensities of Perception': Actors and Victims in *The Portrait of a Lady* and *The Wings of the Dove*" (*SHR* 11:253–65), discusses comparable and differing techniques James uses in the two novels to dramatize "predator-victim relationships." The essay is solid and logical, helpful no doubt to beginning readers of James; but it rehearses tired evidence and should have been cut.

The Princess Casamassima evoked three fine studies this year. In his essay entitled "*The Princess Casamassima*: Suicide and 'The Penetrating Imagination'" (*TSL* 22:162–69), Philip Page shows that just as James uses his imagination to create fiction, so his characters—especially in this novel—penetrate, by acts of the imagination, the past, the future, and each other's minds. When Hyacinth Robinson finds his past unreadable, his future impossible, and his friends indifferent, he chooses suicide as "the final projection, the final imaginative leap." On the other hand, David Seed, in a powerful essay entitled "Hyacinth Robinson and the Politics of *The Princess Casamassima*" (*EA* 30:30–39), first slashes away at and then extends tentative leads from previous critics, and next independently reasons that Hyacinth, "a prig and an egotist" who fails to penetrate London more than visually, evinces no sympathy for the oppressed, initiates no course of positive action, sees himself as "shaped and beautified by his best experience," wants a home and a surrogate mother more than he does sexual love, and is a dependent more than a heroic loner whose suicide is "the ultimate indulgence of his passive nature." Marcia Jacobson's "Convention and Innovation in *The Princess Casamassima*" (*JEGP* 76:238–54) is in large part a study of the ways in which James prepared himself to write his one and only novel about the poor. He probably read much working-class fiction with plots involving "the descent to working-class life and the rise from it." Jacobson then excellently shows not only James's fortunate recoil from "the facile optimism" of the genre, but also his disappointing avoidance of any naturalistic treatment of poverty, specific depiction of the anarchist movement, and dramatizing of labor vs. capital. Given her point of view, Jacobson is right to label *The Princess Casamassima* "a disappointing book."

In "A House Divided: A New Reading of *The Bostonians*" (*CLAJ* 20:459–74), Barry Menikoff likens James's initially unpopular novel to a play of three acts (Books First, Second, and Third), each built around a focal scene (chapters 4–9, 26–28, and 40–42). All of this in order to highlight Basil Ransom's and Olive Chancellor's struggle for Verena Tarrant, with all of its sexual, social, and political overtones. The resulting *psychomachia* finds basic expression "through the dominant pattern of religious and martial imagery." Thus far, this is hardly a new reading. Menikoff's plot summary is too expansive, and then his conclusion is too bald that Verena is a "portrait of . . . [America's] conscience," fought for inconclusively by North (Olive) and South (Basil) during the Civil War and ever since by national—and indeed diversely human—elements which that incompatible pair represents.

A critical essay of major importance is Tzvetan Todorov's "The Verbal Age" (*CritI* 4:351–71)—translated by Patricia Martin Gibby. In it, Todorov brilliantly intermingles dozens of quotations from *The Awkward Age* and his own comments in a discussion of conversational uncertainties in that much-abused novel. He is aware that the meaning of many words used in talk is uncertain, that James further complicates his novel by ellipsis, anaphoric and deictic pronouns, lexical and propositional symbolism, and allusion—sometimes narrow, often almost limitless—and a commenting narrator. Todorov also analyzes the "symbolic deafness" of Tishy Grendon, Aggie, Lord Cashmore, and Edward Brookenham, who seem, respectively, one-track, naive, literal, and stupid. Finally, Tedorov comments on the linguistic complications which follow the habit of Mrs. Brookenham's circle of saying anything they please but never directly, and on certain technical consequences of James's casting *The Awkward Age* as a drama.

John Carlos Rowe's essay, "The Authority of the Sign in Henry James's 'The Sacred Fount' " (*Criticism* 19:223–40), gets my vote for the most needlessly obscure essay of the year on James. The recondite thesis is that "The narrator sustains his voice only by acknowledging his submission to a language that permits him to exist. By deconstructing his own authority, he discovers himself by means of a critical reflection on the nature of signification." Rowe also attempts to relate the partly autobiographical narrator, as he struggles toward social identity, to James as he moves toward his distinctive voice. Rowe's insights will be enjoyed by only a fraction of his potential audience, because of a critical vocabulary which seems almost willfully esoteric.

Stuart Hutchinson's tightly coiled essay called "James's Medal: Options in *The Wings of the Dove*" (*EIC* 27:315–35) takes its title from James's prefatory image of Milly Theale's drama as a medal hung before the reader, a medal with obverse and reverse as options for the spectator. Hutchinson is mainly concerned to offer a reverse to the image which too many critics have polished: Milly as "a Christ-like martyr." He sees her instead, or at least partly, as culpable in her self-serving misinterpreting of Kate Croy and especially as wanting her bequest to Merton Densher to help him idealize the donor.

William Bysshe Stein has struck again. In his naughty, outrageously overwritten essay entitled "*The Wings of the Dove*: James's Eucharist of *Punch*" (*CR* 21:236–60), he persuades the most recalcitrant of Jacobites that Milly is a phony Alice in (and out of) Matcham, looking through Bronzinos and striking poses (with her associates) reminiscent of Puseyites, the subjects of Pre-Raphaelites, Du Maurier victims, Pater patter, *Punch* cartoons, and other *fin de siècle* puncturers of the littry decadent. Thus, Milly is unlovely and morbid, her Susan Shepherd Stringham "the shepherding godmother of an impossible dream," Lord Mark "the Bonehead Peer," and others participants in a parade of *Punch* targets. A sample of Stein's song: "Their [Kate's and Milly's] mutual pillage of fashionable jargon, always gratingly advertised by James's plumagy interpolations, reduces the language of the novel to a meaningless game of ventriloquy." The whole hypnotic essay is so of a piece that it is hard to quote from. To be appreciated, it ought to be read aloud at a department meeting where drinks are served, and Rossetti and Burne-Jones slides projected on a soiled screen.

More essays this year were devoted to *The Ambassadors* than to any other novel by James. Three are reasonably short. In "*The Ambassadors*: The Man of Imagination Encaged and Provided for" (*SNNTS* 9:137–53), Susan M. Greenstein considers Lambert Strether as partly an autobiographical figure, since both he and his creator question their American heritage and wonder whether they have "missed the essence of life." Greenstein neatly differentiates between James's "[i]ronic undercutting" of John Marcher (of "The Beast in the Jungle") and his more pervasive "radical undercutting" of Strether, and also discusses Strether's incomplete, troubling appreciation of foreign places (partly in relation to James's strictures against expatriates Nathaniel Hawthorne and William Wetmore Story). Strether is ultimately seen here as one whose "imaginative capacity" cannot wholly survive what he discovers about Chad Newsome and Marie de Vionnet. John M. Warner's "'In View of Other Matters': The Religious Dimensions of *The Ambassadors*" (*ELWIU* 4:78–94) by contrast suggests that in this novel James "develops a searching critique of both the moral and the aesthetic attitudes toward life," in order to unify aspects of aesthetic vs. moral reality. Warner reviews pertinent evidence from James's Preface and his *Notebooks*, examines Strether's disillusionment with the fascinating but killing Edenic blandishments of life, and concludes that by the end of the novel the hero is beyond merely synthesizing morality and aesthetics and has become different in "kind and perception"—in short, has become a man of positively Kierkegaardian "religious piety." An efficient way of fixing Warner's fine insights in one's mind is to see with the critic that Strether rejects Maria Gostrey because she offers a return to childhood and rejects Marie de Vionnet because she offers a return to the pagan past, and that he then accepts instead a dignified Other—beyond any Either/Or. Edgar J. Burde, in "*The Ambassadors* and the Double Vision of Henry James" (*ELWIU* 4: 59–77), however, sees Strether as remaining basically an imaginative, idealizing visionary whose quixoticism is only temporarily defeated by his confronting sexuality in Chad and Marie. Burde further sees James's purpose in the novel to be the dramatizing of a debate between the world of spirit and that of matter. The critic also suggests that after passing through "confused and disordered ambiguity" in *The Sacred Fount*, James arrived at the controlled and "complex double vision" which is at work in *The Ambassadors*. Burde valuably adjusts his theory to the persistent demands of previous critics who alternately ennoble Strether and ridicule him, and then ingeniously reads his story as a counterpoint of those very tugs.

An ambitious essay is "The Jamesian Dialectic in *The Ambassadors*" (*SoR* 13:468–91) by Daniel Mark Fogel. It is good-spirited and clearly written, and its general thesis is that *The Ambassadors* is "built upon polarities and upon the possibilities for resolving them." The special virtue of Fogel's essay lies in his meticulous adducing of evidence "from the minute structures of phrases, sentences, paragraphs, and chapters to the broad design of [the] whole." Fogel runs through much previous criticism, to gain both reinforcement and target practice. At the end, after beautifully analyzing much evidence from various levels, all in explication of his thesis that the novel is a "generally Romantic dialectic of spiral return supported by bipolar elements," Fogel boldly concludes, *contra* several supposedly high-powered critics, that Strether's "final position[,] . . . as combining the best in his American background and in his European education," is positive. I am not sure that we can ever be quite so certain about this subtly ambiguous novel, but Fogel has given us much to ponder.

The James section of Viola Hopkins Winner's quick, spottily packed essay entitled "The American Pictorial Vision: Objects and Ideas in Hawthorne, James, and Hemingway" (*SAF* 5:143–59) stems partly from her previous book *Henry James and the Visual Arts* (see *ALS 1970*). Here she discusses how James, among others, "adapted and transformed pictorial conventions," and analyzes "what is uniquely American in American pictorialism, of which these are the basic conventions: works of graphic art are not merely described as part of the mise-en-scene but are used to delineate character and to develop theme; descriptions of people, places, or nature reflect identifiable schools or works of art; art works provide structural unity or have inspired a sense of spatial ordering within a temporal form. . . ." As for James, Winner concentrates exclusively here on *The Ambassadors*. In Paris, Strether learns to see, make moral distinctions, and be inductive, unlike Chad and others from Woollett. The idealized Barbizon Lambinet episode—"the richest and most sustained pictorial rendering in James's fiction, indeed in American fiction"—yields to its more hedonistic Impressionist sequel. Winner seems best here when she discusses *The Ambassadors* as "permeated by the ethos of Impressionism," and correlating with Impressionism in its point of view, audience challenge, and (partly) structure.

Finally, *The Golden Bowl* continues to challenge ingenious critics, if not wide audiences. Martha Banta's essay entitled "About America's 'White Terror': James, Poe, Pynchon, and Others" (in *Literature and the Occult*, pp. 31–53) is a tangled, eclectic ramble through the implications of James's reference to Edgar Allan Poe's *Arthur Gordon Pym* at the outset of *The Golden Bowl*. Banta's trip takes us from Herman Melville's white symbolism, through Poe's, Henry Adams's, Emily Dickinson's, and Thomas Pynchon's, to James's Maggie Verver. Her light is positive, good, moral, loving—unlike previous luminosities. Though his realism is "agnostic, this-worldly," and though his characters can neither possess the ideal nor even "be certain what the ideal act ought to be," James shows his Maggie piercing Pym's "great white [American] curtain" and "making occult contact with both 'myself' and the beyondness of the self." As unoccult as can be is the emphasis of Michael T. Gilmore in *The Middle Way*, which includes a short chapter on *The Golden Bowl* (as well as an afterword touching on *The American Scene*). Gilmore shows the continuance into

James of earlier American romancers' discontent with their country's drift, especially after the Civil War, from the admirable Puritan "middle way"—between materialism and other-worldliness—toward capitalistic Calvinism, the worship of progress, and national millenialism. The best Puritans lived in the world without being of it; so does Maggie, in her way, once she sheds her nun-like naivete, enters the fallen world, learns to see reality, and fights to save her marriage.

iv. Criticism: Individual Tales

Only eight of James's short fictional works were considered in separate essays this year, with "The Turn of the Screw" leading the way in popularity.

Carl Wood's "Frederick Winterbourne, James's Prisoner of Chillon" (*SNNTS* 9:33–45) has possibilities but presses. The result is a farfetched comparison of Winterbourne, the narrator of "Daisy Miller," to Bonnivard, Lord Byron's famous prisoner, and of Daisy not only to the prisoner's briefly alighting bird but also to the memory of the prisoner's spirited younger brother.

James L. Babin touches on much in "Henry James's 'Middle Years' in Fiction and Autobiography" (*SoR* 13:505–17) but is finally disappointing. Babin suggests that "The Middle Years," James's short story, and *The Middle Years*, his autobiographical fragment, "share a common concern—the life of the artist." Both discuss how well the artist has done what he attempted and also the value of it. Neither Dencombe in the fiction nor James in his autobiography is concerned with nature or with social surfaces.

Dorothy W. Boland, in "Henry James's 'The Figure in the Carpet': A Fabric of the East" (*PLL* 13:424–29), suggests that Hugh Vereker's work approximates an Oriental vision of life rather than a specific statement; further, that "the characters . . . are each limited to their own perception by pure necessity, or karmic law." Vereker becomes "a spokesman for Vishnu," which George Corvick first perceives and Gwendolyn Erme then instinctively understands. They then successively and perhaps ironically die, thus being "released from all karmas of earthly life," while the obtuse narrator remains blinded by the veil of egocentricity.

Ralf Norrman's "The Intercepted Telegram Plot in Henry James's *In the Cage*" (*N&Q* 24:425–27) cleverly shows that when in chapter

13 of the story the "little spying, meddling telegraphist," who is habitually wrong in her romantic guesses, changes a word in Lady Bradeen's wire, she "changed the wrong word [that is, a name], and thereby, through *not* changing the right word [a code number], . . . did [Captain Philip] Everard a service."

Three 1977 essays belabor "The Turn of the Screw." Shoshana Felman in an essay two thousand words longer than its subject, "Turning the Screw of Interpretation" (*YFS* 55–56:94–207), makes use of a few French literary analogues, the teachings of Jacques Lacan (influential contemporary French psychoanalyst), and previous literary criticism on James's celebrated tale (mostly what is reprinted in Gerald Willen's *Casebook* and the Norton Critical Edition) to show that James's text returns on itself to trap naive and sophisticated readers alike, since it not only both invites and resists psychological interpretations but also lures Freudians and then implicitly comments on their comments. Felman exhaustively defines "a Freudian reading" (via erotic rhetoric, thematic content, and elliptical narration); criticizes opposing critical camps for attempting "to . . . eliminat[e] . . . the heterogeneity of meaning" in "The Turn of the Screw"; splendidly (if prolixly) discusses its prologue and the establishment therein of its title; and considers implications of the fact that the story is a text—in a way, a letter even—by the governess, is thus independent of Douglas, and also becomes "itself a story about letters." The critic then relates the letters in the tale to its ghosts, which are perhaps generated by the governess's seeing—i.e., reading—such letters. Next, the causes of Miles's death are worried over yet again, along with nonliteral implications of such words as *grasp*, *clutch*, *split*, *mast(er)*, *know*, *see*, *screw*, and *turn*. Finally, the immense subtlety of James's constructing "an *amusette* to catch those not easily caught" is illuminated. By contrast, "*The Turn of the Screw* Squared" (*SoR* 13:492–504) by Mary Y. Hallab simply connects James's thriller with traditional fairy tales and finds in it such archetypal elements as child-stealing, revenants, taboos, underworld homes, protective surrogate parents, influential gods, initiation and rebirth patterns, and the like. Such an interpretation starts naively from James's evasive prefatory remark that his story is "a fairy-tale pure and simple" but has—all the same—a legitimate place in the exasperatingly expanding critical "Screw" canon. But let us willingly add to it H. Robert Huntley's "James' *The Turn of the Screw*: Its 'Fine Machinery' " (*AI* 34:

224–37), which suggests that "one way in which James has balanced the possibilities between genuine apparitions and an unreliable narrator lies with that continuing and covert suggestion of some type of identification between governess and apparitions." Huntley shows how James uses all of the characteristics of the Doppelgänger, or double figure, in Western and Slavic literature.

William McMurray theorizes in "Reality in James's 'The Great Good Place'" (*SSF* 14:82–83) that the hero of the fable solipsistically carries his dream-world peace back into the actual world, and that the two worlds then merge. The moral therefore is that "Reality . . . is not something given and independent of man. Rather, it is something created in experience, and man is the creator."

In "Bridegroom and Bride in 'The Jolly Corner'" (*SSF* 14:282–84), Jason P. Rosenblatt sees parallels between Matthew 25 (which concerns the wise and foolish virgins, the parable of the talents, and the Last Judgment) and the story of Spencer Brydon. It is said that in the concluding section of James's story Brydon is likened to the resurrected Christ, Alice Staverton to one of the wise, lamp-trimming virgins, and the property on the jolly corner to a good and faithful servant.

v. Criticism: Specific Nonfictional Works

Into our final category fall essays and chapters having to do with James's nonfictional works, specifically here his criticism, his *Autobiography*, and the ongoing edition of his letters.

David Gervais begins his essay on "James's Reading of *Madame Bovary*" (*CQ* 7:1–26) with the statement that some of the best commentary on Gustave Flaubert has been a "kind of creative adverse criticism" by other fine "writers who felt his art to be incompatible with the art they themselves sought to create." James was such a one. His essay on Flaubert in *Partial Portraits* engages Gervais largely. He takes James to task for charging Flaubert with "so much dryness and coldness," whereas Flaubert really sought "to express a more than personal range of feeling," favored the tragic sense of *King Lear* more than the humanitarian moralizing of *Uncle Tom's Cabin*, and achieved form and characterization by rendering outside action instead of writing as George Eliot and James did.

Carl S. Smith, in "James's Travels, Travel Writings, and the Development of His Art" (*MLQ* 38:367–80), studies James's travel writings, letters, notebooks, autobiographical volumes, and critical prefaces to show "in how many . . . ways his travels and his writing about them trained him as a novelist and helped create the idiosyncratic cast of mind that we distinguish as Jamesian." Smith's essay, a major one on an aspect of the increasingly popular subject of American travel writing, first indicates the ways in which James used travel (it was his main way of "taking life," he wrote many essays and books on his wanderings, and those writings paid off in royalties and further "not only inspired his fictional studies of travelers but also gave him a broader awareness of the processes of observation that has come to be considered as characteristically his own"), and second discusses lessons which James learned by inveterate traveling ("much of what we perceive is influenced by what we intellectually are and have been," he "internalized" his travel adventures, he sought and noted the "composition" of familiar haunts, and he recorded his surprise when new areas sometimes did not square with his preconceptions of them).

James's autobiographical writings are also receiving more attention. In *The Art of Life* Mutlu Konuk Blasing discusses autobiographical materials by several American writers, including James, as they relate to spiritual confession and to stories of worldly success, and as they sometimes mingle these two American streams. Anything is autobiographical here in which hero, narrator, and author have one name. Blasing reads James's critical prefaces as "autobiographical and thus necessarily fictional," since James "is writing from the perspective of mature accomplishment; knowing what he has become, he can interpret the stages of his career as necessary steps in the evolution of the author of [such late works as] *The Ambassadors* and *The Golden Bowl.*"

The thesis of Thomas Cooley's *Educated Lives* is that the autobiographies of certain American authors born around 1840 are different from those which came before. Earlier autobiographies "expressed a fundamentally static view of the psyche," whereas those of Henry Adams, Mark Twain, William Dean Howells, and James are patterned narratives, half-way between history and fiction, of "the fallen self." James is seen as closest to Howells, professionally and psychologically. Cooley curiously calls his fifth chapter "A Sporting Life: Henry James," because James thought that his "pursuit of culture . . . promised a life 'tremendously "sporting" in its way'. . . ." Cooley richly discusses the harmonious subjects of James's *Autobiography*: the cultivation of his actively pitched imagination, the emergence of his aesthetic consciousness, his ever-improving sense of scenic composition, and "the play of his present imagination in the act of recapturing its past history."

A related study, also of great importance, is Adeline R. Tintner's "Autobiography as Fiction: 'The Usurping Consciousness' as Hero of James's Memoirs" (*TCL* 23:239–60), which does three things, and does each well. Tintner alarmingly reveals that James tampered with his brother William's letters to make them say what they ought to have said; thus James, quoting the revisions in his *Autobiography*, fashions "a new form of fiction, creative autobiography." Tintner then intriguingly shows that Proust, with *Du côté de Chez Swann*, was beginning to write similar fictionalized autobiography. Finally she draws parallels between James's memoirs and Joyce's *The Portrait of the Artist as a Young Man*. Such an outline of "Autobiography as Fiction" only begins to indicate its range. Tintner touches on comparisons, leaves them to pursue related topics, and then musically returns to amplify. Thus, she mentions the three authors' parents, their expanding consciousnesses, and their aesthetic use of various sensations. She notes parallels between James's work and works by each of the later writers—various tastes, childish scenes, crumbs and other triggering "clues," forms of inspiring art, family deaths, and dreams. What at first seems like unforgivable tampering by James with his documents figures eventually to be a possible influence upon two other literary titans of our century. I still wonder whether even a devoted brother ought to rephrase his sources to get at the truth of a higher order. Since James did so in his autobiographical volumes, did he also fake his documentation as he wrote *William Wetmore Story and His Friends*? Has anyone ever checked?

And last of all we come to Lyall Powers's "Self-Portrait by Henry James" (*MAQR* 16:113–17), which offers the reader of Leon Edel's ongoing edition of James's letters not only an example of extravagant praise of that editor's work but happily also some valuable insights on the importance to James of Newport as a kind of American Venice.

University of Pittsburgh

8. Pound and Eliot

George Bornstein

Scholars confronting the new periplum of Pound and Eliot studies will find that three features have become increasingly prominent. First, after years of expounding the two poets largely in terms of a critical theory derived from their own prose statements, critics have begun to approach Pound and Eliot more independently and to question their pronouncements both about literature and about the separation of their art and lives. The result at its best has been sympathetic revaluation and more balanced appreciation. Secondly, and partly in consequence, the relationship of Pound and Eliot to the 19th century has emerged with greater clarity. Modern readers may now look beyond earlier assertions of a sharp break to more just appraisal of change, continuity, and transformation. And finally, the major long works—*The Cantos*, *The Waste Land*, and *Four Quartets* —claim an increasingly large share of the commentary. One may add that lack of a standard edition of their complete works continues to obstruct the study of both writers.

i. Pound

***a.* Texts.** Publication of *Ezra Pound and Music: The Complete Criticism* (New York: New Directions), edited by the Canadian composer and music theorist R. Murray Schafer, helps remedy continuing problems of the inaccessibility and unreliability of Pound's texts. The volume groups Pound's surprisingly large amount of musical criticism into four chronological divisions: the early reviews in England to 1917, the pronouncements from 1917–21 under the pseudonym "William Atheling," the statements written in France and Italy, 1921–27, and those from the Rapallo years, 1928–41. Schafer provides full scholarly apparatus and a useful if pedestrian introduction. Particularly valuable are the reprinting of previously uncollected reviews from England, translations of articles for Italian newspapers during the Fascist years, and occasional manuscript materials. Schafer has done a good job, although a listing or tabulation of the individual pieces and their subjects would have been helpful. He projects a second volume dealing with Pound's "chief attempts to realize these ideas in musical compositions."

Of much smaller scope is D. G. Bridson's "Ezra Pound's 'Four Steps'" (*SoR* 13:862–71), a commentary with transcription from a tape of a short statement Pound made at St. Elizabeth's in 1956. As an explanation of the "four steps" that brought Pound into conflict with the American authorities, the statement sounds less "clearly-argued," "dispassionate," or "reasonable and persuasive" than Bridson claims in his introduction to it. "Two Unpublished Pound Letters: Pound's Aid to Dreiser" (*LC* 42:67–70) by Louis Oldani presents two salty letters from Pound to Harold Hersey, who, along with H. L. Mencken, coordinated the campaign against suppression of Dreiser's *The "Genius."* Finally, Margaret Bates reprints a manifesto by Pound against "pseudo-scholarship" in "EP: Maker of Connections" (*Paideuma* 6: 114–15).

***b.* Biography.** The fullest new biographical information appears in Ellen Williams's *Harriet Monroe and the Poetry Renaissance*. Drawing partly on unpublished papers relating to *Poetry* magazine and Miss Monroe, Williams gives the fullest account to date of Pound's early relation to both the magazine and its editor in which she convincingly corrects some of the condescension in Pound's view of his American correspondent. Joseph Parisi provides a convenient summary of the sections of Williams's book relevant to Pound studies in his review essay "Miss Monroe, Mr. Pound, and the Boorzoi" (*Poetry* 131:39–51).

Two articles make substantive contributions. Timothy Materer's "Ezra Pound and Gaudier-Brzeska: Sophie's Diary" (*JML* 6:315–21) usefully supplements traditional views of Pound's friendship with the young artist by culling pertinent passages from Sophie Brzeska's manuscript diary. Conceding that Sophie's continual jealousy of Gaudier's friends weakens her reliability, Materer traces her version of the early admiration and eventual cooling of relations between the two men. The article adds some new facts and a few interesting remarks of Pound on the subject of women and marriage shortly before his own wedding. A source demanding equal caution is David Anderson's translation of Felice Chilanti's 1972 Italian account of "Ezra Pound Among the Seditious in the 1940's" (*Paideuma* 6:235–50). While the properly skeptical scholar will not take at face value all the maneuvers of this self-described "dissident Fascist" to distance himself and Pound from "the *Fascist Fascists*, the real Fascists," Chilanti's account of Pound's involvement with the group surrounding the biweekly journal *Domani* in 1941–42 both clarifies some of Pound's activities during that period and illuminates some obscure allusions in *The Pisan Cantos* as well. Serious students of Pound's life may enjoy relaxing with H. Bibesco's parodic "Lunch with Uncle Ez" (*AtM* Aug:55–58).

c. General Studies. In contrast to recent works focusing on a specific segment of Pound's career, William Harmon offers a synoptic overview in *Time in Ezra Pound's Work* (Chapel Hill: The Univ. of N.C. Press). Tracing the theme of time in separate chapters through the early and late cultural criticism, the poetics, *Personae*, and *The Cantos*, Harmon demonstrates the development and ultimate frustration of Pound's views. While respectful, Harmon avoids the hagiography that has often plagued Pound studies and talks with helpful frankness about the Fascist years; the strictures on *Jefferson and/or Mussolini* for example are worthwhile, as are the speculations on the problem of time in Imagist poetry. Yet partly because he considers "time" in so many senses—as history, as subjective experience, as a characteristic of literary works, and as a category in itself—Harmon often offers a competent survey in place of an exploration in depth. With the poetry, too, Harmon provides more an ordering than an exegesis in which an occasional fine insight like the contrast between cyclical natural time and linear human decline in "Poem by the Bridge at Ten-Shin" mingles with pages of summary of other poems. This book will benefit undergraduate and perhaps graduate students more than advanced scholars. Vincent Miller's wandering essay, "Pound's Battle with Time" (*YR* 66:193–208), is of less use.

Max Nänny's "Oral Dimensions in Ezra Pound" (*Paideuma* 6:13–26) stands out as the year's most provocative general article. Collating a wide range of Pound's remarks on the oral aspects of literature and culture, Nänny argues that Pound's work—especially *The Cantos*—seeks to reverse for the modern world the change from oral to literate tradition in Classical Greece as described in Eric A. Havelock's *Preface to Plato*. Besides illuminating an important aspect of Pound's thought, Nänny generates important insights into the poetry in viewing it by "the standards of the tribal encyclopedists of the oral past." Charles O. Hartman's "Condensation: The Critical Vocabulary of Pound and Eliot" (*CE* 39:179–90) uses the laboratory meaning of "condensation" to interpret Pound's mistaken etymology of Dichten= Condensare and to employ it as the organizing motif of his critical theory. Hartman usefully directs attention from the overt doctrine to the metaphoric basis of the prose principles—a helpful technique with both Pound and Eliot—but does not fulfill his own announced goal, "to find a system behind this proliferation of terms." The poet and critic Theodore Weiss rethinks some of the central issues of Pound's career and reflects on some of his earlier critics in the course of tracing his own developing appreciation in "E. P.: The Man Who Cared Too Much" (*Parnassus* 5:79–119). More narrowly, Richard Luckett's " 'Meaning Motion': Old Music and Some Modern Writers" (*E&S* 30:88–97) touches on Pound and Dolmetsch. The variety of articles in the special Pound number of *Unisa English Studies* 15 testifies to growing world interest in Pound but adds more to the development of his reputation in South Africa than to advanced research.

d. **Relation to Other Writers.** While Pound's pervasive use of allusion links nearly any consideration of his work to that of other artists, a number of studies continue to take broad connections rather than individual works as their chief subjects. This year nearly all such investigations centered on 19th- and 20th-century writers.

The only book in this area, George Bornstein's *The Postromantic Consciousness of Ezra Pound* (Victoria, B.C.: ELS Monograph Series, Univ. of Victoria), extends to Pound studies the increasingly influential critical view of the centrality of Romanticism to modernism. After an early chapter on "Pound as a Critic of Romanticism," which assembles and analyzes Pound's disparate statements to demonstrate his ambivalent attitude toward the High Romantics and more consistent animus against their debased, turn-of-the-century followers, the book focuses on the acts of mind of the various personae in the dramatic monologues, Imagist poems, *Mauberley*, and *The Cantos*. In pursuing their poetic quests, Pound's personae operate within mind-centered paradigms recognizably related to Romantic enterprises in both lyric and epic. Yet in combining innovative technique with inherited tradition, Pound's postromanticism did not repeat but rather transformed his forerunners in service of his characteristic goal of making it new. The book speaks frankly about resultant problems of poetic structure and of the reconciliation between process and product in the verse.

Two articles by eminent Poundians examine further aspects of Pound's uneasy relation to Romanticism. Hugh Witemeyer's "Walter Savage Landor and Ezra Pound" in *Romantic and Modern*, pp. 147–63, carefully traces Pound's developing admiration and utilization of Landor. In a model of careful historical scholarship, Witemeyer concludes that in Landor "Pound admired the literary stance of the civilized man of letters who has inherited a rich tradition from the European past, and is determined to preserve and transmit it to future generations, even at the cost of ostracism and exile." In the same volume (pp. 133–45), Herbert N. Schneidau's "Pound and Wordsworth on Poetry and Prose" manages to illuminate both its overt subject and Pound's particular use of language. Using terms derived from the linguistics of Roman Jakobson, Schneidau argues that Pound crosses the metaphoric and metonomic poles of discourse. The only article on the relation to an earlier writer, Richard Sieburth's "Ideas into Action: Pound and Voltaire" (*Paideuma* 6:365–90), discusses Pound's biographic fascination with Voltaire as a model of the engaged intellectual and then treats Pound's translations of Voltaire in "Impressions of François-Marie Arouet" and use of him in *The Cantos.*

The two best of the five articles on 20th-century figures concern Joyce. Nathan Halper's "How Simple: A Tale of Joyce and Pound" (*PR* 44:438–46) explicates several references in *Ulysses* and *Finnegans Wake* in terms of Joyce's response to Pound's declining admiration of his ongoing work; the words "wonderworker," "Esra," "Maunderin," and "poposterous" receive particular attention. Herbert N. Schneidau's "Style and Sacrament in Modernist Writing" (*GaR* 31: 427–52) contrasts Joyce's stylistic strategy of expansion to Pound's bent for condensation and aligns Joyce with Chomsky's theories and Pound with Jakobson's, as in the article on Wordsworth discussed above. More briefly, Woon-Ping Chin Holaday argues in "Pound and Binyon: China via the British Museum" (*Paideuma* 6:27–36) that

Laurence Binyon's early books on Oriental art may have influenced Pound, while Leon Surette's "A Case for Occam's Razor: Pound and Spengler" (*Paideuma* 6:109–13) disputes Ronald Bush's recent elucidation of analogies between Pound's thought and Spengler's *Decline of the West.* Finally, Douglas Thompson moves from Pound as influenced to Pound as influencing in "Pound and Brazilian Concretism" (*Paideuma* 6:279–94), which shows that Pound has had a major impact on the group of poets around *Noigandres* magazine, especially through his use of the ideogram.

***e*. Studies of Specific Works.** Except for Jo Brantley Berryman's "The Art of the Image: Allusions in Pound's 'Medallion'" (*Paideuma* 6:295–308), the significant work this year focused on *The Cantos.* In the most ambitious project, James J. Wilhelm treats *The Later Cantos of Ezra Pound* (New York: Walker). Wilhelm's enterprise usefully supplements what is still the best book on Pound's epic, Daniel Pearlman's *The Barb of Time*, which stopped with the Pisan cantos, by emphasizing the later *Rock Drill*, *Thrones*, and *Drafts and Fragments* sections. After exploring the importance of Pound's own biography, the ideogrammic method, some particular themes (women and gold), and the complicated contribution of the Troubadours and Dante to the poem, Wilhelm turns to individual chapters on eight central late cantos. He organizes each around a particular theme or figure: banking and politics for 88, nature for 90, Apollonius of Tyre for 94, Byzantium for 96, Confucius for 98–99, Napoleon for 101, and Anselm for 105. The discussions of those cantos will be essential to further work. Wilhelm particularly illuminates Pound's use of often obscure sources, such as Thomas Hart Benton's autobiographical *Thirty Years' View* or Philostratus's *Life of Apollonius of Tyana.* His work would have been even more valuable had he either taken a more balanced view of the success of *The Cantos* or else more convincingly refuted what he calls the trend "in recent reviews of books about Pound to criticize the authors for not being more objectively critical in their approaches, for accepting Pound's work too eagerly in its entirety." Wilhelm too often begs central questions by attacking unnamed "anti-Poundians" instead of analyzing the poem's problems to help appreciate its substantial accomplishments.

M. L. Rosenthal adopts a more judicious view in his interesting article, "The Structuring of Pound's Cantos" (*Paideuma* 6:3–11).

"*The Cantos* are an extreme form of sequence," writes Rosenthal. "They are, in fact, a sequence of sequences." He suggestively compares each new group of cantos to the production of separate volumes of poetry by other poets and sees such groups not as integral parts of a single whole but as a recasting or starting over again, albeit often with common or continuing concerns. The alternate groupings 1–16 and 1–30, both sanctioned by separate publication, receive the most attention. In contrast to Rosenthal, William McNaughton revives the notions of Dantescan and fugal structures for the poem in "A Note on Main Form in *The Cantos*" (*Paideuma* 6:147–52). The chief novelty of his schema is to identify fugal elements corresponding to subject, counter-subject, and stretto within each main section. Considering one motif rather than overall structure, Donald Davie traces the treatment of "Sicily in the Cantos" (*Paideuma* 6:101–7) and concludes that only once (in 109) does Sicily impinge upon Pound perceptually rather than verbally or notionally. From this, Davie draws an unfavorable contrast to Yeats's broader assimilation and delivers some harsh strictures on *Thrones.*

Paideuma's preeminence in Pound scholarship appears most prominently in its eleven separate items on individual cantos. In the interest of economy I shall discuss only the two of those that have wider implications. (The rest explore, sometimes in exhaustive detail, the sources of Cantos 2, 24, 26, 34, 42–43, 49, 54, 74, 93, and 100.) Perhaps the finest article of the year on *The Cantos*, M. L. Rosenthal's "Pound at his Best: Canto 47 as a Model of Poetic Thought" (*Paideuma* 6:309–21), sensitively explicates the canto in terms of both technique and subject as paradigmatic of Pound's poetic strategies. Rosenthal's handling of the Odyssean elements exemplifies his perceptive conclusions about Pound's manipulation of sources: "Canto 47, then, reenacts Homer's Book X but does so by planting Odyssean moments amid disjunct passages of varying tones and intensities. It thus shifts attention from the traditional, myth-based epic to the workings of an alert, subjective modern sensibility completely at home with the older work and to an important degree obsessed by it." He concludes with an interesting placement of that sensibility between Yeats's more traditional monologues on the one hand and the postmodern objectivists like Charles Olson on the other. Wendy Stallard Flory's "Pound's Blake and Blake's Dante: 'The Circle of the Lustful' and Canto 20" (*Paideuma* 6:155–65) traces both details and overall direction of Pound's presentation of Paolo and Francesca to Blake's engraving and painting illustrating Dante's Circle of the Lustful. Her work reminds one both that the visual sources of *The Cantos* need more attention and that Pound's relation to Blake (whom he once called "dippy William") has been studied hardly at all.

Five articles from other journals deserve mention. The two most specific are William Cookson's "Ezra Pound & Myth: A Reader's Guide to Canto II" (*Agenda* 15:87–92) and Peter Shaw's "Ezra Pound on American History" (*PR* 44:112–24). Shaw argues polemically against the accuracy and aesthetic value of the Adams cantos and arraigns previous critics for excusing the excesses of modernism; his remarks on Canto 62 are particularly interesting. Sister Bernetta Quinn's "Light from the East: *The Cantos* and Chinese Art" (*Greyfriar* 18:49–63) pursues a worthwhile topic, as does Stephen J. Adams's "The Soundscape of the *Cantos*: Some Ideas of Music in the Poetry of Ezra Pound" (*HAB* 28:167–88). Shaw expounds his subject in three ways which do not always cohere—as the aural qualities of the verse itself, as an historical component of Pound's paradigm of culture, and as a measure for the values of individual sensibilities; he has a related article on Pound's versecraft, "Pound's Quantities and Absolute Rhythm" (*ELWIU* 4:95–109). Finally, Fred Moramarco's "Concluding an Epic: The Drafts and Fragments of *The Cantos*" (*AL* 49:309–26) offers a competent survey of its subject in terms of Pound's growing acceptance of human limitations.

ii. Eliot

***a.* Biography.** With *Eliot's Early Years* (New York: Oxford Univ. Press) Lyndall Gordon has done the finest recent biographical work on Eliot. Given Eliot's famous proscription of a biography and the unavailability in this century of many central documents, Gordon has wisely opted for a more limited goal: "This book is an attempt to elicit the autobiographical element in Eliot's poetry by measuring the poetry against the life." To that end she marshalls a formidable array of unpublished manuscripts which display the interaction between the art and life up to Eliot's official conversion in 1927. Of the wealth of new material here, I found the account of Eliot's visionary experience during a Boston walk in 1910 and the unpublished poem about it perhaps the most startling, while the long discussion of Eliot's difficulties with women evinces tactful understanding. Gordon successfully demonstrates the importance of religion to the early Eliot, though she goes too far in pushing the turning point of his life back to an alleged near-conversion in 1914 and in identifying "the traditional schemata of the exemplary life" as the key to *The Waste Land*. Perhaps most importantly, she sustains in more detail than anyone else her central contention that the impersonal facade of Eliot's poetry masks an often literal reworking of personal experience. Eliot emerges from her pages as at once a more human, fallible, and sympathetic figure than the old, aloof stereotype.

Two articles offer more modest contributions. Keith Fraser's "*Stepping Heavenward*: the Canonization of T. S. Eliot" (*UWR* 13: 5–17) explores the early friendship and later aloofness between Eliot and Richard Aldington, especially in terms of Aldington's satiric portrait of Eliot in *Stepping Heavenward*. E. W. F. Tomlin agreeably records impressions of Eliot gleaned from 34 years of acquaintance in "T. S. Eliot: A Friendship" (*The Listener* 97:541–43), particularly about Eliot's conduct at Faber and his personal manner. Finally, Ellen Williams discusses Eliot's relation to *Poetry* magazine in *Harriet Monroe and the Poetry Renaissance* (see above, section i).

***b.* General Studies.** To some extent *The Literary Criticism of T. S. Eliot: New Essays*, edited by David Newton-De Molina (London: The Athlone Press), does for Eliot's literary essays what Lyndall Gordon does for his early poetry: it casts off cant about impersonality to reveal both the personal aspect of the work, and the tensions within the work itself. For all their natural disparity, the nine essayists share a revisionist bent sensitive to the vices as well as the virtues of Eliot's criticism and capable of evaluating its problematic impact on subsequent theory. If their tone is sometimes harsher than we have been used to, it is also healthier. In particular, Graham Hough's "The Poet as Critic" explores Eliot's alternate critical personae of the literary condottiere and well-balanced man of letters; Denis Donoghue's "Eliot and the *Criterion*" examines "the distance between Eliot's mind and daily events"; and Sam Hynes's "The Trials of a Christian Critic" traces Eliot's late determination to be a Christian critic and lagging doubt as to what that meant. In the final essay, "Eliot, Arnold, and the English Poetic Tradition," C. K. Stead reconsiders Eliot's relation to 19th-century literature. He convincingly concludes that just as much of Eliot's poetry has been shown recently to continue as much as it casts off from the previous century, so, too, "a great deal of Eliot's criticism, particularly as it bears upon the important question of poetic composition, is likewise Romantic, despite its eye-catching, anti-Romantic declarations."

In his short *"Ulysses," "The Waste Land," and Modernism* (Port Washington, N.Y.: Kennikat Press) Stanley Sultan ambitiously aims to illuminate Eliot's poem in itself, in relation to Joyce's novel, and as a central document of cultural modernism. That is too large a task for only 92 pages, but along the way Sultan presents well-formulated parallels and divergences between his two central texts, and he uses the *Waste Land* drafts to suggest interesting influences of *Ulysses* on the poem. Sultan might have omitted sections like the long and unconvincing argument for the centrality of the *Waste Land* notes, to follow up in greater detail suggestions like the importance of the autobiographic impulse in the two works. J. Birje-Patil's *Beneath the Axle-Tree: An Introduction to Eliot's Poems, Plays, and Criticism* (Delhi: The Macmillan Company of India) is frankly introductory, while Thomas Meighan's even shorter *T. S. Eliot: A Critical Study of His Principles and Achievements* (New York: Vantage Press) may safely be ignored.

Two well-known critics produced the most valuable general articles this year. Denis Donoghue's fascinating "On the Limits of a Language" (*SR* 85:371–91) ponders linguistic limits and the effect of foreign-language tags in exploring Eliot's relation to Dante and to tradition in general. Particularly good on *The Waste Land* and *Four Quartets*, Donoghue sees literary tradition as helping to overcome "the temperamental difficulty which Eliot obviously found in acknowledging the reality of feelings other than his own." In the "Eliot: the Walking Dead" chapter of his *The Mysteries of Identity: a Theme in Modern Literature* (New York: Oxford Univ. Press) Robert Langbaum places Eliot in a continuum showing the decline of romanticist notions of identity from Wordsworth through Arnold to Beckett. Steadily probing the postromantic aspects of Eliot's work, Langbaum shows the value of seeing *The Waste Land* as a Romantic monodrama in which identity emerges out of delivering archetypes from the closed circles of the Bradleyan self and of the immediate historical moment. The remarks on "Prufrock" are apt.

Perhaps the best of the other general essays is Grania Jones's

"Eliot and History" (*CritQ* 18:31–48), which compares Eliot's historical scheme to various others of the 19th and 20th centuries in concluding that "Behind the cover of his modernism, Eliot has carried out an audaciously anachronistic manoeuvre: he has cured himself of the modern disease of obsessive historiography by returning to the simplicity of exemplary history, as it was told and perceived by all traditional societies." In "'A gesture and a pose': T. S. Eliot's Images of Love" (*CritQ* 18:5–26) Martin Scofield argues not altogether convincingly for the centrality of love in Eliot's poetry and traces such recurrent images as the weeping girl. Eben Bass's wandering "Hemingway's Women of Another Country" (*MarkhamR* 6:35–39) discusses Eliot's epigraph from *The Jew of Malta* in "Portrait of a Lady" and Hemingway's allusions to the play in *The Sun Also Rises.* Zohreh Tawakuli Sullivan provides an overview of the early monologues in "Memory and Meditative Structure in T. S. Eliot's Early Poetry" (*Renascence* 29:97–105). Sullivan uses Ignatian and Augustinian paradigms of meditation to locate the cause of failure of the spiritual quests of the early speakers in their inadequate powers of memory. Jack Behar offers less insight into the early work in "Eliot and the Language of Gesture: The Early Poems" (*TCL* 23:487–97). Charles O. Hartman's "Condensation: The Critical Vocabulary of Pound and Eliot" (*CE* 39:179–90) has been discussed above, under Pound.

c. Relation to Other Writers. As with Pound, nearly all Eliot scholarship inevitably mentions sources, allusions, influence, and the like. I have included in this separate section, however, only those items taking such concerns as their principal subject, and have arranged them according to literary chronology.

William Arrowsmith proffers a mixed bag in "Daedal Harmonies: a Dialogue on Eliot and the Classics" (*SoR* 13:1–47), modeled upon Eliot's own "Dialogue on Dramatic Poetry." Arrowsmith argues correctly that Eliotic allusions typically refer to the entire context of a line or phrase and operate by extended analogy. Yet the long and learned discussion of "Dans le restaurant" sometimes seems arbitrary in its identification of references, while the article as a whole reflects a more naive understanding of the relation between Eliot's poetry and prose than that displayed by the contributors to the Newton-de Molina volume. The discussion of Plato's *Philebus* in relation to Phlebus the Phoenecian is particularly good. Focused more exclusively on Virgil, Andrew V. Ettin's "Milton, T. S. Eliot, and the Virgilian Vision: Some Versions of Georgic" (*Genre* 10:233–58) aligns Virgil's *Georgics*, Milton's *Paradise Regained*, and Eliot's *Four Quartets* in terms not of influence but rather of "generic analogue." He sees all three as adopting similar views of nature, language, and heroism to develop a shared central theme of life as a struggle against the tyranny of the external world.

In keeping with the increasing attention to Eliot's 19th-century heritage, the two studies of Eliot and Dante this year both use Shelley as a mediating figure. This accords with Eliot's praise of Shelley's *Triumph of Life* in the "What Dante Means to Me" lecture rather than with the earlier blasts. In his somewhat mistitled "New Verse, Ancient Rhyme: T. S. Eliot and Dante" (*Parnassus* 5:127–46) Thomas Vance discusses the creative responses to Dante by Shelley, Eliot, and (more briefly) Pound. Besides several worthwhile specific insights, Vance provocatively locates the ground of the 19th- and 20th-century rediscovery of Dante in "the insecurity that is the hallmark of the Romantic vision and the ironic modern visions and revisions which descend from it." Glenn O'Malley takes a narrower focus in "Dante, Shelley, and T. S. Eliot" (*Romantic and Modern*, pp. 165–76). He compares the two later writers as translators of Dante, providing a careful treatment of Eliot's prose versions of the *Commedia* in the "Dante" essay. He concludes with an interesting suggestion extending Grover Smith's account of the impact of Shelley on "Sweeney Erect" by tracing the orangutan image to an observation of Eliot's on *Queen Mab*. The chief work on Renaissance roots, James Torrens's "Eliot's Poetry and the Incubus of Shakespeare" (*Thought* 52:407–21) surveys the Shakespearean allusions in Eliot's major poetry; greater awareness of contemporary theories of literary influence might have led to more original conclusions.

A. Walton Litz's "'That Strange Abstraction, "Nature"': T. S. Eliot's Victorian Inheritance," in *Nature and the Victorian Imagination*, edited by U. C. Knoepflmacher and G. B. Tennyson (Berkeley and Los Angeles: Univ. of Calif. Press), pp. 470–88, offers a major reassessment. Pointing out of Pound and Eliot that "it is only in the last few years that we have come to see both writers as natural inheritors of the major nineteenth-century traditions," Litz traces Eliot's early animosity to the Victorians, with its unfortunate effect on subsequent critics, and then delineates his later rapprochement. Litz handles Eliot's relation to Tennyson particularly well, although *Four Quartets* seems to me to exhibit a more uneasy relation to *In Memoriam* than he allows. This fine article opens a host of possibilities for further research.

The falling of two out of the three chief articles in the *T. S. Eliot Review* into this category (relation to other writers) makes it convenient to treat that journal as a whole here. The *Review* has been running a year late, so that the items in this paragraph come from the 1976 double issue. In "Eliot and *Huck Finn*: River and Sea in 'The Dry Salvages'" (3:3–12) Lois A. Cuddy mines Eliot's introduction to the novel for correlations with the poem. Lewis Freed quarrels with previous commentators in "Eliot and Bradley" (3:29–58). Lillian Feder's treatment of "The Death of St. Narcissus" and *The Waste Land* in her "Narcissus as Saint and Dancer" (3:13–20) constitutes perhaps the best contribution to *TSER* this year. An imminent name change to *Yeats Eliot Review* indicates an expansion in scope for this journal.

***d.* Studies of Specific Works: Poetry.** *The Waste Land* received the most attention this year, most prominently in James E. Miller, Jr.'s problematic book *T. S. Eliot's Personal Waste Land: Exorcism of the Demons* (University Park: The Penn. State Univ. Press). Starting from John Peter's claims (1952) for the importance of Jean Verdenal to Eliot, Miller argues that the governing consciousness of the poem reveals a split between a botched relation with a wife and a homoerotic attraction to a dead young man. Despite peripheral (and exemplary) admonitions against reductive uses of biography, the book persistently identifies those characters as Eliot, his first wife Vivienne, and his dead friend Verdenal. Especially with the last claim, Miller runs into trouble: too little is known of Verdenal's role in Eliot's life. As a result, the argument often dissolves into the tendentious devices of controversies based on inadequate evidence, such as the notion that Shakespeare did not write his own plays: claims of "a conspiracy of silence," rhetorical or loaded questions ("Was April cruel because it was perhaps associated with the Gallipoli landings and Verdenal's death?"), and an array of specious terms like "it is possible that," "may well have," "apparently," "perhaps," "would have been natural for," "we might assume," and the like. This is a pity, both because Miller has some excellent incidental insights and because the autobiographic aspects of Eliot's work have been coming into their rightful prominence of late. But the large claims in this book command too little evidence to win the assent of most readers.

The articles tend to relate *The Waste Land* to other works. One of the most substantial, Peter A. Martin's " 'Son of Man' in The Book of Ezekiel and T. S. Eliot's *The Waste Land*" (*ArQ* 33:197–215) reviews the Biblical sources of Eliot's phrase and draws an extended parallel between The Book of Ezekiel and the poem. In "1922 and After: The Poetic Landscapes of Joyce and Eliot" (*CentR* 20:332–50) Shari Benstock generates enough parallels and contrasts between *The Waste Land* and *Ulysses* to swamp the reader. She sees a disparity in tone between Eliot's moral didacticism and Joyce's comic mode as supporting a thematic split between Eliotic movement toward redemption and Joycean concern for common human understanding. More briefly, four contributions to *Notes and Queries* (24: 449–452) concern the phrase "HURRY UP PLEASE ITS TIME," the Sanskrit words at the end, the cry "co co rico," and the lines about Ugolino's tower. Readers in need of respite from the sources of *The Waste Land* will find it treated *as* a source for Samuel R. Delany's recent science fiction novel in "Images of *The Waste Land* in *The Einstein Intersection*" (*Extrapolation* 18:116–23) by H. J. Gardiner.

Four articles concern other poems. Michel Grimaud, in "Hermaneutics, Onomastics and Poetics in English and French Literature" (*MLN* 92:888–921), explores the significance of J. Alfred Prufrock's name in terms of poststructuralist techniques. Grimaud mingles interesting speculation with ingenuity gone amok. Arthur E. Walzer sees the description of the squatting Jew as deriving from a Miltonic description of Satan in "An Allusion to *Paradise Lost* in Eliot's 'Gerontion' " (*NMAL* 2:item 6), while Grace B. Briggs suggests Stevenson's story "The Ebb Tide" as source for "The Hollow Men" (*N&Q* 24:448–49). Finally, Narsingh Srivastava's "The Ideas of the *Bhagavad Gita* in *Four Quartets*" (*CL* 29:97–108) offers an informed survey respectful of Eliot's knowledge.

***e*. Studies of Specific Works: Drama.** Little significant work appeared in this category. H. L. Sharma's commentaries on individual plays in *T. S. Eliot: His Dramatic Theories* (New Delhi: S. Chand, 1976) are rudimentary. At the other extreme, Michael Beehler's "*Murder in the Cathedral*: The Countersacramental Play of Signs"

(*Genre* 10:329–38) is the most fashionably esoteric of Eliot items, heavily derivative of Jacques Derrida. One turns in relief to Carol Weiher's modest correlation of a passage from *Ash Wednesday* with a speech by Becket in " 'Sometimes Hesitating at the Angles of Stairs': Becket's Treasonous Thoughts in *Murder in the Cathedral*" (*NMAL* 2:item 1). Mabel C. Donnelly argues in "The Failure of Act III of Eliot's *The Cocktail Party*" (*CLAJ* 21:58–61) that the urbane and sensitive tone of Acts I and II becomes "chilling" in Act III. She sees the problem as more a failure of the heart than of wit on the part of the would-be Guardians.

The University of Michigan

9. Faulkner

Panthea Reid Broughton

The year's work in Faulkner studies is, again, very uneven in quality. Much is pointlessly redundant; much is vapidly general; yet much is important and arresting. Along with a vast accumulation of unnecessary and regrettable publications, 1977 occasioned the publication of several new materials essential to Faulkner studies and of some critical works which significantly expand our ways of seeing the work of William Faulkner.

i. Bibliography, Editions, and Manuscripts

In 1963 James B. Meriwether published an article entitled "The Text of Faulkner's Books: An Introduction and Some Notes" (*MFS* 9:159–70) (see *ALS 1963*, pp. 73–74). Until now the essay has been the definitive statement on the reliability of different Faulkner texts. But in 1977 Meriwether replaced his previous list with an "up-to-date guide to the reliability of the significant texts of Faulkner's writings published in book form, whether now available or not." Entitled "The Books of William Faulkner: A Guide for Students and Scholars" (*MissQ* 30:417–28), Meriwether's article provides an authoritative guide to editions of Faulkner's books. Also in the special Faulkner issue of *The Mississippi Quarterly* is a collection of correspondence between Faulkner and *The Saturday Evening Post.* Meriwether has edited these documents under the heading "Faulkner's Correspondence with *The Saturday Evening Post*" (*MissQ* 30:461–75). The *Post*'s letters to Faulkner are decorous and polite, while Faulkner's letters are whimsical and serious, desperate and accommodating. The discovery of all but one of these letters in the Wesley Stout collection at the Library of Congress and their publication here is indeed welcome. In "Faulkner's Short Story Sending Schedule" (*PBSA* 71:98–105) Max Putzel offers a number of emendations to Meriwether's appendix to *The Literary Career of William Faulkner* (see *ALS 1971*, p. 105). Putzel finds some lapses and some misleading editorial practices in Meriwether's account of Faulkner's sending schedule; clearly, Putzel's article must be referred to in conjunction with Meriwether's list. Also published this year was *A Catalogue for "The William Faulkner Collection" at the University of Toledo* (Toledo: The Friends of the Univ. of Toledo Libraries). This catalogue lists the first editions, foreign editions, and first magazine publications of Faulkner's works held in the Toledo collection. Major events in Faulkner studies this year were the facsimile publication of *The Marionettes* (see section v) and the concordances to *As I Lay Dying* (see section vi) and *Go Down, Moses* (see section vii).

ii. Biography

No major biographical discussions appeared in 1977. Nevertheless, several interesting and informative pieces, with relevance not only to Faulkner's own life but also to that of his family, are reviewed here. First and most important of these essays is one overlooked last year, Joseph Blotner's "The Falkners and the Fictional Families" (*GaR* 30 [1976]:572–92). Blotner begins by considering two points of view about Faulkner's use of material from "real life": one represented by Faulkner's friend Robert Farley's statement that " 'The reason why Bill's characters are so real is because they were real' "; the other represented by Faulkner's own statement, " 'I improved on God, who, dramatic though He be, has no sense, no feeling for, theatre.' " Blotner marshals evidence to establish, first, similarities between the models in the Falkner family and Faulkner's portrayal of them. Doing so, Blotner presents detailed information about the Falkners from Col. William Clark Falkner to author William Cuthbert Faulkner. This material is essentially a review and condensation of data from Blotner's biography; it is presented here as a focused narrative without footnotes or other scholarly paraphenalia.

That lack of documentation presents some problems. For instance, in the biography Blotner tells a story about the death in 1849 of William Clark Falkner's first wife and the subsequent adoption of the Falkners' approximately six-month old son John Wesley Thompson Falkner by the John Wesley Thompsons. In the biography Blotner attributes the story to Faulkner's cousin Sallie Murry Wilkins (though the index misprints "Williams" for "Wilkins"). Another treatment of the same material, Thomas McHaney's "The Falkners and the Origin of Yoknapatawpha County: Some Corrections" (*MissQ* 25[1972]:249–64), however, says that when Falkner's wife died in childbirth in 1848, the Thompsons adopted the baby. McHaney's essay antedates the biography by two years and this essay by four years, but in neither place does Blotner acknowledge another version of the story. Documentation here might not only have acknowledged the difficulty; it might have resolved it. Instead, the format of the *Georgia Review* article asks us to take on faith the accuracy and authority with which it is written. That is a loss, but there is a gain in the readability and drama with which Blotner writes here.

Blotner's thesis is not only that Faulkner borrowed historical and biographical material but that he transformed it. He writes: "Faulkner had a tendency to make his borrowings larger than life—not that he made them unbelievable, but that he infused into them a degree of passion and a nearly mythic quality that permitted them to carry the emotional freighting he wanted them to bear." That infusion, of course, meant a substantial altering of raw material. It is probably these alterations which are most intriguing for the Faulknerian. Why, for instance, as he duplicated the Falkner family with the Sartoris family, did Faulkner omit a fictionalized version of his own father? And why did he split his own personality into the Sartoris twins? Blotner's essay broaches such questions and presents an appealing review of the relations between life and art in Faulkner.

Another treatment of Faulkner's most famous ancestor is Calvin S. Brown's "Colonel Falkner As General Reader: *The White Rose of Memphis*" (*MissQ* 30:585–95). This article is of interest to the Faulkner student since it establishes, through attention to the remarkable number of allusions in *The White Rose*, how integral to the life of Faulkner's great-grandfather was a vital literary tradition.

A valuable resource for pursuing the question of Faulkner's use of biographical and historical material is to be found in James B. Lloyd's *The Oxford "Eagle," 1900–1962: An Annotated Checklist of Material on William Faulkner and the History of Lafayette County* (Mississippi State: *The Mississippi Quarterly*). Lloyd follows a sensible policy of inclusion or exclusion on this list according to relevance to

Faulkner's life and work. His census deals admirably well with various problems in the *Eagle*'s filing system and offers a highly useful tool for finding pertinent materials.

One item that promised to offer really valuable biographical information is Malcolm Franklin's *Bitterweeds: Life with William Faulkner at Rowan Oak* (Irving, Tex.: The Society for the Study of Traditional Culture); but the book is a disappointment. Its amateurish production is indicative of its problems: occasionally, the type face changes or a sentence ends in the middle of a line while the following sentence is set on the line below. The letters from Faulkner to his step-son Franklin, which serve as an appendix to the book, are printed in an unpaginated muddle in which most of them appear twice. But the real question about this book is not *how* it was printed but *why*. Unfortunately, *Bitterweeds* being almost entirely anecdotal, Malcolm Franklin is not a gifted storyteller. Some few of his boyish learning experiences do suggest something of the character of the man Faulkner, but nothing that Franklin tells us explains the gaps in understanding between himself and his step-father alluded to by Faulkner in a 1943 letter; nor can Franklin exhibit the genuine warmth felt between the two men. Neither can Franklin give us any sense of what his mother was like. Franklin's principal people all get lost among descriptions of customs, food, drink, linen, silver, cutglass, and servants; perhaps a better title for his purposes would have been "gracious living at Rowan Oak." Except for a description of Faulkner's writing habits and a brief account of his drinking bouts and a single mention of his and Estelle's separate bedrooms, Malcolm Franklin's account makes the Faulkners sound like only another undistinguished exemplum of the aristocratic southern family. Franklin's scrambling of tales from his childhood and adulthood confuses the reader and may disguise his omission of details from an extensive period of time. The book may be more remarkable for its omissions than inclusions. For the Faulkner scholar or Faulkner buff, the unpardonable omission is the personality of William Faulkner.

Another item which tells less than we might wish is Meta Doherty Wilde's "An Unpublished Chapter From *A Loving Gentleman*" (*MissQ* 30:449–60). This chapter reviews its author's own family background. In itself, this material has little import for the Faulknerian except when Wilde repeats incidents Faulkner "borrowed" from her experience and retold in his fiction. But as she reports

Faulkner's fascination with all things Southern, we do gain perspective. Of course, it is difficult to tell whether Wilde is exaggerating this issue; and when, in a prefatory note, she writes, "This Southern background accounts for the book's [i.e. *A Loving Gentleman's*] central character, my very dear William Faulkner," we cannot be sure what she means. Nevertheless, her writing sometimes suggests that what these lovers really had in common was homesickness, and even that is a valuable insight.

One item of real biographical and critical importance should be mentioned here. It is the reprint of *Faulkner in the University: Class Conferences at the University of Virginia 1957–58*, edited by Frederick L. Gwynn and Joseph L. Blotner (Charlottesville: Univ. Press of Va.). This second printing is most welcome.

iii. Criticism: General

a. **Books.** Joanna V. Creighton's *William Faulkner's Craft of Revision: The Trilogy, "The Unvanquished," and "Go Down, Moses"* (Detroit: Wayne State Univ. Press) offers an account of the revisions Faulkner made when he incorporated earlier stories into the larger wholes of these novels. Through careful comparisons of every extant version of each tale, Creighton speaks authoritatively about Faulkner's process of revision. Her account convinces us that Faulkner typically and most effectively revised toward further complication of character, incident, and theme, that these revisions always were conducted with an eye to the structure and coherence of the larger work, that Faulkner was painstakingly conscious of the implications of technique, and that (with the exception of the issue of racial injustice in *The Unvanquished*) these revisions evidence a determination to develop thoroughly the moral implications latent in the original short stories. Creighton writes a highly competent descriptive account, but when she occasionally goes beyond her comments on the process of revision to offer interpretive comment on the whole novel, she reveals certain limitations. For instance, she seems to equate novelistic unity with a focus upon a central character; thus she ignores the possibility that *Go Down, Moses* can be a novel unified by motif and theme rather than by the continuing presence of a single central character. Also she seems to think of "the almost categorically unsympathetic treatment" of "generic Snopesism" as an achievement flawed by whatever intimations Faulkner makes that Snopes too are human; yet elsewhere she astutely remarks that "all of Flem's successes are built upon the moral weaknesses—particularly the greed—of others" and that "Snopesian behavior is not restricted to the Snopes family"; thus sometimes she seems to expect a monolithic division between the bad and the good and at other times she knows better. The major limitation in Creighton's appraisal, however, is that this approach calls for the very thing Creighton either cannot or will not attempt: a conclusion which treats the structural and thematic implications of the process which she has so carefully, and, I think, accurately described.

The South and Faulkner's Yoknapatawpha: The Actual and the Apocryphal, edited by Evans Harrington and Ann J. Abadie (Jackson: Univ. Press of Miss.) is a collection of essays and transcripts from the 1976 "Faulkner and Yoknapatawpha" Conference at the University of Mississippi. As engaging overviews or introductions to Faulkner studies, these talks certainly succeeded; they testify to a lively and worthwhile conference; however, their value as serious contributions to Faulkner scholarship is less assured. In a talk entitled "The South in American History" Daniel Aaron provides an historical review of 19th- and 20th-century attitudes about the South both from within and without its boundaries. The issue for Aaron is whether or not the South was seen as an alien section of the country, but Aaron does not associate this issue with Faulkner as he might, for instance, by examining how much Faulkner accepted prevailing assumptions and how much he departed from them. Louis D. Rubin, Jr.'s "Scarlett O'Hara and the Two Quentin Compsons" makes a number of interesting comparisons between two books about the American Civil War which were both published in 1936: *Gone With the Wind* and *Absalom, Absalom!* The comparisons are intriguing, but tell us more about Margaret Mitchell's novel than about Faulkner's.

Darwin T. Turner's "Faulkner and Slavery" points out how "conpicuously missing from Faulkner's depiction of slavery is any picture of physical brutality." In fact, except when there is sexual exploitation, slavery in Faulkner, Turner argues, is comparatively innocent. Turner's attention to the disparity between Faulkner's abstract sense of the curse of slavery and his unwillingness to depict its horrors does remind us of how much the terms of Faulkner's fictional world were shaped by the terms of his actual world. In "Faulkner and (Southern) Women," Linda Welshimer Wagner treats the many strong and capable women in Faulkner. Wagner points out that the "loss of self-determination and the realization of their ineffectuality is the cross most of Faulkner's women carry," but she fails to consider the extent of Faulkner's sympathy toward such women. Without such consideration, it is difficult to describe Faulkner as a feminist (as Wagner is tempted to) or a misogynist. In the space of such a brief talk, however, Wagner can hardly explore in depth the question of Faulkner's ambivalence toward women. In "Nature's Legacy to William Faulkner," John Pilkington associates the hunting stories in *Go Down, Moses* with the American romantic tradition. Pilkington's review of the Edenic metaphor in American letters is interesting and competent, though hardly ground-breaking. His most interesting point, that "both Cooper and Faulkner wish to make the reader sympathetic to the end of the wilderness and with it the Garden of Eden metaphor," requires a defense that Pilkington does not provide.

This volume includes transcripts of several question-and-answer sessions at the conference. Shelby Foote was slated to speak on "Faulkner's Depiction of the Planter Aristocracy," but since Foote believes that "there are no aristocrats in Mississippi," he relieved himself of a speech topic. Instead, Foote answered questions from the audience, as he also did instead of making a formal talk on "Faulkner and War." His responses, especially the personal reminiscences, are entertaining, but certainly not revelatory. Likewise, the transcripts of discussions on "Faulkner and Race" with Turner, Foote, and Harrington and "Faulkner and Women" with Wagner, Harrington, and Victoria Fielden Black (Faulkner's step-granddaughter) do suggest interesting but unremarkable sessions.

The volume includes two talks by Michael Millgate. His "Faulkner and History" suggests that fables, or permanent truths, are "clearly the essential element in what Faulkner understands by history," but that history in a more orthodox sense was not very important to Faulkner. Millgate's caveat against taking any one character's statement as "message" cannot be made too often; for, as he points out, even Gavin Stevens's "The past is never dead. It's not even past" is not unequivocally endorsed in the context of *Requiem for a Nun.* In speaking of history, Millgate makes interesting implications about Faulkner's writing technique; nevertheless, this study, competent as it is, does not significantly add to what Millgate has already said about Faulkner. At the end of the conference, Millgate also spoke on the topic "Faulkner and the South: Some Reflections." His observations on the title *The Hamlet* suggest the way allusion works in Faulkner and finally suggest that Faulkner's South is "not real estate but *paysage moralisé*." Such a distinction between "the actual and the apocryphal" was especially appropriate for this conference on "The South and Faulkner's Yoknapatawpha"; nevertheless, sound and insightful as Millgate's comments are, I feel that most of them, like most of the commentaries in this collection, were better suited to remain speeches than to be reprinted as articles.

Critics are now beginning to study more seriously Faulkner's associations with Hollywood. This year saw the publication of one book, Bruce F. Kawin's *Faulkner and Film* (New York: Ungar), which offers a generalized overview of the topic. The book's title establishes the bounds of its unity; that is, Kawin seems to have set himself the task of dealing, however cursorily, with all topics which somehow connect Faulkner with film. Thus one whole section of the book is a discussion of the filmscripts Hollywood made from Faulkner's fiction. Since Kawin spends a third of his book on that topic, he cannot deal as thoroughly as he otherwise might with the topics at hand in the rest of the book: Faulkner's own work in Hollywood and the influence of his fiction on film history. Of these three divisions in his book, the most valuable is the middle section which clarifies Faulkner's actual contribution to the scripts on which he worked. Kawin's attention to *The Big Sleep*, for example, explains what material was Faulkner's, clarifies how Faulkner's and Hawks's interpretations differed, and manages to decipher much of this almost inexplicable film. Kawin supplements this section with a "Filmography," which is a helpful list, with relevant dates, of the films on which Faulkner worked. Kawin straightens out some misstatements and half-truths about Faulkner in Hollywood and points out thematic carry-overs from fiction to film. He convinces us of Faulkner's professionalism, but not, though he tries, of his commitment to Hollywood endeavors. Kawin is sometimes careless with his Faulkner (he says that Quentin II was locked in her room by her mother!), but he at least addresses himself to the paradox that "Faulkner's novels are cinematic and his screen plays are novelistic." Nevertheless, though Kawin treats an interesting and vital and largely unexplored subject, in most of his book he does so without enough wit or wisdom.

David Williams's *Faulkner's Women: The Myth and the Muse*

(Montreal: McGill-Queen's Univ. Press) treats an important topic with a good bit of sophistication; yet Williams's turgid prose so obfuscates whatever insights he may have to offer that we tend to lose them and he us. For instance, in his first chapter he writes: "Since the feminine-in-man shall be the subject here of a good deal of aesthetic study, some brief account of the modus operandi in art of a psychic factor is by this time imperative." If this is a straightforward introduction to comments on methodology, the discussion of Williams's complex topic promises to be rough going indeed; and it is. Williams's first basic assumption seems to be that it is no longer through religion but through mythic art that the numinous becomes accessible; his second assumption is that the power of Faulkner's fiction is a direct function of his writing in the mythic mode. Williams notes that archetypal presences other than that of the "Great Goddess" are also to be found in Faulkner, but he examines only the "several transpersonal factors which shall be thoroughly defined as the archetypal feminine." Despite the prose, at least this approach does not make the now too familiar mistake of equating Faulkner's women with all that is somehow both innocent and natural. Rather it insists that certain of Faulkner's women possess a dynamic force which testifies to the "suprapersonal power of the anima." One real contribution that Williams makes is his illustration of how the anima can work in Faulkner's fiction for either creative or destructive ends, but Williams is not clear enough about an implied cause and effect relationship between male rejection of the flesh, motion, and life and the anima's retribution for that rejection. Also, he makes a rather too neat division between the male and the female psyche. For instance, it seems to me that Addie Bundren's "house-cleaning" is as abstract and legalistic an approach to life as any invented by a Faulknerian male; Williams, however, sees in it mainly "the increase of life."

Williams's readings of most texts are basically sound (though he rather absurdly wants to read the Reverend Shegog's sermon two ways at once). I think he is right to speak of Faulkner's rewriting of *Sanctuary* in terms of a conscious use of symbols, of Faulkner's own struggle with the anima as source for the power of feminine presences in his novels (though the latter point needs a fuller explanation), and of the decrease in dynamic power of Faulkner's women as a function of their becoming more individuated, socialized, and "realistic." But one basic problem with this book is that its "modus operandi" remains obscure. We do not know how Williams determines which characters are just characters and which are embodiments of the archetypes. And we are frustrated to find that, though Williams says that "the artist who is gripped by an archetype will find that its greatest effect is upon form," he hardly ever talks about form in the novels. And he might have explained more explicitly the need for and the effects of an archetypal presence in art. Another major problem with this book is that Williams does not clearly distinguish moral from aesthetic criteria. He writes that the anima is negatively empowered in Temple Drake and hardly empowered in Linda Snopes Kohl at all since Linda is "the end product of feminine individuation"; somehow, in this, Williams seems to be making a moral judgment on Linda rather than an aesthetic judgment on Faulkner. And, finally, Williams's use of Faulkner criticism is not as thorough, his use of noncritical sources not as illuminating, as they might be. Though this book considers a difficult and important topic with a good bit of care and insight, the topic itself finally seems to elude this rather muddled treatment.

***b.* Articles.** A brief comment by Donald A. Petesch entitled "Some Notes On the Family in Faulkner's Fiction" (*NMW* 10:11–18) serves as a practical antidote to Williams's book. That is, while Williams theorizes about the dynamic power of the archetypal feminine in certain Faulkner novels, Petesch reminds us that "Faulkner's work is a wasteland of twisted and warping family relationships" and that women are basically irrelevant to the process of initiation, which is central to so many Faulknerian novels. The implications of Petesch's comments, however, require a much fuller exploration than he provides here.

The problem with articles on general topics in Faulkner's work is that the medium can contain a message but no proper substantiation of it; that is, authors of such pieces can only generalize, and generalizing about Faulkner is risky business indeed. For instance, one article whose title implies a specific enough focus is John B. Rosenman's "A Matter of Choice: The Locked Door Theme in Faulkner" (*SAB* 41,ii [1976]:8–12); but Rosenman begins by saying that "the social center of Faulkner's fiction consists of rural poor whites who struggle to achieve dignity in the face of upper-class contempt." Even if true, such a statement could hardly be supported in the five pages Rosenman takes for this essay.

In "Faulkner's Use of the Mule: Symbol of Endurance and Derision" (*NMW* 10:19–26), Wayne D. McGinnis offers a helpful caveat against sentimentalizing the patient endurance of the mule and, by analogy, the South in Faulkner's fiction. The topic, however, stubbornly resists being put in such narrow traces.

iv. Criticism: Special Studies

***a.* Ideas, Influences, Intellectual Background.** One very competent influence study and several less successful ones appeared in 1977. Arthur F. Kinney's "Faulkner and Flaubert" (*JML* 6:222–47) is a fine consideration of Flaubert's influence, both in matters of technique and of theme, on Faulkner. Concentrating on the two Temple Drake novels, Kinney hypothesizes that "like *Madame Bovary, Sanctuary* is the secular tracing, as *La Tentation* and *Requiem* are the sacred tracing, of man's inevitable corruptibility." This concentration effectively focuses Kinney's large topic so that he may specifically compare, for example, the two authors' spatialization of sections of narrative. His essay suggests how rewarding would be a full exploration both of Flaubert's influence and of the ways in which "the boldest experimenter in fiction in our country and in our time" transformed that influence.

Joseph Blotner's article "Romantic Elements in Faulkner" in *Romantic and Modern*, pp. 207–21, testifies to the influence of the Romantics on Faulkner. Yet this article is less an influence study than a check list of romantic elements in Faulkner's work, especially in *Sartoris*; thus it remains more a useful catalogue than a thorough assessment of Faulkner's romanticism.

Faulkner's borrowing from southern history is the subject of Hubert McAlexander, Jr.'s "General Earl Van Dorn and Faulkner's Use of History" (*JMiH* 39:357–61). This helpful note reviews the salient facts about Van Dorn's glamorous military career and his unglamorous death and offers some comments about Faulkner's several uses of this historical material. A guide to Faulkner's extensive mining of local historical materials is found in James B. Lloyd's book (see section ii).

Several studies of Faulkner's influence on others indicate how Faulkner's vision has shaped western fiction. Diane R. Leonard's "Simon's *L'Herbe*: Beyond Sound and Fury" (*FAR* 1[1976]:13–30) is a detailed and informative study of relations between two novels. Leonard examines similar situations and themes in *The Sound and the Fury* and *L'Herbe* to establish that Simon does not slavishly imitate but rather accepts and transforms Faulknerian ways of seeing. Another article, Phyllis Zatlin Boring's "Faulkner in Spain: The Case of Elena Quiroga" (*CLS* 14:166–76) applies a similar thesis to one important contemporary Spanish novelist. Boring's study suggests that it is Faulkner's technique, rather than subject matter or theme, which has had the largest impact on Elena Quiroga.

Two essays in Spanish considered, through comparisons between "A Rose for Emily" and Juan Carlos Onetti's "La Novia Robada," Faulkner's influence on Onetti. Corina Mathieu-Higginbotham's "Faulkner y Onetti: Una Visión de La Realidad a Través de Jefferson y Santa Maria" (*Hispano* 61:51–60) examines theme and technique to suggest that both authors use point of view to imply the cause of their protagonists' warped lives. Mathieu-Higginbotham's essay is a fairly comprehensive influence study, while Josefina Ludmer's "Onetti: 'La Novia (carta) robada (a Faulkner)'" (*Hispam* 9[1975]:3–19) is a more detailed technical study. It explores (as its title indicates) double meanings and inversions of Faulkner in Onetti.[1]

Miroslav J. Hanak's paper entitled "Nietzsche, Dostoevsky and Faulkner: Rebellion Against Society in the Light of the New Left" in *Actes du VIe Congrès de l'Association Internationale de Littérature Comparée*, edited by M. Cadot et al. (Stuttgart: Kunst und Wissne/Erich Bieber, 1975) reads like a précis of a longer work; unfortunately, it is not. Instead Hanak summarizes intellectual and political trends with astonishing rapidity to conclude that the three writers under consideration are not reactionary, as the left has labeled them, for all three call for a radical reform of mankind and see in "*dehumanizing* conceptualism" the enemy of that reform. The Faulknerian may find it interesting to read of Faulkner in a European socio/political context, rewarding to see simplistic distortions of Faulkner's work lose another residual remnant of credibility, but distressing to read a paper so divorced from specific attention to any Faulknerian text that it cannot substantiate itself.

Several studies on the subject of time also remain trapped in generalizations. Daniel G. Ford's "Comments on William Faulkner's

1. I wish to thank St. John Robinson for his assistance with the Spanish essays in section iv, a.

Temporal Vision in *Sanctuary, The Sound and the Fury, Light in August, Absalom, Absalom!*" (*SoQ* 15:283–90) can hardly pretend to treat the vast topic announced in his title. Though Ford does make a useful distinction between Proustian involuntary memory and Bergsonian duration, he works by assertion only to say what is already generally known. In "The Metaphysics of Yoknapatawpha County: 'Airy Space and Scope for your Delirium'" (*HSL* 8[1976]:223–40) Francine Ringold presents another overview of the Bergsonian influence with some attention to the ramifications in Faulkner's work of Einstein's theory of relativity. Though generally well written, this paper is not a contribution to new understandings. Similarly Fran Polek's "Tick-tocks, Whirs, and Broken Gears: Time and Identity in Faulkner" (*Renascence* 29:193–200) is another overview which serves to sum up more than to reconsider in any depth how identity may be "correlated to time." One article that does not pretend to be original criticism but rather to be an introductory capsule summary is Seymour Gross and Rosalie Murphy's "From Stephen Crane to William Faulkner: Some Remarks on the Religious Sense in American Literature" (*Cithara* 16:90–108). Gross and Murphy offer a brief but basically sound treatment of Faulkner's sense of a spiritual order. Another introductory overview is to be found in V. R. N. Prasad's "William Faulkner and the Southern Syndrome" in *Indian Studies in American Fiction*, edited by M. K. Naik, S. K. Desai, and S. Mokashi-punekar (Dharwar: Karnatak Univ.; Delhi: Macmillan, 1974). Prasad offers an historical but somewhat romanticized review of Southern philosophy, history, and life and of the relation of other modern Southern writers, as well as Faulkner, to that "syndrome." This is a basically sound introduction, especially for the foreign reader, to Faulkner's southernness and his concern for the survival of the human spirit. Such overviews do have their place, but they have little or nothing to offer to the Faulknerian.

***b.* Language and Style.** In 1977 a few of the articles on individual works treated Faulkner's language and style; none dealt with the subject per se. Probably that is just as well, since few critics seem able to generalize to any point about this topic. One foreign item picked up from 1976 illustrates the problem. Writing on "Faulkner's Technique" in *Studies in American Literature: Essays in Honour of William Mulder*, edited by Jagdish Chander and Narindar S. Pradhan

(Delhi: Oxford, 1976), V. Y. Kantak intends, apparently, to answer F. R. Leavis and Clifton Fadiman. This prolix article relies on such nonstatements as "The triumph of that curious Faulknerian technique is rather to indicate a certain intangible presence in the Southern consciousness"; but Kantak apparently finds that presence too intangible to describe. Another article from India, on the other hand, suggests that it is possible to discuss Faulkner's technical achievement in terms that do not vaporize into airy nothingness. In "The Rhetoric of William Faulkner" (*IJES* 16 [1976]:29–43), D. S. Maini suggests the psychic, philosophical, and historical sources of what he terms Faulkner's "imperial rhetoric." Maini sees Faulkner's rhetoric as an heroic, albeit hubristic, affirmation reenacting the human tragedy. Maini ignores an apparent paradox between his own interpretation and that of James Guetti in *The Limits of Metaphor* (see *ALS 1967*, pp. 33–34), but he does offer fresh insight into the character of Faulkner's rhetoric and its stylistic consequences. Further application of his theories would be welcome; for his essay suggests another way to approach that most neglected of topics in Faulkner studies: language and style.

c. **Race.** Until lately we have had too few influence studies in Faulkner criticism which were not mechanical and superficial. Walter Taylor in "Faulkner: Nineteenth Century Notions of Racial Mixture and the Twentieth-Century Imagination" (*SCR* 10:57–68) sets out to correct that problem with regard to one topic; his concern is with the influence on Faulkner of stereotypical southern depictions of black and racially mixed characters. Taylor effectively classifies the traditional southern literary attitudes towards miscegenation. Though references to 19th-century southern writers are conspicuously absent from Faulkner's comments about his reading, nevertheless Taylor shows how Faulkner's portrayals of persons of racially mixed blood reenact a centuries-old debate. Inasmuch as Faulkner was deferent to "the pseudo-genetics and paranoia of another era," Taylor feels that Faulkner failed his own genius. Like Darwin T. Turner's treatment of "Faulkner and Slavery" (see section iii), Taylor's scholarship establishes with some precision the terms of a limitation in Faulkner's imaginative capacity to transcend the limits of his own time and place. While Taylor's consideration of Faulkner and race is basically empirical, Lee Clinton Jenkins's "Faulkner, the Mythic Mind, and the

Blacks" (*L&P* 27:74–91) is mythic. Using Sigmund Freud, Otto Rank, and John T. Irwin, Jenkins offers an interesting hypothesis about the relation in Faulkner between incest and miscegenation and the frequent association between women and blacks. This poorly proofed essay takes rather too long to get to its point: that the ways in which the conscious mind deals with the unconscious, or the self with its shadow, are reenacted in Faulkner's fiction in the ways whites deal with blacks. The essay does offer an intriguing framework for understanding the personal conflicts in Faulkner's fiction.

v. Individual Works to 1929

This year Faulkner's early work received a great deal of long overdue and much welcome critical attention. *The Marionettes*, with an Introduction and Textual Apparatus by Noel Polk (Charlottesville: Univ. Press of Va.) is a handsomely produced reissue of the Bibliographical Society of the University of Virginia's 1975 limited edition facsimile; now we have a more accessible and affordable edition. There are four known copies of *The Marionettes*; this edition is a reproduction of what apparently was Faulkner's original copy (given to Ben Wasson and now in the Virginia collection); it is the most elaborate of the four hand-lettered, hand-drawn, and hand-bound books. (The other three are substantially identical; two are to be found at the University of Texas; one, which was also issued in a limited edition facsimile in 1975, is at the University of Mississippi.) The extravagant similies, stylized drawings, and elaborate mannerisms of this very early work (*The Marionettes* was apparently written in the fall of 1920) testify to the influence of the Decadents and also to Faulkner's early sense of the artifice of art. Reading *The Marionettes* establishes how pervasive throughout his career was Faulkner's concern with certain central themes: among them nameless, frustrated desires, associations between sexuality and death and stasis and sterility. Polk's introduction, a revision of an earlier article (see *ALS 1973*, pp. 141–42) offers an excellent glance backward to *Marionettes*'s sources and forward to thematic motifs in the fiction. His textual appendices are scrupulously handled, and the volume itself is beautifully produced.

Also in 1920 Faulkner published in *The Mississippian* translations of four poems by Paul Verlaine. In "Faulkner as Translator: His Version of Verlaine" (*MissQ* 30:429–32) Martin Kreiswirth compares these translations with the originals and with translations done by Arthur Symons. Kreiswirth's competent note establishes how dependent Faulkner's translations were upon the English versions of the same poems printed by Symons in *The Symbolist Movement in Literature* (1919). Another of Faulkner's early works has now received the sort of close scrutiny all his writing calls for: Philip Momberger's "A Reading of Faulkner's 'The Hill' " (*SLJ* 9, ii:16–29) offers an excellent analysis of this prose sketch. Momberger's careful reading establishes how the oppositions between hill and valley and withdrawal and engagement which are set forth here remain central in Faulkner's later work. While this reading is in itself contained and thorough, it suggests, as attention to self-revelatory early work often does, how very appropriate a biographical approach would also be.

Two other works in 1977 at least open such discussion. One is Cleanth Brooks's "The Image of Helen Baird in Faulkner's Early Poetry and Fiction" (*SR* 85:218–34). Reviewing Faulkner's 1926–27 relationship with Helen Baird, Brooks shows how her image, tempered by allusions to Cabell's *Jurgen* and Rostand's *Cyrano* especially, appeared and reappeared in Faulkner's writing. Brooks has done considerable literary detective work (particularly impressive is his use of Joan Williams's novel *The Wintering*, 1971), but, as he acknowledges himself, this essay includes little new evidence. It does exhibit a certain familiar hesitancy about the biography; for instance, even while marshalling biographical evidence, Brooks writes, "I am not at all sure that we need to derive Faulkner's special kind of romanticism from events that occurred to him in his personal life." As I have suggested before (see *ALS 1976*, pp. 121–23), I see no reason to ignore Faulkner's personal life, even though we know that we cannot simply "derive" the poetry and fiction from it.

In 1977 Notre Dame Press printed a limited edition facsimile of Faulkner's *Mayday*, another hand-printed, hand-drawn (and *Mayday* also includes hand-painted watercolor illustrations), and hand-bound booklet, which Faulkner dedicated and gave to Helen Baird in 1926. Along with the facsimile Notre Dame has published a brief pamphlet by Carvel Collins entitled "Faulkner's *Mayday*." Like Brooks, Collins traces both biographical and literary sources. Especially impressive are Collins's comparisons between *Mayday* and *The Sound and the Fury*. He finds allusions to other works by James

Branch Cabell beside *Jurgen.* His references to certain formerly unknown biographical details (another stay in New Haven, an unsuccessful love affair, and a 1925 beginning for work which was to become *The Sound and the Fury*) provoke us to ask for more discussion from Collins.

James M. Mellard's "*Soldier's Pay* and the Growth of Faulkner's Comedy" (*Gerber Festschrift*, pp. 99–117) is hampered by his terminology; descriptions and labels like "romantic idealist," "skirting of disaster," and "brilliant understatement" do not provide a true analysis of the structural terms of Faulkner's comedy. Also, Mellard is simply not very precise—as when he says that Margaret Powers "early-on falls in love with" Donald Mahon.

In "Faulkner and Huxley: A Note on *Mosquitoes* and *Crome Yellow*" (*MissQ* 30:433–36), Edwin T. Arnold III traces parallels between the two novels. He presents an impressive list, but he fails to speak of technical or thematic similarities and, finally, to consider the significance of the material he covers. In "The Subjective Intensities of Faulkner's *Flags in the Dust*" (*CRevAS* 8:154–64) Kerry McSweeney concentrates his attention upon Faulkner's style and upon his treatment of sexuality and the past—those "subjective intensities" McSweeney feels criticism of *Sartoris* and/or *Flags in the Dust* has so far ignored. This very fine treatment of style and voice does a great deal to explain the difference between Faulkner's control and his lack of control of his art. McSweeney makes especially sound observations about reasons why "poetic" similes are more successful when they express the power of the past than when they deal with the power of sexuality.

This year once again *The Sound and the Fury* commanded more attention than any other of Faulkner's novels; and again there was enormous disparity in the quality and value of this work. One of the best articles was Judith Slater's "Quentin's Tunnel Vision: Modes of Perception and Their Stylistic Realization in *The Sound and the Fury*" (*L&P* 27:4–15). Slater's thesis—that "Quentin's suicide represents not the breakdown of his defenses but a logical extension of them"—is hardly new. Yet she bases that thesis upon a fresh examination of the pattern of perceptual reorganizations Quentin exhibits. This approach is most fruitful as an analysis of image and syntax. It reveals close psychic patterns of association between women and time and establishes Quentin's sense of the control Dalton Ames and

Gerald Bland have over both. This approach further establishes the psychological dimensions of Quentin's inability to cope with either women or time.

In "Light Imagery in *The Sound and the Fury*: April 7, 1928" (*JNT* 6[1976]:41–50), Roger Ramsey offers an excellent close reading of section I, detailing Faulkner's ironic association of light imagery with death and loss. Grounding itself in the *Macbeth* allusion, this study offers further evidence of the remarkable artistry with which Faulkner constructed this novel.

Another useful article is Boyd Davis's "Caddy Compson's Eden" (*MissQ* 30:381–94). This article is really about garden and tree imagery in Faulkner's early work, with special attention paid to *The Sound and the Fury* and to mythic, historical, and literary uses of garden imagery. Davis's sound scholarship carefully and effectively illustrates how allusions often work in Faulkner. In "The Other Family and Luster in *The Sound and the Fury*" (*CLAJ* 20[1976]: 245–61), Thadious Davis presents a rather romanticized treatment of Dilsey's family. Davis excuses or overlooks Luster's meanness and sees in Luster's attitude toward the Compsons a foretaste of a changing status for blacks. Despite such a combination of under- and over-reading, Davis does offer insight into the ways Faulkner foiled the black Gibsons against the white Compsons in *The Sound and the Fury*. Also Davis's comments upon the use of Italics in Benjy's section are helpful (though they suggest that this matter requires further examination).

Another article which suffers (as several discussed in section iii do) from having first been a speech is William J. Handy's "*The Sound and the Fury*: A Formalist Approach" (*NDQ* 44, iii[1976]:71–83). After spending one third of his essay getting ready to apply Formalist techniques to *The Sound and the Fury*, Handy spends the other two thirds making rather obvious and often shop-worn observations which are not distinctly formalist and which do not probe beneath the surface of the novel. One book which does not have *The Sound and the Fury* as its principal subject but which should be cross-referenced here is Estella Schoenberg's *Old Tales and Talking: Quentin Compson in William Faulkner's "Absalom, Absalom!" and Related Works* (see section vi).

An excellent note, "Jason Compson and the Costs of Speculation:

A Second Look" (*MissQ* 30:437–40), serves as an addenda to William W. Cobau's earlier note on the same topic (see *ALS 1969*, p. 115). Adding further information about the cotton market in 1928, Wayne W. Westbrook enlarges our appreciation of the characterization of Jason Compson. Another note deserves mentioning principally as a warning. In "Similarities Between 'The Waste Land' and *The Sound and the Fury*" (*NConL* 7, i:10–13), Jean Bolen Bridges tries to treat a large and complex topic simply by listing "similarities"; her two and a half pages are crammed with pronouncements without defense or explanation or reference to previous scholarship.

vi. Individual Works, 1930–1939

The year 1977 was an especially good year for scholarship on *As I Lay Dying*. The preeminent event was the publication of *As I Lay Dying: A Concordance to the Novel*, edited by Jack L. Capps, introduction by Cleanth Brooks (Ann Arbor, Mich.: Univ. Microfilms). This is the first of the concordances published by the Faulkner Concordance Advisory Board with the support of the United States Military Academy. Capps's preface refers to roughly a decade which the advisory board has spent determining procedural and textual matters. One of the board's decisions was to use available texts and list variations; another was to break texts into coherent "sense units" rather than divide them into lines. Clearly the board had the utility and convenience of its product in mind; but a full explanation of such determinations would have been welcome in this first concordance. Instead we have only Capps's brief explanation of programming procedure. (There is one egregious error in this preface which I mention in hopes that it will be corrected; Capps dates Faulkner's visit to West Point in 1963 [after Faulkner's death] rather than in 1962.)

Introductory material is brief in this concordance and also in the concordance to *Go Down, Moses* (see section vii). Cleanth Brooks's introduction discusses the usefulness of concordances for literary study in general, for Faulkner's canon, and finally for *As I Lay Dying*. All that Brooks writes is appropriate and welcome, and he makes particularly astute observations about some four sample words from *As I Lay Dying*. ("Thick," for instance, appears 13 times but never modifies a solid object which normally might be described as "thick.") I regret that this introduction does not deal at greater length with this concordance's relevance to *As I Lay Dying*, but I gather that the board's intention was to keep introductory discussions to a minimum. The volume does, however, provide us with notes on the use of the text and with helpful statistical summaries of the vocabulary in the novel: a histogram of vocabulary by word length indicating frequency of occurrence; and a list of words in order of their frequency of appearance. The latter appendix offers certain surprises. *Jewel* appears 303 times while the next most frequent entry for a character's name is *Cash* at 236 entries (neither the word *jewel* nor *cash* appears in lower case form in the novel): *horse* appears 134 times, while *Anse* appears on 132 occasions; *God* appears 59 times, *Christ* once. The concordance itself, of course, makes possible a wealth of information. The 53 entries under *road*, for instance, may be classed into three types: literal and functional references to the road the Bundrens are riding along, descriptions of that road, and figurative uses of the word *road* (the last class comprises almost half of the entries). An even larger percentage of the 85 entries under *eyes* is entirely figurative. Such observations can only begin to suggest the sort of analyses the concordance now makes possible. Obviously, it opens new and very exciting prospects for Faulkner studies.

The year 1977 also saw the publication of two fine articles on *As I Lay Dying*. A speculative treatment of Darl's vision is offered by Watson G. Branch in "Darl Bundren's 'Cubistic' Vision" (*TSLL* 19: 42–59). Branch is convinced that it was the First World War which disheartened Darl and that exposure, while in France, to early modern art movements "provided Darl with a mode for conceiving reality commensurate to the disorientation he felt." Branch's thorough research and careful documentation make such an improbable-sounding argument feasible. Certainly Branch does establish the influence of cubism on Faulkner and Faulkner's use in Darl's section not only of terminology but of ways of seeing derived from cubism. Further evidence that this mode of perception typifies Darl alone could have been established only after the concordance's appearance. In "Faulkner's Folklore in *As I Lay Dying*: An Old Motif in a New Manner" (*SNNTS* 9:46–53) David Middleton suggests that the "grieving husband" formula for certain folk tales was ironically inverted by Faulkner in *As I Lay Dying*. Middleton sees the relationship between Anse and Addie as a struggle for dominance which Anse finally wins by turning Addie's scheme to his own profit. Such an awareness of folkloric motifs is a useful corrective to various sentimentalizations of the Bundrens.

Another rather different treatment of folk materials is offered by Floyd C. Watkins in his *In Time and Place.* Clarifying and verifying customs and mores typical of country Southerners, Watkins in his chapter "*As I Lay Dying*: The Dignity of Earth" (pp. 175–89) offers a useful introduction to the folkways the Bundrens and their kind lived by; certainly, he establishes the authenticity of Faulkner's portraits. The chapter implicitly rests within a framework based on Watkins's assumption that intimate acquaintance with a traditional culture is a necessary condition for genuine achievement in fiction; I find that framework questionable, but my objections are reflections of a different approach to literature which I have expressed elsewhere in my *William Faulkner: The Abstract and the Actual* (1974). A third treatment of legendary or folk materials in this novel, Kenneth Seib's "Midrashic Legend in Faulkner's *As I Lay Dying*" (*NMAL* 2:item 5), simply exhibits the uselessness of notes too brief to establish anything.

This year saw the publication of a fine article on *Sanctuary* by T. H. Adamowski entitled "Faulkner's Popeye: the 'Other' as Self" (*CRevAS* 8:36–51). This sensitive reading solves certain apparent enigmas in Faulkner's portrayal. Refuting the "electric-light-stamped-tin" interpretation of Popeye as a symbol of modernity and the flatly deterministic interpretation of Popeye as a product of his inheritance, Adamowski analyses the fascination Popeye holds over other characters and readers as well. Using Sartre to clarify connections between fascination and indifference, Adamowski argues convincingly for consistency in Popeye's last moments. His reading of this puzzling character is most welcome. Another competent article is Linda Kauffman's "The Madam and the Midwife: Reba Rivers and Sairey Gamp" (*MissQ* 30: 395–401). Kauffman makes a useful comparison not only between characters but between *Sanctuary* and *Martin Chuzzlewit* as well. In "Temple's Provocative Quest: Or, What Really Happened at the Old Frenchman Place" (*NMW* 10:74–79) Judith Wood Angelius argues that Temple is less intentionally flirtatious than readers have assumed, but Angelius fails to establish what difference her reading will make in our understanding of Temple and the novel. "The Four Faces of Temple Drake: Faulkner's *Sanctuary, Requiem for a Nun*, and the Two Film Adaptations" (*AQ* 28 [1796]:544–60) by Pauline Degenfelder does not tell us anything new about the novels, though it is interesting to note that Degenfelder sees the films about Temple Drake, but not Faulkner's novels, as misogynist.

Notes and articles on *Light in August* in 1977 were unremarkable. In "Love's Labors: Byron Bunch and Shakespeare" (*NMW* 10:80–86) Mario L. D'Avanzo does offer useful comparisons between Faulkner's Byron and Shakespeare's Biron; his topic, however, is too large for such a mini-article. In "Byron Bunch and Percy Grimm: Strange Twins of *Light in August*" (*MissQ* 30:441–43) Hugh M. Ruppersburg points out two parallel scenes in the novel, but he hardly knows what to make of the comparison. A longer study, Louise A. Poresky's "Joe Christmas: His Tragedy as Victim" (*HSL* 8 [1976]:209–22) rather tediously reviews the circumstances of Joe's life. She would have done well to delete the review and to defend more thoroughly her assumption that Joe's behavior is motivated by an Oedipal conflict.

Despite the title of Pauline Degenfelder's essay "Sirk's *The Tarnished Angels*: *Pylon* recreated" (*LFQ* 5:242–51), no criticism this year dealt with *Pylon*; for Degenfelder's essay is really about the film and not the novel (the word "recreated" in her title turns out to mean "remade").

Two studies this year offer radically different approaches to the distinction between fact and truth which lies at the heart of *Absalom, Absalom!* One is Estella Schoenberg's *Old Tales and Talking: Quentin Compson in William Faulkner's 'Absalom, Absalom!' and Related Works* (Jackson: Univ. Press of Miss.). Schoenberg's thesis is that in *Absalom, Absalom!* "Sutpen's is not unquestionably the primary story. It is at least as easy—for me much easier—to see the story of Quentin Compson in the foreground of *Absalom, Absalom!* and to hear in the book's title Jason Richmond Compson's grief for his son Quentin." She goes on to assert that "Quentin's working out the story of Sutpen's children in this novel is Faulkner's means of retelling Quentin's story and explaining Quentin's suicide." Schoenberg supports her thesis by a number of questionable arguments. Among them is the assumption that "The Sutpen material in *Absalom, Absadom!* is *im*material—literally. It is inadequate for even short fictional units. . . ." This argument seems to be that because the Sutpen story "failed in every other use" (i.e., earlier versions such as "Evangeline" were not successful), the success of this novel is explained by the presence of Quentin Compson, and therefore this is Quentin's, not Sutpen's, story. Schoenberg considers the same point to be proved by the fact that Quentin's chronology is without mistakes, while Sutpen's is not, and that Quentin's telling "moves straight and steady through two short time spans," while Sutpen's chronology is supposed "to be sloshing about in Bergsonian duration." Finally Schoenberg concludes that because "most of them [the events of the Sutpen story] either did not happen or cannot be proved to have happened," then *Absalom, Absalom!* is not Sutpen's story.

For a critic to discount a fictional story within a story because its "facts" cannot be proved is ludicrous—especially when she is dealing with a novel designed to show how irrelevant are facts and empirical proof. The failure of Schoenberg's study is especially unfortunate because she has given us significant summaries of unpublished, little-known, and largely unavailable material. (She writes a particularly valuable account of "Evangeline," an early story of the Sutpen children which was found among other forgotten papers at Rowanoak in 1971 and is now housed in the Jill Faulkner Summers archive at the University of Virginia.) Also Schoenberg does remind us of how little about Thomas Sutpen we actually can be sure. But though most of her data is accurate, her hypothesis and conclusion are simply unsound.

In contrast to Schoenberg, Carl E. Rollyson, Jr., not only understands the primacy of imaginative truth, but he argues that such an understanding is crucial to the historian as well as the artist. In "*Absalom, Absalom!*: The Novel as Historiography" (*LH* 5:42–54) Rollyson acknowledges, as Schoenberg does, that the "fact" of Bon's black blood is not empirically validated; but while Schoenberg concluded that therefore there was no threat of miscegenation, Rollyson sees that therefore "only through their [i.e. Quentin's and Shreve's] emotional and intellectual transactions do we make the discovery that solves the riddle of the past." Essentially, this article serves to remind us that the "methodology" Quentin and Shreve use is a supremely human achievement, not alien even to such an empirically based discipline as history.

In another article Rollyson makes an interesting suggestion about what Shreve really means when he asks Quentin to tell about the

South. But Rollyson's "Faulkner and Historical Fiction: *Redgauntlet* and *Absalom, Absalom!* (*DR* 56:671–81) simply points out parallels between *Absalom, Absalom!* and Sir Walter Scott's *Redgauntlet.* The article lacks what its title promises: an appraisal of Faulkner's relation to historical fiction.

Similarly, in "Another Possible Source for *Absalom, Absalom!*" (*NMW* 10: 87–94) Edward J. Piacentino traces the parallels (already alluded to by Blotner and Holman) between this novel and T. S. Stribling's trilogy about the Vaiden family. Both Rollyson's study of parallels with Scott and Piacentino's study of parallels with Stribling suggest interesting connections; neither article, however, analyzes the significance of the echoes in Faulkner of other works. In "Sutpen's 'Incidental' Wives and the Question of Respectability" (*MissQ* 30: 445–47) Stuart L. Burns argues that Sutpen's intent is to find not a respectable bride but a lily-white one; Burns fails to define the distinction between these concepts.

Other than the chapter on *The Unvanquished* in Joanne V. Creighton's *William Faulkner's Craft of Revision*, neither that novel nor *The Wild Palms* received any critical attention this year.

vii. Individual Works, 1940–49

In 1977 criticism of *The Hamlet* appeared only in Joanne V. Creighton's book (see section iii) and in a single article on the trilogy (see section viii). Several essays dealt with individual chapters within *Go Down, Moses.* The most valuable of these essays was John L. Cleman's " 'Pantaloon in Black': Its Place in *Go Down, Moses*" (*TSL* 22:170–81). Cleman examines the motifs of love, the "new slavery," and the hunt to show how they function in this story as echoes and inversions of patterns central to the whole novel. Cleman offers a fine reading which no student of *Go Down, Moses* should ignore. Another interesting essay which also treated "Pantaloon in Black" was Eberhard Alsen's "An Existentialist Reading of Faulkner's 'Pantaloon in Black' " (*SSF* 14:169–78). Alsen sees Rider as an existential rather than a tragic hero precisely because Rider recognizes injustice (God, like the white man, has loaded the dice) and because Rider's free choice of the means of death is meaningfully defiant. Except for a rather too easy assumption that only an existentialist stance would bring one "to strike out at degradation and exploitation" while "Christianity demands that man submit himself meekly to God and to human oppressors," Alsen offers a fine reading.

Two essays dealt with "The Bear." One is Wayne Pound's "Symbolic Landscapes in 'The Bear': 'Rural Myth and Technological Fact'" (*GyS* 4:40–52). As another treatment of the civilization and wilderness, machine and garden dichotomy, this essay does not explore new ground so much as it refocuses and synthesizes in a succinct readable manner. J. Edward Schamberger's "Renaming Percival Brownlee in Faulkner's '[The] Bear'" (*CollL* 4:92–94) is a valuable note which not only explains the name "Spintrius" by references to Suetonius, but also suggests the relevance of this episode to the rest of "The Bear."

One publication in 1977 should make it not only easier and more rewarding but almost obligatory to study *Go Down, Moses* as a novel rather than as a collection of stories. That publication is *Go Down Moses: A Concordance to the Novel*, edited by Jack L. Capps, introduction by Michael Millgate (Ann Arbor, Mich.: Univ. Microfilms International). Prefatory materials and appendices are substantially the same as those for the concordance to *As I Lay Dying* (see section iv). Millgate's introduction is brief (as was Brooks's to the first concordance), but especially useful since it illustrates a number of scholarly applications of the concordance of *Go Down, Moses* and suggests the impact this concordance will have. Millgate's comments reveal the "narrative cross-referencing which Faulkner deliberately built into the structure of *Go Down, Moses*." The concordance itself now provides the critic with complete documentation for, say, comparisons between references to *woods* and *wilderness* and to *house*, *room*, and *door* (surprisingly, *wilderness* appears 47 times, *woods* 91, and "house" 176 times); these figures suggest how emblems of civilization are juxtaposed against the wilderness and they establish just how pervasive in all of the novel is the wilderness/civilization dichotomy. Also the high incidence of words like *cage*, *trap*, *fence*, and *tame* invites comparisons throughout the novel with references to *free* and *freedom*. And when we read through the references to *bed* and *cot* we realize how central these images are as symbols and as key plotting signals in the novel. In short, the concordance offers a vast resource for studying Faulkner's vocabulary, his use of symbol and image, and his means of interrelating parts of the novel.

viii. Individual Works, 1950–62

This year *A Fable* received a modest amount of critical attention, all of it welcome. By far the best and most exciting piece was Kathryn A. Chittick's "The Fables in William Faulkner's *A Fable*" (*MissQ* 30: 403–15), which associates *A Fable* with the type of "sacred" literature best exemplified in the Old Testament. Tracing the network of myths which resound throughout *A Fable*, Chittick makes an important contribution to our understanding of the way in which Faulkner's imagination works. She establishes that in Faulkner allusions are not systems of one-to-one equivalences, that they may in fact coexist in a rich pastiche of meanings, and that apparently contradictory associations (as with the General who seems at times to be Christ, or God, or Lucifer) need not cancel each other out, but instead may enrich the resonance of the work as a whole.

In "Eneas Africanus and Faulkner's Fabulous Racehourse" (*SLJ* 9, ii:3–15) Adrienne Bond offers a detailed treatment of parallels between the racehorse story in *A Fable* and its predecessor, Harry Stillwell Edwards's *Eneas Africanus*. This comparison of materials is informative, and Bond makes several valuable observations on differences between Faulkner's and Edwards's tales. Nevertheless, the essay is marred by a failure to explain Faulkner's objectifying and what Bond considers his stereotyping of the black preacher. It is also marred by a final paragraph that reads like a series of non-sequiturs.

The Town and *The Mansion* received attention from Joanne V. Creighton in *William Faulkner's Craft of Revision* (see section iii) and Holly McFarland in "The Mast not Tragic . . . Just Damned: The Women in Faulkner's Trilogy" (*BSUF* 18,ii:27–50). This article is misnamed and too long, but it does conclude with a promising treatment of Linda Kohl and Mink Snopes. And, finally, there was one note in 1977 dealing with *The Reivers*. William E. McCarron's "Shakespeare, Faulkner and Ned William McCaslin" (*NConL* 7:8–9) sensibly explains an allusion to *Richard II* in Faulkner's last novel.

ix. The Stories

Other than the essays on "Pantaloon in Black" and "The Bear" (see section vii) only two essays dealt with the stories. One was Joan D. Winslow's "Language and Destruction in Faulkner's 'Dry September' " (*CLAJ* 20:380–86). As a thematic rather than a technical study, Winslow's essay examines the ways in which words and labels "that have gathered such a powerful emotional force serve to dictate pre-established patterns of behavior." This excellent reading is careful to delineate how both Minnie Cooper and John McLendon are similiarly victims of empty language; and it offers an especially fine treatment of the attempt (by Hawkshaw and two others) to use language positively and referentially.

And finally this year saw the publication of William O. Hendricks's " 'A Rose for Emily': A Syntagmatic Analysis" (*PTL: A Journal for Descriptive Poetics and Theory of Literature* 2:257–95). Hendricks makes a schematic reduction of the story's plot into "two interrelated 'subplots' ": one subplot involves conflicts between Emily, the past, and the present; the other between Emily, Barron, and the present. In Chomskyan terms, the former is the enclosing or *matrix plot*, the latter the enclosed or *constituent plot*. Hendricks is able to subsume all narrative elements into a plot in which "the final image, only implied, of Emily cohabiting with a corpse is a hyperbolic statement of the decadence and extinction of the old aristocratic order." Such a schematization of the plot is valuable in establishing the unity and coherence of what may seem to be a loosely episodic story, but it does not explain the significance of, say, a particular plot reversal which in Hendricks's formula reads first as $\bar{r}$ then as r (these designations mean that Emily first seems to have lost to Homer Barron, but, finally, we discover that, in her own perverse way, she won). Explaining that reversal would be much more valuable than simply diagramming it. Hendricks's documentation is peculiarly narcissistic since it refers mostly to his own work. Furthermore, he could have exposed plot structure and reached these same conclusions much less tortuously. In short, after 38 pages of diagrams and detailed, jargon-ridden preparations and explanations, Hendricks, like Emily, may be accused of overkill.

Louisiana State University

10. Fitzgerald and Hemingway

Jackson R. Bryer

Despite the lack (for the fifth consecutive year) of a full-length exclusively critical book on either Fitzgerald or Hemingway, 1977 did produce a good deal of worthwhile scholarship and criticism. Two valuable textual studies of Fitzgerald novels, a biographical-critical book on Hemingway which paints a clearer portrait of that very complicated man, several good close readings of *The Great Gatsby*, two excellent essays on *A Farewell to Arms*, which also focus on the text, and four new pieces on *Tender Is the Night*, which deal with that novel in a long overdue serious, critical, and complex manner—these are the highlights of a year which also saw the publication of two issues of the *Fitzgerald/Hemingway Annual*. The latter, while somewhat reduced in size, continues to provide—particularly in the areas of textual, bibliographical, and biographical scholarship—much of the most worthwhile material available.

i. Bibliographical Work and Texts

Two very different yet equally valuable full-length textual studies of Fitzgerald novels appeared in 1977. Matthew J. Bruccoli's *"The Last of the Novelists": F. Scott Fitzgerald and "The Last Tycoon"* (Carbondale: So. Ill. Univ. Press) is a detailed and fascinating reconstruction of the successive drafts, with extensive quotations used to illustrate the changes Fitzgerald made as he revised. Much of this material is very technical and is difficult to absorb without an expert knowledge of the text as Edmund Wilson edited it for publication in 1941; but Bruccoli also provides excellent background on the circumstances surrounding the novel's composition as well as some extremely incisive literary analysis of the work. His conclusion—that Wilson's edition "obscures the gestational nature of Fitzgerald's work and misleads readers into judging work-in-progress as completed stages"—emerges gracefully and inescapably from his careful scholarship.

James L. W. West III's *The Making of F. Scott Fitzgerald's "This Side of Paradise"* (Columbia, S.C.: J. Faust & Co.) is less detailed and scholarly than Bruccoli's book, principally because West was unfortunately and inexplicably prohibited from quoting such crucial unpublished Fitzgerald documents as letters, typescripts, and manuscripts. He thus cannot provide the kind of heavily documented tour through the composition of the novel that we get from Bruccoli. But what is sacrificed here in scholarly precision is more than made up for in readability. West's slim book is an extremely suggestive summary of the process which Fitzgerald used in, literally, putting together his first novel using portions of his first draft of the work—which he had called "The Romantic Egotist"—as well as already published stories and playlets and even letters received from friends. West is helpful in accounting for the novel's acknowledged unevenness and cavalier disregard for consistency of point of view in Book 1. He is also making a distinct contribution to further study when he points out that, apparently, an unknown friend of Fitzgerald's (whom West dubs "Grammarian") read through the completed manuscript and made suggestions of changes, many of which Fitzgerald followed and which changed the meanings of several passages. Finally, West's revelation that, in the manuscript, the final line of the novel, Amory Blaine's statement, " 'I know myself, but that is all,' " is followed by a dash rather than the period which completes it in the published version, gives rise to many areas of speculation. Taken together, Bruccoli's and West's books should encourage new and more fruitful attention to two of Fitzgerald's most critically ignored works.

Thomas E. Daniels provides two worthwhile shorter textual pieces. In "Toward a Definitive Edition of F. Scott Fitzgerald's Short Stories" (*PBSA* 71:295–310), he presents a careful, albeit somewhat unrealistic, formula for putting together an edition of Fitzgerald's short stories which would provide "texts as close to Fitzgerald's intention as possible." Given the various versions of many of the stories—holographs, manuscripts, proofs of magazine versions, published versions in magazines, proofs of books, published versions in collections—this represents an immense task which Daniels acknowledges would involve "a great deal of perception concerning Fitzgerald's work—and possibly a little psychic insight." But Daniels answers his own challenge in "The Texts of 'Winter Dreams'" (*FHA 1977*:77–100) by examining three texts of the story and drawing from all of them in suggesting an authoritative version.

As in past years, there is a constant updating, correcting, and adding to the Bruccoli and Hanneman bibliographies of works by Fitzgerald and Hemingway, respectively. In "English Periodical Publications of Fitzgerald's Short Stories: A Correction of the Record" (*FHA 1976*:124–29), Thomas E. Daniels corrects errors of dating and, in one instance, the title of Fitzgerald's stories in English periodicals as listed in Bruccoli's bibliography. Frederic E. Rusch helpfully provides descriptions of four dust jackets of English editions which Bruccoli could not locate (*FHA 1977*:13–18); and, of course, Bruccoli himself contributes annual listings of "Addenda" (*FHA 1976*:251–53; *FHA 1977*:247–49). George Monteiro's "Addenda to Hanneman's *Hemingway: Books on Trial*" (*PBSA* 71:514–15) lists seven reviews or mentions of Hemingway's work from *Books on Trial* and *The Critic*.

Although Linda Welshimer Wagner's *Ernest Hemingway: A Reference Guide* (Boston: G. K. Hall) understandably does not include Monteiro's addenda, it is nonetheless a very useful listing of critical materials. A hasty preliminary comparison of Wagner's volume with the comparable sections of Hanneman's (1967, 1975) suggests that the diligent researcher would do well to consult both books: Wagner deliberately excludes "items relating only to Hemingway's personal life," while Hanneman includes these; but Wagner has updated Hanneman's listings, has added some significant entries, and, above all, has annotated virtually every entry. Among the shorter enumerative compilations, Michael Adams contributes lists of the screen adaptations of Fitzgerald's (FHA *1977*:101–9) and Hemingway's (*FHA 1977*:219–32) works; while Margaret M. Duggan and William White provide unannotated but quite full annual listings of material by and about Fitzgerald (*FHA 1976*:254–59; *FHA 1977*:250–54) and Hemingway (*FHA 1976*:260–72; *FHA 1977*:255–66), respectively.

Of the several new texts by Fitzgerald or Hemingway which surfaced during the year, the most significant is "F. Scott Fitzgerald's Critique of *A Farewell to Arms*" (*FHA 1976*:141–52), which presents the full text of Fitzgerald's notes on Hemingway's novel, carefully edited and footnoted by Charles Mann. In "A Farewell to Machismo" (*NYTM*, 16 Oct.), Aaron Latham provides summaries of several unpublished Hemingway pieces deposited at the Kennedy Library, centering his attention on the novel "Garden of Eden" and its theme of reversed sex roles, a theme which Latham contends gives us a new picture of Hemingway's personality as one "composed of unresolved opposites." A far earlier Hemingway piece, a short story written in 1919, was described by Richard Willing, in "Hemingway Manuscript Revealed" (Washington *Post*, 4 Apr.). Entitled "The Passing of Pickles McCarty" or "The Woppian Way," the story is mentioned and briefly discussed in Baker's biography, but the manuscript apparently had previously been lost.

The other new texts are less important, including as they do a Fitzgerald book review of Heywood Broun's novel *The Boy Grew Older* (*FHA 1977*:9–12), introduced by Margaret M. Duggan; two synopses of movie scenarios which Fitzgerald prepared but apparently never completed, "Ballet Shoes" (*FHA 1976*:3–7) and "The Feather Fan" (*FHA 1977*:3–8); and a facsimile of Hemingway's unused "Author's Preface" for *Torrents of Spring* (*FHA 1977*:113). Fitzgerald's humorous account of a motor trip from Connecticut to Alabama, "The Cruise of the Rolling Junk," which originally appeared in three installments in 1924 in Hearst's *Motor*, was reissued in a handsome book-length facsimile edition in 1976 by Bruccoli Clark Publishers.

ii. Letters and Biography

The only new Fitzgerald or Hemingway letter is a 1940 Hemingway letter to his Loyalist friend Hans Kahle. The letter originally was published in German in *Heute und Morgen* and is here (*FHA 1976*: 187–90) translated and edited by Hans-Joachim Kann.

Scott Donaldson's *By Force of Will: The Life and Art of Ernest Hemingway* (New York: Viking) is the most important new work this year on either Fitzgerald or Hemingway. As its title suggests, it represents a combination of biography and literary criticism and while it succeeds in both areas, it does so most often—although perhaps not most significantly—as biography. Donaldson's stated intention is to "discover and record what Ernest Hemingway thought on a variety of subjects, . . . and then, from these disparate fragments, to construct a mosaic of his mind and personality, of the sort of man he was." He does this by devoting chapters to such Hemingway preoccupations as celebrity, love, money, religion, politics, sports, war, friendship, art, and death. In each case, Donaldson draws skillfully on biographical information, letters (he quotes from many Hemingway letters, despite their author's explicit prohibition against doing so), and the fiction in defining and analyzing his subject's attitudes and opinions on the topics selected. This approach enables Donaldson to make several interesting links between Hemingway's views and his fiction, as when he sees *To Have and Have Not* reflecting its author's rejection of political groups or when he observes that Frederic Henry's treatment of Catherine depicts Hemingway's remorse for his own treatment of his first wife, Hadley. While some may find too little of this sort of critical insight in the book and an abundance of familiar biographical information, Donaldson's style is disarmingly engaging and his book does succeed in producing the portrait of Hemingway that it intends.

By contrast, Lloyd Arnold's *Hemingway: High on the Wild* (New York: Grosset & Dunlap) is more valuable for its many photographs of Hemingway and his hunting and fishing friends than for its text. Lloyd "Pappy" Arnold was Hemingway's guide and friend during the many falls and winters the writer spent at Sun Valley, Idaho, between 1939 and 1961. His account is largely concerned with their hunting and fishing expeditions and with the mixture of Hollywood celebrities, local characters, and hangers-on who gathered around Hemingway during his visits. It is rendered in an often difficult-to-follow colloquial style sprinkled with verbatim transcriptions of conversations; but the reader gets used to the style after a while and the book does have a ring of authenticity which is greatly enhanced by Arnold's photographs.

Of the briefer biographical items, the only one on Fitzgerald is Lloyd Hackl's "Fitzgerald in St. Paul: An Oral History Portrait" (*FHA 1976*:117–22), which briefly describes the ongoing oral history archive being assembled at the Minnesota Historical Society Library through taped interviews with St. Paul contemporaries of Fitzgerald and then focuses on a conversation with Mrs. C. O. (Xandra) Kalman, who knew the author throughout his life.

Two of the biographical pieces on Hemingway deal with his career as a journalist. Dale Wilson's "Hemingway in Kansas City" (*FHA 1976*:211–16) is a lively reminiscence by a fellow *Star* reporter of Hemingway's escapades while employed there in 1917–18. Richard Winslow, in "Greg and Hemmy: Writing For the Toronto *Star* in

1920" (*FHA* 1977:183–93), centers his attention on Hemingway's relationship with Gregory Clark, the features editor of the Toronto *Star Weekly*. A later association, with Sylvia Beach, proprietor of the Shakespeare and Company bookstore in Paris, is covered in Noel Fitch's thorough essay, "Ernest Hemingway—c/o Shakespeare and Company" (*FHA* 1977:157–81). In a brief note, "Uncle Tyler Hemingway" (*FHA* 1977:211–12), Martin Staples Shockley gives information about Hemingway's uncle, with whom he lived in 1917 when he first went to Kansas City. "A Conversation With Mary Hemingway" by David Stewart, Elizabeth Cowan, and Gregory Cowan (*CEA* 40,i:29–33) deals with *The Old Man and the Sea*, which, Mary observes, "just sort of steamed right out onto the paper" and with her husband's decision not to allow his letters to be published, which she regrets because they contain valuable information.

iii. Criticism

***a.* Collections.** The one new collection, Robert O. Stephens's *Ernest Hemingway: The Critical Reception* (New York: Burt Franklin), is an extremely useful gathering of selected reviews of Hemingway's books from *Three Stories and Ten Poems* (1923) to *The Nick Adams Stories* (1972). Stevens provides a succinct introductory survey of Hemingway's reception by reviewers and then reprints a representative number of notices, several drawn from obscure newspapers in remote sections of the United States. Not only does this valuable book include commentary by, among many others, Virginia Woolf, Dorothy Parker, John Dos Passos, William Faulkner, Max Eastman, John Updike, John O'Hara, Evelyn Waugh, and Nelson Algren, it also presents a range of the receptions accorded Hemingway's works as they appeared. This is a full and rich collection which will serve scholars extremely well.

***b.* Full-Length Studies.** Aside from Scott Donaldson's *By Force of Will* (see above) and John S. Whitley's pamphlet on *The Great Gatsby* (see below), the only full-length work on either Fitzgerald or Hemingway this year is the revised edition of Kenneth Eble's 1963 Twayne book on Fitzgerald, *F. Scott Fitzgerald* (Boston: Twayne). This new edition varies from the original only in its inclusion of a new Preface and the addition of a final chapter which briefly summarizes Fitzgerald criticism of the past two decades and indicates the values and weaknesses of his writings as Eble sees them.

c. General Essays. Two of this year's general essays link Fitzgerald and Hemingway. Sister Mary Kathryn Grant's "The Search For Celebration in *The Sun Also Rises* and *The Great Gatsby*" (*ArQ* 33:181–92) is an interesting discussion of the use and function of dancing in the two novels. Dancing in Hemingway "reflects the tension between meaningfully ritual dancing in the bullfight and meaningless, social dancing in the *bal musette* and in the streets"; while, for Fitzgerald, dance "limns the tension between the deep inner need for affirmation and celebration and the 'glimmering' illusory world which proffers only false feasts and surrogate celebrations." In a much briefer piece, "Fitzgerald, Hemingway, and *The Passing of the Great Race*" (*FHA 1977*:215–17), Taylor Alderman suggests that Hemingway's allusion to Madison Grant's book in *The Torrents of Spring* implies a possible connection between that novel and *Gatsby* and between their authors.

Of the five general essays on Fitzgerald, Edwin T. Arnold's "The Motion Picture as Metaphor in the Works of F. Scott Fitzgerald" (*FHA 1977*:43–60) deals with a potentially worthwhile subject in a very discursive and disorganized manner, never satisfactorily establishing how Fitzgerald used cinema as metaphor or, indeed, even defining exactly what that metaphor was. Arnold does, however, stay close to the texts and provides some useful readings. This is not true of William Wasserstrom's "The Goad of Guilt: Henry Adams, Scott and Zelda" (*JML* 6:289–310), which dwells unoriginally on Adams's influence on Fitzgerald and on the mutually destructive and dependent relationship between Scott and Zelda. Wasserstrom's essay is full of incoherent and ultimately meaningless jargon. Much more coherent, and, in a relatively weak group, the most suggestive of the year's general essays on Fitzgerald, is "F. Scott Fitzgerald and the Jacob's Ladder" (*JNT* 7:226–28) by John Ditsky. Ditsky sees a "ladder of social advancement" at the base of Fitzgerald's fiction; and his brief note describing it, while sketchy, is convincingly argued. On the other hand, S. S. Moorty's "Norris and Fitzgerald as Moralists" in *Studies in American Literature: Essays in Honour of William Mulder*, edited by Jagdish Chander and Narindar S. Pradhan (Delhi: Oxford Univ. Press, 1976), pp. 119–26, oversimplifies the themes of both writers with statements like, "If Norris represented the bright moral energy of America in his time, Fitzgerald represented the moral wasteland and the spiritual decay of American society in his." Fran James Polek's "From Renegade to Solid Citizen: The Extraordinary Individual in the Community" (*SDR* 15,i:61–72) rehashes the *Gatsby-Absalom, Absalom!* parallels pointed out by several earlier critics but interestingly adds *The Godfather* in discerning a pattern in which a "young self-proclaimed extraordinary person . . . makes a conscious decision to leave the traditional ethnic, political or religious community" but whose renegade status is "tempered by a repressed but equally strong motivation to eventually regain the traditional community as a fully accepted leader or power figure."

There is an unusual degree of unoriginality and redundancy in the recent crop of general essays on Hemingway. Pieces like John Raeburn's survey of Hemingway's public image, "Hemingway in the Twenties: 'The Artist's Reward' " (*BRMMLA* 29[1975]:118–46) and H. Das Gupta's "Ernest Hemingway and the Spanish Bullfight" (*IJAS* 6,i–ii[1976]:55–64) offer very little that is new on oft-studied topics. Two general studies, Alfred Kazin's "Hemingway the Painter" (*NRep* 176,xxi:21–28) and Leonard Kriegel's "Hemingway's Rites of Manhood" (*PR* 44:415–30), are extremely well written by critics of distinction, but they also essentially deal with familiar material. Kriegel's article is very personal, attempting to justify Hemingway's influence on him; while Kazin's is an overview of the influence of painting and painters on Hemingway but includes typically (for Kazin) insightful remarks on themes and on the enduring values of his greatest work.

Three other general essays propose somewhat fresher vantage points on Hemingway's fiction. In "Hemingway's Novels: The Shift in Orthodoxy and Symbolism" (*ArQ* 33:141–55), William E. Meyer, Jr., sees Hemingway's male characters exhibiting "much the same falling away from orthodox Catholic practice and belief that Hemingway himself does, most significantly in the novels after 1937"; while his female characters' "simultaneous and somewhat paradoxical rise in orthodoxy serves perhaps as an unconscious compensation for the males' decline and also as a conscious device for providing a wider range of character types and actions within individual novels." David M. Wyatt, in "Hemingway's Uncanny Beginnings" (*GaR* 31:476–501), takes a look at *In Our Time, The Sun Also Rises, A Farewell to Arms, Across the River and Into the Trees,* and *For Whom the Bell Tolls,* finding in the first four a "gathering sense of doom" as their "central effect." In *For Whom the Bell Tolls*, however, Wyatt sees the "single obsession which has dominated Hemingway's fiction —waiting for the end—is absorbed into a multiplicity of truths" as its ending "celebrates the power of 'making believe' over fantasies which the traumas of our personal histories make us believe." Robert E. Fleming finds a similarly positive note struck in *For Whom the Bell Tolls*. Fleming's essay, "Hemingway's Treatment of Suicide: 'Fathers and Sons' and *For Whom the Bell Tolls*" (*ArQ* 33:121–32), views the novel as "Hemingway's attempt to purge himself, through his art, of the debilitating psychological effects of his father's suicide," an attempt which, judging from "Jordan's ultimate action and also from Hemingway's later fiction, in which there is scarcely any mention of suicide," was basically successful. David McClellan's note on echoes of the events and people of the Battle of Little Big Horn in Hemingway's later fiction (*FHA 1976*:245–48) is highly conjectural and, at least with respect to *Across the River* and *Islands in the Stream*, unconvincingly argued.

We have only two influence studies. Hans-Joachim Kann's "Ernest Hemingway and German Culture" (*NsM* 28[1976]:16–20) is a brief but thorough investigation of Hemingway's knowledge of and contacts with German culture, in an effort to modify what Kann sees as "the prevailing image of Hemingway"—"the callous, male, hard-boiled 'brute' who, nevertheless, wrote surprisingly good prose." Kann points to Hemingway's references to German music and his admiration of Mann and Remarque as evidence that he was more cultured and intellectual than he is usually credited with being. In "Hemingway Reads Huxley: An Occasion for Some Observations on the Twenties and the Apostolate of the Lost Generation" (*FHA 1976*:154–86), Jerome Meckier is also trying to make a case for Hemingway as an informed reader of one of his leading contemporaries. His thesis appears sound; but, as the pompous title implies, Meckier overwrites and gets bogged down in his own overblown rhetoric.

Finally, we have three quite technical linguistically oriented studies of the famous Hemingway style. In the most interesting of these, "Toward a Stylistic Analysis of Bilingual Texts: From Ernest Hemingway to Contemporary Boricua and Chicano Literature" in *The Analysis of Hispanic Texts: Current Trends in Methodology*, edited by Mary Ann Beck, et al. (Jamaica, N.Y.: York Coll., 1976), pp. 130–49, Gary D. Keller examines in fascinating detail exactly how in *For Whom the Bell Tolls*, without using Spanish words, Hemingway is able to evoke the Spanish language and style of speech. Waldemar Gutwinski's *Cohesion in Literary Texts: A Study of Some Grammatical and Lexical Features of English* (The Hague: Mouton, 1976) is a very technical study which focuses on passages in "Big Two-Hearted River" and James's *The Portrait of a Lady* in great detail. By comparison, the work of E. Nageswara Rao, in "Syntax as Rhetoric: An Analysis of Ernest Hemingway's Early Syntax" (*IndLing* 36[1975]:296–303), seems slight and unimportant.

d. **Essays on Specific Works: Fitzgerald.** The disproportionate amount of attention given to *The Great Gatsby* in comparison to that focused on Fitzgerald's other works continues. In fact, this year's statistics are, regrettably, almost identical to last year's, with 17 essays and notes on *Gatsby*, 7 on *Tender Is the Night*, 2 on *This Side of Paradise*, and 2 on the short stories. Taken as a group, however, the essays—especially those on *Tender Is the Night*—are stronger than usual.

John S. Whitley's *F. Scott Fitzgerald: "The Great Gatsby"* (London: Edward Arnold, 1976) is a 64-page pamphlet in the Studies in English Literature series edited by David Daiches (of 61 titles in print, *Gatsby* is only the third pamphlet on a work by an American author and the first on a modern American writer). Whitley devotes a chapter each to Nick and to Gatsby and while he does rehash a good deal of familiar material—such as color symbolism and time in the novel—he writes well and his discussion of the parallels between Fitzgerald's novel and Keats's poetry, *Heart of Darkness*, *Moby-Dick*, and, more briefly, Poe's poetry, are often illuminating. His comparison of Nick with Marlow and Ishmael is particularly good.

An encouraging trend noted last year, studies of style and close readings of small units of *Gatsby*, happily was sustained in 1977. Leonard A. Podis's "The Unreality of Reality: Metaphor in *The Great Gatsby*" (*Style* 11:56–72), inadvertently included in last year's survey (*ALS 1976*, p. 152), actually appeared this year and belongs with the group of essays to be discussed below.

Four essays discuss limited sections of the novel: all are valuable readings. In "Tragic Inevitability in *The Great Gatsby*" (*CLAJ* 21: 51–57), Edwin Moses does a close examination of Chapter 1, contending that "the pattern of the whole is implicit in the part." Moses sees much of the power of the novel emanating "from the sense of tragic inevitability which Fitzgerald develops in the very first chapter"—which he views as concerned with nemesis: "the inevitable convulsive righting of a balance in nature which the tragic hero has disturbed." Robert Emmet Long's focus is on "The Opening Three Chapters of 'The Great Gatsby'" (*EngR* 26,iv[1975]:85–94) but his point is similar to Moses's in that he sees them intimating the events of the plot which follow and expressing the theme of the novel—the corrupting effect of money on several levels of society. In "*The Great Gatsby*: The Final Vision" (*FHA 1976*:108–15), Christiane Johnson analyzes the famous last page of the novel in great detail, suggesting that the vision at the end gives *Gatsby* "a dimension that has been latent all along" in that "from the temporal and the inessential, we pass on to the timeless and the essential." What these three essays strongly imply, then, is that *Gatsby* is a brilliantly designed artistic creation in which all of the parts fit together with great precision. In the same way, Robert A. Martin, in "Gatsby's 'Good Night' in Chapter 3 of *The Great Gatsby*" (*CEA* 39,iv:12–16), justifies the five "good nights" which Gatsby says on the basis of his need to impress Nick favorably so that the latter can arrange a meeting between Gatsby and Daisy. In making this analysis, Martin takes issue with Jeffrey Hart (see *ALS 1976*, p. 153), who saw Fitzgerald borrowing from Eliot's *The Waste Land*; and he joins those critics determined to show that Fitzgerald planned *Gatsby* carefully, with not a word or phrase simply borrowed or carelessly inserted.

Two of the year's essays concern a much-discussed topic, the narrative technique of the novel; and, not surprisingly, they come to opposite conclusions. In "Gatsby and the Failure of the Omniscient 'I'" (*UDQ* 12,i:303–12), Ron Neuhaus argues that Fitzgerald inconsistently moves from first-person narration to omniscient authorial voice because "the moral authority of first person narrative was not adequate" for "a world which could not provide the fulfillment" of "the desire for moral security." Neuhaus's conclusions are dubious and his argument is not convincingly presented because he too often couches it in generalities rather than turning to the text. Eric Nelson is on far firmer ground in "Commitment and Insight in *The Great Gatsby*" (*RLV* 43:142–52). Here Nelson examines Nick in order to get at what he sees as the greatness of the novel—"a genuine portrayal of the divided sensibility" of American culture. Nelson views

Nick as the embodiment of this sensibility in that he is both a realist and a romantic, noting further that "the defeat of Nick, the man of insight, and Gatsby, the man of commitment, at the end of Fitzgerald's novel suggests that in modern America these qualities stand separate and vulnerable." This commitment-insight conflict runs throughout Fitzgerald's writings, according to Nelson, whose essay is provocative and plausible. As promising in subject matter but much more disappointing in presentation is William Baer's and Steven McLean Folks's "Language and Character in *The Great Gatsby*" (*TLOP* 6:18–25), two attempts to show how Fitzgerald manipulates the reader's attitudes towards characters "by means of the language that he gives these characters to say." Baer deals with Daisy and Folks with Tom; both papers, especially Folks's, are so poorly written that, though they appear to be making accurate assessments, they are difficult to read.

Five other essays attempt, with varying degrees of success, to impose different kinds of patterns on the novel. W. T. Lhamon, Jr., in "The Essential Houses of *The Great Gatsby*" (*MarkhamR* 6:56–60), examines the Buchanans's house, Myrtle's New York apartment, and Gatsby's mansion as manifesting "at a subtle, structural level the seeming variety but underlying unidimensionality that the novel postulates." The three houses, Lhamon points out, symbolize the three classes depicted in *Gatsby*. In a somewhat less original piece, "The Gathering Darkness: A Study of the Effects of Technology in *The Great Gatsby*" (*FHA 1976*:130–38), Kenneth S. Knodt discusses cars, the railroad, telephones, motorboats, motorcycles, guns, and other symbols of a technology which he sees destroying "a simpler, easier, pastoral world" in the novel. Knodt does not go far enough in exploring the implications of this pattern. By contrast, Neila Seshachari's "*The Great Gatsby*: Apogee of Fitzgerald's Mythopoeia" (*FHA 1976*:96–107) is richly suggestive of the many levels of the novel in its claim that "Gatsby may appear to be a mythic character not only because he is impersonalized and appears to be the romantic impulse crystallized in the term American Dream, but also because Gatsby's story offers a complete parallel to the embryonic path of the mythic hero." Her conclusion that, because Gatsby is a mythic hero, his death can be a tragedy "only for the people; it is always a triumph or ultimate victory for the hero himself," while certainly debatable, goes well beyond most previous myth criticism approaches to *Gatsby*. In

David Laird's "Hallucination and History in *The Great Gatsby*" (*SDR* 15,i:18–27), very few original insights emerge from a discussion of the novel's depiction of the individual's struggle "to impose his or her attitudes or goals upon the rush of events, indeed, to bend that rush in a direction which will reclaim a remembered past and thus to transcend time and history." Stephen Zelnick's high personal (and highly questionable) approach to *Gatsby*, in "The Incest Theme in *The Great Gatsby*: An Exploration of the False Poetry of Petty Bourgeois Consciousness" in *Weapons of Criticism: Marxism in America and the Literary Tradition*, edited by Norman Rudich (Palo Alto, Calif.: Ramparts Press, 1976), pp. 327–40, is epitomized in his title and in his view of the novel as "a specific and historically definite portrayal of the American 1920s as it was perceived by a humane and talented writer, whose theme, although he was finally unable to grasp it firmly, is the tortuous contradictions of his own petty bourgeois class."

We have only three source or influence studies of *Gatsby* this year. The best of these is Steven Curry and Peter L. Hays's "Fitzgerald's *Vanity Fair*" (*FHA 1977*:63–75), which traces in great detail the numerous likenesses between *Gatsby* and Thackeray's great work—in narrative technique, parallels between major characters, parallels between settings, in the metaphorical function of setting in each novel, in the thematic usages of "time, the past, and history, especially war," in both, in the indictment "of the materialism and superficiality of its respective age" which each presents, and in the fact that both novels lack a hero. Curry and Hays are thorough and their essay is convincingly presented. They seem much more plausible than Michael A. Peterman does, in his "A Neglected Source for *The Great Gatsby*: The Influence of Edith Wharton's *The Spark*" (*CRevAS* 8:26–35); although Peterman does point to parallels in point of view, narrative mood and tone, characterizations, and structural techniques. Joseph Corso's "One Not-Forgotten Summer Night: Sources for Fictional Symbols of American Character in *The Great Gatsby*" (*FHA 1976*:8–33) searches through the first 27 years of Fitzgerald's own life for experiences and persons which helped shape *Gatsby*, especially the figures of Jay Gatz and Dan Cody. Predictably, some of his discoveries seem far-fetched, others much more probable.

At least four of the seven essays on *Tender Is the Night* move in new directions and assume that Fitzgerald's last completed novel is a complex and carefully textured work, an assumption not present in much earlier criticism. Typically, in "The Aesthetic of Forbearance: Fitzgerald's *Tender Is the Night*" (*Novel* 11:26–39), Maria DiBattista considers the novel within the framework of an aesthetic of forbearance, which "implies a suppression of narrative information and as such represents a guiding principle in the construction of plot" and "demands a canny treatment of history, of character, and of appropriate generic and mythic material to insure that the ironic mystery of its fable is protected against sentimental, moralistic readings." DiBattista's fascinating discussion also leads into suggestions of parallels with *The Odyssey*. Of equal interest is Judith Wilt's "The Spinning Story: Gothic Motifs in *Tender Is the Night*" (*FHA 1976*:79–95), which explores the "peculiarly Gothic narrative strategy . . . of drawing in, often through two or three loops of storytellers, towards the unthinkable act, the unsayable desire, the unbearable bargain, the 'unhuman' mystery that generates the story." Wilt also notes in *Tender* the Gothic element of "Complicity, the desire of the forbidden, desire of the evil, desire of the unnatural, desire of the destructive, the rotten, the dying, desire of death"; and the Gothic setting of "the madhouse, transmuted during the nineteenth century into the laboratory . . . , with its cast of attendant victim-ghouls, and its ambiguously dreadful presiding spirit, the scientist, and above all its constant nightmare dissolving of the boundaries of madness and reason." This a richly rewarding essay.

Raymond J. Wilson's "Henry James and F. Scott Fitzgerald: Americans Abroad" (*RS* 45:82–91) also explores new territory in suggesting "startling similarities"—in descriptions of settings and characters, in the situations which challenge the characters, in the alternatives the characters cannot take, and "not only in the success or failure of the characters, but even in the very criteria by which they expect us to judge success or failure"—between *Tender Is the Night* and *Daisy Miller* and *The American*. Wilson's theory that the similarities result from two very different American writers reacting in parallel ways to experiences in Europe is modestly urged; his article is interesting and well thought out and implies a topic for further exploration. Mary Verity McNicholas's "Fitzgerald's Women in *Tender Is the Night*" (*CollL* 4:40–70) is perhaps less original than the other three essays but it still is a thorough discussion of each of the novel's female characters in relation to Dick's dual nature and Fitzgerald's own dual vision of women. The latter two ideas are are hardly new; but McNicholas's drawing in of female characters besides Nicole and Rosemary and relating them to these ideas is a contribution to our understanding of the novel.

Ruth Perlmutter's "Malcolm Lowry's Unpublished Filmscript of *Tender Is the Night*" (*AQ* 28[1976]:561–74) complements last year's publication of the Lowrys' notes on their planned screenplay (see *ALS 1976*, p. 155) in providing an analysis of the script itself, which Perlmutter calls "a closet film, perhaps never filmable, but capturing within it the spirit of two filmic genres—the legacy to America of the German expressionistic film and the Hollywood epic from Griffith to Welles." She also points out what she sees as "the remarkable affinities between Lowry and Fitzgerald in life and work." In two brief notes on *Tender*, Margaret McBride, in "The Divine Dick Diver" (*NMAL* 1:item 28), and Michael Adams, in "Dick Diver and Constance Talmadge" (*FHA 1977*:61–62), discuss Dick as a Christ figure and the reference in the novel to Miss Talmadge's movie *Breakfast at Sunrise*, respectively.

Fitzgerald's short stories continue to be ignored, as do his other three novels and his essays. Dorothy Ballweg Good's "'A Romance and a Reading List': The Literary References in *This Side of Paradise*" (*FHA 1976*:35–64) is a useful but hardly critically insightful compilation of authors, titles, and other literary references in the novel; while Robert M. McIlvaine's "Thomas Parke D'Invilliers and Villiers de L'Isle-Adam" (*NMAL* 1:item 19) is a very brief and questionable suggestion that the name Fitzgerald chose for the character in *This Side of Paradise* (and for the author of the verses on the title page of *Gatsby*) "is meant to remind the reader of Villiers de L'Isle-Adam and thus heighten the *fin de siècle* atmosphere that pervades the Princeton section of the novel." In contrast to these slight pieces, Anthony J. Mazzella's "The Tension of Opposites in Fitzgerald's 'May Day'" (*SSF* 14:379–85) is an impressive and full explication of the story, which Mazzella views as "structured on the careful modulation of opposites, of integration and disintegration" and "a moving expression of order struggling against approaching chaos." His close examinations of form, tone, structure, images, and plot amply verify this interpretation. Matthew J. Bruccoli's less ambitious piece, "On F. Scott Fitzgerald and 'Bernice Bobs Her Hair'" (*The American Short Story*, pp. 219–22), is clearly written for a nonscholarly audience and primarily states already established criteria for looking at Fitzgerald's fiction.

***e.* Essays on Specific Works: Hemingway.** As usual, the essays on specific Hemingway works are far more evenly distributed through his full canon than are those on Fitzgerald. Thus, there are 5 essays apiece on two of the novels, 3 on one of the other novels, 2 apiece on two other novels, and 23 pieces on some 20 different short stories.

The two most substantial essays on *A Farewell to Arms*, both by Bernard Oldsey, are complementary in that one, "The Genesis of *A Farewell to Arms*" (*SAF* 5:175–85), deals with the beginning of the novel; while the other, "The Sense of an Ending in *A Farewell to Arms*" (*MFS* 23:491–510), is concerned with its final chapter. Both pieces rely heavily and valuably on examination of textual materials; in the second essay, Oldsey reprints and discusses five endings which Hemingway rejected. The first essay includes a close reading of Chapter I, which Oldsey demonstrates consists of "five . . . prose-poem paragraphs arranged in seasonal progression" and of primary imagery clustering "around the weather, the topography, and the historical fact of war." Similarly, Oldsey sees the ending which Hemingway eventually chose for the novel as "characterized by extraordinary dramatic compression, but a succinct recapitulation of leading motifs, by implicative understatement, by a high percentage of negating phrases, and by the final effect of dwindling away to nothing, with a seeming rupture of chronological time." These two essays represent some of the very best close reading of either Hemingway or Fitzgerald that we have had in recent years.

Next to Oldsey's work, the other three pieces on *A Farewell to Arms* seem very slight. Michael Garrety's "Love and War: R. H. Mottram, *The Spanish Farm Trilogy*, and Ernest Hemingway, *A Farewell to Arms*" in *The First World War in Fiction: A Collection of Critical Essays*, edited by Holger Klein (London: Macmillan, 1976), pp. 10–22, rehearses well-worn platitudes about the struggle of "the individual against a society which will dehumanise him and seek his extinction in its ultimate manifestation of a nation at war." In "Dying Without Death: Borzage's *A Farewell to Arms*" (*The Classic American Novel and the Movies*, pp. 297–304), William Horrigan makes some interesting comparisons between the 1929 film and Hemingway's original. Eugene B. Cantelupe's "Statues and Lovers in *A Fare-*

well to Arms" (*FHA* 1977:203–5) claims that "the statue image of Catherine in the daringly muted ending of the novel echoes the mortuary sculpture that Hemingway introduces in the beginning."

The year's four full-length essays on *The Sun Also Rises* all offer interesting new readings. In "Paris and the Expatriate Mystique: Hemingway's *The Sun Also Rises*" (*ArQ* 33:156–64), David Morgan Zehr examines the four types of Americans in Paris depicted in the novel, contrasting them with Jake, who is "not aimlessly drifting like so many others," but "has a job which he enjoys and . . . has a sensitive awareness of a physical, non-Americanized Paris—a city of streets, buildings, cafés, and common people." Zehr concludes that, through Jake, Hemingway justifies his own presence in Paris and qualifies "the mystique of both the dissipated expatriate and a Babylonian Paris." While this last assertion is questionable, the essay is a worthwhile one. Similarly, Gerry Brenner's finding, in "Hemingway's 'Vulgar' Ethic: Revaluating *The Sun Also Rises*" (*ArQ* 33:101–15), that by "vulgarizing ethics, usually the presence of religion and philosophy, Hemingway demonstrates that socially affirmative ethical systems can be derived from debauchery and athletics," is presented convincingly and supported by detail from the text.

Two other pieces on *Sun* compare it with works by other authors; both illuminate Hemingway's novel in doing so. Eben Bass's "Hemingway's Women of Another Country" (*MarkhamR* 6:35–39) draws parallels and contrasts between *Sun* and Marlowe's *The Jew of Malta*, Eliot's "Portrait of a Lady" and the Biblical story of Jacob and Esau. Although this is an ambitious and sometimes overworked idea, Bass is successful when he focuses on Robert Cohn, the Jew "as a dupe rather than a victimizer," a "victim of a world ruled by women," and thus the womanized man feared by both Eliot and Hemingway. In " 'We Could Have Had Such a Damned Good Time Together': Individual and Society in *The Sun Also Rises* and *Mutmassungen über Jakob*" (*MLS* 7,i:82–90), Sara Lennox begins with Uwe Johnson's use of Hemingway's famous concluding line in suggesting that parallels exist between the two novels, "parallels which illuminate each novel's statement regarding the possibility of human happiness within the society which each describes." She feels that the Johnson novel "stands Hemingway's on its head: where Hemingway treats the individual isolated from society, seeking an individual happiness in romantic love, Johnson examines an individual seeking a social solution whom his society totally subsumes." This is a carefully argued and well-written article. As such it is far more convincing than the one note on *Sun*, Robert E. Jungman's "A Note on the Ending of *The Sun Also Rises*" (*FHA 1977*:214), which suggests that Hemingway's reference to the Gran Via at the end of the novel echoes the Biblical evocation of Hell in Matthew 7:13–14 and implies that Brett and Jake are "on the road to Hell."

This year's two short pieces and one longer essay on *For Whom the Bell Tolls* center on the character of Robert Jordan. Herman Nibbelink's "The Meaning of Nature in *For Whom the Bell Tolls*" (*ArQ* 33:165–72) unfortunately fails to live up to the admirable (albeit grandiose) thesis statement of its opening paragraph: "By extended description, metaphoric narration and dialogue, and symbolic action Hemingway uses nature to evoke tone, delineate character, gauge action, and eventually establish an ontology that gives place to the many seemingly contrived references to religion, superstition, and myth." Nibbelink concerns himself primarily with the depiction of Jordan and with the character's final act, "the antithesis of suicide—to become one with nature, stoically willing himself to the Whole." The thesis of this essay requires far more detailed support than is offered here. Walter J. Slatoff's "The 'Great Sin' in *For Whom the Bell Tolls*" (*JNT* 7:142–48) is less ambitious and more convincing in looking closely at passages from the novel which demonstrate that Hemingway viewed killing as a "great sin" and that "what Jordan is fighting for must be fought for and at the same time [the novel] asserts absolutely and without qualification that killing is unjustified and sinful." In his note, "Anselmo, Atonement and Hemingway's *For Whom the Bell Tolls*" (*NConL* 7,ii:7–8), Robert G. Walker suggests that the name Anselmo recalls St. Anselmo of Canterbury (1033–1109) whose most famous work "made atonement the basis for a new explanation of Incarnation and Redemption"—"God became one with man, then the God-man gave his life so that man could once again become one with God." Thus, Walker sees Jordan's integration at the conclusion of the novel as foreshadowed by Anselmo's atonement and Jordan's "at-one-ness" prefigured by Anselmo's. Although brief, Walker's piece is valuable.

The year's one substantial article on *Across the River and into the Trees*, Gerry Brenner's "An 'Imitation' of Dante's *Divine Comedy*: Hemingway's *Across the River and Into the Trees*" (*FHA 1976*:191–

209), is an excellent analysis of Hemingway's novel as a "conscious imitation" of Dante's poem. Brenner cites such Dantean characteristics or parallels as love of a city, encyclopedism, narrative point of view, language, places and figures, the "shared aim of the heroes of both works"—the search for salvation, a common historicity which deliberately mixes nonfiction with fiction, and a common dream dimension. As compelling as Brenner's argument is—and it is very convincing—the questions which he raises at the conclusion of his essay are even more provocative: " 'Do his works reveal structures that are organic or ones that are mechanically dependent upon pre-existing forms?' 'Is his artistic genius continuously autonomous or does it eventually succumb to a life-long penchant for traditions and rituals?' 'Are his fictions motivated out of an authentic compulsion to express a genuine artistic vision or an athlete's desire to compete?' " As much for what it implies as for what it states explicitly, Brenner's article is one of the most important on Hemingway in several years. William Adair's "Death the Hunter: A Note on *Across the River and into the Trees*" (*NConL* 7,i:6–8) views the character of Baron Alvarito as "a symbol of Death and nothingness."

Both new essays on *The Old Man and the Sea* deal with oft-treated topics but they do so satisfactorily. This is particularly true of Sam S. Baskett's treatment of the baseball motif in the novel, "The Great Santiago: Opium, Vocation, and Dream in *The Old Man and the Sea*" (*FHA 1976*:230–42). Baskett's contention that baseball functions ironically "as a symbol of that which is finally inessential to Santiago" and that the latter's greatness lies in his "dream-like act of envisaging a supreme aim beyond entertainment and occupation," of "how to live 'now' in a dimension of the imagination transcending pastime and craft" is urged gracefully and persuasively. G. R. Wilson, Jr.'s reading of the Christian symbolism in the novel, "Incarnation and Redemption in *The Old Man and the Sea*" (*SSF* 14:369–73), seems further from the text than Baskett's piece; but he is probably on firm ground in noting that Christian symbolism "constitutes the basic technique by which Hemingway presents his view of man as a coherent and intrinsically important part of the cosmos in which he must find values."

Two worthwhile essays on *Islands in the Stream* hopefully signal overdue serious critical consideration of that novel. In " 'Bimini' and the Subject of Hemingway's *Islands in the Stream*" (*Topic* 31:41–

51), Joseph DeFalco contends that the novel is an "impressive experiment" in that Hemingway shifted his focus from character to setting in order to exploit the "metaphorical possibilities inherent in the subject matter." DeFalco sees *Islands in the Stream* and *The Old Man and the Sea* as the two surviving parts of an ambitious interlocking series of novels which Hemingway planned in which the sea was to be used metaphorically "to suggest time, life, and experience." He examines the "Bimini" section in detail in order to make his point that Hudson is such a negative character that his responses dominate the story and the metaphorical subject loses its effectiveness. In "The American Pictorial Vision: Objects and Ideas in Hawthorne, James, and Hemingway" (*SAF* 5:143–59), Viola Hopkins Winner links *Islands in the Stream, The House of the Seven Gables, The Marble Faun*, and *The Ambassadors* as works which share a common center: "the conflict between human needs and art, . . . the choice between 'perfection of the life, or of the work.'" Her discussion of Hemingway's novel centers on Hudson's bar painting which "embodies not only Hudson's artistic vision but his moral values."

As usual, there are many essays on Hemingway's short stories. Several deal with more than one story; two are concerned with specific collections and see patterns in those collections. Gilbert H. Muller's "*In Our Time*: Hemingway and the Discontents of Civilization" (*Renascence* 29:185–92) uses Janov's theories in *The Primal Scream* as a reference point: the main characters in *In Our Time* "never scream out at the fragmentation of existence . . . . Rather they become apostles of the sort of stoicisim which Janov finds so self-destructive. These protagonists suffer in silence, and the repressed scream which they carry with them is . . . their final undoing." In "Scrambling the Unscrambleable: *The Nick Adams Stories*" (*ArQ* 33:133–40), Stuart L. Burns argues that Young's ordering of the stories is thematically unsuccessful. Burns offers his own order which emphasizes "more clearly the theme of loss that is a major ordering principle of the stories." This is a clearly presented and, for the most part, a convincing essay.

Joseph M. Flora's note, "A Closer Look at the Young Nick Adams and His Father" (*SSF* 14:75–78), is a useful reading of "Indian Camp" and "The Doctor and the Doctor's Wife," which disputes Linda W. Wagner's view that the stories present " 'the death of Nick's feelings for his parents.' " Flora argues that, while we do question the doctor's character, "love has not died" in either story. Flora depends to some extent in making his point upon "Three Shots," the fragment which Hemingway intended to use as the opening of "Indian Camp" but later discarded. Dick Penner also does so in "The First Nick Adams Story" (*FHA 1977*:195–202), an explication of "Indian Camp" which sees the story as having "two major and interconnected themes: the relation between Nick and his father, and Nick's awareness of death." Penner considers the "ambiguity" of the story's ending the key to understanding it: "On a literal, biological level, Nick's assurance that he will 'never die' is ironic. He will die. On an experiential level, however, the ending is not ironic . . . . To experience death, to meet it head on, as Nick does in 'Indian Camp,' is to know its reality." Kenneth G. Johnston's "The Bull and the Lion: Hemingway's Fables for Critics" (*FHA 1977*:149–56) is a pleasant reading of Hemingway's two 1950 fables for children, "The Faithful Bull" and "The Good Lion," which suggests quite plausibly that they are "thinly disguised, flattering selfportraits, tales of self-justification, probably intended to disarm, forestall and/or anticipate domestic and literary criticism."

Unfortunately, most of this year's pieces on individual stories are slight, either in length or content—or both. We have two notes on "The Light of the World." In one, " 'The Light of the World': Hemingway's Comedy of Errors" (*NConL* 7,v:5–8), James Barbour contends that Hemingway introduced textual and factual errors into the story in order to undercut "the surface or the seemingly 'spiritual' meaning of the narrative"; while in the other, Richard Layman's " 'C. and M.' in 'The Light of the World' " (*FHA 1976*:243–44), the suggestion is made that C and M in the story refers to a mixture of cocaine and morphine. But an article on "The Short Happy Life of Francis Macomber," Robert O. Stephens's "Macomber and That Somali Proverb: The Matrix of Knowledge" (*FHA 1977*:137–47), does at least explore new territory in viewing Macomber's growing awareness through anthropologist Edward Hall's paradigm of "formal, informal, and technical awareness" in *The Silent Language*. Stephens traces Macomber's progression through these three stages and his reading of the story is original and provocative.

In the longer of two pieces on "Hills Like White Elephants," "The Wages of Love: 'Hills Like White Elephants' " (*FHA 1976*:224–29), George Monteiro makes a plausible case that the events of the story and Hemingway's deliberate avoidance of the word *abortion* grew out of the author's fear that his wife was pregnant with what would have been their second child and that this event (the fears eventually proved unfounded) set him thinking about "the personal consequences of an unwanted pregnancy." Somewhat more dubious is Gary D. Elliott's contention, in "Hemingway's 'Hills Like White Elephants'" (*Expl* 35,iv:22–23), that the bamboo-bead curtain in the story functions symbolically in representing a rosary for the young woman "who must certainly be a Catholic" and who "resists an abortion because her religious heritage adamantly opposes it."

Two essays view short stories in the context of Hemingway's other writings. William Adair's "Landscapes of the Mind: 'Big Two-Hearted River'" (*CollL* 4:144–51) is a "comparison-of-texts" reading of "A Way You'll Never Be," *A Farewell to Arms*, *Across the River and Into the Trees*, and "Big Two-Hearted River," which suggests that Hemingway's fiction "incorporates two time periods, the pre-story past and the story's present time; or, the past as it invades and exerts its pressure on time and present." In "'Nobody Ever Dies': Hemingway's Neglected Story of Freedom Fighters" (*KanQ* 9,ii:53–58), Kenneth B. Johnston sees the story as anticipating *For Whom the Bell Tolls* with respect to themes, motifs, characters, and scenes. Johnston's essay is an excellent and balanced reading of the story as well as an intriguing comparison of it with the later novel.

The other essays on the short stories this year are, for the most part, interesting but not exciting or seminal readings. Amberys R. Whittle and Gregory S. Sojka provide close readings of "The Gambler, the Nun, and the Radio" and "Big Two-Hearted River," respectively. In "A Reading of Hemingway's 'The Gambler, the Nun, and the Radio'" (*ArQ* 33:173–80), Whittle sees the story as a parable which "describes the plight of all mankind as it is threatened by world revolution and tyranny." Sojka's "Who Is Sam Cardinella, and Why Is He Hanging Between Two Sunny Days at Seney?" (*FHA 1976*:217–23) suggests that the vignette which divides the two parts of the story in *In Our Time* provides a "brief glimpse of a man who wilts under pressure" and "serves as a graphic contrast to the protagonist of the short story, who is striving valiantly to remain in full control of all his faculties despite his own panic and suffering." Olga K. Garnica's "Rules of Verbal Interaction and Literary Analysis" (*Poetics* 6:155–67) is a very technical linguistic interpretation of "Indian Camp," which focuses on terms of address and sequence types as two aspects of direct speech in the story.

In "Hemingway's Man of the World" (*ArQ* 33:116–20), J. M. Ferguson, Jr., concludes that Hemingway's "true man of the world" is one who has "suffered and learned bitter truths and sometimes despair" but is "essentially sensitive and compassionate." Myra Armistead's "Hemingway's 'An Alpine Idyll'" (*SSF* 14:255–58) attempts to establish a connection between the two parts of the story by pointing out that "just as the Americans have been skiing too long, the valley people have been telling and hearing the tales too long and have become insensitive to the feelings of their fellow men." Anthony Hunt, in "Another Turn for Hemingway's 'The Revolutionist': Sources and Meanings" (*FHA 1977*:119–35), gives a full and valuable analysis of the historical and biographical bases of the story as well as of the tale itself. By comparison, Wolfgang Schlepper's "Hemingway's 'The Killers': An Absurd Happening" (*LWU* 10:104–14) strains too hard to show how Hemingway's story "has some basic qualities in common" with Absurd Drama. Earl Rovit, in "On Ernest Hemingway and 'Soldier's Home'" (*The American Short Story*, pp. 251–55), presents a brief but very full and suggestive reading of the story within the contexts of the post-World-War-I world and Hemingway's own life and style, concluding that it "makes a compelling statement about the problems that divide generations and people of different experience at an historical moment of massive and incomprehensible change." In "Dating the Events of 'The Three-Day Blow'" (*FHA 1977*:207–10), George Monteiro sorts out and dates the baseball references in the story, placing it in 1917 but also noting that Hemingway may have deliberately conflated into a single conversation events which actually occurred during three or four different years. Finally, no year would be complete without a piece (mercifully only a short note this time) on "Perpetual Confusion in 'A Clean, Well-Lighted Place': The Manuscript Evidence" (*FHA 1977*:115–18). Hans-Joachim Kann does at least examine the holograph; but his discussion does not shed very much new light on the issue.

***f.* Dissertations.** Dissertations completed during the year totalled five on Fitzgerald and seven on Hemingway, with three others discussing Fitzgerald along with other writers and one other doing the same with Hemingway. Several titles—"Satire in the Early Works of

F. Scott Fitzgerald," "Sense of Place in F. Scott Fitzgerald," "The Foreign Critical Reputation of F. Scott Fitzgerald," "*The Sun Also Rises*: The Making of a First Novel," "Hemingway's *The Fifth Column*: Background, Publication, Production, Reception"—offer the possibilities of worthwhile future publications.[1]

1. This essay could not have been completed without the research assistance of Ruth M. Alvarez.

Part II

11. Literature to 1800

Robert D. Arner

Another good year for early American studies, 1977 was highlighted by the publication of the late Kenneth B. Murdock's edition of the first two books of Cotton Mather's *Magnalia*, by J. A. Leo Lemay's festschrift devoted to early Virginia literature and dedicated to Richard Beale Davis, and by John Seelye's eccentric but stimulating account of the river as fact and symbol in early American life and literature. Important articles include Charles W. Mignon's announcement of the discovery of a new Edward Taylor manuscript, Emory Elliott's and Mason I. Lowance, Jr.'s excellent chapters in Earl Miner's *Literary Uses of Typology from the Late Middle Ages to the Present* (Princeton: Princeton Univ. Press), Robert Daly's discussion of Puritan poetics, Gustaaf van Cromphout's analysis of Cotton Mather's biographical methods, James A. Rawley's report on the world of Phillis Wheatley, and Walter P. Wenska, Jr.'s elucidation of Hannah Foster's *The Coquette*. Philip Young's *Revolutionary Ladies* ranks as easily the most entertaining study of the year, while William L. Andrews's note on Freneau's "Political Litany" wins the "Most Inconsequential Publication of the Year Award" hands down. More than the usual number of articles eluded my search this year, a situation I blame on the proliferation of journals (and scholars) whose point of origin no one seems to know but the editors and authors themselves, but I happily leave that detective work to my successor next year.

i. Edward Taylor

Certainly the principal event of the year in Taylor scholarship was Charles W. Mignon's deceptively brief "The Nebraska Edward Taylor Manuscript: 'Upon the Types of the Old Testament'" (*EAL* 12: 296–301), a work that confirms many scholarly speculations about the extent and nature of Taylor's typological investigations and provides additional, convincing evidence to support Norman Grabo's theory of a close link between the sermons and the poetry. Other Taylor documents, less important only by degree, were turned up by Thomas M. and Virginia L. Davis in "Edward Taylor's Metrical Paraphrases of the Psalms" (*AL* 48:455–70); the verses are of little poetic but substantial biographical consequence in that they suggest the Hebrew Psalms may have been more influential than Ignation meditation in determining the direction of Taylor's literary career and the shape of his verse. And in the single critical essay on Taylor this past year, " 'The Inward Teacles and the Outward Traces': Edward Taylor's Elusive Transitions" (*EAL* 12:163–76), William J. Scheick presents intricate analyses of Meditations 1.39 and 2.3 in order to demonstrate how Taylor's New England environment and/or "idiosyncratic pattern[s] of association in the poet's mind" can provide clues to the inner coherence of poems that appear to be chaotic and disorganized; Scheick sees his approach to the poet's artistic achievement as the approach of the future, replacing inquiries into Taylor's theology and intellectual heritage.

ii. Puritanism

In a special European scholars' edition of *EAL*, Ursula Brumm courageously tackles once again the pervasive mythology that has grown up around the Landing of the Pilgrim Fathers, offering in "Did the Pilgrims Fall Upon Their Knees When They Arrived in the New World? Art and History in the Ninth Chapter, Book One, of Bradford's History *Of Plymouth Plantation*" (*EAL* 12:25–35), a careful reading of the First Landing passage as "the very apex" of Bradford's book; "writing retrospectively," and seeking to reduce a complex emotional experience to its underlying "simple Trueth," Brumm points out, Bradford had recourse to selected mythical and archetypal images which defined the actualities of the new American environment in terms of the symbolic realities of his own imagination. Another early writer who knew something about archetypes, the irrepressible Thomas Morton, is the subject of Karen Ordahl Kupperman's "Thomas Morton, Historian" (*NEQ* 50:660–64), which does not improve upon Major W. Minor's "William Bradford Versus Thomas Morton" (*EAL* 5[1970]:1–13) as a discussion of the legitimacy of

Bradford's charge of illegal gun-trading with the Indians. Much more consequential is Michael Zuckerman's "Pilgrims in the Wilderness: Community, Modernity, and the Maypole at Merry Mount" (*NEQ* 50:255–77), perhaps the most provocative historical interpretation to date of this trivial episode which spawned a major American romance cycle; even so, however, Zuckerman might have profited from a reading of Robert D. Arner's "Pastoral Celebration and Satire in Thomas Morton's *New English Canaan*" (*Criticism* 16[1974]:217–31) in expanding his interpretation of the symbolic meanings of the differences between Morton's and the Pilgrims' attitudes toward Indians, sex, land, and liberty. Finally, another one of Morton's antagonists, William Wood, was favored with Alden T. Vaughan's fine edition of *New Englands Prospect* (Amherst: Univ. of Mass. Press), the price of which will unfortunately prohibit its otherwise well-deserved adoption for graduate seminars.

One of the most frequently discussed first-generation writers, Roger Williams, occasioned Wallace Coyle's *Roger Williams: A Reference Guide* (Boston: G. K. Hall), like other works in this bibliographical series a highly useful (if sometimes confusingly arranged) research tool that displays the ups and downs of Williams's reputation at a glance. As an addition to any future versions of this volume, there is Hans R. Guggisberg's "Religious Freedom and the History of the Christian World in Roger Williams' Thought" (*EAL* 12:36–48), which examines the sources of Williams's "liberalism" in European polemical literature, particularly in the anonymous *Scriptures and Reasons . . . against Persecution in the Cause of Conscience*; implicitly at least, Guggisberg denies the theory that close contact with the Indians had a profound effect on the tendency of Williams's thought toward greater liberty of worship.

Only two essays in *Literary Uses of Typology* are of immediate interest to early Americanists, but the volume itself is a sophisticated critical study of many aspects of the typological tradition and deserves a place in the library of every serious student of literature. Emory Elliott's "From Fathers to Sons: The Evolution of Typology in Puritan New England" (pp. 204–27) extends and elaborates upon the thesis of generational difference and conflict which Elliott originally articulated in *Power and the Pulpit in Puritan New England* (Princeton: Princeton Univ. Press, 1975), and Mason I. Lowance,

Jr.'s "Typology and Millennial Eschatology in Early New England" (pp. 228–73)is a comprehensive discussion of that infinitely complex subject—the best short treatment, I am tempted to say, yet in print. Typology also figures prominently in Robert Daly's excellent article on "Puritan Poetics: The World, the Flesh, and God" (*EAL* 12:136–62), a tantalizing foretaste of his forthcoming book-length study; in addition to typology, Daly examines the influence of Ramist rhetoric and the impact of Biblical injunctions against idolatry on American Puritan verse.

Among Puritan poets receiving individual attention this year was John Fiske, subject of Astrid Schmitt-v. Mühlenfels's "John Fiske's Funeral Elegy on John Cotton" (*EAL* 12:49–62), which discusses Fiske's knotty verses as an example of Puritan elegies and attempts to differentiate the individual elements of the poem from the merely conventional ones. Anne Bradstreet's poetry prompted Rosamund R. Rosenmeier's " 'Divine Translation': A Contribution to the Study of Anne Bradstreet's Method in the Marriage Poems" (*EAL* 12:121–35), a plausible account of how Bradtreet reconciled the world and the spirit through typological images and figures drawn from the "biblical language of promise"; "like biblical history, her personal history seems to have been a . . . crescendo . . . of relationships, that brought her finally . . . to the experience of integration that she so much desired."

Puritan theologians of the first generation are well represented in Phyllis M. and Nicholas R. Jones's judiciously selected collection of sermons, *Salvation in New England* (Austin: Univ. of Tex. Press), although the introductory discussion of sermon style strikes me as too elementary for the audience to whom the book is presumably addressed. Later theologians, including controversial ones like Nicholas Short and John Davenport, have their say in Michael G. Hall's and William L. Joyce's "The Half-Way Covenant of 1662: Some New Evidence" (*PAAS* 87:97–110), an important article about nine new documents written mostly in refutation of the Synodal position; this collection triples the amount of evidence heretofore available to critics and historians. Another important manuscript by a key figure in early Puritanism has been edited by Mason I. Lowance, Jr., and David Watters in "Increase Mather's 'New Jerusalem': Millennialism in Late Seventeenth-Century New England" (*PAAS* 87:343–408) and provided with an excellent historical introduction that makes clear how Mather's exegesis differs from that of other exegetes of the Apocalypse and—predictably for a project to which Professor Lowance sets his able hand—how deeply Mather's readings are rooted in typology.

Sparked by Sacvan Bercovitch's recent study (now, I think, unfairly being sniped at by critics who seem to miss its overriding significance for reasons that strike me as uniformly petty) and confirmed by the late Kenneth B. Murdock's excellent and long-awaited edition of *Magnalia Christi Americana, Books I and II* (Cambridge: Harvard Univ. Press), the Cotton Mather revival continues. In a first-rate article to follow up last year's insights, Gustaaf van Cromphout explores the classical influences of the style, themes, and structure of *Magnalia* ("Cotton Mather: The Puritan Historian as Renaissance Humanist," *AL* 49:327–37), while Philip F. Gura's stimulating study of "Cotton Mather's *Life of Phips*: 'A Vice with the Vizard of Vertue Upon It'" (*NEQ* 50:440–57) extends both Cromphout's and Jane Donahue Eberwein's (see *ALS 1975*, p. 213) analyses of this highly important biography, clearly a turning point both in Mather's career and in the fortunes of American Puritanism. Two other historical turning points for Mather are discussed in M. Wynn Thomas's "Cotton Mather's *Wonders of the Invisible World*: Some Metamorphoses of Salem Witchcraft," *The Damned Art: Essays in the Literature of Witchcraft*, edited by Sydney Anglo (Boston: Routledge & Kegan Paul), pp. 202–26, and in David Levin's note on "Cotton Mather's Declaration of Gentlemen and Thomas Jefferson's Declaration of Independence" (*NEQ* 50:509–14), which points out parallels between the two documents in "the grievances, the language, and the form."

Two concluding general studies of Puritanism are Eugene F. Quirk's "Early American Literature and the Problem of Cultural Moulds" (*EngR* 18,iii:9–12), in which Emerson is arraigned for rejecting all colonial writing as slavishly imitative and thereby unwittingly setting a trend which American Studies continues to follow, and Sacvan Bercovitch's "How the Puritans Won the American Revolution" (*MR* 17[1976]:597–630), a winsomely—and provocatively—mistitled essay about how Nathaniel Hawthorne, George Bancroft, et al. came to interpret the Puritan contribution of order to the otherwise chaotic revolutionary impulses of the Founding Fathers.

iii. The South

Certainly the most significant event of the year in colonial southern studies, and one of the most significant events for several years past, was the publication of *Essays in Early Virginia Literature Honoring Richard Beale Davis*, edited by J. A. Leo Lemay (New York: Burt Franklin). Organized chronologically around the modestly understated theme that "the number of competent and even excellent literary men produced by early Virginia is one indicator of a flourishing civilization," the book begins with Everett Emerson's survey of "Thomas Hariot, John White, and Ould Virginia" (pp. 1–11)—an essay at whose core lies the questionable claim that Hariot and White "saw what they looked at" rather than what they imagined (surely, for example, Theodore de Bry's engravings merely highlighted White's intentional allusion to the Three Graces in his depiction of "Indians Dancing" in his edition of the *Briefe and True Report*, and surely also Hariot's prose is more highly allusive, both in terms of references to geography and to other literature, than Emerson suggests). Then Lewis Leary takes a look at "The Adventures of Captain John Smith as Heroic Legend" (pp. 13–33), measuring Smith's own version of his travels and exploits against Lord Raglan's 22 archetypal incidents and crediting Smith with ten or eleven. Philip L. Barbour follows with "Samuel Purchas: The Indefatigable Encyclopedist Who Lacked Good Judgment" (pp. 35–52), an account of the four key editions of Purchas's work in its growth toward *Pilgrims* in 1625; Barbour points out that all versions of Purchas's masterwork, while irreplaceable as historical resources, lack the unifying theme of empire which makes Hakluyt's *Voiages* not only an important historical document but also an impressive literary achievement.

One of Purchas's contributors, acknowledged but lamentably truncated in Purchas's editing, was Henry Norwood, subject of Leota Harris Hirsch's "Henry Norwood and His Voiage to Virginia" (pp. 53–72); Norwood wrote what Hirsch correctly describes as "a fast-paced adventure story," an entertaining blend of realism, gothicism, romance, and humor. And in "To Caesar Friend or Foe? The Burwell Papers and Bacon's Rebellion" (pp. 73–90), Wilbur H. Ward rounds out discussion of 17th-century Virginia literature with his careful treatment of John Cotton's prose narrative of the Rebellion and his conjectures that Ebenezer Cooke, author of a versified "History of Colonel Nathaniel Bacon's Rebellion in Virginia," probably had sources other than Cotton's manuscript for his poem.

Eighteenth-century Virginians are represented in Lemay's volume by Wilbur R. Jacobs's cursory and disappointing "Robert Beverley: Colonial Ecologist and Indian Lover" (pp. 91–100) and by Robert D. Arner's "Style, Substance, and Self in William Byrd's Familiar Letters" (pp. 101–20), the first extended treatment of this important aspect of Byrd's literary career. In "The Reverend Samuel Davies's Essay Series: The Virginia Centinel, 1756–1757" (pp. 121–64), J. A. Leo Lemay establishes beyond any reasonable doubt that Davies was indeed the author of that pseudonymous serial, widely reprinted in colonial newspapers, and Homer D. Kemp ("The Reverend John Camm: 'To Raise a Flame and Live in It,'" pp. 165–80) and Jack P. Greene ("A Mirror of Virtue for a Declining Land: John Camm's Funeral Sermon for William Nelson," pp. 181–202) collaborate to make a substantial contribution to our knowledge of this minor but interesting Virginia Tory writer. A. R. Riggs examines the political pamphleteering of the "Penman of the Revolution: A Case for Arthur Lee" (pp. 203–20) and argues that Lee deserves the "Penman" title almost as much as Thomas Paine. William J. Scheick offers an original and illuminating interpretation of "Chaos and Imaginative Order in Thomas Jefferson's *Notes on the State of Virginia*" (pp. 221–34) and is seconded in his efforts to come to terms with Jefferson's imagination by Stephen D. Cox's excellent "The Literary Aesthetics of Thomas Jefferson" (pp. 235–56). Carl Dolmetsch's "Tucker's 'Hermit of the Mountain' Essays: Prolegomenon for a Collected Edition" (pp. 257–76) provides both an end and an implicit rationale for this generally first-rate collection of essays, for in concluding Dolmetsch also reminds us of how much additional work is needed to place Tucker (and by extension virtually every other writer discussed in the book) in his proper historical and cultural context and how badly modern scholarly editions of these neglected Virginia authors are needed.

In separate but clearly related scholarly developments to accompany Lemay's volume, William S. Prince has collected and edited *The Poems of St. George Tucker of Williamsburg, Virginia, 1752–1827* (New York: Vantage), providing an introduction that rivals Dolmetsch's essay for its informational value, its comprehensive view of Tucker's career, and its placement of Tucker within the American poetic tradition. Two interesting notes on early southern authors are Joseph R. Gavlin's "Another Side to William Byrd of Westover: An Explanation of the Food in His Secret Diaries" (*VC* 26: 124–33), which traces Byrd's food-faddism to George Cheyne's *New Theory of Continental Fevers* (1702) and *Essay of Health and Long Life* (1724), and John Davenport Neville's discussion of "The Reverend Hugh Jones and His Universal Georgian Calendar" (*VC* 26:134–43), an account of Jones's unsuccessful attempts to win acceptance of the intricate 13-month calendar he explained in his *Panchronometer* (1753). Appropriately, it is Richard Beale Davis who has the last word in southern studies for the year, offering a brief but invaluable bibliographical overview of "Southern Writing of the Revolutionary Period, c. 1760–1790" (EAL 12:107–20) and tacitly inviting someone to extend the chronological coverage of his own monumental *Intellectual Life in the Colonial South, 1585–1763* (Knoxville: Univ. of Tenn. Press, 1978).

iv. Franklin and the Enlightenment

A scarcity of articles on Franklin marks this year's work (or nonwork) in colonial literary scholarship, with only one essay, Hugh J. Dawson's "Franklin's 'Memoirs' in 1784: The Design of the *Autobiography*" (*EAL* 12:286–93), directly addressing Franklin's writing; Dawson takes a stab at solving the vexing problems associated with Franklin's autobiographical artistry, arguing that Franklin quite skillfully integrates Parts I and II by abandoning "chronology in favor of moral instruction" as his structural device and "repositioning . . . topics [from the original outline] to drive home the lessons." And in "*Carmen Gratitudinis*: A Latin Tribute to President Aaron Burr by Benjamin Young Prime (1751)" (*Humanistica Lovaniensia* 26:228–35), Leo M. Kaiser adds the only other note on Enlightenment writers by editing an important piece that represents Prime's longest Latin poem, a combination of borrowings from Virgil, Ovid, and Horace and passages of striking lyric originality and skill.

v. Edwards and the Great Awakening

Robert L. Berner's "Grace and Works in America: The Role of Jonathan Edwards" (*SoQ* 15:125–34) is a misinformed article that resurrects, among other dead ideas, the old contrast between frontier liberalism and seacoast, urban conservatism in all its original simplicity and that tries unsuccessfully to set Edwards scholarship back at least four decades. Far more substantial—a major contribution, in fact—is Wilson H. Kimnach's "Jonathan Edwards' Early Sermons: New York, 1722–1723" (*JPH* 55:255–66; originally and superiorly entitled "Before Surprising Conversions: The Design of Jonathan Edwards"), in which Kimnach synopsizes the contents of Edwards's New York sermons to trace his development into a preacher of genuine originality and power who had, however, yet to find his central themes of true religious affection and the morphology of conversion when he left New York in 1723. Roland A. Delattre's "Beauty and Politics: A Problematical Legacy of Jonathan Edwards," in *American Philosophy from Edwards to Quine*, edited by Robert W. Shahan and Kenneth R. Merrill (Norman: Univ. of Okla. Press), pp. 20–28, also promises to be of interest, but I was not able to obtain a copy for the purposes of this review and mention it here only as a bibliographical item.

vi. Revolutionary and Early National Periods

The major contribution to literary scholarship in this period during 1977 was Everett H. Emerson's *American Literature, 1764–1789: The Revolutionary Years* (Madison: Univ. of Wisc. Press). Though not up to the standard set by Emerson's earlier collection on *Major Writers of Early American Literature* (Madison: Univ. of Wisc. Press, 1972), this gathering of essays is in some ways a companion piece to that earlier volume, extending its chronological coverage to the close of the Revolutionary War and thus rounding out a kind of literary history of colonial America. All the expected figures are discussed in this book in essays that are generally overviews of existing attitudes rather than original contributions or fresh interpretations. Emerson himself sets the tone in his "The Cultural Context of the American Revolution" (pp. 3–18) and is ably supported by Elaine K. Ginsberg ("The Patriot Pamphleteers," pp. 19–38), Evelyn J. Hinz ("Thomas Paine," pp. 39–58), Charles E. Modlin ("The Loyalists' Reply," pp. 59–72), Robert M. Benton ("The Preachers," pp. 73–86), Calhoun Winton ("The Theater and Drama," pp. 87–104), Mary E. Rucker ("Benjamin Franklin," pp. 105–26), William L. Andrews ("Philip

Freneau and Francis Hopkinson," pp. 127–44), Thomas Philbrick ("Thomas Jefferson," pp. 145–70), Bernard W. Bell ("African-American Writers," pp. 171–94), Patricia M. Medieros ("Three Travelers: Carver, Bartram, and Woolman," pp. 195–212), A. W. Plumstead ("Hector St. John de Crèvecoeur," pp. 213–32), Robert D. Arner ("The Connecticut Wits," pp. 233–52), Robert Bain ("The Federalist," pp. 253–74), and Cecilia Tichi ("Worried Celebrants of the American Revolution," pp. 275–92). This listing is a deliberate rhetorical device meant to indicate both the range of subjects and the survey nature of the essays themselves; Cecelia Tichi's concluding essay rises above the others in the volume in this respect, while Patricia M. Medieros's piece on Carver, Bartram, and Woolman seems likely to win the "missed-opportunities-to-say-something-original" award. All in all, Emerson's book is a good place to brush up on figures with whom long separation may have made us unfamiliar and to locate essential bibliographies to send us back to more specific scholarship.

Several useful specific essays on figures included in Emerson's volume, in fact, appeared in journals during 1977. Arguing that "more interest must be paid to the various characters"—to the wife, "F. B.," Farmer James, and so on, for instance—Jean F. Béranger, in "The Desire of Communication: Narrator and Narratee in *Letters from an American Farmer*" (*EAL* 12:73–85), goes into great detail discussing the incipiently fictional components of Crèvecoeur's book. In "Crèvecoeur: A 'Man of Sorrows' and the American Revolution," *MR* 17[1976]:288–301), A. W. Plumstead explores the dark side of Crèvecoeur's life and Letters, highlighting the Frenchman's theme that "the virtuous common people of the earth suffer most in revolutions" and finding in Crèvecoeur's *Sketches* "not even a potential hero of the rebel cause." Less gloomy is Harold Kulungian's "The Aestheticism of Crèvecoeur's American Farmer" (*EAL* 12:197–201), which identifies the Farmer as a character whose "sensual understanding" is totally dependent on his environment, a condition which either exalts or oppresses him and leaves him no middle ground "between beauty and the absence of it."

Contending that Thomas Paine's *Common Sense* possesses the same impact today that it did in 1776, an historically naive assertion, Elaine K. Ginsberg offers a rhetorical analysis, based upon Paine's use of two-, three-, and four-or-more part series, of that pamphlet in

"Style and Indentification in *Common Sense*" (*WVUPP* 23:26–36). In another essay on Paine, J. Rodney Fulcher ("*Common Sense vs. Plain Truth*: Political Propaganda and Civil Society," *SoQ* 15:57–74) adds nothing to what we already knew about the contrast between Paine's style and that of his Tory, or in the case of John Adams, conservative pamphleteering counterparts. Other articles on Revolutionary propagandists include John G. Buchanan's excellent treatment of the Reverend Samuel Cooper's use of "Whig theory and Puritan theology" to persuade Americans of "The Justice of America's Cause: Revolutionary Rhetoric in the Sermons of Samuel Cooper" (*NEQ* 50:101–24) and Macel D. Ezele's uninformative discussion of "John Dickinson's Identity Crisis" in *Personalities & Policies: Essays on English and European History*, edited by E. Deanne Malpass (Fort Worth: Texas Christian Univ. Press), pp. 50–58. (Incidentally, Gillian B. Anderson also buries Samuel Cooper in "The Funeral of Samuel Cooper," *NEQ* 50:644–5). A better note on Dickinson is Pierre Marambaud's analysis of the Pennsylvanian's persuasive style in "Dickinson's *Letters from a Farmer in Pennsylvania* as Political Discourse: Ideology, Imagery, and Rhetoric" (*EAL* 12:63–72). Yet another Revolutionary rhetorician is the subject of Judy Hample's "The Textual and Cultural Authenticity of Patrick Henry's 'Liberty or Death' Speech" (*QJS* 63:298–310), which concludes that the famous speech has none of the former sort of authenticity but more than enough of the latter variety to make up for any deficiencies. On the other side of the political fence, Leo M. Kaiser discusses the "Tory Classicist: Robert Proud and His Translations from Boethius" (*Humanistica Lovaniensia* 26:179–87), translations that speak directly to Proud's despair as the Revolutionary conflict rises and falls, and, finally, George Selement attempts to bring both Tory and patriot positions into some sort of focus with his "American Revolution or War for Independence: The Conflict Viewed Through the Newspapers of Philadelphia, 1763–1776" (*MichA* 9:299–312). He also concludes that in Philadelphia at least the Tory position soon fell into public disrepute, and the debate began to center on whether the struggle with Great Britain should be viewed simply as a war for separation or as an upheaval in established social patterns.

For poetry written in and around the Revolutionary period, there is, first of all, Vincent Freimarck's "Reader's Reach and Writer's Grasp" (*EAL* 12:302–3), an account of an anonymous verse inscribed

"To the President" and published in *The Massachussetts Magazine* in 1793; a distinguishing feature of the poem is its clever adaptation of Christopher Smart's "Song to David" only two years after the first comprehensive edition of Smart's poetry, still without the "Song," however, had appeared. A far better-known poem is interpreted by Jane Donahue Eberwein in "Freneau's 'The Beauties of Santa Cruz,'" (*EAL* 12:271–76), a reading of the lyric which finds, unconvincingly to this reader, that Freneau was not "an escapist [from the Revolutionary conflict] in 1776." And William L. Andrews hypothesizes in "Freneau's 'A Political Litany': A Note on Interpretation" (*EAL* 12: 193–96) that the refrain "Libera Nos" and the parody of the Book of Common Prayer central to that poem are intimately related to the poet's private life, particularly to his recent rejection of a career in the ministry, whereas the truth is that Freneau had picked up that refrain precisely where he picked up more than a few of his poetic devices, from broadside traditions dating back (in this instance at least) to the Puritan Revolution (see, for example, the broadside verses that begin "From Commonwealth Coblers, and zealous State Tinkers . . . Libera Nos").

One important consequence of the continuing interest in minority contributions to American literature is the close investigation of Phillis Wheatley's life and works, an investigation that has already produced important new poems and letters. Now Phil Lapansky adds to Wheatley's growing canon yet another work, "*Deism*—An Unpublished Poem by Phillis Wheatley" (*NEQ* 50:517–20); probably written around 1770, the poem is a poor performance poetically but gives additional evidence of Wheatley's intense piety. And in a brief but significant note, Muktar Ali Isani locates an early advertisement for Wheatley's *Poems* in Ezekiel Russell's *Censor* and discusses the differences between the titles in this aborted volume and those eventually published in the London edition of 1773 ("The First Proposed Edition of *Poems on Various Subjects* and the Phillis Wheatley Canon," *AL* 49:97–103). Another bibliographical contribution by Isani is "Wheatley's Departure for London and Her 'Farewel to America'" (*SAB* 32,iv:123–29), which analyzes the differences between the 1773 version of that poem and four earlier versions published in New England newspapers. And, finally, James A. Rawley's "The World of Phillis Wheatley" (*NEQ* 50:666–76) makes use of newly discovered material in updating Julian Mason, Jr.'s and M. A.

Richmond's accounts of Wheatley's life, particularly of her connections with John Thornton and the "Clapham Sect" of zealous evangelists (Rawley's essay, for what it's worth, is also my candidate for the worst punctuated article of the year).

Two books on quite different sorts of Revolutionary personalities conclude the scholary contributions of 1977 to our knowledge of this period. First is Kenneth Lynn's excellent little collection of Tory and patriot biographies and his bibliographical essay outlining fashions in historical interpretation of the Revolution, in *A Divided People*, Contributions in American Studies, No. 30 (Westport, Conn.: Greenwood); for both actors and interpreters alike, Lynn takes his motto from Sir Lewis Namier: "A man's relation, for instance, to his father . . . may determine the pattern of his later political conduct . . . ." Lynn is especially provocative, as this motto might suggest, in his discussion of the ubiquitous mother-child and father-son metaphors of Revolutionary pamphleteering.

Another book with a Freudian thesis is Philip Young's *Revolutionary Ladies* (New York: Alfred A. Knopf). An exploration of, among other things, the Circe archetype and sexual intrigue during the War for Independence, it is not directed exclusively to the student of literature (though it refers frequently to popular literature of the period), but it should also delight the historian, the buff of historical romance, and the general literate reader (if there are any of those animals in modern day America) as well. Separate chapters examine the careers and legends of Betsy Loring, Lady Frances Wentworth, and Margaret Moncrieffe, but many more "ladies"—the Van Horne girls, the notorious Apthorps, and Charlotte Stanley, to name but a few—also put in appearances in a book that sparkles from beginning to end. Young's paradoxical motto, borrowed from Simone de Beauvoir in apparent despite of the militant feminism of our times, is that "women who exploit their femininity to the limit create for themselves a situation almost equivalent to that of a man." Alas for that *almost*, however, as the case of poor Ms. Moncrieffe will testify.

vii. Brown and Contemporaries

The first volume in the Bicentennial Edition of the works of Charles Brockden Brown is *Wieland and Memoirs of Carwin*, edited by Sydney J. Krause, S. W. Reid, and Alexander Cowie (Kent, O.: Kent

State Univ. Press). Though there are some questionable readings of minor words, particularly of the "here" versus "there" variety, the editorial apparatus of this volume is above reproach; the work is carefully done and precisely what it ought to be for a CEAA edition. Especially noteworthy is Cowie's "Historical Essay," a very fine discussion of the Brown whose images and symbols reveal an inner world of repressed or suppressed feelings rather than of the Brown whose main concern was with the external world of intellectual traditions and novelistic conventions he exploited with full consciousness as commentaries on the times. Also noteworthy is the typography of this volume, as if the lucidity and cleanness of the world of the margins were deliberately being set in contrast to the tangled web of narrative and narrator(s) in the tale itself. Cowie's reading of the book would find favor, I suspect, with A. Carl Bredahl, Jr., who in "Transfiguration in *Wieland*" (*EAL* 12:177–92) advances an interesting argument that what is really at stake in this novel is a conflict between energy and order, explosive force and form, and that Clara's function as both storyteller (the transformed) and story-telling moralist (the seeker after order and meaning) is a centrally ambiguous one; a stimulating essay, Bredahl's piece is marred by some contradictory, ambiguous, or ill-considered remarks, such as that *Wieland* teaches the moral "that one needs to respond to the evidence of his senses and not impose upon them pre-established intellectual patterns"—a confusing and impossible moral indeed in a world created by double-tongued deceivers and illuminated by half-light at best.

Charles Brockden Brown is also one of the subjects of Charles E. Bennett's "A Poetical Correspondence Among Elihu Hubbard Smith, Joseph Bringhurst, Jr., and Charles Brockden Brown" (*EAL* 12:277–85), which penetrates the pseudonyms of "Ella," "Birtha," and "Henry," who among them wrote some 35 poems published in Fenno's *Gazette* between February and August 1791. Another early novelist, Hannah Foster, found her first good reader in Walter P. Wenska, Jr., whose "*The Coquette* and the American Dream of Freedom" (*EAL* 12:243–55) perceptively ties the work to such later fictional studies of quests for freedom doomed from the start as James's *Daisy Miller* and Kate Chopin's *The Awakening*. And Harrison T. Meserole, in "Some Notes on Early American Fiction: Kelroy Was There" (*SAF* 5:1–12), extols the virtues of the villainess of Rebecca Rush's *Kelroy* (if that mild oxymoron may be permitted) and surveys some of the bibliographical work that needs to be done in the area of early American fiction generally. As if in confirmation of Meserole's call to action, Edward W. Pitcher writes "A Note on 'Azakia': Jack B. Moore's 'Early American Short Story'" (*SSF* 14: 395–96), pointing out that Moore's tale (see *ALS 1976*, p. 190) was in fact written by a Frenchman and originally published in France in 1765.

As for poets of the early national period, James F. Tanner's "The 'Triple Ban' and Joel Barlow's 'Advice to a Raven in Russia'" (*EAL* 12:294–95) explicates that historical allusion as a reference to military conscription in France. A poet of far less consequence is discussed in Leo M. Kaiser's "A Rediscovered Latin Poem of Nathaniel Gardner" (*SCN* 35,i–ii:70), a poem possibly written as early as 1739 but first published in the January 1807 number of *The Monthly Anthology and Boston Review*.

Scholarship on other early American literary genres and their writers was sparse in 1977, with only Harry U. Taylor, Jr.'s bibliography of "The Dramas of August von Kotzebue on the New York and Philadelphia Stages from 1798 to 1805" (*WVUPP* 23:47–58) and Martin Roth's unimaginative and poorly researched "Irving and the Old Style" (*EAL* 12:256–70) breaking the silence to remind us of the flourishing Federal theater and the still more flourishing Addisonian essay. In particular, Roth seems not ever to have heard of the existence of Boston's "Hell-Fire Club," Franklin's "Do-good Papers," and many another early American essay series that antedates Irving's *Salmagundi*.

viii. General and Miscellaneous

One comes to John Seelye's *Prophetic Waters: The River in Early American Life and Literature* (New York: Oxford Univ. Press) prepared by book jacket blurbs and promotional puffs for something of great significance and originality. I was, frankly, disappointed in the work and found most of the readings of familiar colonial texts quite conventional and even conservative at times (when they were not off base altogether, as seemed to me the case with his reading of Beverley's *History and Present State of Virginia*). Further, I was not charmed by Seelye's eccentric style, though many other reviewers appear to have been; it seemed to me an amalgam of Dore Schary's and Diedrich Knickerbocker's styles, and if it worked for me at all, it worked only to remind me that historical vision is always idiosyncratic and that the ancient critical distinction between true and false wit is probably worth resurrecting and maintaining in an age when language is already so fluid that practically everything might just as well be writ on water anyway. There are, it must be said, some good things in Seelye's book, including his discussion of many early works that are not discussed elsewhere but that clearly merit analysis and his interpretations of the symbolic cartography of the early explorers, but I am one reader, I am afraid, who does not find these rare treasures worth digging through the verbiage to uncover.

Taking the contrast between British and American legal situations as his starting point, C. R. Kropf ("Colonial Satire and the Law," *EAL* 12:234–42) examines the far-reaching impact of the Zenger libel case in arguing an interesting but thin case that the absence of governmental restrictions on libel allowed Americans to speak their minds so openly in print that "there was no reason, legal or otherwise, for an author to resort to the indirect approach of satire in his attacks on the government and public figures." Another literary genre is described in Hans Galinsky's "Exploring the 'Exploration Report' and Its Image of the Overseas World: Spanish, French, and English Variants of a Common Form Type in Early American Literature" (*EAL* 12:5–24), which isolates for discussion the journey and quest motifs, the mythic consciousness, and the unavoidable theme of cultural incongruity that have fed into and sustained American literature as a multiethnic, multilingual body of writing. And Marion Barber Stowell, slighting (as usual in early American studies) the southern contribution, nonetheless produces an otherwise commendable account of *Early American Almanacs: The Colonial Workday Bible* (New York: Burt Franklin). The first full-length study of this neglected and fascinating genre—actually a hodgepodge of several genres—Stowell's book is more a sampler than a full-fledged study and is short on literary analysis but long on intrinsic entertainment value; still, despite the good points of the book, another, genuinely critical work on the subject of early almanacs is sorely needed.

Two articles explored the emergence of early American character types during the formative years of the new nation. In an essay that will never do, Beverly Beeton sets out to discuss "The Frontiersman Before Leatherstocking" (*MarkhamR* 7:1–5) but neglects to mention William Hubbard's Maine frontiersmen (or Cotton Mather's, for that matter), John Underhill, Benjamin Church, Dr. Alexander Hamilton's "Buckskins"—etc., etc. And in "The Farmer in Early American Literature" (*Gypsy Scholar* 4,i:17–26), Marilyn Brick Silver presents a similarly slim survey of her subject, failing to mention, for example, John Dickinson's well-known Pennsylvania Farmer or the rural characters who populate the landscapes of Bartram's *Travels*.

An interesting overview of the changing status of women in religious worship and society at large is Lonna M. Malmscheimer's "Daughters of Zion: New England Roots of American Feminism" (*NEQ* 50:484–504), which studies sermons by John Robinson, John Cotton, Cotton Mather, and others to chart the gradual release of pious American women from subjugation and silence within the church to political action without. Another study centered on women is Emily Stipes Watts's *The Poetry of American Women*, an unnecessarily chauvinistic book that appears to assume feminine poetic virtue can best be established by denigrating the efforts of male poets rather than by close analysis of poetic texts. In the first several chapters, which are all that concern us here, Watts treats such writers as Bradstreet, Sarah Kemble Knight, Phillis Wheatley, Ann Eliza Bleeker, and Susanna Haswell Rowson without once acknowledging, for example, that Bradstreet is the only true poet in the group, the only one whose verse will stand up to critical scrutiny. Even in this instance, Watts has, I believe, misunderstood or misrepresented the true sources of Bradstreet's talent, which lay more in her domestic situation than out of it, and I may as well also admit that I find something silly about a critical sensibility that can seriously argue for Mrs. Rowson's poetic ineptitude as a form of experimentation with verse linking her with H. D. and Emily Dickinson. Generally speaking, Watts is a fine critic whose work on Edwards and Hemingway clearly indicates that she knows better than to make such statements, and I can only hope that her study improves as it goes on and Watts finds better women writers with whom to work.

A study of a different sort is Stanford J. Searl, Jr.'s "Perry Miller as Artist: Piety and Imagination in *The New England Mind: The Seventeenth Century*" (*EAL* 12:221–33); Searl presents a rather dully written (and conceived) analysis of Miller's work as "a quest for the inward meaning of American Puritanism" conducted with both the verbal resources and the passion of Melville's quest for hidden epistemological mysteries in *Moby-Dick.*

Two bibliographical compilations bring to an end the year's work in early American studies. William J. Scheick and JoElla Doggett collaborate on *Seventeenth-Century American Poetry: A Reference Guide* (Boston: G. K. Hall), yet another volume in this important bibliographical series; though once again a number of articles have been overlooked, as seems unavoidably the case with undertakings of this sort, this volume appears to have been done with more care than several others in the series and clearly stands as the place to begin research into the subject of early American poetry. And, finally, William S. Ward provides a valuable listing of British responses to early American poems, plays, and novels in "American Authors and British Reviewers 1798–1826: A Bibliography" (*AL* 49:1–21).

One final personal note: in the four years I have been responsible for "Literature to 1800," I have learned many invaluable lessons about the profession, not all of which would be lessons to every reader or which are worth sharing in any case. But I would ask that in the future, all scholars who publish in this area make a special effort to send the author of this chapter, whoever he or she may be, offprints of any pertinent articles. It is difficult to keep tabs on everybody, even on those you know, and this simple professional courtesy should make my successor's task somewhat easier and his or her bibliographical coverage as complete as possible. That would be in the best interest of all of us.

University of Cincinnati

12. 19th-Century Literature

Thomas Wortham

The only unity one should wish to find in the great variety of literary responses this chapter is responsible for surveying is of excellence, and this year one need not be disappointed in this desire. A brilliant new study of Cooper's artistry, an intelligent interest manifested in thoughtful articles on the nation's many regions and their literary spokesmen, a splendid edition of the letters of Bryant in visible progress and of Frederic completed, and a spanking clean text of Howells's *A Modern Instance* are hardly insignificant offerings. If all of the lesser critical and bibliographical performances do not fulfill their announced purposes as fully or as elegantly as one might expect, they nevertheless testify to the generally good health of literary scholarship on 19th-century American literature. Actually little has changed. Cooper retains his place of prominence in the early part of the century, though farther down the road, Stephen Crane steps slightly aside to let his first master, Howells, pass. A good number of the gentler sex bustle by, shoving out of way the "genteel" poets of midcentury. Perhaps the ladies aren't so gentle as the last century supposed. But little has changed. As before, as ever, there rises a still, quiet voice crying above the babble: Ambrose Bierce! Ambrose Bierce! Where are you?

i. General Studies

The important role of the periodical in the development of a national literature during the 19th century has been frequently observed but little studied by scholars. One of the problems the student of the magazine has been faced with is bibliographical, notwithstanding Frank Luther Mott's monumental *History of American Magazines.* Now, with the publication of *An Annotated Bibliography of American Literary Periodicals, 1741–1850* (Boston: G. K. Hall), investigators' work will be made somewhat easier. Masterfully conceived and impressively performed by Jayne K. Kribbs, it is, without doubt, the most useful and needed of the many reference guides to be issued by the Boston publishing firm in the last several years. Kribbs's annotations give not only the expected information—place and period of publication, names of editors and publishers, locations of known copies—but also summarize the contents of most of the 940 journals listed in the bibliography. Five separate indices permit this information to be conveniently rearranged by chronology, geographic region, names of editors and publishers, authors or titles of tales, novels, and drama.

General period studies were again few this year. The best is John P. McWilliams's "Fictions of Merry Mount" (*AQ* 29:3–30), a detailed and illuminating account of the literary response from William Bradford to Robert Lowell to this incident in Puritan history. "From the outset," McWilliams writes, "Merry Mount has provided the historical writer a mirror in which he could find confirmation for his own ethics, for the values of his class, or for assumptions widely shared in his region or generation." Though Hawthorne's "The Maypole of Merry Mount" receives the most detailed consideration, it is viewed against the "recreations" of the story in the 19th century by Lydia Child, Catherine Maria Sedgwick, Longfellow, Irving, Whittier, and, most important after Hawthorne, John Lothrop Motley, whose *Merry-Mount* appeared in 1849. Unlike the others, in McWilliams's view, Motley "was able to break through the encrusted prejudice and repeated phrases of New England historiography to allow Morton's viewpoint, legal and ethical, its first hearing." McWilliams's is comparative analysis at its best; not only are we given "a history of changing cultural fears and values," but, McWilliams argues, "distinctions of genre and profession based upon notions of history and non-history lose their vitality."

In "American Anti-Semitism: A Reinterpretation" (*AQ* 29:166–81), Michael N. Dobkowski examines late 19th- and early 20th-century popular literature and considers the pervasive negative stereotype of the Jews he finds propagated there a major source of antisemitism in America. More specialized is his note, "The End of Confidence: The Patrician Anti-Semitism of John Jay Chapman and William Astor Chanler" (*MarkhamR* 7:14–17), in which he exhibits Chapman and Chanler as representatives of an older, genteel society which focused on the Jew as "the symbol of all they disliked about the new industrial America." Neither essay is especially original in outlook, and it is difficult to determine in what respect Dobkowski thinks his work a reinterpretation. Both essays are also marred by a shrillness of tone one would think no longer necessary or desirable.

ii. Irving, Cooper, and Their Contemporaries

William S. Ward's "American Authors and British Reviewers, 1798–1826: A Bibliography" (*AL* 49:1–21) should be overwhelming proof that few educated Britons could long remain in Sydney Smith's ignorance of American literature during the early decades of the Republic. Of the more than 450 reviews and articles Ward has located, the largest number expectedly were devoted to the works of Irving and Cooper. If such numerical considerations constitute useful literary study, then Ward's checklist is not without merit. One suspects, however, that his findings will not justify a reconsideration of earlier studies of the British response to an emerging American literature, and one is left to wonder the value of such compilations, unadorned as this is by any significant commentary.

With the publication of three volumes this year, "The Complete Works of Washington Irving" (Boston: Twayne) is apparently on sound footing again. *Bracebridge Hall*, edited by Herbert F. Smith, *The Adventures of Captain Bonneville*, the joint work of Robert A. Rees and Alan Sandy, and *Letters of Jonathan Oldstyle, Gent.*, printed in one volume with the *Salmagundi* papers and edited by Bruce I. Granger and Martha Hartzog, follow the format and procedures of the earlier volumes in the series and are each awarded the CEAA seal. Invaluable as the scholarly service of these modern critical editions is, we cannot forget the old editions—the physical objects through which the stories and sketches were first made known. Even subsequent editions sometimes have a value that transcends the mere bibliographical. *Old Christmas*, for example, an 1875 English collection of five of the "Sketch Book" pieces, illustrated by the talented Randolph J. Caldecott, and now reprinted in excellent facsimile and with a cordial introduction by Andrew B. Myers (Tarrytown, N.Y.: Sleepy Hollow Restorations), attests to the binding power of the early illustrations of our popular classics. This is an area of literary analysis that has only recently begun to receive the attention it deserves; that it is a valid area of inquiry for the student of literature as well as the art critic is finely demonstrated by Teona Tone Gneiting in her 1977 UCLA dissertation, "Picture and Text: A Theory of Illustrated Fiction in the Nineteenth Century."

Bruce Granger's claim in the introduction to his edition of the *Letters of Jonathan Oldstyle* that these early pieces foreshadow the more mature work of Irving is challenged by Martin Roth in "Irving and the Old Style" (*EAL* 12:256–70). Roth convincingly argues that in following so closely the English serial tradition established or perpetuated by such writers as Goldsmith, Addison and Steele, Irving failed in the *Letters*: "It was characteristic of Irving in his first period to choose to write in traditional genres that carried with them a heavy burden of moralizing; yet, because of his temperament and talents, the world he projected in his writings was a comic one in which moral and physical evil left no traces." Only when he freed himself in 1807 from this tradition he had failed to understand was he able to "accommodate his immature choice of format to his own nature as a comic writer."

Daniel L. Plung is undoubtedly right in " 'Rip Van Winkle': Metempsychosis and the Quest for Self-Reliance" (*BRMMLA* 31:65–80) in emphasizing differences rather than similarities between Rip and his European counterparts, but Plung's inability to feel any of the haunting reservations Philip Young found in the story nearly twenty years ago enervates his understanding of a story he views merely as "a tale depicting the American quest for individualism and self-reliance." More bold is Wayne Franklin's "The Misadventures of Irving's Bonneville: Trapping and Being Trapped in the Rocky Mountains" (*The Westering Experience*, pp. 122–28). Following the lead of Edgeley W. Todd, Franklin challenges the general opinion that Irving's "western" books, *Astoria* and *Bonneville*, are hackwork, romanticized histories full of inaccuracies. Without denying the play of Irving's imagination in the creation of these books, Franklin sees them as serious historical studies that greatly influenced the later writers of the history of the trans-Mississippi regions: the books "aim at something beyond the truth of their nominal subjects"; they embrace the question of what the "West" is, and, equally important, what the East was to do with it. The answers Franklin hears Irving give are not overly hopeful; the oppression and the destruction of the western empire was already an established fact and would in time spell the end of the wilderness.

Advances in our understanding of Cooper's achievement are moved even further ahead this year with the publication of H. Daniel Peck's excellent critical study, *A World by Itself: The Pastoral Moment in Cooper's Fiction* (New Haven: Yale Univ. Press). Even if Peck's attempt to answer the long argued question—why do we so enjoy reading Cooper?—is not entirely satisfactory, his explanation, arrived at by addressing the problem in literary and aesthetic terms rather than those of social and intellectual history, comes nearer succeeding than any before it. According to Peck, the power of Cooper's novels for the modern reader is located in their landscapes, that ordering of space which evokes in the reader a "timeless vision of simplicity and childhood wonder." Utilizing the theories of modern childhood psychology and the phenomenology of Gaston Bachelard, Peck finds the novels compelling because they enable us to fulfill the need to repossess the lost world of childhood. Furthermore, the heroes of the tales are "distinguished by the power of *observation* rather than by the power of *interpretation*"; they are see-ers, not seers. Unlike Emerson and Thoreau, they do not "possess" the landscape in an abstract or metaphysical sense; instead they capture a fixed, static structure that is sustained by Cooper's pastoral vision, "a still point of the imagination, a place from which [the reader] will never have to leave."

In such a context, Alan L. Steinberg's generic approach to the Leatherstocking Tales strikes one as not only derivative but rather simple-minded. In his "James Fenimore Cooper: The Sentimental Frontier" (*SDR* 15:94–108), Steinberg attributes both the strengths and the weaknesses of the tales to "Cooper's deliberate attempt to utilize many of the standard conventions of sentimental fiction in his treatment of the American frontier experience." Unfortunately, Steinberg's definition of the sentimental tradition is so hazy as to have little critical utility.

Two articles deal with Cooper's attitude toward the American Revolution in his writings. The Loyalist in his fiction is considered together with its counterpart in the stories of Hawthorne and Frederic by Donald G. Darnell in " 'Visions of Hereditary Rank': The Loyalist in the Fiction of Hawthorne, Cooper, and Frederic" (*SAB* 42:45–54).

Notwithstanding the expected differences, there are striking similarities in the three authors' characterizations of the Loyalist: he is artistocratic either in title or character, urbane, committed to a high concept of honor, courageous, steadfast, and serene in his loyalty. Most sympathetic of the three towards the figure, Cooper invariably portrays the Loyalists as "Anglican gentlemen . . . guilty neither of pride of place nor of hauteur." Unwilling to dismiss him as a villain, neither could Cooper (nor Hawthorne and Frederic), as an American writer, wholeheartedly endorse the Loyalist. His ambivalence wavered before an important and real question in postrevolutionary America: "Could a democracy provide the characters for heroic fiction?"

Even more impressive is Mike Ewart's "Cooper and the American Revolution: The Non-Fiction" (*JAmS* 11:61–79). Examining not only Cooper's published nonfiction but also important correspondence, Ewart attempts to locate "an unformulated, but coherent, theory of revolution" which informs Cooper's point-of-view. What he finds is a justification of the American Revolution that is based upon the belief that what was set in place was "a polity whose stability is insured and guaranteed by its form as a constitutional republic, and by the complementary action of its concomitant social structure, whose class system unfailingly offers the fittest leaders of the polity to the people." Because the fundamental assumptions of Cooper's ideology did not change, as did the political actualities of the nation during the first half of the 19th century, Cooper's political texts "became increasingly irascible and dissociated from the reality they purport to chronicle."

Cooper's notions about the gentleman and his essential role in the life of the community have, of course, received much attention in the past, but the gentle-lady has largely been ignored. In "The Education of Elizabeth Temple" (*SNNTS* 9:187–94), Jay S. Paul focuses on the function of Judge Temple's daughter in *The Pioneers* and finds that it is Elizabeth, "a worthy successor to her father," who "provides Cooper's narrative and the community itself the enlightened and personable spirit of the gentry at its best." But the promise of continuity represented by and in Elizabeth was not fulfilled in Cooper's fictional imagination when he took up her descendants in *Home As Found.* The practical failure in this third and last of the Effingham novels of the myth "of the public leader whose authority is resolute and just" is one of the concerns of Eric J. Sundquist in "Incest and

Imitation in Cooper's *Home As Found*" (*NCF* 32:261–84). Not only is *Home As Found* a biting social satire—"one of the best, despite disastrous sections, in American writing"—but it is also, in Sundquist's view, "an absorbing exhibition and defense of Cooper's own psychological vagaries and social tastes." In an engaging reading of this disturbing novel, Sundquist probes both its autobiographical and its cultural meanings to great advantage.

Other concerns of Cooper and his critics which have by now become commonplace are reviewed to no advantage by Mary E. Rucker in "Natural, Tribal, and Civil Law in Cooper's *The Prairie*" (*WAL* 12:215–22) and by Mary Conrad Kraus in "Civilized Law vs. Primitive Law in *The Pioneers*" (*CEA* 39, iii:9–10). A suggestion by Roberta F. Weldon that a figure in Indian myth is the prototype for the character of Tom Hutter is the modest point of her "Cooper's *The Deerslayer* and the Indian Myth of Nanabozho" (*NYFQ* 2[1976]: 61–67). Finally, Rosaly Torna Kurth has assembled "Susan Fenimore Cooper: An Annotated Checklist of Her Writings" (*NYH* 58: 173–93), demonstrating that Cooper's daughter-attendant and literary-aide was "a notably productive author in her own right," but recognizing it is as author of *Pages and Pictures* (1861), a companion volume to her father's works, that she will be remembered.

One would expect after the impressive number of studies of William Gilmore Simms in recent years a falling off, but such is not the case. In his survey of "The Present State of Simms Scholarship" (*SLJ* 10, i:92–7), C. Hugh Holman observes that "after a century of by-no-means benign neglect, . . . Simms is at last beginning to receive the kind of serious, thorough, careful, painstakingly exact, fundamentally scholarly examination which he has long deserved as the most prolific and the leading man of letters of the Old South." Still, unlike Cooper and Irving, Simms, from the evidence Holman himself offers, is mostly able to attract only regional interest. And, as in the recent past, it is as an historical novelist that Simms draws greatest attention.

Holman's 1976 essay on "Simms's Changing View of Loyalists during the Revolution" (see *ALS 1976*, pp. 202–3) works effectively as the foundation for the second chapter of his new book, *The Immoderate Past: The Southern Writer and History* (Athens: Univ. of Ga. Press), reviewed elsewhere in this volume. More general in outlook is John C. Guilds's "Simms's Use of History: Theory and Practice" (*MissQ* 30: 505–11), an essay which delineates well that which the title sets out. But Guilds's claim that "it is doubtful that any other American author of his time made so extensive or so intelligent use of history in his creative writing" as did Simms, while it may be true from a narrow, quantitative point of view, still does little to dispel Hawthorne's charge that "the real treasures of [Simms's] subject have escaped the author's notice."

If it is as novelist of the American Revolution that Simms primarily is to be remembered, then it is regrettable that his Revolutionary War novels are not to be included in the South Carolina Centennial Edition of his writings. Instead, they have been reissued in a reprint edition in eight volumes (Spartanburg, S.C.: The Reprint Co., 1976) with new introductions and explanatory notes. The notes are of a generally impressive quality, but, in Mary Ann Wimsatt's opinion ("Simms's War Novels," *MissQ* 30:297–304), the introductions fail because they do not treat the novels as literature. Certainly Wimsatt is herself capable of treating Simms's writings as literature, as she demonstrates in "Simms's Early Short Stories" (*LC* 41:163–79). These pieces, written during the time the American short story was being developed by Irving, Hawthorne, Poe, and others, reveal not only the diversity of Simms's early interests and the wide range of his reading, but also show him to have been a successful experimenter in the technical aspects of short fiction and worthy of a significant place in the history of its development.

Simms also should be remembered, according to Jack L. Davis, as one who realized early the tragic implications of the white settlers' inability to learn from the native inhabitants of North America whom they eventually conquered. In an interesting but turgidly written essay, "W. Gilmore Simms' 'Oakatibbe' and the Failure of the Westering Imagination" (*The Westering Experience*, pp. 112–21), Davis interprets Simms's 1845 short story, "Oakatibbe, or the Choctaw Sampson," as an oblique protest against the deplorable policy of genocide in his time, and as an attempt "to awaken white Americans to the positive strengths of aboriginal culture."

The second volume of *The Letters of William Cullen Bryant* (New York: Fordham Univ. Press), superbly edited by William Cullen Bryant II and Thomas G. Voss, brings together the letters for the years 1836 through 1849, a period during which Bryant was chiefly involved in the editorship of the New York *Evening Post*. The correspondence is mostly that of a politically minded journalist, but the travel letters from Europe in 1845 and the Great Lake region the following year are frequently illuminating of Bryant's aesthetics and also entertaining. Such fundamental, primary scholarship, done as in this case meticulously and thoroughly, is essential to the fullest consideration of any author's achievement, and perhaps it makes such considerations more attractive, even of Bryant, whose works have existed too long in a critical limbo.

iii. Popular Writers of the American Renaissance

As with the last several years, this section might better be titled "That Damned Mob of Scribbling Women." The female writers of mid-century have come into their own, and there is no indication they will gracefully retire from the critical marketplace to their parlors in the near future. Nor should they when the attention bestowed upon them is so generally sound, as it is today. That critical sophistication in the treatment of their writings has been singularly lacking in the past is dismayingly testified to by an annotated checklist compiled by Jean W. Ashton, *Harriet Beecher Stowe: A Reference Guide* (Boston: G. K. Hall), a useful companion to Margaret Hildreth's primary bibliography of Stowe (see *ALS 1976*, p. 205). To Ashton's list of hundreds of needless articles which have appeared on Stowe can now be added George B. Bryan's "*Uncle Tom's Cabin* and Vermont" (*Vermont History* 45:35–37), which proposes that Stowe's prolonged water-cure at Brattleboro in the 1840s was responsible for her making Miss Ophelia in the novel a Vermonter.

How Stowe came to write *Uncle Tom's Cabin* is, of course, the most important aspect of her life for students of literature, and they will welcome heartily E. Bruce Kirkham's *The Building of Uncle Tom's Cabin* (Knoxville: Univ. of Tenn. Press). Kirkham's thorough research destroys many myths dear to the popular historian about the composition of Harriet's great-big book. It did not, as Stowe afterwards claimed, begin in a vision; it was not the work of a literary amateur, but the effort of a writer who had been schooled carefully in the tradition of domestic sentimentalism in fiction; and Stowe, like any artist who cared at least in part about his craft, did revise. In his lengthy discussions of the manuscript fragments of the novel and of Stowe's subsequent revisions, all which are charted or reproduced in the book, Kirkham documents the growth of the novel from its conception as "a fairly short serialized story" to its publication as a double-decker in 1852. Though Stowe's reconsiderations and revisions were, in Kirkham's opinion, both good and poor, he does see in them an overall improvement. Unfortunately, Kirkham's labors do not reveal to him the source of the novel's immense and enduring power. "Were there no Negroes in the book, no Legrees, no St. Clares or Shelbys, no products of the [slavery] system," Kirkham explains after the fashion of Carl Van Doren thirty years ago, *Uncle Tom's Cabin* "would be just another sentimental novel. But there are, and so it is not." This is the sort of unperceptiveness that has given editorial scholars a poor reputation as literary critics. It doesn't disqualify the merits of Kirkham's book, but it does limit them.

If the prosaic quality of Kirkham's critical insights is not to be admired, the overingeniousness of Elizabeth Ammons is hardly more desirable in that it threatens to undercut the good sense of her article, "Heroines in *Uncle Tom's Cabin*" (*AL* 49:161–79). Ammons proposes that the objections to Stowe's characterization of Tom are primarily the result of misunderstanding. Those critics hostile to Tom mistakenly regard him as an unsatisfactory hero, whereas he should be seen as an important heroine in the novel. Stowe deliberately feminized Tom, not because she was unable to make him assertively masculine, but because she did not wish to do so. Together with the more conventional heroines in the novel, Tom stands as a model "of an alternative, humane ethic which Stowe envisions as the foundation for an enlightened and equitable new era."

The Stowe-Day Foundation of Hartford, Conn., continues through its admirable publication program to make Stowe's writing better known. A handsome reprint edition of *Poganuc People*, intro. by Joseph S. Van Why, and a descriptive guide to the Stowe manuscripts in the Foundation Library, *The Papers of Harriet Beecher Stowe*, compiled by Margaret Granville Mair, were issued this year under its imprint.

Current fashion rather than scholarly need was obviously the reason for the publication of Martha Saxton's *Louisa May: A Modern Biography of Louisa May Alcott* (Boston: Houghton Mifflin). It tells us nothing of importance that has not been told before; nor is this new telling of an old, essentially uninteresting story either graceful in its manner or even fair to all the participants. The portrait of Alcott that emerges is of an obsessed, self-destructive personality who would never, in spite of her far greater popularity, escape the shadow of her father. Advance publicity announced for the book a subtitle, "Her Father's Daughter," and the chief value of Saxton's book is in its account of the tormented but terribly human relationships in the Alcott family. Alcott's best fiction reflects these tensions, none more than *Work: A Story of Experience*, now reissued with a long introduction by Sarah Elbert (New York: Schocken Books). But it is not the book's autobiographical elements that justify our remembrance, according to Elbert: "*Work* deserves a modern audience, not only as an historical document and a modern literary achievement, but also as a key to understanding the commonality of our daily struggles with those of our mothers and grandmothers."

Just as tremendously popular as Alcott in her time was Elizabeth Stuart Phelps Ward, and it would be attractive to have for consideration a new biography of her. Instead, we must be satisfied with an intelligent essay by Barton Levi St. Armand, "Paradise Deferred: The Image of Heaven in the Work of Emily Dickinson and Elizabeth Stuart Phelps" (*AQ* 29:55–72). However unpleasant it is to modern tastes, Dickinson was deeply enamored with the popular culture of "Victorian" America and quite often failed to distance herself sufficiently from its maudlin and sentimental affectation. But she also found significant meaning and comfort in the images and sensibilities of that same culture, and it is from this point of view that St. Armand addresses us. *The Gates Ajar*, Ward's novel, was one of the great sellers of the 19th century, and, according to St. Armand, the sensibility it exhibits is analogous to Dickinson's poems on the same subjects. "It is the searching exploration of the nature of the heaven to come and the substitution of a warm domestic paradise for the cold orthodox stereotype of a city of pearl and jasper which make *The Gates Ajar* increasingly relevant to the parallel development of Dickinson's poetry."

Interest in the "Fireside Poet" has so dwindled that it probably makes little difference that my critical edition of James Russell Lowell's *The Biglow Papers* [*First Series*] (DeKalb: Northern Ill. Univ. Press) was not published until this year (announced as published in *ALS 1975*, p. 245) and that it never was intended to be the premier volume of a new edition of Lowell's writings. Equally wonderful is Thomas H. Pauly's notion that there are critics (certainly not living) who have misread Longfellow's *Outre-Mer*, an error he wishes to correct with his essay, "*Outre-Mer* and Longfellow's Quest for a Career" (*NEQ* 50:30–52). During the slow composition of this, his first book, "Longfellow was laying a valuable conceptual and aesthetic basis for his future career"; the poet he called for in *Outre-Mer*—"the author of popular ballads and adapter of European poetry to American tastes"—would be his own destiny.

Even the qualified praise of the poetry of Whittier by Robert Penn Warren several years ago (see *ALS 1971*, p. 205) would now appear excessive for the scant response it has elicited were it not for Merrill Lewis's "In Praise of Whittier's 'Pictures'" (*ESQ* 23:244–51), an impressively sensitive response not only to Whittier's little-known poem, "Pictures," published in 1852, but to his pastoral poetry in general. One voice, however eloquent, still does not make a revival, and Whittier's declining reputation is the movement unmistakenly charted by Albert J. von Frank in *Whittier: A Comprehensive Annotated Bibliography* (New York: Garland, 1976).

An enormously worthwhile book that ought to be written is a discriminating account of the Hales of Massachusetts. Certainly there is no dearth of archival material concerning the dynamic family, including one recently opened to scholars at the University of Pennsylvania and described by C. E. Crimmins in "An Assemblage of Politicians, Writers, and Hippopotami: The Elsa Noble Collection" (*LC* 42:71–75). Best known of the family for his writings and the exuberant personality they record was Edward Everett Hale, the subject of a new critical biography by John R. Adams, *Edward Everett Hale* (TUSAS 284). While Adams rightly emphasizes Hale's literary career, he does not attempt a reinterpretation, but instead offers a reminder of what Hale meant to his time. So sympathetic is Adams to his subject, and yet so balanced is his judgment, most readers are likely to share Adams's reluctance to admit in the end that Hale's was only a "footnote achievement."

iv. Henry Adams and Late 19th-Century Nonfiction

What most amazes one about Earl N. Harbert's *The Force So Much Closer Home: Henry Adams and the Adams Family* (New York: New York Univ. Press) is that the book was not written long ago. To view the works of the family-conscious Adams in terms of the family heritage as it existed in his ancestors' writings is an approach that guarantees interesting results. Even one little versed in Adams's biography should readily agree with the thesis that Adams's understanding of himself and the world was largely shaped by the principles and active interests passed down to him by his forebears. As Harbert puts it: " 'Family' offered him a special key to self-understanding, a path for exploring the basic causes of his actions and his thoughts and a unique resource which he made use of in both his writings and his life." When Adams addressed himself to the same issues as had his ancestors, "the family mind" was a source of strength; but when led into new areas of thought, unexplored by family members, "a deep distrust of self" pushed Adams into irony and paradox. On the whole, Harbert's discussion is highly satisfying, casting as it does many interesting lights on Adams's writings. The basically chronological approach employed by Harbert, however, does lead to some irritating repetition, a fault made more apparent by Harbert's too frequent reminders of the book's controlling thesis.

A detailed account of Adams's years in England as secretary to his father, 1861–68, and an assessment of their impact on his subsequent career are the tasks William Dusinberre admirably carries out in "Henry Adams in England" (*JAmS* 11:163–86). According to Dusinberre, Adams's English experience "helped to shape the social purpose which informed the earlier part of his literary career, and they strengthened his artistic integrity." In context, these claims are modest, but nevertheless informing. Even more revealing of the character of Adams's thought and its expression is Elizabeth Waterston's "The Gap in Henry Adams' Education" (*CRevAS* 7[1976]:132–38), a "feminist" explanation not only of the twenty-year lacuna in Adams's account of his life in *The Education*, but also of the curious absence of women from Adams's masterpiece, in spite of his "emphasis on the primacy of sex in determining history." This fact, says Waterston, makes it imperative that we "supplement *The Education of Henry Adams* with another study, the history [of his life] composed to fill in its gaps. In doing so we will clarify the important evolution of Henry Adams—sexist historian." This does seem an excessive demand, considering how durable Ernest Samuels's biography of Adams has proven, but interpretations like this of Waterston of the biographical facts will continue to benefit our understanding.

Henry Adams, the "modern" described by John Carlos Rowe last year (see *ALS 1976*, p. 207–8), continues to attract significant attention. Two essayists especially successful in using *The Education of Henry Adams* as a starting point for their analyses of 20th-century writers are William Wasserstrom, "The Goad of Guilt: Henry Adams, Scott and Zelda" (*JML* 6:289–310), and Jamie Robertson, "Henry Adams, Wallace Stegner, and the Search for a Sense of Place in the West" (*The Westering Experience*, pp. 135–43).

Though its subject lies somewhat outside the perimeters of this survey, Bruce Kuklick's magnificent study of the influential philosophers who taught at Harvard between the Civil War and the Depression, *The Rise of American Philosophy: Cambridge, Massachusetts, 1860–1930* (New Haven and London: Yale Univ. Press) should be called to the attention of students of late 19th-century intellectual life in America. William James naturally figures prominently in this history, as do Charles Sanders Peirce, Josiah Royce, and George Santayana, mentioning only those who achieved literary as well as philosophic fame.

Although its authors claim their intention is not to debunk James, that is the flavor left by the essay, "William James—Warts and All" (*AQ* 29:207–21), by George R. Garrison and Edward H. Madden. Objecting to the eulogistic praise of James as "a significant social activist and reformer" in the standard biographies by Ralph Barton Perry, Gay Wilson Allen, and F. O. Matthiessen, Garrison and Madden point out that not only was James an ineffective reformer "in the areas where he extended himself," but, "moreover, he showed unexpected blind spots on the issues of racism, women's rights, British oppression of the Irish, and British imperialism in general." Still, the authors confess after this litany of shortcomings, "none of what we have written detracts a whit from James' genuine helpfulness to almost everyone he knew." Ignas K. Skrupskelis includes in his *William James: A Reference Guide* (Boston: G. K. Hall) a wonderful category overlooked as yet by stylistic critics of James's admirable prose: "James's Spirit Writings . . . alleged to have been communicated by James through various mediums after his death." The rest of the guide follows convention. Finally, Frederick J. Down Scott edits and provides a useful narrative for letters written during "William James' 1898 Visit to California" (*SJS* 3, i:7–22).

Francis Parkman's *The Oregon Trail* (1849) is generally regarded as a classic description of Indian life, valuable in the ethnological study of Native American culture; but, according to L. Hugh Moore,

"Francis Parkman on the Oregon Trail: A Study in Cultural Prejudice" (*WAL* 12:185–97), Parkman's escape from the pallid and emasculate life of the East "was never real; it was merely physical, never intellectual or emotional." As a result of its author's "deep-rooted cultural prejudices," Parkman's book "unintentionally reveals his own culture while it falsifies the other culture he tried to study." The writings of two later travellers in the West, Clarence King and John Muir, are the subjects of several essays in the current volume of *Exploration*, the Journal of the MLA Special Session on the Literature of Exploration and Travel.

v. Local Color and Literary Regionalism

A regional approach to the study of literature has long been established as one of the most fruitful critical methods, even though it is not in vogue today. It is therefore remarkable that the region whose writers dominated American literature between 1870 and 1930 has been so largely overlooked by literary historians and critics. We do not hesitate to talk about the New England mind or about southern literature, but the mind and art of the Midwest go undefined in the imaginations of most of us. No sooner than we recognize this, however, do we find two publications whose intention is to correct this error of omission. The Society for the Study of Midwestern Literature, founded in 1971 and based at Michigan State University, issues an attractively printed annual, *MidAmerica* (Sherwood Anderson's orthography), which, in its first four volumes, leans mostly to the literary. Less belletristic in outlook is *The Old Northwest: A Journal of Regional Life and Letters*, published by Miami University of Ohio, though in the current volume several articles are directed to students of 19th-century literature.

To the field he has made so much his own, Walter Blair returns once again and the result is a brightly written, instructive, yet pleasant essay, "Americanized Comic Braggarts" (*CritI* 4:331–49), which examines the distinctive features of the alazōn or comic braggart as he evolved in American humor. "When the *miles gloriosus* crossed the Atlantic, trudged on to the frontier and became a ring-tailed roarer, he underwent a change: here he was not a poltroon or a sissy. He was a mighty athlete . . . he was tough." It's a shame such vigor doesn't motivate most of the youngsters who follow after Blair. Neil Schmitz is an exception, however, and his "Tall Tale, Tall Talk: Pursuing the Lie in Jacksonian Literature" (*AL* 48:471–91) is one of the finest pieces on Southwestern Humor in years. Using as illustrative (and illustrious) texts a section of Joseph G. Baldwin's *The Flush Times of Alabama and Mississippi* and Thomas B. Thorpe's "The Big Bear of Arkansas," Schmitz demonstrates that it is the attitude, the mode of the speaker, and not the *mythos* or subject of the tall tale that is significant: "colloquial discourse exists as a language spoken with knowledge and filled with meaning, a discourse speaking the world." Not restricted to dialect or tortured misspelling, tall talkers were those whose speech, "whether polished or rude, reflects their alienation, their secret knowledge of what is and what is said." Enter Melville.

An uncollected "Flush Times" sketch, "Joseph G. Baldwin's 'General Gymm and Colonel Burrows'" (*MidSF* 5:31–37), which first appeared after the publication of Baldwin's volume of sketches in 1853, is reprinted with little editorial benefit or critical justification by L. Moody Simms, Jr. Maurice Duke's "John Wilford Overall's *Southern Punch*: Humor in the Rebel Capital" (*Gerber Festschrift*, pp. 43–58), however, does make a lively case for our remembering this humorous periodical published weekly in Richmond, Virginia, during the bleakest months of the War Between the States.

Most impressive quantitatively of the regional publications this year is Donald R. Noble's edition of George Tucker's futuristic comedy of manners, *A Century Hence: or, A Romance of 1941* (Charlottesville: Univ. Press of Va.), completed in 1841, but unpublished until now. If Tucker (1775–1861), a Virginia politician and economist who sometimes turned his hand to fiction, is not readily remembered, then the names of these 19th-century southern writers—Philip Alexander Bruce, Thomas E. Hogg, William Quesenbury, Edmund Ruffin, and William Henry Sparks—who are subjects of articles this year (see *1977 MLA International Bibliography*), are even less likely to mean anything except to very local enthusiasts. Because of the distinction achieved by his great-grandson, William Clark Falkner fares better in our memory. Calvin S. Brown believes that by looking at the literary quotations, allusions, and references in Falkner's 1881 novel, *The White Rose of Memphis*, we can know approximately what litterature a "general reader" of the South actually knew in the decades following the Civil War. One may be skeptical of this method that Brown employs in "Colonel Falkner As General Reader: *The White Rose of Memphis*" (*MissQ* 30:585–95) or surprised in finding Falkner, the author of several books, classified as a common reader, but no one will find remarkable the findings that Shakespeare, the Bible, and Scott were the Colonel's favorite reading.

Because the craft of fiction was in his time practised at a much higher level than it was in Simms's day, George Washington Cable has never enjoyed the national reputation and critical attention he probably deserves. Arlin Turner does briefly consider in "George W. Cable's Use of the Past" (*MissQ* 30:512–16) the effects of an apprenticeship in historical writing on Cable's mature fiction. Like Hawthorne before him, "Cable saw his city and state and region to be products of historical circumstances and forces. . . . He found in the historical past clues he thought valuable for understanding the present and for resolving current issues." In this, of course, he foreshadows Warren and Faulkner, as he also does in his treatment of race relations, the subject of William Bedford Clark's "Cable and the Theme of Miscegenation in *Old Creole Days* and *The Grandissimes*" (*MissQ* 30:597–609). A devoted reformer, Cable saw in fiction a means to help right the wrongs of his region, the greatest of which was the caste system that had survived slavery in the South. The theme of mixed blood, the problem of miscegenation "exerted a very evocative influence over his creative imagination," according to Clark. The fact of miscegenation served Cable "as a convenient emblem for the South's inheritance of racial wrongs"; the theme served as an index to the complexity of this southern problem which would continue to torment many of Cable's followers.

In a lighter vein is J. John Perret's account of a hoax perpetrated on Cable by Sidonie de la Houssaye, a Louisiana French writer who passed off as fact three of her own fictional creations Cable purchased and collected in *Strange True Stories of Louisiana* (1889). Faced with public humiliation should the fraud be revealed, poor Cable resorted to lying. Part of the humor of Perret's article, "Strange True Stories of Louisiana: History or Hoax?" (*SoSt* 16:41–53), seems unintended, arising as it does from Perret's ambivalent attitude toward the two shysters.

Joel Chandler Harris's ambivalence toward the New South Movement is the subject of Wayne Mixon's "Joel Chandler Harris, The Yeoman Tradition, and the New South Movement" (*GHQ* 61:308–17). Wishing to have us see Harris separate from Thomas Nelson Page and the other plantation romancers with whom he is generally associated, Mixon argues that Harris was more of a traditionalist who "hoped the New South would remain the middle class agrarian democracy he believed much of the Old South had been." In order to maintain this desire, Harris cultivated in both the character of Uncle Remus and his stories of the old regime a myth of the yeoman South, "a white man's democracy." Also caught between traditional values and the new order following the Civil War was Grace King, another southerner whose career, as it is recounted by Robert Bush, reminds us that regionalism addressed itself beyond local barriers. According to Bush's "Grace King: The Emergence of a Southern Intellectual Woman" (*SoR* 13:272–88), it was King's acquaintance with Julia Ward Howe, R. W. Gilder, C. D. Warner, and Lafcadio Hearn in the mid-1880s that was most immediately instrumental in launching King into her literary career.

New England regionalists fared less well this year, though a critical study of *Seba Smith* (TUSAS 283) by Milton and Patricia Rickels is a praiseworthy addition to the familiar Twayne series. Anyone who has worked with Smith's dialect texts, especially the Jack Downing letters, will appreciate the Rickels's success in making their cultural, historical, and linguistic meanings more easily available to modern readers. Smith as a thoughtful, perceptive, political critic, not a dialect humorist, is what interests John H. Schroeder in "Major Jack Downing and American Expansionism: Seba Smith's Political Satire, 1847–1856" (*NEQ* 50:214–33). During this later period of Smith's literary career, he extended his satiric criticism in the Downing letters to include the doctrine of Manifest Destiny and the bombastic American nationalism of the day, both of which Smith attributed to the "new democracy" which had followed on the election to presidency of Andrew Jackson.

Though she admits her findings are only tentative, Priscilla Leder asks several perceptive and important questions about American novels written by women in her article, "The Gifts of Peace: Sarah Orne Jewett's Vision of Romance" (*GyS* 4:27–39). Leder's choice of *The Country of the Pointed Firs* to test the well-known theories about

American fiction advanced by Richard Chase, Leslie Fiedler, and others is especially fortunate. Not only does it bring into clearer focus what has seemed to many questionable assumptions about the nature of American fiction, its anti-social bias, for example; but it also brings to our attention a work that "is much more than a collection of local color types and scenery." As Willa Cather realized, *The Country of the Pointed Firs* is a masterpiece of regional literature that speaks importantly to the universal condition of mankind.

Mary Wilkins Freeman's literary reputation is now so slight that a reminder of her "intelligence and acumen" is indeed welcome, especially when accompanied by the critical intelligence and acumen demonstrated by Alice Glarden Brand in "Mary Wilkins Freeman: Misanthropy as Propaganda" (*NEQ* 50:83–100). Brand examines the relationships between the men and women of Freeman's bleak stories and finds their representation timeless, archetypal. Freeman's cynical view of the rural, parochial world she dealt with changed little during her forty-year career; informing that vision throughout was an unsparing misanthropy: "The social order perpetuated itself by controlling every aspect of rural life. Sex roles were inflexible and inviolate. Men and women shared an understandable yet a pathological need to cling to those roles. They orbited around their partners, working, in effect, to ensnare themselves in unhealthy relationships. The relational aberrations in these stories are indiscriminate and pervasive." Freeman, in the role of "civilized critic of destructive human behaviors," was not entirely negative; "by documenting these behaviors she pressed for their eradication."

Several new titles appeared during the year in the Boise State University Western Writers Series, edited by Wayne Chatterton and James H. Maguire, useful, pamphlet-sized studies resembling the old University of Minnesota Pamphlets on American Writers; and, as with earlier numbers, the scope of the series continues somewhat wide of what is conventionally regarded as literary. Robert L. Gale's *Charles Warren Stoddard* (WWS) could have served a valuable service to literary scholarship, but the effort is wasted owing to Gale's unwarranted and unsavory harshness toward his subject. The essay, mostly composed of plot summaries, at which Gale is a proven master, fails as either literary criticism or interpretive biography. Gale is not completely unaffected by Stoddard's infectious personality—Howells described him to Clemens as that "poor, sweet, pure-hearted, good-intentioned, impotent Stoddard"—or his rare charm as a stylist, but he chooses not to emphasize these merits.

vi. Realism and the Age of Howells

Not since Edwin H. Cady's *The Light of Common Day: Realism in American Fiction* (see *ALS 1971*, pp. 167–68) has there appeared so provocative a consideration of American literary realism as Gary Stephens's "Haunted Americana: The Endurance of American Realism" (*PR* 44:71–84). In fact, it addresses a tantalizing problem some felt Cady's book shied off: considering how dreary and "old-fashioned" most of the fiction produced between 1885–1915 unmistakably is, how is it that it still endures? We may not entirely be persuaded of the validity of Stephens's answers, but his critical reasoning, supported by the examples of Howells, Clemens, Garland, and Dreiser, cannot fail to lure us. The dullness as well as the durable intrigue of realism, Stephens proposes, originates from the same source: the realists wished to create a literature that had "a healing power, a power to discover and convey a sense of unity among things." New, personal eschatologies had to be provided in works of fiction to replace the old religious order that was lost. Furthermore, "the realistic writer hoped that his perception of reality would not only become the vision shared by the culture as a whole but that as a consequence of it the world would change." Stephens's argument concludes with the suggestion that "it is the quasi-religious quality of this literature, the possibility of salvation glimpsed even in the most pessimistic vision, that despite the failure of the realists' public goals, and despite their deep private anxiety, gives their writing a power that transcends their failure."

Of all the charges made against 19th-century realistic novels, the most persistent is that they fail to deal adequately with the sexual motive. Joseph Katz, for whom these novels obviously are neither dull nor regrettably old-fashioned, challenges this general view in a spirited, if not entirely original, essay, "Eroticism in American Literary Realism" (*SAF* 5:35–50). According to Katz, the sexual "sterility of American literary realism is only appearance"; the sophisticated, alert reader will see through to the reality hidden by the fig leaf of decorum. In general principle, it cannot be denied that Katz makes good sense when he advises: "To understand the realists' use of eroticism requires, first, the elemental acceptance of the fact that they did indeed use it; and, second, the development of the ability to read as they wrote." Undoubtedly there are academic bluenoses who will cry foul at Katz's practical application of these principles, though the rest of us will be inclined to add Crane's "Why Did the Young Clerk Swear? Or, the Unsatisfactory French" to our students' reading lists.

With the publication of *A Modern Instance* (Bloomington and London: Ind. Univ. Pres), introduction and notes to the text by George N. Bennett, text established by David J. Nordloh and David Kleinman, "A Selected Edition of W. D. Howells" is one volume short of its halfway mark. My own association with this project prevents me from dealing here with the volume in the manner it deserves, but I do venture to say that it will not diminish a whit the splendid editorial record Nordloh and his colleagues have earned this far. It is also attractive to think the Howells editorial project is largely responsible for the increased interest in Howells, evidenced by the growing number of critical responses to his writings. This number is probably somewhat inflated this year owing to a special issue of *ALR* on Howells and pleasantly dedicated to George Arms by his students and friends. But critical concern with Howells is no longer the domain of the convivial few that it was less than a decade ago; it's gone public. Nor is the "tendency to consign Howells once again too exclusively to the ranks of the fuddy-duddies" at all apparent this year as it was last when Warren French noticed it in this chapter (see *ALS 1976*, p. 215). Whether the "really beautiful time" James predicted for Howells's reputation has or will come does not matter; what is important is that his novels and other writings are being read in a manner remarkable even to the most ardent of Howellsians in whose memory the years of neglect are still fresh.

One result of this enlarging focus is that areas of Howells's art, previously neglected, are receiving intelligent notice. George C. Carrington, Jr., whose work on Howells's major fiction is among the best, now calls our attention to "Howells' Christmas Sketches: The Uses of Allegory" (*ALR* 10:242–53), six little-known sketches Howells wrote for Christmas numbers of Harper's periodicals, five during the troubled years of the 1890s, the sixth in 1915. Carrington encourages us to regard these pieces not as essays, but as allegorical sketches whose persona, the narrative "I," is not Howells speaking in his own voice, but an "independent character, farther from Howells than the first-person narrators of *Suburban Sketches* and *Their Wedding Journey*, but closer to him than Basil March usually is." Allegory, a literary technique not usually associated with Howells's art, allowed him in these sketches "to project uncertainties, anxieties, guilt, and other painful feelings into fiction while concealing, when he wished, the fact that he was doing any such thing."

Similar tensions and uncertainties are found by Kermit Vanderbilt, "The Perception and Art of *Literary Friends and Acquaintance*" (*ALR* 10:289–306), to underlie the charm and geniality of Howells's "matchless volume of literary memoirs." Through the techniques of an "inside narrative," resulting from the double perspective with which Howells views his New England past—the eyes of the young, "uncomplicated esthete," and those of the mature novelist—Howells attempted in *Literary Friends* to achieve a unified sensibility, to find in his lived experience a definable form. Plainly, a crude summary like this cannot begin to suggest the care and complexity of Vanderbilt's critical analysis of this hitherto unexamined classic.

None of the other essays in this special number of *ALR* approaches the level of these two, but David L. Frazier's "Howells' Symbolic Houses: The Plutocrats and Palaces" (pp. 267–79) is quite nice in a minor way. The observation that houses frequently serve in Howells's novels as realistic symbols, pointing inward to illuminate the work, is a critical commonplace, but Frazier's application of it is throughout intelligent and reinforcing. Less successful is Ralph F. Bogardus's "A Literary Realist and the Camera: W. D. Howells and the Uses of Photography" (pp. 231–41), which fails to recognize a genuine historical problem—the primitive state of photography during most of Howells's time (the work of Brady, Eickenmeyer, and Stieglitz, notwithstanding). It is therefore not surprising "that ultimately [Howells] never emerged from his life-long ambivalence about the potential of photography itself and as a positive ally of, and influence on, literature." But admitting this does not diminish the intriguing use of photography in Howells's fiction and criticism. Bogardus has simply missed too much in the work of a man who in old age delighted in going off to the movies with T. S. Perry. Finally, William McMurray's "Moral Law and Justice in Howells' Fiction" (pp. 280–88) is so derivative (especially of his own book on Howells:

see *ALS 1967*, p. 142) and superficial that while there is little to fault, there is even less to praise.

Perhaps Allen F. Stein's "Marriage in Howells's Novels" (*AL* 48: 501–24) is a better article than on first reading it appears. Certainly it does not amount to much to observe that Howells was the first American writer to commit himself in his fiction to a "careful exploration" of the institution of marriage. In fact, the danger has long been that Howells will be remembered only as "the marriage novelist." But Stein goes deeper than this; he sees that without a properly informed awareness of Howells's view of marriage, "one cannot fully understand his overriding vision of life," and he sees that Howells's outlook on marriage was an expanding vision. In the early novels, "marriage enables one to deal with disorder that lurks both in the external world and within oneself"; later, the comfort and stability provided by marriage becomes "a potential means of benefiting society." But when Stein describes the marriage of Atherton and Clara Kingsbury in *A Modern Instance* as "successful," the limitations of his work become all too apparent; the fine irony of Howells has evaded still another worthy critic.

This is not true of Gary A. Hunt, whose critical sophistication in "'A Reality That Can't Be Quite Definitely Spoken': Sexuality in *Their Wedding Journey*" (*SNNTS* 9:17–32) is a worthy match for the subtle complexity of Howells's vision. Hunt distinguishes between two "journeys" in the travel-novel; one geographic, the other psychological; the physical journey symbolic of the interior. Hunt notices that "from beginning to end the novel is permeated by a tone of sexual panic and frustration," something Howells could not have been entirely unconscious of. The violent landscapes—storms, plunging rapids, gaping chasms—the newly married Marches encounter on their journey are translated into the subconscious language of unregulated passion to which neither can satisfactorily respond. The importance of the book for Hunt lies in its "exploration of the psychological dynamics of marriage"; like Whitman and James, Howells was able to transcend "the narrow and false idealism of the 'genteel tradition,'" and revealed at the very outset of his career "the suppressed underside of the Victorian mind."

John Crowley, whose work on psychological themes in Howells's writings has made his name respected among Howellsians, continues his investigations this year with four impressive pieces. In "An Interoceanic Episode: *The Lady of the Aroostook*" (*AL* 49:180–91), Crowley summons T. W. Higginson's 1879 distinction between James's "international episodes" and Howells's "interoceanic episodes," the cultural dialogue implied in the latter being between the Atlantic and the Pacific slopes. "As an international episode," Crowley writes, "*The Lady of the Aroostook* expresses Howells's rejection of Europe; as an interoceanic episode, it suggests his disenchantment with his adopted East." Since neither the "licentiousness of Europe" nor the sexual "repression of the East" is adequate to the "conjugal ideal" James Staniford and Lydia Blood embody, the young couple must in the end seek their "Promised Land" in California. Howells's inability, however, to show the existence of this western paradise constitutes for Crowley the novel's major fault. The parallels Crowley finds in the novel with Hawthorne's *The House of the Seven Gables* and his emphasis on Lydia's sexuality are both essential to his reading of this early Howells novel. Less informing, though thoroughly competent, is Crowley's defense of Howells's 1874 novel, *A Foregone Conclusion*, in which the marriage at the end of Florida Vervain and Henry Ferris is usually discounted as an unjustified "romantic flourish," a victory of the sentimental tastes of Howells's readers over his own artistic integrity. Crowley argues in "'A Completer Verity': The Ending of W. D. Howells' *A Foregone Conclusion*" (*ELN* 14:192–97) that the conclusion does function in the context of the novel as a whole; it is neither happy nor unhappy since the "happy ending"—the couple's marriage—is undercut by tones of melancholy and banality, resulting from the relationship of each to Don Ippolito's tragic life.

While on the question of the enervating effect of Howells's audience on his fiction, it will be appropriate to mention Laurel T. Goldman's rambling essay, "A Different View of the Iron Madonna: William Dean Howells and His Magazine Readers" (*NEQ* 50:563–86). The article contains many errors, far too many to be politely overlooked, and, more damaging, its conclusion does not address the problem set out at the beginning. Goldman wishes to refute the charge that Howells was compromised by the middle-class women readers, especially of the magazines, of his time; but during her performance the focus shifts from an aesthetic question to a sociological one: because of Howells's "sense of community," he was more aware of his readers than was any other contemporary author. And because of this awareness or sensitivity "to the sociology of reading in America," Howells is now the best source of information on late 19th-century authorship in America. Certainly this is an important issue, deserving much more study than it has received. We know so little about the reading public and its relationship to serious literature in 19th-century America that we are not even much tempted to overgeneralize on the subject. Before his death in 1966, William Charvat spelled out some of the economic aspects of this problem, but we have progressed little beyond that point. Goldman's article gives every appearance of being work-in-progress, and she certainly should not be dissuaded from her researches. Even if she fails in the end to command her findings, we cannot help but be benefited by the evidence she uncovers.

In company with Charles L. Crow, Crowley turns to Howells's later fiction in "Psychic and Psychological Themes in Howells' 'A Sleep and a Forgetting' " (*ESQ* 23:41–51). The two provide not only a fine explication of Howells's powerful "psychological" story, but also an informed examination of his shifting psychological theorizings and his ambivalent attitude toward the question of immortality. They remind us that among Howells's many other innovations was his pioneering work in fiction dealing with psychotherapeutic relationships, a popular sub-genre in the 20th century. Finally, in "Howells' Minister in a Maze: 'A Difficult Case' " (*CLQ* 13:278–83), Crowley draws our attention to the striking Hawthornian quality of another of Howells's mature stories whose primary inspiration, Crowley believes, was chapter 20, "The Minister in a Maze," of *The Scarlet Letter*. Howells's story seems to affirm "a willed belief in the ideal of love and a commitment to life itself, whatever its mysteries and imperfections," but like most of Hawthorne's best tales, it ends in "calculated irresolution."

Howells's response to Hawthorne's work has been the subject of considerable commentary in recent years, but Kermit Vanderbilt is the first to suggest the larger context of this transmission. In a far-reaching, though not necessarily far-fetched, essay, "From Passion to Impasse: The Structure of a Dark Romantic Theme in Hawthorne, Howells, and Barth" (*SNNTS* 8[1976]:419–29), Vanderbilt speculates "on how the Hawthorne legacy with its Howellsian coloring may have been transmitted into the present century in a representative work like John Barth's *End of the Road*." As Vanderbilt demonstrated some years ago (see *ALS 1968*, p. 150), Howells "reassembled the components" of Hawthorne's *The Scarlet Letter* in *A Modern Instance*, but he did not resist, as had Hawthorne, their dark conclusion: "the exhaustion and soilure of American mind and spirit, with the life-energies of his principal characters working counter to each other." Howells is more devastating than Hawthorne "in rejecting the adaptability of his American characters," or to use the phrase of Henry James, "in sounding 'a terrible sense of human abysses.'" Quoting Atherton's final words in the novel—"Ah! I don't know! I don't know!"—Vanderbilt argues that "had American fiction gone forward from this ending—relativistic, bleak, exhausted, and dehumanized"—long-genre fiction "might have had to self-destruct." But Howells "recharted his course into a somewhat more affirmative, quasi-Tolstoyian esthetic," and the genre survived another seventy years.

Ever since the appearance of Edwin H. Cady's modern edition of *The Shadow of a Dream* in 1962, Howells's novella has gradually achieved a leading place in his fiction. Now, in an illuminating explication, "Howells's *Oresteia*: The Union of Theme and Structure in *The Shadow of a Dream*" (*AL* 49:57–69), Barbara L. Parker demonstrates that Howells's short novel is not an anomaly in the canon of his fiction; its antiromanticism and its moral thrust both render the work thoroughly Howellsian. Parker takes as her point of departure Aeschylus' *Oresteia*, whose elements she sees Howells reshaping "to elucidate his characteristic theme of complicity."

Though it is irresponsible to declare a subject beyond the need of further study, an article like Harry Walsh's "Tolstoy and the Economic Novels of William Dean Howells" (*CLS* 14:143–65) might tempt one to commit such an indiscretion. After reexamining the well-known and well-documented sources of Howells's social philosophy, Walsh arrives at this truly remarkable and absolutely indefensible position (if its terms mean anything at all): "Howells rejected the deterministic doctrines which dominated intellectual life in the second half of the nineteenth century; he represents, through his Tolstoyism, an epigonic outcropping of the perfectibilist substratum which underlay transcendentalism." Alexander Fodor's "The Acceptance of Leo Tolstoy in the United States" (*RS* 45:73–81) does serve a worthwhile service in reminding us that it was not until the 1890s that Tolstoy attained true popularity in America, and then largely as a result of Howells's enthusiasm; before the 1890s, Tolstoy's writings were known only to a few Americans.

Whereas Howells and the Russians appears to the adventuring scholar a well-charted territory, Howells and the Spanish is virtually untrodden. This is especially remarkable when one remembers Howells's youthful passion and his life-long interest in the language and literature of Spain. Though neither of two recent studies in the area of this important topic are satisfactory, they may augur further activity. Angel Capellán Gonzalo brings to his essay, "William Dean Howells and Armando Palacio Valdés: A Literary Friendship" (*REH* 10[1976]:451–71), a thorough knowledge of Spanish literary history of modern times, but his critical acumen is regrettably amateurish. More promising and far more ambitious is the work of Mary Ruth Wisehart, whose dissertation, "A Literary Kinship: William Dean Howells and Six Spanish Novelists" (*DAI* 37:5133A–34A), studies Howells's response to the writings of Cervantes, Blasco Ibáñez, Palacio Valdés, Pérez Galdós, Juan Valera, and Pardo Bazán.

Except for the "monotones" of *Stops of Various Quills*, Howells's poetry has been passed over by the critics, an understandable slight considering the conventional quality of most, though not all, of it. Nor was Howells's poetics any more notable in its originality. One then wonders why Valden Madsen thinks it necessary that we be reminded of "W. D. Howells's Formal Poetics and His Appraisals of Whitman and Emily Dickinson" (*WWR* 23:103–09); he neither offers anything we had not known before nor points out anything we are in the slightest danger of forgetting. Robert Rowlette's saga "William D. Howells' 1899 Midwest Lecture Tour" (*ALR* 10:125–67) has reached its third and presumably last installment. Unfortunately, this detailed account of Howells's tour through the Middle West is badly marred because Rowlette did not consult the unpublished letters Howells wrote while on the road. I have tried in "W. D. Howells' 1899 Midwest Lecture Tour: What the Letters Tell" (forthcoming, *ALR*, Autumn 1978) to correct Rowlette's factual errors.

Unless one has at hand a complete file of *Life*, the old magazine of humor, Robert C. Leitz's "Howells in *Life*, 1883–1920: An Annotated Checklist" (*RALS* 7:53–69) will be practically useless. E. R. Hagemann was able to turn such research into something genuinely amusing and of potential scholarly promise (see *ALS 1968*, pp. 86–

87); Leitz merely shows he has patience, perseverance, and a rather uninspired imagination.

Howells appears significantly in Jules Chametzky's *From the Ghetto: The Fiction of Abraham Cahan* (Amherst: Univ. of Mass. Press), especially the fourth chapter, which examines Howells's role in Cahan's development as a novelist. In light of Chametzky's explicit prejudices, his treatment is exceedingly fair: Howells's boldness in supporting Cahan when no one else came to his defense "helped to broaden and enrich the country's literary heritage." But this achievement is diminished for Chametzky by the ambivalence middle-class Howells felt toward the Jewish immigrants.

On the whole, the year's work on Howells is invigorating. The essays of Crowley, Carrington, Vanderbilt, Hunt, and others begin to make up for the years nobody read Howells and nobody much cared, years when Gordon Milne's chapter on Howells in *The Sense of Society: A History of the American Novel of Manners* (Rutherford, N.J.: Fairleigh Dickinson Univ. Press) might have passed for criticism. But perhaps times were never that bad.

Rebecca Harding Davis's "Life in the Iron-Mills" generally figures in literary histories as an important forerunner of realistic fiction, but Walter Hesford, "Literary Contexts of 'Life in the Iron-Mills'" (*AL* 49:70–85), believes the 1861 story is better appreciated when placed in other literary contexts: the achievement of Hawthorne in the romance; the tradition of the British social novel as represented in the works of Gaskell, Disraeli, and Kingsley; and "the religious, apocalyptic bias of mid-nineteenth-century American literature." As a transitional work, Davis's story could be expected to extend the accomplishments of the past as well as to prepare for those to come, and Hesford's intelligent inquiry advances modestly but genuinely our understanding of this crucial period in American literature when its fiction was searching for new modes of expression. The only other significant contribution this year to the scant scholarship on this neglected period is George Monteiro's edition of "'The Minstrel': An Unpublished Story by John Hay" (*BBr* 25:27–42), a slight piece of juvenilia set in the Middle Ages and probably written in the late 1850s.

Martin Bucco makes the most of the limited space of his *E. W. Howe* (WWS 26) by focusing on the one work of Howe still read, *The Story of a Country Town.* This pioneering study of small-town life "blasted the Jeffersonian garden with the raw winds of Darwinism and Necessity and stressed Western drabness and tragic failure." Especially interesting are Bucco's psychological speculations based on the book's autobiographical elements. Also biographical in its approach is R. Jackson Wilson's "Experience and Utopia: The Making of Edward Bellamy's *Looking Backward*" (*JAmS* 11:45–60). Like other utopian writers of his time (William Morris, for example), Bellamy disguised his fear of industrialism "by an apparent acceptance of technology"; but on close reading of the romance one sees that an Emersonian concept of nature is the mechanism that awakens the desire for a more perfect community. The pastoral, substantially preindustrial landscape that characterizes Bellamy's Boston of A.D. 2000 is one of several indications that Bellamy's utopia was neither futuristic nor technological, "conceived not in hope or expectation but in nostalgia." Wilson locates the origin of this intellectual retreat in Bellamy's own early failure in the marketplace, and he explicates Bellamy's social program in its light. At one point in the essay, Wilson comments: "Bellamy's own perception of the relationship between his biography and the nature of *Looking Backward* was extremely confused and contradictory." It is unfortunate the editors of *SFS* were unaware of this when they decided to reprint without any comment "Documents in the History of Science Fiction: Edward Bellamy. How I Came to Write *Looking Backward*" (4:194–95).

Though largely forgotten, *The Anglomaniacs* (1890) by Constance Cary Harrison is a delightful comedy of manners, and it is pleasant to notice that Elizabeth Hardwick has included it in the list of novels she is responsible for reprinting in a series called Rediscovered Fiction by American Women (New York: Arno). For those who would know more about Harrison, there is Dorothy M. Scura's competent but somewhat pedestrian survey of her life and writings, "Homage to Constance Cary Harrison" (*SHR* 10[Bicent. iss. 1976]: 35–46) Another of Howells's popular contemporaries whose work is remembered this year is E. P. Roe, the author of many religious novels. Cecil Finley's "E. P. Roe: Successful and Sentimental Religious Novels" (*GrLR* 4:26–34) is general in outlook, but "The New and Regenerated Adams of E. P. Roe" (*MarkhamR* 6:21–26) by Dennis E. Minor neatly explicates two of Roe's most successful novels, *Barriers Burned Away* (1872) and *Opening a Chestnut Burr* (1874), in terms of the American Adam "myth."

There were the usual number of articles on late 19th-century pulp fiction, but only a few are sufficiently distinguished to be mentioned. Victor A. Kramer usefully reexamines an explanation advanced some years ago by Robert Falk (see *ALS 1964*, p. 111) of the seemingly curious emphasis in Horatio Alger's stories upon resignation and dependence. Ironically, Kramer points out in "Alger's Call for Resignation" (*MarkhamR* 6:49–54), instead of inspiring their readers to success, Alger's books may have had the reverse effect, "since an awareness of possible defeat is also significant throughout this fiction." "The Indian and Juvenile Novels, 1865–1900" (*Dartmouth Col. Lib. Bull.* 17:53–73) is a somewhat misleading title for an article by Samuel F. Pickering, Jr., since only the stories of Alger, "Harry Castleman" (pseudonym of Charles A. Fosdick), and Edward Ellis are included in the survey. The depiction of the cowboy in dime novels between 1850–1900 is the subject of Clifford Westermeier's "The Cowboy—His Pristine Image" (*S. Dak. Hist.* 8:1–23).

A genuine need for sophisticated critical analysis of the so-called "Genteel Poets" is partly satisfied by Robert J. Scholnick, *Edmund Clarence Stedman* (TUSAS 286). The format of the Twayne books, restricting for so many authors, proves in this instance an advantage. Especially commendatory is the book's fourth chapter, "Between Poe and Emerson: An Aesthetic Theory," in which Scholnick assesses Stedman's major critical work, *The Nature and Elements of Poetry* (1892), in terms of native artistic and intellectual traditions. Scholnick avoids the trap that too frequently ensnares the critic who turns his attention to a minor achievement like Stedman's: he does not diminish the genuine greatness of 19th-century American poetry and poetics by exaggerating Stedman's place in that tradition. Altogether, the book is a model of restraint and critical discrimination.

vii. Fin de Siècle America: Stephen Crane and the 1890s

The best of the year's work on Stephen Crane was primarily focused on his stories about the West, but even this tended to the superficial. Perhaps Crane's slender achievement has been adequately measured for the present time, and all we shall encounter in the near future will be derivative and reiterative work. At least the critical seriousness with which readers approached Crane's writings a decade ago has been replaced by a less strenuous and somewhat peripheral attitude. The year's one important exception, Glen M. Johnson's "Stephen Crane's 'One Dash—Horses': A Model of 'Realistic' Irony" (*MFS* 23: 571–78), supports this impression; not only does the title, with its focus on one of Crane's lesser-known stories, belie the general importance of the article, but the editors of *MFS* relegate the piece to the "Notes and Discussion" section of their journal.

Johnson's is indeed an impressive reading of Crane's 1895 story, the earliest of his published attempts to work with Western materials and forms; but it is even more important as an analysis—at times too sketchy—of "realistic" irony. Setting the story in a context with "The Five White Mice" and "The Bride Comes to Yellow Sky," Johnson arrives at this general observation: "Crane exploits both satire and expressionistic techniques for comic purposes; his goal is the realist's goal of providing usable insights into 'the way things happen.' " Basic to Crane's narrative technique, structured by a dialectical progression, are two levels of perception: the internal, subjective, limited perspective of the characters and the ironic point of view of the narrator; the first utilizing the techniques of literary expressionism, the other of distancing satire.

Crane's discovery of the West was an important event in the development of his talent. Throughout his youthful career, Crane was remarkably responsive to popular legends and traditions, as Donald Vanouse points out in "Popular Culture in the Writings of Stephen Crane" (*JPC* 10[1976]:424–30), but true to his penetrating vision he persisted in seeing through to the sterner reality behind the clichés and easy patterns of popular explanations. The Matter of the Wild West provided Crane's ironic vision with popular materials rich for exploitation in his stories, or as James L. Dean puts it in "The Wests of Howells and Crane" (*ALR* 10:254–66): "The undercivilized West Crane dramatized often allows its characters to remain young and, after a fashion, innocent. These characters seem like child-men, and the West they inhabit is, in some respects at least, an extraordinarily large play area in which frequent skirmishes occur between often boyish men. Though the consequences of the game these men play are sometimes fatal, the games are played with all the seriousness and all the improvised rules common to backyard childhood." But behind the childish adventure lies that "dark something" Crane's characters are rarely far from: "Generally it signals a moment of anguish," Dean explains, "or terror, or the presence of a complex moral situation not understood by innocence. This 'something' also ends the games of childhood and intimates death."

The effort to free Crane's art from the stigma of literary naturalism continues in a generally satisfying piece by Chester L. Wolford, "The Eagle and the Crow: High Tragedy and Epic in 'The Blue Hotel' " (*PrS* 51:260–74). The reason Crane's writings have endured, Wolford argues, is not because he responded only to the passing movements and ideas of his time, but because he drew on the resources of such classical genres as epic and tragedy. It is Wolford's belief "that 'The Blue Hotel' gains much of its universality and greatness from the fact that it draws upon epic and tragedy—epic, generally, in terms of the story's implications about the American West, and tragedy, specifically, in terms of the story's form."

The appeal of Crane's writings to proponents of various critical fads remains sufficiently strong to give us two articles which, failing to advance our understanding of Crane's artistry, at least do not hide his essential power. Shannon Burns and James A. Levernier's "Androgyny in Stephen Crane's 'The Bride Comes to Yellow Sky' " (*RS* 45:236–43) can be recommended to those desiring to pep up their undergraduate lecture notes, but "Stephen Crane's *Maggie*: The Death of the Self" by Robert J. Begiebing (*AI* 34:50–71) is so bemired in psychoanalytic jargon that its defense of Crane's revisions in the story between the 1893 and 1896 texts will probably be too readily discounted by the majority who read the article.

Several short notices provide useful insights into the means of Crane's art. In "The Artful Monstrosity of Crane's Monster" (*SSF* 14:403–05), Ruth Betsy Tenenbaum examines Crane's "indirect method" of conveying the impression, central to the meaning of "The Monster," of the town's monstrous behavior. This Crane does by frequently associating with the townspeople animal and mechanical imagery and by "having the characters use mechanical language." Crane's employment of "The Game of High-Five in 'The Blue Hotel' " (*AL* 49:440–42) assumes symbolic importance for James Ellis and underscores for him the validity of the Easterner's explanation of the events of the story. Though no longer than a conventional note, Paul Witherington's "Public and Private Order in Stephen Crane's 'The Upturned Face' " (*MarkhamR* 6:70–71) is in fact an excellent, brief reading of Crane's last war story and deserves wider attention than it is likely to attract. Finally, Clarence O. Johnson, "Crane's 'Experiment in Misery'" (*Expl* 35:20–21), questions whether Crane knew as much about assassin beetles as Thomas Bonner supposed last year when he wrote about the "bestial characteristics" of Crane's "assassin" in "Experiment in Misery" (see *ALS 1976*, p. 219); the newspaper piece Bonner used as evidence of Crane's knowledge was in fact a literary hoax.

The first volume of the new Frederic edition is *The Correspondence of Harold Frederic*, edited by George E. Fortenberry, Stanton Garner, and Robert H. Woodward, text established by Charlyne Dodge (Fort Worth: Texas Christian Univ. Press), which gathers "all known letters to and from Frederic." That I managed to locate three letters not caught by the editors—two to Talcott Williams dated August 28, 1893, and March 26, 1895, and located at Amherst College, and one to Mr. Schidrowitz, July 14, 1897, owned by the Morristown (N.J.) National Historical Park—only indicates that I am clever enough to use the revised edition of *American Literary Manuscripts* (see "Bibliographical Addendum"), which probably appeared after the Frederic *Correspondence* was in press. It is on all counts an impressive performance, and the editors' rationale in making this the premier volume exemplary; "since neither an adequate biography nor a previous edition of [Frederic's] letters is available" the editors decided to make these documents that will "be called upon time and time again by editors of subsequent volumes" available to all readers from the first.

A story by Frederic, "The Editor and the Schoolma'am," first published in the *New York Times* in 1888, is reprinted with a brief introduction by L. Brent Bohlke (*PrS* 50:306–28); the irony of such a venture as this is that the microfilm edition of the *Times* is probably more readily available to most interested persons than is the *Prairie Schooner*. Much more valuable is "Harold Frederic's Earliest Publications" (*ALR* 10:168–90), an edition by George Monteiro and Philip B. Eppard of five pieces by Frederic on politics and religion that appeared in a quasi-religious weekly, *The Index*, in 1875 and 1876.

Interest in Frank Norris in 1977 was even more meagre, the quietly unpretentious defense of "The Erratic Design of Frank Norris's *Moran of the Lady Letty*" (*ALR* 10:114–24) by Joseph R. McElrath, Jr., being the only item of merit. The promising subject of Joseph J. Kwiat's "The Social Responsibilities of the American Painter and Writer: Robert Henri and John Sloan; Frank Norris and Theodore Dreiser" (*CentR* 21:19–35) is not carried off, the essay rarely rising above the level of commonplace observation.

The renewed interest in midwestern literature noted earlier in this chapter naturally extends to the "Chicago School of Fiction" heralded by Howells as the new future of American literature nearly eighty years ago. Kenny J. Williams points out in " 'The Past Is Prologue'—Chicago's Early Writing" (*MidAmerica IV*, pp. 56–73) that the businessman was already established as cultural hero in Chicago writing long before the appearance in print of Fuller, Herrick, and Dreiser. Still, the conflict between the new "business morality" and traditional ethical and aesthetic concerns weighed heavily on the imaginations of Chicago's leading novelists, as the example of Henry Blake Fuller so brilliantly demonstrates. Those familiar with Fuller's writings know how torn he was throughout his life between the romance of the Old World, especially Italy, and the commonplace realities of the New, for him Chicago. Kenneth Scambray describes this paradox intelligently in "From Etruria to Naples: Italy in the Works of Henry Blake Fuller" (*ItalAm* 3:56–71): "While he yearned to portray the essence of precious Italy in his romances, the Old World's past still remained too intimidating and oppressive for his American characters." What gives substance to Scambray's otherwise tame speculations and observations is his liberal use of unpublished materials in the Fuller collection at the Newberry Library.

While one can easily imagine a more useless piece of "scholarship" than Charles L. P. Silet's *Henry Blake Fuller and Hamlin Garland: A Reference Guide* (Boston: G. K. Hall), to do so does little to redeem the failings of this annotated checklist. Not only is the volume poorly executed, but in conception the work is badly flawed. Especially unfortunate is the compiler's decision not to include contemporary reviews of either author's books, though there are some notable exceptions. This omission is a serious error, especially in the case of Garland whose final importance is likely to be the role he played in what Stephen Crane called "the beautiful war" between the romanticists and the realists. The journalistic response to his writings was one of the important theaters of that literary war, giving Garland a significance far out of proportion to his meager aesthetic worth.

Nancy Bunge's "Walt Whitman's Influence on Hamlin Garland" (*WWR* 23:45–50) seems to approach as near definitiveness as one should expect in an imperfect world, though her conclusions are hardly startling: "Whitman clearly influenced the principles and aspirations of Garland's work, however slight his impact on its form. Garland's later 'disenchantment' with Whitman stemmed not from an abrogation of the ideals he absorbed from him, but from doubts they would ever be realized."

More revealing is an essay by Robert Gish whose interest in "Hamlin Garland's Northwest Travels: 'Camp' Westering" (*The Westering Experience*, pp. 94–105) is "in the disparity between what Garland says or seems to intend to say and how he actually sounds." For example, "intending in *The [Trail of the] Goldseekers* to sound tough and up to the test, a clean liver, a leader of men and horses, a noted author . . . Garland reveals himself in outlandish, hysterical and unintentionally humorous voices of priggish condescensions and gothic garrulity." The effect is that most embarrassing of literary failings, bathos. More talented than either Fuller or Garland, Robert Herrick never has enjoyed the attention they occasionally receive. Friedrich W. Horlacher does at least give us "An Annotated Checklist of Robert Herrick's Contributions to the *Chicago Tribune*" (*ALR* 10:191–210), and for this thorough piece of workmanship future critics of Herrick's writings should be thankful.

Popular interest in Ambrose Bierce continues, just as the critical response to his writings remains slight. Edward Wagenknecht has put together an excellent anthology of *The Stories and Fables of Ambrose Bierce* (Owings Mills, Md.: Stemmer House) obviously designed for general trade; his introduction to the well-chosen selection is nicely balanced, the emphasis quite properly on Bierce's literary productions rather than on his curious biography. B. S. Field, Jr., does try to generate some critical interest in "Ambrose Bierce as a Comic" (*WHR* 31:173–80), but his efforts seem largely unsuccessful. If judged as a comic writer—as he should be—Bierce's "position among the traditions of American literature takes on a new perspective," Field argues; his work is that of "a joker and a practitioner of *humor noir*." F. J. Logan also thinks Bierce is a victim of being misread by the critics, especially in the case of his deservedly well-known story, "An Occurrence at Owl Creek Bridge." "It is unfortunate," Logan writes in "The Wry Seriousness of 'Owl Creek Bridge' " (*ALR* 10:101–13), "that the story should be generally valued for its accidents and not for its essence." It is not "a war yarn with a gimmicky ending," as even such luminaries as Brooks and Warren would have us believe. "Bierce knew what he was doing," Logan explains, "and we can know what he did. . . . The [story's] logic lets us know that we are participating in a hallucination, and that whatever else the reality behind the hallucination may be, it is not tragedy."

George Arms, Warner Berthoff, Kenneth Eble, Per Seyersted, George M. Spangler, and Larzer Ziff are some of the critics who come under Priscilla Allen's spirited wrath in "Old Critics and New: The Treatment of Chopin's *The Awakening*" (*The Authority of Experience: Essays in Feminist Criticism*, edited by by Arlyn Diamond and Lee R. Edwards [Amherst: Univ. of Mass. Press], pp. 224–38). As is usual with this sort of negative criticism, Allen is more successful in pointing out the errors of her predecessors than she is in establishing a reading of her own. "*The Awakening* is a far more revolutionary novel than any of the critics have realized," she tells us. "What gives it its shock effect today (for it still has that power) and its relevance is that it is a portrait of a woman determined to have full integrity, full personhood—or nothing."

Perhaps the cause for so much misunderstanding about the meaning of *The Awakening* is owing to Chopin's own inability to admit to the full consequences of her vision; at least this is the suggestion of Paula S. Berggren in "'A Lost Soul': Work without Hope in *The Awakening*" (*RFI* 3:1–7). Chopin's "great theme is not simple freedom but self-hood, and her writings acknowledge that apparent self-sacrifice may be as sure a road to self-enhancement as frank self-absorption." But if work "is the soul's salvation for many of Chopin's characters," for most of her women "'careerist' self-discipline precludes the possibility of love." In *The Awakening* a happy medium between Mme Ratignolle, the embodiment of motherhood, and Mlle Reisz, the artist, was for Chopin "almost impossible to strike." As a result, Edna's work is aimless, purposeless: "her gestures lack proportion because she lacks commitment."

In "Kate Chopin's *At Fault* and *The Awakening*: A Study in Structure" (*MarkhamR* 7:10–14), Thomas Bonner, Jr., uses the structuring techniques of the two novels to measure Chopin's growth as an artist during the ten years that separated their publication. *At Fault* (1890) "reveals a writer conscious of the form and tradition of the novel, but one unsure of her skills"; whereas *The Awakening* (1899), "with its unified, coherent, and often poetic narrative," exhibits a mature artist in full command of the resources of her craft.

One important technical aspect of the art of fiction—the handling of time—is the focus of Emily Toth's "Timely and Timeless: The Treatment of Time in *The Awakening* and *Sister Carrie*" (*SoSt* 16: 271–76). Though in plot and reception the two novels are superficially similar, they differ significantly in their treatment of time. "The rhythm of *Sister Carrie* is purposeful, causal, and linear, correlating with Dreiser's materialism; *The Awakening* is lyrical, epiphanic, concerned with moments of consciousness rather than upward striving." Would Toth had stopped there, but she does not. "Dreiser's *Sister Carrie* . . . follows a masculine model of incremental public success; Chopin's *Awakening* is more concerned with the private or feminine sphere, with the growth of awareness in its central female character, who in effect gives birth to herself." Perhaps this sort of analysis has some of the elementary virtues of a heuristic device, but finally it seems to confuse more than it reveals. That it is very much in fashion, there can be no doubt.

University of California, Los Angeles

13. Fiction: 1900 to the 1930s

David Stouck

With the exception of Cynthia Griffin Wolff's study of Edith Wharton there was no significant new critical ground broken in the scholarship on individual authors. There were some valuable bibliographies published and some perceptive papers on special topics, but the most stimulating essays in 1977 were on general themes and on the literature of the period as a whole.

In a truly perceptive essay entitled "Haunted Americana: The Endurance of American Realism" (PR 44:71–84) Gary Stephens points out that realists (or naturalists) supplanted the quasi-religious vision of the popular melodramas with a carefully documented view of reality and hoped that by delineating ugliness and injustice in the present they would hasten an age of beauty and progress. But the realists, argues Stephens, could not provide an eschatology to replace the religious reassurances of the melodramas so that their fictions are period pieces, weighted down with great masses of observed detail lacking spiritual significance and haunted by the hopes and dreams they failed to realize. The characters in such fictions, says Stephens, lose faith in the popular myths they live by and are left to confront the void of daily life. Dreiser's *An American Tragedy* is used to exemplify the pattern and Clyde Griffiths's dream of success is deadly when tested against reality, writes Stephens, for it gives way to the electric chair, "the void left by religion and a lost idea of America." Another response was to retreat into fantasy. In "The Land of Oz and the American Dream" (*MarkhamR* 5[1976]:21–24) Barry Bauska argues that when the physical frontier had disappeared by 1900 American writers began inventing new frontiers, and one of these was the Utopia of Baum's *The Wizard of Oz*. Baum's book, says Bauska, was America's first native fairy tale and is characteristically American in that equality, openness, and goodness prevail in Oz.

Linda W. Wagner's "Tension and Technique: The Years of Greatness" (*SAF* 5:64–77) examines collectively the novels written in the early part of the century and searches out their most durable characteristics. She sees American fiction of the "modern" period unified by an obsession with craft, by an absorption with its unique Americanness, and especially by a sense of wonder and promise. The novels of Dreiser, Cather, and Anderson, says Wagner, are rich in characterization, but most lasting are those books like *The Great Gatsby* and Faulkner's novels which center on the process of development rather than on presentation of the character that results. Barry Gross's essay "In Another Country: The Revolt from the Village" (*Mid-America* 4:101–11) looks at some of the same novels and argues that the "revolt" against the Midwest and its culture was largely the impression of outside critics like Mencken and not the feeling of midwestern writers themselves. *Winesburg, Ohio*, observes Gross, is nostalgic for the village, in *The Great Gatsby* the west is the center of security for Nick Carraway, and in Willa Cather's novels the farm and village are deplored only when they have yielded to the false values of progress. One cannot do justice in a summary to the richness of these four essays; they all make valuable contributions to appreciating the literature of this period.

i. Theodore Dreiser

From the vast storehouse of Dreiser's miscellaneous nonfictional prose Donald Pizer has put together a volume entitled *Theodore Dreiser: A Selection of Uncollected Prose* (Detroit: Wayne State Univ. Press) which surveys the full range of Dreiser's ideas and interests, from his earliest journalism in 1892 until 1945, the year of his death. In the introduction Pizer states that he has tried to make available three kinds of writing: material representing major moments in the history of Dreiser's thought; commentary by the author on the origin and nature of his novels; and pieces which display the range of Dreiser's ideas. In his introductory essay Pizer gives consideration to the matter of consistency in Dreiser's thought and suggests that the paradoxes and shifts of emphasis in Dreiser's ideas have a "permanent center in his belief that life is a constant flux in which the individual counts for nought as opposites seek, but never achieve, balance." Pizer traces the kernel of Dreiser's thinking back to Herbert Spencer's idea of equation and reproduces an essay in which Dreiser lavishly lauds the British philosopher. Pizer also points out that two themes —the artist's role and the philosopher's quest for truth—run throughout Dreiser's writing. This will be a useful volume for Dreiser scholars and students. What is especially valuable is to have reproduced here philosophical pieces from *Ev'ry Month*, the now rare magazine which Dreiser edited from 1895–97, and some of the essays written from 1926–45 which have not been available in convenient form before.

While not strictly scholarship, Philip L. Gerber's *Plots and Characters in the Fiction of Theodore Dreiser* (Hamden, Conn.: Archon Books) is a potentially useful research tool, designed to provide scholar and student with quick access to information in Dreiser's novels. In a preface Gerber justifies the need for such a volume by pointing out that Dreiser wrote long, complicated books with significant characters numbering as many as 180 in one book. Moreover, says Gerber, Dreiser's characters, forever rootless and adapting to new situations, often employ aliases (the heroine of *Sister Carrie* for example has five names) and these are more easily accounted for with a reference book of names. The plot summaries are well written, providing much detail in a very economical form. This is a worthwhile addition to Robert L. Gale's "Plots and Characters" series.

Jack Salzman has edited a special Dreiser number for volume 23 of *Modern Fiction Studies* with essays covering a wide range of topics and approaches. The best two essays are both on *Sister Carrie*. In "Carrie's Sister: The Popular Prototypes for Dreiser's Heroine" (pp. 395–407) Cathy N. and Arnold E. Davidson describe the kinds of fiction popular in the late 19th century (the "working girl" novel, the "costume" romance, the Horatio Alger story) and show how in *Sister Carrie* Dreiser controverts almost all the conventional patterns of morality in these types of fiction. In "Dreiser at the World's Fair: The City without Limits" (pp. 369–79) Guy Szuberla argues that in *Sister Carrie* Dreiser reverses the American pastoral myth and shows his protagonist finding a world of infinite possibilities not on the wilderness frontier but in the city. Dreiser's sense of an "urban sublime," says Szuberla, was derived in large part from his experience of the White City at the 1893 Chicago World's Fair.

A good psychoanalytical reading of Dreiser appears in Robert Forrey's "Theodore Dreiser: Oedipus Redivivus" (pp. 341–54). Dreiser's development, argues Forrey, was arrested at a stage when the child rejected his harsh and often absent father and identified with his mother. Thus in Dreiser's early fiction, says Forrey, we find young women such as Carrie and Jennie who are viewed sympathetically by the author and are betrayed by the older men in their lives. In the figures of Frank Cowperwood and Clyde Griffiths, says Forrey, Dreiser poses as the virile, powerful son, but relations with women are haunted by the Oedipal taboo, and like Dreiser himself these characters are caught up in self-destructive pursuits of young women who pose no reminder of the maternal relation. In another psychological study, "Dreiser's Other Tragedy" (pp. 449–56), Frederic E. Rusch tells us that the murder of a girl by an ambitious young man was not the only type of crime that interested Dreiser, but that he was also interested in sex crimes that brought great shame upon a family. In this light Rusch discusses Dreiser's play, *The Hand of the Potter*, relating it to the newspaper account of a twelve-year-old girl murdered in the Bronx in 1912 and to the fictional tragedy of Solon Barnes, whose son is involved in a sex crime in *The Bulwark*. Another less popular work is treated in Dorothy Klopf's "Theodore Dreiser's *The 'Genius'*: Much Matter and More Art" (pp. 441–48). Klopf defends Dreiser's *Künstlerroman* as an effective and influential book and argues that this "study of Eugene Witla's spiritual fall from an ideal to the material comprises Dreiser's most incisive critique of the American Dream."

Less successful are those essays which try to explain inconsistencies and failures in Dreiser's fiction. Such is Paul A. Orlov's essay, "The Subversion of the Self: Anti-Naturalistic Crux in *An American Tragedy* (pp. 457–72). Orlov argues that in *An American Tragedy*, in spite of Dreiser's mechanistic philosophy, man does have genuine individuality and that "the intrinsic reality and importance of identity in Clyde [Griffiths] and Roberta Alden is the source of the tragic import of their lives and deaths." In "Dreiser's Defense of Carrie Meeber" (pp. 381–93) Max Westbrook argues that Dreiser's defense of Carrie does not rest simply in a philosophy of mechanistic determinism, but acquires power from his attack on the Lamarckian version of social evolution, on the country's single-stranded morality, and on an insufficient awareness of the power of environment to influence and usurp individual responsibility. And in "The Disproportion of Sadness: Dreiser's *The Financier* and *The Titan*" (pp. 409–22) John O'Neill argues that Dreiser's great theme was the gap between man's dreams and the reality of the world around him, but that this theme disappears in the Cowperwood novels where we see Cowperwood mechanically mastering both objects and people. *The Financier*, writes O'Neill, dramatizes with some effectiveness the gap in the filial-paternal relationship, but the central themes of *The Titan*, sexuality and the individual in conflict with corporate power, are rendered wholly as abstractions. In addition, this issue of *MFS* (pp. 423–40) prints two chapters from *A Traveller at Forty* that were cut by the editors at Century. The chapters tell of Dreiser's encounter with a German streetwalker by the name of Hanscha Jower. In a prefatory note Thomas P. Riggio suggests that Dreiser "struck a new note in American perceptions of Europe," that he anticipated writers like T. S. Eliot, Hemingway, and Henry Miller for whom a Europe of street corners, cafes, repartee, and women "became a major symbol of modern futility."

Two essays from other journals approach the free will and determinism problem with greater insight than the essays in *MFS*. In "Another Two Dreisers: The Artist as Genius" (*SNNTS* 9:119–33) Thomas P. Riggio looks at this question as it informs Dreiser's portrait of the artist in *The 'Genius.'* Dreiser's development of Witla as an artist, says Riggio, owes much to the 19th-century romantic cult of the genius whose freedom permits his quest after beauty and truth, but later in the novel Dreiser defines Witla's obsessions and failures as predetermined, and the question of Witla's commitment to art (was it just a mood, some indiscernible force in his nature?) remains unresolved. The best of the essays on this subject is "American Literary Naturalism: The Example of Dreiser" (*SAF* 5:51–63) by Donald Pizer, who feels that free will versus determinism is never the central issue of a Dreiser novel, but serves rather as a metaphor of life against which various temperaments can define themselves. Thus in *Jennie Gerhardt* Lester Kane emerges a skeptic and pessimist as he puzzles over man's role in a mechanistic world, while Jennie, equally puzzled, emerges as a woman of positive feelings, grateful for the world's beauty in spite of its mystery and cruelty.

Two essays are concerned with style and revisions. In "The Language of Realism, The Language of False Consciousness: A Reading of *Sister Carrie*" (*Novel* 10:101–13) Sandy Petrey argues that Dreiser's first novel is written in two irreconcilable styles: what he calls social realism and sentimental moralizing. *Sister Carrie* is so structured, writes Petrey, that the moral passages stand as formal parodies of the sentimental tradition although Dreiser clearly did not intend them as such. Petrey calls the moral passages "twaddle," a response which is challenged by Ellen Moers (*Novel* 11:63–69). In "Dreiser's Ant Tragedy: The Revision of 'The Shining Slave Makers'" (*SSF* 14:41–8), Don B. Graham compares the 1901 version of Dreiser's story in *Ainslee's Magazine* with its 1918 publication in *Free and Other Stories* and finds that the approximately 169 revisions not only enhance the struggle for survival theme but especially enhance the mood of melancholy wonder and mystery with which Dreiser characteristically surveyed parallels between man and simple organisms.

Two notes on Dreiser proved to be of some interest. In "Dreiser at the Aquarium" (*DN* 8:1–5) Alan Price traces the lobster and squid episode in *The Financier* back to a short story entitled "A Lesson from the Aquarium" which Dreiser published in *Tom Watson's Magazine* in 1906. And in "Dreiser's Sentimental Heroine, Aileen Butler" (*AL* 48:590–96) Mary Anne Lindborg relates the mawkish attitudes and gestures of Aileen to the sentimental novels she reads and argues that in Aileen, Dreiser "illustrates the futility of trying to live out the old traditions in the world of the new." Finally in "The East-West Theme in Dreiser's *An American Tragedy* (*WAL* 12:177–83) Martin Bucco observes that differences in geography in the novel are superficial, that events in the east and west are parallel and that to change location is to change nothing. This is an interesting point but it hardly warrants the essay being published simultaneously in another collection, *The Westering Experience*, pp. 106–11.

ii. Edith Wharton

Cynthia Griffin Wolff's *A Feast of Words: The Triumph of Edith Wharton* (New York: Oxford Univ. Press) is a remarkable book of literary criticism, certainly the best critical study for the year from this period. Wolff's approach is to relate Wharton's fiction to her psychological development. Her central thesis is that Wharton was emotionally deprived in her relationship to her mother, that her life-long love of words served as an oral substitute for the communication and affection that were denied her in her family relationships. Wharton feared her domineering mother, says Wolff, and as a young woman she approached her mother's world, the society of old New York, with the habit of self-denial and retreat. But eventually through her writing, says Wolff, she was able to free herself from her fears and dependency because serious writing "demanded some permanent capacity to confront her inner self." The novels, as Wolff examines them, bear witness to this process.

Wolff's psychoanalytical account of Wharton's life at first seems reductive and repetitious, but the scheme she constructs proves the basis for a truly brilliant reading of Wharton's major fictions. Wolff sees *The House of Mirth* as the novelist's first successful attempt to deal with her emotional history. The novel, writes Wolff, is about "the psychological disfigurement of any woman who chooses to accept society's definition of her as a beautiful object and nothing more" and bears the stamp of Wharton's own childhood rage at being evaluated this way by her mother's world. Wolff sees Wharton exploring in *Ethan Frome* the horror of retreat to a world of childish dependencies. The New England landscape for Wharton is not the summery, pastoral world of Sarah Orne Jewett, but a sterile winter landscape of frozen emotions and longing for death. Wolff draws attention to the book's narrative structure and points out that Ethan's story is never presented as fact but as a dream vision, a projection of the narrator's own morbid imagination. However, the world of mute longings, postponed sexuality and material dependency, says Wolff, was one that after the affair with Morton Fullerton, Edith was able to leave behind. Her full embracing of contemporary experience, her newly acquired ability to take initiative, are recorded, says Wolff, in *The Custom of the Country*, a novel about energy and about the forces of change always at work in society. Undine Spragg, says Wolff, embodies energy and the American spirit of competition embraced with a voracious appetite. This novel seems to argue "that appetite (or energy) of itself is necessary to life, but that ungoverned and insatiable appetite must be rejected." *Summer*, says Wolff, puts this theme in explicitly sexual terms, but in this novel she finds Wharton for the first time urging the values of society and tradition. In *The Age of Innocence* she sees Edith Wharton coming to terms with and accepting the old New York of her childhood. In the character of Newland Archer she finds Wharton saying that an individual's genuine growth and maturity must proceed from an understanding and acceptance of his background, not a rejection of it. Wharton had for many years rejected her past and Wolff notes that the last works are charged with a feeling of loss, focusing on children and family life which Wharton had never had for herself. Wolff writes with such insight and with such enthusiastic affection that her book makes one want to reread the novels.

Wolff's magnificent study overshadows a book like Richard H. Lawson's *Edith Wharton* (New York: Frederick Ungar), but Lawson's book was intended as an introduction and as such gives the new reader a useful guide to Wharton's major works. Much of Lawson's monograph consists of plot summaries, but occasionally his analyses of the novels are fresh and interesting. For instance he argues that in *The House of Mirth* it is Lily's emerging self-awareness and especially "her unassertive honesty" which prevent her from adapting to the rules of her society and result in her death. Brief mention should be made here of Lawson's more significant study, *Edith Wharton and German Literature* (Bonn: Bouvier [1974]), which has not received notice in *ALS* before. Lawson explores the influences of German literature on Wharton as a corrective to what he feels is the overrated influence of Henry James. He traces Wharton's brief interest in working class reforms, as evidenced particularly in *The Fruit of the Tree*, to her translation of Hermann Sudermann's play, *Es Lebe das Leben.* The heroine of the play, an aristocratic woman of nearly forty who is suffering an intolerable marriage, would have struck a sympathetic chord with Wharton, says Lawson. Lawson also considers the Nietzschean theme in "The Blond Beast," the probable influence of Gottfried Keller on *Summer*, and the possible influence of Goethe's *Bildungsroman* on major books like *The House of Mirth* and *The Age of Innocence* where the protagonist's development is viewed in terms of social activity. More recently, in "Thematic Similarities in Edith Wharton and Thomas Mann" (*TCL* 23:289–98), Lawson suggests that, although there is no documentary evidence, Edith Wharton was likely aware of and read some of Mann's books in the period before World War I. Lawson says the works of both writers reflect their *haut-bourgeois* origins, for the decline of the old nonmercantile society is their basic theme and irony their common mode. The decline of a society is central to David C. Stineback's reading of *The House of Mirth* in *Shifting World* (Lewisburg, Pa.: Bucknell Univ. Press [1976]) where he argues that Lily Bart holds on to her good taste and social distinctions and thereby condemns herself to an early death.

The scope and complexity of Wolff's book is such that it anticipates the arguments found in individual articles on Wharton. There are parallels between Wolff's treatment of the New England fiction and Alan Henry Rose's view of the same works as set forth in his article "'Such Depths of Sad Initiation': Edith Wharton and New England" (*NEQ* 50:423–39). Like Wolff, Rose sees Wharton's New England as a barren setting where the characters are invariably thwarted in the path to mature self-realization. In both *Ethan Frome* and *Summer*, says Rose, there lurks in the landscape a sense of a precultural void, and the characters in fear and awe surrender for protection to incestuous-like relationships, Ethan to Zeena, who had nursed his dying mother, and Charity to Lawyer Royall, who had rescued her from the lawless society of the Mountain and raised her as his daughter. Wolff sees Wharton as repeatedly assessing the customs and values of her past and in "Ironic Reversal in Edith Wharton's *Bunner Sisters*," [*sic*] (*SSF* 14:241–45) Judith P. Saunders views the "Bunner Sisters" as a special kind of *Bildungsroman* in which the heroine discovers the inadequacy of the principles she has lived by, so that "enlightenment depends upon unlearning." Most importantly, says Saunders, the heroine, Ann Eliza, learns that self-sacrifice can be destructive rather than ennobling, for when she arranges that the man she loves marry her sister, she in effect arranges for her sister's illness, abuse, and death. As Wolff's book testifies, no American author has been served better by feminist criticism than Edith Wharton, and Judith Fetterley's "'The Temptation to be a Beautiful Object': Double Standard and Double Bind in *The House of Mirth*" (*SAF* 5:199–211) is another insightful addition to feminist readings of Wharton's works. Fetterley's essay is a study of "sexual politics" in *The House of Mirth* and reveals the many ways in which Lily Bart is the victim of patriarchal culture. By valuing her only in terms of her beauty, says Fetterley, society creates a schism between Lily's real self and her cultural identity, and since her beauty is accidental and something over which she has little control, Lily has an abiding sense of her powerlessness. There are many excellent arguments in this essay, especially on the double standard of social behavior, but perhaps most interesting of all are Fetterley's analysis of marriage as an economic transaction wherein "the beautiful object becomes the possession of that man who has the money," and her observation that the types of marriageable men in the novel are unpleasant, that the novel "is pervaded by a sense of male flesh as repulsive and by a vision of men as gross dull beasts."

iii. Sherwood Anderson

Jack Salzman, who edited the special Dreiser number for *MFS*, is also the editor of a special number on Anderson for *Twentieth Century Literature*, volume 23. Again the essays are varied in subject and approach. One of the best essays is John O'Neill's "Anderson Writ Large: 'Godliness' in *Winesburg, Ohio*" (pp. 67–83), which shows how the long story "Godliness" goes beyond the short epiphany or psychological revelation and provides a historical and sociological framework for the whole cycle of stories. O'Neill observes that "Godliness" combines Anderson's experimental technique, that reveals character in a telling gesture, with more traditional forms of narrative that provide a realistic, historical perspective. An interesting psychological reading of Anderson can be found in "Sherwood Anderson: The Artist's Struggle for Self-Respect" (pp. 40–52) where Mia Klein traces Anderson's ambiguous feelings about the artist to his unresolved relationship with his father. Anderson's "lovable improvident" father was a natural storyteller and Anderson consequently, says Klein, attributed such qualities as childishness, lack of masculinity, even insanity, to the artist type. These insights are pertinent to any reading of *Windy McPherson's Son*, Anderson's novel about the filial relationship. Not surprisingly J. R. Scafidel in "Sexuality in *Windy McPherson's Son*" (pp. 94–101) argues that impotence is the novel's pervasive theme and suggests that the distance between *Windy McPherson's Son* and *Winesburg, Ohio* is not so great if they are viewed in terms of Anderson's treatment of sex. There are good readings of three lesser known stories ("There She Is—She Is Taking Her Bath," "The Yellow Gown," and "The Triumph of a Modern or, Send for the Lawyer") in Paul P. Somers, Jr.'s "Sherwood Anderson's Mastery of Narrative Distance" (pp. 84–93). What Somers demonstrates is how Anderson creates an ironic distance between the sophisticated first-person narrators of these stories and the "implied author," a distance which elicits varying degrees of sympathy from the reader. Somers also observes that "Jamesian elements are prominent in these stories, rather surprisingly, considering Anderson's professed aversion to Henry James."

Anderson's correspondence with three Japanese writers is described in detail by Kichinosuki Ohashi (pp. 115–39), while Mary Sue Schriber describes his critical reception in France between the two world wars (pp. 140–56), including a checklist of French commentary on Anderson between 1919 and 1939. There is an informal essay by Anderson himself entitled "Being A Writer" (pp. 1–16) and a collection of photographs (pp. 17–39), which give a good pictorial representation of Anderson's life.

Ray Lewis White's *Sherwood Anderson: A Reference Guide* (Boston: G. K. Hall) provides Anderson scholars with a definitive bibliography of works about Anderson. This is a splendid reference book, containing more than 2,550 entries and including works from 15 foreign languages. Unlike other bibliographers, White has included obscure newspaper clippings (from the archives at the Newberry Library) because he feels references to the author in the popular press help one to gauge the high and low critical periods that Anderson experienced and that must have influenced his career. After the bibliography was ready for printing, Ray White and Diana Haskell were given access to the libraries of two Chicago newspapers, and they found an additional 97 items which appear in a supplementary list in the November number of *The Winesburg Eagle* (Univ. of Richmond, Va.). Welford Dunaway Taylor, editor of *The Winesburg Eagle*, is the author of *Sherwood Anderson* (New York: Frederick Ungar), a first-rate monograph which describes in a thorough, informed fashion the most significant aspects of Anderson's work and career. Taylor is limited to the "introduction" format but he nonetheless makes some fresh observations on Anderson's writing. Most interesting is his discussion of Old Testament echoes in the narrative voice of *Winesburg, Ohio*, a voice which bespeaks wisdom and sympathy. Taylor selects *Poor White* and *Kit Brandon* as the best of Anderson's longer works and gives a particularly good account of the latter novel.

There were three individual essays on *Winesburg, Ohio*, which remains the most frequently discussed work. One of the best observations to be made about the form of *Winesburg, Ohio* is found in "*Winesburg, Ohio*: A Portrait of the Artist as a Young Man" (*SoQ*

16:27–38) where Samuel Pickering writes that "the short-story structure, partly-told tales, and unclear thematic organization invite critical creativity and make the book a sort of 'unfinished masterpiece.'" Pickering compares Anderson's book to George Moore's *Confessions of a Young Man*, arguing that both books portray the potential artist as aliens in the romantic vein (uncommitted to relatives, family, or women) and that both books rely on the imagination of the reader to complete the narrative gaps. In "*Winesburg, Ohio* as a Dance of Death" (*AL* 48:525–42) David Stouck examines a pattern of grotesque physical movements made by the characters in the Winesburg stories and relates them to the procession of dead and remembered figures in the introductory sketch. Stouck says that when Anderson remembered the lonely and obscure figures of his past, especially his dying mother's, their gestures coalesced in his mind to form a procession like a Dance of Death. The idea of death in Anderson's writing, however, does not simply denote the grave, argues Stouck, but points to the loneliness and frustration of the unlived life and a view of modern society as a form of living death. *The Markham Review* consistently publishes short articles of high quality and Martin J. Fertig's "'A Great Deal of Wonder in Me': Inspiration and Transformation in *Winesburg, Ohio*" (*MarkhamR* 6:65–70) is a good example. Fertig shows how Anderson was able to depict the inner reality of his characters' lives by having their external appearance transformed in the eyes of the narrator, George Willard. Thus, for example, Fertig draws attention to the way the hideous Wash Williams becomes a comely young man with a beautiful voice as he tells his story, and how Elizabeth Willard becomes a lovely woman in death. This fine article points to one of the essential formal patterns in the Winesburg stories.

Three articles are concerned exclusively with the concept of the grotesque as found in Anderson. In "Distorted Matter and Disjunctive Forms: The Grotesque as Modernist Genre" (*ArQ* 33:339–47) Joseph R. Millichap argues that modernist writers concerned with aesthetic form embraced grotesque subjects because their twisted, distorted forms reflected the fragmentation and alienation of the modern world. Millichap sees the form of *Winesburg, Ohio*, with its chapters on isolated individuals, as embodying the disjunctive aspect of the grotesque vision. James Schevill's "Notes on the Grotesque: Anderson, Brecht, and Williams" (*TCL* 23:229–38) is a more impressionistic look at the concept of the grotesque, tracing it back to the repression and violence of evangelical religion, and to the confusion created between the pioneer ideal of independence and the modern technological goal of abundance in America. Distortion, writes Schevill, inevitably emerges in the lives of people who believe they are free and independent but in fact are victims of technology and standardization. An interesting note by Martha M. Park entitled "How Far from Emerson's Man of One Idea to Anderson's Grotesques?" (*CLAJ* 20:374–79) suggests that Anderson in writing *Winesburg, Ohio* might have been influenced by reading Emerson, who wrote in several places that if a man fastens on a single aspect of truth too long, then it becomes a distorted falsehood.

Two other articles look at less frequently discussed books. In "The 'Unkinging' of Man: Intellectual Background as Structural Device in Sherwood Anderson's *Poor White*" (*SDR* 15,i:45–60) Daniel R. Hoeber argues that Freud is not the important influence on *Poor White* but rather Scientific Materialism. The principal story, insists Hoeber, is the mechanization of Hugh McVey, the poor country boy who becomes an inventor, and it is his devotion to technology and machines which is the source of frustration in the marriage between Hugh and Clara Butterworth. Finally, *Dark Laughter* is compared with Updike's *Rabbit, Run* by Rolf Lundén in *SN* 49:59–68 (see chap. 21, v).

iv. Jack London

The abiding interest in London is reflected in two new biographies. That interest has always been strongest outside the United States, and not surprisingly both biographies are by English writers. Robert Barltrop's *Jack London: The Man, The Writer, The Rebel* (London: Pluto Press [1976]) is an affectionate biography with a special interest in London as a socialist. The book is very readable and amply illustrated, but at times its information is sketchy. For instance Eliza London is often mentioned, but her doubtful status as Jack's sister is never explained. Barltrop's book is "popular" biography in the vein of Irving Stone's *Sailor on Horseback* and, writing in *WAL* 12:231–36, Dale L. Walker laments its "dearth of serious research, repetition of old errors, and conclusions based on skimpy (or nonexistent) evidence." A full-bodied, more scholarly biography can be found in Andrew Sinclair's *Jack: A Biography of Jack London* (New York:

Harper and Row). Sinclair has worked closely with the London papers at the Huntington Library and the result is as close to a definitive biography as will likely appear for some time. Sinclair's biography is not marred by partisan interests; he lets the dubious facts about London's birth, his marriages, and his death speak for themselves. Sinclair's book is not as engaging to read as Barltrop's but the scholar will want to consult Sinclair for the facts, such as they are known. Neither biographer attempts literary criticism of London's fiction.

Another important publication is Joan Sherman's *Jack London: A Reference Guide* (Boston: G. K. Hall) where the scholar will now find an annotated bibliography of writings about London covering the period 1900–75. This guide includes major newspaper reviews, scholarly books and articles, poems about London, theses, and manuscript collections. The major exclusion is foreign-language materials, except for those articles available in translation. In an introduction Sherman gives a concise summary of London's critical reputation, which she sees defined as the clash between "high" and "low" culture in America. For many years Jamesian literary values were applied to London and he was found wanting, writes Sherman, but his enormous popularity and the growing critical interest in his writing argue for his importance in American literary history. Sherman's introduction is instructive, her annotations objective. This is another valuable addition to G. K. Hall's excellent reference guide series.

Again *Martin Eden* was the London book most frequently discussed. In "*Martin Eden*: Jack London's 'Splendid Dream'" (*WAL* 12:199–214) Sam S. Baskett puts forth the opinion that in *Martin Eden* "London attempts a more ambitious pattern than he fully accomplishes" and that this is why the novel is not wholly satisfying. Martin's ambition on the one hand, writes Baskett, is to understand "the entire 'scheme of existence,'" like Henry Adams's narrator in *The Education*; on the other hand, like Fitzgerald's Gatsby, he dreams romantically of creating a new self. His failure to take an ironic perspective on these impossible goals results in his suicide, Baskett points out, and in parallel fashion London was unable in the novel to complete the pattern he essayed. The stylistic and ideological inconsistencies of the novel are given a clear appraisal in Richard Morgan's "Naturalism, Socialism, and Jack London's *Martin Eden*" (*JLN* 10:13–22). Morgan points out that while romanticism is Martin's spur to climb socially, he is conceived of by London as a naturalistic hero and his climb is determined by certain social phenomena acting upon him. He argues that London's socialism was also hybrid, an unlikely fusion of Marx and Nietzsche, and that its most characteristic aspect was London's belief in a "man on horseback" who would break the hold of capitalism and lead the people to socialism.

In "American Writing as a Wildlife Preserve: Jack London and Norman Mailer" (*SoQ* 15:135–48) Stephen J. Whitfield connects London and Mailer with a peculiarly American definition of the novelist—"not as artificer but as hero, strident in politics and masculinity . . . embattled and engaged in the turbulence of history." Theirs is a man's world, says Whitfield, a world of rites rather than manners, of male companionship and ordeals, and for both writers art is about "life defined as adventure, romance, and the inevitable flirtation with death." Denouncing this macho myth, Robert Forrey in "Labor's Love Lost" (*JLN* 10:48–51) once again urges that the homosexual question be considered in any serious assessment of London's work (see *ALS 1976*, p. 234), and he cites letters and poems between London and George Sterling as evidence of London's erotic feeling for men. Finally, two of London's stories were given careful readings. Billy G. Collins in "Jack London's 'The Red One': Journey to a Lost Heart" (*JLN* 10:1–6) argues that though London in this late story allows the reader to hope for evolution to a higher stage of human perfection, the story is a cry of despair "with no present hope for happiness left on earth." And in " 'The Wife of a King': A Defense" (*JLN* 10:34–38) Jacqueline Tavernier-Courbier argues that this comic tale about a half-breed woman is not a racist *Pygmalion* but a sympathetic and light-hearted tale of how a native woman becomes both attractive and self-aware.

v. Willa Cather

Cather's stature as a novelist of the front rank is reflected in the increasing number of general studies of American literature in which she is now included. From earlier books such as R. W. B. Lewis's *The American Adam*, Leslie Fiedler's *Love and Death in the American Novel*, or Wright Morris's *The Territory Ahead* women writers were largely omitted, but in fact such perennial American themes as the romantic dream of success, the quest for an innocent pastoral retreat and the idealization of male comradeship are all central to Willa

Cather's fiction. David C. Stineback's *Shifting World* is a study of American fiction in which characters swept up in rapid social progress experience an intense nostalgia for the past. Stineback sees this as a dilemma central to American novels. In his chapter on Cather he argues that in *The Professor's House* the juxtaposition of two mutually incompatible views of life is handled with irony, that the novel represents Cather's renunciation of nostalgia. In order for Professor St. Peter to survive, says Stineback, he must give up his ideal vision of the past embodied in Tom Outland, and turn to a life without delight as symbolized in Augusta. Floyd C. Watkins's *In Time and Place* studies the relationship of fiction to geography and culture and devotes two chapters to Cather. A chapter on *My Ántonia* describes at length the Nebraskan landscape and the varied ethnic backgrounds of the immigrants to this landscape. The most interesting aspect of this discussion is Watkins's argument that landscape determines culture and shapes the course of an individual's life. He relates both the suicide of Mr. Shimerda and the success of Ántonia to nature's control over man. In a chapter on *Death Comes for the Archbishop* Watkins explores the authenticity of Cather's materials and demonstrates that her narratives, though sometimes altered for artistic effect, "are based on actual geography, history and culture." Watkins's study has researched some fresh details, but its general thesis as pertains to Cather is not new.

Willa Cather's first novel, *Alexander's Bridge*, has been reissued as a Bison paperback by the University of Nebraska Press. In an "Introduction" Bernice Slote documents some of the sources for the novel and shows through a careful study of theme and imagery how the book forms an integral part of the Cather canon. Bartley Alexander's dilemma of the divided self, writes Slote, is a theme that runs right through Cather's work with perhaps its most important development in *The Professor's House*. In this first novel, Slote continues, Cather also employed many of her favorite image patterns: moon-myth imagery, the cycle of the seasons, gold colors, and images of drowning. Slote tells us that in the early reviews of the book Cather was linked with Edith Wharton as part of the Jamesian school. The two writers were never associated with each other and with the publication of *O Pioneers!* Cather's career was clearly going in a very different direction from Wharton's, but parallels are drawn between the two writers by Lillian D. Bloom in her review article

"On Daring to Look Back with Wharton and Cather" (*Novel* 10:67–78). Bloom sees conservatism as the major similarity between Wharton and Cather. They both rejected postwar American culture, she points out, as a materialistic noncivilization, and both deplored the disappearance of "good manners" as an index to moral certitude.

Essays on *O Pioneers!*, *A Lost Lady* and *Shadows on the Rock* reflect a continuing interest in the whole range of Cather's canon. In "The Wild Duck Image in Willa Cather and Henryk Ibsen" (*AN&Q* 15[1976]:23–27) Frank W. Shelton points out that while for both authors the wild duck represents the spirit of romance, for Ibsen it was a child's illusion that would be snuffed out by the grimy real world, whereas for Cather in *O Pioneers!* it embodied a reality linked to the reassuring truths of the land and the cycle of the seasons. In "Willa Cather's *A Lost Lady*: The Paradoxes of Change" (*Novel* 11:51–62) Susan J. Rosowski suggests that the theme of *A Lost Lady* is human adaptation to change and shows how Marian Forrester's flexibility allows her to move forward in time while Niel Herbert's pride and idealism threaten to isolate him entirely from the present. To Niel, writes Rosowski, Marian is an aesthetic ideal that has been tarnished, and she cannot be part of his moral-aesthetic until he comes finally to view her with compassion and forgiveness. In "The Hand of the Artist in *Shadows on the Rock*" (*SAF* 5:263–68) John Hinz carefully analyzes the page of Cather's original typescript with its corrections that appeared as a frontispiece to the Library edition of *Shadows on the Rock*. Here, says Hinz, we can see how Cather first composed a narrative in a spontaneous, unchecked manner, but afterwards ruthlessly pruned away all verbal extravagances and imprecision. In her revision, says Hinz, she invariably sought to eliminate explicit statement in order to produce the "overtone divined by the ear but not heard by it."

vi. Gertrude Stein

Stein's experiments with writing will continue, I expect, to intrigue critics. There were three articles dealing specifically with technique. The most comprehensive of these is "Gertrude Stein and Cubist Narrative" (*MFS* 22:543–55) in which Marilyn Gaddis Rose defends the term cubism as a description of Stein's method in certain works. Rose demonstrates that in "The Good Anna" Stein used four different styles (expository, realistic, impressionistic, abstract) the way a painter poises interacting planes against alternating volumes and shifts in perspective. Cubism, says Rose, is "any art form studying its own processes without recourse to representational reality" and this she says is essential to *Lucy Church Amiably* and *Ida* where one analyzes such works not by referring them to reality but by identifying certain objects, noting the frequency of their occurrence and whether they are disposed in a pattern or not. In "Gertrude Stein in Manuscript" (*YULG* 51:156–63) Wendy Steiner approaches the 1923 portrait, "He and They, Hemingway," as a riddle which she tries to solve by relating the text to the cover of the *cahier* in which Stein was writing. The portrait, says Steiner, dramatizes her dealings with Hemingway with a reference to Victor Hugo, whose picture was on the notebook, and illustrates her theory of creativity embracing the sensory experiences of the present moment. Henry M. Sayre's "Imaging the Mind: Juan Gris and Gertrude Stein" (*SHR* 11:204–15) does not put forth new ideas about Stein but illustrates some of the familiar ones clearly. Sayre looks at a short volume titled *A Book Concluding With As A Wife Has A Cow: A Love Story* where language is stripped of both meaning and connotation and becomes a plastic construction, "a sensual thing to be carressed by the ear and the eye." Gris's lithographs for the book, says Sayre, similarly reveal not what is seen, but *how* a thing is seen.

Three articles deal more with theme than technique. In "Fading: A Way. Gertrude Stein's Sources for *Three Lives*" (*JML* 5[1976]:463–80) Lawren Farber proposes that Stein's thesis in the book concerns the state of grace in the world and that by merging a particular historical life with details from other lives she has created a continuous theological interpretation of history. Farber demonstrates that the reader must examine the etymology of names, most of which are German, in order to perceive this allegorical dimension to the narrative. In "Gertrude Stein's *Paris France* and American Literary Tradition" (*SDR* 15,i:7–17) Judith P. Saunders argues that Stein uses France the way Thoreau uses Walden woods—to create a world apart in which she can be free. She believed, says Saunders, that a writer needed two countries, and Saunders compares her withdrawal to France to Thoreau's retreat to Walden and Huck Finn's flight to the river and raft. And in a note entitled "Stein's Four Roses" (*JML* 6: 325–28) Robert F. Fleissner speculates that Stein's famous line might refer to the "multifoliate rose" of T. S. Eliot, with the same mystical insistence on Being as in the Old Testament phrase, "I am that I am."

There is always an interest in Gertrude Stein as a personality. In "Mind, Body, and Gertrude Stein" (*CritI* 3:489–506) Catharine R. Stimpson probes biography to find the various strategies that enabled Stein, a woman, a writer, and a homosexual, to live as a "tainted anomaly." Stimpson also shows how the situation of *Q.E.D.*, her novel about love between women, was rewritten in heterosexual or "coded" terms in "Melanctha." The interest in Stein as an anomalous personality dominates a memoir and collection of letters and photographs published as *Dear Sammy: Letters from Gertrude Stein and Alice B. Toklas* (Boston: Houghton Mifflin). The editor and recipient of the letters is Samuel M. Steward, who befriended Stein and Toklas when they were in their sixties and who remained loyal to the friendship until Toklas's death. The memoir is almost fiction and immensely readable, as fascinating for the implied portrait of Steward as for its picture of Stein and Toklas. But there is something stagey in the scenes recalled by Steward where Stein supposedly discusses in some detail her theories about writing, her literary friendships, and her sexual preferences. Much less pointed are the letters themselves, which are concerned with arranging a second reading tour of America, the possibilities of making a film in Hollywood, and thanking Steward for gifts. Only in two letters does Stein discuss literary matters very seriously: in one dated September 2, 1935, she talks about content without form in much modern writing, and in another dated June 25, 1938, she discusses her reaction to reading Wordsworth and Coleridge after the lapse of many years. The book, however, does reveal an interesting facet of Stein's and Toklas's life: their almost maternal need in later years to surround themselves with young admirers, however meager in talent or intellect.

vii. Glasgow, Cabell

The Mississippi Quarterly published a special number on Ellen Glasgow with four of the essays grouped under the general heading of "the apprenticeship of Ellen Glasgow." Julius Rowan Raper in "Ambivalence Toward Authority: A Look at Glasgow's Library, 1890–1906" (*MissQ* 31:5–16) gives an account of some 200 titles acquired from Ellen Glasgow's personal library by the University of Virginia in 1975 which further support his thesis (see *ALS* 1971, p, 211) that the major intellectual influences on Glasgow were the scientific determinists, Darwin, Spencer, and their followers. But Raper also finds that there were works of mysticism and Transcendentalism in her library, both Eastern and Western, and that their influence is also discernible at points in her fiction. In "The Southern Lady in the Early Novels of Ellen Glasgow" (*MissQ* 31:17–31) Dorothy McInnis Scura observes that the ideal southern woman was the wish fulfillment of men, that she was characteristically beautiful, passive, devoted to the values of the past and also frequently narrow and boring. These traits, says Scura, appear in many of Glasgow's early fictional females, but it was in *Virginia* that Glasgow did her first full portrait of the type. Dorothy Kish in "Toward a Perfect Place: Setting in the Early Novels of Ellen Glasgow" (*MissQ* 31:33–44) makes the obvious point that Glasgow's fiction grew more effective as she related details of her Virginia landscape to the symbolic dimension of character and action, and leaning heavily on the observations of other critics, Edgar MacDonald in "A Finger on the Pulse of Life: Ellen Glasgow's Search for a Style" (*MissQ* 31:45–56) concludes that Glasgow's style came to serve her characters as "an extension of their attitudes rather than a reflection of the author's." Imagery and symbolism in her writing, he suggests, move from the theatrical to the poetically suggestive, knitting together character, time, place, and mood. In this same issue much more interesting is Ladell Payne's discussion of a late Glasgow novel. In "Ellen Glasgow's *Vein of Iron*: Vanity, Irony, Idiocy" (*MissQ* 31:57–65) Payne argues that in the recurring figure of the idiot boy Toby Waters, and of the idiot family in Panther Gap, Glasgow has created a philosophical symbol of life's meaninglessness. The Fincastles, however, endure, says Payne, knowing that life's happiness is an illusion, that existence is idiocy, because they feel endurance is preferable to the oblivion of death.

Julius Raper's "Invisible Things: The Short Stories of Ellen Glasgow" (*SLJ* 9,ii:66–90) is an interesting examination of a group of stories Glasgow wrote between 1916 and 1925. This was a low period in the author's life and career, but Raper shows how these stories represent experiments in which she was finding techniques "for revealing a character's unconscious side by projecting it upon other characters." These experiments, writes Raper, in such stories as "Whispering Leaves" and "Jordan's End" paved the way for Glasgow's psychological masterpieces, *Barren Ground, The Romantic Comedians*, and *The Sheltered Life*. The last novel is the subject of a chapter in David C. Stineback's *Shifting World*. Stineback argues that in this ironic masterpiece Glasgow changes the conflict from the individual's struggle against tradition to a society's struggle against history. The Archbalds and Birdsongs, writes Stineback, live in a diminished world of heroic and romantic illusions, a world that is gradually disintegrating in the face of technological progress from without and evasions and deceptions from within. George Birdsong's personal weakness, concludes Stineback, becomes the occasion for this society's self-destruction.

Critical interest in Ellen Glasgow has been encouraged by the formation of an Ellen Glasgow Society and the publication of a newsletter. The *EGN* reports on new Glasgow research and reprints old reviews, letters, and other Glasgow memorabilia. The growing interest in Glasgow is also reflected in the decision of the Arno Press to publish two Glasgow titles out of print, *The Descendant* and *The Romantic Comedians*.

There is a long article about James Branch Cabell titled "Life Beyond Life: Cabell's Theory and Practice of Romance" (*Genre* 10: 299–327) in which Evelyn J. Hinz and John J. Teunissen examine Cabell's concepts of romance as set forth in *Beyond Life*. Some of the important points they establish are these: that the realist, according to Cabell, is concerned with history whereas the romancer has a cosmic perspective and sees time not as linear but as moving in great cycles; that there are three attitudes to life (the Chivalric, the Gallant, the Poetic) which repeat themselves through history; that "human beings and human living are pretty much the same in most times and stations." These critics point out that because the romancer sees life as cyclical, his interest in the past is not nostalgic but more closely related to myth, and in the rest of the article they demonstrate that Cabell's characters and stories are not conceived of as "archaic," but as describing a mythic heritage which takes man in a great curve "back to the garden." With a similar purpose but very different conclusion, Desmond Tarrant in "James Branch Cabell: Wizard of the Unconscious" (*Kalki* 7:93–99) shows how Cabell's romantic philosophy of a better world, as defined in *Beyond Life*, is "based firmly on the theory of evolution." While in "The Contexts for Cabell" (*Kalki* 7:75–87) Robert H. Canary links Cabell with Barth, Borges, and Vonnegut as "fabulators," writers less concerned with realism and more concerned with ideas and ideals. These writers, he says, are best viewed in the light of romanticism as defined by Irving Babbitt, for their work belongs to the mode of romantic irony.

viii. B. Traven

Judy B. Stone's basic assumption in *The Mystery of B. Traven* (Los Altos, Calif.: William Kaufmann) is that Traven was originally the German anarchist Ret Marut and possibly the illegitimate son of Kaiser Wilhelm II. Nearly half of her book is an account of Marut's life and the political climate of post–World War I Germany. The crucial sequence in Stone's book, however, is the series of interviews that she conducted in Mexico City in 1966 with Hal Croves, who claimed to be Traven's representative, but whom Stone identifies as Traven. There is nothing new here as regards the Traven mystery—these theories have circulated before. Perhaps the widow of Croves, who is supposedly preparing a biography of her husband, will produce some concrete evidence as to the identity of B. Traven. Stone's book is journalism, not scholarship, but it is a very enjoyable book to read. With its short chapters circling around the question of Traven's identity and the tension of interviewing Croves, it is the kind of journalism that itself becomes a fiction. More reliable is Michael L. Baumann's book (*see ALS 1976*, pp. 247–48).

I expect that identity will always be a central issue surrounding this author, but increasingly articles appear which are concerned primarily with Traven's books. These are the pieces which will ultimately determine Traven's status as a writer. In a bracing essay entitled "B. Traven's Death-Ship Commune" (*TQ* 20,iv:59–78) Donald Gutierrez writes that Gerald Gales is very different from the antihero of the modernist novel, for he is conceived of as a normal, healthy individual who must penetrate through the layers of evil that society has secreted over human beings in order to survive. The subject of Traven's novel is not the alienated individual, says Gutierrez, but the group of outcasts that can work together communally and can endure the evil that is eternally part of the human condition. Traven has a dubious status as an American writer since his novels were apparently first written in German, but several critics are at pains to put Traven in the context of American literature (see *ALS* 1976, p. 248). Such is the case of Richard E. Mezo, whose article "A Machine in the Garden" (*TQ* 20,iv:47–58) examines Traven's *The White Rose* in the light of Leo Marx's pastoral thesis. The main theme of Traven's novel, says Mezo, is the extension of industrial society (here an American-based oil company) into the Edenic wilderness of Mexico. The central contrast in the novel, writes Mezo, is between the harmony of the Indian society at Rosa Blanca and the industrial machinery of the United States, "the nuts and bolts monster spawned by the capitalist system . . . running amok, leaving in its wake a path of destruction." Several of Traven's books have been discussed in detail by critics, but Baumann in "B. Traven: Realist and Prophet" (*VQR* 53:73–85) asserts that the relatively obscure *Land des Frühlings*, first published in 1928 but not yet translated into English, is the most important book Traven composed. This photographic essay on South Mexico celebrates realistically the landscape that Traven knew so well, says Baumann, but the text is a veritable source book of Traven's principal ideas—his anarchist's anger at the inequalities of the world, his denunciation of capitalist ambition and agreed, and his curious prophecy that man's salvation lies with the Mexican Indians who are motivated by a communal sense of life.

ix. John Dos Passos

There were three substantial articles on Dos Passos in 1977. In "Dos Passos's *U.S.A.* and the Illusion of Memory" (*MFS* 23:543–55) Jonathan Morse argues that there is a predictability to the plots and characters in Dos Passos's trilogy because the books were written to illustrate a deterministic theory of history derived from Marx and Veblen. Thus, says Morse, seemingly diverse fictional characters lose their individuality and begin to merge as they come together at an appropriate point in time. The object of *U.S.A.*, writes Morse, was "to explain to the age of Fitzgerald that the age's brightest new beliefs—spontaneous generation of capital, freedom of the individual from accountability to historical laws—were illusions," that the dialectic of history would ultimately prevail.

In two closely related articles David L. Vanderwerken examines the thematic implications of language in Dos Passos's major fictions. In "*Manhatten Transfer*: Dos Passos' Babel Story" (*AL* 49:253–67) Vanderwerken suggests that the Babel myth is an organizing principle for *Manhatten Transfer* and shows how the great phrases of the founding fathers ("life, liberty, and the pursuit of happiness") have degenerated into a confused, fragmented language preaching success, fame, and the pursuit of big money. He traces this theme through the narratives devoted to Jimmy Herf. Similarly in "*U.S.A.*: Dos Passos and the 'Old Words' " (*TCL* 23:195–228) Vanderwerken shows how Dos Passos measures the rhetoric and behavior of modern Americans against the great verbal propositions upon which America was founded and finds the "old words" corrupted. In the four structural devices of the trilogy, says Vanderwerken, Dos Passos is concerned with facets of language, and gaps between the original meanings of "old words" and their current use are made visible. Mention finally should be made of *Lost Generation Journal* 5,i, which is devoted largely to short articles on Dos Passos. Papers include a comparison of Dos Passos and Mailer as war novelists, and a study of Dos Passos's and Erskine Caldwell's debt to training in journalism.

x. Lardner, Lewis

Ring Lardner, Jr., who was blacklisted in Hollywood in the 1950s, muses in *The Lardners: My Family Remembered* (New York: Harper and Row [1976]) over his "inability to find a single ancestral line that wasn't Anglo-Saxon." A central theme to his memoir is that the Lardners were a typical middle-class American family, affluent and aggressively self-assured, and that his father's career and alcoholism were part of the story of the middle-class America that expired in 1929. He tells us that Ring Lardner never felt it his destiny to be a writer, that he had "little ambition to be anything beyond a baseball reporter and part-time songwriter." Being assigned in 1913 to take over "In the Wake of the News," a humor column for the *Chicago Tribune*, was the decisive event in Lardner's career, writes his son, for it was there that he developed his semiliterate American style. Later Scott Fitzgerald and Max Perkins, we are told, encouraged the sick Lardner to continue writing. Ring Lardner, Jr., casts a cold eye on his father's career, but his memoir is a valuable addition to the mosaic of impressions necessary to see any writer fully.

Ring Lardner, Jr., thinks some of the baseball stories his father produced at the end of the war are among his very best. These were never reprinted until the 1976 collection, *Some Champions*, edited by

Matthew J. Bruccoli and Richard Layman (New York: Scribner's). This volume reproduces 9 stories and 17 autobiographical "sketches," most of which were written during the last years of Lardner's life. Bruccoli and Layman have also put together *Ring W. Lardner: A Descriptive Bibliography* (Pittsburgh: Univ. of Pittsburgh Press [1976]), an exhaustive listing of primary works. In addition to Lardner's fiction there are listings for sheet music, movie and dramatic work, interviews, and dust-jacket blurbs. This is a handsomely produced volume which includes a number of illustrations for dust jackets, binding, and sheet music.

There has been little work of significance done on Sinclair Lewis in the last two years. Floyd Watkins's *In Time and Place* includes a chapter on *Main Street* in which Watkins compares the fictional town of Gopher Prairie with its historical prototype, Sauk Centre. He argues somewhat pointlessly that Lewis ignored the vitality and cultural sophistication of the Minnesota town in order to satirize America. In "Sinclair Lewis's *Kingsblood Royal*: A Thesis Novel for the Forties" (*SLN* 7–8 [1976]:10–17) Robert L. Coard views *Kingsblood Royal* as a documentary novel about "the Negro problem" wherein Lewis exposes the limitations and prejudices of white, middle-class Americans. Coard notes at the same time that Lewis was not so much a realist as a caricaturist and that while the thesis of racial injustice remains relevant to America the book's dramatic action is crudely rigged and lacking in durable artistry. The only positive note sounded on Lewis's behalf is to be found in "The Reception of the Works of Sinclair Lewis in Hungary" (*HSE* 10[1976]:59–72), where Lászlo Jakabfi gives a detailed account of Lewis's popularity and the critical views of his work in Hungary. *Arrowsmith,* Jakabfi informs us, was Lewis's most popular novel, with nine editions appearing between 1928 and 1971. Critics, he concedes, are divided as to the durability of Lewis's work, but the positive critics compare Lewis's life work, he says, to Balzac's *Comédie Humaine*.

xi. Minor Writers

Studies and editions of minor authors continue to appear as this area of literature is thoroughly scrutinized by critics. John W. Crowley has edited *George Cabot Lodge: Selected Fiction and Verse* for *The John Colet Archive of American Literature* (St. Paul, Minn.: The

John Colet Press [1976]). Crowley sees Lodge as a minor but "symptomatic writer, whose work is a reflection of and key to the literary and intellectual history of the period." Lodge's work, says Crowley, reflects both the stifling atmosphere of America's fin de siècle and the impact of scientific naturalism, Nietzsche, and Walt Whitman. In his introduction Crowley tells us that Lodge, who was a member of the eminent Cabot Lodge family of Boston, devised for himself a philosophy he called Conservative Christian Anarchism, which repudiated materialism and asserted the values of teachers like Buddha, Socrates, and Christ, who sought to be fully human. This romantic philosophy refers Lodge's hitherto unpublished novel, *The Genius of the Commonplace*, back to the 19th century, but the economic naturalism that Lodge presents and attacks aligns the novel at the same time with the work of Norris and Dreiser. The selections of both poetry and fiction, however, make it clear that Lodge was more successful as a poet.

A different kind of transitional figure in American literary history is Abraham Cahan, the Lithuanian Jew who came to New York in 1882 and who, writing in both Yiddish and English, interpreted the richness of American life to Yiddish-speaking immigrants and in turn described the experience of the Jewish immigrants to an American audience. In his study of Cahan entitled *From the Ghetto: The Fiction of Abraham Cahan* (Amherst: Univ. of Mass. Press) Jules Chametzky focuses on the question of language in Cahan's work, for it was in his attention to speech and linguistic expression, says Chametzky, that Cahan most effectively dramatized the clashes between and within cultures. In his first English novel, *Yekl: A Tale of the New York Ghetto*, Cahan graphically illustrates the cultural debasement of his immigrants in the ugliness of their newly mastered English. In his masterwork, *The Rise of David Levinsky*, the characters, insists Chametzky, speak a flat, unremarkable English which constitutes Cahan's indictment of the acculturation process, for in abandoning their mother tongue the characters grow remote from the values of love and human concern intimately associated with their original culture. Chametzky discusses at some length Cahan's life as a socialist and journalist, but gives very little information about his personal life. Howells praised Cahan for his realism and Chametzky concludes his study by comparing *Levinsky* to *The Rise of Silas Lapham* and *Sister Carrie*, novels which treat the theme of success in America. This is the first book-length study of Cahan and though it focuses interestingly on the question of language, as an introduction it leaves many questions unanswered. Jules Zanger's "David Levinsky: Master of Pilpul" (*PLL* 13:283–94) is an overview of Cahan's last novel, focusing on the hero's Americanization.

Upton Sinclair (TUSAS 294) by William A. Bloodworth, Jr., is a sympathetic but critically objective study of "the writer who turned the stomach of a nation." Bloodworth sees Sinclair's place in American literary history as the persistent voice of reform and evaluates his novels as documentary fiction. To measure Sinclair's achievement in *The Jungle* by the standards of James or Faulkner, says Bloodworth, is to miss the significance and power of the novel. Sinclair, he continues, was concerned "to bring working-class life into fiction without censoring any of the oppressiveness of that life as he observed it." The novel's purpose, says Bloodworth, is to present life, not reorder and interpret it according to an artistic vision. At the same time, admits Bloodworth, Sinclair's fiction was shaped by his idealistic sensibility and it was idealism in conflict with an unjust capitalist society which made him such a tireless crusader for social justice both in his life and writing. Bloodworth also points out that this idealism put him at odds with his own personal responsibilities, especially family loyalties. Bloodworth's study is a measured, critically astute account of a difficult literary figure, altogether a first-rate book.

Simon Fraser University

14. Fiction: The 1930s to the 1950s

Margaret Anne O'Connor

The major contributions of 1977 to the study of writers who grew to prominence in the years between 1930 and the early 1950s are a comprehensive bibliography of Thomas Wolfe, a critical analysis of the work of Djuna Barnes, and biographies of Vladimir Nabokov and James Agee—the latter a success in the traditional form and the former an experiment in Nabokovian prose. Beyond these works, the year will be remembered for book-length tributes to Tennessee Williams and Jesse Stuart, as well as for the memorial essays prompted by the deaths of Nabokov, Anaïs Nin, and James Jones. Wolfe and Eudora Welty acquired their own journals, while the *Steinbeck Quarterly* and *Under the Sign of Pisces: Anaïs Nin and Her Circle* continued to flourish. The specialized journals have proliferated to such an extent that this essay can seldom go beyond describing the highlights of the year's publication in each. There were in addition composite studies of the depression years and the South that treat authors of this chapter along with other 20th-century figures. These works will only be briefly noted here, as they are reviewed in chapter 20.

i. "Art for Humanity's Sake"—Proletarians and Others

Literature and art growing from the pressures of the depression years prompted three book-length works in 1977. While Charles A. Jellison records the voices of the times in his anthology *Tomatoes Were Cheaper: Tales from the Thirties*, Charles R. Hearn considers the effect of hard times on the national consciousness in *The American Dream in the Great Depression*. Monty Noam Penkower's *The Federal Writer's Project* gives a detailed description of the government program which employed such diverse writers as John Steinbeck, Nelson Algren, and Eudora Welty early in their careers. Their experiences in the program gave them access to materials that were to influence their fictional worlds. All three works reviewed in chapter 20 attest to the vigorous and continuing interest in fiction of this period.

a. **James Agee.** One of the most important studies to appear this year is Genevieve Moreau's critical biography, *The Restless Journey of James Agee* (New York: William Morrow and Company). Moreau creates a compassionate portrait of a talented writer whose many and varied interests led to unfinished projects and personal dissatisfactions in the midst of many triumphs. Moreau treats Agee's turn from the writing of poetry to prose in a chapter titled "Commitment," and uses his remarks in a review-essay titled "Art for What's Sake," which appeared in the *New Masses* in 1935, as evidence of his personal goals for the future. According to Moreau, "Agee hoped that an alliance could grow up between Surrealism and Marxism" (p. 149), and in his own work he felt committed to furthering the experimentation he lauded in his various reviews. The commitment led ultimately to his most highly regarded work, *Let Us Now Praise Famous Men* (1941). In a final chapter, which serves as an epilogue to the volume, Moreau contrasts the man with "the Agee legend": "If the generation of the thirties had found its reflection in Fitzgerald, Agee's generation recognized itself in that anti-intellectual poet, musician, journalist, screenwriter. . . . For many, Agee embodied a magnificent dream, intensely pursued but never realized: the dream of a world from which all sterility would be banished" (p. 276). Moreau's study includes a thorough bibliography, copious notes, and a comprehensive index; it is as useful as it is readable, an admirable piece of work.

Jonathan Morse draws examples from *Let Us Now Praise Famous Men* to support some far-ranging observations in "James Agee, Southern Literature, and the Domain of Metaphor" (*SAQ* 76:309–17). Finding that "Agee's metaphors do not record or evoke a reality; they abolish its terms of existence and recreate them, in another image, in a purely esthetic domain," Morse sees affinities to other southern writers: "James Agee, James Dickey, and Allen Tate are as far apart as it is possible to be in most of their attitudes, but they all have this in common, through their language: they historicize, they moralize the phenomena of life by turning them into metaphors."

b. **John Steinbeck.** John Ditsky makes frequent reference to Steinbeck's correspondence in the three chapters of *Essays on "East of*

Eden" (Steinbeck Monograph Series, no. 7) to support his belief in the centrality of this 1952 novel to an understanding of Steinbeck's entire career. Finding evidence of the novel's genesis in letters from the early 1930s, Ditsky sees Steinbeck's early career as a "conscious—and unconscious—preparing for the writing of *East of Eden*" (ix). Ditsky sidesteps the issue of the "quality" of the novel, but he argues for its importance biographically as the work in which Steinbeck attempts to resolve the personal and cultural conflicts that threatened his self-esteem and sense of identity. The first essay directly treats these biographical concerns, while the second and third investigate the sexual and cultural polarities warring within the allegorical levels of the novel. Ditsky's collection badly needs a fourth essay to draw together the ideas presented. Since many critics, as Ditsky himself notes, date Steinbeck's "decline" at or before the appearance of this novel, the issue of its quality in terms of his other work should not be ignored.

As usual, the *Steinbeck Quarterly* was the most comprehensive source of information on and analysis of Steinbeck's works in 1977. As the organ of the Steinbeck Society, the journal serves its membership well. Volume 10 contained minutes and papers of the Steinbeck Society meetings held in the United States in 1975 and 1976, two reports on the First International Steinbeck Congress in Fukuoka, Japan, in August 1976, as well as reviews and a continuing international bibliography. Also Linda Ray Pratt treats Steinbeck's neglected 1936 novel in "In Defense of Mac's Dubious Battle" (*StQ* 10:36–44). Pratt discusses the ambiguities in this novel of Communist labor organizers and finds them complicated by Steinbeck's own admitted ambivalences on the subject. It is the reader's lack of "comfortable assurances" from the author that make the work difficult: "In *In Dubious Battle* Steinbeck raises his hardest questions with his most objective perspective." Pratt's implicit plea is for another look at a complex and rewarding work. Louis D. Owens also contributes an excellent reading in his article "Steinbeck's 'Flight': Into the Jaws of Death" (*StQ* 10:103–8). Owens reviews scholarship on various ambiguous points in the story as he posits his own theory as to its relationship to the rest of the Steinbeck canon: "The living mountains and the dying Pepe are inseparable parts of this whole, reflecting the theme of man's 'oneness' with nature which runs through a large portion of Steinbeck's writing."

Outside the pages of *StQ*, criticism centered on Steinbeck's early fiction. Robert H. Woodward cites convincing evidence from Steinbeck's recently published letters and materials in the Steinbeck collection at the University of Texas that suggest his story "How Edith McGillicuddy Met R. L. Stevenson" was composed in 1934. His brief note, "John Steinbeck, Edith McGillicuddy, and *Tortilla Flat*: A Problem in Manuscript Dating" (*SJS* 3, iii:70–73) takes issue with Roy Simmonds's dating of the piece in an earlier issue of *SJS*. James D. Brasch's "*The Grapes of Wrath* and Old Testament Skepticism" (*SJS* 3, ii:16–27) argues that Jim Casy is more akin to the skeptical author of Ecclesiastes than to Jesus Christ whose initials he shares: "Unlike Jesus, Casy knows that there is no new thing under the sun, there is no good news for the morrow and there are only the humors and labours of the people on which to base a structure for survival." Robert Murray Davis's reading of "Steinbeck's 'The Murder'" (*SSF* 14:63–68) is offered as a defense of the work against charges of racism and sexism leveled against it and its author. As Davis sees it, "the story focuses upon psychological rather than physical action and deals, not with Jelka's being pounded into a satisfactory wife, but with Jim's becoming a satisfactory husband and complete human being." Since Jim achieves this level of humanity only after pounding his wife into submission, Davis's shifting of emphasis does little to deflect the criticism he mentions. Herman Jay discusses *The Grapes of Wrath* and *East of Eden* as two novels which were successfully adapted into films in "Hollywood and American Literature: The American Novel on the Screen" (*EJ* 66,i:82–86). Comparing the filmed versions of *The Grapes of Wrath* and *Huck Finn*, Jay finds that the thematic content of Mark Twain's novel was distorted in the 1939 MGM film starring Mickey Rooney, while the 1939 Twentieth-Century-Fox version of Steinbeck's novel remains close to the intentions of the novelist, despite the more hopeful scene chosen for the ending. The most useful aspect of Jay's rather simplistic article is the annotated list of classic American novels that have been made into films. Jay gives the current distributor for the films to make the listings particularly useful for teachers.

Two articles by Jackson J. Benson give a preview of the approach he will take to Steinbeck in the critical biography he is preparing. He discusses the conflicting traditions in which Steinbeck was writing in "John Steinbeck: Novelist as Scientist" (*Novel* 10:248–64). Believing in "scientific philosophy and methodology," Steinbeck the artist could not completely deny free will as could a scientist. Benson clarifies the scientist-artist conflict described biographically here in a second article—"John Steinbeck's *Cannery Row*: A Reconsideration" (*WAL* 12:11–40). Benson terms this 1944 novel "a work of art, a poem" primarily because Steinbeck fuses the scientist and novelist in the character of Doc. By identifying with Doc, the reader participates in the creation of the work: "When the audience participates in some fashion, depending on the art form, that participation in itself becomes creative, artistic activity." Thus the work becomes "a testament to the redemptive possibilities of art" while still true to Steinbeck's attitude toward science and determinism.

c. Jesse Stuart. Two tributes to Jesse Stuart and his work were published in 1977 in recognition of the author's seventieth birthday. Kentucky honored its native son with the ten essays in *Jesse Stuart: Essays on His Work*, edited by J. R. LeMaster and Mary Washington Clarke (Lexington: Univ. Press of Ky.), and the *Jack London Newsletter* devoted its winter issue to his work. These essays ranged broadly over Stuart's many interests: writing poetry, short stories, novels, and children's books; his teaching and student days at Vanderbilt; as well as the particular use of folklore, humor, language, regionalism, and imagery. Perhaps the most esoteric subject discussed is Fatma M. Mahgoub's "Problems of Translating Jesse Stuart into Arabic" (*JLN* 10:110–14). Ruel E. Foster takes on the task of evaluating Stuart's best work in "*Foretaste of Glory*: An Assessment Thirty Years Later" (*JLN* 10:71–77). Foster sees this 1946 novel as Stuart's greatest claim for lasting critical approval. Loose and episodic in structure, this comic piece offers Stuart's natural language and image making their best setting. Foster suggests, however, in "Jesse Stuart's Way With Short Fiction" (*KansQ* 9,ii:21–29), that this novel is not Stuart's *only* claim to lasting fame. Commenting on the extraordinary breadth of Stuart's audience, particularly that reached through his work in *Esquire* under Arnold Gingrichs's editorship, Foster notes "the ambivalent nature of his reputation." While many of the five hundred prose pieces that Stuart has published were written in haste and are consequently quite weak, Foster concludes that "the body of his work, of which the short stories are the finest portion, represents the most significant work of any Appalachian writer."

d. **Henry Roth and Isaac Rosenfeld.** Irving Howe presents his personal perspective on a group of urban American Jewish writers who grew up in the 1920s and 1930s in "Strangers" (*YR* 46:481–500). They "had to make, rather than merely assume America as their native land." The brand of American romanticism they shared was more likely to reach them "through the streets than the schools." While Emerson remained inaccessible, Whitman and Poe became the most popular American writers with immigrant and second generation American Jews. Howe finds the most lasting influence of Jewish writers on contemporary authors to be the mark they left on the American language. Commenting specifically on Henry Roth's lone novel *Call It Sleep*, Howe finds it a distinct "blending of Joyce roughened to the tonalities of New York and deprived of his Irish lilt." As remarkable as the novel is, however, Howe suggests that it has not been very influential: "His work seems so self-contained there is nothing much to do with it except admire." Bonnie Lyons has published a reworking of her 1973 Tulane dissertation as the first book-length critical study of this author, in *Henry Roth: The Man and His Work* (New York: Cooper Square), and concentrates more on the forces influencing Roth than the strains of his work to be detected in later authors. Several portions of this study have appeared previously (see *ALS 1974*, p. 259), but the critical biography sheds new light on Roth. In "Exile and Redemption in Henry Roth's *Call It Sleep*" (*MarkhamR* 6:72–77), Ita Sheres relates the four sections of the novel to the initiation process identified with Lurianic mysticism. Though Roth denied the "Jewishness" of the novel in an interview published in 1975 (see *ALS 1976*, p. 259), Sheres argues persuasively that the tenets of the 16th-century Jewish mystic Isaac Luria form one of the major strains in the novel.

Mark Schechner's "Isaac Rosenfeld's World" (*PR* 43:524–43) presents a portrait of a "second generation Jewish intellectual" who is outside the pattern that Howe describes. A frequent contributor to the *New Republic, Partisan Review, Commentary, New Leader*, and *The Nation* in the 1940s and early 1950s, Rosenfeld's essays were collected in *An Age of Enormity*. This volume, which Schechner praises highly, as well as his melancholy autobiographical novel *Passage from Home* and collection of stories *Alpha and Omega*, are currently out of print. This fact and Rosenfeld's early death lead Schechner to term his career "a recipe for oblivion": He became the sort of Jew and writer that the age demanded. A Trotskyite in Chicago, Rosenfeld found his cultural identity among his own dead, which, "for an American Jew in search of himself in an age of so much enormity, was not so implausible a thing to do."

e. **James T. Farrell.** The work of another urban ethnic writer, James T. Farrell, is the subject of Ann Douglas's "Studs Lonigan and the Failure of History in Mass Society: A Study" (*AQ* 29:487–505). Douglas attributes his unpopularity among critics and the general reading public to the demands he makes on his audience. Writing simply and directly, Farrell "confronts problems other writers evade": The audience is left with the difficult task of confronting and experiencing Farrell's work, not with interpreting it. As a writer whose "fiction does not exhibit . . . criticism dependency," Farrell is seldom introduced into the classroom. Alvin Starr contributes a biographical note with "Richard Wright and the Communist Party—The James T. Farrell Factor (*CLAJ* 21:41–50), crediting Farrell's address to the Communist-sponsored Writer's Congress in 1935 with giving Wright "the strength to keep even his most important ideas from superseding technique in his fiction." Wright followed his advice and made the same decision to subordinate political to aesthetic concerns. Evidence of the decision—and Farrell's influence on it—is then traced in Wright's "Blueprint for Negro Writing" (1937) and in a comparison of *Studs Lonigan* to *Native Son*.

Farrell himself comments on his early work in two interviews published in 1977: Matthew J. Bruccoli's "James T. Farrell" in *Conversations with Writers I*, pp. 23–45, and David T. Michaelis's "Interview with James T. Farrell" (*TR* 58/59:41–47). To both interviewers, Farrell gives brief, clipped responses to questions concerning influences on his work, work habits, and real-life models for his characters. He tells Michaelis, "I consider all my books just one" and that he identifies himself more with the character Danny O'Neill than with any other fictional creation. Michaelis's interview is followed by the first publication of Farrell's "The Fighting Irish," a short story he was discouraged from publishing in the 1930s because one publisher felt that "none of the characters were glamorous enough for his readers." The familiarity of both interviewers with Farrell's work makes the transcriptions of both conversations valuable.

ii. Social Iconoclasts—West and Salinger

The two dissertations on Nathanael West announced in 1977, like most considerations of his work in recent years, emphasize West's innovations in form and technique. Ray Lewis White makes a valuable addition to William White's recent bibliography of West (see *ALS 1976*, p. 260) in "Nathanael West: Additional Reviews of his Work, 1933–57" (*YULG* 51:218–32). White's entries also add to Dennis P. Vannatta's thorough bibliography of secondary materials on West published within the same year (see *ALS 1976*, pp. 260–61). White lists 94 additional reviews as a challenge to William White's statement that West was generally ignored by contemporary reviewers. The compilation displays an impressive job of searching, since most of the reviews are from unindexed newspapers in the Midwest and New England. While Robert M. Hanon, S.J., does little more than belabor the obvious in pointing out the demonic images surrounding the character Shrike in "The Parody of the Sacred in Nathanael West's *Miss Lonelyhearts* (*IFR* 4:190–93), Jeffrey L. Duncan in "The Problem of Language in *Miss Lonelyhearts*" (*IowaR* 8,i:116–28), examines the novel's humor to show why West was "ahead of his time." Duncan suggests that only this novel truly justifies the current high regard in which West is held: "West's novel does disturb us, threaten, because its form makes its theme intensely meaningful, utterly real." West's humor grows from the disparity between his characters who are "malpracticing empiricists" and the author who was a "practicing idealist." André Le Vot lauds the same quality in West's work as he considers West's influence on a later generation of writers: "Disjunctive and Conjunctive Modes in Contemporary American Fiction" (*ForumH* 14,i[1976]:44–55). He identifies a new "lost generation" in a "new wasteland"—John Hawkes, Robert Coover, Donald Barthelme, and William Burroughs—and terms West "the American prophet of the disjunctive mode."

Gerald Rosen considers the Eastern philosophy prevalent in all of Salinger's fiction in *Zen in the Art of J. D. Salinger*, Modern Authors Monograph Series, no. 3 (Berkeley: Creative Arts), a topic which Warren French identifies as the major appeal his work offers to young readers today (see *ALS 1976*, p. 263). In "A Retrospective Look at *The Catcher in the Rye*" (*AQ* 29:547–62), Gerald Rosen suggests that only after the indebtedness of Salinger's later work to Eastern philosophy had been noted could his 1951 novel be truly understood. Rosen's assertion that Holden fears initiation and "success" as the world defines it is certainly not new to criticism on the novel, however. By comparing Holden to "the young Buddha," Rosen does change the degree to which Salinger's reliance on Buddhism has been recognized in the novel. Still, the article and book, both of which contain the same treatment of the novel, offer few strikingly new insights. Two brief notes, in addition, make rather pointless points about the work: Pamela E. Roper sees a desire for protection in the recurring image of "Holden's Hat" (*NConL* 7,iii:8–9) and associates this with the "caul" or birth cap in the hero's name. Onomastics is also the interest of John Matle in "Calling Miss Aigletinger" (*CEA* 39,iii:18–20). He suggests that William Carlos Williams's 1948 poem addressed to a "profound" expounder of philosophy is a likely source for the name Salinger gave to the teacher who takes her classes to the Museum of Natural History each Sunday. In "Reviewers, Critics, and *The Catcher in the Rye*" (*CritI* 3[1976]:15–38), Carol and Richard Ohmann find fault with virtually all of the major critics of the novel, who have ignored what they see as the "political-economic dimension." The reading they offer presents the novel as a direct assault on American life in the early 1950s. One of the critics specifically cited for his failure of vision, James E. Miller, Jr., responds with his own critique of their approach in "*Catcher* in and of our History" (*CritI* 3:599–603). Terming the Ohmanns' revisionist theory as "Marxist or neo-Marxist," Miller rejects their reading, based as it is on "a tidy and clear-cut ideology," in favor of interpretations which confront the more universal issues Salinger deals with. The Ohmanns' response to Miller defends Marxist criticism as a "dynamic and self-critical method" ("Universals and the Historically Particular" [*CritI* 3:773–77]). A stand-off.

While American critics debate the pertinency of the political-economic issues of the novel, European critics are fascinated with the influence of Salinger's passive, alienated Holden Caulfield on the character of Edgar Wibeau, the protagonist of East German writer

Ulrich Plenzdorf's 1973 novel *Die neuen Leiden des jungen W.* Mireille Tabah's 1975 essay (see *ALS 1976*, p. 262) in *Etudes Germaniques* has been followed by Theodor Langenbruch's "Goethe and Salinger as Models for Ulrich Plenzdorf's Novel *Die neuen Leiden des jungen W*" (*PCL* 2,iii [1976]:60–70) and N. L. Thomas's "Werther in a New Guise: Ulrich Plenzdorf's *Die neuen Leiden des jungen W*" (*ML* 57 [1976]:178–82). Aleksandar Flaker must receive the checkered flag in this race, however, with his book-length study *Modelle der Jeans Prosa: Zur literarischen Opposition bei Plenzdorf im osteuropaischen Romankontext* (Kronberg/Ts:Scriptor Verlag, 1975). Flaker's volume traces a series of East European novels written in the idiom of Holden Caulfield and gives his school of fiction the name "Jeans prose" after the distinctive uniform that the protagonists wear. In addition to Plenzdorf, Flaker sees Soviet novelist Vasilij Aksënov and Yugoslavians Ivan Alamnig and Antun Soljan as leaders of the group of writers whose youthful narrators are out of step with the values of their culture. While Flaker, who teaches Eastern European literature at the University of Zagreb, avoids comment on the political implications inherent in the nonconformist youthful hero in a Communist society, Thomas, Langenbruch, and Tabah all see Plenzdorf subtly echoing Salinger's critique of society. Each of these Western European critics also stresses the importance of Goethe's *Werther* as a model for Plenzdorf's novel, while Flaker leaves this subject undeveloped.

iii. Expatriates and Emigreés

The deaths of Anaïs Nin and Vladimir Nabokov in 1977 give a eulogistic tone to many pieces of periodical criticism on these authors. The year also yielded the first biography of Nabokov, a superb book-length study of the work of Djuna Barnes, and a new, though ultimately minor publication by Henry Miller. In addition, Miller, Nin, and Nabokov were each the subject of individual dissertations announced in 1977.

***a.* Henry Miller.** Interest in the work of Henry Miller continues to grow. Elmer Gertz and Felice Flanery Lewis have edited the correspondence of Miller with Gertz, who was his lawyer during the obscenity trials in Chicago after the American publication of *Tropic of*

Cancer in 1961, in *Henry Miller: Years of Trial and Triumph, 1962–1964* (Carbondale: Southern Ill. Univ. Press). Although a significant portion of the correspondence already has been published (see *ALS 1976*, p. 267), Lewis's introduction and the copious notes (primarily by Gertz) make the volume very useful.

Henry Miller's *Gliding into the Everglades and Other Essays* (Lake Oswego, Ore.: Lost Pleiade Press) is an eclectic gathering of six essays, the longest being Miller's record of his 1928 trip to the Florida Everglades during the real estate boom. Written soon after the trip itself, the essay was lost until recently and is published without revision, even though the first page of the manuscript is missing. The youthful narrator of the travelogue makes a strong contrast to the voice in the other essays, the most recent of which deals with the prosaic topic "On Seeing Jack Nicholson for the First Time." Though Miller knowledgeably discusses cinematography in this critique of *Five Easy Pieces*, it is the personality of Jack Nicholson—"lovable" despite the dastardly deeds of the character he plays—that intrigues Miller. Miller's fascination with personalities is the most obvious feature, too, of Roger Jones's "Henry Miller at 84: An Interview" (*QQ* 84:351–65). While Jones judiciously deletes some of the more candid comments Miller makes about Hemingway and several living authors, enough of Miller's strong negative opinions on recent biographers and critics of his own work remain to reveal his still fiery temper. Not surprisingly, he would prefer that only those who know him very well, i.e., perhaps only close friends, should write about him. Of Jay Martin he says, "I'd like to cut his head off!" He also dismisses Norman Mailer's recent anthology/commentary on his work (see *ALS 1976*, p. 266): "I should like Mailer, I ought to be grateful. He's my number one champion here in America at this time . . . [but] he doesn't even know me and he's writing as if he does." He rejects Mailer's thesis that there are two separate Henry Millers—the writer and the man—and prefers to see his life and work approached as an integral whole.

The most substantial pieces of scholarship on Miller to appear in 1977 were two excerpts from Jay Martin's forthcoming biography. In "Remember to Remember: Henry Miller and the Literary Tradition" (*ClioW* 7:75–90), Martin delineates three formative influences on Miller's work—confessional literature, the use of the *Doppelgänger* in 19th-century literature, and 20th-century psychoanalytic case histories. In " 'The King of Smut': Henry Miller's Tragical History" (*AR* 35:342–67), Martin gives a sympathetic overview of the early career of this controversial figure.

***b.* Djuna Barnes.** While Henry Miller's allegiance to the confessional mode of writing has made him one of the most public of American expatriates, Djuna Barnes remains unquestionably the most private. In *The Art of Djuna Barnes: Duality and Damnation* (New York: New York Univ. Press) Louis F. Kannenstine manages the difficult task of respecting this author's almost Garbo-like desire for privacy, while still offering more insight into her work than has any previous critic. Kannenstine's purpose is to destroy the myth that Barnes is a one-book author by giving careful consideration to all her writings over the last 60 years as journalist, poet, novelist, and dramatist. While James B. Scott's recent study of Barnes also treats her entire corpus (see *ALS 1976*, p. 264), Kannenstine's text seems the more complete. Kannenstine thoroughly reviews published criticism on each of the works as he presents his own reading, thus giving a complete history of her literary reputation. Thoroughly researched, lucidly written, carefully documented and indexed, Kannenstine's volume is a credit to its subject.

***c.* Anaïs Nin.** Richard R. Centing, editor of *Under the Sign of Pisces*, selects a passage from Nin's works as an epigraph to the first 1977 number of this journal devoted to "Anaïs Nin and her circle": "Let us celebrate the refusal to despair." He also writes a brief tribute to the author in the form of a review of Robert Snyder's *Anaïs Nin Observed: From a Film Portrait of a Woman as Artist* (Chicago: Swallow Press), a book he recommends as "a treasured remembrance of the spirit of Anaïs Nin." Among the few articles in the journal is Reesa Marcincy's "A Checklist of the Writings of Anaïs Nin, 1973–76" (8,i:2–14), which updates Ben Franklin's 1974 bibliography (see *ALS 1974*, p. 263). The brief checklist also includes several earlier items omitted in Franklin's later book-length bibliography. Paul Brian's "Sexuality and the Opposite Sex: Variations on a theme by Theophile Gautier and Anaïs Nin" (*ELWIU* 4:122–37) compares Gautier's *Mademoiselle de Maupin* (1836) with Nin's *A Spy in the House of Love* (1954) and finds Nin's novel the more satisfying treatment of romance. While Gautier resorts to creating simplified characters in order to make his more universal comments on the nature of love, Nin avoids stereotypes completely in her complex analysis of the subject.

d. **Vladimir Nabokov.** The death of Vladimir Nabokov occasioned many tributes throughout the world, but none was more fitting than that appearing in *TLS*. Alfred Appel, Jr., contributed "Memories of Nabokov" (7 Oct.: 1138–42) as a personal note on the passing of his friend and teacher. Terming Nabokov a "funnanimal," as Joyce established the character type in *Finnegan's Wake*—perhaps closest to a "phenomenal/fun animal" than any other species—Appel describes the spirit in Nabokov's classroom at Cornell in the mid–1950s and relates other anecdotes of his contact with the irreverent Nabokov in his "remarks in the Irish spirit of a wake."

In the first biography to appear on Nabokov, Andrew Field plays Charles Kinbote to Nabokov's John Shade. Like the editor and poet of *Pale Fire*, biographer and biographee in *Nabokov: His Life in Part* (New York: Viking) are virtually inseparable, and readers of either work are struck with the difficulty of extracting the simplest of truths from the double-edged comments of a usually trustworthy source. Field's adeptness at mastering the techniques of Nabokov in creating ambiguity led one of his reviewers, Walter Walkarput in "Nabokov: His Life *Is* Art" (*ChiR* 29,ii:72–82) to suggest: "Andrew Field does not exist. The book recently published under his name . . . is in fact a novel written by Vladimir Nabokov. It is the final and most triumphantly ironic work of one of the most important authors of this century." While Walkarput (whose own identity is questioned in a disclaimer appended to the review by Fiction Editor Brian Stonehill) backs off his thesis somewhat after discussing Field's 1967 volume, *Nabokov: His Life in Art*, the suggestion is hauntingly appealing. In any case, it is hard to argue with Walkarput's observation that " 'Field' appropriates 'Nabokov,' he belittles him, he ridicules him, he makes his life miserable—and makes himself ludicrous in the process. That it has been possible to read this book as a serious biography shows, among other things, how accustomed we have become to mean-spirited critics." As the first book-length biography of Nabokov, Field's work offers more information and insight into his life, particularly the Berlin years, than does any other work; but the volume's form offers a caveat as well, one that Nabokov himself would have assented to: it is impossible to assemble a series of "facts" and find the complete truth. If "new journalism" blurs the distinctions between fact and fiction, Field's "new biography" merely makes more apparent the ambiguities which have always existed. "An astonishing performance," as Walkarput describes it, Field's biography makes an intriguing addition to contemporary scholarship.

To return to the more traditional treatments of Nabokov's work in 1977, Jane Grayson's *Nabokov Translated: A Comparison of Nabokov's Russian and English Prose* (New York: Oxford) usefully surveys Nabokov, the polyglot, and his attitude toward translations. His dissatisfaction with early translations of his own works, his collaboration with native speakers of English when he undertook the English translations of his Russian works, and his surprisingly unsuccessful attempts to convert the American idiom of his later works into Russian are all carefully traced. Grayson's book will serve especially well the need of the bilingual specialists who consult it with specific questions, though her opening chapter gives a fine overview of stylistic variations in the two English novels he translated into Russian. *Nabokov Translated* is an excellent reference text, but an article such as George M. Cummins's "Nabokov's Russian *Lolita*" (*SEEJ* 21:354–65) offers information in a more readable format. While the technical data that Cummins accumulates as he collates the English and Russian editions of *Lolita* coincide with Grayson's findings, his treatment of the effect of the changes suggests that the Russian version, prepared more than a decade after the English edition appeared in 1955, alters the emphases in the work. The Russian translation becomes Nabokov's "Interpretation" of the highlights of the novel. Cummins traces word and color patterns already delineated by critics treating the English version alone and sees in Nabokov's choice of Russian equivalents the deliberateness of Nabokov's allusive language. As this article and Grayson's volume prove, English students of Nabokov's work have much to gain from the work of comparatists.

In "Nabokov's *Bend Sinister*: the Narrator as God" (*SAF* 5:241–53), Richard F. Patteson, discusses the political and perceptual themes he sees in the 1947 novel. As one of Nabokov's two political novels (the other being *Invitation to a Beheading* [1938]), *Bend Sinister* reveals Nabokov's hatred of dictatorships, and in the work he equates communism with fascism as both leading to the establishment of totalitarian regimes. The pervasive narrator in the work plays god in the lives of characters otherwise caught in the viselike grip of the government. Patteson sees an allegorical connection to Genesis in the structure of the novel. Marina T. Naumann also investigates the political implications of Nabokov's work in "Grin's Grinlandia and Nabokov's Zoolandia: Fantastic Literary Affinities" (*GSlav* 2:237–52). Comparing the life and work of Aleksandr Grinevskii (1880–1922) to those of Nabokov, she finds that both Russian writers, the one who stayed after the Revolution and the one who emigrated, create fantasy worlds in the past as retreats from the less fulfilling worlds of the present. Both visions capture "a Russia lost" and are a symptom of the profound change the Revolution had on Russian writers.

A further article and brief note offer opinions on other possible influences on Nabokov's work. Ralph A. Ciancio's "Nabokov and the Verbal Mode of the Grotesque" (*ConL* 18:509–33) contends that while "Nabokov has no direct forebears in the history of grotesque literature," Shakespeare, Laurence Stern, Lewis Carroll, Edward Lear, and James Joyce share Nabokov's ability to use verbal word play "to derange our senses." Ciancio then rather repetitively cites passages from *Lolita* and *Pale Fire* as examples of "the verbal mode of the grotesque." Michael Delizia has a more limited point to make in "Dr. Nabokov and Mr. Thoreau" (*TSB* 142:1–2). Suggesting that Nabokov first read Thoreau in the early 1940s, Delizia finds some Thoreauvian allusions in his work.

iv. The Southerners

Judging by the critical attention paid to its authors of the 1930s to the 1950s period, the South has risen again, and the number of dissertations reported in 1977 promises that interest will remain high. Southern women writers proved the most popular subjects for theses: five on Eudora Welty, three on Carson McCullers, and one each on Caroline Gordon and Katherine Anne Porter. The four dissertations devoted to Robert Penn Warren treat his philosophical views, and the single one on Thomas Wolfe considers his choice of characters. Two dissertations also consider the undeservedly neglected topic of the fiction of Tennessee Williams.

In his discussion of the 25 *Books that Changed the South* (see also chapter 20) Robert B. Downs devotes chapters to several influential 19th-century works of fiction, but includes only Thomas Dixon's glorification of the Ku Klux Klan in *The Clansman* (1905) with the trend-setting nonfiction works he selects as exemplary of the South in the 20th century. His chapter titled "Nostalgia for Never-Never Land" treats the Agrarian manifesto of twelve southerners from Vanderbilt, *I'll Take My Stand* (1930), and is descriptive rather than analytic in purpose. Summarizing each essay in the collection in a brief paragraph, Downs concludes by tracing the critical reception of the work, not by a specifically southern audience, however, but by the American audience at large. Since Downs fails to picture the nature of the South's changed world explicitly, his view of the nature of that society emerges only implicitly in the selection of these particular 25 works. In his five-page introduction, he tantalizes readers with a list of 20 more works which he might have included, works such as *Absalom! Absalom!*, *Tobacco Road*, *Gone with the Wind*, *Native Son*, and *Look Homeward, Angel.* The criteria by which these works were rejected and others selected remain unstated, but clearly a very different book would have resulted from other and equally attractive cullings from even this list of 45. The effect of such a survey as this could be pernicious, distorting the picture of the American South through sheer eclecticism.

The single novel by Fugitive poet Allen Tate is the subject of Anneke Leenhouts's "The Horseman Riding Over the Precipice: George Posey in Allen Tate's *The Fathers*" (*DQR* 7:265–73). Leenhouts joins several critics noted last year (see *ALS 1976*, p. 270) who see the novel as undervalued by current criticism. Louisiana State University Press invites a wider audience for the novel through its 1977 republication of the work, and has also reissued *I'll Take My Stand* with an updating of Louis D. Rubin's introduction to the 1962 edition.

Another figure associated with the Nashville Agrarians and Fugitives is the subject of Jane Gibson Brown's "The Early Novels of Caroline Gordon: Myth and History as a Fictional Technique" (*SoR* 13:289–98). Brown recounts Gordon's delineation of the major techniques to be seen in contemporary fiction as given in her lectures at the University of Dallas in January 1973 and applies these general principles to Gordon's own early stories and novels. "The juxtaposition of modern life against mythology (principally that found in Virgil's *Aeneid*) makes explicit her tragic vision of life" in Brown's view.

Two comparatively minor southern writers received attention this year. James W. Thomas's "Lyle Saxon's Struggle with *Children of Strangers*" (SoS 16,i:27–40) uses the fortieth anniversary of the publication of Saxon's lone novel as the occasion for this long biographical article. Terming Saxon a "lotus-eater," Thomas suggests that he was distracted from the pursuit of fiction by his journalistic interests and his work as head of the Louisiana Federal Writer's Project. "As talented as Saxon was and as wrongfully neglected as he has become, he was not a great writer," Thomas concludes. If this is the single article that is to appear on Saxon—and Thomas does not encourage further treatment—Saxon's novel as well as his biography deserves some consideration. Edward J. Piacentino contributes "T. S. Stribling: A Checklist for His Southern Novels" (*MissQ* 30:639–47) as a useful addition to the meagre bibliography appended to Wilton Eckley's critical biography of the Pulitzer-prize-winning satirist (see *ALS 1975*, p. 310).

a. **Robert Penn Warren.** The early work of Agrarian Robert Penn Warren dominates criticism published on the writer in 1977. Tj. A. Westendorp's "Robert Penn Warren as Critic and Novelist: the Early Phase" (*DQR* 7:274–85) seems to be an excerpt of a longer study dealing with Warren's whole career. It stresses his rejection of the "fatally optimistic vision of the future of America," which was the legacy left to American writers by Emerson and Whitman. Westendorp reads Warren's first novel, *Night Rider* (1939), as an indication of the directions Warren's later writings would take. Jerry A. Herndon in "A Probable Source for the Buffalo-Hunting Episodes in Warren's *Night Rider*" (*Rendezvous* 11:53–62) sees E. Douglas Branch's *The Hunting of the Buffalo* (1929) as the source of Willie Proudfit's stories of hunting in the work. Warren's artistic accomplishment in the novel consists of bestowing symbolic meaning on the step-by-step procedures outlined by Branch. David M. Wyatt finds another distinctive quality in Warren's work in "Robert Penn Warren: The Critic as Artist" (*VQR* 53:475–87). He ranges broadly over Warren's fiction and poetry as he shows the author's penchant for including interpretations of works within his fictions themselves. Concluding that "Warren's novels read like essays about themselves," Wyatt suggests that while Warren has stated that he will write no further criticism per se, his role as a critic figures largely in his achievement as a writer of fiction.

While no new treatments of Warren's best-known novel, *All the King's Men*, emerged in 1977, Robert H. Chamber's *Twentieth Century Interpretations of "All the King's Men": A Collection of Critical Essays* (Englewood Cliffs, N.J.: Prentice-Hall) will make some of the most informative critical pieces on the novel accessible. In the two interviews with Warren appearing in 1977, *All the King's Men* is a central concern. While John Baker's interview appearing in *Conversations with Writers I*, pp. 279–302, and Peter Stitt's for the *Sewanee Review* (85:467–77) echo the structures, and subjects of other recent transcriptions of conversations with Warren, each adds new information, depending on the concerns of the interviewer (see *ALS 1974*, p. 272, and *ALS 1976*, pp. 270–71). Warren's current preference for writing poetry is Stitt's major interest, and Warren's statement that he stopped writing short stories because "I've only written three that I even like" begs for the follow-up question which Stitt fails to ask.

***b.* Carson McCullers.** Three articles on Carson McCullers appearing in 1977 all concentrate on *The Heart is a Lonely Hunter*. Louis D. Rubin's "Carson McCullers: The Aesthetic of Pain" (*VQR* 53:265–83) argues that McCullers, as can be seen in this work in particular, "speaks not to the intelligence so much as to the untutored emotions." What one takes away from her work is "the way that it feels to be lonely." For McCullers, "solitude is inevitable and always painful." While other southern writers such as Flannery O'Connor use "freaks" to make the suspect "normalcy" of other characters more obvious, McCullers has her "freaks" assume the role of everyman. They become the human condition incarnate: "It isn't that freaks are commentaries or criticism on normality; they *are* normality." Again, using *The Heart is a Lonely Hunter* as representative of McCullers's work, Joseph R. Millichap's "Distorted Matter and Disjunctive Forms: The Grotesque as Modernist Genre" (*ArQ* 33:339–47) sees her characteristic themes of "loneliness and fragmentation" emerge in the work. He groups the work and its author with a school of literature that reflects both modernism and a preoccupation with "the Grotesque." The third essay, Nancy B. Rich's "The 'Ironic Parable of Fascism' in *The Heart is a Lonely Hunter*" (*SLJ* 9,ii:108–23), attempts to restore McCullers's original political intent in writing the novel by delineating "an ironic parable of Fascism," as McCullers describes it, at the core of the work: "When the original publisher changed its title from *The Mute* to *The Heart is a Lonely Hunter* . . . he inadvertently shifted its focus from the sought-after to the seekers, thereby effectively restricting the theme to the plight of a few people." The parable, Rich finds, leads to an affirmation of the democratic process in the work.

c. Katherine Anne Porter. Two treatments of Katherine Anne Porter's Miranda Stories reach very similar conclusions. Barbara Harrell Carson finds "the struggle for literal self-possession by the women of the Rhea family" to be a common thread linking the seven stories in *The Old Order* and the two novellas, *Old Mortality* and *Pale Horse, Pale Rider*. In "Winning: Katherine Anne Porter's Women," in *The Authority of Experience: Essays in Feminist Criticism*, edited by Arlyn Diamond and Lee R. Edwards (Amherst: Univ. of Mass. Press), pp. 239–56, Carson analyzes the race imagery prominent in both works and concludes that "a valid selfhood," as the prize sought, and its achievement make for a "painful victory" for Porter's "winners." Rosemary Hennessy's "Katherine Anne Porter's Model for Heroines" (*ColQ* 25:301–15) approaches the same works as offering "innovative images of authenticity for women": "In the Miranda stories Katherine Anne Porter has created a heroine whose journey from innocence to experience embraces universal themes and also offers a positive model for the female *Bildungsroman*." One of the lessons that Miranda learns is that "forfeiting romantic love is the price of self-knowledge," and the mastering of such a hard lesson is certainly an example of the kind of "painful victory" that Carson sees occurring in the stories.

Michael Gessel deals harshly—and rather unfairly—with Porter in "Katherine Anne Porter: The Low Comedy of Sex" (*Gerber Festschrift*, pp. 139–52). Writing as if he were one of Porter's readers, Gessel takes offense at her tactics as a writer as well as what he sees as her warped attitude toward love: "The reader is the butt of the writer, who involves him in order to shake him up. We are likely to find a character with whom we may identify ourselves at the outset of a work—perhaps the character is open and charming—but we are likely to suffer discomfort later in the work when our character hangs out his deformities and in his emotional monstrosities we recognize our own" (p. 139). Angered by such manipulation, Gessel concludes, "I resent Porter"; he does not sustain his case by reference to specific works.

Joan Givner's familiarity with the correspondence of Porter gave her material for three articles published in 1977. Possibly the weakest of the three is "Two Leaning Towers: Viewpoints by Katherine Anne Porter and Virginia Woolf in 1940" (*VWQ* 3,i/ii:85–90) in which Givner compares works by Woolf and Porter written simultaneously—and apparently independently—which coincidentally share the same title. The Leaning Tower of Pisa is the central image in each and both concern "the responsibility of the artist in time of world catastrophes." These similarities lead Givner to draw some dubious biographical parallels between the two women writers: Woolf's suicide finds its match in Porter's 20-year retreat from writing after work on "The Leaning Tower." In " 'Her Great Art, Her Sober Craft': Katherine Anne Porter's Creative Process" (*SWR* 62:217–30), Givner reviews correspondence between Porter and novelist Josephine Herbst carried on while Porter was writing "The Leaning Tower." Using Porter's observations on Germany in the 1930s as a starting point, Givner presents a reading of the story emphasizing the political commentary that is part of the work's symbolic structure. Givner uses a similar technique in "The Genesis of *Ship of Fools*" (*SLJ* 10,i:14–30) as she refers to the 20-page, single-spaced letter that Porter wrote to Caroline Gordon in 1931 about her voyage to Europe that carries the germ of the 1962 novel. While *Ship of Fools* has provided "a fool's paradise for symbol-hunters and analogy-seekers" among previous critics, Givner notes that "few of the names, characters, and events in the novel were invented." Such careful scholarship results in a fine reading of the novel.

As a footnote to work on Porter this year, several minor items should be mentioned. Mary Rohrberger's "Betrayer or Betrayed: Another View of 'Flowering Judas' " (*NMAL* 2:item 10) posits the idea that it is Laura who is betrayed in the story, not that she is the betrayer as other critics have suggested. While Rohrberger's brief note cannot settle the debate, it is at least part of a continuing attempt to resolve a central point in an important work, a quality not shared in a current exchange in *CEA* resulting from Charles W. Smith's assertion that Porter made a grammatical error in the opening sentence of her story "Theft" (see *ALS 1976*, p. 274). Carol Simpson Stern writes intelligently in "'A Flaw in Katherine Anne Porter's "Theft": The Teacher Taught': A Reply" (*CEA* 39,iv:4–8) in defense of the sentence but only manages to provoke Smith's "Rebuttal" (*CEA* 39,iv:9–11), which decries "Porter's apparently intransigent pride and Professor Stern's evident approval of that pride." There seems to be little point in carrying the "debate" further.

d. **Tennessee Williams.** Two very readable articles treat fiction in Jac Tharpe's *Tennessee Williams: A Tribute* (Jackson: Univ. Press of Miss.), a 900-page collection of over 50 critical essays on the author. Ren Draya's "The Fiction of Tennessee Williams" (pp. 647–62) focuses on the characters, themes, and techniques in his fiction which relate to his plays. Thomas J. Richardson's primarily biographical essay, "The City of Day and the City of Night: New Orleans and the Exotic Unreality of Tennessee" (pp. 631–46), gives readings for the 11 stories in *One Arm and Other Stories* (1948), stressing the importance of setting in the works. Unfortunately, the final essay in the collection, S. Alan Chesler's "Tennessee Williams: Reassessment and Assessment" (pp. 848–80) does not even comment on the current reputation of Williams as a writer of fiction, which contributes to the effect left by the impressive collection that Williams's work as a writer of fiction occupies a very small place in his overall achievement.

e. **Eudora Welty.** While no book-length study of Eudora Welty's work was published in 1977, a French journal (*Delta*) devoted to the study of southern American literature published seven essays and an unpublished short story as a special tribute to the author (see chapter 21,ii). This journal and Todd Freeman's interview with Welty in *Conversations with Writers II*, pp. 285–316, offer the year's most sustained presentations on Welty's life and work, but four pieces of periodical criticism also deserve comment. Michael Kreyling, in "Life with People: Virginia Woolf, Eudora Welty and *The Optimist's Daughter* (*SoR* 13:250–71), uses Welty's *Paris Review* interview of 1972 (see *ALS 1976*, p. 252) to support his assertion that Welty's novel owes a large debt to Woolf's *To the Lighthouse*. He also considers an earlier version of Welty's novel appearing in the *New Yorker* in 1969 and suggests that changes made before book-length publication stress the theme of distance, a direct tie between the two novels. In "The Problem of Time in Welty's *Delta Wedding*" (*SAF* 5:213–25), Douglas Messerli agrees with Louis D. Rubin's statement that Welty's characters in general "pretend that it [time] never exists." The "intruders" in *Delta Wedding* are exceptions to this generalization, and by the novel's end, Messerli suggests, some of the Fairchild children have gained an awareness of time that will make it possible for them to participate in the world: "They will live a life attuned to the present but not exclusively of the present . . . they will accept the flux of time and will partake of the legacy of the past, of the future's hope." In his treatment of "First Love" and "A Still Moment," Albert P. Devlin terms the two stories published in 1942 "the highest achievement of Miss Welty's early maturity" ("Eudora Welty's Historicism: Method and Vision" [*MissQ* 30:213–34]). Admiring Welty's "facticity," Devlin investigates the historical basis for both works and finds that of "A Still Moment" the more difficult to establish. He treats this topic in more detail in "From Horse to Heron: A Source for Eudora Welty" (*NMW* 10:62–68) as he describes the notebooks of several of her historical travellers. As influential as these sources are on the work, he finds Robert M. Coates's *The Outlaw Years* (1930) the immediate source of the protagonist and central image in the story. In another note in the same journal, W. U. McDonald, Jr., does more collating (see chapter 21), but his conclusions are less informative. "Eudora Welty's Revisions of 'Pageant of Birds'" (*NMW* 10:1–10) compares the version of Welty's essay concerning a pageant held in a Negro church appearing in the *New Republic* in 1943 with a revision for a limited, signed edition in 1974 to show that "language which was acceptable in a liberal Eastern publication in the 40s is not acceptable to a sensitive Southern writer in the 70s."

Several essays too brief to make much of a stir treat well-known and much-discussed ambiguities in Welty's short fiction. Timothy Dow Adams discusses the demise of the big band era and the racial implications of Welty's story in "A Curtain of Black: White and Black Jazz Styles in '*Powerhouse*'" (*NMW* 10:57–61). Nora Calhoun Graves has less substance to discuss as she wonders "Who is the father of Shirley T.?" in "Shirley T. in Eudora Welty's 'Why I live at the P.O.'" (*NConL* 7,ii:6–7). Roland Bartel, too, treats an old issue in "Life and

Death in Eudora Welty's 'A Worn Path'" (*SSF* 14:288–90), in which he finds the psychological depths of the story to be enhanced by the assumption that the Phoenix's grandson is already dead before she makes her journey to get his medicine: "Phoenix has to make herself and others believe that her grandson lives so that she can endure her hardships and her subconscious awareness of the imminence of her own death." Both of the last notes force clarity on calculated ambiguities in these stories at the expense of more pertinent issues.

***f.* Thomas Wolfe.** An excellent comprehensive bibliography is the major feature of this year's work on Thomas Wolfe. John S. Phillipson's *Thomas Wolfe: A Reference Guide* (Boston: G. K. Hall) annotates almost 600 articles, chapters in books, book-length studies, and dissertations written on Wolfe from 1929 to 1976. For the most part, Phillipson omits reviews of specific works since the most important of these have recently been reprinted (see *ALS 1975*, p. 311) and are therefore readily available. One result that can be hoped for from this compilation is that editors of the journals that receive articles on Wolfe will realize how repetitious some submissions are. Phillipson also edits *The Thomas Wolfe Newsletter*, which began publication in spring 1977. Desiring that the semiannual publication "be neither excessively scholarly nor excessively popular," Phillipson calls for brief papers—1,000–2,000 words—and the eight articles in volume 1 suggest the format will work well. Most of the first year's essays are biographical, with several notes contributed by friends and acquaintances explaining their own contact with Wolfe. The continuing features—"Wolfe Trails," "Wolfe Pack," and "Wolfe Calls"—offer bulletin-board space for announcements and a forum for the exchange of information.

Richard Walser, C. Hugh Holman, and Floyd C. Watkins together account for 50 of the items listed by Phillipson, and each critic is heard from again this year. Richard Walser's biographical study *Thomas Wolfe Undergraduate* (Durham, N.C.: Duke Univ. Press) thoroughly documents Wolfe's career as an undergraduate at the University of North Carolina at Chapel Hill from 1916 to 1920. Appending over 600 notes to his 134-page text, Walser is exhaustive in his treatment of the campus, faculty, and activities. The major effect of the volume is to put to rest the hasty generalization that Wolfe at college shared Eugene Gant's withdrawn, introspective personality.

Though only 15 years of age when he entered the university, Wolfe fitted easily into the social and academic life. A campus leader, he eventually edited the student newspaper, and was selected to deliver the class poem upon graduation. Walser appends fragments of a play that Wolfe wrote in the early 1920s about his favorite philosophy professor, Horace Williams, to show how deeply Chapel Hill had left its mark.

Wolfe's response to place is also the subject of two papers delivered at Wolfe's 75th birthday celebration in his hometown of Asheville, North Carolina, in October 1975. Floyd C. Watkins discusses "Thomas Wolfe and Asheville Again and Again and Again . . ." (*SLJ* 10,i:31–55) as he describes the "esthetic perspective" that life in Asheville gave to Wolfe in his early writings: "Once the native left, neither the going nor the coming back was ever altogether a happy experience," he concludes. C. Hugh Holman treats Wolfe's Whitmanesque epic vision in "Thomas Wolfe and America" (*SLJ* 10,i:56–74). In one letter to Maxwell Perkins which Holman quotes, Wolfe's identification of himself with Whitman—and perhaps with the Boy Scouts of America—rings clear: "Like Mr. Joyce, I have at last discovered my own America, I believe I have found my language, I think I know my way. And I shall wreak out my vision of this life, this way, this world and this America, to the top of my bent, to the height of my ability, but with an unswerving devotion, integrity and purity of purpose that shall not be menaced, altered or weakened by any one." Holman considers the relationship between Wolfe and his Scribner's editor Maxwell Perkins in "The Dwarf on Wolfe's Shoulder" (*SoR* 13:240–49). Lamenting the tendency of critics to blame Wolfe for letting Perkins make important artistic decisions in his works, Holman sees Perkins's expressed desire to become "a little dwarf on the shoulders of a great general" as responsible for the collaboration which weakens Wolfe's reputation as a creative artist. It was Wolfe's "lack of artistic self-confidence" that permitted him to be manipulated by Perkins; still, Perkins is the true culprit, not Wolfe: "The provincial boy from the North Carolina mountains was in this particular conflict no match for the urbane New York editor who sat on his shoulder and directed his finest talents to a vast battlefield not properly shaped for them." The titles of two brief notes on Wolfe are adequate summaries of their contents: Albert E. Wilhelm finds

"Borrowings from *Macbeth* in Wolfe's 'The Child by Tiger'" (*SSF* 14:179–80), while Louise Jackson Wright volunteers the information that "It Was in Paris that I saw Thomas Wolfe" (*LGJ* 5,i:22–23).

Charmian Green contributes an important piece of scholarship in "Wolfe's Stonecutter Once Again: An Unpublished Episode" (*MissQ* 30:611–23), which finds in three of Wolfe's unpublished plays of the early 1920s a record of the emerging character of W. O. Gant in *Look Homeward, Angel.* Green's description of the present chaotic state of these early manuscripts makes one regret anew that her recent death will leave the task of unravelling other problems in these manuscripts to others. She writes with clarity and understanding on an important topic.

v. Popular Fiction

Outside of the work in detective and science fiction, the popular literature of the 1930s to the 1950s received relatively little attention in 1977. Dissertations on James Gould Cozzens (two), James Jones, and Thornton Wilder concentrate on their early works, while the two dissertations on H. L. Davis both focus on his western settings. The single dissertation on Walter Van Tilberg Clark discussed the broad question of "Humanity and Eternity" throughout his works (John Harlan Alt, *DAI* 38:3493A). David Lee Mogen considers a provocative topic in "Frontier Themes in Science Fiction" (*DAI* 38:2792A), which suggests a melding of these two genres of popular fiction.

***a.* Best Sellers.** The two popular novels treated by Floyd C. Watkins's *In Time and Place* do not receive very sympathetic readings, as can be readily seen in the titles of the two chapters that treat them: "Flat Wine from *The Grapes of Wrath*" (pp. 19–32) and *Gone with the Wind* as Vulgar Literature" (pp. 33–50). Decrying the factual errors in both works, Watkins posits that "a writer who does not know a world well should not write about it. But that is precisely what Californian John Steinbeck did . . . when he wrote about Okies, a people he did not know" (p. 19). In a similar critique, "Margaret Mitchell wrote about a past she had both inherited and researched, but she represented both northern and southern cultures falsely, and she created stereotyped characters who are untrue in human as well as historical terms" (pp. 9–10). Watkins does not support these assertions, nor does he explain how Willa Cather, William Styron, and William Faulkner (who receive his praise) managed to treat successfully materials outside of their immediate experience while Steinbeck and Mitchell failed. Someone should arrange a debate between Watkins and Leslie Fiedler, who thinks that *Gone with the Wind* is one of the few novels of the 1930s worth rereading (see *ALS 1976*, pp. 251–52).

Philip Gordon joins the attack on best sellers, but his target has few serious defenders. In "The Extroflective Hero: A Look at Ayn Rand" (*JPC* 10:701–10), Gordon laments "the limitations of Rand's concept of ego" and gives a reading of *The Fountainhead* (1943) to support his assertions. Who would disagree with his statement that "erecting starkly simplistic frameworks highly antagonistic to her own views, Rand winds the key in her heroes' backs and then commands them in rigid opposition"? Until a defender appears, however, such observations only serve to reinforce the general dismissal of her work.

The three authors of *The Yearling* (1938), *The Pilgrim Hawk* (1940), and *The Bad Seed* (1954) were also subjects of periodical criticism this year, but not in reference to these well-known works. (1) Lamar York's "Marjorie Kinnan Rawlings' Rivers" (*SLJ* 9,ii:91–107) discusses the metaphor of the river in her autobiography *Cross Creek* (1942) and draws a questionable parallel between its significance here and a literal attachment to the rivers of Florida, which offered Rawlings creative inspiration. (2) John Stark probes early fiction concerning Wisconsin in "Glenway Westcott's Images of Truth" (*GrLR* 4,i:1–9). In the novels of the 1920s, Stark finds a promising talent, but ultimately his article confirms Gertrude Stein's observation that Wescott "has a certain syrup but it does not pour." Stark attributes Westcott's failure to live up to his early promise to his rejection of modernism. (3) William T. Going's "William March: Regional Perspective and Beyond" (*PLL* 13:430–43) is a useful, well-documented biographical sketch of the author from southern Alabama. Going calls for a full-length study of his six novels and uncollected short fiction as well as for more information on his life: "He was an interesting representative of that unlost Lost Generation of writers who did their major work between world wars." Roy S. Simmonds treats "William March's 'Personal Letter': Fact into Fiction" (*MissQ* 30:625–37) as he compares March's observations on Germany seen in the business letters sent home (signed by his real name William Campbell) with the story which appeared in 1945. As an "anti-Nazi polemic," the story is not as successful as Thomas Wolfe's more moving "I Have a Thing to Tell You," which covers the same subject. Still, the movement from letter to story does show how March employed his own experience in his fiction. Bernard F. Engel plays "Taps for Sergeant Jones" (*SSMLN* 7,ii:6–8), while David Bazelon makes a plea for further study of two of James Jones's neglected novels in "In Memoriam: In Defense" (*Salmagundi* 38/39: 151–52). In his tribute to Jones, David Bazelon terms him "the most obviously successful writer of his generation" because of the popular success of *From Here to Eternity* (1951), which earned him over a million dollars in royalties and movie rights. He finds *Some Came Running* (1957) and *The Thin Red Line* (1962) to be the two novels most deserving of the critical attention denied to Jones's work as a whole.

***b.* Science Fiction.** The quality and quantity of 1977 works appearing on science fiction are impressive. Robert Scholes continues his work in the genre (see *ALS 1975*, p. 452) by collaborating with Eric S. Rabkin on a brief outline of *Science Fiction: History, Science, Vision* (New York: Oxford Univ. Press). The final section, "Vision," is the most pertinent to literary scholarship, as the authors present readings of ten innovative works, Olaf Stapleton's *Star Maker* (1937) and Arthur C. Clarke's *Childhood's End* (1953) among them. Three volumes of collected essays and a fourth historical study give a fine overview of the current state of the genre and its uphill battle to gain critical acceptance. Thomas D. Clareson edits *Many Futures, Many Worlds: Theme and Form in Science Fiction* (Kent, Ohio: Kent State Univ. Press), a collection of 14 essays on various themes developed in works of science fiction. While no essays treat specific authors, the comprehensive index to the volume shows that works of Isaac Asimov, Robert A. Heinlein, and Kurt Vonnegut are frequently discussed. Contributors are scholars of ancient and modern literatures and theology, scientists and current writers of science fiction such as Samuel R. Delany and Beverly Friend. Peter Nicholls's *Science Fiction at Large: A Collection of Essays About the Interface Between Science Fiction and Reality* (New York: Harper and Row) gathers the 11 addresses given by practitioners and theoreticians of science fiction delivered at the Institute of Contemporary Arts in London in 1975. The well-known participants at the conference include Ursula K. Le Guin, Edward de Bono, John Taylor, Harry Harrison, and Alvin Toffler. In "Science Fiction and Mrs. Brown" (pp. 13–34), Le Guin stresses the need for writers of SF to recognize the need to emphasize characterization and not merely dwell within a mechanized distant world populated by machines in human guise. Damon Knight's anthology *Turning Points: Essays on the Art of Science Fiction* (New York: Harper and Row) presents a history of the critical acceptance of the genre by reprinting positive and negative assessments of SF over the last 30 years. Aldous Huxley, Arthur C. Clarke, Robert A. Heinlein, and Isaac Asimov are among the well-known practitioners who are heard from in the volume. In *The Futurians* (New York: John Day) Knight also writes a history of The Futurian Society of New York which flourished from 1933 to 1945 and whose members to a great extent shaped the dimensions of SF writing today. Knight, who was himself a member of the group after 1941, covers the social, political, and literary interests of the organization and members such as Asimov, Cyril Kornbluth, Robert A. Lowndes, Judith Merrill, John B. Michel, Frederik Pohl, and Donald A. Wollheim. He documents his personal histories of these figures and of the magazines they served as writers and editors with excerpts from their letters and material from small journals reviewing their work. It is a fascinating history, well researched and indexed, and Knight's acquaintance with the figures he treats gives added authority to his study.

Isaac Asimov is the subject of the first volume in a projected series of essay collections on "Writers of the 21st Century" which will include Philip K. Dick, Ray Bradbury, Robert A. Heinlein, and Ursula K. Le Guin. *Isaac Asimov*, edited by Joseph D. Olander and Martin Harry Greenberg (New York: Taplinger), includes nine new critical essays treating such subjects as his use of technological metaphors, characterizations, attitude toward computers and robots, narrative structures; in addition there are several articles on his science fiction mystery stories, *Foundation* novels, and recent fiction. Asimov himself contributes "Asimov's Guide to Asimov" (pp. 201–6) in which he responds to specific points brought out in the essays. Hesitant at first, Asimov finally agrees that perhaps the "deep levels" developed in the nine articles might, indeed, exist: "I'm glad of that, even delighted; but, if you don't mind, I intend not to think about it too much. After all, if I ever started *trying* to do all these wonderful things on purpose, I might, in the excitement of it all, forget how to tell a story—and I certainly wouldn't want that to happen" (p. 206). Olander and Greenberg complete their collection with a biographical sketch of Asimov, a bibliography of his nonfiction, novels, collections, and uncollected stories arranged alphabetically by title, and a comprehensive index to the volume. All of these SF works published in 1977 have been prepared with care and are very professional, demonstrating the scholarly respectability of science fiction today.

Philip A. Shreffler's *The H. P. Lovecraft Companion* (Westport, Conn.: Greenwood) is written more for the enthusiast than for the critic. Though Shrefller does treat issues such as "Lovecraft's Literary Theory" (pp. 3–38) and the sources for Lovecraft's images of monsters ("The Mythos Monsters," pp. 153–75), the bulk of the volume consists of plot summaries and an alphabetically arranged annotated catalogue of monsters and major characters in Lovecraft's work. Schreffler appends a Lovecraft essay of 1938, "The History and Chronology of *Necronomicon*" (pp. 181–83) and a selected bibliography of primary and secondary works on Lovecraft, as well as works of the occult which influenced him. August Derleth's "H. P. Lovecraft: The Making of a Literary Reputation, 1937–71" (*BBr* 25:13–25) is a much more informative source of information on Lovecraft's treatment in published criticism, however. John Taylor's "Poe, Lovecraft, and the Monologue" (*Topic* 12:52–62) traces Lovecraft's use of the first person narrator throughout his work and attributes it to Lovecraft's interest in Poe.

c. Detective Fiction. In contrast to the six collections of essays on authors of science fiction, detective fiction seems almost neglected, though Frank MacShane's edition of *The Notebooks of Raymond Chandler and English Summer: A Gothic Romance* (New York: Ecco Press of Viking) brings new primary material into print. Enthusiasts might also be interested in a new "how-to" volume, *Writing Suspense and Mystery Fiction*, edited by A. S. Burack (Boston: The Writer), which includes chapters written by current practitioners, as well as "nut-and bolts" advice on breaking into print. One good feature of the collection is the selection of classic essays on the genre by

Dorothy L. Sayers, S. S. Van Dine, Howard Haycraft, Raymond Chandler, and Ogden Nash. For the real neophyte, the volume also contains a "Glossary of Legal Terms" provided by the American Bar Association (pp. 329–41). Two provocative articles appeared in *ArmD*, Marvin Lachman's brief historical survey of "The American Regional Mystery: Southern California" (*ArmD* 10:294–306) and Zahava K. Dorinson's "Ross Macdonald: The Personal Paradigm and Popular Fiction" (*ArmD* 10:43–45, 87). In an article that is more provoking than provocative, Norman Kiell equates Macdonald with his detective Lew Archer in "The Very Private Eye of Ross Macdonald" (*L&P* 27:21–34, 67–73). Though Kiell does not discuss biographical evidence for his thesis, he suggests "Macdonald himself is obviously caught in the penumbra of an unresolved oedipal conflict and although aware of its mythological and psychoanalytical significance is unable to work his way out through the thicket." Concluding that "his novels are sublimations for his hidden unconscious motives and the hitching post for masochistic repetition of injustice experienced in reality," Keill's eagerness in reading the author into his work will no doubt dissuade his readers from embarking on their own careers as writers of detective fiction.

University of North Carolina at Chapel Hill

15. Fiction: The 1950s to the Present

James H. Justus

Since 1968 the costars of this chapter have most frequently been Mailer and O'Connor. Commentators apparently are now heeding the half-serious call of more than a decade ago for a moratorium on O'Connor criticism, since for the past two years the extraordinary volume has been subsiding. A similar tapering-off in work on Mailer is perceptible for the first time this year. And though studies of Vonnegut, Pynchon, and Malamud are extensive, the most attractive subject is no individual author but a subgenre: science fiction. Abused and tormented as it is by its own custodians, I have noted only representative studies. Among the 53 relevant dissertations reported, multiple authors continue to be popular; and studies of separate writers cluster around Mailer (6), Malamud (5), Kerouac (who with 4 seems to be on the verge of rediscovery), and Hawkes and Pynchon (3 each). The fact that William Gaddis and John Cheever show up as subjects—along with single studies of Paul Bowles, Peter DeVries, Wright Morris, and I. B. Singer—promises some original work in the future. Dissertations on special topics, however, while they may really be solid contributions, sound either depressingly familiar (black humor, "visions of reality," community in southern literature, madness in contemporary fiction) or indulgently creative ("meta-naturalism," "Neo-Romanticism," "Irrealism").

i. General Studies

a. Overviews and Special Topics. The four novelists listed in Frank D. McConnell's *Four Postwar American Novelists: Bellow, Mailer, Barth, and Pynchon* (Chicago: Univ. of Chicago Press) are said to define the essential range of fiction since World War II, and despite their differences they are described as both romantic and "post-Apocalyptic" in their efforts to construct "mythologies of authenticity" which can rebuild a "truly humane city." McConnell calls for literary critics to follow these novelists in reforging connections "between literature and social morality, between literary experiment and the pressures of history." Specific treatments of individual novelists will be noted in appropriate places below.

One of McConnell's questionable theses is that the American novel has been Europeanized since 1945; an essay that both complements and corrects this view is "American and European Makers of the Twentieth-Century Novel," the introductory essay by Harry R. Garvin in his collection, *Makers of the Twentieth-Century Novel.* Despite the emergence of the European tradition of the novel of ideas in Bellow and Barth, Garvin argues that the tide of influence has been largely in the other direction—European novelists have developed "the American sensibility" in order to respond better to the crises of estrangement and discontinuity.

Most of Keith M. May's concern in *Out of the Maelstrom: Psychology and the Novel in the Twentieth Century* (New York: St. Martin's) is with British modernists, although one chapter, "Attack on the Unconscious: Sartre and the Post-War American Novel" (pp. 78–97), covers Updike, Mailer, Salinger, and Bellow. May's investigation of similarities between novelists and psychologists (those disturbed by the loss of comprehensive "Meaning" formerly supplied by religion) is mostly a remapping of familiar terrain; an upbeat conclusion suggests that a return to 19th-century realists might be salutary in our expanding vision of man.

Two novelists tackle some of the problems facing the contemporary writer. In "The Cultural Situation of the American Writer" (*ASI* 15, iii: 19–28), John Updike notes that in the absence of a tradition of craftsmanship the role of writer as priest tends to rise in importance; and the seeming advantages of the American experience (a bias for "the land," Protestantism, and honesty) often turn into failures. In "The State of the Novel: Dying Art or New Science?" (*MQR* 16:359–73), Walker Percy suggests that the novelists are raising questions and establishing models that were the province of psychiatrists a generation ago. Just as art is cognitive (discovering, knowing, telling), the method of the artist is increasingly diagnostic.

Although Melvin J. Friedman's "Dislocations of Setting and Word: Notes on American Fiction Since 1950" (*SAF* 5:79–98) is mostly a descriptive survey of the two groups of contemporary fictionists (traditionalists and experimentalists), its neutral tone makes it an ideal introduction for the cultural contexts of what Jerome Klinkowitz has called "disruptive" and "innovative" fiction. In "Imagination and Self-Definition" (*PR* 44:235–44), Manfred Puetz observes that one of the distinctions between the modernists and postmodernists is how the older writers' use of "subphenomenal framework" of public myth is countered in such writers as Barth, Vonnegut, and Pynchon with eruptive and nonschematic private fantasies.

If, as Puetz suggests, a solemn mythophilia in the modernists is replaced by a sense of wry comedy in their successors, one thread of that pattern is defined in the rich and valuable "Never Mind That the Nag's a Pile of Bones: The Modern Comic Novel and the Comic Tradition" (*TSLL* 19:1–23), in which Ronald Wallace sees many contemporary comic heroes (Barth's Todd Andrews, Hawkes's Skipper, Coover's J. Henry Waugh) deriving from the fusion of the traditional *eiron* and *alazon*: if like the typical *alazon*, the modern comic hero unconsciously exposes himself, like the typical *eiron* he also exposes his society. Harriet and Irving Deer argue that modern satire is grounded in the postexistential assumption that all structures are problematical compared to traditional satire, which could be didactic because fixed structures were a given. "Satire as Rhetorical Play" (*Boundary 2* 5:711–21) illustrates the "self-participatory" nature of contemporary satire in Heller, Vonnegut, and Barthelme. In "Black Humor and the Mass Audience" (*Gerber Festschrift*, pp. 1–11), Hamlin Hill finds that this elusive mode dissolves the barriers between two major categories—high-culture humor ("satiric, fantastic, intellectual, and defeatist") and mass-culture humor ("realistic, optimistic, commonsensical, and unsatiric almost to the point of self-censorship") —and, while losing some of its edge, is now invading the popular media.

In "Women on Women: The Looking Glass Novel" (*UDQ* 11, iii[1976]:1–13), Marianna da Vinci Nichols concludes that a study of current fictions by women (Joyce Carol Oates, Judith Rossner, Allison Lurie) indicates that "exorcising ancient images of the self may be infinitely more difficult than learning a new rhetoric"; most recent heroines emerge from two molds: the liberated woman and the "suffering Eve."

John Hollowell's *Fact and Fiction* (see also chapter 20, i, b) is both a history of these mixed genres and critical readings of Capote's

In Cold Blood, Wolfe's *The Electric Kool-Aid Acid Test*, and Mailer's *The Armies of the Night*—all books "colored with the mood of perpetual crisis" of the 1960s. The coverage is by now familiar and the choice of texts predictable; and though it has none of the energy and contentious theorizing of Mas'ud Zavarzadeh's *The Mythopoeic Reality* (see *ALS 1976*, pp. 287–88), *Fact and Fiction* is solid and informative as a good historical account should be. In his chapter on the New Journalism, though it owes much to Tom Wolfe's own hype, Hollowell extrapolates Wolfe's view of the realistic novel into an unprovable but interesting guess: that had there been a "significant movement in literature," it is unlikely that the New Journalism would have made much impression.

The New Journalists and the newer fictionists are mutually tangential to realism, says John Hellmann in "Fables of Fact: New Journalism Reconsidered" (*CentR* 21:414–32): the surfictionists and irrealists write the "strangely imaginary" and the New Journalists the "strangely factual." Just as both respond creatively to realism, so both show related approaches for solving its "problems." Christopher Booker's speculative "Inside the Bubble: Re-reading Tom Wolfe" (*Encounter* 49, iii:72–77) is an analysis of how Wolfe slips into an empty and chilling identification of himself with the bizarre cultural inanities which he so lovingly depicts. More confessional than critical and studded with mininarratives, Morris Dickstein's *Gates of Eden* features separate chapters on the New Journalism, Black Humor, Black Writing, and Rock Music and itself falls somewhere between the New Journalism and the nonfiction novel; it is a survivor's hectoring documentary (for more detail, see chapter 20, i, b).

A clutch of gathered interviews must be noted. Wilfrid Sheed introduces the fourth series of interviews in the George Plimpton anthology, *Writers at Work: The "Paris Review" Interviews* (New York: Viking, 1976), two of the most interesting of which are Ted Berrigan's "Jack Kerouac" (pp. 365–95) and Charles Thomas Samuels's "John Updike" (pp. 431–54). Among the 13 interviews in *Conversations with Writers I* are those with Vance Bourjaily, James Dickey, William Price Fox, and John Gardner. Although the original tapes of these interviews are being preserved as "part of a permanent archive of oral history," the quality of both questions and answers varies wildly. *The Author Speaks: Selected PW Interviews, 1967–1976* (New York: Bowker), a compilation by editors of and contributors to *Publishers Weekly*, is uniformly chatty in substance and casually expository in form. In the cheerful tumble of the good, bad, and indifferent, a few moments stand out: E. L. Doctorow explores the concept of narrative energy, Jerzy Kosinski is lucidly relevant on the useful power of a second language, and Mary McCarthy dispatches the bitchiness of her critics in her best bitchy manner.

***b.* The New Fiction: Theories and Modes.** Jerome Klinkowitz's *The Life of Fiction* (Urbana: Univ. of Ill. Press) is another attempt to put distance between the Modernists and their continuators (Barth, Pynchon) and the newer fictionists, who require from readers a personal response unanticipated by earlier writers. "SuperFiction" is aggressively American in its influences (film comedians, jazz, rock music, comics, detective novels); its practitioners, who are "out to create a good time," are expressive rather than descriptive, both "self-reflective and self-reflexive." *The Life of Fiction*, with graphics by Roy R. Behrens, contains 12 chapters of interspersed commentary and anthologized selections; a succinct summary, together with the fine introduction, clarifies and generalizes the aims and continuing achievements of the newer fiction. Some of the writers represented are Jonathan Baumbach, Steve Katz, Walter Abish, and Ronald Sukenick.

In his own "Fiction in the Seventies: Ten Digressions on Ten Digressions" (*SAF* 5:99–108), which usefully complements Klinkowitz's book, Sukenick refuses to call the varied and "mistaken" strategies of American postwar fiction "fallacies"; nevertheless, his quarrels are with both obvious competitors—"parodists" like Barth and "journalists" like Wolfe—and esoterically named ones—"hermeticists" and "collagists." Reviewing in "Zone of Remission: Current American Fiction" (*MR* 18:357–72) the avid polemical insistence by Robert Scholes and Raymond Federman that innovative fictionists shed the conventionally real, Shaun O'Connell argues for critics also to develop greater tolerance for the varied forms, showing how such writers as Don DeLillo, Ishmael Reed, and Vonnegut "both contain and transcend the 'real.' "

Some of the results of a 1976 symposium on "postmodern literary theory" are gathered in *Boundary 2* (5, ii). Despite its title, Charles Altieri's "The Qualities of Action: A Theory of Middles in Literature" (pp. 323–50; 899–917) is in large part another indictment of the heritage of the New Criticism, this one focusing on its "debilitating tension between a vision of intense literary experience and a formalistic model of explaining that experience," a legacy which Altieri sees in the two poles of contemporary theory: the nonreferential, nondiscursive experience of literary texts against their complex rhetorical explanation. Richard E. Palmer ("Postmodernity and Hermeneutics," pp. 363–93) gives a sensible survey of the varied attempts at rebellion against Modernism and argues that this revolt is part of a larger transformation which is marked by a loss of faith in systems and rationality itself and the affirming of such alternative realities as proposed by R. D. Laing and Carlos Castaneda. Richard Wasson in " 'The True Possession of Time': Paul Nizan, Marxism, and Modernism" (pp. 395–410) cuts through most of the fog by the simple expedient of common sense and the more complex expedient of emphasizing Marxist historiography; in his attack on the newest new criticism, "blindness is insight, true reading is insightful misreading; criticism becomes de-creation of the text." In his essay on Heidegger's destruction of the ontological tradition, "Breaking the Circle: Hermeneutics as Dis-closure" (pp. 421–57), William V. Spanos argues for giving ontological priority to "temporality" rather than "form" as in earlier systems.

David Henry Lowenkron sketches the historical antecedents and formulates a theory of "The Metanovel" (*CE* 38[1976]:343–55), which he sees not as a negative example of inbreeding or elitism but an aesthetic analogue "for metaphysical concerns" central to our time. As the exploitation of the conflict between imagined invention and actuality, Gide's *The Counterfeiters* is the central text, but Lowenkron cites similar examples by Philip Roth, Ronald Sukenick, and Barth. "Naive Narration: Classic to Post-Modern" (*MFS* 23:531–42) is Philip Stevick's exploration of the relations between "the experiencing voice" of a younger self and the mature voice of present narration, with special emphasis on Leonard Michaels, Richard Brautigan, and Vonnegut. Stevick concludes that naiveté is not inevitably funny or tactically useful but "attractive in itself, as a way of being in the world."

Robert Detweiler cites four "Theological Trends of Postmodern Fiction" (*JAAR* 44[1976]:225–37): the need "to let language speak itself," the disappearance of the "subject," the evocation of "presence," and the shaping of alternate worlds. While no one would question these characteristics, most critics would see them oriented toward linguistic, philosophic, and aesthetic values rather than theological.

ii. Norman Mailer

If such Mailer "cheerleaders" as Richard Poirier and Jimmy Breslin project the novelist as profound philosopher and prophet of sexual liberation, McConnell consciously emphasizes the writer's "left conservatism," in "Norman Mailer and the Cutting Edge of Style" (*Four Postwar American Novelists*, pp. 58–107). He correctly describes the quintessential moment in Mailer's fiction as the destruction of ideological politics and the reestablishment of a "primordial, visionary politics" in its place. His affair with the novel has been largely a concern for a style that will allow him to "act out the 'neat terrorism' imagined by the doomed Hearn" of *The Naked and the Dead*; despite the "masking, self-disguising powers of fiction," Mailer also sees it as an agent of "imaginable and personal salvation."

McConnell's provocative suggestion that *An American Dream* is the story of "a kind of imaginative suicide" is strangely corroborated by J. Michael Lennon in "Mailer's Radical Bridge" (*JNT* 7:170–88), who sees Mailer in that work consciously exercising his "powerful autobiographical impulse" for the first time—occasioned largely by his battle with publishers over the supposed obscenity of *The Deer Park*. In building his bridge (from Marx to Freud), Mailer allowed his private sensibility to become public event, and the great works of nonfiction all display the ongoing process of creating a persona equal to the complexities of fictional personae.

Andrew Gordon believes that while the compressed action of *An American Dream*, with its reliance upon symbols and magic rather than rational connection, is a "disguised fulfilment of infantile erotic wishes" and therefore totally egoistic, that work also represents the "repressed dream life of the nation" through Mailer's depiction of the hero. In "The Modern Dream-Vision: Freud's *The Interpretation of Dreams* and Mailer's *An American Dream*" (*L&P* 27:100–5), Gordon concludes that despite the psychological candor, the force of Mailer's novel probably derives paradoxically "from precisely those things which Mailer *refuses* to admit." In another psychological reading, "Norman Mailer: The Family Romance and the Oedipal Family" (*AI* 34:277–86), Howard Silverstein uses *An American Dream* along with *Barbary Shore, The Deer Park*, and "The Time of Her Time" to illustrate his thesis that the romantic triangles in this fiction tend to be "family" affairs because the characters have all failed to resolve their oedipal conflicts.

A skimpy little entrée which is heavily mantled in a sauce of Kesey, Heidegger, Mark Twain, and Hawthorne, "Norman Mailer's *Moby-Dick*" (*NMAL* 1:item 26) is Raymond Benoit's comparison of Melville's whale and Mailer's Pentagon. Designating Queequeg, Tashtego, and Daggo as "Melville's flower children" is one measure of the seriousness of this piece. A spirited and more thoughtful comparison is Stephen J. Whitfield's "American Writing as a Wildlife Preserve: Jack London and Norman Mailer" (*SoQ* 15:135–48), which articulates these novelists' shared notion of the writer "not as artificer but as hero, strident in his politics and his masculinity, direct and imperious in his relationship to his readers, embattled and engaged in the turbulence of history." The art of London and Mailer, who both show a kind of ringside immediacy because they equate writing and fighting, is about life defined in a "muscle-flexing reductionism" of adventure and romance.

That kind of reductionism is more ominously interpreted by Helon Howell Raines, who studies "The Time of Her Time" in "Norman Mailer's Sergius O'Shaugnessy, Villain and Victim" (*Frontiers* 2, i:71–75): because the protagonist is fearful of the androgynous in his psyche he is driven to degrade and dominate women; furthermore, there is "a close identification between the author and his narrator-hero in moral, emotional, and intellectual values."

Yet another comparison-contrast which might have earned kudos in a composition class in 1969 is George Stade's "Mailer and Miller" (*PR* 44:616–24), a self-indulgent look at two self-indulgent self-promoters by way of the gulf separating the person and the personae it constructs. Such notions that Mailer is charged and changed by history while Henry Miller is "infra- and supra-historical" are elegantly imagined, but their actual rendering—in a breathless rat-a-tat-tat of pithy antitheses—leaves the reader nostalgic for old-fashioned exposition.

J. Michael Lennon in a second piece this year traces the writer's attitude toward and involvement in the media in "Mailer's Sarcophagus: The Artist, the Media, and the 'Wad'" (*MFS* 23:179–87). For this avatar of Whitman's mythological "bard of democracy" each book since the mid-1960s is "an attempt to parallel the media's coverage of some of the most important events of our time," not as objective chronicles but as "stereoscopic reports, attempts to link public event and private sensibility." His repertoire of personae (Aquarius, Ruminant, Director, Acolyte) is both a reflection of Mailer's imaginative stances and the attempt to control his own metamorphoses.

iii. Kurt Vonnegut

In the best of the new work on Vonnegut, Richard Giannone contends that the large narrative we read in all the novels is the working out of the notion that, contrary to Vonnegut's remarks in 1970 ("humanity is at the center of the universe"), men "feel eccentric in the universe; and when they do find a place, their success is a qualified victory replete with failure." *Vonnegut: A Preface to His Novels* (Port Washington, N.Y.: Kennikat Press) means what it says: patient, thoughtful, suggestive of the text it prefaces, and rendered in a manner which displays admiration for the subject without the embarrassing compulsion to compete with it. Giannone is sensible and perceptive on all the fiction, but he is particularly acute in his comments on the cosmic sweep of *The Sirens of Titan*, with its "double mood" of creating both innocent wonder and a sense of dignity for the "petty experience of contemporary life"; on how setting (a Jerusalem jail) and mind (Campbell's) become interchangeable in *Mother Night*; and on how Vonnegut's spiritual autobiography, *Slapstick*, is also a parodic narrative imitating another imitation (Laurel and Hardy films). Giannone supplies a useful epilogue dealing with the quality of mind emerging from the novels, especially the nature of Vonnegut's changing narrating voices and masks and his theory of fiction "as a living process of progressive relation to an involved, evolving reader."

In contrast, Clark Mayo's *Kurt Vonnegut: The Gospel from Outer Space (or, Yes We Have No Nirvanas)* (San Bernardino, Calif.: Borgo Press) belongs to the Cute Kurt school of works aggressively designed to stroke the more mindless of the Vonnegut cult. Mayo apparently believes that the Tralfamadorian perspective of *Slaughterhouse-Five* is the naive vision which the novel as a whole affirms. There are much talk of "Gestalt fiction" without much illustration and assertions of how Vonnegut's conscious choice of naiveté and wonder "develops" in successive novels. Mayo's book is filled with tautologies ("The vision of *Player Piano*'s dystopia is largely a negative one"), unpersuasive analogies (Eliot Rosewater and Faulkner's Isaac McCaslin), and potentially perceptive issues that are never explored (*Mother Night* as a drama about the problems of the creative artist). The "naive vision" which Vonnegut certainly has still waits for satisfactory critical treatment.

James Lundquist's *Kurt Vonnegut* (New York: Ungar) is an uneven mix of banalities and fresh perceptions. Like everybody else, Lundquist cites Vonnegut's practical writing experience at Indianapolis's Short Ridge High School (has any writer, or his admirers, made more of his high school than Vonnegut?); he sees the "fragmented idiom" and structural discontinuities as a "formal approximation of the experience of watching television"; and he appreciates antielitist readers because Vonnegut's unsophistication suggests "that he may even be right there, where they are and where it's at." Despite the tiresome reminder that *Slaughterhouse-Five* is another novel "about writing novels," Lundquist's treatment of this work is satisfyingly succinct and perceptive. Lundquist is also commendably clear-eyed in the influence of science fiction on Vonnegut, who in this view transforms a cultist form into an "astral jokebook."

According to editors Jerome Klinkowitz and Donald L. Lawler, the purpose of *Vonnegut in America: An Introduction to the Life and Work of Kurt Vonnegut* (New York: Delacorte/Seymour Lawrence) is to move "the compassionate satirist" from his position as spokesman for a counterculture to the embodiment of "the authentic idiom of a whole culture." Klinkowitz's own biographical essay emphasizes the novelist's unique ability "to fashion a work of art out of an ordinary middle-class life," and his "A Do-It-Yourself Story Collection by Kurt Vonnegut" surveys some of the early stories from the mass circulation magazines. Lawler contributes a rambling essay, "*The Sirens of Titan*: Vonnegut's Metaphysical Shaggy-Dog Story," about how the extended joke structure deflects the reader's expectations of meaning through devices long understood only in surrealism and expressionism. Willis E. McNelly once again claims a reluctant Vonnegut for the serried ranks of science fictionists ("Kurt Vonnegut as Science-Fiction Writer"). Conrad Festa in "Vonnegut's Satire" sees this mode as dominant, Menippean, and "sustained." William Veeder argues that the formal innovations to be seen in two novels ("Technique as Recovery: *Lolita* and *Mother Night*") help the reader "recover his best self by recovering his bond with all mankind," and both novels share not only situations, themes, and techniques but also an emphasis on "our common guilt." Peter J. Reed concentrates on "The Later Vonnegut," especially such devices as the intrusive I-narrator, curt phrasing, and repetitive clusters; in the process he gives the best reading yet of *Breakfast of Champions*. Donald M. Fiene supplies an annotated checklist of translations of Vonnegut works and Soviet criticism with his contribution, "Kurt Vonnegut as an American Dissident: His Popularity in the Soviet Union and His Affinities with Russian Literature." (Fiene demonstrates the influence of Dostoevsky on Vonnegut also in an addendum, "Vonnegut's Quotations from Dostoevsky" [*NMAL* 1:item 29].) Klinkowitz updates a primary and secondary bibliography of Vonnegut items in this volume which equals the usefulness of *The Vonnegut Statement* (see *ALS 1973*, pp. 279–81).

In her imaginatively conceived and executed essay, "Bringing Chaos to Order: The Novel Tradition and Kurt Vonnegut, Jr." (*Genre* 10:283–97), Mary Sue Schriber argues that four novels are really "a single work that explores the novel's relationship to reality and truth and, consequently, its contemporary value." Vonnegut's achievement in *Mother Night* and *Cat's Cradle* (using conventional novelistic form) and *Slaughterhouse-Five* and *Breakfast of Champions* (which are departures) provides a paradigm of the dilemma of the modern novelist who subscribes to novel-writing as the truthful imitation of reality without wanting to break faith with a broad middle-class audience.

The most satisfying piece yet to clarify the philosophical and attitudinal contradictions between the narrator's "Earthling message" and Billy Pilgrim's "Tralfamadorian message" is Dolores K. Gros Louis's "*Slaughterhouse-Five*: Pacifism vs. Passiveness" (*BSUF* 18, ii:3–8), which describes how "Tralfamadorianism is the hyperbolic antithesis" of the authorial recollections and Vonnegut's antimilitarism. Edward A. Kopper, Jr., discusses symbolic patterns of orange and black in "Color Symbolism in Vonnegut's *Slaughterhouse-Five*" (*NMAL* 1:item 17). Robert Merrill, in "Vonnegut's *Breakfast of Champions*: The Conversion of Heliogabalus" (*Crit* 18, iii:99–109), finds Vonnegut-the-protagonist of this novel less appealing than the one in *Slaughterhouse-Five*—in part because the earlier persona protests social attitudes which lead to war and the later one explores the idea that our attitudes are irrelevant to such events.

The fact that "Kurt Vonnegut: The Art of Fiction LXIV" (*ParisR* 69:56–103) is a composite of four separate interviews going back over a decade perhaps explains the tired familiarity of some of the comments; only the hard-core buff will find this necessary.

iv. Thomas Pynchon

Despite an oddly dated eagerness to redeem Pynchon from the charges of psychotic obsessiveness and a relentless effort to freeze him within what he calls the "Terrible Decade" (1963–73), McConnell's "Thomas Pynchon and the Abreaction of the Lord of Night" (*Four Postwar American Novelists*, pp. 159–97) is saved by the critic's sensitive feeling for *Gravity's Rainbow*. The concern for topicality is at once heightened and transcended when McConnell notes the Virgilian irony with which Pynchon transforms his book into a continuing myth on the same theme as the *Aeneid*, "the chances for reestablishing civilized life in the midst of brutality and the inhuman." Summoning up Goethe and Dante as parallels for the simultaneous ascending and plummeting motions in *Gravity's Rainbow* may be a trifle heady, but these are domesticated somewhat by a citation of other influences: Noam Chomsky, the Bible, Wallace Stevens, and the film version of *The Wizard of Oz*. Sanford S. Ames dips into the French "intertextualists" for further parallels in Pynchon's fiction, showing in "Pynchon and Visible Language: Ecriture" (*IFR* 4:170–73) how it makes visible an oppressive ideology which condemns man "to a vision of unscribbled and unscrambled redemption."

In "Third Story Man: Biblical Irony in Thomas Pynchon's 'Entropy'" (*SSF* 14:88–93), John Simons sees Miriam as a "would-be Mary figure" who opposes Saul, an "ironic parody" of the apostle Paul speaking for "the new science of decline and decay." "Love and Death: Variations on a Theme in Pynchon's Early Fiction" (*JNT* 7:157–69) is, among other things, David Cowart's fruitful comparison of "Under the Rose" and chapter three of *V*. Cowart also believes that the frequent allusions to Puccini's *Manon Lescaut* suggest not only romantic love and the death that thwarts it, but also "the love of a good man for all of humanity."

In "Thomas Pynchon's *V.* and Mythology" (*Crit* 18,iii:5–18),

Joseph Fahy links the novelist's apocalyptic strain to "an intricate mythology" derived perhaps from Robert Graves's *The White Goddess*; the evidence includes the profusion of names and titles and the emphasis on holocaust in the final chapters. Mark A. Weinstein's historical survey of the formal and philosophical distinctions between history and the novel in "The Creative Imagination in Fiction and History" (*Genre* 9[1976]:263–77) ends with Pynchon's *V.* Stencil, a "hero of thought" who trusts the relevance of the past but is willing to create meaning where it does not exist, is identified as R. G. Collingwood's "artist-historian who must create 'a web of imaginative construction' out of the flimsiest materials." Most readers, however, understand Pynchon's depiction of those materials as profuse, dense, and undifferentiated—which is one of the points made in "Fiction as History, History as Fiction: The Reader and Thomas Pynchon's *V.*" (*SCR* 10, i:4–18) by Donald J. Greiner, who suggests that *we* may be Stencil: drawn into a pattern-seeking plot in which the imagination generates creations "which finally ensnare the creator."

"Oedipa as Androgyne in Thomas Pynchon's *The Crying of Lot 49*" (*ConL* 18:38–50) is Cathy N. Davidson's account of how Pynchon's protagonist saves herself by becoming an androgyne descending into the underworld—an unpersuasive reading which is also unduly affirmative. "The Form and Meaning of Pynchon's *The Crying of Lot 49*" (*ArielE* 8,i:53–71) may be a good antidote. Seeing the apologue as crucial to this novel because of its indifference to psychological realism and its hospitality to digression, repetition, and loose structure, Robert Merrill suggests that the novel tries to resolve some basic issues about modern America rather than its heroine's personal problems, and as such the novel is darker and more rightist than many critics have realized.

One article which attempts to lift this novelist out of the encapsulated critical hothouse where most critics tend to keep him is Robert Rawdon Wilson's "Spooking Oedipa: On Godgames" (*CRCL* 4:186–204). *Godgame* is defined as a kind of literary illusion in which a victim attempts to think his way out of a confusing web of incidents and whose process of thinking may be "from the inside as a succession of states of consciousness." This subgenre, baroque in origin and related to other uses of literary illusion and perspectivism, occurs in the work of Hesse and Borges, but Pynchon's variation is to make the experience of consciousness actually modify the characters' natures, not simply to reveal potentiality. Close attention to patterned motifs distinguishes "The Entropic Rhythm of Thomas Pynchon's Comedy in *The Crying of Lot 49*" (*HSE* 11:117–30) from previous readings; in it Zoltán Abádi-Nagy skillfully and persuasively abstracts "comic moments" which arrange themselves in three thematic "rhythms" (those relating to closed systems, death, and the quest) to demonstrate that entropy thematically operates on a comic level.

Finding rewarding parallels between "Pynchon's *The Crying of Lot 49* and the Paintings of Remedios Varo" (*Crit* 18, iii:19–26), David Cowart believes the surrealistic mood and technique of Pynchon's novel may be a verbal version of the paintings of a Spanish exile whose works enjoyed a retrospective in Mexico City in 1964, the year after her death. James I. McClintock says in "United State Revisited: Pynchon and Zamiatin" (*ConL* 18:475–90) that Eugene Zamiatin's *We* was obsessed with entropy 50 years before *Gravity's Rainbow*; and both works share concepts, subject, myths, symbols, and a general sensibility.

Ambiguity, not deterministic certainty, is the "essential fuel" for the reader's proper openness to Pynchon's third novel, says Mark R. Siegel in "Creative Paranoia: Understanding the System of *Gravity's Rainbow*" (*Crit* 18, iii:39–54). Unless the rocket is seen as important as Slothrop, many sections of the novel are irrelevant; and metaphors which suggest all the potential shapes of reality tend to make Pynchon's vision not one of despair but of possibility. The most viable option for the self in that novel, however, is given to Roger Mexico, according to Joseph W. Slade in "Escaping Rationalization: Options for the Self in *Gravity's Rainbow*" (*Crit* 18, iii:27–38), because he is a scientist who wants to "get beyond cause and effect," to reembrace paradox. Unlike those in traditional romantic novels, Pynchon's characters look outward, asking questions of perception and interpretation, not of identity.

A generic interpretation by Speer Morgan, "*Gravity's Rainbow*: What's the Big Idea?" (*MFS* 23:199–216), locates Pynchon's book among Northrop Frye's anatomies, where real energies are supplied by "intellectual abundance"; its symbolic pattern, though similar to that of the first two novels, is more literal and less simply allegorical. Lawrence C. Wolfley sees neo-Freudianism as a pervasive influence in "Repression's Rainbow: The Presence of Norman O. Brown in Pynchon's Big Novel" (*PMLA* 92:873–89), with the fictive manipulation of "dialectical consciousness" played against "the dead hand of dualism." Pynchon's style, says Wolfley, shows a fascination with man's freedom located finally in language as "an irreducibly intuitive symbolic process." An even better essay is "'And How Far-Fallen': Puritan Themes in *Gravity's Rainbow*" (*Crit* 18, iii:55–73), in which John M. Krafft traces Pynchon's use of the Puritan tendency to extend theologically based categories into "secular classification which assumed, for secular ends, theological sanctions" in such matters as the relationship of the Elect and the Preterite (we and they) and the nature and function of the Word.

Finally, Donald Skarzenski in "Enzian and the Octopus: Fact in Pynchon's Fiction" (*NAML* 1:item 35), contends that the squid and octopus serve as symbols for evil machinations, and Enzian of *Gravity's Rainbow* is named for an actual German rocket which incorporated a "tumescent plastic."

v. Saul Bellow, Bernard Malamud, and Philip Roth

One of the results of Bellow's winning the Nobel Prize is a series of overviews and reassessments of his career. In his thoughtful "Saul Bellow, On the Soul" (*Midstream*, Dec.: 47–59), Alvin H. Rosenfeld surveys the heuristic design of the career from *Dangling Man*, whose introspections outpace the narrative in a journal form that fittingly reflects a soul turned in upon itself, through the last four novels, in which the protagonists' thinking processes give the narratives an Emersonian edge. Rosenfeld believes that Bellow's development has been shaped by two diverse urgencies: a need to reaffirm faith in rationality and the notion of human life as a received "bond" and a need to rely upon the "spell-prone" or "mediumistic" impulses associated with magical thinking. (In "Strangers" [*YR* 66:481–500], Irving Howe calls attention to the "shy, idealistic, ethicized" aspect of Bellow and other Jewish-American fictionists of the 1950s, a romantic sensibility that somehow offered a counter to the nativist strain of romanticism deriving from Emerson.)

In "Saul Bellow and the Terms of Our Contract" (*Four Postwar American Novelists*, pp. 1–57), McConnell traces the career from preeminence in the 1950s to what he views as decline in the 1960s—and Bellow's own resistance to the development of fiction in the last decade he sees as a significant chapter in the history of taste. Mc-

Connell, largely eschewing the faddish anti-Bellovians of the *Partisan Review*, credits Bellow with the difficult insistence that we know our responsibility "to make the City of Man its own best hope for Godhead." Although it is a mistake to see Bellow only as a continuator of the realistic novel, the confrontation with the inhuman in Bellow is realistically articulated within a human context.

"Saul Bellow and the Nobel Prize" (*JAmS* 11:3–12) is Malcolm Bradbury's account of the tendency of American laureates to fall into a "post-Nobel note of uncomfortable over-affirmation," although Bellow's use of the novel as a vehicle of "moral capaciousness" predates the award. A more aggressively blunt defense of the novelist's moral voice is incorporated in *The Sweeter Welcome: Voices for a Vision of Affirmation: Bellow, Malamud and Martin Buber* (Needham Heights, Mass.: Humanitas Press, 1976), a book written expressly against a "modern literature of icy estrangement" by Robert Kegan. Both Bellow and Malamud are discussed in terms of Hasidism, Buber's revisionism, and "the diverse exercises of the modern soul we now call existentialism." Kegan admits his unconcern with form, since the "spirit" of these authors (i.e., the relation between their work and the reader) is what counts.

In "Brueghel and Augie March" (*AL* 49:113–19), following up a description of Pieter Brueghel's "The Misanthrope" in chapter 10 of *The Adventures of Augie March*, Jeffrey Meyers convincingly shows that the three figures of the painting—the misanthrope, the cutpurse, and the shepherd—represent alternatives for dealing with a hostile world; Augie ponders the implications of all three without committing himself to any. Mark M. Christhilf's "Death and Deliverance in Saul Bellow's Symbolic City" (*BSUF* 18, ii:9–23), while overargued, is a perceptive and convincing essay. In the "introverted" novels the city is transformed from a concrete narrative setting (*The Victim*) to a higher, abstract plane (*Mr. Sammler's Planet*); in the "extroverted" novels the city functions "as a paradigm for structural organization" (*Augie March* and *Humboldt's Gift*); in both the spirit-destroying city is an extension of man's own evil potential.

In "Bellow's' Gift" (*NUQ* 31:288–304), an attempt to place Bellow in context with his contemporary rivals, Seymour Epstein interprets Sammler's words over his nephew's corpse as Bellow's refinement of his long-standing interest: "Ideas themselves will not save us, but the capacity of man to *have* ideas might." If the grand theme is "the failure of Western civilization to sustain the individual," a more pointed related theme is that it is endangered by "default of its best people." Although none of his contemporaries has made his themes yield more, for Bellow a plethora of means and materials and "repetitive improvisations" results often in trivializing the important questions which the novelist himself has brought up.

Suzanne F. Kistler ("Bellow's Man-Eating Comedy: Cannibal Imagery in *Humboldt's Gift*, *NMAL* 2:item 8) suggests that the cannibal metaphor implicitly condemns Humboldt's and Citrine's complicity in adopting the mores of capitalist America instead of rejecting its corruption. On the basis of one story, Constance Rooke in "Saul Bellow's 'Leaving the Yellow House': The Trouble with Women" (*SSF* 14:184–87) generalizes that women are unworthy of respect or sympathy in Bellow's fiction "if their aspiration or presumption directs them to overstep" their traditionally assigned roles.

Jo Brans is a sprightly questioner in "Common Needs, Common Preoccupations: An Interview with Saul Bellow" (*SWR* 62[1976]:1–19), but the novelist is sprightly himself as he waxes indignant at academic critics who turn such masterworks as *Moby-Dick* into Marxist, existentialist, or Christian symbolist documents. Bellow also notes the lack of a literary community in America outside (but sometimes within) the academy and the "scandalous" level of critical articles in magazines. In the most valuable part of her *Saul Bellow: His Works and His Critics, An Annotated International Bibliography* (New York: Garland) Marianne Nault provides a comprehensive list of the published work "up to the point at which this typescript was completed" and describes those Bellow papers, mostly at the University of Chicago, which are "accessible to the scholar with the author's permission."

Leslie Field calls him a "Marginal Jew." Admitting his own "cribbed' praise, Ihab Hassan speaks mostly of the "knot of resistance" he encounters when he reads him. And a few other contributors to *The Fiction of Bernard Malamud*, edited by Richard Astro and Jackson J. Benson (Corvallis: Ore. State Univ. Press), regard varied aspects of the novelist with restraint in a volume supposedly celebratory. Hassan's "Bernard Malamud: 1976, Fictions Within Our Fictions" (pp. 43–64) may not be the most aggressive of paracriticisms, but it is pretentiously self-regarding enough to qualify. Field's "Bernard Malamud and the Marginal Jew" (pp. 97–116) relates the novelist's work to that of other Jewish-Americans who rejected much of their past to embrace "enlightenment"; Malamud is finally "timid." In "The Many Names of S. Levin: An Essay in Genre Criticism" (pp. 149–61), Leslie Fiedler also finds Malamud timid, especially in his creation of the ambiguously heroic protagonist of *A New Life.* Scraping together some of his past preoccupations in one more version, Fiedler first defines a "true Western" (a tale of transitory love between a white male refugee from civilization and a nonwhite member of a group which has been exploited by his lover's people) and then decides that Malamud is "not sufficiently misogynist to write a real Western," thereby flubbing his chance to write the first "real Jewish anti-Western."[1]

Despite buttressing by quotations from Camus, Buber, and other modern philosophers, W. J. Handy's "The Malamud Hero: Quest for Existence" (pp. 65–86) is a familiar exercise coming to a familiar conclusion: the typical Malamud hero is placed squarely in the naturalistic world, and the effort to extricate himself from meaninglessness becomes "a quest for a new life." The big virtue of Ben Siegel's "Through a Glass Darkly: Bernard Malamud's Painful Views of the Self" (pp. 117–47) is its book-by-book survey, which emphasizes the novelist's commitment to "absurd man and his comic condition" and his appreciation of the humane values rooted in Talmudic lore and the realities experienced by the Jews of the Diaspora. In "Malamud's Yiddish-Accented Medieval Stories" (pp. 87–96), Peter L. Hays finds Chrétien de Troye's treatment of Lancelot as "The Knight of the Cart" an early parallel with and possibly a source of the novelist's heroes who are excessively reviled for "the crime of love." Donald Risty completes the Astro-Benson volume with "A Comprehensive Checklist of Malamud Criticism" (pp. 163–90).

A gathering of four essays in *LNL* 2, iii, features presumably what editor Bates Hoffer calls for in Malamud criticism: "more careful and precise analyses of each story on its own terms." His own contribution, "The Magic in Malamud's Barrel" (pp. 1–26) is mostly a contentious litany of other critics' deficiencies; his modest point is that Malamud's Leo becomes "the great Law-Breaker" as an ironic parallel to the Hero of the Pentateuch. Kristin Kliemann demonstrates in "A Perspective on Bernard Malamud's 'Idiots First' " (pp. 27–40)

1. This logic is easier to follow in Fiedler's shorter version, "Malamud's Travesty Western" (*Novel* 10:212–19).

that non-Jews can with some background study appreciate Malamud's story "more fully." Her own research shows that the concept of Sheol is built into the structure of Malamud's story. In "The Levels of Allegory in 'The Loan'" (pp. 41–57), Tricia Peterson also researches Jewish customs and finds parallels between Malamud's story and the Moses story, only to conclude that "modern Judaism and the modern Jew are not capable of upholding God's law." Laurel Canham suggests that Orthodox Jews may be selling Malamud short, since at least four stories (including "Take Pity" and "Angel Levine") show the importance of not only Jewish thought but also the Torah, the Mishnah, and the Talmud.

In "Nature in Bernard Malamud's *The Assistant*" (*Renascence* 29: 211–23), Arnold L. Goldsmith sees a purposeful ambiguity in the mythic underpinnings of this novel; a study of imagery (moonlight, flowers, birds) reveals evocative and legendary dimensions rather than mimetic realism, but the possibility of failure tends to undercut Alpine's final role as moral benefactor.

In "The Tenants in the House of Fiction" (*SNNTS* 8[1976]:458–67), Steven G. Kellman sees Malamud's most self-conscious work pervaded by urban decay and racial warfare. Although it probes the nature of literature and the social conditions from which it arises, *The Tenants* fails to compose the "unresolved tensions of contemporary society" and to fix the novel's "relationship to life"—which seems to be asking a lot of any novel. Discussing "The Endings in Malamud's *The Tenants*" (*NMAL* 1:item 5), George E. Hatvary finds four contradictory conclusions (naturalistic, happy, tragic, and experimental open-ended); more should surely be made of this insight.

Except for Irving Malin's "Looking at Roth's Kafka; or Some Hints About Comedy" (*SSF* 14:273–75), relating Philip Roth's essayistic "Looking at Kafka" to the novelist's own life and style, the work this year on Roth consists of overlapping and repetitive essays by Pierre Michel, some of which in turn repeat some of his observations last year (see *ALS 1976*, p. 299). In "What Price Misanthropy? Philip Roth's Fiction" (*ES* 58:232–39), Michel sees a narrowing of tone ("too grating for genius") and vision and chastizes Roth for the Pynchon-like hopelessness with which he views "the problems of contemporary America, those that plague society, or the city, or the minorities. . . ." "'On the Air': Philip Roth's Arid World" (*EA* 29 [1976]:566–60) concentrates on the "unbridled fantasy" of this 1970 story, which, though it is a logical continuation of *Portnoy's Complaint*, smudges the line between the character's obsession and the "acrimonious fancies" of the author.

vi. Flannery O'Connor and J. F. Powers

The finest essay on O'Connor to appear in a long time is "Grotesque Conversions and Critical Piety" (*FOB* 6:17–35), in which Melissa Hines shows how the Georgian's uniqueness lies in the union of matter (conversion to orthodox religious faith) and manner (unorthodox manipulation of the grotesque mode). Both subject and style are "experiences" that turn on a "transformation of the perceptions in the face of an indissoluble mystery which provokes a characteristically ambivalent response." Hines sees in "Parker's Back," her central example, a telescoping of the whole history of the term *grotesque*, a tour de force which "reenacts the technical development of the mode in an example of its operation."

In "Flannery O'Connor in the American Romance Tradition" (*FOB* 6:83–98), Virginia F. Wray consults occasional writings, letters, and interviews to support her contention that O'Connor is the inheritor of the American Renaissance romancers. Like Hawthorne and Melville, O'Connor's interest is in "the theoretical aim and practical means of metaphor to fuse the knowable and the directly unknowable realms of human experience into a single realm."[2] O'Connor's links with Poe, however, will have to wait, since in his brief excerpt from a study in progress, "Vision and the Eye for Detail in Poe and O'Connor" (*FOB* 6:36–46), Marion Montgomery spends considerably more time on Poe's "William Wilson" than on any O'Connor title.

John F. Desmond in "Mr. Head's Epiphany in Flannery O'Connor's 'The Artificial Nigger'" (*NMAL* 1:item 20) cites a Dantean analogue to explain why Mr. Head's epiphany occurs after his return to the country—the "true starting place from which the journey to supernatural perfection can begin." As indicated by his title, "Flannery O'Connor's Company of Southerners: or, 'The Artificial Nigger' Read as Fiction Rather than Theology" (*FOB* 6:47–71), Louis D.

2. Wray also reports "An Authorial Clue to the Significance of the title *The Violent Bear It Away*" (*FOB* 6:107–8) in the novelist's glossed copy of Emmanuel Mounier's *Personalism* (1952).

Rubin, Jr., writes a badly needed "corrective" piece emphasizing the author's depiction of her time and place. Her middle Georgia plain folk follow a tradition—Faulkner, Wolfe, Agee, the Southwestern Humorists—which theological exegetes tend to overlook. Comedy, says Rubin, derives from a contrast in language, "which is also a contrast in viewpoint and in culture," and finally moral vision. In trying to counter the bad press given to Julian's mother in "Everything That Rises Must Converge," Doreen Ferlaino Fowler discovers that "Mrs. Chestny's Saving Graces" (*FOB* 6:99–106), though less obtrusive than her complacency, are suggested by the imagery of martyrdom and childhood, which in turn suggests "avenues to grace."

Mary S. Strine, in "Narrative Strategy and Communicative Design in Flannery O'Connor's *The Violent Bear It Away*" (*Studies in Interpretation II*, pp. 45–57), concentrates on "the narrator as a personality," a device which in its varied points of view contributes to the coherence of theme and plot. The "conjectural description" in the novel becomes a running commentary indicating norms, especially the use of the sun and the absence of light as the emblems of virtue and vice.

The editor of the forthcoming O'Connor letters, Sally Fitzgerald, defines the key term of her essay, "The Habit of Being" (*FOB* 6:5–16), as "an excellence not only of action, but of interior disposition and activity that increasingly reflected the object, the Being, which specified it, and was itself reflected in what she said and did." The letters will attest to this, whatever new light on the fiction they may shed. Robert E. Golden and Mary C. Sullivan's *Flannery O'Connor and Caroline Gordon: A Reference Guide* (Boston: G. K. Hall) is not, as the title might suggest, a collaborative enterprise but a publishing convenience. Golden's O'Connor segment (pp. 1–189), chronologically arranged and descriptively annotated, includes more-or-less complete critical commentary in books and articles through 1973; it is less complete after that.

In "On the Revisions of *Morte D'Urban*" (*SSF* 14:84–86), Eleanor B. Wymard contends that a study of revisions of chapters first published as stories shows that J. F. Powers understood well the distinctive demands of both the short story and novel forms. Wymard illustrates her thesis with a *New Yorker* story, "The Green Banana," later revised as the opening chapter of the novel. Arlene Schler, in "How to Recognize Heaven When You See It: The Theology of St. John of the Cross in J. F. Powers' 'Lions, Harts, Leaping Does'" (*SSF* 14: 159–64), interprets Didymus's final hours as a conscious representation of the soul's ascent to God according to the theological system of the Spanish mystic; the "illuminative life," the final stage, is symbolized in the story by the images of the ladder of light and the dark night.

vii. John Barth and John Hawkes

In his overview, "John Barth and the Key to the Treasure" (*Four Postwar American Novelists*, pp. 108–58), McConnell sees Barth's position somewhere between the sustaining cultural traditions emphasized by Bellow and the personal existentialism of Mailer. His is a self-consciousness which, though it insists upon the primacy of tradition, strenuously searches for the "radical articulation of the individual mind, the outsider's vision, which can at once corrode and refine (or redefine) the structures of the humane tradition." Among his readings of the individual novels, the most piquant comes in his citation of *Giles Goat-Boy* as Barth's "war novel (to parallel *The Naked and the Dead, Dangling Man*, and *Gravity's Rainbow*).

In "Beauty as Good: A Platonic Imperative in John Barth?" (*SoQ* 15:335–44), Jac Tharpe attempts to distinguish between "ethics in the work of John Barth" and "John Barth's ethics," using existentialism as his guide; but his major effort is to define the potential value of performance under adverse conditions, a stance which after two decades Barth still precariously maintains.

Daniel V. Fraustino believes "a quick reading" of *The Country Wife* is necessary for enjoying Barth's second novel in his extravagant but plausible "*The Country Wife* Comes to *The End of the Road*: Wycherley Bewitches Barth" (*ArQ* 33:76–86): both works share a common surname (Horner), typed characters, the figure of a doctor-confidant, the themes of adultery and cuckoldry, and the imagery of the hunt.

While others have cited the Moebius strip as a generative image for Barth, two critics have explored the matter more deeply. Victor J. Vitanza, in "The Novelist as Topologist: John Barth's *Lost in the Funhouse*" (*TSLL* 19:83–97), argues that the inability to create new forms and subjects—the substance of this novel—is represented by the topologist, who is concerned with ways in which surfaces can be "twisted, bent, pulled, stretched, or otherwise reformed from one shape into another." All the segments of *Funhouse* are seen as homologues of "Frame-Tale." Anyone who reads "Barth's *Lost in the Funhouse*: The Anatomy of Nothing (–,O," ")" (*LNL* 2, i:68–106) will need a text of the work before him, for Bates Hoffer's analysis is detailed, not to say tedious, as it takes the Moebius strip analogue stage by stage through every section of the book.

In "Reader, Critic, and the Form of John Hawkes's *The Cannibal*" (*Boundary 2* 5:829–44), Thomas W. Armstrong concerns himself with the reader-text relationship—i.e., Heidegger's "hermeneutical circularity." The text gradually discloses itself to the reader simultaneously as something he has always known and as a mystery; form becomes a matter of both consciousness and text.

Despite Hawkes's claim that he considers the enemies of the novel to be plot, character, setting, and theme, Carey Wall asserts that the conventional plot of *Second Skin* identifies the experiences of his characters, supplying "correspondences" which test the reader's faith in moral categories and the nature of reality. "Solid Ground in John Hawkes's *Second Skin*" (*Makers of the Twentieth-Century Novel*, pp. 309–19) is a workmanlike reading whose virtues are clarity and commonsense. Wall is particularly good in contrasting the larger implications of Skipper's two worlds, the dark one of violence and ineffectual ritual and the golden world of connection and love where death is a natural part of life.

Reconciling the conflicting views of Skipper as transcendent victim and self-serving villain, Bruce Bassoff in "Mythic Truth and Deception in *Second Skin*" (*EA* 30:337–42) argues that the "unanimity of violence" against Hawkes's hero as well as his godlike activities can be explained by the fact that violence is "the secret heart of the sacred, and Skipper's god-like transcendence [is] the metamorphosis of this violence." Similarly, in "The Hero as Artist in John Hawkes's *Second Skin*" (*IFR* 4:119–27) Patrick O'Donnell sees a recurring pattern by which the transformation of demonic objects and symbols into their sanctified, beneficent counterparts makes Skipper both hero and artist. More or less persuasively, Ronald Wallace traces the comic movement of the plot in "The Rarer Action: Comedy in John Hawkes's *Second Skin*" (*SNNTS* 9:169–86); if initially Skipper's response to violence seems comic, in the context of his humorous society, it becomes heroic—like Prospero, this hero transforms "the seeds of death into the seeds of life."

"The Reader's Voyage Through *Travesty*" (*ChiR* 28,ii:172–87) is a literal guide to *Travesty*, which Paul Emmett sees as a blend of epistemology, myth, and humor unique among the other artifacts of the new fiction. Robert M. Scotto believes *Travesty* to be a parodic rendition of the French *récit* (like Camus's *The Fall*) and in "A Note on John Hawkes's *Death, Sleep & The Traveller* and *Travesty*" (*NMAL* 1:item 11) he argues that both recent works parody "a diary of a madman and a note from underground." These two later works are discussed rather freely in Paul Emmett and Richard Vine's "A Conversation with John Hawkes" (*ChiR* 28,ii:163–71), but the novelist also touches on the autobiographical aspect and the so-called "poetic effects" of his prose.

viii. John Updike, Joyce Carol Oates, and John Cheever

In her provocative "John Updike: 'The Rubble of Footnotes Bound into Kierkegaard' " (*JAAR* 45:1011–35), Sue Mitchell Crowley finds that the Danish philosopher's notion of the self as a synthesis of finitude and infinitude is freely appropriated by Updike as a thematic pattern as he moves his characters from despair to hope. More significantly, some of the stories ("The Astronomer" among them) are themselves formal recapitulations of the Kierkegaardian method for achieving existential certitude.

William H. Shurr, in "The Lutheran Experience in John Updike's 'Pigeon Feathers' " (*SSF* 14:329–35), links the adolescent hero to Rip Van Winkle and Ike McCaslin as solitary hunters facing "the darkness within," but he finds Updike's story unique in that its religious details specifically recall Martin Luther's transformation. Robert E. Waxman follows those who see the influence of Karl Barth in Updike's fiction, especially the theologian's scorn of metaphysical proofs and his reliance upon faith in Christian revelation. However, in "Invitations to Dread: John Updike's Metaphysical Quest" (*Renascence* 29:201–10) Waxman argues that in his two groups of "fragment-stories" Updike reveals a struggle between Barth's insistence upon God's wholly transcendent nature and Pascal's approach to God through anxiety, disillusionment, and despair.

Paul Borgman argues that the central conflict in *Rabbit, Run* is between the hero's intimations of "motions of grace" and the world of silent compromise, represented by Eccles, a rationalist who would "demythologize Rabbit's imagination." Rabbit is "The Tragic Hero of Updike's *Rabbit, Run*" (*Renascence* 29:106–12) because his motions of grace are realized only within his own skin, "limited to the present tense of his frightening, shrinking sense of time and space."

Suzanne H. Uphaus demonstrates in "*The Centaur*: Updike's Mock Epic" (*JNT* 7:24–36) how the novelist's juxtaposed use of classical mythology and realistic detail reflects the ostensible meaning of the novel: "The thematic loss of Christianity parallels the artistic loss of classical faith," which means the decline of faith into good works and the decline of myth into naturalism. In another essay, "The Unified Vision of *A Month of Sundays*" (*UWR* 12,ii:5–16), Uphaus finds this recent work Updike's first in which his familiar dichotomy (this world apprehended through the senses and the "other world" apprehended by faith) does not appear as mutually exclusive possibilities. Whereas Uphaus sees Marshfield's career as Updike's reinterpretation of American religious history, Lloyd Spencer Thomas, in "Scarlet Sundays—Updike vs. Hawthorne" (*CEA* 39,iii:16–17), asserts that Updike's transformation of Hawthorne's "grave world of Puritan Boston into a contemporary vaudeville" results in a "ludicrous diminution of Hawthorne's theme."

In William B. Wahl's "Updike's World and *Couples*" (*Hillway Festschrift*, pp. 256–95) limp observations pass for sauciness ("The novel lapses into idiocy here and there") and saucy observations pose as aggressive common sense ("I wonder if Updike's wife, after reading *Couples*, tried to get him to see a psychoanalyst?"). Tangling querulously with other critics upon whom he nevertheless depends, Wahl is even weaker when he lurches into technical analysis: that the point of view in *Couples* "seems the usual sort for novel-length fiction" is no more helpful than in saying that the "little man" is Updike's chief concern.

In "The Center of Violence in Joyce Carol Oates's Fiction" (*NMAL* 2:item 9), Leonard J. Leff contends that feminine destructiveness, resulting from spiritual narcissism, prevents Oates's male characters from living meaningfully. Charlotte Goodman recognizes the same tendency in her "Women and Madness in the Fiction of Joyce Carol Oates" (*W&L* 5,ii:17–28), but the female characters dramatize some of the real-life factors "that contribute to the despair and psychological disintegration of contemporary women."

Rose Marie Burwell argues that in *With Shuddering Fall* the theme of "Joyce Carol Oates' First Novel" (*CanL* 73:54–67) is neither madness nor violence but the "complex drive of the human organism toward psychological wholeness." Though marred by excessive plot summary, this essay is informed by Burwell's perceptive use of a Jungian tension between individuation and societal forces.

"From Jimmy Gatz to Jules Wendall: A Study of 'Nothing Substantial' " (*DR* 56:718–24) is James R. Giles's comparison between the heroic dreams of Fitzgerald's character and the figure in *Them*, a cynic who will likely succeed in California. Sanford Pinsker finds that Oates's third work is "more a study in comic nihilism, in suburban emptiness, than it is a seriously rendered psycho-drama." In his sensible and deftly written "Suburban Molesters: Joyce Carol Oates' *Expensive People*" (*MQ* 19:89–103), he points out that illusion and reality are intertwined in such a "reflexively absurd" world that the work becomes a Nabokovian romp "in the art-and-craft of confessional narration." In "Her Brother's Keeper" (*SHR* 11:195–203), William T. Liston argues that Oates's "In the Region of Ice" is a reworking of *Measure for Measure*, dramatizing the existential fact that a Christian cannot practice her religion by withdrawing from the world.

If John C. Moore detects a perceptible movement from Cheever's realistic depiction of the surfaces of bourgeois America to "fables of heroism" in the recent fiction ("The Hero on the 5:42: John Cheever's Short Fiction," *WHR* 30[1976]:147–52), Robert Detweiler stresses Cheever's "new assertiveness" with which the old absurdities are treated and an increased mastery of form joined by a slackened faith in American resiliency; though "John Cheever's *Bullet Park*: A World Beyond Madness" (*Hillway Festschrift*, pp. 6–32) is primarily a rhetorical study of narrating speech and fluid perspectives, Detweiler relates the pervasively religious setting to a Blakeian vision of madness as a "preparation for a greater clarity and sanity" beyond.

As the first full-length study of this author, Samuel Coale's *John Cheever* (New York: Ungar) suffers from unimaginative organization in early chapters in which glosses on arbitrarily selected stories turn into simple plot summaries, but commentary on the longer fiction is more serious. While this novelist's characteristic lyricism works best in *The Wapshot Chronicle*, Coale believes *The Wapshot Scandal*, with its darker mood, is Cheever's most inventive novel, especially in the calculated use of Christian imagery. *Falconer* he sees as the breakthrough novel, since Cheever jettisons his familiar suburbia and its spurious pastoralism for a setting which perfectly fits the theme—"the confinement of the spirit in, and the attempts of the spirit to free itself from" materialistic society. Coale's is hardly the last word to be heard on the ways Cheever's transfiguring language works, but this brief study handles the subject briskly and effectively.

ix. William Styron, Walker Percy, and Other Southerners

A final chapter in Richard Gray's *The Literature of Memory* (pp. 257–305) takes up the "problem of survival" of post-World War II authors who find the long shadow of Faulkner growing longer each year (see also chapter 20,i,b). Failures are Tennessee Williams and Truman Capote (because of decadent local color and debased gothicism); modest successes are Carson McCullers and Flannery O'Connor, whose idiosyncratic visions prevent consideration of such large problems as "history and society, tradition and modernity." Since these are precisely the issues which Styron grapples with, he is given the lion's share of attention. Gray is particularly acute in analyzing the language of the fiction—the "self-reflexiveness" of *Lie Down in Darkness* and the meditational idiom of *Nat Turner*. In the latter novel, he detects the conversion of traditionalism into a carefully formulated form of radicalism akin more to Emerson or Eldridge Cleaver than to Robert Penn Warren or Faulkner.

Life can be "deeply human and true whether or not it is fact," says Floyd C. Watkins in his superb chapter from *In Time and Place* ("*The Confessions of Nat Turner*: History and Imagination," pp. 51–70). Watkins stresses Styron's achievement in creating credible psychological portraiture out of sparse materials, beginning with the very opening set of images. Showing little patience with the ideological urgencies of Styron's black critics, Watkins asserts that the novelist creates a man markedly human rather than one who is heroic; even slave narratives, he reminds us, are interpretations—accounts of lives summoned up from the thoughful perspective of the present.

A study which need never have been undertaken is Roberta Zipper Gunod's "An Anomaly of 'And'" (*LNL* 2,ii:19–42), which announces that a "real linguistic difference" exists between *Nat Turner* and two works by American black authors and that the key to the difference is the heavy use by Ralph Ellison and Claude Brown of the connector *and*, derived from the blacks' knowledge of biblical rhythms (presumably unavailable to whites). In his surprisingly convincing essay, "A Rose Is a Rose Is a Columbine: *Citizen Kane* and William Styron's *Nat Turner*" (*LFQ* 5:118–24), Bruce M. Firestone pursues the novelist's admission that the Orson Welles film helped him with a narrative problem by proposing that the scene of Nat as a young boy spelling "Columbine" is equivalent to Welles's "Rosebud"—a clue to the inner man.

Ray Ownbey's "Discussions with William Styron" (*MissQ* 30: 283–95) is particularly interesting because the novelist speaks at length about *Sophie's Choice*, his novel-in-progress which will breach the barriers between autobiography and fiction just as *Nat Turner* smudged the lines between history and fiction. James L. W. West III's *William Styron: A Descriptive Bibliography* (Boston: G. K. Hall) is a superb and meticulous work which includes editions in English (including paperbacks) and French, unpublished and republished contributions to books, published letters, interviews, and some translations. Styron also contributed a preface.

In "Existential Modes in *The Moviegoer*" (*RS* 45:214–23), Anthony Quagliano continues the investigation of those critics who take Percy's essays on philosophy and psychology as serious clues to the essence of his fiction. He again cites Percy's three modes (alienation, rotation, repetition) without contributing anything compellingly new. In "Walker Percy and Modern Gnosticism" (*SoR* 13:677–87) Cleanth Brooks points out the parallel diagnoses of the present state of culture in the novelist's works and Eric Voegelin's magisterial *Order and History*. What Percy's Thomas More calls "angelism"—man's impatience with his own mortal limitations—becomes full-blown in *Lancelot*, in which the hero, like a first-century heretic, is confident "that he knows how to reform a corrupt world and [is] willing to kill if he cannot cure."

Susan S. Kissel's thesis in "Walker Percy's 'Conversions'" (*SLJ* 9, ii:124–36) is that the first three protagonists are depicted as having found more than just a method of discovery—they are portrayed as "actually having *made* discoveries which lead to final reversals in the directions of their lives." Same valuable cultural observations can be found in Edward J. Cashin's "History as Mores: Walker Percy's

Lancelot" (*GaR* 31:875–80), especially on the kind of "internalized" history common to the southern imagination. The fourth novel conveys a kind of "consensus history," which Cashin traces back to two strains: the commercial (stemming from old Charleston) and the Dixie Puritan (filtering down from the Great Awakening).

In his comprehensive survey of James Dickey's career, "After a Long Silence: James Dickey as a South Carolina Writer" (*SCR* 9,i [1976]:12–20), Richard J. Calhoun stresses in his segment on the lone novel Dickey's dramatization of " 'deliverance' *in* the wilderness but also *from* the wilderness in a more meaningful return to existence in the city." Barnett Guttenberg's imaginative use of Wordsworth's notion of the visionary moment which transforms one's "place" into spiritual communion leads to a fine reading in "The Pattern of Redemption in Dickey's *Deliverance*" (*Crit* 18,iii:83–91). Gentry becomes a Romantic poet-prophet whose journey to "partial victory over a fallen world" becomes an exemplum: the vital river links nature and society, a "redeemed microcosm" incorporating love, identity, and freedom.

A less Wordsworthian nature is suggested in the novel, however, by Eugene M. Longen in "Dickey's *Deliverance*: Sex and the Great Outdoors" (*SLJ* 9,ii:137–49). The state of unconcern which characterizes the homosexual rape also characterizes the forces of nature—"the chilling impersonality of the outdoors as a milieu in which to survive." Coming to grips with the rugged Georgia terrain is equated to recognizing the submerged darker self of violence and unreason. Although disappointingly vague in its conclusions, Donald Monk's "Colour Symbolism in James Dickey's *Deliverance*" (*JAmS* 11:261–79) centers on the recognition of "what is in the visible," and Gentry's "paranormal" awakening is rendered by symbolic uses of sight and its limitations. Like Dickey's poem "Madness" the novel seeks to explore the limits of the rational and the beauty of natural violence.

"Cormac McCarthy: The Hard Wages of Original Sin" (*AppalJ* 4:105–19) is the first overview of a novelist sometimes accused of writing overwrought "late Southern Gothic." William J. Schafer traces the "ameliorated version of hard primitivism" of *The Orchard Keeper* (1965) to the progressively harsher worlds of *Outer Dark* (1968) and *Child of God* (1973). In "William Price Fox: The Spirit of Character and the Spirit of Place" (*SCR* 9,i[1976]:30–35), Joan Bobbitt gives the first substantial notice to a regional writer who, if his work develops according to his most recent novel, *Ruby Red* (1971), "will soon warrant consideration" by more readers outside South Carolina. "A Garland for Peter Taylor on His Sixtieth Birthday" (*Shenandoah* 28,ii) is comprised of memoirs, remembrances, and criticism by such contemporaries as Robert Penn Warren, Allen Tate, Brainard Cheney, Andrew Lytle, and Ashley Brown.

x. Wright Morris, Wallace Stegner, and Other Westerners

Two superb essays in *The Westering Experience* that are at once theoretical and hortatory should be required reading for both serious Western writers and their critics: Jack Brenner's "Imagining the West" (pp. 32–47) and Dan D. Walker's "Who Is Going to Ride Point?" (pp. 23–31). The first discusses how the curious insistence upon the myth of "authentic experience" leads to scorn for the "distorting" power of fiction—stemming in part, says Brenner, from the fact that the West was frozen into stereotype and legend "almost before it was settled." Citing the "timidity" of Western historians and their fictional imitators, Walker pleads for responsibility among Western writers in the ultimate way—"of being makers of important fictive worlds."

The full range of a commemorative volume, *Conversations with Wright Morris: Critical Views and Responses*, edited by Robert E. Knoll (Lincoln: Univ. of Nebr. Press), is more accurately suggested by the subtitle. It is composed of three lectures, records of four conversations, an essay by Morris himself, and a bibliography. In paying homage to "Wright Morris Country" (pp. 3–13), John W. Aldridge is more spendthrift than critic, but Wayne C. Booth ("Form in *The Works of Love*," pp. 35–73) is surely right in stressing not Morris's themes, some of which are banal, but his "power as a teller of tales." Morris comments to David Madden on style ("The Dictates of Style," pp. 101–19) as well as his general feelings about Bellow, Mailer, and others. Peter C. Bunnell's "The Photography of Wright Morris: A Portfolio" (pp. 121–39) and Robert L. Boyce's "A Wright Morris Bibliography" (pp. 168–206) round out this rich volume.

Of the three contemporaries mentioned in his thoughtful article, "D. H. Lawrence and the Immediate Present: Kurt Vonnegut, Jr., Ken Kesey, and Wright Morris" (*DHLR* 10:103–41), G. B. Crump finds Morris the most profound Laurentian, with his emphasis on process and expansion, his use of the road as a metaphor for a dynamic universe, and his stern suspicion of transcendental impulses. Jack Hafer believes the Plains setting becomes "the sacred center of the universe" in "Setting and Theme in Wright Morris's *Ceremony in Lone Tree*" (*HK* 10,iii:10–20) as a means of countering this violence-drenched book (he counts 14 human deaths), and because its setting is mythically imagined as "the navel of the world" the novel becomes a "religious chronicle."

The Rocky Mountain West, with its frustrated yearnings for permanence and stability, is identified with another western author in Forrest G. and Margaret G. Robinson's *Wallace Stegner* (TUSAS 282). One important chapter is devoted to Stegner's nonfiction, including the essays on the conditions confronting western writers (the twin traps of inadequate intelligence and the aggressive championing of eastern values). As the Robinsons convincingly demonstrate, this writer's concept of "the middle ground," the imaginative rendering of milieu, is central to his fiction since that rendering embraces values relevant to both history and literature. A chapter on the critical writing along with a brief discussion of the short fiction is followed by deeper and more thoughtful analyses of the novels, with special emphasis on Stegner's skill in point of view. An epilogue suggests "lines of kinship" (Bernard De Voto, Willa Cather, Mark Twain). The Robinsons write a remarkably graceful and effective prose, firm and casual simultaneously, and their insights are acute.

The Robinsons' contention that the difficult reconciliation of past and present is Stegner's recurring theme is confirmed by Jamie Robertson's "Henry Adams, Wallace Stegner, and the Search for a Sense of Place in the West" (*The Westering Experience*, pp. 135–43), which links *Wolf Willow* and Adams's *Education.* The generic mix of Stegner's book suggests that a sense of place is a "poetic creation" explaining our relationship to both place and past. Kerry Ahearn, who takes a different tack in "Heroes vs. Women: Conflict and Duplicity in Stegner" (*WHR* 31:125–41), believes that the novels chart the spiritual journey of a man who, though seeing himself as a son of the West, is burdened by the Puritan spirit. Because they are "prophetesses of reduced expectations, of objectivity, of the desire to live by controls," Stegner's females suffer, whether as young victims, rebels, or "old partners." Both *Angle of Repose* and *The Spectator Bird* are generously covered in this fine essay. "Cellars of Consciousness: Stegner's 'The Blue-Winged Teal' " (*SSF* 14:180–82) is a brief analysis of an initiation story centered on the symbolic uses of red and blue.

Tracing the fortunes of Thomas Berger's "Indian Book" in "The Second Decade of 'Little Big Man' " (*Nation* 225:149–51), Frederick Turner asserts that its distinct departure from most western literature, the dramatic cultural dialogue between whites and Plains Indians, stems from Berger's extensive reading of first-hand narratives generally ignored by most western writers. But, Turner concludes, Berger's novel is also a seminal product of the 1960s in its drive to develop structures, styles, and ways of thinking beyond "any version of ethnocentrism." In his evaluation, "The Radical Americanist" (*Nation* 225: 151–53), Brooks Landon sees Berger's protagonists as "observing Ishmaels" who, though they may trick and betray one another, are relentlessly convinced that the world as it is makes pretty good sense. Though Jack Crabb is one of these notable "survivors," Carlo Reinhart may be Berger's most skillfully portrayed character. John W. Turner's "*Little Big Man*, the Novel and the Film: A Study of Narrative Structure" (*LFQ* 5:154–63) shows that complex contrasts between savagery and civilization are important to both the novel and Arthur Penn's movie, though the latter's structure is too frail to sustain the weight of the materials, partly because their rendering depends so much on "the discursive and metaphoric aspects of language."

In their separate studies of N. Scott Momaday's famous novel, both Lawrence J. Evers and Floyd C. Watkins deal with the techniques for creating cultural landscapes. In "Words and Place: A Reading of *House Made of Dawn*" (*WAL* 11:297–320), Evers contends that despite Momaday's characterization of his hero ("a man without a voice" because he is separated from the oral traditions of his people), the novel is structured, like many oral narratives, around a cyclic movement from discord to harmony. Watkins reminds us in "Culture versus Anonymity in *House Made of Dawn*" (*In Time and Place*, pp. 133–71) that the novel treats an older scheme of things, an ancient vision of evil, good, and the world which the white man cannot fathom. Watkins's long and valuable essay, mingling personal experience, interviews, and traditional scholarship, concentrates on the symbolic appropriateness of native legends, ceremonies, and chants.

In *Larry McMurtry* (TUSAS 291), Charles D. Peavy credits his subject with the invention of the "urban western," a mode incorporating satire, black humor, and the frank exploitation of sex to depict the stagnation of the small town—which suggests that Sherwood Anderson perhaps needs rethinking. Peavy traces the themes (mostly initiation), attitudes (mostly cynical), and techniques of characterization (mostly stereotypical—for strong females and aging patriarchs) without notably persuading us that McMurtry is really worth the effort. A useful 15-page bibliography includes notes on the novelist's papers at the University of Houston.

xi. Others

***a.* Donald Barthelme, Robert Coover, and Other Innovators.** In "Remarks Re-marked: Barthelme, What Curios of Signs!" (*Boundary 2* 5:795–811), John Leland is especially perceptive on *Snow White*, in which the codes and forms of the fairy tale have passed into latency; cyclic structure degenerates into serial form, and Snow White must exist within "structures of reduplication" replacing the closed structure of myth. In "Bartheme's *The Dead Father*: Analysis of an Allegory" (*LNL* 2,ii:43–119), Barbara Maloy argues that statistical analysis can conquer the "fragments" of contemporary fiction and reveal "conscious and unconscious elements affecting its totality." What we learn about the novelist's theme—the love-hate relationship between father and son—is that the geographical spread of place names and allusions to five global newspapers "convey to the reader that the father-son conflict is universal." Particularly valuable is *Donald Barthelme: A Comprehensive Bibliography and Annotated Secondary Checklist* (Hamden, Conn.: Archon Books), compiled by Jerome Klinkowitz, Asa Pieratt, and Robert Murray Davis, who include descriptions of books, stories (some pseudonymous or unsigned), essays, dramatic adaptations, sound recordings, interviews, and even the juvenilia. This updating covers material available through 1976.

The most interesting part of her "The Man Behind the Catcher's Mask: A Closer Look at Robert Coover's *Universal Baseball Association*" (*UDQ* 12:165–74) is Judith Wood Angelius's argument that Henry Waugh appears in the last chapter as Paul, whose final transformation reinforces role-entrapment as a theme. Jessie Gunn speculates that Coover's themes (birth, growth, and death) as well as his authorial comments on creativity suggest that the "need for redesign" is a major impulse behind arrangements of his stories. Leisurely connected to the first part of "Structure as Revelation: Coover's *Pricksongs and Descants*" (*LNL* 2,i:1–42) is a long section on "The Sentient Lens," in which Gunn establishes the helix as the basic structure.

"Tri(y)log" is a conversation among Mas'ud Zavarzadeh, Joseph Hynes, and Raymond Federman (*ChiR* 28,ii:93–109), in which the new fictionist differentiates his group from that of Barth, Hawkes, and Gass and links himself ("I am trying to create a non-style") with Ronald Sukenick and Steve Katz. All three comment on the problem of writing a criticism to match such fiction. In Thomas LeClair's "William Gass: The Art of Fiction LXV" (*ParisR* 70:61–94), a revealing and bouncy interview, Gass would tend to agree with Federman—though his categories are between those who write "performatively" and those who do not. In "Words, War, and Meditation in Don DeLillo's *End Zone*" (*IFR* 4:68–70), Anya Taylor contends that this novel about the decline of language "under the bombardment of terms from thermonuclear warfare" attempts to revive language through an aesthetically disciplined "ritual of silence and self-loss through football."

***b.* Joseph Heller and Ken Kesey.** The most substantial essay on Heller this year is James Nagel's bibliographical study of the novelist's note cards, kept during the composition of *Catch-22*, on the structure and characters. The existence of "The *Catch-22* Note Cards" (*SNNTS* 8[1976]:394–405), now housed at Brandeis University, serves to refute earlier charges that the novel was chaotically organized and to corroborate more sophisticated readings in the last five years. "Joseph Heller: Something Happened to the American Dream" (*CEA* 40,i:34–38) is Nicholas Canaday's character sketch of the protagonist of *Something Happened*, the Willy Loman of the 1970s. Slocum shows his creator's "nostalgic yearning for youthful energy and confidence" common to an earlier America. George J. Searles would agree that the principal theme is the bankruptcy of the middle-class experience, typified by Slocum's preoccupation with lost innocence and integrity; but to judge from "*Something Happened*: A New Direction for Joseph Heller" (*Crit* 18,iii:74–82), the novel's chief interest seems to lie in its "total dissimilarity from Heller's first novel."

Searles also contributes "McMurphy's Tatoos [*sic*] in Kesey's

One Flew Over the Cuckoo's Nest" (*NMAL* 1:item 24). Noting that the poker hand tattooed on McMurphy's shoulder—aces and eights—is known colloquially as the "dead man's hand," Searles concludes that the tattoo prefigures the hero's inevitable extinction. Kesey shows up badly in Joseph M. Flora's "Westering and Women: A Thematic Study of Kesey's *One Flew Over the Cuckoo's Nest* and Fisher's *Mountain Man*" (*HK* 10,ii:3–14), although precisely why Kesey's novel should be chosen to emphasize the undeniable strengths of Vardis Fisher is not clear. That Kesey's females tend to be either the whore or "the maternal emasculator" is both true and trite; and if *Mountain Man* is a tribute to "wifely and motherly love," it does not necessarily follow that Kesey's novel fails to be moral, responsible, and adult. In "Straws for the Cuckoo's Nest" (*JPC* 10[1976]:199–202), Edward Stone suggests that Kesey's literary raids included Melville (the theme of monomania), Mark Twain (the figure of the con man), and Faulkner (the tragic vision). Marsha McCreadie's "*One Flew Over the Cuckoo's Nest*: Some Reasons for One Happy Adaptation (*LFQ* 5:125–31) and Elaine B. Safer's " 'It's the Truth Even If It Didn't Happen': Ken Kesey's *One Flew Over the Cuckoo's Nest*" (*LFQ* 5:132–41) are both detailed articles on the adaptation of Kesey's novel into the Milos Forman film.

***c.* John Gardner and E. L. Doctorow.** Gardner's two complementary pieces, "Moral Fiction" (*HudR* 29[1976]:497–512) and "The Idea of Moral Criticism" (*WHR* 31:98–109), unapologetically plead for models of decent behavior and critics that defend "the Good, the True, and the Beautiful." Arguing against Gass's theory of fiction as mere language, Gardner asserts that the writing of fiction is "a mode of thought because by imitating we come to understand the thing we imitate" and that the true writer of criticism, while he may address himself to techniques, is ultimately concerned with ends, since art is important precisely because it affirms values. A good introduction is "Settling for Ithaca: The Fictions of John Gardner" (*SR* 85:520–31) in which Bruce Allen reads the stories (in the order in which he believes they were written) as "initiatory journeys toward knowledge" informed by the medievalist poets' unswerving belief in human imperfection. David A. Dillon's "John C. Gardner: A Bibliography" (*BB* 34:86–89, 104) includes the novelist's scholarly works and comprises items "up to May 1977."

Discussing the Melvillean vision in E. L. Doctorow's fiction, in "Marching Backward into the Future: Progress as Illusion in Doctorow's Novels" (*SWR* 62:397–409), David Emblidge detects in all three novels a central motif of history as a repetitive process in which man is an unwilling pawn easily seduced into a belief in progress. Quests for revenge, the narrative conduits for that motif, are attempts "to make things the way they were, and in so doing reenact a common pattern of fruitless human behavior." Another critic has detected the presence of Heinrich von Kleist in *Ragtime* (see *ALS 1976*, p. 313): Peter F. Neumeyer in "E. L. Doctorow, Kleist, and the Ascendancy of Things" (*CEA* 39, iv:17–21) suggests that unlike the obsessed but larger-than-life figure whose fall is tragic in *Michael Kohlhaas*, the "ficto-historical" characters in *Ragtime* are emblematic of the "American apotheosis," in which the focus is not on one person, but on the makers, inventors, and financiers of "things."

***d.* Detective, Popular, and Science Fictionists.** Lew Archer takes his place on the couch in "The Very Private Eye of Ross Macdonald" (*L&P* 27:21–34, 67–73), in which Norman Kiell relates the pervasive use of the eye and its functions to unresolved oedipal conflicts in the detective hero (and presumably his creator), "anxieties incurred by fantasies of the primal scene, and the inevitable search for identity exemplified in the search for the father."

For his fascinating but finally indecisive essay, "A River of Blood and Time: Images of Jewish-Gentile Relations in Contemporary Pulp Culture" (*SAQ* 76:12–30), Dennis E. Showalter dips into airport newsstands, soap opera, the Disney matinee, and the Johnny Carson Show for evidence of what he calls a "pattern of absorption"—the Jew's ambiguous accommodation to the larger social community. The second edition of A. Grove Day's *James Michener* (TUSAS 60) differs little from the first (see *ALS 1964*, p. 175). Though both *The Source* and *Centennial* have recently enhanced Michener's popularity, the novelist's friend and biographer finds nothing significantly altered.

Clarence A. Andrews surveys "The Comic Element in Iowa Literature" (*Gerber Festschrift*, pp. 119–37), including Richard Bissell's bawdy and witty Mississippi River books. John G. Cawelti's analysis of *Mad* magazine in "The Sanity of *Mad*" (*Gerber Festschrift*, pp. 171–88) shows that while it became an exponent of liberation from middle-class anxieties through mockery and satire, it also promoted a "running critical examination" of the new morality.

If the early novel is about "the emergence of character" because it reflects actual social phenomena, so contemporary science fiction is about the disappearance of character, a mirror of our regimented and rationalized society in which individuals feel anonymous: this is the thesis of Scott Sanders's "Invisible Men and Women: The Disappearance of Character in Science Fiction" (*SFS* 4:14–24), an essay richly illustrated by examples from Pynchon, Mailer, and standard science fictionists.

In his provocative "Discontent in American Science Fiction" (*SFS* 4:3–13), Gérard Klein suggests that the human desire for unity, frustrated politically and socially, is displaced in science fiction by "a desire for fusion on the biological level." Luk De Vos contends in "Science Fiction as *Trivial-literatur*: Some Methodological Considerations" (*CLS* 14:4–19) that this subgenre is historically valuable because it reflects social structures less ideologically conditioned than mainstream literature. Charles Elkins, however, in "An Approach to the Social Functions of American SF" (*SFS* 4:228–32) argues flatly that the task of this kind of writer is to find resolutions to the role conflicts which vex society by creating images of the past and future which may serve as models for action in the present. On different grounds in "Cosmology and Science Fiction" (*SFS* 4:107–10), Stanislaw Lem berates the "miniscule, simplified and lukewarm" nature of most science fiction because its creators are hostile to scientific study not already media-sanctioned.

Two sociological studies of interest are Linda Fleming's "The American SF Subculture" (*SFS* 4:263–71)—which calls for further work in the way this specialized reading community develops its own channels of communication, recruiting methods, and rewards—and Albert I. Berger's "Science-Fiction Fans in Socio-Economic Perspective: Factors in the Social Consciousness of a Genre" (*SFS* 4:232–46)—an elaborate statistical report which generally confirms the view that science fiction readers have of themselves (better educated and more involved in professions and technology than the average reading community). In "A Feminist Critique of Science Fiction" (*Extrapolation* 18:6–19), Mary Kenny Badami charges that these writers' treatment of women characters panders to bondage fantasies and sadomasochism in teenage boys. She admits she is not much concerned with the quality of such books: "principally I am judging the books on their message (truth)—whether they conform to the way I believe life is and ought to be." For those interested in accepting Badami's criteria, "A Checklist of SF Novels with Female Protagonists" follows her article.

According to Sam N. Lehman-Wilzig's somewhat rambling "Science Fiction as Futurist Prediction: Alternative Visions of Heinlein and Clarke" (*LitR* 20:133–51), extrapolating present problems into future nightmares "borders on mania" in Robert Heinlein's simplistic vision; Arthur C. Clarke, however, responds with "emotional placidity" since he suggests that no individual hero but "mankind in toto" will be our savior. In a Marxist reading, "Ideological Contradiction in Clarke's *The City and the Stars*" (*SFS* 4:150–57), Tom Moylan finds this work, balanced precariously on the edge of subversion and socializing, finally ending as a "mechanism of bourgeois ideology."

Four pieces this year are on Ursula K. Le Guin. Martin Bickman, in "Le Guin's *The Left Hand of Darkness*: Form and Content" (*SFS* 4:42–47), sees in this work the embodiment of insights from Pynchon, Nabokov, Gaddis, Borges, and other mainstream fictionists who view the commonsensical idea of the world as arbitrary. Some of the same themes also show up in her stories, according to Thomas J. Remington's "A Touch of Difference, A Touch of Love; Theme in Three Stories by Ursula K. Le Guin" (*Extrapolation* 18:28–41)—namely, loneliness, the need to understand the self by disinterested love. In "Le Guin's 'Aberrant' Opus: Escaping the Trap of Discontent" (*SFS* 4:287–95), Gérard Klein sees in the Hainish cycle possibilities of hope and change lying in "the experience, the subjectivity of the other." Elizabeth Cummins Cogell, in "Setting as Analogue to Characterization in Ursula Le Guin" (*Extrapolation* 18:131–41), also concentrates on the Hainish stories, the settings of which are used to characterize native species of other worlds.

"The Surreal Translations of Samuel R. Delany" (*SFS* 4:25–34) is a stylistic analysis by Peter S. Alterman, who focuses on "tortured time" sequences, shifting points of view, fluid narrators, and non-linear logic. In "Images of the Waste Land in *The Einstein Intersection*" (*Extrapolation* 18:116–23), H. Jane Gardiner discovers that Delany's 1966 book utilizes the myth of the Grail Quest. Russell Letson, in "The Face of a Thousand Heroes: Philip José Farmer" (*SFS* 4:35–41), demonstrates that Farmer extends the boundaries of space opera formulas especially in his use of the double hero—the ordinary man who must act the hero and the ordinary man who is transformed into a superhero. In "The Worlds of Philip José Farmer" (*Extrapolation* 18:124–30), Letson also qualifies Leslie Fiedler's Freudian reading of Farmer's work (see *ALS 1975*, p. 358).

***e.* Miscellaneous.** A significant essay on William Gaddis is "To Soar in Atonement: Art as Expiation in Gaddis's *The Recognitions*" (*Novel* 10:127–36) by Joseph S. Salemi, who finds the aesthetic center of this novel analogous to Pound's in *Hugh Selwyn Mauberley*: the novel betrays bitterness over a world gone rotten with oversimplification, moral relationships, latitudinarian religion, and undisciplined art.

In "Hugh Selby's *Last Exit to Brooklyn*: The Psychodynamics of Person and Place" (*AmS* 22:137–51), Eberhard Kreutzer relates the confined setting to rhetorical devices which suggest the immobility of the characters; an "additive" style, paying less attention to differentiation than to the "rhythms of typical behavior," mingles realism and symbolism in the manner of Crane's *Maggie*. The structure of Jack Kerouac's *The Dharma Bums* may be as "surprisingly subtle" as Keith N. Hull claims in "A Dharma Bum Goes West to Meet the East" (*WAL* 11:321–29), since the "backsliding" progress of its hero to achieve the Zen ideal is objectified in narrative events, but for all that, as Hull lamely concludes, the reader may be the butt of a joke—"if there is one."

William J. Schafer reads three historical novels, including *The Sin of the Prophet* (1952), in "Truman Nelson: Heeding the Voices of Revolution" (*MinnR* 7[1976]:66–82) as an anatomy of radical reformist sensibility in New England before the Civil War, which constitutes a "guidebook to our revolutionary heritage." William M. Chace's "*The Middle of the Journey*: Death and Politics" (*Novel* 10:137–44) is a plea for ignoring Lionel Trilling's novel as political; death, which gives character to all the main events, is the real theme. Larry McCaffery's "Stanley Elkin: A Bibliography, 1957–1977" (*BB* 34:73–76) does not purport to be "totally exhaustive," but it helpfully lists all the important short fiction and novels (including published excerpts), uncollected short fiction, essays, reviews, and the scant handful of critical commentary on Elkin.

David Seed's "The Fiction of Isaac Bashevis Singer" (*CritQ* 18, i:73–79) will serve only minimally for those already acquainted with the work of the recent Nobel laureate and seems to have been written mostly to mark the British publication of recent Singer titles. In discussing one of Singer's rare stories set in Israel in "I. B. Singer's 'The Captive': A False Messiah in the Promised Land" (*SAF* 5:269–75), Julian C. Rice finds a profound skepticism toward the Messianic aspects of that country, whose citizens are now "psychological captives of the value systems of their former oppressors."

In "Witness to the Absurd: Elie Wiesel and the French Existentialists" (*Renascence* 29:170–84), Mary Jean Green argues that Wiesel is not so much an " 'ethnic' novelist whose limited message is directed toward a limited group," but, like Sartre and Camus, uses the novel as a vehicle for explaining the most fundamental of modern philosophical issues.

Indiana University

16. Poetry: 1900 to the 1930s

Richard Crowder

i. General

In 1977 *Expl* published only three items related to this chapter, all on Frost. A new periodical similar in purpose is *Notes on Modern American Literature* (*NMAL*), which in volume 1 presents discussions of poems by Ransom, Cummings, Sandburg, Frost (2), and Stevens (3). These mini-essays vary in usefulness, but the reader can find suggestions for further exploration. *AN&Q* carries an occasional brief comment on a poet of our period. Janet McCann, in "Wallace Stevens' 'Esthetique du Mal,' Section X" (15:111–13), says that Stevens pictures Baudelaire as forerunner of "the shaken realist" who, however, can take a cautiously affirmative view.

DAI (vol. 37, nos. 7–12 and vol. 38, nos. 1–6) abstracts 29 dissertations totally or in part concerning our poets. MacLeish's literary essays are the subject of one thesis. Of the three on Robert Penn Warren two are on his fiction. John G. Neihardt is considered as critic and reviewer. Among the ten other poets treated at least as part of a study are the following: Sandburg, Masters, Lindsay, and Ransom, one each; Crane, Cummings, Tate, and Donald Davidson, two each; Frost, four; and Stevens, ten. Ransom's uncertainty in 1951 as to whether to put Stevens into the major or the minor category would seem to have been solved by our graduate students, as well, of course, as by our professional critics.

In the following pages the reader will find mention of 23 relevant books. Adelaide Crapsey's work, presented in full, is accompanied by helpful notes and essays. Harriet Monroe and *Poetry* magazine is the subject of a book. Full-length studies of Elinor Wylie and Sara Teasdale have been reissued. John Dewey's poems are published with helpful apparatus. We are picking up a 1976 study of George Cabot Lodge. There are books about Warren, Ransom, Jeffers, and Santayana (this latter with a chapter on Stevens). Stevens is the subject of four solid books, one from 1974. Finally Frost is central to five books: a collection of reviews, the third volume of his biography, a critical study, the brief record of a conversation, and a book of pictures.

ii. Women Poets (and Fletcher)

For the first time Crapsey's poems are brought together—both good and bad—by Susan Sutton Smith in *Complete Poems and Collected Letters of Adelaide Crapsey* (Albany: SUNY Press). We know the poet as the inventor of the haiku-like "cinquain," but she is here revealed as a craftsman of widely ranging technique. Nearly 100 pages of letters show her as a charming, courageous person with a strong sense of humor. The letters date from 1893, when she was a student at Kemper Hall, to September 1914, about a fortnight before her death. The editor's 47-page introduction presents the few known facts of the poet's life, reviews criticism of the poetry to date, undertakes a new evaluation, and delineates the textual problems the editor encountered. Eight pages of photographs are interesting and helpful. A careful and scholarly set of appendices and an index are at the back of the book. Though minor, Crapsey has, as Yvor Winters said, "great distinction."

In "A Doll's Heart: The Girl in the Poetry of Edna St. Vincent Millay and Louise Bogan" (*TCL* 23:157–79), Elizabeth P. Perlmutter analyzes work of both poets to prove that they used the undeniably female voice "as a formal principle for invigorating and intensifying lyric speech." "God's World," "Passer Mortuus Est," and other poems illustrate Millay's Girl both as subject matter and as adrenalizing power. Both Millay and Bogan discovered at last that the Girl was a mere doll (a lie), for true rewards (peace, joy, etc.) would come only to the Woman. Another in a usable series of bibliographical helps in the study of American writers is Judith Nirman's *Edna St. Vincent Millay: A Reference Guide* (Boston: G. K. Hall). Included are book titles and information about reviews, critical articles, and parts of books year by year from first mention to the near present. There is a full and skillfully conceived index, including comparisons with other authors, themes, techniques, etc.

By analyzing John Gould Fletcher's "The Skaters" and H. D.'s "Oread," John T. Gage determines that they function similarly:

skaters in terms of swallows, waves in terms of trees (or *vice versa*?). In "Images and Critical Method" (*Style* 11:355–74) he says that both poems "*control* our experience of . . . comparisons" but can only "*occasion* our experience of some mental image." From the reader's view, so-called images are more useful if they are considered as structures of thought rather than simple visualizations, the Imagists' creed to the contrary notwithstanding.

A rich and readable history of *Poetry* from its beginnings through the following decade is Ellen Williams's *Harriet Monroe and the Poetry Renaissance*, a volume that has considerable relevance for the poets of this chapter. The author draws on the *Poetry* papers and various Monroe files at the University of Chicago as well as relevant materials and correspondence from a wide range of sources, including quotations and paraphrases from many magazines and books. She gives undeniably authentic extension to our portrait of Ezra Pound and adds important details to our understanding of Amy Lowell, Alfred Kreymborg, Alice Corbin Henderson, and other figures of the period—editors, critics, and poets. An introduction and four lengthy chapters evaluate the issues of *Poetry* as they appeared. The author concludes that 1914–15 were "the great years," that Monroe did not possess the necessary vision and sensitivity to keep the momentum rolling. An appendix on finances, a long bibliography, and a full index complete this rewarding volume.

Two reprints are of some importance to us, for the publishers are obviously betting on a continued interest in their subjects. Greenwood Press (Westport, Conn.) has brought out Nancy Hoyt's 1955 biography of her sister, *Elinor Wylie: The Portrait of an Unknown Lady*. Pentelic Press (Norfolk, Va.) has reissued Margaret Haley Carpenter's *Sara Teasdale: A Biography* (first ed., 1960).

iii. New York and New England

Jo Ann Boydston has written an extensive introduction (over 40 pages) to her edition of *The Poems of John Dewey* (Carbondale: Southern Ill. Univ. Press). Placing the poems in their biographical perspective, discussing, for example, the relationship of Dewey with Anzia Yezierska, who thought of him as "an intellectual New Englander," of herself as an "exotic Oriental," Boydston works out some of Dewey's themes: determination to persevere, appreciation of traits of dauntlessness, problems of society, etc. She also explores dominant images from nature and other sources. A section of "Textual Apparatus" describes the appearance of the texts (even the typewriters used), explains the "Editorial Method," and catalogues the alterations and emendations for each of the 98 poems.

F. Richard Thomas, in "Hart Crane, Alfred Stieglitz, and Camera Photography" (*CentR* 21:294–309), detects three elements in Stieglitz's practice of photography which relate to Crane's aesthetic: the use of a machine, the ability to eternalize a given moment, and the capacity for conveying meanings beyond his surface subjects. Crane differed from Stieglitz, however, in not submitting to "the machine culture." Thomas concludes that Crane's most successful poems are the shorter ones that closely relate to Stieglitz photographs. Washington Augustus Roebling, the engineer responsible for the building of the Brookyn Bridge, had, not surprisingly, a personal reaction to the famous Crane poem, as Vivian H. Pemberton reveals in "The Roebling Response to Hart Crane's *The Bridge*: A New Letter" (*OQ* 20:155–57).

Eric J. Sundquist's "Bringing Home the Word: Magic, Lies, and Silence in Hart Crane" (*ELH* 44:376–99) is a study of the poet's constant struggle with language as magic, with the supernatural capacity for being filled with symbolic importance. The author's argument relies on Crane's peculiar problems. He sees Crane in the constant act of bringing home the Word, stealing language which never held together as he tried to shape it to his own uses. At last, suicide was the the only answer—"an original, unindebted performance." Placing Crane firmly in the Romantic tradition, Robert Combs finds an inherent skepticism in the poems. His *Vision of the Voyage: Hart Crane and the Psychology of Romanticism* (Memphis: Memphis State Univ. Press) connects Crane's technique with Hegel's *The Phenomenology of the Spirit.* Combs sees Crane's career as seriate experimentation based metaphorically on his subjective life. The problems and ambiguities are without bounds. The book is well indexed. In 1963 Samuel Hago published *Hart Crane: An Introduction and Interpretation*, which has now been reissued as *Smithereened Apart: A Critique of Hart Crane* (Athens: Ohio Univ. Press). The balanced discussions of the chief poems and an undaunted confrontation of difficult passages are accompanied by a new preface and a bibliography brought up to date.

In an essay-review of *Selected Poems of S. Foster Damon* called "Damon's Poetic Testament" (*MQR* 16:323–29), Laurence Goldstein claims that by 1929 Damon had shown himself to be a sound, if not a leading, writer. This was the year of *Tilted Moons*, which brought together some of his best poetry. After this date he was distracted by scholarly research unworthy of his abilities, although he did later become also a well-known Blake scholar. His best verse was written out of an intelligence critical and creative, at the same time as he aimed "to haunt his fellows," to be "hectoring and pungent." In the same issue of *MQR* (16:308–22) "S. Foster Damon, Demonologist," by Barton Levi St. Armand, studies the poet's occult interests and his experiments (sometimes with Robert S. Hillyer) in psychic experience. The last nine pages contain Damon's own "A Spiritualist Diary" (1920–21).

Last year we inadvertently omitted John W. Crowley's *George Cabot Lodge* (TUSAS 264). In addition to publishing Lodge's *Selected Fiction and Verse* (see *ALS 1976*, p. 333), Crowley has issued this book-length discussion of Lodge's work, not claiming a major position for the Harvard-educated poet, but finding him nevertheless worth working with for his stance in the first decade of this century as a Conservative Christian Anarchist and a transcendental optimist. The author suggests that Lodge and his contemporaries anticipated T. S. Eliot's "revolution."

There has been a noticeable falling off of Robinson criticism this year, possibly because the *Colby Library Quarterly* has at least temporarily turned its attention elsewhere, though other journals have been equally diffident. Joan Manheimer presents a study of the poet's story-telling technique in "Edwin Arlington Robinson's 'Eros Turannos': Narrative Reconsidered" (*LitR* 20:253–69). She focuses on Robinson's use of rejected figures and the nature of the speaker's voice and attitude, then more briefly shows similar limitations in speakers in other poems. Robinson, she says, recognizes that to think the speaker could be omniscient would be an illusory point of view. In *IJAS* 7:54–66 G. P. Thakur discusses the controversies about the origin of "Tilbury Town" and its position in appreciation of the poetry ("Tilbury Town as Region: A Study of the Poetry of E. A. Robinson").

Nancy Cummings De Forêt gives a daughter's intimate view of her famous father in *Charon's Daughter: A Passion of Identity* (New

York: Liveright Publishing Corp.). Included are nine e. e. cummings poems never before published. Here is another volume to add to the library of daughters' appraisals to shelve alongside books by Holly Stevens and Leslie Frost—not to be overlooked in the final analysis. We have recently had a little burst of studies about Cummings as a college man. Richard S. Kennedy continues what he began last year (see *ALS 1976*, pp. 330–31). His new contribution is "E. E. Cummings at Harvard: Verse, Friends, Rebellion" (*HLB* 25:253–91). When Cummings entered Harvard he was already in the habit of writing poems, some of them quite good. S. Foster Damon became his mentor in the modern arts—music, painting, sculpture, as well as literature. Cummings established friendships with John Dos Passos, Scofield Thayer, and other men who were destined to achieve at least some reputation. Kennedy pictures his eventual breakthrough into the society of girls as he realized freedom from home restraints. There are several paragraphs on his differences with his father. (The understanding and appreciation came years later.) The reader is introduced to the courses he took as an undergraduate, including English Versification. The author explicates a number of the poems. This is an important and fascinating contribution to the picture of the growth of the poet.

Gary R. Stolz, in "Santayana in America" (*NEQ* 50:53–67), recounts the events of the poet-philosopher's 40 years in America. Drawing on material from his forthcoming book, Stolz says the American years were "intellectually enriching," though Europe was a welcome change in 1912. Only then, ironically, did the man begin to gain a reputation for excellence here. Lois Hughson's *Thresholds of Reality: George Santayana and Modernist Poetics* (Port Washington, N.Y.: Kennikat Press) portrays Santayana as a bridging figure from late Victorianism to literary modernism, in which Eliot and Stevens were the leaders. Santayana, says the author, sorely needed to master and then shape childhood losses and deprivations in his writing. "Displacement of action by imagination" is the thesis of the book, in which Santayana and Yeats are shown as transitional, Eliot and Stevens as "figures of fulfillment." Four chapters focus on Santayana: his lyric poetry, the limits of his skepticism, his sense of beauty, and the supremacy for him of the imagination. The following three chapters are devoted to Yeats, Eliot, and finally Stevens, of principal interest here. Called "Stevens and the Sufficiency of Reality," this chapter shows how Stevens exploited ordinary experience as poetic image: he would impose on each viewer of the world the responsibility of poet ("maker"). In other words, "the imaginative act" is not "an expression of poetic personality," but "the creation of order and determinate form." Within its self-imposed limits, this is an interesting and suggestive book.

iv. Midwesterners, Californians, and Southerners

John E. Hallwas devotes much of his time to the Illinois poets Lindsay, Masters, and Sandburg. (He is the author of the item on Sandburg in *NMAL* mentioned in the opening paragraph.) His "Poetry and Prophecy: Vachel Lindsay's 'The Jazz Age'" (*IllQ* 40:30–37) explains that this uncollected poem is actually expressing a desire for culture different from the jazz age—"simple, secure and replete with national and religious heroes to lend inspiration." Hallwas speculates that it may also express the poet's "desire to escape from the pressures and frustrations" of a declining reputation and unnoticed cultural proposals. Hallwas also studies "Masters and the Pioneers: Four Epitaphs from *Spoon River Anthology*" (*ON* 2[1976]:389–99), demonstrating how Edgar Lee Masters gave poetic significance to the lives of his own ancestors, linking himself, with great respect, to the pioneers of the past, who contrast sharply with the often frustrated and weak-willed residents of the modern Spoon River. Another Masters article appears in *ELWIU* 4:212–20, this one of biographical interest. Using chiefly Masters's heretofore undeciphered letters in the Newberry Library, Herb Russell ("Edgar Lee Masters' Final Years in the Midwest") corrects Masters's own (deliberate?) misstatements about his life in Chicago to 1923 and outlines his travels to Egypt and Paris. His love affairs and subsequent divorce are not slighted. The author analyzes the sonnet sequence based on the poet's temporary return to his wife before their divorce and his departure for New York. Russell also connects the *Spoon River* books with Pope's satirical *Dunciad* in "Edgar Lee Masters' 'Spooniad': A Source and Its Significance" (*MarkhamR* 6:26–27). Masters, along with Sherwood Anderson and Sinclair Lewis, was in revolt, not from the village itself, but from the myth of the village as innocent, virtuous, and democratic. Masters testified, "The best years of my life were spent back there in Illinois." Barry Gross thus reports in "The Revolt That Wasn't: The Legacies of Critical Myopia" (*CEA* 39,ii:4–8).

After outlining the opinions of two Sandburg critics in "Carl Sandburg as Poet—an Evaluation" (*SSML Misc.* 5:1–11), Frederick C. Stern refutes their view that "When Death Came April Twelve, 1945" is one of the poet's best later works. The author concludes that, in contrast to his youthful attitude, nowadays he loves Sandburg's poetry more than he admires, thinks about, or even reads it. It will continue to be a good introduction to poetry for teen-agers, but serious readers will soon go beyond it. On the other hand, Louis D. Rubin, Jr., has been a loyal supporter of Sandburg since his review of *Complete Poems* in *NewRep* in 1951. Now in "Not to Forget Carl Sandburg . . ." (*SR*:181–89) he writes appreciatively of the poet's language as "vernacular in an organic way, not as tour de force or demonstration." Sandburg opened up new experiences not usually submitted to aesthetic contemplation. Rubin sees the Lincoln books not as biography so much as an addition to Lincoln folklore. He predicts long life for Sandburg's work. John T. Flanagan writes of "Carl Sandburg, Lyric Poet" in *MidAmerica* 4:89–100. He admits that Sandburg may have written much too much and may have failed to explore the depths possible in imagery, but he maintained his lyricism throughout his writing career. Especially devoted to clear and accurate imagery, he also was knowledgeable in the use of other lyric devices such as onomatopoeia and alliteration without ever departing from "the spirit and idiom of the American people."

Thomas A. Zaniello discusses "The Early Career of Yvor Winters: The Imagist Movement and the American Indian" (*SIH* 6,i:5–10). In his early poems Winters used "Indian-like perceptions" paralleling the precision of Imagists. He was dissatisfied, however, with the stress on details in association. He came to believe that "post-symbolism" was the answer ("controlled associationism and precision of reference"). Zaniello says that Winters found in the closing lines of Stevens's "Sunday Morning" a brilliant illustration of his point.

Thanks in large measure to the persistent labors of Robert J. Brophy as editor of the *Robinson Jeffers Newsletter*, Robinson Jeffers's reputation has been kept very much alive. *RJN* has continued its extended coverage of Jeffers scholarship and other activities this year. *RJN* 48 reprints an article by Horace D. Lyon called "The Little People of the Santa Lucias" (supernatural beings purportedly inhabitants of Jeffers country) and publishes a poem "For Robinson Jeffers" by Bill Hotchkiss (the insights of poets are not to be overlooked), an ambitious Jeffers checklist from 1934 on, and a catalogue of the holdings in the Berg Collection of the New York Public Library. *RJN* 49 follows the same format. "Una Jeffers: Correspondent" continues, here presenting "Excerpts from Letters to Blanche Matthias, 1927–1934," filled with intimate views of the life and thought of both Una and her husband. A chapter abstract from a Brown dissertation recounts Mabel Dodge Luhan's relation to Jeffers's extramarital affair and Una's attempted suicide.

Frederic I. Carpenter has of recent years turned his mature attention to Jeffers. In "Robinson Jeffers Today: Beyond Good and Beneath Evil" (*AL* 49:86–96) he provides a chronological study of the rebirth of interest in the Jeffers canon, mentioning articles and books published since 1962, the date of Jeffers's death, including the reprinting of three books heretofore unpopular: *The Double Axe, Dear Judas* (Carpenter thinks this one "the best"), and *The Women at Point Sur.* He concludes that Jeffers's poetic world "is not beyond evil, but beneath (or before) evil." In " 'Post Mortem': 'The Poet Is Dead' " (*WAL* 12:3–10) Carpenter defines the poet's greatness as based in his unflinching confrontation of opposing values. The result is emotions almost pornographic in their sexuality. At the other end are "frustrations and guilt" so clearly delineated that the reader must almost conclude that the poet was obsessed with morality. In looking at Jeffers's "Post Mortem" (1927) and William Everson's "The Poet Is Dead" (written after Jeffers's death in 1962), the author points out that Everson used Jeffers's very words and phrases in trying to relate him to the world he found so repulsive.

Marlan Beilke's *Shining Clarity: God and Man in the Works of Robinson Jeffers* (Amador City, Calif.: Quintessence Publications) interprets the shorter poems in roughly chronological order so that the reader can follow the poet's developing perception of the themes of God and man. The book also includes recollections of Jeffers by Horace D. Lyon (see *RJN* 48, above) and is livened by many portraits and illustrations. Man and God are also the subject of "Spinoza and Jeffers on Man in Nature" by George Sessions (*Inquiry* 20:481–528). Spinoza's view of the cosmos is the basis for this discussion of the way man is related to God and nature. Sessions, however, makes it clear that Jeffers also sees man as part and parcel of his environment as opposed to "the man-dominant Resource Conservation and Development paradigm" on the one hand and "absolute subjectivism" on the other.

Individual long works are scrutinized in two articles. Barbara S. Nadel's "Robinson Jeffers' *Cawdor*: The Emergence of Man's Tragic Beauty" (*JAAR* 5:225–72) concludes that, though Jeffers is damning man's destructive egocentrism as Cawdor follows the path to hell, yet he introduces modifying images later in the poem which turn accusation into compassion. In "Jeffers' *Medea*: A Debt to Euripides" (*RLV* 42[1976]:620–23), Catherine Georgoudaki points out that both Jeffers and Euripides treat of the end results of passion, but, whereas in Euripides destruction comes from love, in Jeffers the cause is violent hatred. The author's conclusion is that the world created by Euripides is more positive than that of Jeffers.

M. Catherine Harris updates R. D. Stallman's 1952 work with "Conrad Aiken's Critical Recognition, 1914–76" (*BB* 34:29–34 [pt. 1]; 137–40, 156 [pt. 2]). Part 1 catalogues the writer's biographies and poetry; part 2 details his fiction and drama, his literary criticism and editorship, and critics' comments on his prose and poetry. Harris has been conscientious in the preparation of this bibliography, but, modestly and generously admitting to the immensity of the task, she invites additions and corrections. Lawrence Kingsley's "The Texts of Allen Tate's 'Ode to the Confederate Dead'" (*PBSA* 71:171–89) is divided into three parts. Part 1 quotes the varying opinions on the "Ode" from Ransom, Warren, and Donald Davidson. Part 2 traces the printing history of the various revisions. Part 3 undertakes to prove that Tate's judgment in making changes was not influenced by praise or criticism. Though he has made no revisions in many years, he feels his poem must remain unfinished.

"The Sword Between Them: Love and Death in 'The Equilibrists'" by W. Potter Woodbery (*SLJ* 9,ii:51–65) draws on the Manichaean idea that sexual union is abhorrent as one yearns for union with the Absolute, a theme John Crowe Ransom borrowed from Provençal lyric poetry. Passion never satisfied keeps one reaching for the Transcendent. "The flames and ice of the equilibrists easily translate into the hot and cold flashes so symptomatic of the Provençal love anguish." George Core gives a biographical account of Ransom with extended critical comment in "A Naturalist Looks at Sentiment" (*VQR* 53:455–74). Core says that Ransom always maintained his relationships with humanity and avoided the stance implicit in *ars gratia artis.* His gentle but firm opinion was that "Life must come first."

Mississippi Quarterly, vol. 30, no. 1, is a special issue devoted to Ransom. Eight substantial essays consider Ransom from as many points of view. Robert Buffington in "Overlooking the Last Infirmity" (pp. 5–27) studies the poet's obsession with revision in his advanced years. William Pratt's "Metamorphosis of a Poem" (pp. 29–58) analyzes the changes over a period of 45 years as "Tom, Tom, the Piper's Son" became "The Vanity of Bright Boys," after which Ransom simply abandoned the poem. The theses developed in *The World's Body* and *The New Criticism* are the subject of Thomas Daniel Young's "Ransom's Critical Theories: Structure and Texture" (pp. 71–85). "The Function of the Person in Ransom's Critical Prose" (pp. 87–100) by Marcia McDonald portrays the personality behind the writing: the "earthiness," the "occasional light tone," the "wit," the "graciousness." In "Ransom's Quest for Value" (pp. 101–10) Eugénie Lambert Hamner shows how the poet continued to relate aesthetic values to religious: as late as 1970 he was supporting the heart (the "Spirit") as the source of mythic insight. In an opposing view Wayne A. Knoll, S.J., traces the poet's experiences with religion from his Methodist background to his final position of divorcing religion and moralistic ideology from aesthetics—"the elevation of taste." "Summer's End" (pp. 137–53) is a personal recollection by Ransom's granddaughter, Robb Forman Dew. The concluding section of the issue brings Mildred Brooks Peters's 1968 bibliography through another decade: "John Crowe Ransom: A Checklist, 1967–1976" (pp. 155–68) lists books and separately published poems and essays as well as books about Ransom, items collected, periodical articles, and dissertation topics. This entire issue is a rich mine for Ransom scholars and other readers.

For several years we have had tantalizing essays from Thomas Daniel Young reminding us that a Ransom biography was in the making. Here it is—*Gentleman in a Dustcoat: A Biography of John Crowe Ransom* (Baton Rouge: La. State Univ. Press)—readable, reasonable, ordered, clear—just right for the subject. Without riding a hobby, the author paints an open picture of Ransom year by year. His sources are numerous and deep; the details are richly satisfying in all phases of the story, whether Young is disclosing his subject as teacher, theorist, purposefully "minor" poet, critic, theologue, philosopher of agrarianism, or, towards the end, tinkering reviser. Extensive notes and a full index add to the value of this sound work on an important man of American letters.

William Tjenos close-reads Robert Penn Warren's "Homage to Emerson" to demonstrate how the poet turns a shapeless perception into a conception. The author says, however, in "The Poetry of Robert Penn Warren: The Art to Transfigure" (*SLJ* 9,i[1976]:3–12), that the pattern is not inflexible in all the poems, which develop individually in line with the experience they spring from. The consistency lies in the confrontation of a "world of flux" and seeking in it a response to human desire. Stanly Plumly characterizes the three editions of Warren's *Selected Poems* (1944, 1966, 1977) in "Warren Selected—An American Poetry, 1923–75" (*OhR* 18,i:37–48). The first reenacts and pays for the past, which is now a dream—"a little like folk history and folk wisdom—deadly, fierce, and all-illuminating." In the second Warren emerges from "a rhetorical bind" with cleaner rhythms, purer language, and self-assured voice. The third, with the most recent poems placed first, stresses present knowledge, wisdom, joy, and delight, but it would be misleading to present Warren as anything but "angry, alluvial, *there*." In reviewing this most recent (third) edition, William Spiegelman, "The Poetic Achievement of Robert Penn Warren" (*SWR* 62,iv:vi–vii,411–15), says the arrangement lets the reader move "upstream to the source." He points out vigorously that Warren's thinking differs from Stevens's faith in the "thing itself" and from Shakespeare's "unaccommodated man" in that Warren has a constant feeling of "the envelope of consciousness, custom, or the past." For him innocence is simply unblessed ignorance. "We cannot resign from history." In his review, Guy Rotella zeros in on one neglected book—"Robert Penn Warren's *You, Emperors, and Others*" (*Descant* 21,iv:36–48). Examining the five poems of the sequence "Mortmain," he concludes that for Warren "the tragic vision and inclusive view are the mode of [his own struggle for meaning as man and artist] and the enablers of what joy it produces." In still another review, David M. Wyatt sees the reverse arrangement as a "profound act of criticism." "Robert Penn Warren: The Critic as Artist" (*VQR* 53:475–87) calls it "a rebellion against the priority of an earlier self." The result is that "the critic/son" is at last "the artist/father." The drama of the arrangement lies there: in the gradual assumption of "fatherhood."

All these reviews prompted by Warren's latest collections offer refreshing insights into the work of a man now taking his place with Stevens and Frost at the forefront of the poets of this century. In fact, says Warren, "I want to write a couple more novels that are in my head, but I really enjoy writing poetry more now." This statement was made in a fascinating and informative conversation recorded by Peter Stitt in "An Interview with Robert Penn Warren" (*SR* 85:467–77). Interrogation brought out some intimate facts of his life at Vanderbilt with the Fugitives as well as a number of experiences Warren had as poet.

Neil Nakadate, in "Voices of Community: The Function of Colloquy in Robert Penn Warren's *Brother to Dragons*" (*TSL* 21 [1976]: 114–24), points out that in this poem about the axe murder of a black man "R.P.W." is the questioner, definer, and director of intellectual analysis. Involved are Thomas Jefferson (his nephews have been the murderers) and others through whose voices (and his own) Warren arrives at "a revelation of complicity, necessity, and the direction of fulfillment" leading to facing up to life. Knowledge and reconciliation make the difference.

"The Ballad of Billie Potts" is Warren's central poem, surpassing all others in imagery, "sound texture," and thematic synthesis: the passage from innocence into "the world's stew of time and loss; the sudden discovery of the depraved, "dirty" self which this passage brings; the final unification of these opposites. This is the observation of Victor H. Strandberg in *The Poetic Vision of Robert Penn Warren* (Lexington: Univ. Press of Ky.), his second sound book on Warren as poet (see *ALS 1976*, pp. 214–15). Here Strandberg cites comments of critics through the years, then takes a close look at a number of other poems before concluding that in "Billie Potts" the poet reached his maturity as artist and thinker, publishing no more poems till *Brother to Dragons* a decade later, a book which, says the author, is Warren's most masterful study of the undiscovered self. Strandberg shows how profoundly the thought of William James has influenced Warren, whose fifty years as poet give him rank "among the finest and most fertile talents of his age." *The Poetic Vision* is a well-structured book in almost excessive praise of Warren.

v. Robert Frost

Linda W. Wagner, with her customary assiduity, has edited *Robert Frost: The Critical Reception* (New York: Burt Franklin) and supplied a descriptive introduction. The book reprints the American reviews of Frost's major collections in order of publication. (A few British reviews are included, especially of the two earliest volumes.) Where appropriate, checklists of additional reviews are appended to the chapters. An index lists the reviewers and the periodicals in which appraisals were printed. This book will save a great deal of time and labor.

The third volume of Lawrance Thompson's *Robert Frost* is subtitled *The Later Years, 1938–1963* (New York: Holt, Rinehart and Winston). R. H. Winnick completed the book from Thompson's materials after Thompson's death. (The two preceding volumes were reviewed in *ALS 1966*, p. 190, and *ALS 1970*, pp. 288–89.) The story recounts the virtually daily movements of the old curmudgeon as he collected honors, medals, and laurels—irascible, egotistical, ungenerous—all the time bearing personal tragedy as his wife died, his son committed suicide, and one of his daughters became insane. A rather uncharacteristic gesture was his reconciliation with T. S. Eliot. There is evidence of considerable incompatibility between Frost and his biographer. If one recalls other accounts of the poet's life, he will realize that definitive assessment will rest on much more than this frequently gloomy portrait, for Frost seems to have become somewhat less vicious and self-centered in his last years than indicated here.

Reviews of this biography are numerous. S. Maloff, in "Poetry and Power" (*Commonweal* 104:215–18), reports that Thompson told him emphatically that he had "scars" from "getting too close" to Frost. Maloff's conclusion, however, like any serious reader's, is that Frost's best poems (before his final period) are tragic, terrifying, born of a sense that the universe, made up of contraries, is absolutely desolate. "Transfigured Dead" by Edward Hirsh (*Commentary* 63,iii:86–90) says that Frost draws out and expands the imagination of his readers by electrifying and disclosing the peculiar aura of America itself and making richer and more stimulating the American view of nature, which can never be the same now because of him.

Cyril Clemens's *A Chat with Robert Frost* (Folcroft, Pa.: Folcroft Library Editions) continues a series of conversations with various writers. (The author has "chatted," for example, with Housman and Hardy.) This pamphlet is not of great scholarly consequence. Also of tangential interest to scholars is a book of chiefly scenic photographs with captions from Frost poems called *Robert Frost Country* (New York: Doubleday), compiled by Betsy and Tom Melvin, with a foreword by William Meredith. Further stories about the poet include John Ciardi's "Robert Frost: Two Anecdotes" (*SatR*, Sept. 3:48). The first shows how Frost would often refer to one's conversational phrase only after examining it for possible offense. The second relates an incident showing how the poet, in his later years, was always "on stage" in public. Donald Hall's "Vanity, Fame, Love, and Robert Frost" (*Commentary* 64,vi:51–61) is excerpted from a forthcoming book, *Remembering Poets.* Hall at 16 first encountered the poet at Bread Loaf. He had contact with Frost again and again—at Harvard, Stanford, Michigan, Frost's Vermont cabin. These are vivid recollections to add to the many anecdotes stored in Thompson's biography and elsewhere.

Andy J. Moore studies the influence of Frost on Robert Lowell in the latter's sonnet "Robert Frost," e.g., the midnight setting as symbolic of both poets' feeling of emptiness, both being acquainted with the night, both beset by family problems. His article is entitled "Frost and Lowell at Midnight" (*SoQ* 15:291–95). In regard to individual poems, some few studies have come out, notably five articles and an impressive book. Roy Scheele connects one important poem to the English tradition of flower poetry in "Sensible Confusion in Frost's 'The Subverted Flower'" (*SCR* 10:89–99). Archibald Henderson performs a psychoanalytical operation on "Robert Frost's 'Out, Out—'" (*AI* 34,i:12–27). He sees the buzz-saw as suggesting the Reality Principle and also the model of the boy's Ego, which keeps him from carrying out his Oedipus impulses. (The boy is conforming to the rules of the world.) The saw also serves as provocation to masturbate. Ridden by guilt which breaks his spirit, the boy commits suicide, sacrificing himself to the saw as totem. This is a very complicated interpretation of the poem. Some readers will say it goes too far. Another article discusses with elaborate explication the ambiguities presented in one of the poet's terrifying pieces about suffering and put-upon women: Constance Rooke's "The Elusive/Allusive Voice: An Interpretation of Frost's 'A Servant to Servants'" (*CimR* 30:13–23).

Helen Bacon, chairman of the Department of Greek and Latin at Barnard College, continues to give us refreshing studies of Frost and the classics. (See *ALS 1975*, p. 365.) This year she offers "For Girls: From 'Birches' to 'Wild Grapes,'" (*YR* 67:13–29). She has discovered that Frost, being told that "Birches" was a poem for boys, set out to write "Wild Grapes" with a girl's experience in mind. She sees parallels with the Sermon on the Mount and especially with the *Bacchae* of Euripides. (Both the play and Frost's poem involve "several kinds of knowledge, or wisdom.") "Birches" and "Wild Grapes" each say that rebirth (in the one poem, for men; in the other, for women) is achieved through "linking heartbeats and footbeats," that is, by the path of poetry. Joan St. C. Crane has come forward with another of her invariably interesting and inventive bibliographical studies—"Robert Frost's 'Kitty Hawk'" (*SB* 30:241–49). She notes the differences in four versions: as a 1956 Christmas card, in the *Atlantic*, in the *Saturday Review*, and in *In the Clearing* (1962).

The book we mentioned is Richard Poirier's *Robert Frost: The Work of Knowing* (New York: Oxford), in which the author comes at Frost from Emerson through William James. (We have already noted the alleged influence of James on Robert Penn Warren, above.) Poirier sees definite Jamesian influence in "Design" and finds *Pragmatism* to be the source of a number of Frost metaphors. He is not afraid to point out Frost's sentimental lapses or to leave him a popular poet albeit not to be read too literally, but rather as a constant maker of tropes. In the matter of "walls," for example, Poirier sees them as "an elementary or vulgar expression of the human need for form, of which poetry is a masterly example." He confronts a number of poems readers have taken for granted and finds in them unsuspected profundity. This is a major contribution to Frost explication, for some critics the best yet to appear. The author gave us a preview in *GaR* 31:286–315. "Soundings for Home: Frost's Poetry of Extravagance and Return" is an excerpt from chapter 3, about wandering and coming home as metaphor of the human plight.

vi. Wallace Stevens

Stevens is engaging more attention these days than any other of our poets dealt with in this chapter. Unlike Frost, he does not invite biographical divulgence (except for his daughter's important book reviewed here on his very young manhood). A rare exception is James Rother's "The Tempering of *Harmonium*: The Last Years of Wallace Stevens's Apprenticeship, 1908–1914" (*ArQ* 33:319–38). This article tells the story of the poet's final strides into maturity: his absorption of the *Symbolistes*, Mallarmé in particular, and the adoption of the Pierrot figure. All the while, he was trying to achieve "a fluid medium comprised of ambiguous imperatives and impersonal forensics." Rother gave us, in 1976, another essay—on "Wallace Stevens as a Nonsense Poet" (*TSL* 21: 80–89), which suggests that the poet used nonsense to differentiate between varieties of both fact and "rational truth." Refining what he found in Lewis Carroll and Mallarmé, he would shift from a reader's expectations to some surprising elements, as illustrated, for example, in "Bantams in Pine-Woods" and "The Comedian as the Letter C." Eleanor Cook also looks at this latter poem in "Wallace Stevens: 'The Comedian as the Letter C' " (*AL* 49:192–205) and finds it concerned with "the way language lets us perceive through our eyes and ears." The conclusion of the poem is open-ended, for Stevens sees that the imagination is always struggling with external reality.

Mario L. D'Avanzo examines another *Harmonium* poem in "Emerson and Shakespeare in Stevens's 'Bantams in Pine-Woods' " (*AL* 49:103–7), in which he sees Emerson's symbolic pine tree from "The Poet" transformed into a "ten-foot poet" attacked by an argumentative rooster. The idea of the sun as "blackamoor" D'Avanzo traces to *Love's Labour's Lost*, the sun here too being a slave merely assisting the supreme poet. The short, mortal poet reduces the Emersonian ideal to "what is possible." Carol Kyros Walker, in "The Subject as Speaker in 'Sunday Morning' " (*CP* 10:25–31), argues for a single persona in that poem—a woman—in spite of apparent propositions and counter-propositions otherwise.

Michael T. Beehler's "Meteoric Poetry: Wallace Stevens' 'Description without Place' " (*Criticism* 19:241–59) is interesting and closely argued. For Stevens, says Beehler, language is "description without place," that is, nonrepresentational. Linguistic depth is illusory: "the vacant signs of language" seem to name a thing and so go beyond structure and syntax; they constitute "an empty but expedient metaphor." Michel Benamou continues his studies of Stevens and the *Symbolistes* with "Displacement of Parental Space: American Poetry and French Symbolism" (*Boundary 2* 5:471–86). Only the last part of the article actually deals with Stevens's poetry itself. Benamou here states that Stevens in his final poems proposes "mere being" as the end—an innocence that repays all the poet's deconstructions. What matters, then, is not the origin (not the "egg") but space and end. "Thesis and Anti-Thesis in Wallace Stevens's Concept of Metaphor" (*GyS* 4:96–122) is the title of Kathleen Dale's article in which she pursues the poet's maneuvers into and out of the "phenomenological attitude."

Several articles appear in the new *Wallace Stevens Journal* (*WStJ* 1). Among them, Lisa Steinman examines briefly the long poems in terms of intellectual effort to cope with the difficult so that one can fit into a "world not his own" but control the shaping of his very self ("Figure and Figuration in Stevens' Long Poems," pp. 10–16). George Bornstein's "Provisional Romanticism in 'Notes toward a Supreme Fiction'" (pp. 17–24) shows how this later work is the ultimate expression of the poet's mature journey from the old to the "new romanticism." William Ingoldsby gives a brief description of the Huntington Collection and summarizes its most important holdings in "The Wallace Stevens Manuscript Collection at the Huntington Library" (pp. 41–48). Included also is a section on "Current Bibliography" (pp. 32–36, 87–88). This new periodical should serve scholars working on Stevens as well as *RJN* serves Jeffers students.

"Credences of Summer" is a summing up of the poet's early experiments and a fingerpost toward the work of later years. This is the observation of Robert J. Bertholf in "The Revolving toward Myth: Stevens' 'Credences of Summer'" in the new *BuR*'s *Twentieth Century Poetry, Fiction, Theory*, pp. 208–29 (hard-back with no volume numbering). In this poem Stevens decides against settling exclusively in the North (as he has said he would in the early "Farewell to Florida"). Bertholf inspects the several parables of the poem about "the source of energy of the imagination's life." Stevens, he discovers, has transferred opposites like North and South into the glory of the imagination at work: "in 'Credences of Summer' he found the central power, and with it an abundance of joy." Incidentally, this is Bertholf's third good article on Stevens in three years. (See *ALS 1975*, p. 370, and *ALS 1976*, p. 329.)

According to Robert N. Mollinger, in "Wallace Stevens' Search for the Central Man" (*TSL* 21[1976]:66–79), Stevens wavers between negative and positive positions on what the essentials are for the "central man." Early poems see him as the man of the masses; the middle period pictures him as hero; the late poems, as they try to reconcile these two views, portray him finally as a realistic "major man." Richard Eberhart's "Reflections on Wallace Stevens in 1976" (SoR 13:417–18) reveals that the author's generation of poets was glad to be able to shift belief to Stevens after years of enduring Eliot! Stevens "was my specialist of the exquisite, the refined, and he was my expert in the grand, the noble, the generous, a poet of large statements and design." No schizoid, he made a good living and also worked at his poetry. Eberhart expresses a present need for "a poetry of the people" written by "a man as big as the continent we live in . . . a poet of universal, not particular consciousness." This is not to say that Stevens, in his own way, was not universal, but American poetry must move ahead.

"Hermit in a Poet's Metaphors: Wallace Stevens as 'Satirist' " is Edward Neill's contribution to *AWR*, 26,lix:61–68. Neill quotes from various poems to ilustrate his point that Stevens was capable of "deft buffoonery and satirical thrust" as he confronted mankind's basic underdog status. In nine brief "notes and observations," Robert Pawlowski supports such statements as the following: "No one poem seems to be more central to Stevens's work than any other." "The only human action he seems to allow is the mind's action. . . . the poems emerge often with a valid dramatic structure." The author concludes his essay, "The Poetry of Wallace Stevens" (*TQ* 20,iii:62–70), with statements of dissatisfaction over such dicta as "the poet's subject is his sense of the world." Pawlowski solves no problems but suggests much for further cogitation. David Howard, in "Wallace Stevens and Politics" (*RMS* 21:52–75), contends that, just as the poet's use of Christianity's language and overtones is his method of refutation of conventional faith, so he combats Communism, the currently "dominant threat to human energies," by taking over its vocabulary. "Thirteen Ways of Looking at a Blackbird," according to Robert S. Ryf, is "the first complete formulation of . . . Stevens' governing poetic theme." "X Ways of Looking at Y: Stevens' Elusive Blackbirds" (*Mosaic* 11,i:93–101) calls to witness several Stevens essays in support of a close examination of each of the 13 stanzas, which are more than just a collection of images: "the process of looking-at requires a great deal of looking into."

Robert M. Browne quarrels with Samuel Jay Keyser over the latter's method of interpreting Stevens's "The Snow Man" (see *ALS 1976*, pp. 327–28). In "Regarding 'The Snow Man': Some Comments for S. J. Keyser" (*CE* 39:220–23), Browne accuses Keyser of jumping illegitimately from "structure to reading process," neglecting "the rhetorical aspect." Keyser's rejoinder—"Reply to Robert M. Browne (1977)" (*CE* 39:223–26)—emphasizes the error implicit in ignoring the syntactical process: it is fatal, he asserts, to think of the structure of a poem as accidental.

A. Walton Litz has contributed "Wallace Stevens' Defense of Poetry: *La poesie pure*, the New Romantic, and the Pressure of Reality" to *Romantic and Modern*, pp. 111–32. Litz traces the poet's growth of confidence in his deep feeling that the true romantic temper is not an escape from reality but the profoundest proof of the validity of the imagination. Litz begins with "The Snow Man" and "Tea at the Palaz of Hoon" (1921) to show Stevens's "extreme coordinates" (bare landscape and exotic detail). He quotes at some length from *The Necessary Angel* and *Opus Posthumous* in support of his point—that by 1951 Stevens was able to state unequivocally that, whereas in "pure poetry" style and poem are identical, now in his own understanding of romanticism "the style of man is man himself," not in a precious but in a truly transcendental sense. This is a very important essay.

An exceptionally unsentimental and unprejudiced portrait of her father by a daughter is Holly Stevens's *Souvenirs and Prophecies: The Young Wallace Stevens* (New York: Knopf). She uses various sources: the early poems (including some painful Harvard efforts); the badly altered journals begun at Harvard in 1898 and continued intermittently to 1912; letters to his fiancée; family conversations; scanty records from his birthplace, his college town, and New York (before the move to Hartford). She pulls no punches in disclosing the young Stevens as unskillful reporter and unpolished lover. She shows how he read incessantly and developed into an absolute aesthete. With judgment and insight, she reveals some of her father's early bad verse as the foundation for the solid work of his mature years, though she does not undertake to explain why and how he suddenly began the composition of his great poems in 1915. We are fortunate to have such a fair estimate from a devoted daughter.

I want to mention a book which we missed in 1974—Lucy Beckett's *Wallace Stevens* (New York, London: Cambridge Univ. Press), a lucid study based on the poet's relentless search through the years for belief in a world where religion has disintegrated. The author uses other poets as background for Stevens's problems and solutions, from Keats, Wordsworth, and Emerson to Santayana and, above all, Eliot. The poetry argues successfully for "the progress of the soul." Beckett's work is a book of considerable insight and interest.

Another readable and concise examination of the poems is *Wallace Stevens: An Introduction to the Poetry* (New York: Columbia Univ. Press), by Susan B. Weston. After an imaginative foreword by John Unterecker, Weston proceeds to develop chapters on "the gaiety of language," "introspective exiles," and "hero-hymns." She devotes 27 pages to "Notes toward a Supreme Fiction," stating, as Stevens's conclusion, that heaven amounts to what is imagined well here on earth and communicated through words. And it is "The World of Words" that brings the book to a close, examining the last works to demonstrate how difficult it was for him to get at reality. To close *The Collected Poems* with "Not Ideas about the Thing but the Thing Itself" was courageous—accepting as possible "that our every definition of reality is a regulative and saving fiction." This is a valuable book for tyro and old hand alike.

We have known for some time that Harold Bloom was working on *Wallace Stevens: The Poems of Our Climate* (Ithaca, N.Y.: Cornell Univ. Press). Now it is before us, providing not only detailed information on the poems but an extension of Bloom's thinking on the American Romantic movement. He holds Stevens's poetry in highest esteem, but pays little attention to such matters as linguistics and syntax. Instead, he is constantly riding his hobby (not universally supported) that all modern American literature descends from Emerson. Bloom's chapters are ingenious and complicated, based on a theory of three "crossings": Election, Solipsism, and Identification—experiencing sensations, acting in a symbolic world, and communicating with readers. (There is some problem in making the theory work with a few poems, but a fine critic must take chances.) The 12 chapters of explication are at once complex and clarifying, leading to a compassionate understanding of the poet's final "transcendentalism." (See Litz, above.) One of Bloom's successful procedures is the tracing of key words throughout the poet's complete work. This book is bound to be widely read and thoroughly digested by graduate students, scholars, and critics of every level and persuasion.

Purdue University

17. Poetry: The 1930s to the Present

James E. Breslin

i. General

In the late seventies American poetry continues to draw upon the surge of energy that erupted and transformed our poetry in the late fifties and early sixties. The rising reputations of the present decade —Ammons, Ashbery, Merwin, Merrill, O'Hara—belong not to younger poets but to neglected figures from the generation that began to write in the Age of Eisenhower. No younger poets—either singly or in concerted movement—have offered serious challenge to these now forty-ish writers, so that if we look around for a "revolutionary anthology," we must turn to Donald Allen's *The New American Poetry*, now almost 20 years old.

This attenuation of inventive energy may make us uneasy; but it may also yield the literary critic a certain comforting sense of shape, of definition, to something as inchoate as a "contemporary literary scene." For the critic of contemporary writing is situated—along with the writers themselves—*inside* an *ongoing* process. How, then, to carve a manageable topic and a credible argument out of the surrounding formlessness? As if in nervous reaction to the threat of chaos, three of the book-length general studies of contemporary poetry published in 1977 are strikingly brief; their brevity seems all the more curious given their inability to define and limit the scope of their concerns in any convincing way. Karl Malkoff's *Escape from the Self* (New York: Columbia University Press) is the only one of the three to offer a general thesis about contemporary poetry. The "defining characteristic" of poetry in our time, according to Malkoff, "is its abandonment of the ego—the conscious self—as the inevitable perspective from which reality must be viewed." This contention, however, is at once too broad and too narrow; the transcendence of the ego has been a poetic project at least since Romanticism, yet it is one that hardly characterizes all current poetry. Malkoff's instances are mainly drawn from Projectivist and Confessional verse; but Plath's regressive and self-destructive abandonment of the ego has radically different human and literary consequences from the attempt of an Olson to get rid of "the lyrical interference" of the ego. Moreover, the brevity of Malkoff's discussions of particular poets suggests that he is content to use the poets to "prove" his thesis rather than to use the thesis to open up the works of the poets. One exception to this is the section on *Life Studies.*

In *Modern American Lyric* (New Brunswick: Rutgers Univ. Press), Arthur Oberg studies "the transformation of lyric and love" he finds in the work of Lowell, Berryman, Creeley, and Plath. Yet neither lyric form nor the theme of love is defined with sufficient clarity for us to understand why these four poets have been included, why many others have been excluded. The chapters on specific poets often wander from consideration of the love lyric, and the writing often drifts into impressionistic generalities, though Oberg has some interesting things to say about the way Plath's absolutism generates a distrust of the poetic image—and language generally.

The autobiographical impulse—or "how individuality or temperment emerges as poetic form"—provides the central concern of David Kalstone's *Five Temperaments* (New York: Oxford Univ. Press). But this definition of his scope eliminates almost no poet after Wordsworth and thus makes Kalstone's particular choices—Bishop, Lowell, Merrill, Rich, Ashbery—seem arbitrary. A modest book, *Five Temperaments* attempts no overview of contemporary poetry; but Kalstone does offer exactly what Malkoff and Oberg do not: rich, careful readings of the poems, subtly attentive to the workings of literary language—the readings themselves written in an elegant, evocative prose. Analyses of particular poems become the solid ground upon which acute studies of each poet's growth are built. Kalstone is perhaps strongest in talking about the way Merrill "twins a witty surface with the poet's power to discover the veined patterns of his life" and Rich's search for a language "true to the movement of the feelings."

The problem of shaping an overall argument never arose for Laurence Lieberman in *Unassigned Frequencies* (Urbana: Univ. of Ill. Press); a collection of essays and reviews of American poetry written between 1964 and 1977, the book records the ongoing encounters between an attentive reviewer and 45 contemporary poets. But how can one justify pulling these pieces together into a book? No persistent theme or even set of concerns emerges; Lieberman can only claim that the poets he writes about are "*representative* of the remarkable variety and sweep of poetry in the United States today"—an uplifting statement but one that reveals the book's lack of center. Many of the reviews are all-too-brief encounters; but Lieberman is a strenuous, enthusiastic reader who is at his best in the sections on Dickey, Merwin, Strand, Waggoner, and Ashbery.

Two ambitious essays—the one historical, the other comparative—do make important and provocative general statements about contemporary poetry. In "Symbolism/Anti-Symbolism" (*Centrum* 4:69–103), Marjorie Perloff argues that "modernism" is not a monolithic concept but embodies "two rival strains" which she calls "symbolism" and "anti-symbolism"; the antisymbolic mode predominates in contemporary poetry. In the work of Yeats and Eliot "we find an elaborate network of symbols that point beyond themselves to another reality"—a poetry that "demands" interpretation; but in the "anti-symbolic" mode—illustrated by Ashbery and Rothenberg—we find a poetics of presence that seeks to subvert interpretation. Rimbaud is cited as the origin of the antisymbolic strain, and Perloff's essay closes with a brilliant analysis of "Villes I" from his *Illuminations*. Lawrence Kramer, in "The Wodwo Watches the Water Clock: Language in Postmodern British and American Poetry" (*ConL* 18:319–42), also finds a poetics of presence at the core of recent American poetry. He demonstrates "that postmodern American poets have by and large kept up the passionate belief in language as mediation—in the ability of language to confront, interpret, and even to reenact experience"—whereas recent British poets "seem deeply distrustful of the intersection between language and reality, and appear to see the process of using language as a hard struggle against what seems its futility or vulnerability." Kramer defends this thesis by detailed, densely argued analyses of poems by Larkin, Hill, Hughes, Ammons, Lowell, and Ashbery.

Many critics have found a distinctive feature of recent poetry in its adoption of a "personal voice"—a problematic term. In "Modern American Literature: The Poetics of the Individual Voice" (*CentR* 21:333–54), Linda Wagner argues that the personal voice in contemporary poetry continues a strain in both 19th-century (Whitman,

Dickinson) and early modern (Williams, Hemingway, Stein) writing. She argues that what distinguishes contemporary work is its "move away from the literary personal to the personal as myth" and the desire to "focus on the process of actualization, of becoming."

ii. W. C. Williams, Marianne Moore, H. D., Louise Bogan

For readers of contemporary poetry William Carlos Williams clearly remains a dominant figure, as the length of Linda Wagner's *William Carlos Williams: A Reference Guide* (Boston: G. K. Hall) attests. Building on the work of Emily Wallace, Jack Hardie, and Paul Mariani, Wagner provides a chronological, annotated list of critical works about Williams from 1909 to 1975. No book-length critical study of Williams appeared in 1977, but the number and energy of the essays affirm the continuing vitality of Williams scholarship.

Two excellent essays on *Kora in Hell*—Ron Loewinsohn's "'Fools Have Big Wombs': William Carlos Williams' *Kora in Hell*" (*ELWIU* 4:221–38) and Thomas P. Joswick's "Beginning with Loss: The Poetics of William Carlos Williams's *Kora in Hell: Improvisations*" (*TSLL* 19:98–118)—demonstrate that energy and, in their subtle but basic differences, they define key issues in current critical debate about Williams. The "underlying" structure of *Kora* is, according to Loewinsohn, "a cycle, made up of cycles, that destroys historical, linear time while simultaneously affirming the value and immediacy of each moment," and Loewinsohn goes on to show how this principle informs *Kora* from the level of the sentence on up to the work as a whole. Joswick, on the other hand, concludes that in *Kora* "writing subverts itself and its 'meaning' as it goes along, and the poet will already know 'the fleeting nature of his triumphs before they come,' because he cannot rest in any closing of the circle." Joswick's essay offers a carefully argued theoretical analysis of the idea of form in *Kora*. Loewinsohn assumes that *Kora in Hell* does embody *immediate* experience and that it does so in an *achieved form*—both of which propositions Joswick questions, though he seems to assume that form is always a matter of *arrest*.

Two 1977 essays deal with the relations between Williams's poetry and painting, James E. Breslin's "William Carlos Williams and Charles Demuth: Cross-Fertilization in the Arts" (*JML* 6:248–63) reads a Williams poem ("The Pot of Flowers") based on a Demuth watercolor ("Tuberoses") and a Demuth painting ("I Saw the Figure 5 in Gold") based on a Williams poem ("The Great Figure") and identifies "cubist realism" as the core of the many affinities between poet and painter. Juxtaposing Williams's "The Hunters in the Snow" with John Berryman's "Winter Landscape"—both poems based on Brueghel's "The Hunters in the Snow"—David M. Wyatt measures "the willingness of each poet, working in a temporal medium, to see its limits transgressed or affirmed" (*CLQ* 13:246–62). Wyatt's powerful readings of the two poems allow him to show how Williams offers the reader an experience of ongoing yet endless process ("the activity of reading such a poem, of looking at such a painting, is never complete"), while Berryman creates "a structure of static harmony," of "ultimate arrest."

Early influences on Williams are debated in two short essays appearing in the *William Carlos Williams Newsletter*. In "Whitman's Voice in 'The Wanderer'" (3,ii:17–22), Jessie D. Green argues for specific thematic and verbal echoes of Whitman in Williams's early poem, while Stuart Peterfreund's "Keats's Influence on William Carlos Williams" (3,i:8–13) questions the conventional notion that Williams early on freed himself from the influence of Keats: Peterfreund contends that *Paterson* revises *Endymion*, moving the epic from "hellenized gorgeousness to 20th-century workaday reality."

The general neglect of Williams's plays may be justified, but Kurt Heinzelman, in "Staging the Poem: William Carlos Williams' *A Dream of Love*" (*ConL* 18:491–508), makes a persuasive case for the literary, if not the theatrical, values of the play. Heinzelman formulates Williams's dramatic theory and acutely applies it to a reading of *A Dream of Love* that argues that the play dramatizes the creative process: "the play is the dream of the dramatist achieving living form."

Reviewing some of the established general resemblances between Joyce and Williams—"the mythic patternings of the male hero and of his female counterpart" in *Paterson* and *Finnegans Wake*—Stephen Tapscott argues in "Paterson A'Bloom: Williams, Joyce, and The Virtue of 'ABCEDMINDEDNESS'" (*ArQ* 33:348–66) that a deeper connection between the two writers can be found in their reliance on "the objective power of the word" as the means of marrying inner and outer experience; this notion of language, however—one held by many modern artists—is hardly specific enough to link Joyce and Williams convincingly. The new configuration of attitude and style in Williams's poetry of the fifties is the subject of Marc Hofstadter's "A Different Speech: William Carlos Williams' Later Poetry" (*TCL* 23: 451–66): "Its edges softened, his poetry takes on a gentle, meditative, embracing quality that allows him to increase his range and to sum up his lifelong efforts at expression."

Two books—a bibliography and a critical study—and half of an article constitute the chief contributions to the study of Marianne Moore in 1977. With its thorough, chronological listing of all the poet's writings, Craig S. Abbott's *Marianne Moore: A Descriptive Bibliography* (Pittsburgh: Univ. of Pittsburgh Press) documents the extensiveness of Moore's literary activities and provides a way of studying her frequently substantial revisions of her published work. Pamela White Hadas's *Marianne Moore, Poet of Affection* (Syracuse: Syracuse Univ. Press) is disappointing in major ways. Hadas does not place her own work in relation to previous criticism, chiefly because she has no thesis that would allow her to align her work with what has already been said. "I have tried," Hadas writes, "to characterize the style of Marianne Moore's literary productions as motivated by a number of intents, primarily survival, conversation, discovery, and selfhood." But how can "conversation" or "selfhood" be an intent? And for style? Moreover, these terms do not generate any unifying argument, only some rather disparate subjects for discussion. A long section called "Styling a Style" is followed by chapters on "Taming Animals," "Fighting Affections," and "Apprehending Heroes," but the rationale for selecting these topics and a sense of how they work together into an organized whole are never clarified. The writing, moreover, is often prolix, depending on enthusiastic generalities and quite spare with particulars. But when she does descend to specific texts—when she analyzes Moore's diction, syntax, her use of proverb, quotation, riddle, her syllabics, and her rhythms—Hadas is consistently fresh, penetrating, and precise; her readings of particular poems in the later chapters—especially of "Marriage"—are careful and acute.

Interest in Moore continues to be reflected in the *Marianne Moore Newsletter*, which is now a semiannual publication of the Rosenbach Foundation in Philadelphia. Each issue contains a dozen or so fairly short items, and the journal thus serves as a place for scholars to publish their briefer insights. A longer article that deals with both Moore and H. D. is Margaret Newlin's "'Unhelpful Hymen': Marianne Moore and Hilda Doolittle" (*EIC* 27:216–30), which begins by quoting Robert Graves and others as saying that women cannot really be poets. In the face of such chauvinism, Newlin maintains that H. D. ("a swaying sapling") and her friend Marianne Moore ("slim, tall, graceful") were splendid poets. Whereas H. D. was rapturous and vacillating—in constant emotional conflict, Moore declined marriage offers and remained reticent and guarded.

For the past several years a reconsideration of the work of H. D. has slowly been under way—one emphasizing her later rather than her Imagist work. No major contribution to this reassessment was made in 1977. But by a reading of autobiographical and mythical levels, Vincent Quinn, in "H. D.'s 'Hermetic Definition': The Poet as Archetypal Mother" (*ConL* 18:51–61), persuasively argues this late poem to be a self-conscious meditation on its own composition, the poet's transformation of an actual and temporal love experience into the timeless realm of art. Metamorphosis provides the starting point as well for Susan Friedman's "Creating a Women's Mythology: H. D.'s *Helen in Egypt*" (*WS* 5:163–97); H. D.'s epic, according to Friedman, attempts a "reexamination of existing cultural traditions and the rediscovery and creation of a women's mythology." Via Helen, H. D. transforms the woman from dangerous other into "authentic selfhood."

The poetry of Louise Bogan was studied in two essays in a special issue of *Women's Studies* devoted to women's poetry. In a short and rather generalized essay—"Louise Bogan: To Be (Or Not To Be?) Woman Poet" (5:131–35)—Gloria Bowles examines the way Bogan's ambivalent feelings about her femininity affect her poetics and her development as a writer, while Jaqueline Ridgeway, concerned with the "constant conflict between will and authority" ("The Necessity of Form to the Poetry of Louise Bogan," 5:137–49), studies the literary expression of that psychic conflict in Bogan's tension between a formal severity and the powerful emotions that are revealed in her symbolic language. Both Bowles and Ridgeway view Bogan as victim of the social and literary constraints of her era, but a much more complex and stronger image of Bogan emerges from Elizabeth Perlmutter's "A Doll's Heart: The Girl in the Poetry of Edna St. Vincent Millay and Louise Bogan" (*TCL* 23:157–79). In this carefully researched and closely reasoned essay, Ms. Perlmutter contends that both Millay and Bogan began with the lyric persona of The Girl, "a figure of enchantment, poised briefly by the course of nature between maidenly hope and womanly disillusionment." But "whereas Millay's lyric language continued to conjure as make-believe, theatrical world, with the poet spotlighted as mere-slip-of-a-Girl, Bogan's language was uttered by a Girl increasingly intent upon subordinating her personality and experience to the discipline of language itself." See also Jane Couchman, "Louise Bogan: A Bibliography of Primary and Secondary Materials, 1915–1975" (*BB* 33:73–77, 104; 33:111–26, 147; 33:178–81).

iii. Delmore Schwartz, John Berryman, Theodore Roethke, Robert Lowell, Elizabeth Bishop

Many of the poets of this "middle generation" have long been regarded as failures whose intense rivalry with their immediate predecessors led variously to overweening ambition, bitter frustration, drinking problems, mental breakdown, and suicide. Delmore Schwartz provides the prototypical case, and it is fitting that the best book in 1977 dealing with one of these poets is not a critical study but a biography of Schwartz: *Delmore Schwartz: The Life of an American Poet*, by James Atlas (New York: Farrar, Straus, Giroux). In fact the only weakness of Atlas's superb book lies in its too-impressionistic attempts to make some case for Schwartz as a poet. The characterization of Schwartz—emphasizing his drive for fame, his wild oscillations between self-love and self-hatred, the paranoid delusions of his later years—is a familiar one. But what makes Atlas's biography so compelling is the rich and vivid detail of his narrative, which gives the often-mythologized figure of Schwartz a moving, concrete reality. The effect on the poet of his parents' disastrous marriage, of his Jewishness, of his astonishing early success, of the New York literary scene of the forties is fully documented and shrewdly assessed. Given the abundance of unpublished material made available to him, Atlas could easily have written a biography that got bogged down in insignificant detail; given Schwartz's life, Atlas could have aimed at sensational effect or sentimentality. Instead, his sympathetic understanding of Schwartz's life is conveyed with a firm and intelligent control. In "Self and History in Delmore Schwartz's Poetry and Criticism" (*IowaR* 8,iv:95–103) David Zucker finds a tension between the poet's melancholy "determinism" and his "romantic lyricism," but this brief essay really only formulates this notion rather than applies it to a rigorous reading of Schwartz's work.

As with Schwartz, Berryman's harrowing life has preoccupied his critics as much as his work. Steven Barza, in "About John Berryman" (*ColQ* 26,iii:51–72), raises general questions about art and suicide and particular questions about Berryman's suicide, makes speculative gestures in the direction of answering both, but finally leaves this reader dangling uncertainly. But in what appears to be a section of a full-length biography—"Drink As Disease: John Berryman" (*PR* 44:565–83)—John Haffenden moves away from simple mythologizing of the life in a carefully researched and perceptive account of Berryman from late 1969, when he briefly thought he had conquered alcoholism, through his return to drinking and subsequent treatment (described in his *Recovery* [1973]), in an AA program in the spring of 1970.

With his *John Berryman: An Introduction to the Poetry* (New York: Columbia Univ. Press)—a book in a series that includes studies of Pound, Stevens, and Moore—Joel Conarroe makes an important contribution to the "canonization" of one middle-generation poet. Conarroe's admiration for Berryman is all the more convincing because, unlike most Berryman critics, Conarroe maintains a critical distance from his subject. Berryman, in Conarroe's estimate, is a master of the personal lyric of separation or loss. In this developmental study, then, Berryman's career, like that of so many of his contemporaries, becomes a "process of liberating his voice." This voice is lost in the stiff rhythms, inflated diction, and general derivativeness of the early work—especially the political poems; but it becomes the energizing source of Berryman's art in his major achievements, the *Homage to Mistress Ann Bradstreet* and the *Dream Songs*. Conarroe deals with these long, complex poems by raising the critical questions an initial reader might entertain, then answering them in concise discussions of theme, language, and form that are focused upon representative passages. There is also a strong section on Berryman's *Sonnets* and a provocative case made for the evolving unity of *Love and Fame*. Sometimes the series' limits of space make Conarroe move too fast, especially in the last chapter; but the book does provide a substantial and judicious way of entry into Berryman's poetry.

A double issue of *John Berryman Studies* (3,i–ii) prints a symposium on the last *Dream Song*. None of the contributions uses the occasion to address the question of the *theory* of the poem's form, but the issue does contain much vigorous analysis of its set text and the way it echoes earlier sections of the poem. Gary Q. Arpin examines Berryman's earliest poetry in "Establishing a Tradition: John Berryman's Student Verse" (*JBS* 3,iv:11–16) and a supplement to Richard Kelley's checklist of critical writings about Berryman appears in *JBS* 3,iii:36–48.

Little work was done on Theodore Roethke in 1977, the main contribution being a marking of what already has been written: Keith Moul's *Theodore Roethke's Career: An Annotated Bibliography* (Boston: G. K. Hall). The book lists chronologically all works by and about Roethke, with concise annotations of the secondary material. William Heyen's "The Yeats Influence: Roethke's Formal Lyrics of the Fifties (*JBS* 3,iv:17–64) precisely defines the Yeatsian impact (in rhythm, image, form) on the poems in *The Waking* and *Words for the Wind*; Heyen also makes convincing judgments about when the influence of Yeats is working creatively, and when it is not.

Once considered the preeminent poet among his contemporaries, Robert Lowell's position is now less certain; his death in 1977 is likely to provoke further debate about his achievement, but no major statement emerges from last year's criticism. J. D. McClatchy, in "Robert Lowell: Learning How To Live in History" (*APR* 6,i:34–38), shows how the *Selected Poems*, its inclusions, omissions, rewritings, "provides Lowell's own sense of his career"; this incisive and vigorously written essay is rich both with specific insights into the poems and general notions about Lowell's development. Lowell's own review of Philip Larkin's *Oxford Book of Twentieth-Century English Verse* is also reprinted in this issue of *APR*.

Lowell's career is provocatively juxtaposed with that of Ginsberg by Charles Molesworth in "Republican Objects and Utopian Moments: The Poetries of Robert Lowell and Allen Ginsberg" (*APR* 6,v:35–39). The "fullest voices" of both poets, says Molesworth, "were achieved by their ability to make the public events they often deplored into something like private musings." In characterizing their modes of speech, their development, Molesworth remains aware of basic differences: "Lowell is a poet haunted, and Ginsberg is a poet wishing"; yet both, in their recent work, have arrived at a bleak despair about our historical moment.

In honor of his sixtieth birthday, a special issue of *Salmagundi* (no. 37) is devoted to the work of Lowell. Included are a memoir by Philip Booth and essays, many of them by young poets, on single poems by Lowell. The best of these are the contributions by Helen Vendler and Robert Haas. Postulating that "lyrics are mostly meditative poems," Vendler powerfully argues that Lowell gives life to the clichéd triangular situation in "Ulysses, Circe, Penelope" by moving the lyric from reflection to action. The action, the killing of the suitors, is viewed as fated, yet Lowell makes "moral judgment" coexist with the "certainty that things could not have been otherwise." The Haas essay brilliantly combines autobiography and subtle literary analysis to convey his sense of the "formal risks" and expressive power of "The Quaker Graveyard in Nantucket." Other essays in this *Salmagundi* deal with "Domesday Book," "Near the Ocean," "Waking Early Sunday Morning," "End of the Year," and "Fall Weekend at Milgate," with Lowell's own "After Enjoying Six or Seven Essays on Me" closing the discussion. Steven G. Axelrod's "Lowell's *The Dolphin* as a 'Book of Life'" (*ConL* 18:458–74) defends Lowell's late poem by arguing that it is not a confessional account of "changing marriages" but about the mind itself: "the real text is [Lowell's] mind in the act of grasping at the bare events and turning back upon itself, converting them and itself to fiction—the necessary fiction of consciousness and the closely related fiction of poetry."

A "Homage to Elizabeth Bishop" in *World Literature Today* (51,i) contains nine essays, plus several brief statements by writers ranging from Octavio Paz to Frank Bidart. These, along with five additional essays and Kalstone's excellent chapter in *Five Temperaments*, establish that a major revision of Elizabeth Bishop's work is in progress. Not all of this work, however, is substantive. Ashley Brown's "Elizabeth Bishop in Brazil" (*SoR* 13:688–704) combines memoir and impressionistic criticism in a gracefully trivial essay, while Candace Slater examines "Brazil in the Poetry of Elizabeth Bishop" (*WLT* 51:33–36) to find Brazil represented—not too surprisingly—in the landscapes and characters of many poems; and Eleanor Ross Taylor, in "Driving to the Interior: A Note on Elizabeth Bishop" (*WLT* 51:44–46), briefly examines some of the implications of Bishop's idea of the poet as explorer. The focus of "Elizabeth Bishop's 'Songs for a Colored Singer'" (*WLT* 51:37–40) is limited, but Anne R. Newman studies these poems to show Bishop's "sensitivity to particular intonations, forms and themes of black music."

More valuable are those essays which question the conventional designation of Bishop as a "descriptive" poet and attempt to define her imaginative vision. "Elizabeth Bishop: The Delicate Art of Map Making" by Sybil Estess (*SoR* 13:705–27) argues that Bishop's "empiricism" is "tempered by a highly individualized perception," but this unique view of Bishop's is never fully specified. Two further essays by Estess focus on particular poems: "Cape Breton" in "Toward the Interior: Epiphany in 'Cape Breton' as Representative Poem" (*WLT* 51:49–52) and "At the Fishhouses" in "Shelters for 'What Is Within': Meditation in Elizabeth Bishop" (*MPS* 8,i:50–60); both essays—with a fair amount of repetition between them—find a movement toward epiphany and a vision of life emerging from decay and death in the poems they concentrate upon. Two essays by Lloyd Schwartz locate Bishop's vision in "differences, contrasts, and contradictions." In "The Mechanical Horse and the Indian Princess: Two Poems from *North & South*" (*WLT* 51:41–44), Schwartz explores "contrasting attitudes" to be found both within and between "Cirque d'Hiver" and "Florida," while in "One Art: The Poetry of Elizabeth Bishop, 1971–1976" (*Ploughshares* 3,iii–iv:30–52), he argues a self-conscious continuity between *North & South* and *Geography III*: "as they insist on their *similarity* to the earlier works," the later poems "reveal" the earlier "to be 'felt,' less 'objective,' more 'serious' than we may have assumed."

Another account of Bishop's development—Jerome Mazzaro's "Elizabeth Bishop's Particulars" (*WLT* 51:46–49)—shows how her changing use of detail marks a changing vision: from "direct apprehension to relational awareness." Beginning with an analysis of Bishop's story "In the Village," Marjorie Perloff, in "Elizabeth Bishop: The Course of a Particular" (*MPS* 8,i:177–192), views the poet's concentration upon physical detail as a psychological as well as a literary strategy: "discrimination, careful discernment of sameness and difference—these become quasi-religious rituals that distance despair"—just as Kalstone in *Five Temperaments* contends that "Bishop's precise explorations become a way of countering and encountering a lost world." The contradictions of Bishop's vision are stressed in general appreciations written by two poets. "It is this continually renewed sense of discovering the strangeness, the unreality of our reality at the very moment of becoming conscious of it *as* reality, that is the great subject for Elizabeth Bishop," according to John Ashbery (*WLT* 51:9–11), while Howard Moss similarly observes the "sense of normalcy and oddness in tandem," the intermingling of the homely and the fantastic in Bishop's verse (*WLT* 51:29–33). An observation very like this—of "the interpenetration of the domestic and the strange"—provides the starting point for Helen Vendler's "Domestication, Domesticity and the Otherworldly" (*WLT* 51:23–28), but Vendler pushes this insight toward a powerful and intricate reading of the poems which emphasizes "the reserves of mystery which give, in their own way, a joy more strange than the familiar blessings of the world made human."

iv. Charles Olson, Robert Creeley

In 1977 surprisingly little work was done on these "Projectivist" poets. Olson, the elder of the group, was the subject of four essays, all of them thematic studies of the *Maximus* poems, and only one of these—by Sherman Paul—of real consequence. Rosmarie Waldrop, in "Charles Olson: Process and Relationship" (*TCL* 23:467–86), argues that Olson, opposed to the separation of reality into discrete objects, proposes a vision of process and interconnection. Olson's poetry, therefore, moves toward relations of contiguity, metonymy. None of this will astonish readers of Olson, though there are some good illustrations from *Maximus*. In "Charles Olson's *Maximus*: Glouster as Dream and Reality" (*TQ* 20,iii:20–29), Paul Christensen identifies the ideal of "human community," based on a "restoration of individual consciousness," as the core of Olson's epic, but the brief discussions of each of the three volumes of *Maximus* seldom push beneath the surface. "Descent into Polis: Charles Olson's Search for Community" (*MPS* 8,i:13–22) by Philip E. Smith II examines Olson's notion of the polis in a more delimited and detailed way—mainly by studying Olson's essay on Ernst Robert Curtius and Olson's poems to and about Ranier Maria Gerhardt. In his "*Maximus*: Volume 3 or Books VII and After" (*Boundary 2* 5,ii:557–71) Sherman Paul, drawing on his wide reading in American poetry, carefully places the third volume of *Maximus* both in relation to the first two and to Olson's "life-long project"; this essay contains a power and precision of insight and a range of reference that is lacking in the other three studies of Olson's major work.

Olson, The Journal of the Charles Olson Archives (no. 7) prints the poet's "Journal of a Swordfishing Cruise, July 1936," a bibliography of Olson's writings published posthumously, and a supplement to an earlier checklist of Olson's reading, while no. 8 contains unpublished writings from and an interview with Olson about the Black Mountain period.

Arthur Oberg, in "Robert Creeley: And the Power to Tell Is Glory" (*OhR* 18,ii:79–97)—an essay quite different from the Creeley chapter in Oberg's *Modern American Lyric*—emphasizes the "geography of pain and loss" in Creeley's writing and uses Creeley's doubts "whether distances can ever be bridged, whether words can ever be more than holes aching to be filled" to distinguish him from Williams. More problematic than the thematic issues raised by Oberg are the formal questions raised by a poetry, like Creeley's, that claims to be "open." Aptly focusing on endings, Terry R. Bacon's "Closure in Robert Creeley's Poetry" (*MPS* 8,iii:227–47) pursues this difficult structural question on both theoretical and practical levels; through its precise distinctions, this essay defines a variety of ways Creeley has evolved for making his poems integral, open, yet complete.

v. Allen Ginsberg, Gary Snyder, Jack Spicer, William Everson

Is Ginsberg primarily a public figure or a literary artist? Our uncertainties on this issue are reflected in the differing approaches of the two essays—one biographical and psychoanalytic, the other mildly formalistic—published about Ginsberg in 1977. Drawing upon unpublished materials in the Ginsberg papers at Columbia, James E. Breslin's "Allen Ginsberg: The Origins of 'Howl' and 'Kaddish'" (*IowaR* 8,ii:82–108) unfolds the dynamics of Ginsberg's relations with his poet-father and his mother, who spent much of her life in mental institutions. "Howl" and "Kaddish" are then viewed as attempts to assert a separate, autonomous personality, but both poems, for all their rebellious energy, end by submitting to parental influence, notably in the poet's wish (in "Kaddish") to fuse with the lost figure of the mother. In "Remembering and Rereading 'Howl'" (*Ploughshares* 2,iv:151–63), Donald Gertmenian names changes in the poet's voice as the best way to understand the structural relations among the three main parts of "Howl," although this provocative suggestion is not applied in great detail.

Gary Snyder is another poet who is also a public figure but one whose work continues to receive considerable critical attention, some of it—as in the two essays done in 1977 by Robert Kern—of a high level. Kern's "Clearing the Ground: Gary Snyder and the Modernist Imperative" (*Criticism* 19:158–77) ostensibly adopts a narrow focus: *Riprap*. But Kern views Snyder's first book in its historical context—as a work "necessarily concerned with initiating a career and establishing a poetic identity at a time (the middle and late 1950s) when the literary environment is still dominated by a modernism that is nevertheless in the process" of breaking up. Paradoxically, *Riprap*, in repudiating tradition, is repeating the basic gesture of modernism, but Snyder's style, with its "literalism, referentiality and metonymic tendencies," breaks with the modernist notion of the autotelic poem. "Recipes, Catalogues, Open Form Poetics: Gary Snyder's Archetypal Voice" (*ConL* 18:173–97), also by Kern, similarly focuses upon a paradox: that Snyder's attempts to open his poetry to immediate experience lead to the creation of a poetic voice that is anonymous—as if a place were speaking, through the poet/medium—yet is simultaneously the personal voice of the poet. Kern does not show how poems in open forms avoid formlessness, but his essay does provide a valuable meditation on the presuppositions behind and problems raised by such forms for both poets and critics.

In "Wordsworth and Snyder: The Primitivist and His Problem of Self-Definition" (*CentR* 21:75–86), Laurence Goldstein places Snyder in the context not of modernist or contemporary poetics but of romanticism. The romantic poet claims that his "Word comes to us as the essential expression of his being" yet also recognizes "that language betrays its originating spirit." Snyder pushes toward a state of pure being, yet the very representation of this condition in language pulls him back toward the alien modes of history, culture, literature. This notion is impeccable, but rather than being the conclusion it ought to have been the starting point for a reading of Snyder's poetry; in fact, Kern's notion of "archetypal voice" proposes one solution to the dilemma Goldstein identifies. Most critics approach Snyder as a poet of immediate experience; but Bert Almon, in "Buddhism and Energy in the Recent Poetry of Gary Snyder" (*Mosaic*

11,i:117–25), argues "a metaphysical dimension" to the poetry, but the author goes on not to examine Snyder's ontology but his shifting allegiances—from Zen to the Vajrayana sect—within Buddhism.

In "Whose Mountain Is This?—Gary Snyder's Translation of Han Shan" (*Renditions*, 7:93–102) Ling Chung studies Snyder's *Cold Mountain Poems* as translations and shows how Snyder "experimented with the English language by deliberately adopting Chinese grammatical and metrical patterns." At the same time, many of Snyder's changes of physical detail insert a tension between man and nature that is basically different from the sense of harmony to be found in the Chinese original.

Jack Spicer, the little-known west coast poet whose *Collected Books* appeared in 1975 (ten years after his death), is the subject of an entire issue of *Boundary 2* (6,i). Philosophical in manner and post-Structuralist in approach, these ambitious essays are sometimes dizzyingly abstract, seldom willing to make concessions to the uninitiated reader; they veer from the merely pretentious to the truly profound. The general—but by no means unanimous—view is that Spicer's work, based on the elimination of the subject (the "I") and a theory of composition as dictation, is a "poetry of absence," grandly identified as calling into "question the metaphysical or logocentric forms that have dominated" the Western literary tradition from the time of the Greeks. Clayton Eshleman discusses the translations in *After Lorca*; Peter Riley the narratives of *The Holy Grail*; James Liddy the *Books of Magazine Verse*. Stephanie A. Judy employs Victor Zuckerkandl's theory of music as an approach to Spicer's subversions of meaning, and in the longest and most opaque of the contributions, Colin Christopher Stuart and John Scoggan take up Saussure and Derrida to unfold Spicer's theory of language. Most valuable, perhaps, are the essays by Michael Davidson on *The Heads of the Town up to the Aether* and by Jed Rasula on "Spicer's Orpheus and the Emancipation of Pronouns." Davidson does find a strange kind of incarnation in Spicer's work. *Heads of the Town*, "presenting random voices without a narrative frame or objective correlative," "records its own process of trying to speak"; the book thus incarnates "a trying-to-speak by a voice that has been separated from a body." Focusing on the evolution of Spicer's esthetic down to *Heads of the Town*, Rasula shows the shift from a "simplistic" theory of language as reference to a theory of language as "a play of substitutions"—a development that effects "a reversal of the roles of writing and reading."

Lee Bartlett and Allan Campo's *William Everson: A Descriptive Bibliography, 1934–1976* (Metuchen, N.J.: Scarecrow Press) presents a complete chronological listing of all publications by Brother Antoninus/William Everson, plus a selected checklist of secondary criticism.

vi. Sylvia Plath, Anne Sexton, Adrienne Rich, Denise Levertov, Muriel Rukeyser

Is confessional poetry an identifiable genre? What happens when an autobiographical writer also seeks *literary* effect? What is the relation between speaker and author in confessional verse? Such questions continue to engage critics of recent poetry, though their pursuit of them has not, unfortunately, been affected by current theoretical writings about autobiography, to be found in such journals as *New Literary History*. The simplest conception of confessionalism is that stated in "Anne Sexton: Poetry as a Form of Exorcism" (*ABR* 28: 102–11) by Lawrence S. Cunningham, who calls such writing "logotherapy," though he has no illusions about its effectiveness. Critically examining M. L. Rosenthal's criteria for confessional poetry, Jon Rosenblatt, in "The Limits of the 'Confessional Mode' in Recent American Poetry" (*Genre* 9:153–59) persuasively argues that these criteria are inadequate to distinguish contemporary from "previous lyric practice"; in fact, Lowell, Plath, and Berryman "use lyric forms that can best be understood in the context of Romantic and modern attitudes toward the self rather than in relation to special kinds of autobiographical revelations."

Sandra Gilbert stipulates the confessional as a mode of self-definition in " 'My Name Is Darkness': The Poetry of Self-Definition" (*ConL* 18:443–57); she goes on to argue that, as such, the confessional "may be (at least for our own time) a distinctively female poetic mode." The male writer, "even while romantically exploring his own psyche," can objectify himself as a "representative specimen" and ironically assess his sufferings "because he considers his analytic perspective on himself a civilized, normative point of view." But such ironic self-scrutiny is "totally unavailable" to the woman poet, who "feels eccentric, not representative; peripheral, not central." "To define her suffering," Gilbert provocatively asserts, "would be to define her identity, and such self-definition" is the "goal," not the "starting point" for writers such as Plath, Sexton, Rich, Levertov, and Wakoski.

Radically different from each other—and from Gilbert—are Carol H. Cantrell's "Self and Tradition in Recent Poetry" (*MQ* 18:343–60) and Joan Bobbitt's "Lowell and Plath; Objectivity and the Confessional Mode" (*ArQ* 33:311–18). Cantrell finds not an active search for self-definition but a "passivity" at the core of both *Life Studies* and *Ariel*, while Bobbitt contends that Lowell and Plath objectively distance themselves from their subject matters. Neither of these short essays, however, is equal to the scope and depth of the complex issues they raise.

In "Sylvia Plath and Confessional Poetry: A Reconsideration" (*IowaR* 8,i:104–15), however, M. D. Uroff contrasts Plath with Lowell by characterizing the different relations between speaker and author in their work. In *Life Studies* the speaker examines painful experiences in order to arrive at self-knowledge, but the personae of Plath's poems, "far from speaking for the poet," "stage crazy performances which are parodic versions of the imaginative act." Because they resist self-understanding, Plath's "superbly controlled" poems "reveal truths about the speakers that their obsessive assertions deny."

Concentrating on Plath's "Daddy" and Levertov's "During the Eichmann Trial," Sophie B. Blaydes, in "Metaphors of Life and Death in the Poetry of Denise Levertov and Sylvia Plath" (*DR* 57: 494–506), discovers—not too surprisingly—that while Plath's work is dominated by metaphors of death, Levertov's offers metaphors of life.

Like Gilbert, Rachel Blau DuPlessis attempts to define a special awareness of women's poetry in "The Critique of Consciousness and Myth in Levertov, Rich, and Rukeyser" (*FemS* 3,i-ii:199–221). All three writers, she states, "enact a personal awakening to political and social life" and seek "the invention of self-exploratory and reevaluative myths." So, of course, do many other women, and even some men; but the essay deals perceptively with these three poets and the argument that "their myths are critical of prior mythic thought; they are historically specific rather than eternal; they replace archetypes by prototypes" is an extremely interesting one.

Most of Rich's critics—like the poet herself—have seen her career as a progressive unfolding, moving gradually toward elimination of the separation between speaker and poet that characterized her early work and toward the vision of androgynous wholeness in her recent writing. Characteristic of this trend is "Adrienne Rich and an Organic Feminist Criticism" (*CE* 39:191–203) by Marilyn Farwell, who uses Rich's criticism to evolve a literary theory based on a "feminist philosophy." The "key" to all of Rich's criticism, according to Farwell, "is a desire for wholeness"—"which attempts to relate ethics and language, text and artist, creation and relation, and ultimately art and life." Basically revising the conventional view, Susan R. Van Dyne, in "The Mirrored Vision of Adrienne Rich" (*MPS* 8,ii:140–73), locates the poet's artistic consciousness not in personal or political unity but in a "blended, double awareness—of identifying and distancing, of being both I and Other," a vision that remains constant beneath all the changes in Rich's poetry.

vii. Frank O'Hara, John Ashbery, W. S. Merwin, A. R. Ammons, James Wright, Galway Kinnell, James Merrill, Richard Howard

Marjorie Perloff's distinguished *Frank O'Hara: Poet Among Painters* (New York: George Braziller) begins defining O'Hara's poetic project by viewing it in historical context. Reacting against the predominant Symbolist poetics, O'Hara developed a poetry of presence, in poetic structures that are "always changing, shifting, becoming." This characterization, supported by Perloff's wide reading in modern poetry, both in English and French, and her careful attention to O'Hara's texts, will make it difficult to sustain the common view that O'Hara's work is charming but trivial. Early in his career, Perloff shows, O'Hara's repudiating of Symbolism pushed him in two opposed directions: toward the "clotted, somewhat mannered Surrealist mode" of *Oranges*, and toward a "natural, colloquial, whimsical, lighthearted mode" derived from Williams. After an excellent chapter dealing with O'Hara's relations with the visual arts, Perloff analyzes the syntax and voice, the transformation of such genres as the autobiographical lyric, occasional poem, ode, and love poem in the work of O'Hara's "great period" (1954–61). In these poems, fantasy and literalism, surrealist image and American idiom fuse in a poetry of process. Her closing chapter treats the diminished achievement of the last five years of O'Hara's life as well as the question of his literary influence.

The astonishing rise of John Ashbery's reputation itself becomes a subject for speculative analysis in Charles Molesworth's " 'This Leaving-Out Business': The Poetry of John Ashbery" (*Salmagundi* 38–39:20–41). In this skeptical review of Ashbery's development, the early poetry is viewed as "a poetry of inconsequence," motivated by a "fear of the banal" and a "craving for the truly fresh" that leads to the mixing of the mundane and the mysterious in surrealism. But Ashbery has slowly moved his work toward "the traditions of prose discourse"—not to offer statement but "a most tenuous, unassertive language."

As with Ashbery, W. S. Merwin and A. R. Ammons were the subject of only one essay each in 1977, but the high quality of these pieces testifies to the ability of these poets to attract critics with real intellectual power. Cary Nelson's "The Resources of Failure: W. S. Merwin's Deconstructive Career" (*Boundary 2* 5,ii:573–98) identifies Merwin's work as "a poetry that inherits the despair of the century but gives it a prophetic new form, a form that ruthlessly deconstructs its own accomplishments." Philosophical in approach, this brilliant essay probes deeply into Merwin's evolving poetic and makes the "rebirth out of willful failure" that begins with *The Moving Target* the crucial turn in Merwin's career.

Similarly developmental, Frederick Buell's " 'To Be Quiet in the Hands of the Marvelous': The Poetry of A. R. Ammons" (*IowaR* 8, iv:67–85) is more concerned with specifically literary issues, such as voice and style, than Nelson is. Buell discusses the stark absolutism of Ammons's first book, then shows how all subsequent work expands in two directions. Ammons brings his work "closer to the American commonplace, and he opens it to a broad eclecticism of knowledge and wisdom." "Corsons Inlet," *Tape for the Turn of the Year*, and "Essay on Poetics" are the representative texts Buell examines to define Ammons's evolving poetic. An excellent analysis of "Corsons Inlet" appears in " 'Ghostlier Demarcations, Keener Sounds': A. R. Ammons' 'Corsons Inlet' " by Guy Rotella (*CP* 10,ii:25–33).

Critical discussions of James Wright's career usually stress his liberating break from "traditional" to "open" forms in *The Branch Will Not Break*. In his terse yet suggestive "The Continuity of James

Wright's Poems" (*OhR* 8,ii:44–57), William Matthews characterizes Wright as "a profoundly traditional poet" who "discovered his personal uses for literary tradition through rhetorical forms, rather than through stanza forms or rhyming patterns." Wright's key models, according to Matthews, are less the surrealists than the King James Bible and the "plain talk" of Robinson and Frost. Thus the main value of this essay derives from its suggestion that as Wright's language became "simpler," his poetry did not become less but "more successfully formal" and traditional. David C. Dogherty's "James Wright: The Murderer's Grave in the New Northwest" (*ON* 2,i:45–54) stresses Wright's vision of his native Midwest, the change from the bitter "love has changed to wrath" of the early poems to the "fuller, more complex and compassionate" view of *Two Citizens.*

A special issue devoted to Wright, *Ironwood* (no. 10), includes essays by Steven Orlen on *The Green Wall*, by Madeline DeFrees on *St. Judas*, by Jane Robinett on two versions of "At the Executed Murderer's Grave," by Shirley C. Scott on Wright's ongoing attempt to neutralize his imagination, by Phillis Hoge Thompson on Wright's "kindness," by Dave Smith on the language of *Two Citizens*, by Leonard Nathan on the traditional "melancholy man" as the speaker of Wright's poetry and by Peter Stitt on the "continual evolution" of Wright's career. There is also a general appreciation of Wright's work by William Heyen; but the most powerfully argued of these essays is Robert Haas's revisionary account of Wright's development. Citing a cult of "the isolated inner world"—of sensitivity separated from intelligence and true imagination—as the special temptation of Wright's writing, Haas finds this form of decadence marring even *The Branch Will Not Break*—whereas the later poems "reflect a determination to face 'the black ditch of the Ohio' and not be killed by it."

In "The Poetry of Galway Kinnell" (*Meanjin* 36:228–239), Andrew Taylor discovers "a transformational process"—moving from "a death of the self" through "a withdrawal to a prehuman or preconscious state" and ending with a "rebirth," a return to life—at the core of all of Kinnell's poetry. Unfortunately, Taylor does not try to see transformational processes at work in Kinnell's language or forms, and he makes no comparisons that would allow us to distinguish Kinnell's version of this process from, say, Wright's.

In "James Merrill's *The Book of Ephraim*" (*Shenandoah* 27,iv:63–

91;28,i:83–110), Henry Sloss provides a detailed reading of Merrill's dazzling poem. Sloss's prose is often overwrought, but he has some interesting things to say about the poem's narrator, who requires from the reader "both submersion in and resistance to the other-worldly revelation in the poem," and about the poem as recording Merrill's "conversion" from nonchalant dismissal to courageous determination "to take on the other world."

Sloss's "*Cleaving and Burning*: An Essay on Richard Howard's Poetry" (*Shenandoah* 29,i:85–103) sets forth a theory about the differences between Howard's third and fifth books (*Untitled Subjects* and *Two-Part Inventions*) on the one hand, and his fourth and sixth collections (*Findings* and *Fellow Feelings*) on the other. In the latter two, "where the world is closed to the poet, language is open to him; lexicography and linguistics take up when afflatus leaves off"; but Sloss moves too quickly through all six of Howard's volumes to make his argument convincing.

viii. Younger Poets

Writing about unrecognized poets challenges us to convert our excited impressions into substantive arguments—that must be made to an audience that is likely to be indifferent to, may even be vaguely hostile toward, and will certainly be ignorant of the work of our "discoveries." The year 1977 did not, unfortunately, produce any essays that succeed in establishing young poets as figures who *compel* our attention. "For Bill Knott: In Celebration and Anticipation of His *Selected/Collected Poems*" (*Ploughshares* 4,i:25–37) conveys Thomas Lux's enthusiasm for Knott but not much else. Sentences such as "his best work re-affirms that poetry can be something that does more than lie on a page. The poems come alive with an energy and a clarity made possible by the substance of his risks" illustrate the occupational disease of such writing: they are vague enough to be inserted into an essay about any poet we might happen to admire.

Victor Contoski's "Charles Simic: Language at the Stone's Heart" (*ChiR* 28,iv:145–57) may not convince us that Simic offers "some of the most strikingly original poetry of our time," yet it does evocatively pursue the "relationship between the animate and inanimate" in Simic's five books to date. Jean Rosenbaum's "You Are Your Own Magician: A Vision of Integrity in the Poetry of Marge Piercy" (*MPS*

8:193–205) makes no great claims for the importance of Piercy's work, but the essay amply documents the desire "for a world of wholeness and completeness" as the poetry's basic motive, while Victor Contoski's "Marge Piercy: A Vision of the Peaceable Kingdom" (*MPS* 8:205–16) shrewdly analyzes the dangers of Piercy's commitment to social reform and argues that her best work breaks down the simple "them" versus "us" dichotomy of her political writing and explores the way social injustices have been internalized by the poet herself.

University of California, Berkeley

18. Drama

Winifred Frazer

i. From the Beginning

Leading off the year's work on the history of American drama is Walter J. Meserve's first volume of a proposed long study—*An Emerging Entertainment: The Drama of the American People to 1828* (Bloomington: Ind. Univ. Press). A carefully researched description of the written drama (not the theatrical history), Meserve's book begins with the earliest native colonial drama and concludes with the year 1828, when Edwin Forrest's Prize Play Contests began to encourage native American playwrights. His point of view, that American drama did not emerge full blown in 1920, but was preceded by a long period of slow growth, is seconded by Laurence G. Avery in "A Proposal Concerning the Study of Early American Drama" (*ETJ* 29:243–50). Avery claims that the religious and sentimental drama of the 17th and 18th centuries, continuing into the 19th under the influence of neoclassicism and German idealism, must be restudied in the light of its pragmatic purpose rather than, as Krutch and other modern critics have, for its mimetic skill.

An annotated edition of *The Disappointment* or *The Force of Credulity* by Andrew Barton (pseudonym of Thomas Forrest), edited by David Mays (Gainesville: The Univ. Presses of Fla., 1976), supplies the kind of data which abets Meserve's study. Although it was withdrawn two days before its opening at the Southwark Theatre near Philadelphia in 1767, Mays claims that *The Disappointment* should supplant *The Prince of Parthia*, which replaced it at the Southwark, as the first original drama by a native American. Influenced by *The Beggar's Opera*, it may have satirized local dignitaries and contained too many ribald ballads for the puritanical public of the time. Mays, in "Theatre Can't Get Here from There: A Brief Production History of Florida's First Play," in *Eighteenth-Century Florida: Life on the Frontier*, edited by Samuel Proctor (Gainesville: Univ. Presses of Fla., 1976), also speculates on why theatre was so late in coming to St. Augustine. In 300 years of Spanish rule and two decades of British no play was performed, until in 1783, for the benefit of Royalist refugees from the Revolution, Farquhar's *The Beaux' Stratagem* was produced in Government House by a group of amateurs. Martin Staples Shockley in a well-illustrated volume, *The Richmond Stage 1784–1812* (Charlottesville: Univ. Press of Va.), gives a thoroughly researched season-by-season documentation on the plays, the companies, the physical theatres, and the critical reactions to performances during nearly three decades in Richmond. Well-indexed and inclusive, the work is also of value to students of other early American theatres. In *Monarchs of the Mimic World* or *The American Theatre of the Eighteenth Century through the Managers—The Men Who Made It* (Orono: Univ. of Maine Press), James S. Bost provides much documentation concerning actors, actresses, and theatre entrepreneurs, as well as managers and the tastes of the audiences of the time. The volume adds lively detail to the history of the American theatre and is of supplementary aid even to those with a bent for the history of playwriting.

The towering 19th-century figure of Dion Boucicault frequently figures in essays on American theatre history. In "Slavery and Melodrama: Boucicault's *The Octoroon*" (*MarkhamR* 6:77–80), Frank S. Galassi explains how this master of the stage could, on the eve of civil war in 1859, portray the love of partly black Zoe and the heir of Terrebonne Plantation without involving himself in disastrous politics. In "Society, Souvenir, and Celebration 1876: The Two-Hundredth Performance of Daly's *Pique*" (*SoT* 20,iv:3–13), Gretchen Schneider reveals the New York theatre scene in the centennial year, when Augustin Daly provided sterling silver commemorative tickets to all the ladies (900 were made up) at the 200th performance at Daly's 5th Avenue Theatre of *Pique*, a drama which he created to stress American virtues over European. His gesture, besides being a symbol of patriotism, extolled capitalistic achievement and his own munificence as well as the respectability and elegance of the top-hatted and bejeweled audience.

That Shakespeare was important during our first one hundred years is testified to by Charles H. Shattuck's extensively illustrated *Shakespeare on the American Stage: From the Hallams to Edwin Booth* (Washington, D.C.: Folger Shakespeare Library, 1976). That

Shakespeare is a continuing part of the American theatre scene is illustrated (literally by many photographs) in the Spring issue of *Shakespeare Quarterly* (vol. 28, no. 2), which contains a number of comprehensive critical articles on Shakespearean festivals and repertories during the bicentennial year in many states from Oregon to New York and from California to Alabama.

ii. Late 19th, Early 20th Century

In "Frederick B. Warde: America's Greatest Forgotten Tragedian" (*ETJ* 29:333–44), Alan Woods supplies many details of Warde's career, during which he brought eagerly received Romantic tragedies and Shakespeare to numerous cities and towns until the popularity of realistic drama forced him into the Lyceum circuit as a lecturer. Three better-known actors of the American stage are the subjects of books. *Great Times Good Times: The Odyssey of Maurice Barrymore* (Garden City, N.Y.: Doubleday) by James Kotsilibas-Davis relates the story of this theatre idol between the time of his arrival from England in 1875 to his descent into madness in 1901. Famous like-father, like-son John is the subject of another volume, *Damned in Paradise: The Life of John Barrymore* (New York: Atheneum) by John Kobler, which also testifies to the hazards of fame. In *Bright Star of Exile: Joseph Adler and the Yiddish Theatre* (New York: Crowell) Lulla Rosenfeld tells her grandfather's story through his youth in Odessa and his poverty in London's East End to the golden years in New York City, where in the late twenties, besides fourteen on the road, there were twelve flourishing Yiddish theatres.

Bill Smith in *The Vaudevillians* (New York: Macmillan, 1976) recounts the successes and failures of many lesser lights, who nonetheless provided the American public with an extremely popular mode of entertainment. Thirty of those still living reminisce about the past decades, during which the epitome of success was playing The Palace in New York.

Not so American as vaudeville, but part of the American scene, are ethnic theatre groups. Students of medieval drama will be interested in Raymond J. Pentzell's illustrated "A Hungarian Christmas Mummer's Play in Toledo, Ohio" (*ETJ* 29:179–98). With its oral origin in medieval Hungary, the play has been performed by successive generations of parishioners of St. Stephens each year since the 1880s. Chicano theatres like El Teatro Bilingue (an outgrowth of the drama program at Texas A. and M.) perform plays of literary merit, as did the Spanish language theatres which existed in the Southwest when the Anglos arrived, according to John W. Brokaw in "Teatro Chicano: Some Reflections" (*ETJ* 29:535–44). Luis Valdez and his El Teatro Campesino, however, perform revolutionary dramas which appeal to workers such as those in agriculture in California, but which lack artistic merit. Visiting America for the St. Louis World's Fair of 1904 were members of the Dublin Theatre, who engaged in controversy with those who remained in Ireland. Mary M. Lago tries to sort out the causes of friction and their effect on American audiences and on the future Abbey Theatre in "Irish Poetic Drama in St. Louis" (*TCL* 23:180–94). A single visitor, but more influential in urging original, artistic drama for America is described by Norman H. Paul in "Jacques Copeau Looks at the American Stage, 1917–1919" (*ETJ* 29:61–69). During a two-year engagement at the Garrick Theatre, the director of the Théâtre du Vieux-Columbier visited and gave encouragement to many of America's struggling little theatres of the time.

iii. 20th Century

Most important of several historical studies of individuals who have made 20th-century American theatre is Ben Iden Payne's autobiography, which he finished just before he died at the age of 91. *A Life in a Wooden O* (New Haven: Yale Univ. Press) recounts his experience in staging Shakespeare in Britain and America, his life as a Broadway director and as an educator at Carnegie Tech and the University of Texas, where the theatre which bears his name was dedicated in 1976. A short anecdotal introduction by Stephen Sondheim adds personal praise to the subject of Hugh Fordin's *Getting to Know Him: A Biography of Oscar Hammerstein II* (New York: Random House), a volume filled with pictures of family, friends, and numerous productions, from *Show Boat* to *The Sound of Music*, for which Hammerstein wrote lyrics, book, or adaptation. Directors and writers require producers, of whom Cheryl Crawford has been one of America's most important during the past half century. In *One Naked Individual* (Indianapolis: Bobbs-Merrill), the title taken from her childhood misunderstanding of "one nation indivisible," Crawford relates the pitfalls of producing with the Group Theatre of the thirties, the Maplewood Theatre of the forties, the Actors Studio Theatre of the sixties, as well as in private Broadway ventures in some of which she lost her shirt but always kept her hope of another success.

ETJ has reprinted the December, 1976, Special Issue, *A Self-Portrait of the Group Theatre*, in which Crawford's reminiscences are included among such others as Odets, Strasberg, and Clurman. Richard J. Dozier in a note, "Odets and 'Little Lefty'" (*AL* 48:597–98), cites a cartoon character from the *Daily Worker* as a source of Odets's hero in *Waiting for Lefty*, and the same writer, in "The Making of *Awake and Sing*" (*MarkhamR* 6:61–65), compares the original, entitled *I Got the Blues*, with the performed version and justifies his conclusion that the second is more rich and complex and not more revolutionary and hortatory, as has been claimed. Another leftist relates in "'No Man's Land': A Chapter from the Unpublished Autobiography of John Howard Lawson" (*LGJ* 5,ii:12–13,20), edited by Mandy Lawson, how as an ambulance driver in France in 1917 (an experience which affected his life) he began the play, *Roger Bloomer*.

Documentation on theatre during the thirties is also supplied in *The Theatre of Orson Welles* (Lewisburg: Bucknell Univ. Press) by Richard France, which describes the direction, the staging, and the audience reaction to some eight successful plays, including *Doctor Faustus*, *The Cradle Will Rock*, and *Danton's Death*, along with photographs, lists of casts, and a useful bibliography. In the Theatre and Social Action Issue of the *Drama Review* (*TDR*), John S. O'Connor writes on the importance of the Federal Theatre Project's very popular *Living Newspaper* documentary, *Spirochete*, in augmenting the national campaign against syphilis ("Spirochete and the War on Syphilis," 21:91–98). In addition Gregory Mason in "Documentary Drama from the Revue to the Tribunal" (*MD* 20:263–77) makes the interesting point that the *Living Newspapers* of the thirties, influenced by Erwin Piscator (1894–1966), involved the audience emotionally, while such a drama as *In The Matter of J. Robert Oppenheimer* in the sixties required Brechtian distance, historical perspective, and a sense of inquiry.

Lillian Hellman arouses strong emotions in Sidney Hook for her book, *Scoundrel Time*. In "The Case of Lillian Hellman" (*Encounter* 48:82–91) he criticizes her actions in defying the House Unamerican Affairs Committee and Joe McCarthy and engaging in what he considers pro-Stalinist activities. Echoes from midcentury in a less acrimonious vein occur in Kenneth W. Rhoads's "Joe as Christ-type in Saroyan's *The Time of Your Life*" (*ELWIU* 3:227–43), which makes a case for Joe as more than a befuddled dipsomaniac. More importantly, Maxwell Anderson, besides inspiring the USAS Twayne volume of last year by Alfred S. Shivers (see *ALS 1976*, p. 362), is the subject of Laurence G. Avery's *Dramatist in America: Letters of Maxwell Anderson, 1912–1958* (Chapel Hill: The Univ. of N.C. Press). Along with a chronology into which the letters fit, Avery provides excellent notes, a short biography of Anderson and of the main recipients of his letters, as well as the location of many documents not included, the largest collection being at the University of Texas. The G. K. Hall (Boston) bibliographical publication, *Maxwell Anderson and S. N. Behrman: A Reference Guide* by William Klink, also provides scholars with further aid for research on America's most prolific playwright, as well as on Behrman, one of her most popular.

iv. Eugene O'Neill

O'Neill elicits the usual number of articles of varying degrees of originality. Four are concerned with technique: In "From the Exotic to the Real: The Evolution of Black Characterization in the Plays of Eugene O'Neill" (*ForumH* 13:56–61) Roger W. Oliver illustrates the playwright's progress toward realism from Brutus Jones through Jim Harris to Joe Mott. In "From Loving to the Misbegotten: Despair in the Drama of Eugene O'Neill" (*MD* 20:37–53), James R. Scrimgeour in a rundown of despairing characters from John Loving to James Tyrone makes the also not-very-original point that the last is more realistically characterized than the first. In "The Ending of O'Neill's *Beyond the Horizon*" (*MD* 20:293–98), William J. Scheick notes that Rob speaks with eloquence of his dreams at the start, but appropriately is inarticulate as he dies seeking them beyond the sunrise. In still another study of technique, "Eugene O'Neill and George Pierce Baker: A Reconsideration" (*AL* 49:206–20), Paul D. Voelker proves from close analysis of early plays that O'Neill learned from Baker, who was not the negative influence critics have claimed.

In "O'Neill's Use of Realism in *Ah, Wilderness!*" (*NMAL* 1:item 10) Ben Lucow sees an implied criticism of the happy American small town in the character of young Richard, who, although still free, must, like all individuals, give up wilderness for civilization, human personality for society. Joyce Deveau Kennedy's enlightening article, "O'Neill's Lavinia Mannon and the Dickinson Legend" (*AL* 49:108–13) makes a good case for Emily Dickinson and her sister Lavinia as models for O'Neill's character, proving the revived general interest in this 19th-century poet and O'Neill's interest at the time he was writing *Mourning Becomes Electra.* In "A New Look at Mary Cavan Tyrone" (*SoT* 21,i:11–27), Philip G. Hill follows Louis Sheaffer's interpretation that O'Neill hated his mother and shows further by numerous citations that Mary Tyrone is the "scheming, vindictive" villain of *Long Day's Journey.*

Although more concerned with British writers, William R. Brashear in *The Gorgon's Head: A Study in Tragedy and Despair* (Athens: Univ. of Ga. Press) contrasts O'Neill as the voice of will and intuition to Shaw, the voice of the intellect, and to Arthur Miller, a social rather than tragic dramatist.

Of interest to O'Neillians is the production of *Ah, Wilderness!* and *Long Day's Journey into Night* by the Milwaukee Repertory Theater Company and the brochure *Prologue* (3,ii) with its articles on the two plays by some of the best O'Neill scholars. Also of interest is the effort to make O'Neill's home, Tao House, a major center for theatre arts, which continued with benefit performances there of *The Hairy Ape* in July and *A Moon for the Misbegotten* in September. Now a National Historic Site and owned by the state of California, operation and maintainance are the responsibility of the Eugene O'Neill Foundation, Danville 94526. The tri-yearly *Eugene O'Neill Newsletter* under the editorship of Frederick Wilkins, Suffolk University, Boston 02114, continues to carry critical and production items of interest to all O'Neill scholars, such as the January issue's debate by the experts on "Which Plays Will Survive?" The series *The Literature of Death and Dying* (New York: Arno) under the editorship of Robert Kastenbaum includes this year under the title *Return to Life* a reprint of O'Neill's *Lazarus Laughed.*

Of the seven Ph.D. dissertations on O'Neill, "The Research Library of Eugene O'Neill" (*DAI* 38A:259–60) by Kathy Lynn Bernard is likely to prove most fruitful to scholars in illustrating how extensively the playwright made use of his library—now at C. W. Post College and Yale University—in the creation of his dramas. A published dissertation in the series *The Irish-Americans*—Harry Cronin's

Eugene O'Neill: Irish and American (New York: Arno Press, 1976)—covers the areas of O'Neill's Catholic and Irish background, which John Henry Raleigh treated so admirably more than a decade ago.

Pat M. Ryan, in reviewing the history of O'Neill's plays in Sweden in "Stockholm Revives Eugene O'Neill" (*ScanR* 65,i:18–23), makes it seem no wonder that he received the Nobel Prize. Beginning with *Anna Christie* in 1923, fourteen of his plays were produced by the Royal Dramatic Theater in the succeeding forty years—four of them as world premieres. O'Neill's admiration for Strindberg was reciprocated by that of the Swedish people, whose enthusiasm for O'Neill, unlike America's for more than two decades, never faltered.

v. Tennessee Williams, Arthur Miller, Edward Albee

America's most prolific living playwright is the subject of three books. The massive, nearly 900-page *Tennessee Williams: A Tribute*, edited by Jac Tharpe (Jackson: Univ. Press of Miss.), consists of hitherto unpublished essays by more than 50 critics, under such headings as "Themes," "European Contexts," "Techniques," and the titles of particular plays. The publication of the fifth volume of Williams's plays by New Directions last year makes possible consistent references to quoted passages. Although inevitably repetitious, a number of essays provide new insights which make the book a must for students of Williams. In *Tennessee Williams and Film* (New York: Frederick Ungar) Maurice Yacowar covers 15 successful films from *The Glass Menagerie* in 1950 to *Last of the Mobile Hot-Shots* in 1969, which illustrate changes in America as well as in the playwright, who has always been attracted to this medium. The third, which is biographical—*Tennessee Williams' Letters to Donald Windham, 1940–1965* (New York: Holt, Rinehart and Winston)—supplements Williams's own recent *Memoirs*. Windham has edited the letters, which in the main are rather spirited, though somewhat caustic. Revealing a character whose affection for Windham was obviously great through those years, the letters are written as Williams moved from place to place in this country and to Mexico and Cuba, sometimes depressed but often happy in observing others and in commenting movingly on his own situation to his friend.

Williams as usual is the subject of a number of essays: Charles Watson in "The Revision of *The Glass Menagerie*: The Passing of

Good Manners" (*SLJ* 8,i[1976]:74–78) compares the library edition (New York: New Directions, 1949) with the acting version (New York: Dramatists Play Service, 1948) of Williams's first important play and finds that he softens harsh references to the South and gives Northerner Jim more polite responses in the less-known acting version. Edmund A. Napieralski, in "Tennessee Williams' *The Glass Menagerie*: The Dramatic Metaphor" (*SoQ* 16:1–12), praises the drama's performability. The metaphor of Amanda, including archetypal, religious, and mythical connotations, as stage manager of her life and of her children's is carried out in action—the essence of drama and the reason the play endures. In the "Twentieth Century Views" series Stephen S. Stanton has edited *Tennessee Williams: A Collection of Critical Essays* (Englewood Cliffs, N.J.: Prentice-Hall) including 16 previously published essays on such subjects as Williams's language, his characters, and his themes. "*Orpheus Descending*" (*Players* 52:10–13) by S. Alan Chesler, like some of those in *A Tribute*, plows old ground in noting the levels from realistic to mythical on which Williams operates. John Satterfield, however, in "Williams's *Suddenly Last Summer*: The Eye of the Needle" (*MarkhamR* 6:27–33), pays deserved tribute to this play, "a synthesis of syntheses," of fantastic richness, which forces an expansion of the needle's eye to allow passage of a "multihumped camel."

In "Arthur Miller and Tennessee Williams" (*ELWIU* 4:239–49) Peter L. Hays points out similarities between *Death of a Salesman* and *The Glass Menagerie*, as well as the important impression which the production of *Glass*—illustrating life as texture rather than event—made on Miller. Besides the conflict of generations and the implied criticism of American business and values, both plays dramatize naturalistic material expressionistically and are not as different as critics suppose. *The Crucible* comes in for consideration from three angles. Jeanne-Marie A. Miller in "Odets, Miller, and Communism" (*CLAJ* 19:484–93) compares Odets's anti-Nazi *Till the Day I Die* (1935) with Miller's anti-McCarthy *The Crucible* (1953), both of which dramatized a social current and warned the American public of demagogy. To Robert A. Martin ("Arthur Miller's *The Crucible*: Background and Sources" *MD* 20:279–92) the success of the play on the stage today is evidence that Miller's careful research on the Salem witchcraft trials made of the play far more than a propaganda piece of the fifties. In "Production as Criticism: Miller's *The Crucible*"

(*ETJ* 29:354–61) N. Joseph Calarco describes his direction of the Wayne State University's Hilberry Repertory Theatre's production of the play, involving the cast from the first reading in a magic circle of witchcraft played out in a courtroom.

In "Theatre of the Mind in Miller, Osborne and Shaffer" (*Renascence* 30:33–42) C. J. Gianakaris compares Miller's technique to that of two British playwrights. In *After the Fall*, *Inadmissable Evidence*, and *Equus*, Arthur Miller, John Osborne, and Peter Shaffer make their heroes, each in a courtroom structure, examine "the inside of his head" in a Hamlet-like self-assessing "theatre of the mind." The playwright expresses his views to Christian-Albrecht Gollub in "Interview with Arthur Miller" (*MQR* 16:121–41) on various subjects from O'Neill to the radical theatre of the thirties to why the commercial theatre fails to produce the best plays.

As for Albee, Robert B. Bennett in "Tragic Vision in *The Zoo Story*" (*MD* 20:55–66) makes the point that although the play is modest, Jerry's heroic effort to realize an idea of kinship makes the audience experience the affirmation of tragedy. In a short note, "Albee's *Who's Afraid of Virginia Woolf?*" (*Expl* 35,iv:10–11), Kai-Ho-Mah explains that George's line ". . . ice for the lamps of China. . . ." is appropriate, since a common Chinese lamp has an inner moving shade which gives the illusion of horses running in a circle—both illusions and circles applying to Albee's characters.

vi. Contemporary

Theories of playwriting, directing, and stage production of avant-garde drama are as usual treated in several books and articles. Whether or not large numbers of people view such drama, it is the subject of much discussion and of numerous issues of the *Drama Review* (*TDR*) and is no doubt of interest to those working in more traditional theatre. Moreover, many experimentors are American, no longer looking for innovation from abroad. The *Drama Review* (vol. 21, no. 4) portrays seven American playwrights—Richard Foreman, Maria Irene Fornes, Adrienne Kennedy, Sam Shepard, Megan Terry, Jean-Claude van Itallie, and Robert Wilson—photographed in the act of describing their individual creative processes.

Since in the modern view the creative process of the dramatist is only part of the phenomenon of drama, which is supplemented by the creative process of the audience in experiencing the play, the issue complements a volume, *The Theatre of Images*, edited by Bonnie Marranca (New York: Drama Book Specialists), and consisting of three play scripts, which in the postliterate age concentrate on visual and aural images rather than on dialogue. Richard Foreman's ontological-hysteric play *Pandering to the Masses: A Misrepresentation* dramatizes thinking processes in a highly complex series of images. Robert Wilson's *A Letter for Queen Victoria*, an opera without singers, tests the sense perception of the audience in a continuous present freed from "the constraint of syntactic logic." And *The Red Horse Animation*, composed by Lee Breuer and Mabou Mines, appears in the comic book form in which it was produced. In *Essays on Performance Theory* (New York: Drama Book Specialists) Richard Schechner, in seven essays written between 1970 and 1976, contrasts mimetic or illusionist drama, which tries to conceal the seams with which it is sewed, to modern performance theory, which favors audience involvement, modification of the script in performance, group reaction, and theatre as a process in which the seams hang out. Schechner calls on anthropology, ethnology, and primitive ritual in working towards a "poetics of performance."

In its Annual Performance Issue, the *Drama Review* (vol. 21, no. 3) describes the performances (among many from around the world) of two American theatre groups at the annual New Theatre Festival in Baltimore. Soon 3 (San Francisco) presented *Black Water Echo*, in which it is illustrated that performed tasks alter the landscape, and The American Contemporary Theatre (Buffalo) presented *Preface*, involving audience movement into the circle of players. In "Physics and the Theatre: Richard Foreman's *Particle Theory*" (*ETJ* 29:395–404), Florence A. Falk tries to relate Foreman's play, presented by the O-H Theatre Company at the Theatre for the New City, in 1973, to the question of whether physical phenomena have any underlying structural reality and to the nature of the mind which asks. The nine-page text, which takes two and half hours playing time because of the many repeats and pauses, breaks up bits of experience by the scientific method into "discrete elements of observational data." One wonders if Meserve, when he concludes the last volume of his monumental history of American playwriting, will think his efforts worthwhile, in view of some of the final products which hypothesize that drama can only be experienced in performance and not preserved in script.

More understandable is "The Theatrical Style of Tom O'Horgan" (*TDR* 21:59–78), in which Bill Simmer describes the methods of the director of *Hair*, *Lenny*, and *Jesus Christ Superstar* on Broadway and of Arrabal's *The Architect and the Emperor of Assyria* at La Mama in 1976 and 1977. Being called gimmicky or vulgar has not diminished O'Horgan's efforts, by new theatrical effects, to involve the audience in intense response to theatre through a "high level of energy on stage." In "American History on Stage in the 1960s" (*QJS* 63:405–12) Carol Weiher is concerned with more intellectual drama—the revisionist plays of the 1960s, claiming that Martin Duberman's *In White America*, Robert Lowell's *The Old Glory* and Arthur Kopit's *Indians* went beyond back-patting melodrama to prove that we cannot escape the guilt that accompanies glory.

The present interest in roots finds expression in Tennessee, as explained by Saundra Keyes Ivey in "Ascribed Ethnicity and the Ethnic Display Event" (*WF* 36,i:85–107). Staged in a rustic open-air theatre at Sneedville, *Walk Toward the Sunset* stresses the uniqueness of the Melungeon people, whose mixed-blood origin is uncertain. Kermit Hunter's pageant has improved the community self-image and given the Melungeons (vague as the classification is) something to be proud of. Still another type of theatre is complimented by Barry Goldensohn in "Peter Schumann's Bread and Puppet Theater" (*IowaR* 8,ii:71–82). Originally a sculptor, Schumann makes all of his puppets in sizes from six inches to twenty feet and puts them into scripts, propagandistic, political, or religious, and as different as is the Noh adaptation of *The Birdcatcher in Hell* from the religious *Easter Play*.

In a practical vein Patrick Chmel complains in "The Business of Directing on Broadway" (*Players* 52:24–29) that the director is so squeezed between the requirements of the producer-manager and the various unions of Actors, Stage Employees, Musicians, Designers, and others that he has little scope for artistic creativity. Stephen Langley has edited a book in which the producers give their side of the story. In *Producers on Producing* (New York: Drama Book Specialists, 1976) two dozen producers and managers (in essays originally prepared for a seminar at Brooklyn College, CUNY) explain their essential role in getting theatre onto the American stage. A successful manager-director is described in Michael W. Gamble's "The Queen Mother: Clare Tree Major's Theatre for Children" (*Players* 52:18–23). An unpopular autocrat who underpaid her actors and demanded exemplary behavior and dress of her companies, Major nevertheless between 1923 and 1954 kept as many as six companies touring coast to coast nine months of the year and in all produced some 60 plays for children.

"The Renovation of the Yale Repertory Theatre" (*ETJ* 29:375–84) by William B. Warfel is of interest to educators in the field of drama. The innovative Yale School of Drama works closely with and is complemented by this professional Repertory company, which is housed in a former Baptist church near campus, renovated with a modern open stage for presentational theatre. A useful volume called *The Critics* (New York: Macmillan, 1976) by Lehman Engel contrasts the daily reviews of Clive Barnes (New York *Times*), Douglas Watt (New York *Daily News*), and Martin Gottfried (*Women's Wear Daily* and now *Saturday Review*). Treating older greats as well—such as Brooks Atkinson, Walter Kerr, George Jean Nathan, Richard Watts, Jr., and George Oppenheimer—Lehman makes the case that the power of the daily critic to make and break plays should not be abused. On the other hand he has no use for wishy-washy critics who straddle the fence.

Although foreign scholarship is covered elsewhere, one collection that may be of interest for its essays on modern American playwrights was omitted last year: *American Literature in the 1950s* (Tokyo: Annual Report, Toyko Chapter of the American Literature Society of Japan, 1976). The volume includes essays on Albee, Miller, Odets, Chayefsky, MacLeish, McCullers, Inge, and various aspects of American theatre in the fifties.

vii. Reference Works

A second edition of *Contemporary Dramatists*, edited by James Vinson and D. L. Kirkpatrick (New York: St. Martin's Press), includes a biography, a listing of all plays, and details of first productions of some 300 English-language playwrights. Also included are important recently deceased dramatists and another hundred who work in radio, television, and film. Daniel Blum's *A Pictorial History of the Amer-*

ican Theatre 1860–1976 (New York: Crown) in its fourth edition is, as formerly, useful for its brief summary and its innumerable pictures of each season. *The National Playwrights Directory*, edited by Phyllis Johnson Kaye (Waterford, Conn.: O'Neill Theatre Center), includes biographical and professional details about 400 living American playwrights and mention or synopsis of over 4,000 plays.

Broadway and the Tony Awards, edited by James C. Jewell with Thomas Howard (Washington D.C.: Univ. Press of America), includes details on 31 Tony Award Ceremonies and winners, along with summaries of theatrical trends evidenced thereby. *Nonprofit Repertory Theatre in North America 1958–1975: A Bibliography and Indexes to the Playbill Collection of the Theatre Communications Group*, edited by Laura J. Kaminsky (Westport, Conn.: Greenwood Press), serves as a guide to the large playbill collections of this national service organization in New York. Arranged by city and indexed by theatre, play titles, dramatists, and directors, the guide makes for easy reference to the entire collection which is available to libraries on microfiche for nearly a thousand dollars. One hundred and ninety new collections are indexed in the sixth edition of *Ottemiller's Index to Plays in Collections*, edited by John M. and Billie M. Connor (Metuchen, N.J.: Scarecrow Press, 1976), which includes British and American plays between 1900 and 1975.

How to Locate Reviews of Plays and Films, edited by Gordon Samples (Metuchen, N.J.: Scarecrow Press, 1976), is a bibliography of reference guides to newspapers, indexes, leading theatre periodicals, and critical reviews.

A number of theatre collections are now available to scholars of American drama. The largest collection of material from the Federal Theatre Project of the thirties is now open at the Research Center for the FTP at George Mason University in Fairfax, Virginia. It includes 700 scripts, numerous graphics, thousands of photographs, and over 750 bound notebooks of production details.

The Hedgerow Theatre Collection, consisting of photographs, production books, drawings, and woodcuts of the theatre, many articles and speeches of Jasper Deeter, transcripts of his acting classes, and other items concerning the more than half century of Hedgerow's history, has been placed on permanent loan in Boston University's Twentieth Century Archives.

A large collection of historical memorabilia of over 200 early

Texas theatres—the McCord Theatre Collection—is housed in the Fondren Library, Southern Methodist University, and administered by Curator Edyth Renshaw. The collection is a depository for daybooks, diaries, photographs, posters, books, and manuscripts of community and educational theatres throughout Texas.

The Robert Cushman Butler Collection at Washington State University includes fourteen hundred playbills, posters, and letters concerning Charlotte Cushman's stage career, and 200 monographic works on the 19th-century stage.

To conclude on a most optimistic note with that annual compendium of statistics and evaluation of New York and regional theatres—*The Best Plays of 1976–1977*, edited by Otis L. Guernsey, Jr. (New York: Dodd, Mead)—theatre on Broadway and off-Broadway had much the most prosperous season in history. Of the ten best plays, six originated in regional theatre, testifying to the health of the theatre throughout America, and this "playwrights' season" included "new talent cropping up all over the place," so good that many plays might have been selected as the best.

University of Florida

19. Black Literature

Charles Nilon

The efforts of the critics of black literature appear more and more to be carefully focused. They are concerned to give careful consideration to early authors, to describe the black literary tradition, and to show both how it came into existence and how modern and contemporary black authors have used it. This often involves them in tracing the relationships that exist among black history, black community, and the black literary tradition. Defining the task of the critic of black literature and providing adequate critical methods and tools (bibliography and literary history) for his work continue to be assigned high priorities among black critics, and the theoretical considerations that are dealt with in these areas may, in not too many years, result in an adequate theory of black literature and aesthetic modes that are generally satisfactory. The concern to develop a black aesthetic, to evalute the Black Aesthetic, is highly evident in the essays and books that are mentioned here. Although these informally agreed-upon tasks, and a few others, are dominant among the concerns of many black critics, there also appears to be a growing tolerance of difference of opinion and of practices which some years ago would perhaps have been rejected, because they were not politically or ideologically prudent.

Special issues of journals devoted to black literature such as the autumn and winter issues of *The Massachusetts Review*, which published a collection of fiction, poetry, criticism, and art (*Chains of Saints: A Gathering of Afro-American Literature, Art, and Scholarship*, edited by Michael S. Harper and Robert B. Stepto) give evidence of the health and energy of black literary criticism. Another instance of this kind that is of significance is the formal "Symposium on Harold Cruse," which appeared in *The Journal of Ethnic Studies* (5:2–68). These essays are mainly devoted to assessing the significance of Cruse's *The Crisis of the Negro Intellectual* (New York:

Morrow, 1967) and are written by William Eric Perkins, Ernest Allen, and Arthur Paris. A related evidence of the energy and health of black criticism is the confidence it inspires that results in the publication of new journals such as *Minority Voices*, an interdisciplinary journal of literature and the arts that is published at Pennsylvania State University and edited by Elaine D. Woodall.

i. General Bibliography

Helen Ruth Houston's *The Afro-American Novel 1965–1975: A Descriptive Bibliography of Primary and Secondary Material* (Troy, N.Y.: Whitston) is a list of primary and secondary materials for study of Afro-American novelists who have written since 1964. The entry for each author has four sections: a brief biographical statement, a list of the novels the author has written since 1964, a list of critical books and articles by and about the author and a list of the reviews of the author's novels that have been published since 1964. Critical notice of novels written before 1964 that have been published after that year is included in the third section of an author's entries. Curtis W. Ellison's and E. W. Metcalf, Jr.'s *Charles W. Chesnutt: A Reference Guide* (Boston: G. K. Hall) shows the way in which Chesnutt's works were received and describes his activities. It lists treatments of Chesnutt that appear in histories, book reviews, introductions to books, newspapers, journal and periodical articles, historical and critical works about literature, and other sources. The materials are chronological and the guide is indexed. The introduction is a serviceable tool for the guide's use. James A. Page's *Selected Black American Authors: An Illustrated Bio-Bibliography* (Boston: G. K. Hall) is a good tool for quick reference. It is arranged alphabetically and includes authors in a variety of fields.

Dan S. Green's "Bibliography of Writing about W. E. B. DuBois" (*CLAJ* 20:410–21) contains entries on DuBois's life and work. It is extensive, although the author says it is not comprehensive or exhaustive. Green's "W. E. B. DuBois: His Journalistic Career" (*Negro History Bulletin* 40:672–77) is a brief discussion and bibliographic essay devoted to information about *The Moon*, *The Horizon*, *The Crisis*, *The Brownies Book*, and *Phylon*—five journals that DuBois founded and edited. Paul G. Partington has printed "W. E. B. DuBois: A Bibliography of His Published Writings" (73205 Getna Avenue,

Whittier, California 90606) privately. It indexes magazines that DuBois edited, lists newspaper articles and columns, lists books including foreign-language editions, and lists some articles that are published in foreign-language journals.

A catalog of the Glenn Carrington Collection, *The Glenn Carrington Collection: A Guide to the Books, Manuscripts, Music and Recordings* (Washington, D.C.: Moreland-Spingarn Research Center, Howard Univ.) includes collections of the works of Langston Hughes and of Alexander Pushkin in many languages and one of the most complete collections of works by and about LeRoi Jones (Baraka). It also includes periodicals, manuscripts, and letters that are valuable in the study of Afro-American literature.

Ernest Kaiser's "Recent Books" (*Freedomways* 17:55–64, 117–29, 182–99) covers new books well and is annotated. Charles H. Rowell's "Studies in Afro-American Literature: An Annual Annotated Bibliography, 1976" (*Obsidian* 3:80–191) includes interviews, reports, general studies; studies in poetry, fiction, drama, autobiography, studies of individual authors, and bibliographical sources. Vattel T. Rose, Virginia Barrett, Enid Bogle, Dorothy Evans, Lorraine Henry, Jennifer Jordan, and Loeta Lawrence are the compilers of "An Annual Bibliography of Afro-American, African, and Caribbean Literature for the year 1976" (*CLAJ* 21:100–157). The bibliography contains primary and secondary works in black literature with entries under nine headings. There are annotations and cross-references.

ii. Fiction

***a.* Chesnutt.** Arlene A. Elder's essay, "Chesnutt on Washington: An Essential Ambivalence" (*Phylon* 38:1–8), is well documented and judicious in its support of her argument that Charles Waddell Chesnutt was ambivalent in his attitude toward Booker T. Washington despite their lifelong friendship. Elder supports this opinion through an examination of Chesnutt's responses to their personal contacts, and with evidence from his nonliterary essays which are specific in their statements about Washington's social and political stances and in which he states those positions of his that are different from Washington's. Chesnutt reviewed Washington's "The Future of the American Negro" (*Saturday Evening Post*, 20 Jan. 1900) favorably and, after a visit to Tuskegee, published a complimentary article about the Tuskegee experiment in the *Cleveland Leader* ("A Visit to Tuskegee," 31 March 1901). In "The White and the Black," which appeared in the *Boston Transcript* (20 March 1901) he appears to prefer DuBois's position on black education to Washington's. His essay for *The Negro Problem: A Series of Articles by Representative Negroes of Today* (New York: James Post and Company, 1903) in which essays by Washington and DuBois appeared, opposed Washington's political position, but he refused to join DuBois in public attacks on Washington. Chesnutt considered the amalgamation of the races inevitable, and as his conviction grew, his respect for Washington declined, although his friendship continued. A difference in attitude toward the color line may have fixed the ambivalence in Chesnutt's attitude. Eugene Terry argues in "Charles W. Chesnutt: Victim of the Color Line" (*Contributions to Black Studies* 1:15–43) that the color of Chesnutt's skin (he appeared to be white) interferes with adequate critical appraisal from black and white critics of his work. He examines the work of representative black and white critics in some detail in support of this opinion. Because of the color barrier, he feels that adequate appraisal of Chesnutt's work must deal more precisely with Chesnutt's aesthetics and with the formal characteristics of his work. He attempts to provide an example of the effect of this critical approach in an analysis of "The Bouquet," a story from *The Wife of His Youth.* William L. Andrews's " 'Baxter's Procustes': Some More Light on the Biographical Connection" (*BALF* 11:75–78, 89) agrees with Robert Hemenway's " 'Baxter's Procustes': Irony and Protest" (*CLAJ* 8:172–85) that this story probably had its source in a specific racial slight that Chesnutt encountered from a men's club in Cleveland. Presenting evidence which complements Hemenway's and showing the effectiveness of Chesnutt's use of satire, Andrews says that Baxter, the hoaxer in the story, "is Chesnutt's most elaborate self-dramatization"—a demonstration of his own artistic situation in 1904 when he was "an unsucessful author who is patronized, summarized, and categorized by an ignorant, commercially-minded, pseudo-literary readership." C. O. Ogunyemi compares a Chesnutt story with a tale by the African Amos Tutuola in "The Africanness of *The Conjure Woman* and *Feather Woman of the Jungle*" (*ArielE* 8: 17–30.) To indicate the Africanness of *The Conjure Woman,* he uses as touchstones the description of what is characteristically African in Tutuola and its counterpart in Chesnutt. He shows in this way that the raconteurs in the two works are characteristically African, that there is an oral quality in both stories, and that the African mode is flexible. Ogunyemi does not argue that Afro-American folklore, the source of Chesnutt's story, contains African survivals, but his essay supports that opinion.

The serious study of Chesnutt, which has been evident for several years, may be aided considerably by Ellison's and Metcalf's reference guide, listed above.

***b.* Hughes, Turpin, Hurston, Motley.** Langston Hughes's five books of stories about Simple have considerable appeal because of their humor and wisdom and because of the accuracy of their social perception. A concern with social perception is responsible for Melvin G. Williams's asking in "The Gospel According to Simple" (*BALF* 11:46–48) how typical Simple's attitudes toward God, the Bible, and the church are. He concludes that they may be typical of many transplanted southerners living in Harlem who, like Simple, say they grew up on the Bible and sometimes live by it. Like Simple, most of these persons recognize that the church is socially useful. Religion, however, serves Simple most in the stories as metaphor, as an aid to fantasy, and as a source of reference.

Waters Turpin may be, except among his former students, professional associates, and friends a forgotten novelist. Nick Aaron Ford's essay "Waters Turpin: I Knew Him Well" (*CLAJ* 21:1–18) is both an appreciation and an evaluation of his novels—*These Low Grounds, O Canaan!*, and *The Rootless*, which was privately printed. Ford says that Turpin "—more than any other novelist of the period [thirties and forties], undertook with considerable success the task of a sensitive literary sociologist" of the sort that Leo Lowenthal describes in "Literature and Sociology" in James Thorpe's *Relations of Literary Study* (New York: MLA, 1967). He compares Turpin's novels to Claude McKay's and finds that he is sincere and not condescending in his portrayals. The essay contains a careful criticism of *The Rootless* that Ford prepared for Turpin when that novel was in manuscript, which may have influenced the revisions that Turpin made in the novel before he published it.

Lillie P. Howard's "Marriage: Zora Neale Hurston's System of Values" (*CLAJ* 21:256–58) is a study of women in marriage situations and an attempt to determine the characteristics and importance of the good marriage in Hurston's fiction. Three of Hurston's stories, "Spunk," "John Redding Goes to Sea," and "Sweat," and two of her novels, *Jonah's Gourd Vine* and *Their Eyes Were Watching God*, are examined. It is possible that Hurston's training in anthropology, although Howard does not mention it, may influence the portraits of marriage in her fiction.

The importance of the Willard Motley Papers, which are now on loan to Northern Illinois University, to a change in the critical opinion of Motley the novelist is evident in N. Jill Weyant's "Willard Motley's Pivotal Novel: *Let No Man Write My Epitaph*" (*BALF* 11:56–61). Weyant suggests that the novel's reputation may have been affected by its being a sequel to *Knock on Any Door* and because it was written, perhaps hastily, to make money. Weyant shows that the novel is important in judging Motley's literary reputation in spite of its weaknesses. She says that it reveals a transitional stage in Motley's development. His loss of innocence and his growing awareness of racism is revealed both in the attention given to black life in America in the text of the novel and in materials found in the private papers that indicate his changing attitudes toward race. In the novel Motley alternates between black and white characters and manifests black pride for the first time in his fiction. His showing the correspondences between drug addiction and racism in *Epitaph*, Weyant believes, indicates that he was using his overt social protest as a vehicle for covert racial protest. Criticism such as this, in which evidence from the Motley Papers is used to establish circumstances and to make Motley's purposes clear may result in changes in his literary reputation. Indeed a significant step in that direction is signaled in the conclusion of M. E. Grenander's essay, "Criminal Responsibility in *Native Son* and *Knock on Any Door*" (*AL* 49:221–33), a thought-provoking, carefully argued piece, at the end of which she asserts that *Knock on Any Door* (and *Native Son*) "can be numbered among those artistic works that extend the range of understanding by which we exercise those choices that make us more fully human."

***c.* Wright, Baldwin, Ellison.** Although most of the criticism of Richard Wright's fiction is as affirmative as Grenander's is, Wright's use of and relationship to the black literary tradition and his attitude toward the black community continue to be questioned. Evidence of this is shown in James R. King's "Richard Wright, His Life and Writings" (*Negro History Bulletin* 40:138–43) in which there is an attempt to show the effects on Wright's personality of his experiences as a southern black person and the effects of those experiences in his writing. The appearance of his *American Hunger* (New York: Harper and Row), which was excluded from publication as part of *Black Boy* (1945), provides new evidence with which to support judgments that have been made or from which new ones can be made. Gerian Steve Moore judges it and finds evidence in it that Wright "has very little good to say about the black community." His essay, "Richard Wright's *American Hunger* (*CLAJ* 21:79–89), asserts that the work is a clear reflection of Wright's alienation and estrangement from "the rhythm and tempo" of the black community. He argues that Wright wanted to be validated by white people, that he was grateful to the Communist party for providing him a way to understand his experience, that the party prevented him from understanding the nature of that experience, that his character portrayal was limited by his dependence upon the party's ideology, and that his characters are extensions of his ideas—ideas which are not rooted in his understanding of black people. It is significant that Moore does not say that Wright did not understand black people. Wright's stance results in what Moore calls a critical ambivalence toward his work of a kind that is best illustrated in Ralph Ellison's "Richard Wright's Blues," an essay from *Shadow and Act* (New York: Random House, 1964). In Robert B. Stepto's "I Thought I Knew These People: Richard Wright and the Afro-American Literary Tradition" (*MR* 18:525–41) certain of Moore's concerns about Wright's use of black materials are given careful scrutiny. Stepto says that Wright is a fine, perhaps great writer, but that it is difficult to describe his place in the Afro-American Literary Tradition. In his provocative essay Stepto raises and considers four questions: "What was Wright's posture as an author, and how did it correspond with models provided by the tradition? How do his works correspond with models provided by tradition? And what has been his effect on our contemporary literature and culture?" *American Hunger* does not contain much that can be used satisfactorily in answering these questions. Near the end of the book Wright says, "Well, what had I got out of living in the city? What had I got out of living in the South? What had I got out of living in America? I paced the floor knowing that all I possessed were words and a dim knowledge that my country had shown me no examples of how to live a human life. All of my life I had been full of a hunger for a new way to live . . ." [In the text this passage ends with a suspension point.] Such passages satisfy the concerns of neither Stepto nor Moore.

Barry Gross's discussion of "Intellectual Overlordship: Blacks, Jews and *Native Son*" (*JEthS* 5:51–59) is, perhaps, not unrelated to the questions that are discussed by Moore and Stepto. Gross argues that Bigger Thomas is aware and rejects Max at the end of *Native Son* as an assertion and a realization on his part that he was more than a downtrodden suffering being—that he was a "thinking individual able to deal with the crisis that had come in his life." Gross says that the conclusion of the novel indicates Wright's break with the Communist party and his realization that he was not regarded as having worthy cultural resources or dealing intellectually with those problems of the party on which decisions must be made. Bigger's response to Max and Wright's perception of his relation to the party are presented as examples that illustrate Harold Cruse's response to his experiences in the Communist party as he presents them in *Crisis of the Negro Intellectual* and in certain of his essays, but they are also related to Wright's concern about himself and to his attitude toward black history and community and have some relationship to the issues that Moore and Stepto raise.

Findley C. Campbell would agree with Gross's assumptions, but he probably would not agree with a good deal that Moore says about Wright and the Communist party. He develops the opinion in "Prophet of the Storm: Richard Wright and the Radical Tradition" (*Phylon* 38:9–23) that Wright's essential importance arises out of "his literary identification with a specific sociological vision of the life and destiny of black people in particular and human kind in general, a vision with which he consciously identified himself in his early literary career and from which he never strayed throughout his later fiction and nonfiction." The vision ascribed here to Wright belongs to what Campbell calls social humanism as it was practiced in the radical tradition. Campbell uses the term *social humanism* as it is partly defined by Edmund Wilson in *To the Finland Station* (Garden City, N.Y.: Doubleday, 1953, pp. 197–98). He also calls attention to the fact that

Wright used the term *personalism* in a speech in 1936, that he regarded himself as a personalist and argued that for the personalist all liberation began with the private destruction of the idols of his own life.

Katherine Fishburn in her book *Richard Wright's Hero: The Faces of a Rebel-Victim* (Metuchen, N.J.: Scarecrow Press) and John M. Reilly in "Richard Wright's curious thriller, *Savage Holiday*" (*CLAJ* 21:218–23) are primarily concerned with explanations of Wright's craft. Fishburn says that she studies Wright's hero in fictional rather than real time; by this she means that she orders the books logically and does not study them in the order in which they were written. This ordering permits her, she argues, to move from the story of an innocent victim to that of a metaphysical rebel. She argues convincingly that *Black Boy* (1945) and *The Long Dream* (1958) help to explain the truncated lives of the heroes in *Lawd Today* (published in 1963 but written sometime before 1940) and *Native Son* (1940); these two books of latent and open rebellion, in turn, shed light on the existentialism of *The Outsider* (1953) and "The Man Who Lived Underground" (1944). Through this ordering of the novels Fishburn believes that it can be made clear that the final hero, Fred Daniels ("The Man Who Lived Underground"), draws all of the others together "under his mantle of love and brotherhood." Fred, who has suffered and been despised as all of Wright's heroes are, "becomes representative of all men." The six heroes typify the development of the metaphysical rebel turned prophet. Fishburn's analysis of Wright's fiction, although it is not as good as it might be, is intelligent and she makes several valuable observations about Wright's relation to his heroes employing, as she does this, what Wayne Booth calls the "implied author." Fishburn's book is interesting but not a major contribution to the study of Wright's fiction. Reilly's intention, like Fishburn's, is to show how Wright achieves a particular technical success in a novel that is inferior to his earlier fiction. He demonstrates in *Savage Holiday* that Wright has mastered distinctively a form of the detective story and that he has written a dual narrative. One level is constituted by overt action represented by dialogue and Wright's description of character behavior and the other is represented by the story of the crime.

Alfred A. Ferguson examines Richard Wright's *The Outsider* and

James Baldwin's *Another Country* to determine how black men are affected by life in large cities. His essay, "Black Men, White Cities: The Quest for Humanity by Black Protagonists in James Baldwin's *Another Country* and Richard Wright's *The Outsider*" (*BSUF* 18,ii: 51–58), shows the failure of black protagonists who strive for and fail to achieve humanity.

Donald C. Murray's "James Baldwin's 'Sonny Blues': Complicated and Simple" (*SSF* 14:353–57) is a discussion of man's need to find his identity in a hostile world and of the narrative techniques that Baldwin employs in the story. The best contribution of the year to Baldwin scholarship is *James Baldwin, a Critical Evaluation* (Washington, D.C.: Howard Univ. Press), a collection of 21 essays, edited by Therman B. O'Daniel. In the collection there are seven essays on Baldwin's novels, four on his stories, three on his plays, three on his raps and dialogues, and one which treats him as a scenarist. O'Daniel ends the volume with a classified bibliography.

W. J. Weatherby's *Squaring Off: Mailer vs. Baldwin* (London: Mason/Charter) does not contribute directly to an understanding of Baldwin's work. It describes with color and verve a literary relationship, presents incidents, anecdotes, opinions, issues, conversations, and conflicts. It is interesting and does well what it attempts.

John F. Calahan's "Chaos, Complexity and Possibility: The Historical Frequencies of Ralph Waldo Ellison" (*BALF* 11:130–38) shows that Ellison uses history partly from a comic perspective and that his characters, who are always defined by some act of will, are not defined by history and ideology. Perhaps Calahan's most significant comment is that Ellison combines the myth-maker's imagination and the instinct of the historian for specific acts of the past. Shelby Steele makes an assessment of Ellison's concept and use of blues through an analysis of his essay, "Richard Wright's Blues" (from *Shadow and Act*), and of *Invisible Man* in "Ralph Ellison's Blues" (*JBS* 7:151–68) and shows interestingly that through the dynamics of the blues Ellison ties himself and his race to mainstream cultures, thus making the blues a means of transcendence and a means "to the freedom of an existential stance." In a note, "The Wasteland in Ellison's *Invisible Man*" (*NConL* 7:5–6), Leonard J. Deutsch discusses Ellison's acknowledgment in *Shadow and Act* of debt to Eliot's *The Wasteland* and the ways in which he incorporated certain of the poem's formal properties in *Invisible Man.*

***d.* Himes, Gaines, Major, Reed, Morrison, A. Walker, M. Walker.** Ralph Reckley presents psychological explications of two of Chester Himes's novels. His "The Use of the Doppelganger or Double in Chester Himes's *Lonely Crusade*" (*CLAJ* 20:448–58) is the more useful of the two for the person who is interested in Himes as a literary artist and adds to an understanding of the novel. Reckley's observations about the oedipal complex and conflict caused by color values in "The Oedipal Conflict and Interracial Conflict in Chester Himes' *The Third Generation*" (*CLAJ* 21:275–81), are sound, but they do not add much to a reader's understanding of the novel.

Jack Hicks's "To Make These Bones Live: History and Community in Ernest Gaines's Fiction" (*BALF* 11:9–19) and William L. Andrews's " 'We Ain't Going Back There': The Idea of Progress in *The Autobiography of Miss Jane Pittman*" (*BALF* 11:146–49) complement each other in showing the importance of history and community in the novels of Ernest Gaines. Hicks shows that, as Gaines's interest in and use of black history and community increase, there appears to be an evolution of vision that grows increasingly through the four novels. He believes that the value of history and community is best realized and of most significance as it contributes to meaning and structure in *The Autobiography of Miss Jane Pittman.* In order to demonstrate the particular quality of this novel Hicks discusses *Catherine Carmier* (1946), *Of Love and Dust* (1967), and *Bloodline* (1968) in the order of their composition and compares their achievement with what is achieved in *Miss Jane Pittman.* Andrews devotes his attention to Miss Jane Pittman and through his discussion shows that she learns that she and other black people cannot escape to freedom by leaving the South. She accepts, he suggests, a "do-not-run and do-fight" point of view and invalidates the idea of freedom outside the South. Miss Jane Pittman learns what she does through her own efforts and through the actions and experiences of other characters in the novel; she learns because she has community and history and is reassured and given strength by these. With these aids, Andrews says, she develops a progressive awareness, makes sociological progress, and cannot be held back by white repression.

Clarence Major and Ishmael Reed, who write fiction that is consciously experimental and perhaps avant garde, are consciously aware of black history and community and use them in ways that are special and significant. Jerome Klinkowitz includes these two authors in his

The Life of Fiction (Urbana: Univ. of Ill. Press). He says that Clarence Major's fiction is pitted against conventional realistic fiction and against "the commercially received black fiction which has been restricted to the form of social realism." Major, he says, focuses on language and has found a way to treat recognizable subject matter without having it turn into a stereotyped notion of the documentary world. The chapter on Major (pp. 95–104) contains Klinkowitz's comments about him, quotations from his fiction and other works, and gives an accurate description of what his fiction and aesthetic values are. It is through these that a sense of the importance of history and community in Major's work is conveyed.

His chapter (pp. 117–28) on Ishmael Reed reveals more clearly the importance of black history and community than their importance is revealed in the chapter on Major. Klinkowitz suggests, although Reed rejects European forms, that resources from the black world (American and African) give him faith in America and allegiance to an indigenous art form. He mentions but does not explain Reed's neo-hoodoo aesthetic, which Reed takes from black history and community and which is the key to the metaphysical purpose in his art. For Reed the artist is a conjurer or a necromancer who captures an essence rather than renders a photograph. Reed says that he takes cues from the vaudeville stage. It is significant that these two black writers, and others (Klinkowitz treats the novelist Charles Wright briefly), who are a part of the tradition of Afro-American literature, are at the same time examples of the "newer fictionists" among whom Klinkowitz says Beckett is as traditional as Joyce.

Although Toni Morrison's novels may not correctly be called avant garde, they contain technical experiments and are markedly new in their presentation of the black woman in history and in the black community. *First World* published an essay on each of Morrison's novels in its winter issue. Each of the essays considers the form and content of the novel it treats and, because of the uses of history and community that are made in the novels, expresses some concern about adequate critical approaches to the novels. The persons who wrote the essays appear to be concerned in varying degrees that the Black Aesthetic may not be a good means of treating the novels adequately. Philip M. Royster says in "*The Bluest Eye*" (1:35–43) that Toni Morrison's first novel is a pessimistic narrative concerning the situation, condition, and problems of society's scapegoats. He finds a flaw in the author's use of history and community, although he does not call it that. He says, "The novel's weakness lies in the failure of the narrator-*persona*, who has achieved a remarkably sensitive awareness on her journey from childhood ignorance to adult knowledge and responsibility, to focus on crucial moments that wrought changes in her awareness"; but he praises its structure, its precise and imaginative prose, chapters that are constructed on ideas like essays, and its novelistic perspective and short-story focus. Odette C. Martin in "*Sula*" (1:35–44) says that that novel's chief literary function is prophetic or crucial in that it points to the danger of "special negritude" which might produce a dangerous form of ethnocentrism in both black life and art. This is a concern about the use of history and community. As Royster suggests about *The Bluest Eye*, *Sula* is a novel of ideas. It is also justifiably described in this essay as an allegory of black literary history and a social criticism of black life and art. *Song of Solomon* is Toni Morrison's most distinguished effort in the novel form. In Jabari Simama's "Acute Depiction of Bourgeois Reality" (1:45–48), he says the novel's strength lies in the achievement mentioned in his title. It is about, he says, myths (community and history) and it treats the theme of woman's intrinsic worth and "the virtues of the need to explore one's past and history." Simama points out the effects of the novel's failure to render an adequate critique of bourgeois reality, its failure to emphasize the political economy of race, and its failure to present the subtle implications of class division.

Trudier Harris's "Folklore in the Fiction of Alice Walker: A Perspective of Historical and Literary History" (*BALF* 11:3–8) uses Walker's "The Third Life of Grange Copeland" and stories from *In Love and Trouble* to show how a tradition of black folklore uses is perpetuated. She shows, for example, how voodoo is used by Walker much as it is used by Charles W. Chesnutt and as it is described by Zora Neale Hurston in *Mules and Men*. She shows that Walker uses folklore traditionally to advance plots, to characterize, to provide structure, and to raise questions about the nature of society. The essay shows also that the traditional use of black folklore is consistent with certain of the theoretical assumptions about the use of folklore in America that are held by Allen Dundes and Hennig Cohen.

Three essays on Margaret Walker's *Jubilee* call attention to her use of black history and literary traditions. Phyllis Rauch Klotman explains Walker's intention to write a folk novel using oral history—

the experience of slavery as her grandmother had told her about that experience. In " 'Oh Freedom'—Women and History in Margaret Walker's *Jubilee*" (*BALF* 11:139–45), Klotman shows that the novel emerges from the literary traditions of the slave and oral narrative and that its origin is evident in its thematic material and in its structure. Like the slave narrative, it has tripartite structure—bondage, escape, and freedom. Bertie J. Powell shows by comparison in "The Black Experience in Margaret Walker's *Jubilee* and Lorraine Hansberry's *The Drinking Gourd*" (*CLAJ* 21:304–11) the different ways in which the two writers use black history, their portrayals of slavery, and how slave persons struggled to find meaningful lives for themselves. The slave world in both works is presented as a world in which community is achieved and contributes to a sustaining quality of mind and life.

iii. Poetry

***a.* Wheatley, Hughes, Brooks, Hayden, Baraka.** As scholars continue to add to what is known about Phillis Wheatley, her significance as a writer increases and the importance of her life becomes clearer. James A. Rawley's "The World of Phillis Wheatley" (*NEQ* 50:666–77) provides a partial summary of Wheatley scholarship since Julian D. Mason's *The Poems of Phillis Wheatley* (Chapel Hill: Univ. of N.C. Press, 1966) and contributes to the knowledge that exists about her. The essay describes the circumstances of her composing a poem to the Earl of Dartmouth and of the publication of her book in England. It contributes to what is known of Susan Wheatley's influence in her life and rather fully to what is known of her relationship with an Anglo-American group of evangelicals. Some of the letters quoted from in the essay are written by Wheatley. Knowledge of the effort to publish Wheatley's poems is increased considerably by Mukhtar Ali Isani's "The First Proposed Edition of *Poems on Various Subjects* and the Phillis Wheatley Canon" (*AL* 49:97–103). Isani discovers that efforts were made to publish *Poems on Various Subjects, Religious and Moral* by subscription in 1772 and that Ezekiel Russell, editor of the Boston *Censor*, proposed the publication in his paper. The list of poems proposed for the American edition is of major importance, because the dates of composition of the first sixteen poems are given.

Edward J. Mullen's anthology, *Langston Hughes in the Hispanic World and Haiti* (Hamden, Conn.: Archon Books) is a valuable contribution to Hughes scholarship. The essay, "The Literary Reputation of Langston Hughes in the Hispanic World and Haiti" (pp. 15–46) documents an important Hispanic influence and contribution to the beginning of his career, describes his life with his father, tells about his association with Mexican writers and artists, and shows how he was affected by life in Cuba, Spain, and Haiti when he visited those countries. The essay discusses the regard of the writers and artists in these countries for Hughes. Some evidence of that regard is shown in the bibliography, "Langston Hughes's Works Translated into Spanish" (pp. 47–68). Four essays by the Hispanic persons José Antonio Fernández de Castro, Nicolás Guilten, Salvador Novo, and Rafael Lozano constitute the third section of the book and give a good sampling of Hispanic opinion of Hughes. The anthology proper contains the prose pieces and poems that Hughes wrote about Mexican, Cuban, Spanish, and Haitian subjects. As a whole the book contributes to a knowledge of Hughes's importance in the larger sphere of international black literature. The Haitian attitude toward him is conveyed better in Claude Souffrant's "Idéologies Afro-Américaines du developpement: Langston Hughes et le cas d' Haiti" (*Présence Africaine* 103:129–44). Souffrant, who is influenced in his critical method by Roland Barthes's *Sade, Fourier, Loyola* (Paris: Sevil), begins his discussion of Hughes with a discussion of the relation of literature and sociology and a list of Hughes's works that treat Haitian subjects. They represent several genres, but the list, as is indicated in Mullen's work, is not long. Souffrant uses as a focus for his examination of Hughes the statement from Hughes's journal, "It was in Haiti that I first realize [*sic*] how class lines may cut across color lines within a race, and how dark people of the nationality may scorn those below them." The analysis of Hughes's writing is done in the section of the essay that is titled "Le paysan comme va-nu-pieds ou l' exclusion sociale."

Two essays by William H. Hansell, "The Poet-Militant and Foreshadowings of a Black Mystique: Poems in the Second Period of Gwendolyn Brooks" (*CP* 10:37–45), and "Essences, Unifyings, and Black Militancy: Major Themes in Gwendolyn Brooks's *Family Pictures* and *Beckonings*" (*BALF* 11:63–66) are evaluations of her stance as a poet in her second and third periods. Brooks has said that there are three periods in her work. The second period includes the "New Poems" section of *Selected Poems* (New York, 1963), "The Sight of the Horizon" (1963), and "In the Time of Detachment, in the Time of Cold" (1967). The poems of this period are characterized by changes in her portrayal of the role of the poet and of the function of art, and her gradual adoption of attitudes which foreshadowed a mystique of blackness. Hansell says that in this period Brooks advocated the political function of art and militancy for the poet and layman and believed that the poet's role in the revolution was intended to bring about a rededication to American ideals. He says that, in this period, she believed the poet had to deal with the immediate environment in order to retain integrity and authenticity. For Hansell "Riders to the Blood-Red Wrath" is perhaps the most explicit portrayal of the second period sense of the politically militant poet. The two collections of Brooks's poems that have been published in the seventies, *Family Pictures* and *Beckonings*, when considered thematically and stylistically, Hansell finds, are very much like collections of her poems published in the late 1960s in the second period. They call for militancy and communal unity and for the celebration of blackness and black heroes. In these poems Brooks continues to instruct her audience as she did in *In The Mecca* and in *Riot*. Sue S. Parks's essay, "A Study in Tension: Gwendolyn Brooks's '*The Chicago Defender* Sends a Man to Little Rock'" (*BALF* 11:32–34), presents an analysis of a poem to show how tension is achieved and works in it, but, more important than that, she demonstrates how Brooks turns raw material into art and that her poetry has power and "polished technique." Parks refers to a statement in which Brooks said that black poets have three "impressive advantages": subjects that are moving, authoritative, and humane; great drive; and "inspiriting emotion like tied hysteria." Brooks feared, Parks says, that, because of these advantages, black poets might yield to the temptation to write with "no embellishment, no interpretation, no subtleties." She has never done this.

The concept of a black literary tradition and how it is perceived by white literary critics is crucial in Lewis Turco's essay, "Angle of Ascent: The Poetry of Robert Hayden" (*MQR* 16:199–219). Turco's title is misleading, for he says little that is of interest or value that adds to the appreciation and understanding of Hayden's poetry. Something, however, is told of Hayden. More is told of Turco's opinion of Stephen Henderson's claims in his *Introduction to Understanding the New Black Poetry* (New York: Morrow, 1973). Turco's "quarrel" in this essay is with Henderson's use of the phrase "language techniques" and with his use of the terms *theme*, *structure*, and *saturation*. Speaking of Hayden, Turco says, "I intend to examine his work in the light of Stephen Henderson's codification of what constitutes 'Black Poetry' as distinguished from 'White Poetry.' At the same time I will refute Henderson's arguments that there are such things as ethnic 'techniques.' I propose to show that, in fact, Henderson's techniques are elements of ethnic black styles, and that Hayden having written in many of these styles is a paradigmatic poet of the English language who has been true to his roots and history, though not circumscribed by, or limited to, what is merely racial, ethnic, or personal." Henderson could, perhaps, agree with Turco's last sentence, because Turco appears in his use of the phrase "roots and history" to be aware of the black literary tradition and of Hayden's place in it. The "quarrel" perhaps is a product of perception, labels, and feelings. Henderson accepts the fact that there are black history and black community and that a black literary tradition has developed as a part of their coming into existence. In his Introduction he attempts to tell how black poets do certain things, or what their writing habits are, and to give these things names that can be used to describe them in literary discourse. Turco asks, "Where does Henderson imagine that Rev. Dr. King got his oratorical style, if not from the Bible" or from the English language tradition? The question is a good one; Henderson might say that he got it from listening to preachers, some literate and some not, in the black community or from listening to politicians in the South. Certainly the Bible is a source, but it can be asked what are the sources of its linguistic character and, ridiculously perhaps, suggested that the Bible's sources are the origin of King's oratorical style.

Wilbur Williams, Jr., suggests that the bipolar extremes of Hayden's poetic genius are the symbol and history. Explaining this as his essay "Covenant of Timelessness and Time, Symbolism and History in Robert Hayden's *Angle of Ascent*" (*MR* 18:731–49) develops, he says Hayden's "symbolistic imagination is intent on divining the shape of a transcendent order of spirit and grace that might redeem a world tragically bent on its own destruction" and that in doing this he balances the claims of the ideal and the actual in his preoccupation with the relationship between natural and spiritual facts. The essay is valuable because of the way it attempts to put Hayden into the Emersonian tradition. Williams and Howard Faulkner both attempt to judge the character and success of Hayden's *Angle of Ascent* (New York: Liveright, 1975). Faulkner attempts to show that Hayden has found the theme that he sought. His essay, " 'Transformed by Steps of Flight': The Poetry of Robert Hayden" (*CLAJ* 21:282–91), develops the idea that each of Hayden's poems can be reduced to a single pair of words from which the surface structure of the poem is generated. The paired words, he says, that underlie the surface structure of individual poems include walking/dancing, blooming/dying, thriving/twisting—a small number of pairs that, as they are focused, generate and embody transformation which Faulkner believes is Hayden's central theme. Faulkner's analysis of the function of verbs in Hayden's poems contributes a good deal to the understanding of Hayden's prosody.

Houston A. Baker, Jr., traces through references to ideas and statements in Imamu Baraka's poetry and criticism the progress of his social and political ideas and suggests that his present stance, in which he appears to endorse "Marxist-Leninism-Mao-Tse Tung thought," is not incompatible with and is a logical step from the stances that came before it. This essay, " 'These Are Songs If You Have the Music': An Essay on Imamu Baraka" (*Minority Voices* 1: 1–18) contains an excellent reading of some of Baraka's poems.

***b.* White, Yerby, Stuckey.** Roger J. Bresnahan calls attention to a black poet who is of historical significance in "Charles Fred White: A Forgotten Black Poet" (*Negro History Bulletin* 40:659–61). In the essay Bresnahan gives a brief critical appraisal of White's one volume of poems, *The Plea of the Negro Soldier and a Hundred Poems* (1908) and a summary of his biography. The poetry is judged to be of the quality of those poets who are included in Joan R. Sherman's *Invisible Poets: Afro-Americans of the Nineteenth Century* (Urbana: Univ. of Ill. Press, 1974). Alan C. Lupacks's note, "Frank Yerby's 'Wisdom'" (*NConL* 7,iv:8), provides an analysis of Frank Yerby's "Wisdom" in which he shows how the poem's form and content are used to make its meaning. It may not be known that Yerby has written poems. Elma Stuckey's poems have appeared in *Black Lines, Freedomways, The Pan-Africanist*, and the *Journal of Black Studies*. David R. Roediger's short essay, "Elma Stuckey: A Poet Laureate of Black History" (*Negro Hist. Bul.* 40:690–91) traces the career of a poet first published when she was 69 and notes the effective use of black history in her poems, which she says are a synthesis of folk and scholarly traditions. *The Big Gate* (Chicago: Precedent, 1976) is her first book.

iv. Drama—Dodson, Baraka, Kennedy, Bullins

Owen Dodson's essay "Who Has Seen the Wind? Playwrights and the Black Experience" (*BALF* 11:108–16) contributes obliquely to an understanding of the black literary tradition and something to the knowledge of what he feels about his own plays. It provides delight and information. It has no thesis, but it suggests—or better amplifies—the idea in Harold Taylor's quotation with which it is begun: "The ideals of the spirit of humanism are carried, not in manifestoes, catalogues, or proclamations, but in the hearts, and minds and hands of the creative artists." Dodson's contrast of the plays about black life that were written by Ridgely Torrence, Eugene O'Neill, Paul Green, and Marc Connelly—plays that he has studied and directed—with representative plays by Ed Bullins, Imamu Baraka, Edgar White, Garland Lee, Adrienne Kennedy, Ntozake Shange, Langston Hughes, Owen Dodson, Lorraine Hansberry, Leslie Lee, and Phillip Hayes is provocatively reassuring. Jeanne-Marie A. Miller sees changes in the black literary tradition in the treatment of black women. She examines plays that are written by Alice Childress, Lorraine Hansberry, Ed Bullins, and Adrienne Kennedy in her essay, "Images of Black Women in Plays by Black Playwrights" (*CLAJ* 21:494–507), and finds that in their work black women receive varied treatment and that their images, for the most part, are positive.

John V. Hagopian in "Another Ride on Jones's Subway" (*CLAJ* 20:269–74) gives additional testimony of the quality and complexity of Jones's *Dutchman.* He describes the play as more than an attack on the black person who does not affirm his blackness and tries earnestly to explicate something of what is "fascinating and ultimately ambiguous" in it. His speculations about Lula, who, Jones says, is not Eve or Lilith, examine the significance of her unrealistic character and suggest several possibilities of interpretation. Hagopian does not find an exact parallel between Jones's plot and forms of the Flying Dutchman legend. His consideration of the use of the subway in the play is not unrelated to what Thaddeus Martin says about its use in "*Dutchman* Reconsidered" (*BALF* 11:62), although Martin's statement is perhaps more straightforward: "The subway is a metropolis, a way of life, a giant melting pot where human cargo is scrambled together, yet scooped out separately." Like *Dutchman*, Adrienne Kennedy's plays are not easily understood. Her essay, "A Growth of Images" (*TDR* 21:41–48), tells something about her work. She says she thinks about things for years and keeps notebooks in which she describes images, ideas, and dreams. She thinks that she writes best in fantasy and discusses *Funny House of a Negro* as an example of her method.

Warren R. True's "Ed Bullins, Anton Chekhov and the 'Drama of Mood'" (*CLAJ* 20:521–32) lists the dramaturgical similarities of the plays of Chekhov and Bullins—persuasive disconnected dialogue, an obscure development, and circularity of plot shape—in order to show that the dominance of these elements in both playwrights' work creates stasis in the action of their plays. True does not intend to suggest that Bullins is influenced by Chekhov but to suggest that he has not moved away from European reference for his art.

v. Criticism, Literary History, and Language

Alvin Aubert, in "Agonizing Act of Auto-Exorcism" (*First World* 1: 39–40), a critical review of Addison Gayle, Jr's. *Wayward Child: A Personal Odyssey* (New York: Anchor) begins his discussion of the autobiography by pointing out that the paradigm (Metaphor) which Gayle uses in his critical work, *The Way of the New World* (1975) "works, but is inadequate. . . ." "A case in point," Aubert says, "is Gayle's somewhat thesis-focused reading of James Weldon Johnson's *The Autobiography of An Ex-Coloured Man*, which leads to a neglect of the ironic dimension of Johnson's narrator-protagonist, and to a too facile equation of the narrator and his creator as regards the character's values." The approach nearly obliterates what the reader should perceive of Johnson's grasp of the complexity in making sense of a life of 'double-consciousness. . . .'" This review of an autobiography is mentioned in this section on criticism, because it is one of a good number of instances in which a critic this year has used, or tested, or commented on the Black Aesthetic which very largely was formulated by Addison Gayle. The autobiography itself provides a good introduction to Gayle's thought on black literature and to his view of the Black Aesthetic. Several of those persons who have used, or judged it, have not found it adequate, although most of those who criticized it understand how it came into existence and the service, not necessarily aesthetic, that it has given to the study of black literature. Deborah M. Austin's criticism of Gayle's study of the black novel in America, *The Way of the New World*, is a careful examination of his aesthetic theories. In her "Addison Gayle's Theory of Fiction" (*Obsidian* 3:70–79), she examines the strengths and weaknesses of Gayle's theory as it works in his study of the novel. She finds the theory "in many ways unequal to the task" of tracing the development of black fiction from 1853 to the present. Jerry W. Ward's "N. J. Loftis's *Black Anima*: A Problem in Aesthetics" (*JBS* 7:195–210), like the essays mentioned above, asserts rather dogmatically that the Black Aesthetic is not aesthetics. He says, "For some years now we have been talking with varying degrees of generality and specificity about the 'Black Aesthetic,' but in searching through all the writing devoted to this protean phenomenon, one's attempt to find discussion of the *aesthetics* [Ward's italics] which inform the Black Aesthetic is a hopeless undertaking." Ward recognizes the inadequacy of the Black Aesthetic clearly when he recognizes that Loftis's poem, *Black Anima* (New York: Liveright, 1973), offers special aesthetic challenges. He says, "The specific syndrome of factors in the poem that governs our appreciation brings attention to some aesthetic realities that theorists of the Black Aesthetic have failed to treat rigorously" and calls the reader's attention to David Dorsey's "Formal Elements of the Black Aesthetic in Poetry" (*CAAS*, Occasional Paper no. 9, Atlanta University, 1972) as an example of a kind of criticism that is needed. A rather detailed criticism of the Black Aesthetic is presented in Charles H. Rowell's "Diamonds in a Sawdust Pile: Note to Black Southern Writers" (*Black Scholar* 8:25–31). The essay contains both criticisms of and suggestions of ways to provide an adequate black aesthetic. He says the Black Aesthetic's creators and advocates and the aesthetic itself created an anti-art atmosphere, overemphasized politics at the expense of craft, failed to articulate a clear concept of aesthetics, misinterpreted the concept of functionalism in black art, separated the artist and the man in the street, ignored the middle class, frustrated or silenced many of those writers whose sensibilities were not shaped entirely by a folk community, and did not tolerate the notion that black people should develop many kinds of writers.

While the Black Aesthetic has not satisfied the needs of black critics in ways that are mentioned above, it has served well to focus literary attention on the importance of black history, black community, and the black literary tradition. It may also be responsible, perhaps only in a small way, for certain of the critical observations about history, community, and tradition in the group of essays that follow.

Donald B. Gibson's "Individualism and Community in Black History and Fiction" (*BALF* 11:123–29) supports, or accepts, a thesis that Herbert Gutman develops in *Slavery and Freedom, 1750–1925* (New York: Random House, 1976). Like Gutman, Gibson suggests that slaves made a world for themselves and created a community, a sense of which they brought with them from Africa and adapted to the conditions of the new world. The fiction that Gibson studies (Paul Laurence Dunbar's *The Sport of the Gods*, James Weldon Johnson's *The Autobiography of an Ex-Coloured Man*, Jean Toomer's *Cane*, Ralph Ellison's *Invisible Man*, James Baldwin's *Another Country* and *If Beale Street Could Talk*, Richard Wright's *Native Son* and *Outsider*, and Maya Angelou's autobiographical *I Know Why the Caged Bird Sings*) permits him to study the possibilities and limits of individualism as they are typically presented in fiction and to conclude that community is better than individualism. Some of his observations are quite close to those that Klotman makes above and support her reading of Walker's *Jubilee*. His observations about community, based largely on distinctions of a kind that are clear in Angelou's book, are, to an extent, confirmed in David Nelson's study of black novels and poetry in *Black Ethos: Northern Urban Negro Life and Thought, 1890–1930* (Westport, Conn.: Greenwood Press). The relationship of the African experience to the thematic and other uses of community in black literature is stressed in Melvin Dixon's "Black Literature and Community" (*MR* 18:750–69). Dixon compares René Maran's *Batouala*, Claude McKay's *Banjo*, and Jacques Roumain's *Masters of the Dew*, novels by writers of the African diaspora in which the idea of racial community is explored for theme, imagery, and characterization. He also discusses literary movements—the Harlem Renaissance in the United States, Negritude in Africa, and the Indigenist in Haiti—as an additional means of showing the significance of community in black literature. Although her book tries to do too much and shows not gracefully its dissertation origin, Marion

Berghahn's *Images of Africa in Black American Literature* (Totowa, N.J.: Rowman and Littlefield), in chapters on W. E. B. DuBois, Richard Wright, Ralph Ellison, and James Baldwin does show that the use of Africa and African images is thematically effective and functions well in suggesting community.

H. Bruce Franklin's essay, "The Literature of the American Prison" (*MR* 18:50–78), discusses mainly the literature produced by black writers who were prisoners—Malcolm X, Eldridge Cleaver, George Davis, Ethridge Knight, Bobby Seale, and T. J. Reddie. He believes that their writing, particularly the poetry, is like the slave songs and functions as they did; the slave songs were unifying, a communal product, produced (in a sense) by history and recorded by it. Obliquely, this essay shows a good deal of prison as a kind of metaphorical creator of community. It is interesting that Angela Davis is not included among Franklin's list of prisoner writers.

The importance of community to the black writer is well expressed in a quotation from Wallace Thurman's *Infants of Spring* that is used in Charles Scrugg's "'All Dressed Up But No Place to Go': The Black Writer and His Audience During the Harlem Renaissance" (*AL* 48:543–63). In the quotation Thurman calls attention to the futility of an aesthetic movement that is "cut off from communal soil, whose artists gather in houses to wither and die." Scrugg's essay examines published articles by James Weldon Johnson, Alain Locke, Jean Toomer, Sterling Brown, Claude McKay, Walter White, and William Stanley Braithwaite that show their frustration because they felt shut off from their community. The content of Okon E. Uya's "Race Ideology and Scholarship in the United States: William Styron's *Nat Turner* and Its Critics" (*ASI* 15:63–81) and of Henry G. La Bree, III's "The Black Press 150 Years Old" (*Negro History Bulletin* 40:705–7) is important to an understanding of black history and community, although the essays are not primarily concerned to do that.

The books and the essays that have been mentioned in this section contribute something to an understanding of the existence of a tradition of black literature. Reinforcement of that understanding is given in Darwin T. Turner's "Black Fiction, History and Myth" (*SAF* 5: 109–26), which is an examination of several black historical novels—Dunbar's *Fanatics*, Bontemps's *Black Thunder*, Hurston's *Moses, Man of the Mountain*, DuBois's *The Black Fire*, Yerby's *The Foxes of Harrow*, Walker's *Jubilee*, Gaines's *The Autobiography of Miss Jane*

Pittman, and Reed's *Mumbo Jumbo*—each of which uses black history or is in a traditional or generic sense a historical novel. In some of these novels history becomes myth and symbol.

John Wideman's "Defining the Black Voice in Fiction" (*BALF* 11: 79–82) shows with illustrations from Charles W. Chesnutt, Phillis Wheatley, and Gayl Jones, that one of the problems of black literature is the task of charting the evolution of black speech "into a self-sufficient independent literary code." Wideman's essay attempts to trace the route by which the art of the oral poet or the folk artist's technique becomes adequately represented in written literature as it could not be in Phillis Wheatley's poetry. This achievement, he feels, is evident in the writing of Gayl Jones. Her *Corregidora*, he says, illustrates the relationship between literate and oral traditions and ". . . implicates a significant dimension of her style." He says that in *Corregidora* black speech as a literary language has become *Creolized* [his italics] and has become the principal language of a speech community. The core of his discussion is that black writers have created their own code of discourse from resources in the oral tradition and the models of American literature. Wideman's observations about Gayl Jones's use of language are given support by what she says about her mother's speech and by what may be observed in her writing in the interview with her mother that is listed below. What Wideman says about black speech is related to Geneva Smitherman's discussion of black language in *Talkin an Testifyin: The Language of Black America.* (Boston: Houghton Mifflin). She feels that insufficient attention is given to the study of the elements of black American dialect, and its historical and sociocultural development. She gives her attention to these neglected areas, and her discussion of the African world view and the Afro-American oral tradition contribute to an understanding of black community and the literary tradition. J. L. Dillard's *Lexicon of Black English* (New York: Seabury Press), although it is perhaps not a lexicon, contributes a good deal to the study of black language. Michael G. Cooke's "Naming, Being, and Black Experience" (*YR* 47:167–86) stresses the importance of names ". . . a means of locating, extending, and preserving self in the human community" and the great loss it is to shed the sense of a name. His discussion of names is in particular a discussion of language. In his essay he writes about Ralph Ellison's *Invisible Man*,

Michael Harper's *Nightmare Begins Responsibility*, Alice Walker's *Meridan*, and several other authors' work.

Phyllis Rauch Klotman's *Another Man Gone, The Black Runner in Contemporary Afro-American Literature* (Port Washington, N. Y.: Kennikat Press) establishes the presence of the running-man metaphor and theme in western literature and places the black runner —from the slave narrative to contemporary black fiction—within that framework. Klotman's observations are judicious and give evidence of knowledge and understanding. Her reading of novels by James Baldwin, Ralph Ellison, William Melvin Kelley, John A. Williams, and Chester Himes are enlightening. The significance of the runner in the slave narrative and the origin of that genre is treated in Frances S. Foster's "Britton Hammon's *Narrative*: Some Insights into Beginnings" (*CLAJ* 21:179–86). *A Narrative of the Uncommon Sufferings and Surprising Deliverance of Britton Hammon, A Negro* (1760) is the earliest prose work by a black person in North America and is significant, among other reasons, because it is a direct antecedent of the slave narratives and is a precursor to Afro-American autobiography.

Maria K. Mootry's essay, and the introduction to Peter Bruck's anthology, are good discussions of the pastoral and of the black short story. In her "Love and Death in Black Pastorals" (*Obsidian* 3:5–11) Mootry uses as a definition of black pastoral the quotation, "Even in death, there may be arcady," which is taken from Erwin Panofsky's "Et in Arcadia Ego" (*From Philosophy and History* [Oxford: Clarendon Press], pp. 295–320) as a key to her discussion of Richard Wright's "Big Boy Leaves Home," Leon Forest's *There Is a Tree More Ancient than Eden*, Albert Murray's *Train Whistle Guitar*, and two paintings—Aaron Douglas's "Idyll of Deep South" and Horace Peppin's "Holy Mountain III." Her interpretation of the black pastoral, as she defines it, allows her to conclude that the fiction and painting examined in her essay are critiques of American society, "its ideals and the failure to achieve these ideals." Peter Bruck's *The Black American Short Story in the 20th Century* (The Hague: Mouton) is an edited collection of essays placed together to examine a genre that is perhaps neglected by critical attention. The volume's introductory essay discusses the sources of the black short story and traces the history of its development beginning with Paul Laurence

Dunbar's stories. The essay treats a representative number of stories that were written between 1889 and 1965. A selected bibliography lists the authors and titles of collections of short stories published between 1898 and 1977.

vi. Biography, Interviews

Robert Hemenway's *Zora Neale Hurston: A Literary Biography* (Urbana: Univ. of Ill. Press) is an excellent literary biography and perhaps the most useful work on Hurston that now exists. There is much about the book that deserves special praise.

As the list below may suggest, a good many interviews with persons of literary significance have appeared in journals this year. Most of these convey impressions of the person who is being interviewed and frequently information about his artistic values and work that are useful to the literary scholar. Too often, however, interviews are less valuable than perhaps could be. In an unsigned interview that appears in *Black Scholar* (8:44–53) Maya Angelou talks about the masterpiece syndrome, the attitude of the black community toward the artist, her concept of liberation, John Coltrane's music, her attitude toward work, and other things. Gloria T. Hull and Posey Gallager in "Update on *Part One*: Interview with Gwendolyn Brooks" (*CLAJ* 21:19–40) intend to discover what Brooks has thought about and done with her art since *Part One* (1972), her autobiography, was published. Brooks tells them about her effort to write a new, more simple poetry, poetry which has the quality and effect of "We Real Cool" that could be read by ordinary readers and which she might, if she chose, read in taverns. She feels that her effort in *Beckonings* (1975), her most recent book of poems, did not achieve this end. In the middle section of the interview Brooks discussed the social and artistic effects of her decision to become a people's poet and its consequences. Brooks's comments bear a strong resemblance to some of the things that are said about her in the essays that are listed in the section on poetry. The topics that are treated in Michael Harper's and Robert Stepto's "Study and Experience: An Interview with Ralph Ellison" (*MR* 18:417–35), like those in the interview with Gwendolyn Brooks, range not too widely, and both of these interviews have a coherence beyond mere talk with a writer. The Wright-Ellison relationship, older and younger writers, the Black Aesthetic, and Ellison's response to the issue of *Black World* that was devoted to his work are the topics of the interview. Perhaps the most interesting part of Maria K. Mootry's "If He Changed My Name: An Interview with Leon Forest" (*MR* 18:631–42) is his response to a question about his novel, *There Is a Tree More Ancient Than Eden* (1973), and the talk about style and influence that grew from that question. Gayl Jones tries to tell Michael Harper, whose student she was, how she learned to write in "Gayl Jones: An Interview" (*MR*: 692–715). She says she learned by listening to people talk and from her mother who wrote stories. She tells a good deal about the writing of *Corregidora* and concludes that writing classes provided her guidelines. Her interview with her mother, "Interview with Lucile Jones" (*Obsidian* 3:26–35), not only presents her mother distinctively, but it tells things that are important about Gayl Jones's writing style, her use of voice, and provides in her view of her mother a suggestion of the source of some of the materials that appear in her fiction. The interview introduces Lucile Jones and her writing. Two stories by Lucile Jones (pp. 43–53) are published in the same issue of *Obsidian*. Paul Lehman's "The Development of a Black Psyche: An Interview with John Oliver Killens" (*BALF* 11:83–89) supports the idea that people throughout the world, based on their cultural and historic backgrounds, have different psyches. Killens discusses his novels as a part of his discussion of the black psyche. Toni Morrison was working on *Song of Solomon* at the time of her interview with Robert Stepto. The interview, " 'Intimate Things in Place': A Conversation with Toni Morrison" (*MR* 18:473–89), tells about Morrison's sense of place, her concern with good and evil, her interpretation of male-female relationships, and a good deal about her novels—*The Bluest Eye*, *Sula*, and the novel on which she was working. Stepto's questions are good ones.

University of Colorado

20. Themes, Topics, Criticism

Michael J. Hoffman

After half a decade of writing this chapter for *ALS* and of reading all the books needed to prepare it, I have come to appreciate the wide variety of intellectual disciplines involved in the practice of literary criticism, history, and theory. Of all the scholarly assignments I have undertaken, none has offered me a better education than the continuing challenge of this one; nor has any been so continuous a source of enjoyment.

The year 1977 saw a very high level of activity in American literature, particularly in the publication of general overviews of that field. Of the many books published, however, only a few were works of genuine distinction. Nonetheless, only a few were so negligible as to be unrewarding. About some of those I have decided that the best mercy is silence.

In the more general areas of literary activity, 1977 seems to have been a less active year than some in the recent past. Most of the fine books to have appeared were translations of European classics in what we are now coming to call the "new" criticism, as distinguished from the late American version of the New Criticism.

i. American Literature

a. Literary History. I think it is fitting to open a section on literary history with a collection by the dean of American literary historians, Robert E. Spiller: *Milestones in American Literary History* (Westport, Conn.: Greenwood Press). This is a collection of some 31 reviews of books done by Spiller throughout part of his long career, from 1922 to 1960. (Another collection could surely be done of books he has reviewed since that time.) The book has been edited by Robert Walker, but the reviews to be included were chosen by Spiller himself and printed with a short note before each review to set its context.

The reviews are mostly of books that have since become known as important works in the field, such as Brooks's *The Flowering of New England*, Cowley's *Exile's Return*, Gabriel's *The Course of American Democratic Thought*, and Matthiessen's *American Renaissance* (two reviews of it). In all of these reviews there is a shock of recognition that renders them fascinating historical documents as well as testimonies to the commitment that Spiller gave to the developing study of American literature. There are also five essays relating to the *Literary History of the United States* and *The Cycle of American Literature* which provide further evidence as to how those two related books were put together. Spiller's writing is, as one would expect, always lucid and to the point.

A comprehensive study of American poetry is Emily Stipes Watts's *The Poetry of American Women*, to my knowledge the only book that surveys American women poets so comprehensively. Watts begins with Anne Bradstreet and ends with Muriel Rukeyser, and one realizes that another good-sized volume could now be written about the American women poets who have emerged since 1945. While Watts does not try to prove that American women write verse in a unique fashion, she does claim that "American women poets have developed their own themes, prosodic techniques, types of poems, and particular images" (xv). Since most studies of American poetry are predominantly about men, they do not give much place to more than a few women poets. This book intends to rectify that omission.

While I like the book, I am not convinced that the subject matter and techniques of American women poets are much different from those of their male counterparts. Nonetheless, most of the individual chapters are well done, and the book is useful as a reference work. The writing is clear, the scholarship solid. Critically, the book is derivative, however, and the capsule summaries of most of the poets need to be supplemented elsewhere.

One of the ambitious attempts of 1977 is *The American Idea* by Everett Carter. This is a well-written attempt to restate the Parringtonian vision of American culture that has "been submerged under the negations of a 'modernism' that has become the orthodox position toward the arts" (3). While Carter has clearly experienced the culture of Modernism himself, he nonetheless states his intention to write a deliberately old-fashioned book in order to define what he calls the "American Idea." The American idea, according to the author, has primarily two attributes: (1) an unfailing belief in progress, which includes a "rejection of the past, its acceptance of the present, its hopes for the future"; (2) "the basis for these hopes: a belief in the value of man and in his fundamental virtue" (5).

The introductory chapter on Colonial literature presents the historical development well, although its context is thinner than elsewhere in the book. The meat of Carter's exposition lies in his discussions of the major 19th-century authors, all of whom are discussed at length except for Emily Dickinson, perhaps because she does not fit easily into the thesis. Most of the discussions are full ones, although I find the patterning to be a bit repetitious. I was less convinced by the book as I read on in it, although I do think it an important study that has long needed doing. I am disturbed, I must confess, by what I feel is a tone of bland, almost dogmatic self-assurance, as well as what seems to be a willingness to subsume all evidence to fit the author's thesis. The possibility that many 19th-century writers could be complex enough to fit both Carter's thesis and its antithesis is rarely acknowledged. Still, this book represents the definitive treatment of its subject and will have to be dealt with seriously by all future writers on the same subject.

Another definitive treatment of its subject—this one being my choice as the best book of 1977 on an American literary topic—is Ann Douglas, *The Feminization of American Culture* (New York: Knopf). This is a marvelous work, well written, thoughtful, and erudite. Douglas is a fine scholar who has planned and constructed her book carefully and offers many fresh insights into 19th-century American culture. Her general thesis is that a dual "disestablishment" took place during the early 19th century, which involved, on the one hand, a reduction of the clergy in its function from an active, politically conscious role to that of being simply the moral and emotional shepherds of their flocks; on the other, a reduction in the status of women from the productive roles they played in colonial days to the passive consumerism of the 19th century, a consumerism that is now a main basis of American culture and society. Douglas examines both the development of this disestablishment and also the pervasive ways it influenced 19th-century American culture.

Douglas traces the "feminization" of America through the areas of theology, history, death, the press, motherhood, and the development of a new reading public. She writes fascinating case studies of Margaret Fuller and Herman Melville as two failed rebels against this growing feminization. This is a wise book, I think, and one that has a great deal to teach all of us who deal with American literature.

Two books were published in 1977 that are primarily concerned with 19th-century American autobiography. Mutlu Konuk Blasing in *The Art of Life* is less interested in formal autobiography than in the autobiographical impulse that governs such works as *Walden*, *Song of Myself*, Henry James's Prefaces, and Henry Adams's *Education*. Blasing extends her analysis into our own century to such works as *Paterson* and Frank O'Hara's poetry. In Blasing's pragmatic definition, "'autobiographical' refers to works in which the hero, narrator, and author can be identified by the same name" (p. xi). She develops this definition further by stressing that autobiography exemplifies in three ways the interaction of form and history: (1) "the subject of autobiographical writing is the self becoming conscious of itself in and as history" (p. xiv); (2) "the inclusive form of autobiography embodies the interaction of history and consciousness" (p. xiv); (3) "style is not only self-expressive but has a historical function as well . . . it is style that makes the 'I' an 'I'—a continuous, publicly enduring entity" (p. xv). Blasing's critical method is strongly influenced by French thinkers such as Starobinski and Barthes, and her use of some of the jargon of the French school makes that influence seem to be not always well assimilated. As a result, the introduction—which is the best chapter in the book—contains a number of good ideas, but because they are often ponderously presented it is sometimes difficult to separate the important ones from the unimportant.

Still, my overall assessment is positive. The book's basic idea works, and individual chapters—particularly the ones on Whitman and James—develop a number of excellent insights. In fact, the very idea of treating James's Prefaces as autobiographical documents is a fascinating new way of opening up these much-discussed writings.

Thomas Cooley's *Educated Lives* studies the new form that American autobiography took at the end of the 19th century. It focuses on such major figures as Henry Adams, Mark Twain, W. D. Howells, and Henry James, with shorter chapters on three 20th-century figures—Lincoln Steffens, Sherwood Anderson, and Gertrude Stein. The thesis is that autobiographies are "modes of self-expression that take their narrative contours from their authors' preconceptions of the fallen self" (pp. ix–x). The opening chapter presents a brief theory of autobiography, showing how it changed in American letters as the 19th-century concept of human psychology moved from the "faculty" theory (McCosh) to a more behaviorist one (William James). While not as imaginative as the book by Blasing, Cooley's is a more solid performance, each of its chapters based on good scholarship and written in clear, straightforward prose. The chapter on Gertrude Stein, for instance, is excellent, judging the lesser-known *Everybody's Autobiography* to be a more significant contribution to the genre than the famous *Autobiography of Alice B. Toklas.*

Moving into the 20th century, we find a biography of an eminent literary historian, James Hoopes's *Van Wyck Brooks: In Search of American Culture* (Amherst: Univ. of Mass. Press). Hoopes states his "agreement with Brooks on two fundamental points: (1) that the United States did not have in his time (and still lacks in ours) a culture adequate to its needs and (2) that such a culture must not be genteelly removed from, or merely reflective of social reality, but rather, critically engaged with it" (pp. xi–xii). The author has had access to Brooks's papers and cooperation from his widow and children. There are no real biographical surprises here; nor in fact is the biography itself very interesting as a life. Hoopes does provide the reader, however, with some insights into how Brooks's ideas developed and were presented within the context of his life and times. This is a decently written, moderately frank book which suffers a bit from its overly respectful tone, but it is a good summary of Brooks's essential ideas.

One of the more exciting books of the year is from the pen of an even greater man of letters, Edmund Wilson, *Letters on Literature and Politics: 1912–1972*, selected and edited by Elena Wilson (New York: Farrar, Straus, and Giroux). The book contains an excellent introduction by Daniel Aaron and has been adequately edited by the author's widow. The letters themselves are organized by decades, although not on the strictest chronology. Mrs. Wilson interposes quotations from some of Wilson's books to lend greater context to the letters. Each section (or decade) is headed by a chronology. The footnoting is unfortunately minimal, perhaps to reduce the length of this substantial volume. One wishes for more information, however. Nonetheless, the letters are marvelous. Wilson's austere sense of literary commitment and integrity appear everywhere, and his prose is, as always, measured and utterly lucid. These are not, by and large, terribly personal documents, but they do provide a literary history of the age, since Wilson knew everyone, corresponded with most of the leading literary figures of his times, and read everything. One can dip into this book anywhere and lose oneself almost instantly. A literary event. I hope that a fuller, more complete edition will someday be forthcoming.

Brief mention must go to Robert M. Crunden's *The Superfluous Men: Conservative Critics of American Culture, 1900–1945* (Austin: Univ. of Tex. Press), a collection of writings by leading American conservatives of the first half of this century. Included are writings by such well-known figures as Walter Lippmann, George Santayana, Irving Babbitt, H. L. Mencken, and Allen Tate, arranged topically. This is a good collection, far ranging and carefully chosen to give a full, sympathetic sense of the quality of conservative thought. Crunden's introduction is useful. Overall, this is a good survey of the field.

The Damned and the Beautiful: American Youth in the 1920s (New York: Oxford), by Paula S. Fass, is a historical study of the 1920s that will be useful to the literary scholar and teacher of that period. A study of the mores of youth in that legendary decade, the book is historical in its approach and sociological in its method. Fass focuses on how the young of that period became socialized, on how they adapted to the furious changes demanded of them by their environment. There are good chapters on such topics as the family, sexual mores, cultural politics, and "symbols of liberation." The sections that have to do with literary matters are well done, although literature in this book is examined primarily for its documentary value. While Fass's sociological bent occasionally involves her in prolixity and jargon, the book is, as a whole, readable and extremely informative.

The thirties are the subject of the next three books. The first is by Charles R. Hearn, *The American Dream in the Great Depression* (Westport, Conn.: Greenwood), a study of how the American dream survived its collision with the economic realities of the Great Depression. The study is based on many diverse sources, "including how-to-succeed guidebooks and inspirational works, fiction and nonfiction from popular magazines, sociological studies, gangster, tough-guy, and proletarian novels, and the drama and fiction of major writers" (p. ix). Hearn begins by establishing his version of what the American Dream stands for, then traces some of the history of that persistent image, especially of how it functioned in the 1920s, "in a period of prosperity." The remainder of the book describes how the various social realities of the Great Depression challenged the optimism of that dream and called its viability into question. Hearn is excellent in demonstrating how the image of the dream functioned as both a fantasy and a ritual, as well as a delusion, and how for some writers it became a nightmare. This is a solidly researched book in the classic American Studies mode.

Charles A. Jellison's *Tomatoes Were Cheaper: Tales from the Thirties* (Syracuse: Syracuse Univ. Press) is a kind of anecdotal history. Jellison has written in semifictional form a story to represent each year of the 1930s. The stories are historically based and run a gamut of different types of historical event ranging from the disappearance of Judge Crater to a sketch about Paul and Dizzy Dean with the 1934 St. Louis Cardinals. Jellison's intention is to give the reader the flavor of the decade, and in this intention he succeeds admirably. The stories are well written, historically accurate, and fun to read. This is a good book for introducing students to the period, and it is a pleasure even for those more knowledgeable about the time.

The Federal Writers' Project: A Study in Government Patronage of the Arts (Urbana: Univ. of Ill. Press) is Monty Noam Penkower's history of the Federal Writers' Project. It is a straightforward, detailed work, full of much carefully garnered fact. Although the book is not long, it gives the impression of being encyclopedic, and it is more a book to be dipped into than one to be read from beginning to end. The style is clear, but the heavy use of detail slows down the narrative. For a comprehensive overview of the Writers' Project this is not as good a book as Jerre Mangione's *The Dream and the Deal* (1972). Penkower focuses mainly on the years 1937–39, however, the time when the bulk of the American Guide Series was written, and he has interviewed a number of the surviving writers who took part in the Project.

One of the first comprehensive overviews of the 1960s appeared in 1977, Morris Dickstein's *Gates of Eden: American Culture in the Sixties* (New York: Basic Books). This is a well-written book, composed in a tone of personal concern and commitment that reflects an attitude of moral questioning. Dickstein is concerned with the values represented by cultural events and artifacts. I found the book absorbing to read throughout, although I also found myself disagreeing with much of what Dickstein concludes about the decade. I think finally that the book is an interesting failure, but not a negligible one.

The author offers some good insights into the 1950s and the transition from that decade to the next. He also has a number of intelligent perceptions about the "new journalism," although he tends to undervalue the contributions to that genre by Truman Capote and Tom Wolfe and the achievement of Norman Mailer as a spokesman for the culture of the 1960s. When Dickstein presents an analysis of rock culture he is not convincing. Although he did live through the period, he was not really part of that culture's temperament. It is in the latter part of the book, where he turns almost exclusively to literary analysis, that he is most convincing. One has the sense that Dickstein sees himself as a young Lionel Trilling, an erudite, sophisticated, and graceful moralist who also swings. He may yet become such a critic, but, ironically, the book would have been even better had it been more freely confessional and personal. When he plays the role of confessee, Dickstein exercises too much restraint.

***b.* Fiction.** Four interesting books were published about American fiction during 1977, two of them focusing on the 19th century and two of them on the development of the "non-fiction novel" in the 1960s. In *The Middle Way* Michael T. Gilmore develops the thesis that the Puritan theory of "the ideal of the middle way" was the controlling force that underlay the American prose romance of the 19th century. His Introduction establishes this point clearly, and he continues in a chapter called "The Puritans" to develop the concept of the middle way convincingly to show how it developed in Puritan society. In "Mather and Franklin" Gilmore explores the tension that underlay the search for a middle way, showing Mather to be a strong defender of the Puritan tradition at the end of its major thrust and Franklin to be a deracinated Puritan who drops the theology but maintains the work ethic.

Once these poles are established, Gilmore uses the tensions of the middle way as a metaphor for what goes on in Hawthorne, Melville, and James. He is best on Hawthorne, less convincing on Melville, and not as original on James, who seems almost too easy a mark for this kind of treatment. On the whole, however, this is a fresh and provocative book, a well-written contribution to the theory of American fiction.

Perhaps an even better book is William C. Spengemann's *The Adventurous Muse*, which attacks 19th-century American fiction from quite a different perspective. Spengemann divides the fictional poetics into two streams, the "poetics of adventure" and the "poetics of domesticity." The former arises from the long tradition of travel writing that extends back at least to the time of Columbus. The poetics of domesticity stems from a more recent tradition, that of the domestic novel in English and American fiction. Its subcategories include the sentimental, picaresque, gothic, historical, and adventure novels. The history of the 19th-century American novel is a dialectic in which these two traditions interact dynamically. In two long opening chapters Spengemann explores each of these traditions in leisurely depth. He applies his categories critically to Royall Tyler's *The Algerine Captive* and Poe's *The Narrative of Arthur Gordon Pym*, then composes chapters on Hawthorne, Melville, Twain, and James. All the chapters are good, but the one on Hawthorne is particularly so. Spengemann sees James as the culmination of the dialectic because his work embodies strongly both traditions in a unique amalgam. This book may well turn out to be a major contribution to the theory of American fiction.

John Hollowell's *Fact and Fiction: The New Journalism* (Chapel Hill: Univ. of N.C. Press) attempts to describe and define a new fictional genre, that of the nonfiction novel as it evolved in the 1960s. This is a solid, well-written piece of scholarship that contains a number of valid insights into the culture of the decade, although it does not really attempt to make a contribution to theory. It has a series of general chapters that establish a good overview which are followed by long chapters on Capote, Mailer, and Tom Wolfe. While not a speculative book, *Fact and Fiction* does chronicle the history of the new phenomenon and contributes a number of solid readings of works such as *In Cold Blood, The Armies of the Night*, and *The Electric Kool-Aid Acid Test*.

A more serious attempt to develop a theoretical structure for dealing with the same set of works is Mas'ud Zavarzadeh, *The Mythopoeic Reality: The Postwar American Nonfiction Novel* (Urbana: Univ. of Ill. Press). Zavarzadeh studies these new forms (including most of the same writers as Hollowell) by dividing them into categories that fit an elaborate theoretical structure based on the assumption that contemporary reality outstrips anything the so-called fictional mind can imagine. Writers who wish to deal directly with our age, according to Zavarzadeh, must find a form capable of containing contemporary "reality." For him, the three major modes of the nonfiction novel are the Exegetical Nonfiction Novel, the Testimonial Nonfiction Novel, and the Notational Nonfiction Novel. The first is represented by *In Cold Blood*, the second by *The Electric Kool-Aid Acid Test*, and the third by Oscar Lewis's *La Vida*.

Zavarzadeh has an inordinate fondness for jargon, using words like "narratology," "metatheorem," and "fictuality," to name just a few. Occasionally his puns work, as in his notion of "faction." Most of the time, however, the language grates and seems like warmed-over French critical verbiage. Still, the book is worth wading through because it has many stimulating things to say and it demonstrates the author's surprisingly deep understanding of the contemporary scene. While I disagree with Zavarzadeh's feeling that there is an important difference between the "real" facts and persons used in a nonfiction work and the same facts and characters if they were simply "made up," I do find that *The Mythopoeic Reality* makes a major step toward defining the outlines of a theory adequate for dealing with a major new genre.

***c.* The South.** The subject of the American South brought forth in 1977 four books of interest to students of American literature. Limited mention should go to Robert B. Downs's *Books That Changed the South* (Chapel Hill: Univ. of N.C. Press), a book that contains the author's summaries of 25 "seminal books [that] have played key roles in shaping the South as it exists in the twentieth century" (p. xiii). The books selected are presented in chronological order and range from Captain John Smith's *Generall Historie of Virginia, New-England, and the Summer Isles* through Mark Twain's *Life on the Mississippi* to C. Vann Woodward's *Origins of the New South: 1877–1913*. Each chapter puts the book into a historical context, summarizes its contents, says something about the author, and tries to measure the book's influence on the South. The criteria for inclusion seem not to be too rigid, however, and I do not understand how such a volume can exclude *Uncle Tom's Cabin.*

Carl N. Degler's *Place Over Time: The Continuity of Southern Distinctiveness* (Baton Rouge: La. State Univ. Press) was first given as the Walter Lynwood Fleming Lectures in Southern History at

L.S.U. Degler writes as a northerner, and certainly not as an apologist for the region. He has a love of the South, however, and he writes out of that love and a lifetime of scholarship. It is his theory that the South does not have a distinctive culture, but he does believe that there are certain southern regional characteristics that are genuinely distinctive (but which do not add up to a separate civilization). These characteristics have a historical basis, stemming from the fact that the South was the primary slaveholding area of the country, that its economy was deeply dependent on that institution, and that the South worked to justify its maintenance of slavery even to the point of civil war. While a basically conservative book, this is a well-written, thoughtful, and convincing work, worth the time of any reader with an interest in the South or in southern writing.

C. Hugh Holman's *The Immoderate Past: The Southern Writer and History* (Athens: Univ. of Ga. Press) was also given as a series of lectures, the 1976 Lamar Lectures at Wesleyan College. Although another brief book, this one is also a genuine contribution to the study of southern literature. Holman writes about the South's obsession with history, and his main subject is the way in which Southern writers have used the historical novel "to create serious exempla for their readers" (p. 12). He focuses on three principal areas: "How writers before the Civil War used the classic form of the historical novel as Scott developed it to show how, during the American Revolution, the region contributed essentially to the making of the nation. How writers, emphasizing the novel of manners aspect of the realistic movement, set out to describe and define the texture and quality of the life of past ages. And, finally, how novelists have utilized modern experimental techniques to explore the problems of the historical South and the guilt we all inherit from our past" (p. 12). This well-written, balanced book is convincing in its treatment of all three of these areas.

Richard Gray, in a major work entitled *The Literature of Memory: Modern Writers of the American South* (Baltimore: Johns Hopkins Univ. Press), attempts to write the definitive statement about contemporary southern literature. This is basically a critical history of that literature written by an Englishman who brings an intelligent outsider's perspective to his subject. Gray believes in a Hegelian theory of history which believes that history produces its most interesting literature in a situation of dialectic, conflict, and tension. After the First World War southern writers had to come to terms with their distinctive regionalism in a time of unprecedented social, economic, and cultural change. It was this tension that produced the major body of work which came forth from such figures as Wolfe, Tate, Warren, Caldwell, Faulkner, Styron, and Welty, to name but a few writers Gray treats. (Faulkner gets a whole long chapter that is a first-rate summary of his work and its importance.) Gray concludes with a long discussion of Styron's *Confessions of Nat Turner*, which attempts to show how that much-maligned novel fits in with the best and strongest 20th-century southern traditions as found in the work of Faulkner. In my opinion, *The Literature of Memory* establishes itself immediately as the leading overview of 20th-century southern literature.

***d.* Cultural Studies.** Three books comprise this section. The first is a collection edited by Luther S. Luedtke, *The Study of American Culture: Contemporary Conflicts* (Deland, Fla.: Everett/Edwards), which consists of essays contributed by a number of important figures in American Studies. All but two of the essays were given at or in response to lectures presented at the American Studies Institute at the University of Southern California in 1973. But this book is better than most such "proceedings." It provides both those inside the discipline and those outside it with a substantial overview of the best thinking in that field. The essays range from the more traditional approaches of Daniel Aaron and Roderick Nash to popular culture (John G. Cawelti) to an attempt to find a new rationale for the discipline (Jay Mechling) to an attempt to put the study of American culture to the uses of revolution (Robert Meredith). The collection provides an up-to-date indication of where American Studies finds itself at the moment.

Martin Green is an Englishman who teaches at Tufts and has lived many years in the United States. His *Transatlantic Patterns: Cultural Comparisons of England with America* (New York: Basic Books) is a collection of essays that compare the two cultures in terms of such institutions and characteristics as marriage, eroticism, humor, detective fiction, Marxism, and Freudianism. Green is not much of a theorist, but his essays are studded with good insights that arise from his fine sensibility rather than from any systematic approach to the comparative study of culture. Green focuses largely on literary matters, and mostly on British writers. The book is well written but not terribly memorable. It does not live up to the promise of its title.

Dexter Fisher has edited a proceedings entitled *Minority Language and Literature: Retrospective and Perspective* (New York: Modern Language Association). All the papers published in this slim volume were first solicited by the MLA's Commission on Minority Groups and the Study of Language and Literature and were presented at a national symposium on minority literature held in New York City in November 1976. The major theme of the collection is the relationship of minority literature to the American literary mainstream. Since the study of ethnic literatures has become a major new field in American colleges and universities, these essays are important insofar as they summarize the fields as they now exist and set the stage for further study. The pieces here are not terribly innovative and they vary in quality. The best essays are on Chicano literature, but there are also good pieces of a more general nature by Walter J. Ong and the late Michel Benamou.

***e.* The Media and Popular Culture.** A number of interesting books dealt with various aspects of the media and popular culture, indicating that studies in those fields are becoming increasingly sophisticated. In *The American Monomyth* (Garden City, N.Y.: Doubleday) Robert Jewett and John Shelton Lawrence present the thesis that there is a basic American myth underlying most of our popular culture about a superhero who rescues society in its time of distress. While this is not so terribly new an idea, Jewett and Lawrence make an interesting case about the ways in which recent productions of the mass media give dramatic presence to this myth.

The myth itself has a number of varieties about which the authors go into some detail, each of the varieties being embodied in a particular type of story told in television, films, and popular magazines. The myth is often parodied in some of the most successful of the tales, such as in the recent film *Star Wars* (which was released too late to be treated in this book). The authors do examine such elements of popular culture as the movies *Death Wish* and *Jaws* (the first version), Walt Disney, *Playboy*, the television show *Little House on the Prairie*, and *Zap Comics*. Although mythic in their approach, the authors are neither heavily Jungian nor Structuralist. This fine book —while not reactionary—nonetheless does not accept the liberal belief that the subject matter of the media has no lasting effect on human consciousness and behavior.

Jeremy Tunstall's *The Media Are American: Anglo-American Media in the World* (New York: Columbia Univ. Press) is a more sober scholarly survey of the development and influence of the Anglo-American mass media. For the author the model, all-inclusive medium is the daily newspaper. Only recently has television been able to duplicate in one package all the various kinds of things the newspaper has to offer. Tunstall tries to show the ways in which the American mass media have had a profound political and sociological influence around the world. His concern is not with the individual response but with the larger response of a political entity or society. Tunstall's orientation is Marxist and sociological, and the book is laden with carefully chosen facts. Its research base is excellent and it contains a number of highly useful tables showing how frequently, for instance, American television programs are being replayed in various countries around the world. The writing is unfortunately a bit dry.

William H. Read's *America's Mass Media Merchants* (Baltimore: Johns Hopkins Univ. Press) is a study of a somewhat similar kind. The author concentrates on the internationalization of such American mass media as television, films, the United Press, the Associated Press, *Time, Newsweek, The Reader's Digest.* The book is more a survey than a thesis and its author takes no moral position. Rather he suggests simply that the American media have found it profitable to go abroad to sell their wares. Read, nonetheless, is quite aware of how American politics and attitudes have affected other cultures through the exportation of our media software. He also recognizes that the effects of the media are scarcely a matter of indifference. Here in the United States we have come to take the all-pervasive effect of the media for granted. Other countries, however, often resent our encroachments on their cultural sovereignty.

John M. Phelan's *Mediaworld: Programming the Public* (New York: The Seabury Press) is a much livelier book, with a moral tone reminiscent of Daniel Boorstin's *The Image.* For Phelan "mediaworld" refers to a total culture created and manipulated via the mass media. It is his contention that we now live in such a world, that the very consciousness we bring to almost any kind of perception has been shaped by the media in ways we cannot possibly escape.

Phelan was obviously influenced by McLuhan, although his tone is much more full of moral urgency. He feels that McLuhan was wrong in thinking we are becoming a "global village." Mediaworld has, to the contrary, made us all more fragmented and atomistic, isolating us as individual human beings in terms of our moral commitment to community and yet fostering in all of us a kind of one-dimensionalism of values in our roles in a consumer society. Phelan's debt here is to Marcuse, although he does not mention that writer by name. This is a well-written book with a somewhat unconvincing upbeat ending, given the Cassandra-like tone that has dominated it most of the way. The book lacks a bibliography and an index.

The translation of one medium into another is the subject of *The Classic American Novel and the Movies.* Part of the Ungar Film Library, this is a collection of essays written by many different hands about films that have been made from major American novels. Twenty-one of the essays have been written for this volume and have never before been published. Clearly there have been a very large number of films made from classic American novels, a fact that should tell us something of the independence of film as a medium. Most films made from these novels have not been artistically successful; some—like the recent *Great Gatsby*—have been disastrous. The failures have more than outweighed the few successes like *Greed* (based on *McTeague*) or *The Grapes of Wrath.* It seems to take a very special kind of novel—one with a deep sense of the popular mood, like *Gone With the Wind*—to translate well into film. At any rate, the level of the essays in this volume is surprisingly high, and it is an interesting book to dip into. It will be rewarding both to those who love the American novel and those who love American films. It will be doubly rewarding to those who love both.

The best book in this section, however, is John G. Cawelti's *Adventure, Mystery, and Romance: Formula Stories as Art and Popular Culture* (Chicago: Univ. of Chicago Press), a book that should in fact go down as one of the best books of the year on a literary topic. It is a work of genre theory in the classic University of Chicago mode, but it is much more than simply that. Cawelti defines a formula as "a combination or synthesis of a number of specific cultural conventions with a more universal story form or archetype. It is also similar in many ways to the traditional literary conception of a genre" (p. 6). He spends the first few chapters defining the uses and modes of various formulae and then turns to specific forms such as the detective story, the western, and the melodrama. He is especially good on detective stories and has marvelous insights into such writers as Simenon, Chandler, Christie, and Hammett. This well-written, witty book has many important things to say about American culture and the ways in which our literary formulae express our basic cultural needs and aspirations.

ii. General Literary Works

***a.* The Profession.** There are two works in this general category, each of which attempts to address a specific set of circumstances currently faced by our profession. Dorothy K. Bestor deals with the problem of the unemployed M.A. or Ph.D. trained in English in *Aside from Teaching English, What in the World Can You Do?* (Seattle: Univ. of Wash. Press). The great majority of us now established in the profession never considered a career other than college teaching, and many of us went into teaching when there were more jobs than candidates. Now that enrollments have stabilized or are beginning to decline, we are training more Ph.D.'s than can find jobs. Bestor has worked in job placement and has had some success in finding alternative employment for graduate students of English. The abilities most in demand for which literary training is a good background are writing and problem analysis, the ability to do research, and the ability to treat problems in a historical perspective.

This very practical book reflects most of the questions being asked by our unemployed graduates. Should I take a second degree (e.g., in law or business)? For what jobs am I "overqualified"? What kinds of nontraditional teaching positions are available (e.g., teaching English as a second language, scientific writing, children's literature)? What possibilities are there for teaching outside the continental United States? What is the market for Continuing Education? What other kinds of campus positions are available, such as jobs in Student Affairs or administration? Bestor also explores the possibilities outside the academy altogether, such as in editing, the various media, advertising, book publishing, business writing, and working in the various levels of government. There are lots of helpful tips about job sources and publications. The book should be available for easy reference to all of our graduate students.

Walter Kaufmann's *The Future of the Humanities: A New Ap-*

proach to Teaching Art, Religion, Philosophy, Literature and History (New York: Reader's Digest Press) deals with the problem many of us are attempting to face about the future of the humanities in our universities. To readers familiar with Kaufmann's many works on Existentialism, Nietzsche, and Hegel, his polemical tone will not come as a surprise. He is a moralist who is dissatisfied with the way the humanities are now being taught. For Kaufmann we are too scholastic. He wants teachers to be more Socratic. He wants us to be visionary or at least able to respond to the visionary.

For Kaufmann the study of the humanities is a moral enterprise that should be a part of a philosophical and religious education in a spirit of critical inquiry. Students should study foreign languages and learn something of what he calls the ethics of translation. He espouses a commonsense approach to editing in opposition to the current American fetish of "definitive" editions. As this summary may show, Kaufmann has no novel solutions to propose. Perhaps there are none. Nonetheless, the book is worth reading and should make most of its readers give some second thoughts to the way they act as scholars and teachers.

***b.* Composition.** Two books about the teaching of composition are among 1977's stimulating books. In *The Philosophy of Composition* (Chicago: Univ. of Chicago Press), E. D. Hirsch, Jr.—well known for his work in literary interpretation—self-consciously borrows a title from Edgar Allan Poe in a book that attempts to create a philosophical underpinning for teaching composition. Hirsch, when he stepped down as chair of the English Department at the University of Virginia, voluntarily took on the directorship of composition because it was his belief that English departments were not taking seriously what is perhaps their most important function, that of maintaining the literacy of their students. In the course of the practical side of running a freshman composition program, Hirsch brought his habits of scholarship to a study of the linguistic bases for writing as well as for our responses to the written and spoken language. As a result, *The Philosophy of Composition* is not a how-to-do-it handbook but a serious attempt to present the results of research that will lead to better understanding and better teaching of writing.

That Hirsch has maintained an up-to-date understanding of linguistics is indicated by his chapter titles which stress both the primacy of writing over speech and the essential role of the reader as respondent: "Distinctive Features of Written Speech," "The Normative Character of Written Speech," "Progressive Tendencies in the History of Language and of Prose," "Refining the Concept of Readability," "The Psychological Bases of Readability." The final two chapters, "Some Practical Implications" and "The Valid Assessment of Writing Ability," propose a set of practical solutions that seem sensible and pragmatic. Overall, this book is a good example of how scholarly training can be used by a teacher of good will to work on that most unglamorous but necessary of pedagogical areas, the teaching of writing. It is well-written and sensible and of a much higher level than we are accustomed to in a book about this subject.

An even more useful book is Mina P. Shaughnessy, *Errors and Expectations: A Guide for the Teacher of Basic Writing* (Oxford: Oxford Univ. Press), surely the best book on basic writing skills I have ever read. Shaughnessy had to develop her techniques for teaching basic writing at the City University of New York after they adopted their open admissions program. Since most of us teach in institutions that have on some level adopted such a program—certainly American society as a whole now demands that all have access to higher education—this book has much to say of practical value.

The author's common-sense approach deals with writing in categories familiar to everyone. Her chapter titles indicate this but tell little about the sophistication of her approach: "Handwriting and Punctuation," "Syntax," "Common Errors," "Spelling," "Vocabulary," "Beyond the Sentence," Expectations." Every one of these chapters contains new insights into their hackneyed subjects. Shaughnessy has high standards, but she has also taken a hard look at the relevant realities. This well-written book operates on her proven premise that you *can* teach people to write, even supposed "illiterates." It is full of good insights into both writing and teaching, and it should serve in many ways as the best early statement about the transition many professors of literature are now being forced to go through because of the dramatically decreased enrollments in literature courses and the burgeoning enrollments in courses in writing.

c. Major Figures and Collections of Essays. Robert M. Adams's *Bad Mouth: Fugitive Papers on the Dark Side* (Berkeley: Univ. of Calif. Press) is a series of thematically connected essays on various types of negative and hostile uses of language. It was stimulated, no doubt, by changes in the styles of public speech that began to be heard in the 1960s and have continued increasingly during the present decade. Adams's subject is the various ways language can be used beyond its immediate lexical meaning to convey hostility, aggression, gamesmanship, and political tactics. Adams is an accomplished stylist and informal essayist. The book is clever—a bit tongue-in-cheek, yet serious at the same time—mixing rhetoric and personal openness with an ironic tone in such chapters as "Bad Mouth and Other Second Games," "The New Arts of Political Lying," "Dirty Stuff," and "Rags, Garbage, and Fantasy." A minor book, but lots of fun.

A good short monograph on the work of Lionel Trilling is Robert Boyers's *Lionel Trilling: Negative Capability and the Wisdom of Avoidance* (Columbia: Univ. of Mo. Press), an essay on the significance of Trilling's critical vision, rather than a survey of his work. The book focuses on Trilling's theory of tragedy and the influence on his thought of Keats's notion of negative capability. Boyers examines closely only a few of Trilling's writings in order to distill the essence of his vision, primarily his story "Of This Time, Of That Place," his essay on *The Princess Casamassima*, his essay on Keats, and his story "The Other Margaret." Trilling is presented in this book as a restrained moral humanist, and although Boyers seems genuinely to admire Trilling, he does betray ambivalence about some of the values Trilling stood for. I wish he had followed this ambivalence a bit farther and dealt with some of the harsh criticism —justified or not—that has been made of Trilling recently by more radical critics.

The prolific Denis Donoghue is author of a collection of essays entitled *The Sovereign Ghost: Studies in Imagination* (Berkeley: Univ. of Calif. Press) unified primarily by their common concern with the "poetic imagination." The essays range widely, from critical theory in "The Essential Power" and "The Sovereign Ghost," to more practical criticism in "Nuances of a Theme by Allen Tate," to the following-out of an American cultural and literary theme in "The American Style of Failure." While the book is pleasant to read, well written, graceful, and erudite, it offers less in the way of theory than it does in the way of exposure to a fine literary mind and sensibility.

A collection of Simon O. Lesser's essays has been prepared by Robert Sprich and Richard W. Nolan in *The Whispered Meanings:*

Selected Essays of Simon O. Lesser (Amherst: Univ. of Mass. Press). *Fiction and the Unconscious* is the work for which Lesser is best known, and he is considered one of the leading American Freudian literary critics. The essays in this collection are primarily applications of Lesser's theory of ego psychology to major works of literature; they extend the theory the author developed in *Fiction and the Unconscious.* Some of the works about which Lesser writes are *Hamlet, Macbeth, The Trial,* "My Kinsman, Major Molineux," "Sailing to Byzantium," and *The Idiot.* The writing is surprisingly restrained in its use of psychoanalytic jargon. A useful introduction by the editors places Lesser's work within the context of the history of Freudian literary criticism.

Another prolific author, Father Walter J. Ong, has a new collection of essays called *Interfaces of the Word: Studies in the Evolution of Consciousness and Culture* (Ithaca: Cornell Univ. Press), all of them written in the 1970s. Along with such critics as Marshall McLuhan, Ong has long been interested in the theory of communication. For him the roots of communication lie in an oral tradition, but he is also concerned with the various media and the contexts within which works of art are received by the perceiving public. For Ong literary perception is a transaction, and the reader's response as well as the surrounding contexts of presentation must all be taken into account. He is a polymath whose subjects are as various as the reader's response to literature, "The Poem as a Closed Field," "Voice and the Opening of Closed Systems," and "Media Transformation." There is variety and penetration to his intellect, and he is well informed about all sorts of things. This is a very learned book.

***d.* Theory of Fiction.** I begin this section with *Towards a Poetics of Fiction*, edited by Mark Spilka (Bloomington: Ind. Univ. Press), a collection of essays chosen from *Novel: A Forum on Fiction*, all of them published between 1967 and 1976. Contributors include such well-known critics as Wayne Booth, Leo Bersani, Frank Kermode, Robert Scholes, Ian Watt, and Raymond Williams. The general level of individual essays is high, as readers of the journal would expect. Looking over the essays as a group, however, does not convince one that a new poetics of fiction has yet emerged. Organized into the following categories—"Towards a Poetics of Fiction," "Second Thoughts on Theory," "Reappraisals," "Biography and Theory," "History and

Culture," and "Language and Style"—the essays seem disparate; the collection lacks a certain coherence.

Alan Spiegel's *Fiction and the Camera Eye: Visual Consciousness in Film and the Modern Novel* (Charlottesville: Univ. Press of Va., 1976) studies the influence of photography and especially cinematography on the forms of fiction from the mid-19th century to the present. The book begins by examining how photography helped shape the form of Flaubert's novels. It moves through a brief consideration of other figures from the late 19th- and early 20th-century realists and naturalists, spends some time on Proust, then studies the work of Joyce as premier exemplar of the influence of photography, both still and moving, on the novel. This is the most fully documented study yet produced of how Joyce was influenced by and made extensive use of cinematic techniques, particularly in *Ulysses.* Any Joyce enthusiast—indeed, any enthusiast about the novel—will find these pages fascinating. American authors that Spiegel treats include Dos Passos, Faulkner, and Barth. The book would have benefited from a careful consideration of the work of Thomas Pynchon, whose *Gravity's Rainbow* (1973) makes the most extensive use of cinematic techniques and references of any novel I know.

***e.* Science Fiction.** This is a field whose importance in literary study grows larger each year. Two 1977 books deserve some mention. A high-level handbook to introduce both students and scholars to the field has been produced by Robert Scholes and Eric S. Rabkin in *Science Fiction: History, Science, Vision* (New York: Oxford). The book begins with an extended history of science fiction in literature which the authors claim grew out of humanity's need for an explanatory myth in order to deal with its sense of wonder. It then turns to the various sciences used in science fiction stories, after which it treats the forms and themes found in such stories. The final chapter includes brief discussions of ten major science fiction novels from throughout the tradition, from Mary Shelley's *Frankenstein* (1818) to John Brunner's *The Shockwave Rider* (1976). This is a literate, well-written book that surveys the field and is an ideal supplementary text for courses in the subject.

Thomas D. Clareson has edited a collection entitled *Many Futures, Many Worlds: Theme and Form in Science Fiction* (Kent, O.: The Kent State Univ. Press), which attempts to establish a variety of philosophical and critical perspectives for studying science fiction. All the essays are general in nature and are not by well-known writers, but they bring together much of the better thought in this relatively new field of study. Not as good perhaps as a text for courses in science fiction, *Many Futures, Many Worlds* is still a substantial book for someone to turn to who wants to know more about where the field is heading.

***f.* Modernism.** Matei Calinescu's *Faces of Modernity: Avant-Garde, Decadence, Kitsch* (Bloomington: Ind. Univ. Press) is one of the more interesting recent works on the subject of Modernism. The book attempts to define the concept of "the modern" through the key terms in its subtitle. Calinescu studies the literary history of each of these words since the Renaissance (in the case of Modernism) and since the 19th century (in the case of the others). It is the best discussion I have read of how the concept of modernism developed historically. Calinescu carefully distinguishes between "modernism" and "modernity" as ideas. He also draws careful distinction between the "modern" and the "contemporary" and between the concepts of "modernism" and "post-modernism." All of this is done sensibly with both ideological savvy and poetic sensibility (the author is in fact a poet). The discussion of the avant-garde is good, although Renato Poggioli remains the authority here, and the discussion of decadence is excellent. I was a bit disappointed in the discussion of kitsch. All in all, however, this is a very stimulating book which should provide much material for future critics and scholars.

Another stimulating discussion of Modernism appears in a collection of essays by David Lodge called *The Modes of Modern Writing: Metaphor, Metonymy, and the Typology of Modern Literature* (Ithaca: Cornell Univ. Press). The book's first part consists of a set of essays designed to demonstrate that "we need a comprehensive typology of literary discourse—that is, one capable of describing and discriminating between all types of text without prejudging them" (p. ix). In part 2 Lodge attempts to use Roman Jakobson's distinction between metaphor and metonymy as one of the ways such a typology might be developed. The third part applies Lodge's theories to a critical reading of a number of Modernist writers or schools of writers. The book does have a kind of coherence, although most of its individual parts are discrete. Lodge has a deep understanding of 20th-century fiction that comes through very well, particularly in his readings of individual authors.

A disappointing book is Stanley Sultan, *"Ulysses," "The Waste Land," and Modernism* (Port Washington, N.Y.: Kennikat Press). Author of one of the more interesting books on *Ulysses*, Sultan has little new to say about either of the works in his title. This short book is a descriptive rather than a theoretical study, focusing mostly on *The Waste Land.* The author also stresses heavily the catalytic agency of Ezra Pound on both Joyce and Eliot. At the end of the book he attempts to develop a theory of modernism, but it does not really add anything to what we already know about the subject.

g. Miscellaneous. A very useful book is *Phenomenology and Literature* (West Lafayette, Ind.: Purdue Univ. Press) by Robert R. Magliola. It is an attempt to explain for American readers the phenomenological schools of criticism of both Geneva and Heidegger. Magliola is thoroughly versed in the writings of Husserl as well as the various proponents of what is loosely called the Geneva School. He explains the various programs well and offers his own critical assessments of their validity. He has a good chapter on the confrontation between phenomenological criticism and Parisian Structuralism.

The second half of the book explores the applicability of Phenomenology to literary theory, with chapters on E. D. Hirsch and Husserl, Roman Ingarden, Mikel Dufrenne, and a study of the Heideggerian theory of meaning. As a whole, the book does a good job of demystifying a way of looking at the world that has its primacy in both the intentionality of the literary object and in the consciousness of the artistic perceiver. It is both a good survey of the field and a useful introduction for sophisticated beginners.

In Robert Weimann, *Structure and Society in Literary History: Studies in the History and Theory of Historical Criticism* (Charlottesville: Univ. Press of Va.), we have the attempt of a Marxist scholar to develop a new theory of literary history. Although the book is a collection of essays, it does cohere. Weimann spends a great deal of time trying to redefine a concept of tradition which he says is a way of relating the genesis of a work of art to the social function of literature. Weimann's method of reasoning is dialectic, his style heavily Germanic. An interesting section of the book contains his attempt to absorb structuralist theories into his historical methodology. Especially interesting to readers of *ALS* is a long section called "Past Origins and Present Functions in American Literary History."

A book that I found quite disappointing was Raymond Williams's *Marxism and Literature* (Oxford: Oxford). Written as a kind of sophisticated handbook to introduce students to Marxist literary theory, this book does touch all the right bases in a theory of Marxist thought. It manages to clarify certain issues, but it is written in a pedestrian fashion that is disappointing from an author who is normally so exciting to read.

A much more interesting book is by Theodore Ziolkowski: *Disenchanted Images: A Literary Iconology* (Princeton: Princeton Univ. Press), a study of the use of supernatural images in literature and throughout literary history. Ziolkowski defines an iconic image as follows: "An iconic image in literature, then, can function as theme, motif, or symbol depending upon the circumstances. To the extent that the image is tied to a specific figure whose story it constitutively defines, the image functions as theme. To the extent that the image supplies merely one element of a larger action or situation, it functions as motif. And to the extent that the image signifies something other than itself, it functions as symbol" (pp. 14–15). Ziolkowski's strategy is to take three major iconic images, "Venus and the Ring," "The Haunted Portrait," and "The Magic Mirror," and to follow them through four historical stages through which he claims all such images go: (1) the conventional acceptance of magic; (2) rationalization; (3) psychological internalization; (4) ironic usage or parody. "The iconological question that I hope to answer is this; how did these images make their way out of magic into literature and, long after the disappearance of the faith that originally justified their supernatural powers, survive in . . . modern works. . . ?" (p. 17). The process whereby this takes place Ziolkowski calls "disenchantment." To watch the author take one of his images and follow it through the process of disenchantment is a delight that all readers will want to enjoy.

***h.* Linguistics and Structuralism.** Linguistics is coming to be increasingly important in literary criticism because it relates so directly to our present interest in literature as a communication system. A number of works have recently been published that propose linguistic theories of interpretation which often form the basis of structuralist theory. I should like to treat three such works in this section to distinguish them from the more purely "structuralist" works with which I shall deal next.

A name that has become increasingly familiar in recent years is that of Jan Mukařovský, one of the original and most distinguished members of the Prague Linguistic Circle, who died in 1975. Now a collection of his essays on linguistics has been published in English as *The Word and Verbal Art: Selected Essays* by Jan Mukařovský, translated and edited by John Burbank and Peter Steiner (New Haven: Yale Univ. Press), with a short foreword by René Wellek. A second volume, *Structure, Sign, and Function* has also been announced. It is good to have these works in English at last, although much of their subject matter is foreign to the English reader. Since the linguistic essays concentrate so heavily on Czech texts, they don't always translate with relevance. Still, the basic outlines of Mukařovský's work indicate his closeness in emphasis to the work of Roman Jakobson and his influence on Wellek. Those readers who wish to understand more fully the importance of the Prague Linguistic circle to contemporary literary thought would do well to read some of this book.

Mary Louise Pratt's *Toward a Speech Act Theory of Literary Discourse* (Bloomington: Ind. Univ. Press) is a deliberate attempt to use modern linguistics to establish a theory of literary discourse. Pratt states quite early her disagreement with a basic tenet of orthodox Structuralism: "the belief that literature is formally and functionally distinct from other kinds of utterances and the concomitant belief that literature is linguistically autonomous. It then becomes necessary to consider literary discourse in terms of its similarities to our other verbal activities rather than in terms of its differences from them" (p. xii). The bulk of the book is Pratt's attempt to work out a way of talking about "literary utterances in the same terms used to describe other types of utterances" (p. xiii). Her arguments are strong, I think, and her manner of working them out convincing. Particularly interesting in this regard is her long chapter entitled "The 'Poetic Language' Fallacy." I should like to see further work done toward bringing linguistics and literary analysis into a closer, more symbiotic relationship.

R. H. Stacy, in *Defamiliarization in Language and Literature*

(Syracuse: Syracuse Univ. Press), attempts to define for English readers a key term from the Russian linguist and critic Victor Shklovsky, that of *ostranenie* or defamiliarization. Literally, the term means "making strange," and it is Stacy's claim that basic to Shklovsky's theory is "that it is the function of art to make the familiar unfamiliar; that 'art exists to make one feel things, to make the stone *stony*. The purpose of art is to impart the sensations of things as they are perceived and not as they are known' " (p. ix). The intention of the book is to introduce the English-speaking public to a full understanding of Shklovsky's theory of *ostranenie* and also to make it clear how that theory can be applied. In the course of the book Stacy refers to many literatures and writers, from Russian authors, to Proust and Gertrude Stein, to medieval Latin texts. The book is erudite and interesting, although it is not always convincing.

***i.* Structuralism and Post-Structuralism.** A good introductory text that explains the projects of both structuralism and semiotics is Terence Hawkes's *Structuralism and Semiotics* (Berkeley: Univ. of Calif. Press). While not attempting to make an original contribution, this book may well be the best text to introduce the novice to what the "new" criticism is all about. The scholarship is up-to-date and the text is not only well written, it deliberately tries to demystify the difficult. I think Hawkes now supersedes Scholes's excellent introductory text of a few years back. Following exposure to Hawkes, the reader should turn next to Jonathan Culler's excellent *Structuralist Poetics* (see *ALS* 1975, p. 470).

In *Script into Performance: A Structuralist View of Play Production* (Austin: Univ. of Tex. Press) Richard Hornby applies structuralist categories to dramatic productions. Hornby's somewhat loose "structuralist" definition says that "a Structuralist method of interpretation is one that 1. Reveals something hidden; 2. Is intrinsic; 3. Incorporates complexity and ambiguity; 4. Suspends judgment; 5. Is wholistic" (p. 24). His opening section, entitled "Theoretical Discussion," discusses current theories of performance, Aristotle, and various critical methods. His second section applies his theory to Shelley's *The Cenci*, Ibsen's *A Doll House*, and Pinter's *The Homecoming*. In applying Structuralist theory Hornby says we must do the following: "1. Isolate the playscript. 2. Treat it as a space-time complex; 3. Analyze it in detail; 4. Allow for complexity and ambiguity; 5. Find a unifying principle; 6. Test the principle against the text" (p. 114). Although not really a contribution to Structuralist theory, this book is an interesting attempt to make a practical application of it to the theater.

A number of important figures associated with Structuralism and its aftermath were represented by books in 1977. In *Roland Barthes by Roland Barthes*, translated by Richard Howard (New York: Hill and Wang) we have the first English version of a kind of autobiography published by Roland Barthes in 1975. It is similar in structure and style to *The Pleasure of the Text* in its use of fragments or what Barthes has called ideomorphs. Not a continuous story of Barthes's life, it rather probes his various essential characteristics within certain predetermined categories. What we find throughout this short, fascinating book is a continual recurrence by the author to various aspects of his life, such as his childhood and his mother. It is an erotic but not an intimate book, for Barthes keeps us at bay with his predilection for indirect statement and his love of puns. He alludes to many things about himself, but he rarely makes direct statements. Still, one finishes the book with a definite sense of the author that seems authentic and not at all superficial. Certainly anyone interested in this major figure of French structuralism should read this work.

Another book translated into English for the first time is Jacques Derrida's *Of Grammatology*, translated and introduced by Gayatri Chakravorty Spivak (Baltimore: Johns Hopkins Univ. Press), first published in French in 1967. This classic text of French critical and philosophical thought almost defies translation, but Spivak's version is excellent, given Derrida's propensity for punning and jargon, and the Introduction, while lengthy and difficult, does situate Derrida's work, and particularly *Of Grammatology*, within contemporary French and European thought. Rather than try to summarize this very difficult book (I should like to read it one or two more times myself), I shall just state one of its most important and elementary assumptions.

Derrida's thought runs counter to one of the traditions of linguistics in saying that writing rather than speech is basic to language. He focuses on the very act of filling empty pages with words in an effort to get at what is not only basically human in language but what is also constitutive to anything we know as human society.

Derrida's ideas have already achieved some currency in the work of such American critics as Paul De Man, Edward Said, and Joseph Riddell, and they will increasingly be taken seriously as more and more readers confront them first hand. *Of Grammatology* is a sometimes maddening book, to which most American-trained academics will bring furious resistance. Based on Hegel and Nietzsche, the book runs counter to the pragmatic frame of reference in which almost all of us were trained. Still, we must not be so culture bound as to reject out of hand a way of seeing the world and experiencing the written word that is at first foreign to our sensibilities.

Another major figure of contemporary French thought, Michel Foucault, is represented by two books in 1977, only one of which I shall comment on (*Discipline and Punishment* is a brilliant book, but one outside the scope of this essay). *Language, Counter-Memory, Practice: Selected Essays and Interviews by Michel Foucault*, edited and translated by Donald F. Bouchard and Sherry Simon (Ithaca: Cornell Univ. Press) brings together a number of fugitive pieces that are basic to understanding Foucault's concept of the "archaeology of knowledge." Foucault generally chooses as the subject of an essay a historical point at which there is a kind of disjunction between one world view and another. It is about these disjunctions that he writes his history of ideas. The essays and interviews in this book are all occasional pieces, but all are first-rate examples of Foucault's method. The Introduction is helpful in situating Foucault's work, and some of the essays—such as "What is an Author?" and "Nietzsche, Genealogy, History"—are brilliant. Foucault, however, does not write in the discursive fashion to which we are accustomed. He builds by a series of relevant examples, he circles his subject, and then he seals the argument without constructing it dramatically. Still, for the reader not familiar with Foucault's work this volume might provide an easier entrée than some of his full-length books such as *The Order of Things* or *The Archaeology of Knowledge*.

Tzvetan Todorov's *The Poetics of Prose*, translated by Richard Howard (Ithaca: Cornell Univ. Press), was first published in French in 1971. This collection of essays shows Todorov at his most erudite and accessible. Todorov is equally at home writing about English, French, Russian, or Italian subjects. He can treat Henry James or *The Arabian Nights* with equal facility. In addition, he is one of the easiest of the Structuralists for an American reader to encounter, for he uses a traditional discursive style. Todorov is primarily interested in genre theory, poetics, and theory of narrative. The emphasis on the latter two in this book deserves some explanation, for what Todorov means by poetics is not quite what the reader might at first think. In his very useful Foreword, Jonathan Culler provides the following explanation: "We have been accustomed to assume that the purpose of theory is to enrich and illuminate critical practice, to make possible subtler and more accurate interpretations of particular literary works. But poetics asserts that interpretation is not the goal of literary study. Though the interpretation of works may be fascinating and personally fulfilling, the goal of literary study is to understand literature as a human institution, a mode of signification. When poetics studies individual works, it seeks not to interpret them but to discover the structures and conventions of literary discourse which enable them to have the meanings they do" (p. 8). Since so much of contemporary French critical thought reflects the practice Culler describes, I recommend that the reader keep this passage in mind not only when reading Todorov but when reading the work of any number of other critics of the same school.

The Johns Hopkins University Press has begun publishing an annual volume called *Glyph*, the first of which appeared in 1977. This collection of essays contains work that emanates primarily from the work of French critics such as Foucault, Derrida, Deleuze, and others like them. The first volume has essays by such critics as Paul De Man, Jacques Derrida, and John Searle (who replies to Derrida's essay). *Glyph* represents one of the serious attempts to incorporate the new French critical thought into the American academy. The first volume contains a great deal of interesting work, particularly the essays by De Man and Derrida. How much effect *Glyph* will ultimately have on American critical thought remains to be seen.

The final book treated in this section collects essays that attempt to present the most up-to-date thought of American writers on the subject of semiotics. It is *A Perfusion of Signs* (Bloomington: Ind. Univ. Press), edited by Thomas A. Sebeok, a veteran editor of such collections. Some of the essays are fairly technical, but many are accessible to the general reader interested in current thought about communication systems. The essays apply semiotic principles to a wide variety of areas, such as poetics, the circus, culture, and medicine. Clearly any discipline that studies the totality of communication systems has some relevance for the study of literature.

***j.* Conclusion.** To sum up, this was neither a distinguished nor a mediocre year for literary criticism and for overviews of American literature. Only a few books stand out as ones that will surely be read in another decade. The year's work conveys the feeling that literary studies are going through a period of transition. It is clear that American critics are trying on a broader and broader scale to absorb and disseminate the lessons of the European linguistic, semiotic, and structuralist schools of criticism. In works that deal primarily with American literature there seems to be a greater turning by scholars toward broad cultural matters. This also reflects much of what is going on in the restructuring of the curriculum in higher education, as well it should. Universities are more and more reflecting the multiethnic character of American culture, the contemporary stress on gender, and the understanding that much of our higher culture is dependent on formulas developed and reinforced by popular art forms and the mass media. It will be interesting to follow these trends over the next few years as the humanities and humanists live through an extended period of trial.

University of California, Davis

21. Foreign Scholarship

i. East European Contributions

F. Lyra[1]

Scholarship in American literature in East European countries during 1977 was less colorful, varied, and overlapping than in the preceding year. Take, for instance, the Soviet Union alone: In 1976 there were two books on William Faulkner, one by Nikolai Anastasyev (Moskva: Khudozhestvennaya Literatura), the other by Boris Timofyeyevich Gribanov (Moskva: Molodaya Gvardia), which was printed in 100,000 copies; there was a book on William Saroyan by N. A. Gonchar, *Vilyam Saroyan i yego rasskazy* (Erevan: Izdatelstvo Erevanskogo Universiteta); another monograph on Upton Sinclair by V. N. Bogoslovski, *Epton Sinkler* (Moskva: Vysshaya Shkola); Tamara Denisova published *Sovremenni amerikanski roman: Socyalnokriticheskiye tradicii* (Kiyev: Naukova Dumka), in which, applying traditional Soviet criteria, she discussed, among others, the works of Norman Mailer, Joseph Heller, Kurt Vonnegut, James Baldwin, John Killens, Phillip Bonosky, Truman Capote. The same year also brought *20th Century American Literature. A Soviet View* (Moscow: Progress Publishers)—a collection of 34 essays and articles of 21 Soviet Americanists. After Carl R. Proffer's *Soviet Criticism of American Literature in the Sixties* (Ann Arbor, [1972]), the collection constitutes the second survey of Soviet views on American literature in English. Unfortunately, the group of contributors is composed entirely of Moscovites. In the Preface, Yury Kovalev offers embarrassing explanations for excluding contributions from other parts of the country. While the volume is symptomatic of the enormous interest of Soviet scholars and critics in 20th-century American literature, it generates the false impression that Russian and Soviet scholarship on earlier American literature was miniscule and insignificant, which is not true as evidenced in Valentina Abramova Lib-

1. Because of the abundance of material on the one hand and the limitations of space on the other, Professor Lyra reports only on book-length publications.

man's *Amerikanskaya literatura v russkikh perevodakh i kritike: Bibliografia, 1776–1975* (Moskva: Nauka)—clearly the most important Soviet publication of 1977 in the field. Meritorious and commendable as the work is, any scholar interested in the reception of American literature in Russia and the Soviet Union will find the bibliography irritatingly deficient. Libman excludes Russian translations of the following authors: Edward Bellamy, Sinclair Lewis, O. Henry, Mark Twain, Howard Fast, noting only criticism of the writers. As for Jack London, she reports Soviet criticism after 1966. The bibliographer justifies the omissions by stating that Russian translations of all these authors were documented in separate earlier publications by A. N. Nikololyukin (Bellamy), I. M. Levidova (S. Lewis, O. Henry, Twain, Fast), B. M. Parchevskaya (London). Yet she is inconsistent in including criticism on Twain which has been already covered by Inna Levidova's *Mark Tven. Bibliograficheski ukazatel russkikh perevodov i kriticheskoi literatury na russkom yazike 1867–1972* (Moskva: Kniga, [1975]). The inconsistency is deepened by the fact that Libman has included material relating to 20th-century American literature she has covered in another bibliography of hers, *Bibliografia: Literatura SSHA v russkikh perevodakh (XX vyek)* (Moskva, [1970]). Besides, *Amerikanskaya literatura v russkikh perevodakh i kritike* is not as comprehensive as the title suggests: of about 700 American authors whose works appeared in Russian translation and were written about by Russian and Soviet critics, she selected 230 for bibliographical description, settling upon "those writers whose work is for us of historical or actual interest" (p. 8).

In terms of individual American authors in the Soviet Union, the year belongs to Samuel Clemens, just as the preceding one belonged to Faulkner. Anna Sergeyevna Romm produced *Mark Tven* (Moskva: Nauka). Her book deviates from traditional Russian criticism in that she does not treat Clemens as a children's author, except in her interpretation of *The Adventures of Tom Sawyer*. It should be stressed also that Anna Romm's book is not a biography, but a competent study of Twain's artistic and philosophical evolution based on a selected corpus of his works; yet true to the tradition of Soviet scholarship, Twain looms large in the book as a critic of bourgeois civilization in the United States. Judging from the impressive number of copies issued (170,000), her study is bound to exert a substantial impact on the image of Twain in the Soviet Union.

By and large, preoccupation with 20th-century literature continued to dominate in Soviet scholarship in 1977. The prolific and indefatigable Moris Mendelson published yet another book on the contemporary American novel, *Roman SSHA sevodnya* (Moskva: Sovyetski Pisatel), bringing up to date his earlier work *Sovremenni amerikanski roman* (Moskva: 1964). Mendelson's latest book divulges further mellowing of his position as a critic of American literature. As if answering the American scholar Deming Brown, who maintains that Soviet critics dwell on the dark side of American literature, Mendelson reminds his readers emphatically that the authors' works discussed by him contain bright and optimistic elements (p. 375). Besides three chapters about Hemingway, Steinbeck, and Faulkner respectively, Mendelson devotes the main part of his book (nine chapters) to a wide spectrum of writers and literary phenomena, apologizing for not paying sufficient attention to such authors as James Jones, Robert Penn Warren, Jack Kerouac, Bernard Malamud, Flannery O'Connor, Carson McCullers, and others. Subject to his analyses are Herman Wouk and other representatives of "mass literature," novelists of the absurd, satirists; Kurt Vonnegut, "satirist-fantast," gets a whole chapter, as do John Updike, Joyce Carol Oates, Norman Mailer, and the New Journalists. Probably to assure some kind of ideological and esthetic balance, Mendelson devotes an entire chapter to Lars Lawrence. In between he throws in a chapter on "Racists and the fight against racism."

The close connection between literature and sociopolitical life is demonstrated in *Amerikanskaya literatura i obshchestvenno-politicheskaya borba 60-e—nachalo 70-kh godov XX vyeka* (Moskva: Nauka). The book consists of eight articles by five Soviet Americanists: A. S. Mulyarchik, who contributed three articles, A. M. Zveryev, who wrote two, Yu. V. Goncharov, M. P. Tugucheva, and O. M. Kirichenko, who authored one each. Despite the ominous title of the book, the authors discuss its themes in a balanced tone without the obtuse view and style so characteristic in Soviet criticism of American literature in the 1950s.

Preoccupation with 20th-century American literature among Soviet scholars is corroborated in *Literatura SSHA XX vyeka* (Moskva: Nauka). Regretfully, the book has not reached me in time for this survey; neither has Mendelson's study of Walt Whitman in its English version, which had been announced for publication in 1977.

It speaks well for the publishing firm Sovyetski Pisatel to have reissued nine essays on American literature by Ivan Kashkin. They deal with the works of Hemingway, Ambrose Bierce, Erskine Caldwell, Emily Dickinson, Robert Frost, Carl Sandburg, and American poets of the beginning of the 20th century. Published in a volume entitled *Dlya chitatelya-sovremiennika,* along with studies of British authors and articles on a variety of literary subjects, the book constitutes a telling manifestation of Kashkin's stature as interpreter, scholar, and translator of American literature. The pieces cover a period of nearly 30 years (1936–63) of his interest in American literature, although he had begun to write about it as early as 1926.

Apart from 10 articles on 20th-century American literature and 2 on Emily Dickinson and Henry James respectively, Polish Americanists managed to produce only 2 book-length studies, both dissertations. Adela Styczyńska's *The Art of Henry James's Nouvella: A Study of Theme and Form* (Lódź: Acta Universitatis Lodziensis) is a fine piece of academic scholarship. Her exposition of the subject, however, is old-fashioned; the main body of the dissertation deals with the international theme, the position of the artist and James's vision of evil. Her conclusions are valid, meaningful, albeit not quite original when she maintains, for example, that James achieved synthesis of dramatic and epic forms and then states that James builds his novellas like well-made dramas.

The other Polish dissertation was produced by Teresa Kieniewicz, *Recepcja literatury amerykańskiej w Polsce w dwudziestowieczu międzywojennym* (Warszawa: Uniwersytet Warszawski). The study demonstrates that during the period between the First and Second World Wars, Polish publishers' response to American literature was largely determined by commercialism. Polish critics' call for translations of Faulkner's works, for instance, remained unheeded. The brisk narrative section of the book is followed by a bibliography of Polish translations and criticism of American literature published during that period. Unfortunately, the usefulness of the data contained in both sections is impaired by numerous errors.

The year's best contribution to the history of American literature in Eastern Europe is *Dictionar cronologic literatura americană* (Bucuresti: Editura ştiinţifica şi enciclopedică) by Dan Grigorescu, dean of Rumanian Americanists. Impressive in volume (782 pages), published handsomely, the book contains a year-by-year-chronicle of literary events in America from the beginning up to 1976, concluding with Norman Mailer's *Genius and Lust.* Notwithstanding the factual character of the text, the author's narrative style and his comments make it a highly readable book. Apart from the chronicle, the *Dictionar* contains a synoptic table (pp. 650–741) designed to place American literary events in context with world history, American history, American culture, and world literature. The index of authors (pp. 745–83) is very good, but the selected bibliography (pp. 742–44) is below par.

University of Warsaw

ii. French Contributions

Maurice Couturier

In the last few years American literary studies in France have started to develop in two opposite (but hopefully complementary) directions: toward the thorough investigation of a writer's work, in doctoral dissertations which are often too bulky to reach publication; but also toward short studies of mostly contemporary fiction writers, often inspired by structuralist and post-structuralist criticism, which appear in new reviews sponsored by associations, universities, or the National Center of Scientific Research (CNRS).

The doctoral dissertations the French scholars are now producing with "egg-laying regularity" deal particularly with contemporary writers. Until a few years ago it was impossible to defend a dissertation unless the writer was already in the grave. Unfortunately, these dissertations, which contain anywhere between 600 and 1,500 pages, are rarely published, except in the limited offset editions of the University of Lille.

This year only one dissertation has been published in American literature, *La création romanesque chez Thomas Wolfe* (Paris: Didier), by Monique Decaux. This is an important study about a very important novelist who has too long been neglected in France, partly as a result of Faulkner's overriding popularity. Monique Decaux has thoroughly reassessed Wolfe's life and work in the light of Bachelard, Mauron, and Durand's theories. In the first part she has analyzed the psychological case of the novelist through his writings, paying particular attention to his narcissism and to his inner conflict between the mother and the father images, in an attempt to trace the creative energy to its origins. In the second part she has focused her attention upon Wolfe's imaginary vision, exploiting Durand's distinction between the "nocturnal" and the "diurnal" in the collective unconscious. This book is, of course, bound to please the Jungians a great deal more than the Freudians, since it is largely based upon the anthropological definition of symbols. Nonetheless, I am confident, with Roger Asselineau, who introduced the book, that it will remain a major contribution to the study of Wolfe.

Professor Asselineau also has contributed an illuminating essay on "The Impact of American Literature on French Writers" (*CLS* 14:119–34), which surveys its subject from Benjamin Franklin to the present. "French readers and writers have always preferred the Red Indians to the Pale Faces of American literature, Fenimore Cooper, Whitman, and Faulkner to Hawthorne and James, but they have had blind spots as far as humor and poetry are concerned, and they have made exceptions to the rule in favor of Franklin for ideological reasons and Poe because his paleness was so great and so interesting."

The most important scholarly work published this year in France in American literary studies is, no doubt, the first volume of *Faulkner: Oeuvres romanesques* (Paris: Gallimard, Pléiade), edited by Michel Gresset, who is one of the prominent specialists on Faulkner. This is not simply a new French edition of *Sartoris, The Sound and the Fury* (with Faulkner's "Appendix"), *Sanctuary*, and *As I Lay Dying*. Michel Gresset has substantially revised the translations made previously by R. N. Raimbault and H. Delgove and slightly also those of M. E. Coindreau, trying to harmonize them where necessary. In his abundant notes, covering 500 pages, he provides all the background materials and a wealth of variant readings patiently unearthed from manuscripts, typescripts, and galley proofs. He abundantly uses *Flags in the Dust* in his notes on *Sartoris*. Never, so far, had such extensive research been made to edit Faulkner's novels. Michel Gresset has also established a very thorough chronology which will serve as the only reliable biography of Faulkner in French so long as Blotner's work remains untranslated. All those who, on both sides of the Atlantic, believe like Michel Gresset, that "the truth of Faulkner is in his manuscripts" (p. xvii) will be grateful to him for undertaking such an ungrateful work; at long last, all the important pieces of this gigantic puzzle have been gathered in one place, and we can reread Faulkner in a less naïve, and in a more creative manner. Currently, Michel Gresset is working on the translation in French of Faulkner's letters.

At the other end of the research spectrum, one finds an ever-increasing number of reviews that started to come out a few years ago, and around which small teams of researchers are actively working, especially in the field of contemporary fiction. This is largely due to the fact that many of the most seminal works of criticism in France in the last ten years (Barthes, Genette, et al.) have dealt with modern and postmodern fiction, and that American fiction is at the present time of great interest to those who are used to the works of Robbe-Grillet or Butor.

The *Revue Française d'Etudes Américaines* (10, rue Charles V, 75004 Paris) whose first issue, in 1976, was conspicuously about postmodern fiction, has now become the chief arena for American studies in France, both in literature and civilization. The April issue (*RFEA* 3), presented by Robert Silhol, offers a plurality of approaches to literature. In "Psychanalyse et critique psychanalytique" (pp. 29–46), Norman N. Holland describes the main stages psychoanalytical literary criticism has gone through. Then, following Lacan's distinction between "imaginaire" and "symbolique," Régis Durand, in "Les signes de la vérité" (pp. 47–59), examines the problem of interpretation in "Benito Cereno," and insists particularly on those signs that Cereno "fails to decipher and interpret correctly" (p. 47). In a similar vein, Nancy Blake breaks fresh ground in the study of James's novels with "Henry James: All Around the Primal Scene" (pp. 61–69), by showing that "James' fictional web is woven around a mental block" (p. 62). The next two articles investigate the ideological dimension of literature. First Jacques Abbou, in "Literature and Ideology" (pp. 73–78), emphasizes our dependence, as readers, upon our historical environment; then Jean Raynaud, in "Science fiction et critique de l'aliénnation" (pp. 79–92), suggests that present-day "soft-core" science fiction constitutes "an existential cry of warning" (p. 79). This issue ends with two notes: first a study of the changes made by Hemingway before the publication of his stories and novels, "On Some Technical Aspects of the Manuscripts of Ernest Hemingway" (pp. 95–110), by Geneviève Hily-Mane; finally Raymond Federman's plea for a new system of literary production, "Death of the Novel or Another Alternative" (pp. 111–14), in which the novelist claims that the Fiction Collective marks the beginning of a new era in the publishing world.

The October issue (*RFEA* 4) is entirely devoted to American humor, which was the subject of the Association Française d'Etudes Américaines's annual conference. It was prepared by Daniel Royot and Rolande Diot, who also provided excellent introductory articles, "Native Humor: the Giggle for Life" (pp. 5–11), and "From Chaos to Confusion: Little Men and Little Women" (pp. 12–15) respectively, in which they tried to provide the historical background. In the following articles a team of young researchers tried to define humor, and more specifically American humor, with the help of their elders, especially Robert Escarpit, who also contributed an essay, "Réévaluation de l'humour" (pp. 17–22), in which he gave a reassessment of his well-known views of the subject. Three distinct approaches can be identified: first, the psychoanalytical one, particularly in the section in which women's humor is discussed by Noëlle Batt, Nancy Blake, Harry Blake, Kathleen Hulley, Fred Misurella, Catherine Rihoit, and Olga Schérer. Their reflections center on Emily Dickinson, Grace Paley, Gertrude Stein, the Mae West phenomenon, and Henry James; in her concluding article Noëlle Batt pertinently says that humor poses a difficult problem to women in that it implicates them in a discursive system invented by men. The second approach, which is both linguistic and rhetorical, is represented by Maurice Couturier's "Nabokov's Laughter" (pp. 115–22), Rolande Diot's "S. J. Perelman et la *Dementia Praecox School of Humor*" (pp. 91–102), and Jean Raynaud's "Des mécanismes du jeu de mots" (pp. 23–30); this approach is not fundamentally different from the first one, but it gives precedence to textual analysis. The third approach is more sociological: James C. Austin studies western humor in "Gold Dust, Dust Bowl and Gopher Prairie" (pp. 31–37) and Judith Stora Jewish humor in "Paroles de Shlemil" (pp. 80–90). All these articles, rather short on the average, constitute a crazy quilt through which the very subject of humor seems to roam at will, never to be caught.

Delta (Université Paul Valéry, 34 032 Montpellier) is now in its third year, and continues to publish very interesting dossiers about southern writers. The May issue (*Delta* 4) deals entirely with Shelby Foote; it will probably remain a landmark for those who are interested in this author, and will contribute to introduce him in France where he has not received the recognition he deserves. For this issue Editor Claude Richard has gathered around him a team of young scholars who are chiefly concerned with a rhetorical, thematic, and psychoanalytical approach to the works of Shelby Foote, and more particularly to *Jordan County*. Shelby Foote, like Faulkner, is both a novelist and a historian; in a letter quoted by Richard, he acknowledges the twin label: "I believe that history can be written, much as a novel is written, the difference being that in the novel, the writer gets his 'facts' out of his head whereas the historian gets them out of documents . . ." (p. 1). For this issue of *Delta*, which deals with his fiction, Foote offered a passage from *The Civil War* about the assassination of Lincoln. In the concluding article of the issue, Michel Gresset echoes Foote's statement, in an article entitled "L'aval du texte" (pp. 177–80): he analyzes the ambiguity of Foote's discourse as both fiction and history, in "Sacred Mount." The bulk of the issue deals with the general structure of *Jordan County* (Philippe Jaworski's "Terre promise, terre conquise, terre vaine" [pp. 25–44]), its historical import or rather its dependence upon history (A. Gallet's "Tragique et témoignage dans *Jordan County*" [pp. 45–54]). More specifically, it contains a detailed analysis of three stories: "Rain Down Home," "A Marriage Portion," and "Pillar of Fire." Two articles seem to me of particular significance: Richard's "Deux yeux au plat ou les jeux récit et du discours dans 'Rain Down Home' " (pp. 55–70), and Claude Fleurdorge's " 'A Marriage Portion' ou comment l'esprit vient aux filles" (pp. 83–128). Both make ample use of the neorhetorical categories established by G. Genette in *Figures III* to study Foote's fictional discourse; they also make a careful investigation of the semantic fields to discover the dynamic core of the stories. The bibliography, at the end of this issue, owes much to James E. Kibler's bibliography published by the *Mississippi Quarterly* in 1971; but it will be a useful instrument for the study of Shelby Foote in Europe. I believe this is one of the best issues of *Delta* so far.

The November issue (*Delta* 5) deals again with a southern writer, Eudora Welty. Though it contains some interesting articles, it lacks the unity which characterized the former issue. It begins with an unpublished story of Eudora Welty called "Acrobats in a Park," which must have been written around 1935, and with a tentative reading of it by Kenneth Graham (pp. 13–18) as a performance rather than a tale. Four other stories, "June Recital," "The Burning," "First Love," and "Shower of Gold" are studied by Neil Cormoran, Edward Gallaput, A. M. Bonifas-Masserand, and Danièle Pitavy respectively. W. U. MacDonald, Jr., on the other hand, studies the changes made by Eudora Welty in "Flowers for Marjorie" between the first and the second publication (pp. 35–48), showing how she improved her style and deleted external facts at crucial points. This may be the most valuable article in the issue. The last item is an inventory of "The Eudora Welty Collection at the Humanities Research Center of the University of Texas at Austin" (pp. 83–88) established by Alain Blayac. Incidentally, *Delta* 5 also contains an epilog to the former issue, an article about "A Marriage Portion," in which Frédéric Monneyron questions some of Fleurdorge's conclusions.

Close to *Delta* in its critical approach, there comes a new review, called *TREMA*, published by the Research Center on Contemporary American Literature of the University of Paris III. The first issue, which came out in 1976, but was only privately circulated, was about fragmentation in contemporary fiction. This year's issue (*TREMA* 2) deals with a number of theoretical problems connected with postmodernism, especially in the field of fiction. In his introduction, Editor André Le Vot investigates some of the reasons behind the emergence of the new fiction, characterized by its fragmented, nondiscursive nature. He has developed his reflection much further in a very interesting article, published this year also, in *RANAM* 10, called "Contre l'entropie: les stratégies de la fiction américaine post-moderniste" (pp. 298–319). In the first article of *TREMA* 2, "Mutilation and Rebirth in Contemporary Fiction" (pp. 11–17), Nancy Blake tries to assess the psychoanalytical significance of fragmentation in the works of Barth, Barthelme, Burroughs, Hawkes, and Sukenick. This brings Maurice Couturier, in "Les discours du roman" (pp. 19–33), to enquire upon the linguistic significance of the novel since its origin as the "laboratory of discourse," which remains largely true of the postmodern fiction (Coover, Barthelme). Then, in an article inspired by Bakhtin, "Texte-Contexte-Prototexte-Métatexte" (pp. 35–44), Olga Schérer studies present fiction as a set of interdependent texts. There follow five interesting articles on contemporary writers: "*The Devil Tree* et la linéarité" (pp. 47–57), in which Monique Armand scrutinizes the plot of

Kosinski's novel; "Bitextualité dans l'oeuvre de William Burroughs" (pp. 59–70), by Noëlle Batt, which traces the principle of duality in Burroughs's fiction; "Le'erre (Déplacements chez Barthelme)" (pp. 71–80), in which Régis Durand questions "the possibility of a poetics of Barthelme's prose" (p. 71); "Allen Ginsberg's *Howl*: Fragments of a Study" (pp. 81–96), an ambitious analysis of Ginsberg's work by Henri Justin and Marc Chénetier in the Jakobsonian tradition; finally, "Gaddis and the Novel Entropy" (pp. 97–107), a study of *JR* by Johan Thielemans. This issue, like the first one, contains original materials: an interview of James Purdy by Marie-Claude Profit (pp. 111–26), and three fictions or fragments of fictions: "Family Circle" by Peter Spielberg (pp. 129–38), "Not to Knot" by Harry Blake (pp. 139–42), and an extract from *The Fortune Teller* by Ronald Sukenick (pp. 143–46). This collection of articles will be followed, in 1979, by a double issue of *Delta* on Barthelme, Coover, Gass, and Pynchon. For this team of researchers, the study of new forms goes along with the exploration of new critical approaches.

The second issue of *Annales*, published by the Center of Research on English-Speaking America (CRAA) of the University of Bordeaux (33 405 Talence) contains four papers on literature (and more specifically on American literature) which were given in a 1976 seminar. In the first one, "Les femmes dans le théâtre d'O'Neill: essai d'interprétation féministe" (pp. 131–58), Ginette Castro examines the part played by women in three plays (*Desire Under the Elms*, *Strange Interlude*, and *Mourning Becomes Electra*), more in a thematic than in a sociological perspective. Régis Durand's essay, "La voix et le dispositif théâtral" (pp. 159–66) is not specifically about American literature: it explains how the theatre is helping to change human discourse and to create new fictional modes. In "People as They Seem to Me" (pp. 167–81), Toni H. Oliviero tries to assess the importance of determinism and morality in the construction of Stephen Crane's novels, as well as the conflict between literary creation and didacticism. Finally, Guy-Jean Forgue, in "H. L. Mencken et le Sud" (pp. 183–95), studies Mencken's connection with the South and his influence upon southern literature, concluding that Mencken has made it easier to acknowledge such writers as Wolfe, Faulkner, and Caldwell.

This year *Etudes Anglaises* has also published some interesting articles on American literature. Among contributions by French scholars is Olga Schérer's "Faulkner et la fratricide: pour une théorie des titres dans la littérature" (30:407–19), which examines *Absalom, Absalom!* to see how much of the meaning of the novel is encoded in the title. While the titles of simple novels often supply a built-in reading, she believes that the complexity of Faulkner's work renders the title suggestive rather than precise. In a short note, "Autour des manuscrits de 'The Sea Change'" (30:207–9), Geneviève Hily-Mane finds a confirmation, in Hemingway's manuscripts, that the main theme of the story is that of vision. The most interesting article may be J. M. Bonnet's "Nom et renom dans *The Crucible*" (30:179–83): it focuses on the name of Proctor and the concept of name in the play, concluding that "*Proctor meurt pour préserver ce nom*" (p. 183).

This year's harvest is abundant and diversified. On the whole, it is more concerned with the problems of literature and literary studies than with American literature per se. This corresponds exactly with the opening of French universities to the ideas of the structuralists and poststructuralists. This renewal of the critical discourse is a good thing; it provides a new arsenal of concepts and allows us to read new forms of fiction and poetry in a more creative manner. Some people will probably inveigh against this trend, however, because it momentarily does away with the historical approach which had prevailed so far in French universities. This revolution may be short-lived: it poses for the academic world disturbing problems and arouses senseless fears.

Université de Nice

iii. German Contributions

Hans Galinsky

In 1977 interest in subjects cutting across period boundaries intensified remarkably. Attention given individual periods was spread more evenly. Along with French and Swiss colleagues German specialists in colonial literature, an expanding field, enjoyed the hospitality of *Early American Literature*'s first "European Number," competently edited by Ursula Brumm. Large-scale cooperative enterprises continued. They include *The Black American Short Story in the 20th*

Century, edited by Peter Bruck (The Hague: Mouton), *Die amerikanische Literatur der Gegenwart*, edited by Hans Bungert (Stuttgart: Reclam), and *Amerikastudien: Theorie, Geschichte, interpretatorische Praxis*, edited by Martin Christadler and Günter H. Lenz (Stuttgart: Metzler), a "special number" of the biannual *AmS*. A volume of essays from several hands, *Literaturen in englischer Sprache*, edited by Heinz Kosok and Horst Priessnitz (Bonn: Bouvier), broke new ground by viewing American literature in the context of non-British world literatures in English. Publication of "readers," reprinting American or American and German pertinent essays, covered such topics as *Amerikanische Romane des 19. Jahrhunderts*, edited by Martin Christadler (Darmstadt: Wissenschaftliche Buchgesellschaft), and *Deutschlands literarisches Amerikabild*, edited by Alexander Ritter (Hildesheim: Olms). Two recently founded monograph series specializing in or including American literature, *Anglo-American Forum* and *Neue Studien zur Anglistik und Amerikanistik*, have been making rewarding progress. Of around 120 items this year, book-length monographs increased notably.

a. **Literary History—General.** The spirit of revolt from colonial times to the present is the common denominator, explicitly for Dirk Hoerder's useful bibliography *Protest, Direct Action, Repression: Dissent in American Society from Colonial Times to the Present* (Munich: Verlag Dokumentation), and implicitly for Brigitte Scheer-Schäzler's "Das Experiment und seine Tradition in der amerikanischen Literatur." The latter introduces her bilingual collection of specimens representative of, as its title has it, *Experimentelle amerikanische Prosa* (Stuttgart: Reclam). While Hoerder's bibliography takes in voices of protest regardless of their literary quality, Mrs. Scheer-Schäzler confines herself to belles-lettres without neglecting their cultural background. Hers is a panoramic view of "revolt" from established models by experimenting on new ones, with A. B. Paulson figuring as the latest experimenter. Her account (pp. 5–35) is balanced enough to admit the traditionality of this "quest for new forms and potentialities of the imagination."

Less extensive as to its range from early republican times to the present is the same author's survey, "Die amerikanische Lyrik von 1800 bis zur Gegenwart," a concise essay contributed to Kosok's and Priessnitz's *Literaturen in englischer Sprache*, pp. 66–83. It presents present-day categorizations of the history of American poetry from Taylor to recent "confessional poets," and tests their applicability to three central figures, Emerson, Whitman, and Dickinson. Tennyson's "Come into the garden, Maud" serves for paradigmatic contrast. Reducing the range of his choice in favor of close interpretation, Armin P. Frank explores a subtype of poetry, the 'poetological poem,' in "'A Poem Should. . . . Be': Mimetic and Didactic Modes of Poetry on Poetry" (*Bul. of the Dept. of Eng., Univ. of Calcutta* (12 [1976–77]:1–17). Frank deals with a topic of genre. Its treatment includes its American tradition, with examples drawn from more than one period but with MacLeish's well-known poem serving as point of departure. Spanning slightly more than the whole of the 19th century, Martin Christadler's selection of novels interpreted in *Amerikanische Romane des 19. Jahrhunderts* extends from Charles Brockden Brown's *Edgar Huntly* to Henry James's *The Wings of the Dove.* Interpreters assembled in this "reader" comprise only 20th-century critics, mostly American, one British. In his perceptive introduction (pp. vii–xv) Christadler justifies his choice as meant "to document the interest of literary scholars and critics in the historicity of the novel." According to him, most Americans, among them, e.g., Leslie Fiedler, H. N. Smith, A. N. Kaul, Walter A. Bezanson, Charles H. Foster, Richard Chase, Leo Marx, and Richard Poirier, are "indebted to a common theory of culture," whereas John Goode, the English contributor, stands for "a literary and moral phenomenology apparently shared by the American C. A. Dryden."

As to other, more particularized, subjects of general significance, Herbert Foltinek offers "Some Observations on Character in the American Novel" (*SalSEL* 65:33–57). Dieter Schulz in "Die *Romance* als eigenständige amerikanische Erzählform" (*Literaturen in englischer Sprache*, pp. 97–111) turns to a question of genre. He applies "the perspective of chivalry" to the definition of the "romance" in 19th-century America. American narrative prose from Brown through Melville is considered as "a step in the disintegration of the romance of chivalry," a step that does not lead to the realistic novel in terms of "Bildungsroman." This transfer of European, especially German, general concepts of the history of narrative prose will probably remain controversial. Less disagreement will be encountered by Helmut Bonheim's application of linguistic tools to the analysis of the short story: "Mode Markers in the American Short Story" (*Proceed-*

ings of the Fourth Congress of Applied Linguistics, edited by Gerhard Nickel [Stuttgart: Hochschulverlag, 1976], pp. 541–50), which escaped this reporter's ken last year. Based on the author's "Theory of Narrative Modes" (*Semiotica* 14 [1975]:329–44) this essay, by way of "mode markers," studies the varying distribution of such narrative modes as speech, report, description, and comment. Authors discussed range from Irving to Bellow and Updike.

***a-1.* Colonial, Revolutionary, and 19th Century.** Moving only within one period continues to be characteristic of most contributions. Those covering the 16th and 17th centuries, and published together in *Early American Literature* (12:3–62), are prefaced by Ursula Brumm. She rightly stresses the fact that "if these early writers are those furthest removed from contemporary America, they are in a sense the ones nearest to Europe" (p. 3). Hans Galinsky's "Exploring the 'Exploration Report' and Its Image of the Overseas World: Spanish, French, and English Variants of a Common Form Type in Early American Literature" (pp. 5–24) interprets selected passages from Castañeda's *Relación de la jórnada de Cibola*, Champlain's *Les Voyages*, and Hariot's *Virginia*. An analysis of the common constituents of the form type is followed by their contributions, thematic and formal, to later genres of American literature. Ursula Brumm's "Did the Pilgrim Fathers Fall upon Their Knees When They Arrived in the New World? Art and History in the Ninth Chapter, Book One, of Bradford's History *Of Plymouth Plantation*" (pp. 25–35) concentrates "on the interdependence of experience and the literary account of this experience." A sensitive interpreter and specialist in the domains of "history and literature" as well as of Puritanism, the author convincingly proves her point that "images and literary devices place Bradford's interpretation of his experience in the great tradition of the thought, feeling, and conviction to which it belongs, that of the Protestant faith."

With Hans R. Guggisberg's "Religious Freedom and the History of the Christian World in Roger Williams's Thought" (pp. 36–48) the historian proper takes over and thoroughly inspects Williams's ideas and their sources. His "familiarity with the textual sources of the history of the Christian world" is found to be "less extensive than his many quotations from ancient and modern authors seem to indicate." This is accounted for by "life in the wilderness." Guggisberg admits, however, that "we cannot ascertain what he read and studied when he was in England."

Source study gives way to interpretation again when Astrid Schmitt-v. Mühlenfels explicates "John Fiske's Funeral Elegy on John Cotton" (pp. 49–62). Her revision of the text's transcription from the manuscript is convincing. Author of a standard work on New England's funeral elegy, she brings to her detailed analysis the expert knowledge needed to convey to the modern reader her impression that "by accepting the set form of the genre and excelling in it Fiske seems to offer the poetical equivalent to the life of a saint who excels in orthodox stature."

The late colonial part of the 18th century inspired no research whereas its early republican phase is represented by a book on the Loyalists, a topic rarely touched upon in German research. Barbara Krüger's *Die amerikanischen Loyalisten: Eine Studie der Beziehungen zwischen England und Amerika von 1776–1802*, Europäische Hochschulschriften, ser. III, vol. 73 (Frankfurt: Lang) emphasizes the political aspect of the subject without neglecting its literary implications. Linking the end of the 18th century to the first half of the 19th, Heinz Kosok throws light on another theme usually left in the dark by German Americanists. In "Vorstufen des amerikanischen Dramas: 1790–1860" (*Literaturen in englischer Sprache*, pp. 84–96) Kosok sets up a sequence of four steps toward a genuinely American drama: (1) a specifically American figure in the context of the English dramatic tradition, (2) the use of native American subject matter, (3) the combination of steps 1 and 2, (4) the introduction of specifically American problems. Tyler's *The Contrast*, Dunlap's *André*, Barker's *The Indian Princess*, and Boucicault's *The Octoroon* are employed as paradigms.

Reviving interest in Irving shows in Waldemar Zacharasiewicz's "Skizzen eines Reisenden: Bemerkungen zu einem bestimmenden Thema im Werk Washington Irvings" (*Salzburg Studies in English Literature* 65:296–325). The theme of travel is followed through a fascinating series of variations. Overlooked in 1976, Horst Breuer's "Wahnsinn im Werk Edgar Allan Poes: Literarkritisch-psychoanalytischer Versuch" (*DVLG* 50:14–43) bids fair to be the most intelligent German attempt to date to make use of psychoanalytical methods for a study in madness as given literary shape by Poe.

New England's Renaissance receives its customary share of attention, with Emerson, Hawthorne, and Melville solidly in the foreground. In "Des Dichters Dilemma: Ralph Waldo Emerson und der mexikanisch-amerikanische Krieg" (*AmS* 22:261–68) Herwig Friedl dissects the well-known dilemma of the poet as citizen, and the citizen as poet. He succeeds in thoughfully reinterpreting Emerson's "Ode: Inscribed to W. H. Channing" on the basis of Emerson's progress-oriented view of history and its final goal. Not as a seer of history's development, but as an educator does Emerson figure in Claus Rüdiger's *Die pädagogischen Ansätze amerikanischer Transzendentalisten: Erziehungswissenschaftliche Studien zu Amos Bronson Alcott, Ralph Waldo Emerson und Henry David Thoreau 1830–1840*, Anglo-American Forum 8 (Frankfurt: Lang). The decade selected is an excellent choice for its formative relevance and abundance of source material, especially as regards Alcott. Hawthorne was fortunate in finding congenial cotranslators in Hannelore Neves, Siegfried Schmitz, and Hans-Joachim Lang. The last also proves a knowledgeable commentator and empathetic interpreter. The new volume of 732 pages contains a representative selection of 26 tales, 3 sketches, 7 prefaces, and 4 reviews: Nathaniel Hawthorne, *Erzählungen, Skizzen, Vorworte, Rezensionen* (Munich: Winkler) was preceded by Ruth and Hans-Joachim Lang's translation of *The Scarlet Letter* and *The Blithedale Romance* (see *ALS 1975*, p. 480). An "Appendix" to the present volume informs about the textual basis and includes annotations as well as a "Postscript" (pp. 711–29). It achieves a consummate description and critique of a prose-artist's career in the sociocultural context of an author's relations to publisher, reader, and critic.

Melville is approached from three directions. One concerns a larger group of works, two relate to one individual piece each. Melville's novels are analyzed along the thematic line of man and fate. A specific problem in one of his novels, the character of the Cosmopolitan in *The Confidence Man*, is solved by equating the Cosmopolitan with a contemporary author. "The Apple-Tree Table" is examined in terms of communication theory. Ludwig Rothmayr's *Der Mensch und das Schicksal in den Romanen Herman Melvilles*, Regensburger Arbeiten zur Anglistik und Amerikanistik no. 10 (Frankfurt: Lang), resumes discussion of a familiar topic. Focusing on the attitudes of protagonists toward cosmic order, and on verbal cues such as providence, necessity, chance and fate, he pursues his subject through its many religious, philosophical, and structural ramifications. As successfully as on previous occasions Hans-Joachim Lang and Benjamin Lease cooperate in detecting sources and models. In "Melville's Cosmopolitan: Bayard Taylor in *The Confidence Man*" (*AmS* 22:286–89) a case is presented for Taylor as a contributor of decisive traits to the character of Cosmopolitan. It rests on (1) "the thought and phraseology of Taylor's Preface to his *Cyclopaedia of Modern Travel*" being "echoed in Melville's Masquerade," (2) "genial" in an editorial note of *Putnam's Magazine* recurring "as a key word in Melville's work," (3) "Taylor's glowing pictures of California and Californians in *Eldorado*" underlying in part Melville's "dashing and all-fusing spirit of the West." Reminding us that "The Apple-Tree Table" belongs in the immediate vicinity of *The Confidence Man*, Helmbrecht Breinig's "Symbol, Satire, and the Will to Communicate in Melville's 'The Apple-Tree Table'" (*AmS* 22:269–85) marshals the tools of communication theory in order to illuminate the work's complex meaning. Relying on literary allusion as "one of Melville's favorite means of conveying a specific message," Breinig finds in the "Conclusion" of Thoreau's *Walden* two features of importance to the interpretation of "The Apple-Tree Table," the combined "garret" and "insect" motifs, and "Thoreau's version of a symbolist theory of language." Both traits are developed in such a way that " 'The Apple-Tree Table' becomes some sort of ironic commentary not only on Transcendental metaphysics but also on Transcendental theory of communication."

Of later 19th-century authors, Dickinson, Twain, Bellamy, Donnelly, Howells, and Herrick attract the most attention. With "Emily Dickinson: Kunst als Sakrament" (*Literaturwissenschaftliches Jahrbuch der Görres-Gesellschaft*, n.s. 17 [Berlin: Duncker and Humblot, 1976], pp. 129–89) Franz Link published an outstanding essay, which, due to an oversight, went unnoticed last year. Based on a full awareness of international Dickinson scholarship, it is the only article dedicated to 19th-century poetry. In a series of closely interpreted poems Link unfolds the significance of religion in Dickinson's poetry. Art is shown to have become not a substitute for faith but a personal way of expressing belief in immortality as an esthetic reality, without Dickinson claiming for it absolute validity.

The new edition of Mark Twain in German translation reached completion with its ninth volume (Munich: Hanser). Klaus-Jürgen

Popp, its editor, is also responsible for the annotations and a succinct postscript.

In Heinz Ickstadt's "'Fiction Shows Fact the Future': Amerikanische Utopien des späten 19. Jahrhunderts" (*AmS* 22:295–308) literary and social studies fuse with linguistics. The author's own neat abstract pinpoints his interdisciplinary basis: "Recent criticism of utopian literature has tended to regard the utopian novel exclusively as *langue* removed from its specific historical and social frame reference. . . . usually denounced as a blueprint for totalitarian society. In contrast this essay includes the utopian novel in a pragmatic theory of fiction. In its double function as 'substitution and preparation for action,' fiction (whether utopian or other) cannot be separated from its communicative context." Edward Bellamy's *Looking Backward*, Ignatius Donnelly's *Caesar's Column* and *The Golden Bottle* as well as Howells's *A Traveler from Altruria* exemplify a "model" comprising basic features of American utopias published between 1880 and 1900.

Friedrich W. Horlacher has two Herrick items to his credit. He furnishes "An Annotated Checklist of Robert Herrick's Contributions to the *Chicago Tribune* (*ALR* 10:191–210). In "American Beauties and the Robber Barons" (*AmS* 22:291–94) he points up the parallel use of "American Beauties," "a particularly precious variety of the family of roses," in Henry B. Fuller's novel *With the Procession* and Herrick's *The Memoirs of an American Citizen*. The motif's basic function of suggesting "social attitudes of American plutocracy around the turn of this century" is held to be identical, but the symbolist content would seem to be different, "conspicuous consumption" (Veblen) in the former, social Darwinism in the latter.

Fiction of the turn of this century goes on exercising its appeal. Klaus Ensslen's "'Literature Against the Citadel': Schwarze Schreibstrategien auf dem weissen Literaturmarkt um 1900" (*AmS*, Special Number, pp. 248–71) traces Black participation in the production and publication of literature. Charles W. Chesnutt, Paul Laurence Dunbar, and Sutton E. Griggs are chosen to represent three "strategies" open to the Black novelist: "adapting himself to viable literary modes," "undermining the citadel of socially dominant concepts about the black group," "pacing himself completely outside the precepts of the literary market, at the risk of suspending literary communication." One of these authors is presented as a short-story writer in Hartmut W. Selke's "Charles Waddell Chesnutt, "The Sheriff's Children" (1889), a contribution to *The Black American Short Story*, pp. 21–38.

Heinz Ickstadt's "Öffentliche Fiktion und bürgerliches Leben: Der amerikanische Roman als kommunikatives System" (*AmS*, Special Number, pp. 223–47) casts its net among white authors like S. Weir Mitchell, Howells, Owen Wister, Herrick, and London. The basic concept of "fiction" (in the epistemological sense) links it to Breinig's study in Melville's "The Apple-Tree Table" and the author's above-mentioned article about late 19th-century utopias on the one hand, and Arno Müller's "Illusionsbildung und Illusionsabbau: Zur Vermittlungsproblematik im englischsprachigen Entwicklungsroman um die Jahrhundertwende" (*Sprachkunst* 8:104–17) on the other. The fiction-reality contrast, though as old as Plato, lately tends to be rediscovered somewhat too often.

***a-2.* 20th-Century Poetry, Drama, and Fiction to 1945.** Totally neglected by research on the 18th and 19th centuries in 1977, poetry may celebrate its come-back to 20th-century scholarship. Surprisingly, it is even more in the foreground than pre-1945 drama and fiction. Ezra Pound commands the central position. Max Nänny draws attention to "Oral Dimensions in Ezra Pound" (*Paideuma* 6: 13–26). In the same periodical (6:329) Franz H. Link's "A Note on Samothrace in Pound's *Hugh Selwyn Mauberley*" finds two lines each of the poem—"The age demanded an image/Of its accelerated grimace" and "Even the Christian beauty/Defects—after Samothrace"—preconnected in a passage from F. T. Marinetti's first *Futurist Manifest*: "une automobile rugissante, qui a l'air de courir sur la mitraille, est plus belle que la Victoire de Samothrace." Susanne Vietta's "Zum Verhältnis von Subjektivität und Zeitlichkeit" (*AmS* 22:147–66) views Pound and Charles Olson from the angle of their "sharing an equal concern for the disintegrated state of the modern mind." The concept of time is employed "as a criterion for distinguishing the mode and degree in which both poets try to reintegrate man in his world and thus to reestablish his identity." Linking up with Frank's above-mentioned essay, " 'A Poem Should . . . Be,' " a study treating the poetological theme more generally, Gottfried Weiler resumes it more specifically in examining *Die poetologische Lyrik*

Archibald MacLeishs (Frankfurt: Haag & Herchen). Reinhard Schiffer takes up a subject long neglected in "Die Poetik und Lyrik der Objektivisten" (*Die amerikanische Literatur der Gegenwart*, pp. 89–111), which introduces the reader to the poetry of George Oppen, Louis Zukofsky, and Charles Reznikoff.

Drama to 1945 has its only scholarly spokesman this year in Kurt Müller: *Konventionen und Tendenzen der Gesellschaftskritik im expressionistischen Drama der zwanziger Jahre*, Neue Studien zur Anglistik und Amerikanistik, no. 9 (Frankfurt: Lang) sums up and supplements research in a field particularly close to the history of German drama. The conventional ingredients of what used to impress the contemporary spectator as strikingly new in the presentation of tensions between the individual and society as well as of social and political group conflicts receive particular attention and sober evaluation.

Scholarship in fiction is more varied but only slightly greater. The short story comes up for interpretation in Udo Jung's "Jean Toomer, 'Fern' " (*The Black American Short Story*, pp. 53–69), and in a book-length monograph, Heide Ziegler's *Existentielles Erleben und kurzes Erzählen: Das Komische, Tragische, Groteske und Mythische in William Faulkners "Short Stories,"* Amerikastudien, Monograph Series, no. 45 (Stuttgart: Metzler). The latter maintains that the existential mode of experience, by virtue of its exemplary character, has a strong affinity to short fiction. The thesis is tested in two ways: (1) by detailed interpretation of three short stories, each exemplifying the comic, tragic, grotesque, and mythical modes of experience as given artistic shape at the levels of character, situation, and "world," (2) by comparing each mode of experience as to its expression in the short story and in the novel. This subtly reasoning study ranks among the year's best.

The more popular field of the crime story is investigated in Hans-Martin Braun's *Prototypen der amerikanischen Kriminalerzählung: Die Romane und Kurzgeschichten Carroll John Dalys und Dashiell Hammetts*, Regensburger Arbeiten zur Anglistik und Amerikanistik, no. 11 (Frankfurt: Lang). Analysis, comparison, and definition of the prototypical value are carried out methodically. The book meets the need for a competent introduction to Daly whereas Hammett has found a good many German interpreters already.

***a-3.* Literature since 1945: General and Fiction since 1945.** Two attempts have been made to survey the whole area. They cover, however, different, shorter or longer, time spans. There are many more efforts to gain an overview of various sections of the narrative domain just as there are plenty to examine individual fiction writers or appreciate particular works. The survey-type publications occupy two different positions, one extra-, another intraliterary. Returning to a subject taken up in 1976 (see *ALS 1976*, p. 444), Hansjörg Gehring in "Literatur im Dienst der Politik: Zum Re-education-Programm der amerikanischen Militärregierung in Deutschland," Literaturmagazin, no. 7, edited by N. Born and J. Manthey (Reinbek: Rowohlt), pp. 252–70, evaluates the post-1945 functions of literary works, partly written before, and partly contemporaneous. Hans Bungert, editor of *Die Amerikanische Literatur der Gegenwart: Aspekte und Tendenzen*, offers a more extensive view. It also includes part of the pre-1945 scene but reaches forward to the immediate present. It serves as introduction to this team-work enterprise (pp. 7–17). As to classification, lines of development, emphasis on major talents, and placement of works within the American literary tradition, it is instructive to compare this German view with that in Robert E. Spiller's, the only American contributor's, essay " 'Time Present': Amerikanische Literatur seit 1945" (pp. 18–27).

Forming but a part of Bungert's overview, black literature becomes a unified whole of its own in Bernhard Ostendorf's essay "Die afro-amerikanische Literatur nach 1945: Tendenzen und Aspekte" (pp. 128–53). It is both well organized and instructive in that it sets the literary works against a background of political tendencies, the "double vision" of black authors and actual speech forms in black dialogue, and oral interaction for artistic purposes. Ostendorf contributes a similarly informative and soberly evaluative article, "Contemporary Afro-American Culture: The Sixties and Seventies" to *RANAM* (10:131–53).

As usual, responses to fiction since 1945 are considerably more numerous than to drama and poetry. A specialist in the genre, Peter Freese critically follows the somewhat confusing development of the short story in an essay provocatively titled "Die Story ist tot, es lebe die Story" (*Die amerikanische Literatur der Gegenwart*, pp. 228–51).

Time-oriented as well but limited to certain sections of the whole post-World-War-II period are Martin Schäfer's thoughtful and discriminating book, *Science Fiction als Ideologiekritik: Utopische Spuren in der amerikanischen Science Fiction-Literatur 1940–1955*, Amerikastudien, Monograph Series, no. 48 (Stuttgart: Metzler) and Manfred Pütz's succinct article "Imagination and Self-Definition: American Novels of the Sixties" (*PR* 44:235–44).

Formal interests determined the choice of such a complex subject as *Experimentelle amerikanische Prosa*, in which Brigitte Scheer-Schäzler has edited a most instructive volume including prose pieces (and their German translations) published between 1968 and 1973. Authors selected range from John Cage and Bernard Malamud as oldest representatives via W. S. Merwin and Anne Sexton as spokesmen of the generation of the 1920s, and John Barth, Donald Barthelme, Glen Meeter, Gail Godwin, and Joyce Carol Oates as voices of the 1930s to such recent talents of the 1940s generation as Carl Krampf and the afore-mentioned A. B. Paulson.

More specialized, form-directed attention turns to the "documentary novel" and the technique of "fragmentation." The former finds an outlet in Peter Bruck's "Fictitious Nonfiction: Fiktionalisierungs- und Erzählstrategien in der zeitgenössischen amerikanischen Dokumentarprosa" (*AmS* 22:123–36). Truman Capote's *In Cold Blood*, Norman Mailer's *The Armies of the Night*, and Tom Wolfe's *The Electric Kool-Aid Acid Test* supply the works to be examined. The latter, fragmentation as an artistic design, is carefully analyzed in Richard Martin's "Forming Fragmentation: A Function of Fiction Today" (*DQR* 7:162–68). Together with Scheer-Schäzler's anthology, this article gets us closest to the most recent tendencies in American fiction.

Not only genres and trends but also individual authors and particular works inspire research. A case of "elective affinities" between intellectuals at both sides of the Atlantic, both groups sharing a "European tradition," seems to prevail when Vladimir Nabokov and John Barth prove especially attractive. Herbert Grabes's well-received *Erfundene Biographien: Vladimir Nabokovs englische Romane* (see *ALS 1976*, p. 483) came out in an English translation as *Fictitious Biographies: Vladimir Nabokov's English Novels* (The Hague: Mouton). Manfred Pütz, who contributed a penetrating review of the German original to *AmS* 22:220–23, is the author of "Vladimir Nabokov's *Pale Fire*: The Composition of a Reading Experience" (*LWU* 10:31–40). John Barth's *Lost in the Funhouse* and its stylistic signal of initial negation are investigated and explained along lines of communication theory in Hartwig Isernhagen's "Die 'verworfene Erwartung' als Infragestellung der Kommunikation" (*Anglia* 95:139–43). Pütz critically elucidates the uses of mythopoesis in "John Barth's *The Sot-Weed Factor*: The Pitfalls of Mythopoesis" (*TCL* 22:454–66).

More sporadic is research on Malamud, Selby, Vonnegut, and Oates. A fundamental problem of Malamud's novels, their roots in the Bible, is dealt with in Ernst Engelbert's *Die Bedeutung der Bibel in Romanwerk Bernard Malamuds*, Mainzer Studien zur Amerikanistik, vol. 7 (Frankfort: Lang). Covering Malamud's production from *The Natural* through *The Tenants* and resting on a most extensive bibliography of secondary sources, this book testifies to both the ideational and the structural significance of the Bible. Redemption by God's mercy, not justification by man's works, is recognized as the ultimate barrier between full Biblical Christianity and Malamud's "humanism with a Bible-oriented ethic." Calling us back to the neorealism of the 1960s, Hubert Selby's *Last Exit to Brooklyn* furnishes the title of Eberhard Kreutzer's essay (*AmS* 22:137–45). Its subtitle, "The Psychodynamics of Person and Place," appropriately defines the perspective applied by the critic. As for clarity, coherence, and detective skill this is a most remarkable interpretation of a single work. Circularity of the protagonists' development, "spatial symbolism," language "reflecting the conditions of the characters on various levels with particular directness," and the widening of perspective due to a "framework of allusive and symbolical titles and universalizing Bible mottoes" are among the noteworthy results.

Walter Hölbling's "'Dystopie der Gegenwart': Science Fiction und Schizophrenie in Vonneguts *Slaughterhouse-Five*" (*AAAm* 2: 39–62) signals continued interest in a novel particularly meaningful to Germans. A related subject, although placed in a different, non-German, setting, "Joyce Carol Oates in Search of the Sense in Human Life" (*AAAm* 3:39–66) receives discriminating treatment by Siegfried Kraus. It is among the very few articles devoted to this younger American writer in Germany over the last years.

***a-4.* Drama and Poetry since 1945.** After publication of three comprehensive collections of essays on either contemporary American drama or its history in 1972, 1974, and 1976 curiosity seems to be satisfied for a while. The 1977 harvest consists of two survey articles only. A brilliant intellectual achievement, Rudolf Haas's "Das moderne Drama in Amerika als amerikanisches Drama" (*Literaturen in englischer Sprache*, pp. 112–21), reveals American characteristics of a universal genre in its modern shapes. The context of the American theater, its organization and its audiences as well as its interrelations with the European theater and drama are carefully sketched in. According to Haas two major trends constitute the Americanness of the genre before and after 1945: the persistent self-criticism of America, and the expression of modern American life in terms of mythology. Herbert Grabes's "Das amerikanische Drama nach O'Neill" (*Die Amerikanische Literatur der Gegenwart*, pp. 28–48) divides its subject into four, occasionally overlapping, sections: (1) "The psychological drama and its extension in the 1950s" (O'Neill, Miller, Williams), (2) "Edward Albee and the crisis of the Broadway theater" (Inge, Albee, Kopit), (3) "The American drama of 'The Other Theater' off- and off-off Broadway" (Gelber, Garson, van Itallie, Terry, Wilson, Owens), (4) "The American drama of the 'Black Theater'" (Lorraine Hansberry, Adrienne Kennedy, Ossie Davies, Douglas Turner Ward, James Baldwin, LeRoi Jones, Ed Bullins, Ron Miller, Richard Wesley). As the march of names indicates, this survey is meant to be informative rather than interpretive. It covers the 1940s to the 1960s, and concludes with Wesley's *Black Terror* (1970) at the beginning of the present decade.

Post-1945 poetry has to its credit a translation by Manfred Pütz of *Selected Poetry of Patti Smith* (Cologne: Turske), as well as an author- and a theme-oriented study. Passed over in previous collections of essays on the history of American poetry or on contemporary literature in general, Denise Levertov receives from Rudolf Halbritter's "Zur Inhalt-Form-Problematik in Denise Levertovs engagierten Gedichten" (*AmS* 22:167–89) what seems to be the first long German article that treats exclusively of this woman poet of Welsh and Russian-Jewish descent. Focusing on poems of political commitment, mainly selected from *Sorrow Dance*, *Rehearsing the Alphabet*, and *To Stay Alive*, Halbritter arrives at a balanced judgment on successful confessional poems of personal concern, and unsuccessful ones, e.g., such as try to "define" revolution. With Reinhold Schiffer's "Antike Mythologie und moderne amerikanische Lyrik: Bemerkungen zu einigen Rezeptionsweisen" (*Die amerikanische Literatur der Gegenwart*, pp. 112–27) interest shifts from an author to a theme.

Schiffer brings to its discriminating development a sound knowledge of classical mythology and post-1945 poetry. Poems by Allen Tate, Robert Lowell, Richard Wilbur, Ezra Pound, W. D. Snodgrass, Kenneth Rexroth, Denise Levertov, Charles Olson, Allen Ginsberg, and Robert Duncan are chosen to exemplify the various contextual uses—as figures, personifications, symbols, allusions, themes or motifs—classical mythology has been put to. Bordering on comparative literary studies, the treatment of this topic links up with our last section.

***b.* Literary Criticism and Theory, Comparative Studies.** Each of these fields shows a gratifying expansion, with comparative approaches toward American literature ranking first.

Literary criticism and theory are dealt with jointly in Armin Paul Frank's "Neuere Entwicklungen in der amerikanischen Literaturtheorie und Literaturkritik" (*Die amerikanische Literatur der Gegenwart*, pp. 271–310). Deciding on 1941, the year of publication of Ransom's *The New Criticism*, Burke's *The Philosophy of Literary Form*, Wilson's *The Wound and the Bow*, and Matthiessen's *American Renaissance*, as his point of departure, Frank is a reliable and amusing guide of a *tour d'horizon.* It visits eight "countries" including the New Criticism, sociological, psychoanalytical, and American culture-oriented (American Studies-directed) criticism, myth criticism, the Chicago Aristotelians, the New Historicism, and linguistics-based criticism. A demanding and controversial subject is handled fairly. Personal preferences and their reasons are candidly stated. Likewise, "I'll take my stand" could be the motto for Frank's volume of essays, *Literaturwissenschaft zwischen Extremen: Aufsätze und Ansätze zu aktuellen Fragen einer unsicher gemachten Disziplin* (Berlin-New York: de Gruyter). Though falling into the category of general literary studies, this provocative volume draws heavily on American material.

Literary criticism as separate from literary theory is the subject of two publications. Both deal with the critical reception of particular works, yet pursue different purposes. In the shape of a critique of critiques Hans-Joachim Lang's "Der Schatten von Melville's 'Benito Cereno': Überlegungen zur literarischen Kritik" (*AmS*, Special Number, pp. 272–87) is a warning not to put attitudes first when confronted with the interpretation of a literary work such as "Benito Cereno" that does not conform to one's personal attitude. Representative tendencies in the history of its critical reception are competently outlined, and reasons, both extrinsic and intrinsic, for the rise of the critics' dilemma are skillfully disentangled. Lang's essay, one of the most thoughtful of the year, "accepts 'Benito Cereno' as a serious, though incomplete and even flawed, statement concerning slavery." Regina Diehl's *"The Waste Land" and the Poet Critics: Die Rezeption von T. S. Eliots 'The Waste Land' durch die Poet Critics John Crowe Ransom, Allen Tate, Conrad Aiken, Edwin Muir and Stephen Spender in Literaturtheorie und Dichtung* (Grossen Linden: Hoffmann) examines critical reception and productive influence. The choice of three American poet-critics, a Scottish poet-translator, and an English poet and prose writer, critic, and translator provides for variety of talent among the authors selected. It also suggests a comparative method of study.

Literary theory expanding into theory of art is investigated in Ulrich Horstmann's "Die Transzendenz des Konkreten: Anmerkungen zur Kunsttheorie Henry David Thoreaus" (*AmS* 22:247–60). It develops Thoreau's changing positions to the final conclusion that his "anti-transcendentalist 'concretism,' which foreshadowed a positivistic methodology, involuntarily ended in a secularized mysticism of its own." With Hemingway unexpectedly following Thoreau, once again a literary author's own theory comes up for discussion. Romeo Giger's *The Creative Void: Hemingway's Iceberg Theory*, Swiss Studies in English, no. 93 (Bern: Francke) is the first book-length monograph inquiring into the well-known metaphor of Hemingway's, whose interpretation has produced a good deal of disagreement.

Another book is unique in investigating "the concept and the function of the (literary) intellectual" in the Western world by means of such American examples as Randolph Bourne, Herbert Croly, Max Eastman, V. F. Calverton, and Michael Gold. Olaf Hansen's *Bewusstseinsformen literarischer Intelligenz*, Amerikastudien, Monograph Series, No. 47 (Stuttgart: Metzler) tackles a comprehensive subject by linking esthetic, and with it literary, theory to the sociology of the intellectual. This union of disciplines is required by a study that aims at a "criticism of the literary intelligentsia with regard to its interpretation of social reality." The value of this clearly and painstakingly reasoning book is enhanced by the first publication, in an appendix, of five Bourne manuscripts.

Literary theory as applied to the old problem of how to periodize literary history and delimit one's own contemporary stage, is at the center of three interrelated articles. In a joint paper, Gerhard Hoffmann, Alfred Hornung, and Rüdiger Kunow inspect "'Modern,' 'Postmodern' and 'Contemporary' as Criteria for the Analysis of 20th-Century Literature" (*AmS* 22:19–46, with bibliography on pp. 40–46). Michael Köhler's "'Postmodernismus': Ein begriffsgeschichtlicher Überblick" (*AmS* 22:8–18) traces the history of the concept and term from Arnold Toynbee via Irving Howe and Harry Levin to Leslie Fiedler, Ihab Hassan, William Spanos, and David Antin. Jürgen Peper's "Postmodernismus: *Unitary Sensibility* (Von der geschichtlichen Ordnung zum synchron-environmentalen System" (*AmS* 22:65–89) subjects postmodernism to stringent criticism from the viewpoint of a theory of culture that puts the conscience-directed individual first.

In spite of their intensified appeal literary criticism and theory rank second to the study of American literature in comparative contexts. Comparison of whole genres and their theories, of themes and motifs, reception and influence research as well as "imagology," the inquiry into the literary image of one country in the literature of another or several others, are flourishing as never before. American and British drama since around 1880 are juxtaposed in Paul Goetsch's *Bauformen des modernen englischen und amerikanischen Dramas* (Darmstadt: Wissenschaftliche Buchgesellschaft). British and American theories of the short story are collected and bibliographied in Alfred Weber's and Walter F. Greiner's *Short-Story-Theorien (1573–1973)* (Kronberg: Athenäum). Another useful "reader" enabling instructive comparisons, *Der Detektiverzählung auf der Spur: Essays zur Form und Wertung der englischen Detektivliteratur* (Darmstadt: Wissenschaftliche Buchgesellschaft) was compiled by Paul G. Buchloh and Jens Peter Becker. It includes essays by T. S. Eliot, J. W. Krutch, Edmund Wilson, Raymond Chandler, and other Americans. The same publisher also has brought out a three-cornered comparison, American, British, and Anglo-Irish, by Klaus Lubbers, *Typologie der Short Story*. The sections on structural designs and techniques of suggestion and cross-reference are of particular value to the comparatist.

The comparative context of American literature widens again when its study is conducted in the framework of world literatures in

English. Such a view is attempted in Hans Galinsky's "Entwicklung und Perspektiven der literaturwissenschaftlichen Forschung zu den englischsprachigen Literaturen ausserhalb Englands" (*Literaturen in englischer Sprache*, pp. 239–60). Even more multifaceted are the comparisons which Franz H. Link's *Dramaturgie der Zeit* (Freiburg: Rombach) invites. Extending from ancient Greek and Indian drama to contemporaries like Thomas Bernhard, this outstanding study finds room for American dramatists' handling of time, examples ranging from Upton Sinclair's *Singing Jailbirds* to van Itallie's *The Serpent.* Especially O'Neill, Wilder, and Williams are circumspectly integrated with this international survey.

The theme of an ever-increasing reduction of the outer world marks the point of convergence between contemporary American and German poetry in Waltraud Mitgutsch's " 'Weltverlust' in der zeitgenössischen Lyrik" (*Sprachkunst* 8:251–72). Sylvia Plath and Paul Celan furnish examples. Motif constituents of a famous medieval Celtic tale from the Arthurian cycle, which have been transformed by a modern American fiction writer, are detected by Franz Schmitt-v. Mühlenfels in " 'Four Sides of One Story': Tristan and Isolde bei John Updike" (*GRM* 27:98–113). The motif of the "doppelgänger" as used by Poe and Dostoevsky is examined in Horst Brinkmann's fascinating essay, "Zum Doppelgängermotiv bei E. A. Poe ('William Wilson') und F. D. Dostojevskij ('Dcojnik')," *Festschrift für Heinz Wissemann*, edited by Herbert Jelitte and Rolf-Dieter Kluge, *Beiträge zur Slavistik*, vol. 2 (Frankfurt: Lang).

Reception and influence studies juxtapose one American and one German author and accompany three other American authors across Germany. With *Ralph Waldo Emerson und "Die Natur" in Goethes Werken: Parallelen von "Nature" (1836) und "Nature" (1844) mit dem Prosahymnus "Die Natur" und sein möglicher Einfluss*, Mainzer Studien zur Amerikanistik, vol. 8 (Frankfurt: Lang) Rüdiger Els devotes a whole book to an old intriguing question. Painstaking research yields only the possibility of influence, and this in indirect forms like stimulation, support, and clarification of Emerson's own ideas. *Mark Twain in Germany*, edited by Klaus-Jürgen Popp (Munich: Hanser) is a crowning event after Popp's successful completion of the already mentioned nine-volume edition of Twain's works in German translation. The editor's essay, "Mark Twain, der Arglose in Deutschland," stands out for its knowledge and sense of humor. Friedel H. Bastein's *Die Rezeption Stephen Cranes in Deutschland*, Anglo-American Forum, vol. 3 (Frankfurt: Lang) has filled one of the more conspicuous gaps in the history of American literature's reception in Germany. So has Horst Oppel's *Thornton Wilder in Deutschland: Wirkung und Wertung seines Werkes in deutschen Sprachraum*, Abhandlungen der Akademie der Wissenschaften und der Literatur in Mainz, Klasse der Literatur, no. 3 (Wiesbaden: Steiner). Particularly ambitious is Angelika Schmitt-Kaufhold's *Nordamerikanische Literatur im deutschen Sprachraum nach 1945: Positionen der Kritik und Kriterien der Urteilsbildung*, Europäische Hochschulschriften, ser. 14, vol. 47 (Frankfurt: Lang). Divided into "areas of interest," "Genre Problems," and "Basis of Comparison," it successfully attempts to define fundamental positions of criticism and both recurrent and variable criteria of judgment. Limited to narrative prose and to the Federal Republic of Germany as reception area, Hans Bungert's essay, "Zur Rezeption der zeitgenössischen amerikanischen Erzählliteratur in der Bundesrepublik" (*Die amerikanische Literatur der Gegenwart*, pp. 252–62), conveniently serves as a sensitive instrument of control as to the results reached by the preceding book in the narrative field.

The youngest branch of comparative studies, literary imagology, has produced two major books. *Deutschlands literarisches Amerikabild: Neuere Forschungen zur Amerikarezeption der deutschen Literatur*, edited by Alexander Ritter (Hildesheim: Olms) is a "reader" of more than 600 pages. It reprints earlier essays from 1945 to 1975 but also includes two original contributions, a bibliography of 346 items by the editor and a research report by Hans Galinsky, "Deutschlands literarisches Amerikabild: Ein kritischer Bericht zu Geschichte, Stand und Aufgaben der Forschung" (pp. 4–27). Marion Berghahn's *Images of Africa in Black American Literature* (London: Macmillan) clearly distinguishes, and accounts for, the manifold aspects and changing backgrounds of a subject of more than literary significance.

Selective, to the complete exclusion of didactics and popular culture, this year's report testifies to the existence of a whole spectrum of scholarly activity, continuously vigorous and increasingly varied.

Johannes Gutenberg Universität, Mainz

iv. Italian Contributions

Rolando Anzilotti

Italian scholarship slowed its pace this year. The large variety of books and articles that distinguished last year's production was not repeated in 1977, almost as if Italian scholars had to draw their breath, preparing for a new jump forward, or almost like a field that has to lie fallow before growing and ripening a new harvest.

Black literature and culture is one of the categories that fared well because of two interesting books: *Il ponte sullo Harlem River* (Roma: Bulzoni) by Mario Materassi and *Bianchi e neri nella letteratura americana* (Bari: De Donato) by Alessandro Portelli. Materassi's volume is a chronicle of the emotional and ideological itinerary of a white European who, profiting from a long, first-hand experience, is able to shed some personal light on many aspects of the culture, the literature, and the recent history of the Afro-American. Apart from a few pieces of more strictly scholarly nature (e.g., the two Bontemps's novels and Baldwin's "A Note of a Native Son," which received due notice in *ALS 1975*, p. 489), the materials gathered here are articles, notes, and reviews written between 1962 and 1975. Frequently overlapping, and at times dated, or limited in their scope by the exigencies of the occasion, they still make up a valuable and engagingly written volume. The struggle of the blacks, both in life and art, to obtain full recognition as human beings is observed and examined by the writer with genuine sympathy, moral passion and intellectual honesty.

The relationship between blacks and whites in America as seen in literature is the theme of Portelli's study. The author writes as a Marxian scholar intent on analyzing a phenomenon that is fascinating in its very complexity; he is not interested in easy accusations or apologetics, and when he does fall into a loose judgment, it almost appears like an oversight. His subtitle, "The Dialectic of Identity," immediately takes the discussion beyond the American sociological context to a more profound psychological level: the constant dialectic between oppressor and oppressed throughout human history, and even within a single human personality. On this level, where oppressor and oppressed are afraid of being each other and in reality are both, the best documents are those found in the literature that springs from the tension between being white and being black. Portelli sensitively focuses his attention not only on the usual black texts and authors (from Gustavus Vassa to Baldwin and Malcolm X) but also brings Melville, Twain, and Faulkner into the discussion.

Among other books that deserve to be noticed for critical acumen and remarkable industry Barbara Lanati's *L'avanguardia americana: Tre esperimenti* (Torino: Einaudi) is certainly one. Lanati tries to delineate the guiding principles of the American avant-garde as they reveal themselves in Faulkner's *As I Lay Dying*, in Gertrude Stein's work, and in W. C. Williams's *In the American Grain*. The lack of discussion and definition of the concept of avant-garde makes it difficult to relate Faulkner's novel to the other works under examination, so that the first essay merely seems to be a perceptive and intelligent reading of *As I Lay Dying*, which has not much to do with demonstrating the author's thesis. The other two essays reach plausible and interesting conclusions: the linguistic techniques by which Stein tried to involve the reader in the creation of the artistic product are now used by the media to condition the individual; Williams's confrontation of the American intellectual with his own past is a journey *into* America that, instead of leading to an objective vision of history, ultimately becomes a journey towards a point of no return. The value of Lanati's book does not reside in its argument, which appears rather disjointed, but in the keen insights and observations that are contained in it.

Piero Sanavio's *Ezra Pound* (Venezia: Marsilio) is the fruit of many years of familiarity with the poet's entire work and of repeated encounters with the man over a long period. Sanavio, a writer and novelist, but also an Americanist with a long record as a Pound scholar, decided at last to exorcise in a book the great figure that he had always admired for his achievement and always hated for his aberrant political ideas. His purpose, as he states, has been to interpret and explain Pound's work and thought in order to furnish a guide to the reading of what the artist has created. Following the poet's journey from the early literary experiments and discoveries up to the composition of the last *Cantos*, Sanavio proceeds with an analysis that combines verse explication and Marxian investigation of the artist's ideas on art, politics, economics, history, and culture. Not questioning the value of Pound's great poetical achievement, especially the *Cantos*, the discussion of the ideological and cultural background of his compositions is conducted with knowledge and competence, and the poet's allegiance to fascism, though frankly demonstrated and condemned, is explained and made comprehensible in the light of the literary motivations that determined it. Interest in the subject and a personal style make this book intensely readable. This last phrase could also be applied to Barbara Nugnes's *Invito alla lettura di Fitzgerald* (Milano: Mursia), a clear, well-written monograph in a series designed to introduce contemporary authors. Nugnes delineates the writer's career and achievement, describing and analyzing his works with critical ability and sound judgment.

To complete this account of books published in 1977 I shall also mention Lina Unali's *Rivoluzioni a Harvard: capitoli della storia culturale della Nuova Inghilterra, 1800–1850* (Firenze: La Nuova Italia), a slim volume that introduces representative men whose belief in human values threatened, weakened, and eventually changed the religious and theological foundations of Harvard College, and Tommaso Pisanti's *Lo specchio e il ragno: Letteratura americana delle origini* (Napoli: Guida), an informed outline of colonial literature with an anthology of 17th-century poetry translated by the author.

Articles and essays on poetry were almost entirely concerned with 20th-century authors, the only exception being Maria P. Camboni's "La molteplicità del messaggio in 'Roots and Leaves Themselves Alone' di Walt Whitman" (*Lingua e stile* 12:21–24). Camboni traces the structural connotations of the three major themes of the poem as they develop into three parallel arguments: the relationship between poet and reader, between man and nature, and between the present and future of American democracy. She shows that the message of the poem, crammed into ten lines, is conveyed through recurring syntactic and semantic structures, while its complexity results from the semantic and metaphoric multisignificance of words and sentences. Massimo Bacigalupo in "Sofocle e la danza tragica: le Trachinie di Pound" (*Paragone* 334:60–69) competently demonstrates that Pound in *Women of Trachis* approaches Sophocles' *Trachiniae* as if it were a Nō play, blending one alien culture with another and transferring the present into the myth. In this way the poet achieves a "liberation" of language and a partial deconstruction of the "persona." Comparing Eliot's early poetry with that of Montale in "La crisi esistenziale dell'uomo contemporaneo nelle prime poesie di Thomas Stearns Eliot ed Eugenio Montale" (*Otto/Novecento* 1:77–96), Carla Apollonio finds that the two poets, though sharing a similar existential view of the world, and though starting from a similar cultural background (French symbolism and imagism) come to two different solutions of modern man's predicament: Eliot proposes the regenerating vision of religious salvation, whereas Montale accepts and faces the tragedy of our world. Sixteen sonnets from Robert Lowell's *The Dolphin* were presented in translation by Rolando Anzilotti in the annual contemporary poetry selections issued by Mondadori (*Almanacco dello Specchio* 6:129–49). In the brief introduction the translator examines Lowell's volume in the light of the poet's description of it ("the story of changing marriages, not a malice or sensation, far from it"), pointing out the faults of structure and the merits of verse and language. Ginevra Bompiani has contributed a well-written, highly perceptive psychological study of the mythological dimension that is at the core of Plath's poetry. Her "Sylvia Plath, le figure del mito" (*Prospettive Settanta* 1:62–85) aptly focuses on the images and dichotomies that make up the poet's personal mythology, on their reference to her personal history, and on their development in the span of her career.

Scholarly response to fiction has been limited to a few authors. In her "Proiezione dell'io in una fittizia autobiografia del '700,' " *Memoirs of Carwin, the Biloquist*, e la metafora del *biloquismo*" (*Trimestre* 10:45–65) Lina Unali compares C. B. Brown's work to Franklin's *Autobiography* and Fox's *Journal* in order to emphasize the novelist's deviations from the Quaker norm. The protagonist's "second voice" is taken as a satirical metaphor of that inner voice (God's voice), which is perceived by any truly spiritual person; on the strength of this interpretation, which does not consider Brown's rationalist bias revelant, *Carwin* is found to be satanic, impious, and immoral in the light of the traditional values of the time. Satanism is the basic theme of Angelica Palumbo's "Alchimisti e scienziati satanici in tre racconti di Hawthorne," a contribution to the fifth volume of *Il superuomo e i suoi simboli nelle letterature moderne*, edited by Elémire Zolla (Firenze: La Nuova Italia), pp. 139–71. The essay examines three types of Lucifer-like scientists in "Rappaccini's Daughter," "The Birthmark," and "The Artist of the Beautiful." Although some of the copious references to alchemic and occultist lore may enlarge one's views of Hawthorne's culture, they will not modify significantly the way in which these tales have been interpreted so far. Of greater importance for Hawthorne scholars is " 'The innocent abroad': intention and achievement in Hawthorne's *The Marble Faun*," (*Itinerari* 1 [n.s.]:29–74) where Gabriella Micks La Regina takes issue with the many critics who have judged Hawthorne's last completed romance a failure because of faults in structure and characterization. An attentive consideration of Hawthorne's poetics enables La Regina to assert for *The Marble Faun* a structural unity which allows, however, of a multiplicity of interpretive possibilities. The characterization of Hilda is convincingly shown to be plausible as well as functional to the complexities of meaning underlying the overall symbolic pattern of the romance. Well-documented and closely (if not always lucidly) reasoned, this essay should not be overlooked by future students of *The Marble Faun*. "La scrittura di Edgar Allan Poe: dal *flatus voci* alla *littera*" (*Lingua e stile* 20:45–88) is a long essay by Arnaldo Ceccaroni on Poe, the great "mannerist" of the written word ("the letter"). Relying strongly on Derrida, Lacan, Ong, McLuhan and Havelock, Ceccaroni analyzes "Loss of Breath" and "Ms. Found in a Bottle," arguing that Poe's themes must be reinterpreted in terms of the "writing process," which the writer both enacts and experiences. The very fact that the author uses Italian translations for his analysis shows that he is more concerned with the theory of writing than with Poe himself. Guido Morsiani's "Un anarchico fallito" (*Paragone* 324:115–24) briefly deals with *Princess Casamassima* and its protagonist as the projection of James's conscience: Hyacinth, who partakes of refined but politically reactionary aristocracy and of raw, proletarian anarchism, finally refuses political commitment and opts for James's own aesthetic values. An intelligent study of Dostoevsky's influence on Miller in Gabriella Morisco's "Henry Miller: oltre il sottosuolo" (*Spicilegio moderno* 7:138–53). Morisco demonstrates how the American writer was attracted to Dostoevsky's works not out of passive admiration but through some sort of affinity with him. Miller's thematic development was fostered by Dostoevsky, who acted as a constant stimulus towards the acquisition of the experience of the inner self that functions as "the catalyst of the multiple and unconfessed needs of contemporary man." Franco La Polla traces the connection between the language and the epistemology of the characters in *Omensetter's Luck* in "William Gass: la parola dopo l'Eden" (*Paragone* 330:94–106). La Polla finds that the protagonist's vision is edenic and integrated and that he needs no words to express his mode of being. The other characters, instead, experience a post-lapsarian dissociation: their words have no connection with objects and what they evoke is a sense of loss. In his "*The Confessions of Nat Turner* di W. Styron: La polemica sul romanzo storico e il movimento degli anni '60" (*Annali Istituto Orientale di Napoli* 20,i:7–41) Ludovico Isoldo concurs in most of the strictures leveled at Styron by the Ten Black writers in 1968 and criticizes him for not creating his Nat Turner according to Georg Lukács's theory of the historical novel. He also argues that, in order both to warn and reassure the American white audience of the 1960s, Styron shaped his protagonist as an analogue of Malcolm X in his early, utopian Black Muslim phase. Marred by oversimplifications and inconsistencies, the essay suffers also from the author's dogmatism and, of course, from his complete disregard of Styron's existentialist concerns.

Two essays belong to literary history. Giuliana Gigli's "Ideologia letteraria e sinistra americana nella Depressione: la *Partisan Review* (1934–1936)" (*Lavoro critico* 11–12:45–91) is a lengthy study of the role played by this review during the first two years of its life in the debate through which the American Left tried to elaborate a Marxian theory of literature. Unfortunately, whatever conclusions the author was aiming at will remain quite obscure to the majority of readers; in fact, not only does the discussion develop on the most abstract level, but also description and comment are too often inextricably entangled, and Gigli's faith in the communicability of the Leftist shibboleth she so exclusively relies upon is all too absolute.

The myth of America, as a virgin land where man will find his material and spiritual regeneration, is the object of a thoughtful essay by Mario Materassi. In his "Letteratura anglo-americana: una alternativa al mito" (*Il Ponte* 33:495–508) Materassi identifies the aim of all American literature as an effort to describe American reality through the use of a "communicative model": the conflict between "new" and "old," between "static" and "dynamic," "eternal" and "ephemeral." Though not always clearly argued, Materassi's investigation of the function of the myth is both interesting and stimulating.

University of Pisa

v. Japanese Contributions

Keiko Beppu

The academic circle in this country is as alert as ever to literary activities in the States. And our publishers thrive on promoting translations of American writers regardless of periods or ethnic backgrounds. The following rundown of translations which appeared in 1977 shows a close relationship between commercial publishing and scholarship in this country: Alex Haley's *Roots* (Tokyo: Shakaishisosha), Doctorow's *Ragtime* (Tokyo: Hayakawa), Heller's *Catch 22* (Tokyo: Shueisha), Bellow's *Dangling Man* and *Humboldt's Gift* (Tokyo: Kodansha), Roth's *Goodbye, Columbus* (Tokyo: Shueisha), Vonnegut's *The Sirens of Titan* (Tokyo: Hayakawa), Nabokov's *Lolita* (Tokyo: Kawade), Salinger's *Nine Stories* (Tokyo: Shueisha), James Baldwin's and Nikki Giovanni's *A Dialogue* (Tokyo: Shobunsha), Dos Passos' *U.S.A.* (Tokyo: Iwanami), three editions of Fitzgerald's *The Last Tycoon* (Tokyo: Kadokawa, Hayakawa, and Mikasa), Hemingway's *Men Without Women* and *Winner Take Nothing* (Tokyo: Kodansha), and *Islands in the Stream* (Tokyo: Shinchosha); Twain's *Huckleberry Finn* (Tokyo: Iwanami), James's *"Madame de Mauves" and Other Stories* (Tokyo: Yashio). Most noteworthy in the list are translations of *The Journal of John Woolman*, contemporary of Haley's Kunta Kinte (Tokyo: Seibunsha), and of Thoreau's major writings in the *Classic American Literature Series*, Vol. IV (Tokyo: Kenkyusha), with an excellent introductory essay by Shunsuke Kamei.

Reflections of Japanese public taste and the marketplace are found in Yokichi Miyamoto's *America Bungaku o Yomu* [*American Authors and Japanese Readers*] (Tokyo: Shueisha). Miyamoto's essays and reviews here collected have appeared for the past eighteen years in our leading literary magazines and scholarly periodicals—*The Shincho*, *The Gunzo*, or *Eigo Seinen* [*The Rising Generation*]. Miyamoto's reviews are not uniform in critical principle or accuracy. Yet, written closely following the publications of novels in the States—with the exception of *The Catcher in the Rye*—the reviews have a highly journalistic value and are a good indicator of the voracious appetite of the reading public in Japan. Besides, in hindsight, the essays dealing with Henry Miller and Sherwood Anderson turn out to be a landmark which illustrates trends and vicissitudes in modern American literature and since. *American Authors and Japanese Readers* shows the amount and variety of Japanese translations of contemporary American writers.

In scholarship the year 1977 was most productive especially in the field of fiction. *America Shosetsu no Tenkai* [*The Development of the American Novel*], edited by Iwao Iwamoto and Katsuji Takamura (Tokyo: Shohakusha), is a collection of essays on major novelists (from the 18th century to the present) contributed by noted scholars now familiar to the readers of *ALS*. (To name a few: Tetsuji Akasofu, Iwao Iwamoto, Shoichi Saeki, Masayuki Sakamoto.) *The Development of the American Novel* provides a historical perspective on the American novel with commentaries on individual writers who represent each of five eras: the 18th century, the Romantic period, and the ages of realism, modernism, and postmodernism. The anthology attempts, as Richard Chase's *The American Novel and Its Tradition* did in 1957, to establish the genre as independent of European tradition. *The Development of the American Novel* serves as a sort of sequel to Chase's book; postmodernist writers are Mailer, Salinger, Bellow, and Barth, but no black writer is represented.

Two other general studies of American fiction are Nobuyuki Hayashi's *America Bungaku Ronko: Symbolism, Irony, Identity Tansaku no Bungaku* [*Studies in American Literature: Literature of Symbolism, Irony, and Search for Identity*] (Tokyo: Hokuseido) and Motoo Takigawa's *America Bungaku no Mondai Ishiki* [*Major Themes in American Literature*] (Tokyo: Nan'undo). Due attention should be paid to the considerable space given to the novels of Robert Penn Warren in Hayashi's book; other than that its thesis is self-explanatory from the subtitle. Takigawa's exploration on the subject consists of three parts with "interludes" inserted in between. Takigawa contends that relations between God and men constitute the traditional "pattern" in American literature. The first part discusses this major theme in the writings of 19th and 20th century authors: Hawthorne, Melville, Faulkner, Hemingway, and Styron. In the second part, the dialogue with God changes to that with the self in the works of Salinger, Updike, Bellow, and Malamud. Least satisfactory is the third section, "Communication with Society," which examines Sinclair Lewis, Sherwood Anderson, Dreiser, Farrell, and Dos Passos. Takigawa's critical stance is distinctly subjective; still he is encumbered with literary clichés and ism's—his definition of realism in the introduction to section three is confusing. And too much self-vindication mars the otherwise astringent tone of his critical remarks, which are often provocative, as in the case of Updike's *Rabbit, Run.*

The works above surveyed are general explorations of the American novel; curiously enough, the novelists selected for examination overlap, and in most cases they correspond to those writers whose books have been translated into our language.

Recurring themes in American literature noted in the general studies aforementioned receive a more careful treatment and further analysis in research done on individual novelists. In *Herman Melville's Tragic Ambiguity and Beyond* (Tokyo: Kobianshobo), Taizo Tanimoto goes beyond the demigod Ahab and his losing battle with God, and finds in *Billy Budd* the novelist's final reconciliation with God. Tanimoto shows a profound understanding of Melville's works, supported by his close reading of the Scripture—*The New Testament* in particular. His commitment to the novelist's philosophical and moral position at the end of Melville's career is such that to Tanimoto Melville's reconciliation to "the mystery of iniquity" is not a matter of speculation but a revealing truth of Melville's work and his life. *Herman Melville's Tragic Ambiguity and Beyond*, written in English, is a valuable contribution to Melville scholarship. Here an article on *Moby-Dick* deserves mentioning. In "Is Ishmael, Ishmael: An Anatomy of *Moby-Dick*" (*SELit* [Eng. no.]54:73–94), Toshio Yagi questions the accepted identity of the narrator, and argues for the possibility of a late insertion of "Ishmael" in the text of *Moby-Dick.*

Interest in the American novel is also reflected in the Tohjusha's *American and British Writers Series.* The Series in American writers features, in alphabetical order, Bellow, Cather, Faulkner, Fitzgerald, Hawthorne, Hemingway, James, Malamud, Melville, Poe, Salinger, Steinbeck, Twain, T. Williams, and Richard Wright. Of these 15, 4 studies came out in 1977: Hawthorne, Cather, Salinger, and Faulkner. It is unusual in a project of this kind that the books in the series are original studies by experts on the respective novelists; they are equipped with well-prepared bibliographies.

Masayuki Sakamoto, author of *Writers of American Renaissance* (1974), probes into Hawthorne's mental and emotional complex in *Hawthorne: Ingasekai eno Tabi* [*Hawthorne: A Descent into the Blackness of Darkness*] (Tokyo: Tohjusha). Hiroko Sato's *Cather: Bi no Saishi* [*Cather: A Devotee to Beauty*] (Tokyo: Tohjusha) is an affectionate "portrait" of the novelist. The book is different from Ohmori's *The Novels of Willa Cather* (1976), which discusses Cather's works in rigidly chronological order. Sato's interest lies in the *artist* from the Midwest, whose life was dedicated to art. She emphasizes Cather's earlier writings, and points out a certain limitation in biographical approaches to Cather's works. *Cather: A Devotee to Beauty* is solid in research, judicious in the use of former studies on Cather, easy and fluent in style. One may have some reservation about the subtitle; all the same the book is a major addition to Cather scholarship here and abroad.

In view of scarce book-length studies on Salinger in this country, Yukio Rizawa's *Salinger: Seijuku eno Dokei* [*Salinger: A Case of Arrested Development*] (Tokyo: Tohjusha) is an invaluable contribution. Rizawa maintains that the virtue of a novel, everything considered, depends on its character; he places for examination Holden Caulfield among the long list of "American Adams." Which, the critic contends, may serve as measurement in determining the literary value of *The Catcher in the Rye*. His discussions of *Nine Stories* are clear-cut and illuminating. His comparison of "A Perfect Day for Bananafish" and Masuji Ibuse's story, "Sanshouo [A Giant Salamander]" is appropriate to clarify the difference between the Western and Oriental attitude toward religion. Rizawa concludes that Holden is no Adamic figure; and raises a question as to the accepted kinship between Holden and Huck Finn. Thus, his ultimate assessment on the durability of *The Catcher in the Rye* remains muted.

Faulkner has always been the center of critical attention among our scholars; two important additions are Tetsuji Akasofu's *Faulkner: Gendaishi o Ikiru* [*Faulkner: A Life in His Time*] (Tokyo: Tohjusha) and Kenzaburo Ohashi's *Faulkner Kenkyu I* [*Faulkner Studies I*] (Tokyo: Nan'undo). Akasofu's psycholinguistic approach to literature noted in the same author's *The Fate of Logos* (1974) is further developed in his *Faulkner: A Life in His Time*. It discusses the mechanism of language and "notlanguage" in Faulkner's fiction. In the introductory chapter, Akasofu demonstrates how *Soldier's Pay* differs from Hemingway's stories about veterans of two world wars; and then shows how Faulkner transports historical incidents to the level of metaphysics—meditations on time, space, the Jungian earth mother, and on language. The exploration throws light on the novelist's obsession with words, rhetoric, and the dynamics of language, which Akasofu defines, in the concluding chapter, as symbology of writing. *Faulkner Studies* by Kenzaburo Ohashi, distinguished scholar and prolific translator of Faulkner's novels, will be a monumental accomplishment in Faulkner scholarship in this country. Since two other volumes are still in preparation, let it suffice for the present to mention his article related with the research, "Reading Names Right," in (*EigoS* 123:244–46). It gives a glimpse into the scope of Ohashi's life work.

The year 1977 saw some significant publications on American drama and poetry, though the amount or variety is not so overwhelming as that in fiction. Shuji Suzuki's *Gendai America Engeki* [*Modern American Drama*] (Tokyo: Hyoronsha) is an excellent survey of modern American drama *and* theater. The chronological table of plays staged and the thorough, up-to-date bibliography at the back, which takes up one-sixth of the book, are of special interest to scholars as well as to students. In this connection *A Bibliography of Texts and Scholarship on New England Puritanism*, edited by Ken Akiyama et al. (Kyoto: Doshisha American Studies Center) deserves attention. It is a well-prepared bibliographical guide, which introduces foreign scholarships and some 20 books on Puritan writers published by our scholars from 1960 through 1970.

Two readable works on American poetry are Hisao Kanaseki's *America Gendaishi Noto* [*Essays on Modern American Poetry*] (Tokyo: Kenkyusha) and the same critic's *America-Indian no Uta* [*American Indian Poetry*] (Tokyo: Chuokoronsha). The first mentioned is a collection of essays previously published in several academic journals. Kanaseki's intense "curiosity" about modern American poets—the early Pound, imagist poets, and advocates of the imagist movement—extends itself to some contemporary poets, American and Japanese: Marianne Moore, Gary Snyder, Allen Ginsberg, Yoko Danno, Taeko Tomioka, and anonymous Indian poets—as his book on their poetry will show. Kanaseki's discussions of these poets *are* essays in the best sense of the word. The author is well versed not only in poetry but in other cognate fields, even though one may be deceived by his facile prose style. However apologetic he may be about an amateurish approach to his subject, *The Essays on Modern American Poetry* is one long meditation on poetics—a poetics which emphasizes the vitality of words and their magic spell. His poetics is unique and at the same time as traditional as Shelley's *Defense of Poetry.* Such mental flexibility as Kanaseki's is to be valued in scholarship.

All of these virtues go into the making of Kanaseki's original study on Indian poetry and culture. *American Indian Poetry* is delightful reading, well documented by historical and anthropological researches of American Indians. Kanaseki's attachment to the American language is fully rewarded by his discovery of Indians' poems and songs some 20 years ago. Kanaseki turns these poems into beautiful Japanese poems—the best translations, as he says, he has ever attempted. In their poetry words *are* images, not signs but "pictures" of thoughts. The poems are scattered throughout the book as examples illustrating Kanaseki's theses on Indian poetry. Besides these examples, the poems and songs are collected in two "anthologies" within the book, each of which contains 16 poems. And through his research on American Indians and their culture the author begins to see in their simple and wholesome life style the panacea for pollution of various kinds in society. Thus, *American Indian Poetry* becomes a profound critique of our civilization as well.

Among numerous articles on American literature, the following deserve at least mention here. Sylvia Plath and Walt Whitman are taken up respectively in Toshiko Oshio's "The Romantic Agony?" (*EigoS* 123:166–67) and in Kuniko Yoshizaki's "Whitman's 'Soul' in the Light of Zen" (*SALit* 14:18–31). Suzuo Oka's "*Meian* and *The Golden Bowl*" (*EigoS* 123:68–69) is a rejoinder to the literary debate between Mihoko Mori and Yasuko Tanimoto concerning the relationship between James and Sohseki—(see *ALS 1976*, p. 459). Citing Sohseki's letter to one of his readers, Oka proposes that Sohseki might have learned the Jamesian "point of view" from *The Golden Bowl*, which Sohseki read ten years before the writing of *Meian.* Oka gives the benefit of the doubt to the hypothesis, as he finds no other external evidence.

Oka's rejoinder anticipates problems involved in comparative studies, because the penchant for this critical approach seems to be on the increase among scholars in this country. As in all cases, good thoroughgoing scholarship and proper methodology must needs be established.

Kobe College

vi. Scandinavian Contributions

Rolf Lundén

Scandinavian Americanists have usually displayed a preference for fiction compared to other genres. During 1977, however, poetry and drama also received their share of attention, with a special focus on Eugene O'Neill. By tradition, scholars in Scandinavia have also devoted themselves to 19th-century literature, but this year all the contributions concerned works produced after 1890.

Only one general literary history appeared during 1977, Kristian Smidt's *An Outline History of English Literature in Britain and the United States* (Oslo: J. W. Cappelens Forlag). It is geared towards college students and attempts the impossible task of presenting English and American literature in 168 pages, 40 of which cover the literature of the United States. The result must of consequence be meager. The period 1620–1820 is discussed in two pages. Howells is treated in four lines; so is Gertrude Stein. Garland is not mentioned at all. The book also neglects the contemporary scene. There was evidently no space for writers like Gelber, Snyder, Bly, Barth, Hawkes, or Pynchon. But, of course, a literary history like this may serve its purpose of being an introduction and an eye-opener to those who know little or nothing of American literature.

By far the best contribution during 1977 was Ralf Norrman's *Techniques of Ambiguity in the Fiction of Henry James* (Åbo: Åbo Akademi). Throughout the book Norrman shows a masterly command of his elusive material. The study not only encompasses James's complete *oeuvre*, but also shows how ambiguity functions in the works of several other writers from Shakespeare to Melville. Norrman chooses as a focal point James's art of the late 1890s, particularly *The Turn of the Screw* and *In the Cage*. He holds that in the middle period James comes to master his use of ambiguity, while he later loses control over it. The dissertation is divided into two main parts. After a general discussion on the function of ambiguity, the first part is devoted to various ambiguity-creating devices used by James. Norrman deals in turn with "incomplete reversal," where one clue to an interpretation is negated by another which is not strong enough to provide a foundation for a new interpretation; with "blanks" such as gaps in the narrative and "self-erasing combinations"; with "code" and "symbol"; and with "misunderstandings." The second part of the book contains analyses of these devices in a context. With admirable sensitivity Norrman goes through *In the Cage* and *The Turn of the Screw*, showing how ambiguities in details underline the thematic ambiguities. The reader leaves the dissertation knowing not only more about James's fictional technique but also more about the nature and function of literary ambiguity in general.

Dreiser's literary technique is far afield from the subtleties employed by James, but Dreiser's personality seems on the other hand characterized by ambiguity, to say the least. In *Dreiser Looks at Scandinavia* (Uppsala: Almqvist & Wiksell International) Rolf Lundén gives a miniature portrait of Dreiser in the midtwenties. After two chapters on Dreiser's personality and his life during the first half of the 1920s, the main part of the book depicts Dreiser's visit to Scandinavia in 1926. The description is primarily based on Dreiser's unpublished diary, which reveals his complex character and his impressions of the Scandinavian landscape, people, and culture. The book ends with a survey of how the Scandinavian readers and critics received Dreiser's novels.

In *O'Neill och Dramaten* [O'Neill and the Royal Dramatic Theater; with a summary in English] (Stockholm: Akademilitteratur) Tom J. A. Olsson tells the story of another American writer's relationship to Scandinavia. The Royal Dramatic Theater of Stockholm played a pioneering part in the performance history of O'Neill's plays. For his descriptive study Olsson has had access to the theater's files, which has resulted in many illuminating pieces of information. He gives a detailed account of how it came about that the Royal Dramatic Theater started to stage O'Neill's plays as early as 1923. But the greater part of the dissertation is quite logically devoted to the exciting theater history which started when Dag Hammarskjöld helped secure the performance rights for *Long Day's Journey into Night.* Olsson faithfully reproduces the correspondence between Carlotta O'Neill and the head of the theater, Karl Ragnar Gierow. The thesis goes on to depict how *A Touch of the Poet* and *Hughie* had their first performances in Stockholm and how they were received. The complex history of how *More Stately Mansions* grew into the stage version that Gierow prepared is interesting reading. Unfortunately, however, Olsson's study suffers under the burden of excessively numerous and lengthy quotations.

One of the O'Neill plays to have its world première at the Royal Dramatic Theater of Stockholm was *A Touch of the Poet.* In his study, *A Role: O'Neill's Cornelius Melody* (Stockholm: Almqvist & Wiksell International), Lennart Josephson also draws on material in the theater's archives. The book is a close reading not only of Cornelius Melody's part but of the whole play. Josephson becomes so meticulous in his analysis, however, that he sometimes ends up stating the obvious. The best sections of the study deal with Melody's behavior and character and with his models from life. Much of the discussion centers on the end of the play and the question whether Melody's metamorphosis is sincere or not. Josephson is of the opinion that Melody only enters another role, the role of the Irish peasant, and he bases his argument on an unpublished scene from *More Stately Mansions,* where O'Neill states that Melody never finds peace, that he becomes one of the living dead. Josephson's readings of the play are often penetrating, but he relies too often on Swedish critics and newspaper reviewers, whose views are of limited interest.

Scandinavia's best-known O'Neill scholar is presumably Egil Törnqvist. This year he published a solid article, "O'Neill's Work Method" (*SN* 49:43–58), which sheds light on the fact that work was life to O'Neill. After a presentation of the playwright's working environment and his daily routine, the article discusses such phenomena as length of composition and O'Neill's ruthless self-criticism. Using much unpublished material, Törnqvist then draws general conclusions about how the plays grew from initial idea to published product.

Helge Normann Nilsen holds in "Hart Crane's *The Bridge* and the Poetics of Faith" (*Edda* 4:237–42) that Crane's poem must be understood in the context of the movement around Waldo Frank, William Carlos Williams, and Alfred Stieglitz, to whom art should embrace and affirm the American experience and reveal the beauty and purpose within it. Nilsen sees Crane's poetic method as an Emersonian act of bridging, which is expected to reveal the divine order in the world.

Crane's optimism in the 1920s was partially shared by Sherwood Anderson, which Rolf Lundén exemplifies in "*Dark Laughter* and *Rabbit, Run*: Studies in Instinctive Behavior" (*SN* 49:59–68). In the first part of the article Lundén points to several similarities between Anderson's and Updike's novels, such as the protagonist's running away south, his belief in his feelings and instincts, his self-fulfillment in gardening. But Lundén shows that in spite of the similarities *Rabbit, Run* could well have been written as a counterstatement to *Dark Laughter*. Contrary to Anderson, Updike makes clear that the optimistic belief in naturalness and primitivism leads not to self-liberation but to loneliness and destruction.

Romanteori og romananalyse [The Theory and Analysis of the Novel], edited by Gerlach-Nielsen, Hans Hertel, and Nøjgaard (Odense: Universitetsforlag) contains two contributions which in part discuss contemporary American fiction. Peter Hallberg's article on New Journalism gives a background to this genre, pointing at such precursors as Defoe (*The Journal of the Plague Year*), Zola and Strindberg. Hallberg sees New Journalism in its international context, comparing Capote's *In Cold Blood* and Mailer's *The Armies of the Night* to what is happening in the same field in Germany and Scandinavia. Hans Hertel has submitted a Marxist analysis of the "crisis" of the novel. Hertel also devotes some space to New Journalism but discusses more recent writers like John Sacks and Tom Wolfe. He regrets the polarization that he discerns in the United States between realists and fabulators, and true to his conviction he seems to take a stance in favor of the former.

Within the field of contemporary poetry Ingegerd Friberg made a rather uneven contribution, *Moving Inward. A Study of Robert Bly's Poetry*, Gothenburg Studies in English, vol. 38 (Gothenburg: Univ. of Gothenburg). Contrary to most previous critics, Friberg takes Bly's poetry as a starting point, not his poetic theory, and approaches the poems through the imagery. She draws on an admirable wealth of published and unpublished material. Friberg sees in Bly's poetry a continuous moving inward from outer physical descriptions to a symbolic inner quest, and her dissertation quite logically follows a similar pattern. She starts out with a chapter on "The Minnesota Heritage," where she scrutinizes images of movement, snow, field, and barn, and one chapter on the more general existential imagery of place, time, and life energy. These two chapters become a partially mechanical running through of, for instance, snow images in the poems, and the conclusions are rather fuzzy. One has difficulties understanding why "movement" is part of the Minnesota heritage, and one disagrees now and then with Friberg's readings of individual poems. Apart from the conclusion, which is superficial, the second half of the book carries more weight. Studying the "Voyage of the Unconscious" and the "Lady of the House," she is here much more coherent and manages to integrate Bly's poetry into her discussion. Relying on Jungian concepts, she gives perceptive insights into such themes in Bly as spiritual rebirth and the dichotomy of masculine and feminine. Since each of the four chapters is devoted to one specific aspect of Bly's poetry, the same poem may crop up in all the chapters, which gives a somewhat fragmented impression. Under such circumstances an index becomes imperative, but unfortunately Friberg has neglected to include one.

University of Uppsala

Bibliographical Addendum

James Woodress

In 1977 when I was editing *ALS 1975* I called attention in my foreword to a handful of new reference books of special interest to scholars in American literature. The only place in *ALS* where bibliographies, checklists, and the like can logically go is Chapter 20 ("Themes, Topics, Criticism"), but this chapter has more material to cover now than it has space for. My coeditor, J. Albert Robbins, and I now have decided to add a bibliographic addendum in order to review new reference works. Herewith begins what we expect will be a regular feature of this volume.

The most noteworthy bibliographical event of 1977 was the appearance of the second edition of *American Literary Manuscripts* (Athens: Univ. of Ga. Press). Ten years in preparation under the editorship of J. Albert Robbins, this volume replaces the first edition, which has served scholars since 1960. The new volume reflects large library acquisitions of manuscripts since 1960 and includes 400 more authors and 327 more libraries. It not only covers academic, historical, and public libraries, but also surveys holdings of museums, foundations, and authors' homes. The format is basically the same as the earlier edition, but the revision, which was computer-assisted, now is stored on tape for future use. The revisions also contain some added features that make it more useful than its predecessor: listing of proof sheets, audio, video, and film reproductions, memorabilia, references keyed by number to an appendix of printed checklists in various libraries, and a bibliography of other works useful to users of this volume. This book is an essential volume for all research libraries.

Two volumes have appeared that contain primary bibliographies of American writers. The first is Gary Lepper's *A Bibliographical Introduction to Seventy-five Modern American Authors* (Berkeley, Calif.: Serendipity Books, 1976), which lists first editions, variant states of first editions, revised editions (see also *ALS 1976*, p. 341).

The title is a misnomer, however, as all the writers included are post-modernist, that is, post-1945. Compiled by Lepper alone, the work is a considerable achievement, and the errors are few. There is no index unfortunately, but the compilation rivals for the authors it covers the much more ambitious project edited by Matthew Bruccoli, C. E. Frasier Clark, Richard Layman, and Benjamin Franklin, V: *First Printings of American Authors: Contributions Toward Descriptive Checklists* (Detroit: Gale). Volume 1 came out in 1977, volumes 2 and 3 in 1978, volume 4 in 1979. This work covers 500 authors from colonial times to the present and is compiled for collectors, dealers, librarians, and others who need accurate information about first editions.

The range of authors is wide—from Edith Wharton to Sheila Graham, from Thoreau to Betty Smith. In addition to the editors on the title page, more than 50 scholars, collectors, librarians, and dealers cooperated in this project. Although the information given is minimal, it is enough, and there are recorded for the first time some previously unknown errors in first printings. There are three parts for each author: main works (books, pamphlets, broadsides); secondary works (books edited, translations, books with introductions); references including principal biographies, bibliographies, works of criticism. The entries were printed as they were prepared so that each volume ranges through the entire alphabet. There is, however, an index provided with the final volume. This is a handsome series, accurately done, with many reproduced title pages and, for some authors, portraits. Unfortunately only affluent individuals and institutions can afford its price: $140 for the set.

Two volumes appeared in 1977 dealing bibliographically with literary periodicals: Edward E. Chielens's *The Literary Journal in America, 1900–1950* (Detroit: Gale) and Jayne K. Kribbs's *An Annotated Bibliography of American Literary Periodicals, 1741–1850* (Boston: G. K. Hall). The former is another of Gale's useful volumes in its information guide series to American literature. The editor, who previously published a similar volume in the same series on the literary journal before 1900, follows his earlier format. This is a guide to books and articles about the journals and is organized into general studies, literary periodicals of large circulation, little magazines, regional journals, radical periodicals, and academic quarterlies. The plan, rationale, definitions, and procedures are clearly spelled out in the editor's thoughtful introduction. Kribbs's bibliography is a compilation of periodicals only, but the annotations are lucid and useful. They summarize briefly the contents of the periodicals, and they list major contributors and types of literature published. The compilation will be a valuable research tool for the 940 periodicals listed. It goes far beyond the information available in the *Union List of Serials*, gives two locations for each journal, and keys its entries to Poole's *Index* and Frank Luther Mott's *A History of American Magazines*.

Two useful bibliographies of secondary material dealing with special topics also have been issued. They are *Southern Literature, 1968–1975: A Checklist of Scholarship* (Boston: G. K. Hall) and Barbara A. White's *American Women Writers: An Annotated Bibliography of Criticism* (New York: Garland). The former is a conflation by Jerry Williams of the annual checklists appearing in the *Mississippi Quarterly*. It is a continuation of the selective bibliography of southern literary scholarship that Louis D. Rubin, Jr., edited in 1969, though it is an *omnium gatherum* rather than selective and contains more than 11,000 items. Although the wheat and the chaff appear together, the items are annotated. It covers 250 writers from John Smith to the present in listings that range from single items on some obscure figures to over 1,500 entries for Faulkner. White's bibliography is highly selective and runs to only 126 pages, but it is an effort to go beyond the earlier feminist bibliographies that dealt with individual writers to cover works on women writers in general. Its 413 items are all annotated and there is an index.

An unusual and very interesting reference work for scholars who like to chart trends in public taste and literary reputations is Joseph Trimmer's *The National Book Awards for Fiction: An Index to the First Twenty-five Years* (Boston: G. K. Hall). For each year since the awards began in 1950 the compilation lists the winner, the judges, the Pulitzer Prize winner, the best fiction of the year (as selected by editors of the New York Times *Book Review*), fiction appearing on best-seller lists for the year, the position of the winner on the best-seller lists, reviews and critical comment on the prize-winning novel. The 25 winners all are distinguished writers who continue to generate a considerable amount of interest in the academic journals. Compared with the Pulitzer Prize Committee, the National Book Award judges have a better track record in picking books that still seem important.

Another guide to reference works for students of English and

American literature has appeared: Robert C. Schweik and Dieter Riesner's *Reference Sources in English and American Literature: An Annotated Bibliography* (New York: Norton). This bibliography covers 1,217 major research works and takes its place with similar bibliographies: Richard D. Altick and Andrew Wright, *Selective Bibliography for the Study of English and American Literature*, which is lightly annotated and contains 495 items; Donald F. Bond's *A Reference Guide to English Studies*, which contains 1,549 items, also lightly annotated; Philip H. Vitale's *Basic Tools of Research*, which has approximately 500 items, well annotated. The Schweik-Riesner volume is the best annotated of all these and it is the most up-to-date. Since there is a paperback edition at $4.95, it is a good buy.

Another reference tool that has been a desideratum for some time is the new *MLA Handbook*. The old *MLA Style Sheet* long had needed expanding and amplifying, and the new handbook will serve admirably the needs of beginners, with its sections on "Research and Writing," "The Mechanics of Writing," "Preparing the Manuscript," and veterans, with its very detailed models of documentation and bibliography and tables of abbreviations.

Older members of the profession may remember the large Historical Records Survey of the New Deal's Works Progress Administration, which produced a huge bibliography of works by and about some 600 major and minor American authors who published between 1850 and 1942. This project remained nearly forgotten and inaccessible on 250,000 file cards in the library of the University of Pennsylvania for the past 35 years. It now has been published in eight volumes at $670 as *Literary Writings in America: A Bibliography* (Millwood, N.Y.: KTO Press). A team of 50 persons under the supervision of Edward O'Neill of the University of Pennsylvania Department of English worked on this project for five years. This will be an important bibliographic tool.

Another useful reference work has been compiled by Elmer Borklund in *Contemporary Literary Critics* (New York: St. Martin's Press), which contains short essays on 115 modern British and American literary critics. Each essay is preceded by a section similar to a curriculum vitae. There is a chronology with crucial dates, followed by a list of publications. Borklund then presents us with a discussion of the critic's work that sums up the career as well as the basic critical ideas. All the major living figures in literary criticism have a place here, and the summations as well as the factual information all seem well done.

Finally I would like to call attention to the continuing publication of *Literary Research Newsletter* (Manhattan College, Bronx, N.Y. 10471), which completed its third volume in 1978. It is a fertile source for news and reviews of bibliographies and reference works of interest to American literary scholars and should be in research libraries.

Author Index

Aaron, Daniel, 140, 437, 444
Abadie, Ann J., 140
Abádi-Nagy, Zoltán, 316
Abbott, Craig S., 370
Abbou, Jacques, 469
Abernethy, Peter J., 75
Adair, William, 181, 184
Adamowski, T. H., 155
Adams, John R., 218
Adams, Michael, 165
Adams, Richard P., 71
Adams, Robert M., 450
Adams, Stephen J., 126
Adams, Timothy D., 23, 294
Adler, Joyce S., 53
Ahearn, Kerry, 333
Ahluwalia, Harsharan S., 72
Akasofu, Tetsuji, 502, 503
Akiyama, Ken, 503
Alderman, Taylor, 169
Aldridge, John W., 332
Allen, Bruce, 337
Allen, Donald, 365
Allen, Ernest, 406
Allen, Gay W., 220
Allen, Jeanne T., 103
Allen, Priscilla, 242
Almon, Bert, 379
Alsen, Eberhard, 158
Alt, John H., 297
Alterman, Peter S., 340
Altick, Richard D., 514
Altieri, Charles, 307, 308
Ammons, Elizabeth, 216
Anastasyev, Nikolai, 463
Anderson, Charles R., 9, 13, 14, 99, 104, 105
Anderson, David, 121
Anderson, Gillian B., 199
Anderson, Quentin, 70
Andrews, Clarence A., 338
Andrews, William L., 96, 189, 197, 200, 408, 415
Angelius, Judith W., 155, 335
Anglo, Sydney, 193
Angelou, Maya, 430
Appel, Alfred, Jr., 285
Apollonio, Carla, 496
Armand, Monique, 472
Armstrong, Thomas W., 325
Arner, Robert D., 191, 195, 198
Arnold, Edwin T., III, 151, 169
Arnold, Lloyd, 167
Arpin, Gary Q., 374
Arrowsmith, William, 129
Ashbery, John, 377
Ashton, Jean W., 215
Asimov, Isaac, 300
Asselineau, Roger, 87, 468
Astro, Richard, 319
Atlas, James, 372
Aubert, Alvin, 424
Austin, Deborah M., 425
Austin, James C., 470
Autrey, Max L., 39
Avery, Laurence G., 389, 394
Axelrod, Steven G., 375

Babić, Ljiljana, 66
Babin, James L., 114
Bacigalupo, Massimo, 495
Bacon, Helen, 358
Bacon, Terry R., 378
Badami, Mary K., 339, 340
Baer, William, 174
Bain, Robert, 198
Baird, James, 45
Baker, Houston A., Jr., 422
Baker, John, 290
Bales, Kent, 23
Banta, Martha, 113
Barber, Patricia, 50, 60
Barbour, James, 56, 61, 183
Barbour, Philip L., 194
Bargainnier, Earl F., 100
Barltrop, Robert, 257, 258

Barrett, Virginia, 407
Bartel, Roland, 294
Barthes, Roland, 459, 469
Bartlett, Lee, 381
Barton, Andrew, 389
Bartsch, F. K., 81
Barza, Steven, 373
Baskett, Sam S., 181, 258
Bass, Eben, 129, 179
Bassan, Maurice, 21
Bassof, Bruce, 325
Bastein, Friedel H., 492
Bates, Margaret, 120
Batt, Noëlle, 470, 473
Baumann, Michael L., 266, 267
Bauska, Barry, 245
Bazelon, David, 299
Beauchamp, Andrea R., 99
Beck, Mary A., 171
Becker, Jens P., 490
Beckett, Lucy, 363
Beehler, Michael T., 132, 359
Beeton, Beverly, 204
Begiebing, Robert J., 238
Behar, Jack, 129
Behrens, Roy R., 307
Beilke, Marlan, 351
Bell, Bernard W., 198
Benamou, Michel, 360
Bender, Bert, 99, 107
Bennett, Charles E., 202
Bennett, George N., 227
Bennett, Robert B., 398
Benoit, Raymond, 310
Benson, Jackson J., 95, 276, 277, 319
Benstock, Shari, 132
Benton, Robert M., 197
Béranger, Jean F., 198
Bercovitch, Sacvan, 193
Berger, Albert I., 339
Berggren, Paula S., 242
Berghahn, Marion, 426, 492
Bergmann, Johannes D., 53, 61
Bernard, Kathy L., 395
Berner, Robert L., 196
Berrigan, Ted, 306
Berryman, Jo B., 124
Bersani, Leo, 452
Berthold, Dennis, 95
Bertholf, Robert J., 360, 361
Bestor, Dorothy K., 448
Bezanson, Walter E., 54, 61, 476
Bibesco, H., 121
Bickley, R. Bruce, Jr., 59
Bickman, Martin, 46, 80, 340
Bidart, Frank, 375
Birdsall, Eric R., 71
Birje-Patil, J., 128
Black, Stephen A., 57
Black, Victoria F., 141
Blair, Walter, 92, 221
Blair, William T., 32
Blake, Harry, 470, 473
Blake, Nancy, 469, 470, 472
Blanding, Thomas, 4
Blasing, Mutlu K., 117, 436, 437
Blayac, Alain, 472
Blaydes, Sophie B., 382
Bloodworth, William A., Jr., 271
Bloom, Harold, 363
Bloom, Lillian D., 260, 261
Blotner, Joseph, 136, 145, 158, 468
Bluestein, Gene, 26
Blum, Daniel, 401
Bobbitt, Joan, 331, 382
Bogardus, Ralph F., 228
Bogle, Enid, 407
Bogoslovski, V. N., 463
Bohlke, L. Brent, 239
Boland, Dorothy W., 114
Bollinger, Lee C., 60
Bompiani, Ginevra, 496
Bond, Adrienne, 160
Bond, Donald F., 514
Bonheim, Helmut, 476
Bonifas-Masserand, A. M., 472
Bonner, Thomas, Jr., 239, 242
Bonnet, J. M., 474
Booker, Christopher, 306
Boorstin, Daniel, 446
Booth, Philip, 375
Booth, Wayne C., 332, 452
Borgman, Paul, 327
Boring, Phyllis Z., 146
Borklund, Elmer, 514
Born, N., 484
Bornstein, George, 122, 360
Bost, James S., 390
Bouson, J. Brooks, 79
Bowden, Larry R., 15
Bowles, Gloria, 371
Boydston, Jo Ann, 345

Boyers, Robert, 451
Bradbury, Malcolm, 317
Brain, Paul, 284
Branch, Watson G., 154
Brand, Alice G., 225
Brans, Jo, 319
Brasch, James D., 276
Brashear, William R., 395
Braun, Hans-Martin, 483
Bredahl, A. Carl, Jr., 202
Breinig, Helmbrecht, 60, 480, 482
Brenner, Gerry, 179, 180, 181
Brenner, Jack, 332
Breslin, James E., 368, 378
Breslin, Jimmy, 309
Bresnahan, Roger J., 422
Breuer, Horst, 478
Brian, Paul, 284
Bridges, Jean B., 153
Bridson, D. G., 120
Briggs, Grace B., 132
Brinkmann, Horst, 491
Broderick, John C., 9
Brodhead, Richard H., 55
Brodtkorb, Paul, Jr., 56
Brokaw, John W., 392
Brooks, Cleanth, 150, 153, 242, 330
Brooks, Van Wyck, 94
Brophy, Robert J., 350
Brown, Ashley, 375
Brown, Calvin S., 137, 222, 223
Brown, Deming, 465
Brown, Jane G., 288
Browne, Robert M., 362
Bruccoli, Matthew J., 163, 165, 177, 269, 279, 512
Bruck, Peter, 429, 475, 485
Brumm, Ursula, 190, 474, 477
Brunette, Peter, 97
Bryan, George B., 215
Bryant, William Cullen, II, 214
Bucco, Martin, 234, 250
Buchanan, John G., 199
Buchloh, Paul G., 490
Buckingham, Willis, 76
Budd, Louis J., 88
Budick, E. Miller, 41
Buell, Frederick, 384
Buell, Lawrence, 4, 14
Buffington, Robert, 353
Bunge, Nancy L., 22, 75, 241
Bungert, Hans, 475, 484, 492
Bunnell, Peter C., 332
Burack, A. S., 301
Buranelli, Vincent, 38
Burbank, John, 457
Burde, Edgar J., 112
Burke, Kenneth, 75
Burns, Shannon, 238
Burns, Stuart L., 158, 182
Burwell, Rose M., 328
Busch, Frederick, 13
Bush, Ronald, 124
Bush, Sargent, Jr., 92

Cadot, M., 146
Cady, Edwin H., 226, 232
Calahan, John F., 414
Calarco, M. Joseph, 398
Calhoun, Richard J., 331
Calinescu, Matei, 454
Camboni, Maria P., 495
Campbell, Findley C., 412
Cameron, Kenneth, 6
Campo, Allan, 381
Canady, Nicholas, 336
Canary, Robert H., 265
Cantelupe, Eugene B., 178
Cantrell, Carol H., 382
Capps, Jack L., 153, 159
Cardwell, Guy A., 90, 91
Carlson, Jerry W., 102
Carpenter, Frederic I., 351
Carpenter, Margaret H., 345
Carrington, George C., Jr., 227, 234
Carson, Barbara H., 291
Carter, Everett, 91, 434
Castro, Ginette, 473
Cavell, Stanley, 13, 14
Cawelti, John G., 338, 444, 447
Ceccaroni, Arnaldo, 497
Centing, Richard R., 284
Chace, William M., 341
Chaffin, J. Thomas, Jr., 70
Chamber, Robert H., 290
Chametzky, Jules, 234, 270
Chander, Jagdish, 147, 169
Chari, V. K., 69, 71
Charvat, William, 231
Chase, Richard, 476
Chatterton, Wayne, 225
Chénetier, Marc, 473

Chesin, Martin F., 71
Chesler, S. Alan, 293, 397
Chielens, Edward E., 512
Chilanti, Felice, 121
Chittick, Kathryn A., 160
Chmel, Patrick, 400
Christadler, Martin, 475, 476
Christensen, Paul, 377
Christhilf, Mark M., 318
Chung, Ling, 380
Ciancio, Ralph A., 287
Clareson, Thomas D., 299, 453
Clark, C. E., Jr., 20, 21, 512
Clark, Mary W., 277
Clark, William B., 223
Clarke, Arthur C., 299, 340
Cleman, John L., 158
Clemens, Cyril, 357
Clendenning, John, 43
Cluck, Nancy, 84
Coale, Samuel, 24, 328, 329
Coard, Robert L., 269
Cobau, William W., 153
Cody, John, 77
Cogel, Elizabeth C., 340
Coindreau, M. E., 468
Collins, Billy G., 259
Collins, Carvel, 150
Combs, Robert, 346
Conarroe, Joel, 373
Conner, John M., 402
Conner, Billie M., 402
Contoski, Victor, 386, 387
Cook, Eleanor, 359
Cooke, Michael G., 428
Cookson, William, 126
Cooley, Thomas, 117, 436, 437
Cormoran, Neil, 472
Corso, Joseph, 175
Couchman, Jane, 372
Couturier, Maurice, 470, 472
Cover, Robert, 60, 62
Cowan, Elizabeth, 168
Cowan, Gregory, 168
Cowart, David, 314, 316
Cowen, Walker, 52
Cowie, Alexander, 201, 202
Cox, James M., 89
Cox, Stephen D., 195
Coyle, Wallace, 191
Crane, Joan St. C., 358
Crawford, Cheryl, 392, 393
Creighton, Joanna V., 139, 158, 160
Crimmins, C. E., 218
Cronin, Harry, 395
Crossley, Robert, 41, 42
Crow, Charles L., 231
Crowley, John, 229, 230, 234, 269, 347
Crowley, Sue M., 326
Crump, G. B., 332
Crunden, Robert M., 438
Cuddy, Lois A., 131
Culbert, Gary A., 73
Culler, Jonathan, 461
Cummins, George M., 286
Cunningham, Lawrence S., 381
Curry, Steven, 175

Dahl, Curtis, 51
Daiches, David, 172
Dale, Kathleen, 360
Daly, Robert, 189, 192
Daniels, Thomas E., 164, 165
Darnell, Donald G., 32, 211
Das Gupta, H., 170
Dauber, Kenneth, 17, 18, 19, 55
D'Avanzo, Mario L., 8, 15, 81, 359
Davenport, Guy, 70
Davidson, Arnold E., 247
Davidson, Cathy N., 247, 315
Davidson, Edward H., 19, 35, 42
Davidson, Michael, 380
Davie, Donald, 125
Davis, Boyd, 152
Davis, Jack L., 214
Davis, Richard B., 189, 194, 196
Davis, Robert M., 276, 335
Davis, Thomas M., 190
Davis, Virginia L., 190
Dawson, Hugh J., 196
Day, A. Grove, 338
Deamer, Robert G., 12
Dean, James L., 237
de Castro, Antonio F., 419
Decaux, Monique, 467
Dedmond, Francis, 4
Deer, Harriet, 305
Deer, Irving, 305
Deery, Patricia, 9
DeFalco, Joseph, 182
De Forêt, Nancy C., 347
DeFrees, Madeline, 385

Degenfelder, Pauline, 156
Degler, Carl N., 442, 443
Delattre, Roland A., 197
Deleuze, Gilles, 461
Delgove, H., 468
Del Grecco, Robert, 66
Delizia, Michael, 287
De Man, Paul, 461
Denisova, Tamara, 463
Derleth, August, 301
DeRosa, Janet E., 81
Derrida, Jacques, 133, 459, 460, 461
Desai, S. K., 147
Desmond, John F., 322
Detweiler, Robert, 308, 328
Deutsch, Leonard J., 414
Devlin, Albert P., 294
De Vos, Luk, 339
Dew, Robb F., 353
Diamond, Arlyn, 60, 242, 291
DiBattista, Maria, 176
Dickstein, Morris, 306, 439
Diehl, Joanne F., 83
Diehl, Regina, 489
Dillard, J. L., 428
Dillingham, William B., 58, 59, 60
Dillon, David A., 337
Diot, Rolande, 470
Ditsky, John, 169, 274, 275
Dixon, Melvin, 426
Dobkowski, Michael N., 208
Dodge, Charlyne, 239
Dodson, Owen, 423
Doggett, JoElla, 206
Dogherty, David C., 385
Dolmetsch, Carl, 195
Donaldson, Scott, 166, 167, 168
Donnelly, Mabel C., 133
Donoghue, Denis, 127, 128, 451
Dorinson, Zahava K., 302
Dorsey, David, 425
Douglas, Ann, 279, 435
Downs, Robert B., 288, 442
Dozier, Richard J., 393
Drake, William, 14
Draya, Ren, 293
Dressman, Michael R., 74, 79
Dryden, C. A., 476
Dryden, Edgar A., 17, 18, 19, 24, 56
Duban, James, 30, 52, 58
Duggan, Margaret M., 165, 166
Duke, Maurice, 222
Duncan, Jeffrey L., 280
DuPlessis, Rachel B., 382
Durand, Régis, 469, 473
Dusinberre, William, 219

Eberwein, Jane D., 193, 200
Eble, Kenneth, 168
Eberhart, Richard, 361
Eckley, Wilton, 289
Edwards, Lee R., 60, 242, 291
Egan, Michael, 94
Eiseley, Loren, 14
Elbert, Sarah, 217
Elder, Arlene A., 407
Elkins, Charles, 339
Elliott, Emory, 189, 191
Elliott, Gary D., 184
Ellis, James, 238
Ellison, Curtis W., 406, 409
Ellison, Ralph, 411
Els Rüdiger, 491
Emblidge, David, 338
Emerson, Everett, 194, 197
Emmers, Amy P., 49
Emmett, Paul, 326
Engel, Bernard F., 299
Engel, Lehman, 401
Engel, Wilson F., III, 74
Engelbert, Ernst, 486
Ensslen, Klaus, 481
Eppard, Philip B., 88, 239
Epstein, Seymour, 318
Erkkila, Betsy J., 75
Escarpit, Robert, 470
Eshleman, Clayton, 380
Estess, Sybil, 376
Ettin, Andrew V., 130
Evans, Dorothy, 407
Evans, Walter, 42
Evers, Lawrence J., 334
Everson, William, 351
Ewart, Mike, 212
Ezele, Macel D., 199

Fabricant, Carole, 57
Faderman, Lillian, 77
Fadiman, Clifton, 148
Fahy, Joseph, 315
Falk, Florence A., 399
Falk, Robert, 236

Farber, Lawren, 262
Farwell, Marilyn, 383
Fass, Paula S., 438
Faulkner, Howard, 422
Feder, Lillian, 131
Federman, Raymond, 307, 336, 469
Feldman, Shoshana, 115
Fendelman, Earl, 14
Ferguson, Alfred A., 5, 413
Ferguson, J. M., Jr., 185
Ferlazzo, Paul, 76
Fertig, Martin J., 256
Fetterley, Judith, 253
Fiedler, Leslie, 259, 298, 320, 340, 476
Field, Andrew, 285, 286
Field, B. S., Jr., 241
Field, Leslie, 319
Fiene, Donald M., 313
Finley, Cecil, 235
Firestone, Bruce M., 330
Fish, Stanley, 57
Fishburn, Katherine, 413
Fisher, Benjamin F., IV, 40
Fisher, Burton, 30
Fisher, Dexter, 445
Fisher, Marvin, 58, 59, 60
Fitzgerald, Sally, 323
Flaker, Aleksandar, 282
Flanagan, John T., 350
Fleck, Richard, 4
Fleissner, Robert F., 262
Fleming, Linda, 339
Fleming, Robert E., 171
Fleurdorge, Claude, 471
Flora, Joseph M., 182, 337
Flory, Wendy S., 125
Floyd, Nathaniel M., 62
Fodor, Alexander, 232
Fogel, Daniel M., 112
Fogle, Richard H., 27, 59
Folks, Steven M., 174
Foltinek, Herbert, 476
Foner, Philip S., 94
Foote, Shelby, 141
Ford, Daniel G., 146, 147
Ford, Nick A., 409
Fordin, Hugh, 392
Forgue, Guy-Jean, 473
Forman, Milos, 337
Forrey, Robert, 247, 248, 259
Fortenberry, George, 82, 239
Foster, Charles H., 476
Foster, Elizabeth S., 59, 61
Foster, Frances S., 429
Foster, Ruel E., 277
Foucault, Michel, 460, 461
Fowler, Doreen F., 323
France, Richard, 393
Francis, Richard L., 8
Frank, Armin P., 476, 488
Franklin, Benjamin, V, 284, 512
Franklin, H. Bruce, 55, 427
Franklin, Malcolm, 138
Franklin, Wayne, 210
Franzosa, John, 60
Fraser, Keith, 127
Fraustino, Daniel V., 324
Frazier, David L., 228
Freed, Lewis, 131
Freeman, Todd, 293
Freese, Peter, 484
Freimarck, Vincent, 199
French, Roberts W., 72
French, Warren, 227, 281
Friberg, Ingegerd, 508, 509
Friedl, Herwig, 8, 470
Friedman, Melvin J., 304
Friedman, Susan, 371
Frost, Leslie, 348
Frye, Northrop, 72, 316
Fulcher, J. Rodney, 199
Fuller, Dan, 97

Gage, John T., 344
Gaines, Kendra H., 56
Galassi, Frank S., 390
Gale, Robert L., 225, 247
Galinsky, Hans, 204, 477, 491, 492
Gallager, Posey, 430
Gallaput, Edward, 472
Galligan, Edward L., 95
Gamble, Michael W., 401
Garber, Frederick, 9, 10
Gardiner, H. Jane, 132, 340
Gardner, John, 337
Gargano, James W., 39
Garner, Stanton, 52, 239
Garnica, Olga K., 184
Garrety, Michael, 178
Garrison, George R., 220
Garvin, Harry R., 304
Gatta, John, Jr., 31
Gavlin, Joseph R., 196

Gayle, Addison, Jr., 424, 425
Gehring, Hansjörg, 484
Gelpi, Albert, 80
Genette, Gérard, 469
Georgoudaki, Catherine, 352
Gerber, Philip L., 247
Gerlach-Nielsen, Merete, 508
Gertmenian, Donald, 378
Gertz, Elmer, 282, 283
Gervais, David, 116
Gessel, Michael, 291, 292
Gianakaris, C. J., 398
Giannone, Richard, 311
Gibby, Patricia M., 110
Gibson, Donald B., 426
Giger, Romeo, 489
Gigli, Giuliana, 498
Gilbert, Sandra, 381, 382
Giles, James R., 328
Gilman, William H., 5, 50
Gilmore, Michael T., 17, 18, 54, 57, 113, 440
Ginsberg, Elaine K., 197, 198
Gish, Robert, 241
Givner, Joan, 292
Gneiting, Teona T., 210
Goetsch, Paul, 490
Going, William T., 298
Golden, Robert E., 323
Goldensohn, Barry, 400
Goldman, Laurel T., 230
Goldsmith, Arnold L., 321
Goldstein, Laurence, 347, 379
Gollin, Rita K., 24
Gollub, Christian-Alprecht, 398
Gonchar, N. A., 463
Goncharov, Yu. V., 465
Gonzalo, Angel C., 233
Good, Dorothy B., 177
Goode, John, 476
Gordon, Andrew, 309
Gordon, Lyndall, 126
Gordon, Philip, 298
Gozzi, Raymond, 10
Grabes, Herbert, 485, 487
Grabo, Norman, 190
Graham, Don B., 250
Graham, Kenneth, 471
Granger, Bruce I., 209
Grant, Sr. Mary, 169
Grant, William, 29
Graves, Nora C., 294
Gray, Richard, 329, 443
Grayson, Jane, 286
Green, Charmian, 297
Green, Dan S., 406
Green, Eugene, 4
Green, Jessie D., 369
Green, Martin, 27, 444
Green, Mary J., 342
Greenberg, Martin H., 300
Greene, Jack P., 195
Greenstein, Susan M., 111
Greiner, Donald J., 315
Greiner, Walter F., 490
Grenander, M. E., 410
Gresset, Michel, 468, 469, 471
Gribanov, Boris T., 463
Gribben, Alan, 89
Grigorescu, Dan, 466
Grimaud, Michel, 132
Griska, Joseph M., Jr., 93
Gros Louis, Dolores K., 313
Gross, Barry, 246, 350, 411
Gross, Seymour, 147
Grunes, Dennis, 82
Guernsey, Otis L., Jr., 403
Guetti, James, 148
Guggisberg, Hans R., 191, 477
Guilds, John C., 213
Guilten, Nicholás, 419
Gunn, Jessie, 335
Gunod, Roberta Z., 329
Gura, Philip F., 11, 15, 193
Gustafson, Judith A., 28
Gutierrez, Donald, 266
Guttenberg, Barnett, 331
Gutwinski, Waldemar, 172
Gwynn, Frederick L., 139

Haas, Robert, 375, 385
Haas, Rudolf, 487
Hackl, Lloyd, 167
Hadas, Pamela W., 370
Hafer, Jack, 333
Haffenden, John, 373
Hagemann, E. R., 233
Hago, Samuel, 346
Hagopian, John V., 423
Halbritter, Rudolph, 487
Hall, Donald, 357
Hall, Michael G., 192
Hallab, Mary Y., 115
Hallberg, Peter, 508

Halliburton, David H., 41, 46
Hallwas, John, 349
Halper, Nathan, 123
Hamner, Eugénie Lambert, 353
Hample, Judy, 199
Hanak, Miroslav J., 146
Handy, William J., 152, 320
Hanneman, Audre, 165
Hanon, Robert M., 280
Hansell, William H., 419, 420
Hansen, Olaf, 489
Hansen, Sr. Regina, 12
Harap, Louis, 39, 40
Harbert, Earl N., 218, 219
Hardie, Jack, 368
Harding, Walter, 15
Hardwick, Elizabeth, 235
Harmon, William, 121
Harper, Michael S., 406, 430, 431
Harrington, Evans, 140, 141
Harris, John, 95
Harris, M. Catherine, 352
Harris, Trudier, 417
Harrison, Constance C., 235
Hart, Jeffrey, 173
Hartman, Charles O., 122, 129
Hartsock, Mildred, 99, 106
Hartvary, George E., 321
Hartzog, Martha, 209
Haskell, Diana, 255
Hassan, Ihab, 319
Hatvary, George E., 321
Hauser, Helen A., 58
Havelock, Eric A., 122
Hawkes, Terence, 458
Hayashi, Nobuyuki, 500
Hayford, Harrison, 55, 61
Hays, John Q., 90
Hays, Peter L., 175, 320, 397
Hearn, Charles R., 273, 438
Heinzelman, Kurt, 369
Heffernan, Thomas F., 52
Hellman, John, 306
Hellman, Lillian, 393
Hemenway, Robert, 408, 430
Henderson, Archibald, 357
Henderson, Harry B., III, 55
Henderson, Stephen, 421
Hendrick, George, 11, 12
Hendricks, William O., 161
Hennessy, Rosemary, 291
Henry, Lorraine, 407
Herbert, T. Walter, Jr., 50, 54, 56, 63
Herndon, Jerry A., 289
Hertel, Hans, 508
Herzberg, Gay S., 96
Hesford, Walter, 33, 234
Heyen, William, 374, 385
Hicks, Jack, 415
Hildreth, Margaret, 215
Hill, Hamlin, 88, 305
Hill, Philip G., 395
Hily-Mane, Genevieve, 469, 474
Hines, Melissa, 322
Hinz, Evelyn J., 45, 197, 265
Hinz, John, 261
Hirsch, David, 40
Hirsch, E. D., Jr., 449
Hirsch, Leota H., 194
Hirsh, Edward, 356
Hodgson, John A., 47
Hoeber, Daniel R., 257
Hoerder, Dirk, 475
Hoffer, Bates, 320, 325
Hoffman, Gerhard, 490
Hoffman, Michael J., 54, 55
Hofstadter, Marc, 370
Holaday, Woon-Ping C., 123
Hölbling, Walter, 486
Holland, Norman N., 469
Hollowell, John, 305, 306, 441
Holls, F. W., 5
Holman, C. Hugh, 158, 213, 295, 296, 443
Hook, Sidney, 393
Hoopes, James, 437
Horlacher, Friedrich W., 241, 481
Hornby, Richard, 458
Hornung, Alfred, 490
Horrigan, William, 178
Horstmann, Ulrick, 12, 489
Hotchkiss, Bill, 351
Hough, Graham, 127
Houston, Helen R., 406
Howard, David, 361
Howard, Leon, 61
Howard, Lillie P., 409
Howard, Richard, 459, 460
Howard, Thomas, 402
Howe, Irving, 278, 317
Hoyt, Nancy, 345
Hughson, Lois, 348

Hull, Gloria T., 430
Hull, Keith N., 341
Hull, Raymond E., 20
Hulley, Kathleen, 470
Hunt, Anthony, 185
Hunt, Gary A., 229, 234
Hunter, Lloyd A., 90
Huntley, H. Robert, 115
Hutchinson, Stuart, 110
Hynes, Joseph, 336
Hynes, Sam, 127

Ickstadt, Heinz, 481, 482
Idol, John L., 21
Ingoldsby, William, 360
Isani, Muktar Ali, 200, 418
Isernhagen, Hartwig, 486
Isoldo, Ludovico, 498
Ives, Charles, 14
Iwamoto, Iwao, 500

Jacobs, Robert D., 35, 45, 46
Jacobs, Wilbur R., 195
Jacobson, Marcia, 109
Jakabfi, Lászlo, 269
Janssen, James G., 22
Jaworski, Philippe, 471
Jay, Herman, 97, 276
Jelitte, Herbert, 491
Jellison, Charles A., 273, 439
Jenkins, Lee C., 148
Jerome, Robert D., 90
Jewell, James C., 402
Jewett, Robert, 445
Johnson, Barbara, 43
Johnson, Clarence O., 239
Johnson, Glen M., 237
Johnson, Paul D., 14
Johnston, Kenneth G., 183, 184
Jones, Buford, 22
Jones, Dan B., 57
Jones, Daryl E., 96
Jones, Grania, 128
Jones, Nicholas R., 192
Jones, Phyllis M., 192
Jones, Wayne Allen, 20, 21, 22
Jordan, Jennifer, 407
Josephson, Lennart, 507
Joswick, Thomas P., 368
Joyce, William L., 192
Judy, Stephanie A., 380
Jung, Udo, 483
Jungman, Robert E., 180
Justin, Henri, 473

Kai-Ho-Mah, 398
Kaiser, Ernest, 407
Kaiser, Leo M., 196, 199, 203
Kalstone, David, 366, 375, 376
Kaminsky, Laura J., 402
Kanaseki, Hisao, 503, 504
Kann, Hans-Joachim, 166, 171, 185
Kannenstine, Louis F., 284
Kantak, V. Y., 148
Kashkin, Ivan, 466
Kastenbaum, Robert, 395
Katz, Jonathan, 54, 68
Katz, Joseph, 226
Kauffman, Linda, 155
Kaufmann, Walter, 448
Kaul, A. N., 476
Kawin, Bruce F., 142
Kaye, Phyllis J., 402
Kazin, Alfred, 170
Kegan, Robert, 318
Kehler, Joel R., 73
Keller, Gary D., 171
Kelley, Richard, 374
Kelly, Erna E., 73
Kellman, Steven G., 93, 321
Kemp, Homer D., 195
Kennedy, Adrianne, 424
Kennedy, Frederick J., 50, 51
Kennedy, Joyce D., 50, 51, 58, 84, 395
Kennedy, Richard S., 348
Kermode, Frank, 452
Kern, Alexander C., 61
Kern, Robert, 379
Keyes, Saundra, 400
Keyser, Samuel J., 362
Kher, Inder Nath, 77
Kibler, James E., 471
Kiell, Norman, 302, 338
Kieniewicz, Teresa, 466
Killingsworth, Myrth J., 73
Kimnach, Wilson H., 197
Kinghorn, Norton D., 89
Kinkead-Weekes, Mark, 71
King, James R., 411
Kingsley, Lawrence, 352
Kinney, Arthur F., 145
Kirichenko, O. M., 465

Kirk, Carey H., 57
Kirkham, E. Bruce, 215
Kirkpatrick, D. L., 401
Kish, Dorothy, 264
Kissel, Susan S., 330
Kistler, Suzanne I., 319
Klein, Gérard, 339, 340
Klein, Holger, 178
Klein, Mia, 254
Kleinman, David, 227
Kliemann, Kristin, 320
Klink, William, 394
Klinkowitz, Jerome, 305, 307, 312, 313, 335, 415, 416
Klopf, Dorothy, 248
Klotman, Phyllis R., 417, 418, 426, 429
Kluge, Rolf-Dieter, 491
Knight, Damon, 300
Knodt, Kenneth S., 174
Knoepflmacher, U. C., 130
Knoll, Robert E., 332
Knoll, Wayne A., S.J., 353
Kobler, John, 391
Köhler, Michael, 490
Kolb, Harold, 89
Kolbenschlag, M. Claire, 12, 13
Kolinsky, Muriel, 68
Kopper, Edward A., Jr., 313
Korenman, Joan S., 106
Kosok, Heinz, 475, 478
Kotsilibas-Davis, James, 391
Kotzin, Michael C., 101
Kovalev, Yury, 463
Krafft, John M., 317
Kramer, Lawrence, 367
Kramer, Victor A., 236
Kraus, Mary C., 213
Kraus, Siegfried, 486
Krause, Allison, 62
Krause, Sydney J., 201
Kreiswirth, Martin, 150
Kreutzer, Eberhard, 341, 486
Kreyling, Michael, 293
Kribbs, Jayne K., 208
Kriegel, Leonard, 170
Kroll, Barbara, 74
Kropf, C. R., 204
Krüger, Barbara, 478
Kuklick, Bruce, 220
Kulungian, Harold, 198
Kummings, Donald D., 70, 72
Kunow, Rüdiger, 490
Kupperman, Karen O., 190
Kurth, Rosaly T., 213
Kwait, Joseph J., 240

Labiance, Dominick A., 74
LaBree, Henry G., III, 427
Lachman, Marvin, 302
Lago, Mary M., 392
Laird, David, 175
Lanati, Barbara, 494
Landon, Brooks, 334
Lang, Hans-Joachim, 61, 479, 480, 488, 489
Lang, Ruth, 479
Langbaum, Robert, 128
Langenbruch, Theodor, 282
Langley, Stephen, 400
Lapansky, Phil, 200
La Polla, Franco, 497
Lardner, Ring, Jr., 268
La Regina, Gabriella M., 497
Latham, Aaron, 165
Lawler, Donald L., 312
Lawrence, John S., 445
Lawrence, Loeta, 407
Lawson, John H., 393
Lawson, Mandy, 393
Lawson, Richard H., 252
Lay, Mary M., 101
Layman, Richard, 183, 269, 512
Leary, Lewis, 7, 194
Lease, Benjamin, 26, 61, 480
Leavis, F. R., 148
Lebeaux, Richard, 9, 10, 14
LeClair, Thomas, 336
Leder, Priscilla, 224
Leenhouts, Anneke, 288
Leff, Leonard J., 327
Lehman, Paul, 431
Lehman-Wilzig, Sam N., 340
Leitz, Robert C., 233
Leland, John, 335
Le Master, J. R., 277
Lemay, J. A. Leo, 189, 194, 195
Lennon, J. Michael, 309, 310
Lennox, Sara, 179
Lenz, Günter H., 475
Lepper, Gary, 511, 512
Leonard, Diane R., 145, 146
Letson, Russell, 340, 341
Levernier, James A., 238

Levidova, I. M., 464
Levidova, Inna, 464
Levin, David, 193
Le Vot, André, 280, 472
Lévy, Maurice, 44
Lewis, Felice F., 282, 283
Lewis, Merrill, 218
Lewis, R. W. B., 259
Leyda, Jay, 49, 59
Lewis, Paul, 32
Lhamon, W. T., Jr., 174
Libman, Valentina A., 463, 464
Liddy, James, 380
Lieberman, Laurence, 366, 367
Lindborg, Mary Anne, 250
Link, Franz, 480, 482, 491
Lippitt, Noriko M., 36
Lips, Roger, 3, 5
Liston, William T., 328
Litz, A. Walton, 130, 362, 364
Ljungquist, Kent, 46
Lloyd, James B., 137, 145
Lodge, David, 454
Loewinsohn, Ron, 368
Logan, F. J., 241
Long, Robert E., 173
Longen, Eugene M., 331
Longenecker, Marlene, 62
Loving, Jerome, 67, 68, 73
Lowance, Mason I., Jr., 189, 191, 192, 193
Lozano, Rafael, 49
Lowenkron, David H., 308
Lowenthal, Leo, 409
Lozynsky, Artem, 67
Lubbers, Klaus, 490
Luckett, Richard, 122
Lucow, Ben, 394
Ludmer, Josefina, 146
Luedtke, Luther S., 4, 444
Lundén, Rolf, 257, 506, 507, 508
Lundquist, James, 312
Lupack, Alan C., 422
Lux, Thomas, 386
Lycette, Ronald L., 107
Lynn, Kenneth S., 94, 201
Lyon, Horace D., 350
Lyons, Bonnie, 278

Mabbott, T. O., 46
Mabry, Sharon C., 84
McAlexander, Hubert, Jr., 145
McBride, Margaret, 177
McCaffery, Larry, 341
McCann, Janet, 344
McCarron, William E., 160
McCarthy, Paul, 15, 54
McClatchy, J. D., 374
McClellan, David, 171
McClintock, James I., 316
McConnell, Frank D., 303, 304, 309, 314, 317, 324
McCreadie, Marsha, 337
McCullough, Joseph B., 96
MacDonald, Edgar, 264
McDonald, John J., 22
McDonald, Marcia, 353
McDonald, W. U., Jr., 294, 472
McElrath, Joseph R., Jr., 239
McElroy, John H., 57
McFarland, Holly, 160
McGinnis, Wayne D., 145
McGrath, Anne, 15
McHaney, Thomas, 137
McIlvaine, Robert M., 177
McNaughton, William, 125
McNelly, Willie E., 312
McNicholas, Mary V., 176
McMurray, William, 116, 228
MacShane, Frank, 301
McSweeney, Kerry, 151
McWilliams, John P., Jr., 25, 26, 208
Madden, David, 332
Madden, Edward H., 220
Madsen, Valden, 75, 233
Maes-Jelinek, Hena, 54
Magat, J. A., 7
Magiola, Robert R., 455
Maguire, James H., 225
Mahgoub, Fatma M., 277
Mailloux, Stephen J., 53
Maini, Darsham S., 108, 148
Mair, Margaret G., 216
Malin, Irving, 321
Malkoff, Karl, 365, 366
Malmscheimer, Lonna M., 205
Maloff, S., 356
Maloy, Barbara, 335
Malpass, E. Deanne, 199
Mandell, Marvin, 62
Mangione, Jerre, 439
Manheimer, Joan, 347
Mann, Charles, 165
Manthey, J., 484

Marambaud, Pierre, 199
Marcincy, Reesa, 284
Mariani, Paul, 368
Marinetti, F. T., 482
Markels, Julian, 52
Marranca, Bonnie, 399
Marshall, Donald G., 43
Marshall, Margaret W., 52
Martin, Jay, 283, 284
Martin, John S., 7, 8
Martin, Odette C., 417
Martin, Peter A., 132
Martin, Richard, 485
Martin, Robert A., 173, 397
Martin, Terence, 23
Martin, Thaddeus, 424
Martin, Willard E., Jr., 69
Marx, Leo, 9, 476
Mason, Gregory, 393
Mason, Julian D., 200, 418
Materassi, Mario, 493, 498
Materer, Timothy, 120
Matheson, Terence J., 28
Matle, John, 281
Matthews, William, 385
Matthiessen, F. O., 220
Mathieu-Higginbotham, Corina, 146
Matlack, James H., 21
May, Keith M., 304
May, Rollo, 62
Mayo, Clark, 311, 312
Mays, David, 389
Mazzaro, Jerome, 376
Mazzella, Anthony J., 177
Mechling, Jay, 444
Meckier, Jerome, 171
Medieros, Patricia M., 198
Meighan, Thomas, 128
Mellard, James M., 151
Melvin, Betsy, 357
Melvin, Tom, 357
Mendelson, Maurice, 66, 69, 465
Menikoff, Barry, 109, 110
Meredith, Robert, 444
Meredith, William, 357
Meriwether, James B., 135
Merrill, Kenneth R., 197
Merrill, Robert, 315
Meserole, Harrison T., 202, 203
Meserve, Walter J., 389, 399
Messerli, Douglas, 294
Metcalf, E. W., Jr., 406, 409
Meyer, Michael, 9, 10
Meyer, William E., Jr., 170
Meyers, Jeffrey, 318
Mezo, Richard E., 267
Michaelis, David T., 279
Michaels, Walter B., 14
Michel, Pierre, 321
Michelson, Bruce, 93
Middleton, David, 154
Mignon, Charles W., 189
Milder, Robert, 56
Miller, Edwin Haviland, 65, 66
Miller, James E., Jr., 131, 281
Miller, Jeanne-Marie A., 397, 423
Miller, John C., 37, 38
Millgate, Michael, 141, 142, 159
Millichap, Joseph R., 256, 290
Milne, Gordon, 234
Miner, Earl, 189
Minor, Dennis E., 235
Minor, Major W., 190
Misurella, Fred, 470
Mitgutsch, Waltraud, 491
Mixon, Wayne, 224
Miyamoto, Yokichi, 499
Modlin, Charles E., 197
Mogen, David L., 297
Mokashipunekar, S., 147
Moldenhauer, Joseph, 42
Molesworth, Charles, 374, 384
Moller, Mary E., 13
Mollinger, Robert N., 361
Momberger, Philip, 150
Monk, Donald, 331
Montgomery, Marion, 322
Monteiro, George, 53, 76, 77, 84, 88, 100, 165, 183, 185, 234, 239
Moore, Andy J., 357
Moore, Gerian S., 411
Moore, Hastings, 79, 80
Moore, John C., 328
Moore, L. Hugh, 220
Moore, Rayburn S., 74
Moorty, S. S., 169
Mootry, Maria K., 429, 431
Moramarco, Fred, 126
Moreau, Genevieve, 274
Morgan, Richard, 258
Morgan, Ricki, 96
Morgan, Speer, 316
Mori, Mihoko, 504
Morisco, Gabriella, 497

Morris, Wright, 259
Morse, Jonathan, 83, 267, 274
Morsiani, Guido, 497
Moses, Edwin, 172
Moss, Howard, 377
Mott, Frank L., 207, 513
Mott, Wesley T., 13
Moul, Keith, 374
Mourier, Maurice, 44
Moylan, Tom, 340
Mudge, Jeane McClure, 77
Mukavovský, Jan, 457
Mullen, Edward J., 419
Müller, Arno, 482
Müller, Kurt, 483
Muller, Gilbert H., 182
Mulyarchik, A. S., 465
Murdock, Kenneth B., 189, 193
Murphy, Rosalie, 147
Murray, Donald C., 414
Murray, Henry A., 49, 51, 52, 62
Myers, Andrew B., 209
Myerson, Joel, 3, 4, 5

Nadel, Barbara S., 352
Nagel, James, 336
Naik, M. K., 147
Nakadate, Neil, 355
Nänny, Max, 121, 482
Napieralski, Edmund A., 397
Nash, Roderick, 444
Nathan, Leonard, 385
Nault, Marianne, 319
Naumann, Marina T., 287
Neill, Edward, 361
Nelson, Cary, 384
Nelson, David, 426
Nelson, Eric, 173
Nettels, Elsa, 99, 100, 101
Neufeldt, Leonard, 6, 7
Neuhaus, Ron, 173
Neumeyer, Peter F., 338
Neves, Hannelore, 479
Neville, John D., 196
Newberry, Frederick, 28, 32
Newlin, Margaret, 371
Newman, Anne R., 376
Newton-DeMolina, David, 127, 129
Nibbelink, Herman, 180
Nichols, Marianna da V., 305
Nickel, Gerhard, 477
Nikololyukin, A. N., 464
Nilsen, Helge N., 507
Nirman, Judith, 344
Noble, Donald R., 222
Nolan, Richard W., 451
Nordloh, David J., 227
Norrman, Ralf, 114, 505
Novo, Salvador, 419
Nugnes, Barbara, 495

Oberg, Arthur, 366, 378
O'Connell, Shaun, 307
O'Connor, John S., 393
O'Daniel, Therman B., 414
O'Donnell, Patrick, 79, 325
Ogunyemi, C. O., 408, 409
Ohashi, Kenzaburo, 502, 503
Ohashi, Kichinosuki, 255
Ohmann, Carol, 281
Ohmann, Richard, 281
Oka, Suzuo, 504
Olander, Joseph D., 300
Oldsey, Bernard, 178
Oliver, Roger W., 394
Oliviero, Toni H., 473
Olsson, Tom J. A., 506, 507
O'Malley, Glenn, 130
O'Neill, Edward, 514
O'Neill, John, 248, 254
Ong, Walter J., 452
Oppel, Horst, 492
Orlen, Steven, 385
Orlov, Paul A., 248
Orth, Ralph H., 5
Oshio, Toshiko, 504
Ostendorf, Bernhard, 484
Owens, Louis D., 275
Ownbey, Ray, 330

Packard, Hyland, 54
Packer, Barbara, 8
Page, James A., 406
Page, Philip, 109
Pallikunnen, Augustine G., 74
Palmer, James W., 103
Palmer, Richard E., 308
Palumbo, Angelica, 496
Panagakos, William C., 91, 92
Panek, LeRoy L., 43
Parchevskaya, B. M., 464
Paris, Arthur, 406
Parisi, Joseph, 120
Park, Martha M., 9, 257

Parker, Barbara L., 232
Parker, Hershel, 35, 53, 58
Parks, Sue S., 420
Parsons, Coleman O., 89
Partington, Paul G., 406
Patteson, Richard F., 286
Paul, Jay S., 212
Paul, Norman H., 392
Paul, Sherman, 9, 14, 377
Pauly, Thomas H., 217
Pawlowski, Robert, 361
Payne, Ben I., 392
Payne, Ladel, 264
Paz, Octavio, 375
Pearlman, Daniel, 124
Peavy, Charles D., 334
Peck, H. Daniel, 211
Pemberton, Vivian H., 346
Penkower, Monty N., 273, 439
Penn, Arthur, 334
Penner, Dick, 183
Pentzell, Raymond J., 391
Percy, Walker, 304
Perkins, William E., 406
Perlmutter, Elizabeth F., 78, 344, 371
Perlmutter, Ruth, 177
Perloff, Marjorie, 367, 376, 383
Perret, J. John, 223
Perry, Ralph B., 220
Peter, John, 131
Peterfreund, Stuart, 369
Peterman, Michael A., 175
Peters, Mildred B., 353
Peterson, Tricia, 321
Petesch, Donald A., 144
Petrey, Sandy, 249, 250
Pettit, Arthur G., 92
Phelan, John M., 446
Philbrick, Thomas, 198
Phillipson, John S., 295
Piacentino, Edward J., 158, 289
Pickering, Samuel F., Jr., 236, 256
Pieratt, Asa, 335
Pilkington, John, 141
Pisanti, Tommaso, 495
Pitavy, Danièle, 472
Pitcher, Edward W., 203
Pizer, Donald, 246, 249
Plimpton, George, 306
Plumly, Stanly, 354
Plumstead, A. W., 198
Plung, Daniel L., 210
Podis, Leonard A., 172
Poirier, Richard, 309, 358, 476
Polek, Fran J., 147, 170
Polk, Noel, 149
Pollin, Burton R., 36, 46
Popp, Klaus-Jürgen, 481, 491
Poresky, Louise A., 156
Portelli, Alessandro, 493, 494
Pound, Wayne, 159
Powell, Bertie J., 418
Powers, Lyall, 118
Pradhan, Narindar S., 147, 169
Prasad, V. R. N., 147
Pratt, Linda R., 275
Pratt, Mary L., 457
Pratt, William, 353
Price, Alan, 250
Priessnitz, Horst, 475
Prince, William S., 195
Proctor, Samuel, 389
Proffer, Carl R., 463
Profit, Marie-Claude, 473
Puetz, Manfred, 305
Pugh, Scott, 74
Purdy, Strother B., 99, 103, 104
Putt, S. Gorley, 106
Pütz, Manfred, 485, 486, 487
Putzel, Max, 135, 136

Quagliano, Anthony, 330
Quinn, A. H., 38
Quinn, Patrick, 35
Quinn, Sr. Bernetta, 126
Quinn, Vincent, 371
Quirk, Eugene F., 193

Rabkin, Eric S., 299, 453
Raeburn, John, 170
Raimbault, R. N., 468
Raines, Helon H., 310
Raleigh, John H., 396
Ramsey, Roger, 72, 152
Rao, E. Nageswara, 172
Raper, Julius R., 263, 264
Rasula, Jed, 380
Rawley, James A., 189, 200, 418
Raynaud, Jean, 469, 470
Read, William H., 446
Reckley, Ralph, 415
Reed, Michael D., 72
Reed, Peter J., 313
Reed, Walter L., 62

Rees, John O., 14
Rees, Robert A., 209
Reeves, William J., 74
Reid, S. W., 201
Reigstad, Tom, 93
Reilly, John M., 413
Remington, Thomas J., 340
Renshaw, Edyth, 403
Rhoads, Kenneth W., 394
Ricardou, Jean, 44
Rice, Julian C., 342
Rich, Nancy B., 291
Richard, Claude, 44, 471
Richardson, Thomas J., 293
Richmond, M. A., 201
Rickels, Milton, 224
Rickels, Patricia, 224
Ridgeway, Jacqueline, 371
Riesner, Dieter, 514
Riggio, Thomas P., 249
Riggs, A. R., 195
Rihoit, Catherine, 470
Riley, Peter, 380
Rimmon, Shlomith, 105, 106
Ringold, Francine, 147
Ritter, Alexander, 475, 492
Rizawa, Yukio, 502
Robinett, Jane, 385
Robbins, J. Albert, 511
Robertson, Jamie, 220, 333
Robinson, David, 3, 8
Robinson, Forrest G., 333
Robinson, Margaret G., 333
Robinson, St. John, 146
Rodgers, Audrey T., 78
Rodríguez-Seda, A., 54
Roediger, David R., 422
Rohrberger, Mary, 292
Rollyson, Carl E., Jr., 157, 158
Romm, Anna S., 464
Ronda, Bruce A., 15
Rooke, Constance, 358
Roper, Pamela E., 281
Rose, Alan H., 90, 253
Rose, Marilyn G., 261, 262
Rose, Vattel T., 407
Rosenblatt, Jon, 381
Rosen, Gerald, 280, 281
Rosenbaum, Jean, 386
Rosenblatt, Jason P., 116
Rosenfeld, Alvin H., 317
Rosenfeld, Lulla, 391
Rosenman, John B., 144
Rosenmeier, Rosamund R., 192
Rosenthal, M. L., 124, 125
Rosowski, Susan J., 261
Rotella, Guy, 354, 384
Roth, Martin, 203, 210
Rother, James, 359
Rothmayr, Ludwig, 479
Roundy, Nancy, 60
Rouse, Blair, 25
Routh, Michael, 99, 108
Rovit, Earl, 185
Rowe, John C., 44, 110, 219
Rowell, Charles H., 407, 425
Rowlette, Robert, 233
Royot, Daniel, 470
Royster, Philip M., 416
Rubin, Louis D., Jr., 140, 288, 290, 294, 323, 350, 513
Rucker, Mary E., 96, 197, 213
Rudich, Norman, 39, 175
Rüdiger, Claus, 479
Ruland, Richard, 13
Ruppersburg, Hugh M., 156
Rusch, Frederic E., 165, 248
Rusk, Ralph, 5
Russell, Herb, 349
Ryan, Pat M., 396
Ryf, Robert S., 361

Saeki, Shoichi, 500
Safer, Elaine B., 337
Safferson, Muriel, 76
St. Armand, Barton Levi, 36, 42, 53, 76, 77, 79, 80, 81, 82, 83, 217, 347
Sakamoto, Masayuki, 500, 501
Salemi, Joseph S., 341
Salzman, Jack, 247, 254
Samuels, Charles T., 306
Samuels, Ernest, 219
Sanavio, Piero, 494
Sanders, Scott, 339
Sandy, Alan, 209
Sato, Hiroko, 501, 502
Sattelmeyer, Robert, 61
Saucerman, James R., 93
Saunders, Judith P., 13, 253, 262
Satterfield, John, 397
Saxton, Martha, 216, 217
Sayre, Henry M., 262
Sayre, Robert F., 9, 10
Scafella, Frank, 95

Scafidel, J. R., 254
Scambray, Kenneth, 240
Schäfer, Martin, 484
Schafer, R. Murray, 119
Schafer, William J., 331, 341
Schamberger, J. Edward, 159
Schechner, Mark, 378
Schechner, Richard, 399
Scheele, Roy, 357
Scheer-Schäzler, Brigitte, 475, 485
Scheick, William J., 68, 190, 195, 206, 394
Schérer, Olga, 470, 472, 474
Schevill, James, 256, 257
Schiffer, Reinhard, 483, 487, 488
Schleiner, Winfried, 4
Schlepper, Wolfgang, 185
Schler, Arlene, 323
Schmitt-Kaufhold, Angelika, 492
Schmitt-v. Mühlenfels, Astrid, 192, 478, 491
Schmitz, Neil, 221
Schmitz, Siegfried, 479
Schneck, Jerome M., 57
Schneidau, Herbert N., 123
Schneider, Gretchen, 390
Schneider, Suzanne B., 72
Schoenberg, Estella, 152, 156, 157
Scholes, Robert, 299, 307, 452, 453
Scholnick, Robert J., 53, 66, 236
Schriber, Mary Sue, 255, 313
Schroeder, John H., 224
Schulz, Dieter, 476
Schunck, Ferdinand, 61, 62
Schwartz, Lloyd, 376
Schweik, Robert C., 514
Scofield, Martin, 129
Scoggan, John, 380
Scott, F. J. D., 220
Scott, James B., 284
Scott, Shirley C., 385
Scotto, Robert M., 326
Scrimgeour, James R., 394
Scrugg, Charles, 427
Scura, Dorothy M., 235, 264
Sealts, Merton M., Jr., 8, 59, 60
Searl, Stanford J., Jr., 205
Searle, John, 461
Searles, George J., 336
Sebeok, Thomas A., 461
Seed, David, 99, 109, 341
Seelye, John, 5, 91, 189, 203
Seib, Kenneth, 155
Selement, George, 199
Selke, Hartmut W., 482
Seshachari, Neila, 174
Sessions, George, 351
Sewall, Richard B., 77
Sewell, Elizabeth, 37
Shahan, Robert W., 197
Sharma, H. L., 132
Shattuck, Charles H., 390
Shaughessy, Mina P., 450
Shaw, Peter, 25, 126
Sheaffer, Louis, 395
Sheed, Wilfrid, 306
Shelton, Frank W., 261
Sheres, Ita, 278
Sherman, Joan, 258, 422
Sherwood, William R., 79
Shivers, Alfred S., 394
Shneidman, Edwin S., 51, 52, 62
Shockley, Martin S., 168, 390
Showalter, Dennis E., 338
Shreffler, Philip A., 301
Shriver, M. M., 31
Shurr, William H., 326
Sieburth, Richard, 123
Siegel, Mark R., 316
Sihol, Robert, 469
Silet, Charles L., 240
Silver, Marilyn B., 205
Silverstein, Howard, 309
Simama, Jabari, 417
Simmer, Bill, 400
Simmonds, Roy S., 276, 298
Simms, L. Moody, Jr., 222
Simons, John, 314
Simpson, Alan, 88
Simpson, Claude M., Jr., 19, 20, 93
Simpson, Lewis P., 25
Sims, Diane M., 27
Sinclair, Andrew, 257, 258
Sinclair, David, 38
Sitter, Deborah A., 28
Skaggs, Calvin, 103
Skarzenski, Donald, 317
Skrupskelis, Ignas K., 220
Slade, Joseph W., 316
Slater, Candace, 375
Slater, Judith, 151
Slatoff, Walter J., 180
Sloss, Henry, 386
Slote, Bernice, 260

Smidt, Kristian, 505
Smith, Bill, 391
Smith, Carl S., 99, 116
Smith, Charles W., 293
Smith, Dave, 385
Smith, Grover, 130
Smith, Henry N., 103, 476
Smith, Herbert F., 13, 209
Smith, L. Neal, 20
Smith, Philip E., II, 377
Smith, Susan S., 344
Smitherman, Geneva, 428
Snyder, Robert, 284
Sohseki, Natsume, 504
Sojka, Gregory S., 184
Somers, Paul P., Jr., 254
Sondheim, Stephen, 392
Souffrant, Claude, 419
Soule, George H., Jr., 82
Spanos, William V., 308
Spengemann, William C., 44, 55, 92, 441
Spiegel, Alan, 453
Spiegelman, William, 354
Spielberg, Peter, 473
Spilka, Mark, 452
Spiller, Robert E., 433, 484
Spivak, Gayatri C., 459
Sprich, Robert, 451
Srivastava, Narsingh, 132
Stacy, R. H., 457
Stade, George, 310
Stafford, William T., 99
Stallman, R. D., 352
Stanton, Stephen S., 397
Stark, John, 298
Starr, Alvin, 279
Stead, C. K., 127
Stein, Allen F., 229
Stein, William B., 99, 111
Steinberg, Alan L., 211
Steiner, Peter, 457
Steiner, Wendy, 262
Steinman, Lisa, 360
Stelzig, Eugene L., 108
Stephens, Gary, 94, 226, 245
Stephens, Robert O., 168, 183
Stepto, Robert B., 405, 411, 430, 431
Stern, Carol S., 293
Stern, Frederick C., 350
Stern, Madeline, 4
Stevens, Holly, 348, 362
Stevick, Philip, 308
Steward, Samuel M., 263
Stewart, David, 168
Stimpson, Catherine R., 263
Stineback, David C., 252, 260, 265
Stitt, Peter, 290, 355, 385
Stolz, Gary R., 348
Stone, Edward, 27, 337
Stone, Judy B., 266
Stonehill, Brian, 285
Stora, Judith, 470
Stouck, David, 256
Stowell, Marion B., 204
Strandberg, Victor H., 355
Strine, Mary S., 323
Stronks, James, 76
Stuart, Colin C., 380
Styczyńska, Adela, 466
Sukenick, Ronald, 473
Sullivan, Mary C., 323
Sullivan, Zohreh T., 129
Sultan, Stanley, 128, 455
Sundquist, Eric J., 212, 346
Surette, Leon, 124
Suzuki, Shuji, 503
Szuberla, Guy, 247

Tabah, Mireille, 282
Takamura, Katsuji, 500
Takigawa, Motoo, 500
Tanimoto, Taizo, 501
Tanimoto, Yasuko, 504
Tanner, James F., 203
Tanner, Stephen, 13
Tanselle, G. Thomas, 51
Tapscott, Stephen, 369
Tarrant, Desmond, 265
Tavernier-Courbier, Jacqueline, 259
Taylor, Andrew, 385
Taylor, Anya, 336
Taylor, Eleanor R., 375
Taylor, Harry U., Jr., 203
Taylor, John, 301
Taylor, Linda J., 81
Taylor, Walter, 148
Taylor, Welford D., 255
Tenenbaum, R. Betsy, 79, 238
Tenney, Thomas A., 87
Tennyson, G. B., 130
Terry, Eugene, 408
Teunissen, John J., 45, 265
Thakur, G. P., 347

Tharpe, Jac, 293, 324, 396
Thielemans, Johan, 473
Thomas, Amelia F., 4
Thomas, F. Richard, 346
Thomas, James W., 289
Thomas, N. L., 282
Thomas, M. Wynn, 193
Thompson, Douglas, 124
Thompson, G. R., 42
Thompson, Lawrance, 356
Thompson, Phillis H., 385
Thorp, Willard, 55
Thorpe, James, 409
Tichi, Cecilia, 198
Tintner, Adeline, 33, 99, 100, 102, 118
Tjenos, William, 354
Todd, Edgeley W., 210
Todorov, Tzvetan, 110, 460
Tokunaga, Masanori, 92
Tomlin, E. W. F., 127
Törnqvist, Egil, 507
Torrens, James, 130
Toth, Emily, 243
Trail, George Y., 72
Trimmer, Joseph, 513
True, Warren R., 424
Tugucheva, M. P., 465
Tunstall, Jeremy, 446
Turco, Lewis, 420
Turner, Arlin, 223
Turner, Darwin T., 140, 148, 427
Turner, Frederick, 334
Turner, John W., 334
Twitchell, James, 43

Unali, Lina, 495, 496
Updike, John, 304
Uphaus, Suzanne H., 327
Uroff, M. D., 382
Uya, Okon E., 427

Van Cromphout, Gustaaf, 189, 193
Van Doren, Carl, 216
Van Dyne, Susan R., 383
Van Why, Joseph S., 216
Vance, Thomas, 130
Vanderbilt, Kermit, 228, 231, 234
Vanderwerken, David L., 95, 267, 268
Vannatta, Dennis P., 280
Vanouse, Donald, 237
Vaughan, Alden T., 191
Veeder, William, 312
Vendler, Helen, 375, 377
Vessella, Carmella M., 50
Vietta, Susanne, 482
Vine, Richard, 326
Vines, Lois, 36
Vinson, James, 401
Vitale, Philip H., 514
Vitanza, Victor J., 324
Voelker, Paul D., 394
Von der Lippe, George B., 42
von Frank, Albert J., 218
Voss, Thomas G., 214

Wadlington, Warwick, 55
Wagenknecht, Edward, 241
Wagner, Linda W., 140, 141, 165, 182, 245, 246, 356, 367, 368
Wahl, William B., 327
Waite, Robert, 54
Waldron, Randall H., 66
Walkarput, Walter, 285, 286
Walker, Carol K., 359
Walker, Dale L., 257
Walker, Dan D., 332
Walker, Robert G., 180, 433
Wall, Carey, 325
Wallace, Emily, 368
Wallace, Ronald, 305, 325
Walser, Richard, 295, 296
Walsh, Harry, 232
Walter, James F., 24, 29
Walzer, Arthur E., 132
Ward, Jerry W., 425
Ward, Wilbur H., 194
Ward, William S., 206, 209
Warfel, William B., 401
Warnicke, Wayne, 15
Warner, John M., 111, 112
Warren, Austin, 27
Warren, Robert Penn, 218, 242
Wasserman, Renata R., 42
Wasserstrom, William, 169, 220
Wasson, Richard, 308
Waterston, Elizabeth, 219
Watkins, Floyd C., 155, 260, 269, 295, 296, 297, 298, 329, 334
Watson, Charles, 396
Watt, Ian, 452
Watters, David H., 82, 192
Watts, Emily S., 205, 434
Waxman, Robert E., 326
Weatherby, W. J., 414

Weber, Alfred, 490
Weiher, Carol, 133, 400
Weiler, Gottfried, 482
Weimann, Robert, 455
Weinstein, Mark A., 315
Weiss, Theodore, 122
Weldon, Roberta F., 31, 213
Wellek, René, 457
Wells, Daniel A., 44, 53
Wenska, Walter D., Jr., 189, 202
West, James L. W., III, 164, 330
West, Harry C., 32
Westbrook, Max, 248
Westbrook, Wayne W., 153
Westendorp, Tj. A., 289
Westermeier, Clifford, 236
Weston, Susan B., 363
Weyant, N. Jill, 410
White, Barbara, 513
White, E. B., 14
White, Fred D., 73
White, Peter, 30
White, Ray L., 255, 280
White, William, 66, 76, 165, 280
Whitfield, Stephen J., 259, 310
Whitley, John S., 168, 172
Whittle, Amberys R., 184
Wideman, John, 428
Wilbur, Richard, 35, 42
Wilde, Meta D., 138
Wilhelm, Albert E., 296
Wilhelm, James J., 124
Wilkins, Frederick, 395
Willen, Gerald, 115
Williams, David, 142, 143, 144
Williams, Ellen, 120, 127, 345
Williams, Jerry, 513
Williams, Kenny J., 240
Williams, Melvin G., 409
Williams, Raymond, 452, 456
Williams, Wilbur, Jr., 421, 422
Willing, Richard, 166
Wilson, Dale, 167
Wilson, Edmund, 163, 437
Wilson, Elena, 437
Wilson, G. R., Jr., 181
Wilson, R. Jackson, 235
Wilson, Raymond J., 102, 176
Wilson, Robert R., 315
Wilt, Judith, 176
Wimsatt, Mary Ann, 214
Winner, Viola H., 113, 182
Winnick, R. H., 356
Winslow, Joan D., 30, 160
Winslow, Richard, 167
Winters, Yvor, 344
Winton, Calhoun, 197
Wisbey, Herbert A., Jr., 90
Wisehart, Mary R., 233
Witemeyer, Hugh, 123
Witherell, Elizabeth, 5
Witherington, Paul, 238
Wolff, Cynthia G., 102, 245, 250, 253
Wolfley, Lawrence C., 316, 317
Wolford, Chester L., 238
Wood, Carl, 114
Woodall, Elaine D., 406
Woodbery, W. Potter, 352
Woods, Alan, 391
Woodson, Thomas, 56
Woodward, Robert H., 239, 276
Wray, Virginia F., 322
Wright, Andrew, 514
Wright, Louise J., 297
Wright, Nathalia, 55, 56
Wyatt, David M., 170, 171, 289, 354, 369
Wyeth, N. C., 14
Wymard, Eleanor B., 323

Xigues, Donez, 71

Yacowar, Maurice, 396
York, Lamar, 298
Yoshizaki, Kuniko, 504
Young, Philip, 189, 201, 210
Young, Thomas D., 353, 354

Zacharasiewicz, Waldemar, 478
Zanger, Jules, 271
Zaniello, Thomas A., 350
Zavarzadeh, Mas'ud, 306, 336, 441, 442
Zayed, Georges, 36
Zehr, David M., 179
Zelnick, Stephen, 175
Ziegler, Heide, 483
Ziolkowski, Theodore, 456
Zolla, Elémire, 496
Zucker, David, 372
Zuckerman, Michael, 26, 191
Zveryev, A. M., 465

Subject Index

Abish, Walter, 307
Adams, Charles F., Jr., 25
Adams, Henry, 75, 76, 101, 113, 117, 169, 218, 219, 220, 258, 333, 436; *The Education*, 219, 220, 258, 333, 436
Addison, Joseph, 210
Adler, Joseph, 391
Aeschylus: *Oresteia*, 232
Agee, James, 274, 323; *Let Us Now Praise Famous Men*, 274
Aiken, Conrad, 352, 489
Aksënov, Vasilij, 282
Alamnig, Ivan, 282
Albee, Edward, 398, 401, 487; *Who's Afraid of Virginia Woolf?*, 398; *The Zoo Story*, 398
Alcott, Amos Bronson, 15, 479
Alcott, Mrs. Bronson, 4
Alcott, Louisa May, 216, 217; *Work*, 217
Aldington, Richard: *Stepping Heavenward*, 127
Alger, Horatio, 236, 247
Algren, Nelson, 168, 273
Ammons, A. R., 365, 384; "Corsons Inlet," 384; "Essay on Poetics," 384; *Tape for the Turn of the Year*, 384
Anderson, Maxwell, 394
Anderson, Sherwood, 9, 246, 254–57, 335, 349, 436, 499, 500, 507, 508; *Dark Laughter*, 257, 507, 508; *Kit Brandon*, 255; *Poor White*, 255, 257; "There She Is–She Is Taking Her Bath," 254; "The Triumph of a Modern," 254; *Windy McPherson's Son*, 254; *Winesburg, Ohio*, 9, 246, 254, 255, 256, 257; "The Yellow Gown," 254
Angelou, Maya, 426, 430; *I Know Why the Caged Bird Sings*, 426
Antin, David, 490
Appleton, John, 20
Aquinas, Saint Thomas, 27
The Arabian Nights, 460
Arichandra: The Martyr of Truth, 52
Arms, George, 242
Arnold, Lloyd, 167
Arnold, Mathew, 127
Arrabal, Fernando: *The Architect and the Emperor of Assyria*, 400
Ashbery, John, 365, 384
Asimov, Isaac, 299, 300, 301; *Foundation*, 300
Augustine, Saint, 27, 129

Babbitt, Irving, 266, 438
Bachelard, Gaston, 211, 467
Bacon, Francis, 27
Bacon, Nathaniel, 194, 195
Baker, George Pierce, 394
Bakhtin, Mikhail M., 472
Baldwin, James, 414, 426, 427, 429, 463, 487, 493, 494, 499; *Another Country*, 414, 426; *If Beale Street Could Talk*, 426; "Sonny Blues," 414
Baldwin, Joseph G.: *The Flush Times of Alabama and Mississippi*, 222
Balzac, Honoré de, 100, 101, 104, 269; *Comédie Humaine*, 269
Bancroft, George, 193
Barker, James: *The Indian Princess*, 478
Barlow, Joel: "Advice to a Raven in Russia," 203
Barnes, Clive, 401
Barnes, Djuna, 273, 282
Barnum, P. T., 14
Barrymore, John, 391
Barrymore, Maurice, 391
Barth, John, 103, 231, 232, 265, 303, 304, 305, 307, 324–25, 453, 472, 485, 486, 500, 505; *End of the Road*, 232, 324; *Lost in the Fun-*

house, 324, 325, 485; *The Sot-Weed Factor*, 486
Barth, Karl, 326
Barthelme, Donald, 280, 305, 472, 473, 485; *The Dead Father*, 335
Barthes, Roland, 419, 436, 459, 469; *Sade, Fourier, Loyola*, 419
Barton, Andrew: *The Disappointment*, 389
Bartram, William, 198, 205; *Travels*, 205
Baudelaire, Charles, 36
Baum, L. Frank: *The Wizard of Oz*, 245, 314
Baumbach, Jonathan, 307
Bayle, Pierre, 52
Bazán, Pardo, 233
Beach, Sylvia, 168
Beauvoir, Simone de, 201
Beckett, Samuel, 103, 104, 128, 416: *Waiting for Godot*, 104
Behrman, S. N., 394
Bellamy, Edward, 235, 464, 480, 481; *Looking Backward*, 235, 481
Bellow, Saul, 303, 304, 317–19, 324, 332, 499, 500, 501; *The Adventures of Augie March*, 318; *Dangling Man*, 317, 324, 499; *Humbolt's Gift*, 318, 319, 499; *Mr. Sammler's Planet*, 318; *The Victim*, 318
Benton, Thomas H.: *Thirty Years' View*, 124
Berger, Thomas: *Little Big Man*, 334
Bernhard, Thomas, 491
Berryman, John, 366, 369, 373–74, 381; *Dream Songs*, 373, 374; *Homage to Mistress Ann Bradstreet*, 373; *Love and Fame*, 373; *Love Sonnets*, 373; *Recovery*, 373; "Winter Landscape," 369
Berthoff, Warner, 242
Beverly, Robert, 195, 203; *History and Present State of Virginia*, 203
Bhagavad Gita, 132
Bierce, Ambrose, 207, 241, 242: "An Occurrence at Owl Creek Bridge," 241
Bingham, Millicent T., 76
Binyon, Laurence, 123, 124
Bishop, Elizabeth, 366, 375–77; "At the Fishhouses," 376; "Cape Breton," 376; "Cirque d' Hiver," 376; "Florida," 376; "In the Village," 376; *North & South*, 376
Bishop, Jonathan, 8
Bissell, Richard, 338
Black, Victoria F., 141
Blake, Harry: "Not to Knot," 473
Blake, William, 125, 126, 328
Blatchford, Robert, 12
Bleeker, Ann E., 205
Blitzstein, Marc: *The Cradle Will Rock*, 393
Bly, Robert, 505, 508, 509
Boethius, 199
Bogan, Louise, 344, 371–72
Bonaparte, Marie B., 38
Bonosky, Phillip, 463
Bontemps, Arna, 427, 493; *Black Thunder*, 427
Borges, Jorge Luis, 265, 315, 340
Borzage, Frank, 178
Boucicault, Dion: *The Octoroon*, 390, 478
Bourjaily, Vance, 306
Bourne, Randolph, 489
Bowles, Paul, 303
Bradbury, Ray, 300
Bradford, William, 25, 190, 191, 208, 477; *Of Plymouth Plantation*, 477
Bradley, Francis Hubert, 128, 131
Bradstreet, Anne, 192, 205, 434
Brady, Matthew, 228
Braithwaite, William S., 427
Branch, E. Douglas: *The Hunting of the Buffalo*, 289
Brautigan, Richard, 308
Brecht, Bertolt, 256
Breuer, Lee: *Animation*, 399
Breuer, Miles: *The Gostak and the Doshes*, 104
Bringhurst, Joseph, Jr., 202
Bronzino, Agnolo di Cosimo, 105
Brooks, Gwendolyn, 419, 420, 430; *Beckonings*, 419, 430; *Family Pictures*, 419; *In the Mecca*, 420; "In the Time of Detachment," 420; "Riders to the Blood-Red Wrath," 420; *Riot*, 420; *Selected Poems*, 420; "The Sight of the Horizon," 420
Brooks, Van Wyck, 90, 94, 434, 437; *The Flowering of New England*, 434

Broun, Heywood: *The Boy Grew Older*, 166
Brown, Ashley, 332
Brown, Charles Brockden, 201–2; *Edgar Huntly*, 476; *Wieland*, 201, 202, 496
Brown, Claude, 330
Brown, John, 13
Brown, Norman O., 316
Brown, Sterling, 427
Browne, William H., 38
Browning, Deborah, 66
Browning, Robert: "A Light Woman," 100
Bruce, Philip A., 222
Brüchner, Georg: *Danton's Death*, 393
Brueghel, Pieter, 318, 369; "The Hunters in the Snow," 369; "The Misanthrope," 318
Brunner, John: *The Shockwave Rider*, 453
Bryant, William Cullen, 214, 215
Brzeska, Sophie, 120
Buber, Martin, 318
Bucke, Richard M., 67
Buddha, 270
Bullins, Ed, 423, 487
Burke, Kenneth: *The Philosophy of Literary Form*, 488
Burr, Aaron, 196
Burroughs, William, 280, 472, 473
Bush, James: *Spock Must Die!*, 104
Butor, Michel, 469
Byrd, William, 195, 196
Byron, George Noel Gordon, Lord, 114

Cabell, James Branch, 150, 151, 263–65; *Beyond Life*, 265; *Jurgen*, 150, 151
Cable, George Washington, 223; *The Grandissimes*, 223; *Old Creole Days*, 223
Cage, John, 485
Cahan, Abraham, 234, 270–71; *The Rise of David Levinsky*, 270; *Yekl: A Tale of the New York Ghetto*, 270
Caldwell, Erskine, 268, 288, 444, 473; *Tobacco Road*, 288
Calverton, V. F., 489
Camm, John, 195
Campbell, Thomas: "Battle of the Baltic," 52
Camus, Albert, 342
Capote, Truman, 305, 306, 329, 440, 441, 442, 463, 485, 508; *In Cold Blood*, 306, 441, 442, 485, 508
Carlyle, Thomas: *German Romance*, 43
Carpenter, Edward, 12, 68
Carroll, Lewis, 37, 287, 359
Carson, Johnny, 338
Carver, Jonathan, 198
Castaneda, Carlos, 308
Castañeda, Pedro de, 477
Cather, Willa, 225, 246, 259–61, 298, 333, 501, 502; *Alexander's Bridge*, 260; *My Ántonia*, 260; *Death Comes for the Archbishop*, 260; *A Lost Lady*, 261; *O Pioneers!* 260, 261; *The Professor's House*, 260; *Shadows on the Rock*, 261
Celan, Paul, 491
Cervantes Saavedra, Miguel de, 233; *Don Quixote*, 95
Champlain, Samuel de: *Les Voyages*, 477
Chandler, Raymond, 142, 301, 302, 448, 490; *The Big Sleep*, 142
Chanler, William A., 208
Chapman, John J., 208
Chase, Richard, 225, 500; *The American Novel and Its Tradition*, 500
Chaucer, Geoffrey, 74
Chauncy, Charles, 30; *Seasonable Thoughts . . .*, 30
Chayefsky, Paddy, 401
Cheever, John, 303, 328–29; *Bullet Park*, 328; *Falconer*, 328; *The Wapshot Chronicle*, 328
Chekhov, Anton, 424
Cheney, Brainard, 332
Chesnutt, Charles W., 406, 407–9, 417, 428, 481, 482; "Baxter Procustes," 408; "The Bouquet," 408; *The Conjure Woman*, 408; "The Sheriff's Children," 482; *The Wife of His Youth*, 408
Child, Lydia, 25, 208
Childress, Alice, 423
Chomsky, Noam, 104, 123, 161, 314

Chopin, Kate, 202, 242, 243; *At Fault*, 242; *The Awakening*, 202, 243
Christ, 270
Christie, Agatha, 448
Church, Benjamin, 205
Clark, Gregory, 168
Clark, Walter Van Tilburg, 297
Clarke, Arthur C., 299, 300, 340; *Childhood's End*, 299
Cleaver, Eldridge, 329, 427
Clemens, Olivia, 90
Clemm, Maria, 37
Clurman, Harold, 393
Cohen, Hennig, 417
Coleridge, Samuel Taylor, 101, 263
Coltrane, John, 430
Connelly, Marc, 423
Conrad, Joseph, 99, 100, 172; *Heart of Darkness*, 172
Cooke, Ebenezer, 195
Cooper, James Fenimore, 23, 80, 141, 207, 209, 211–13, 468; *The Deerslayer*, 213; *Home As Found*, 212, 213; *Leatherstocking Tales*, 80; *The Pioneers*, 212, 213; *The Prairie*, 213
Cooper, Samuel, 199
Cooper, Susan Fenimore: *Pages and Pictures*, 213
Coover, Robert, 280, 335–36, 473; *Pricksongs and Descants*, 336; *Universal Baseball Association*, 335
Copeau, Jacques, 392
Copland, Aaron, 84, 85
Cotton, John, 192, 194, 205, 478
Cowley, Malcolm: *Exile's Return*, 434
Cozzens, James G., 297
Cranch, Christopher, 4, 8
Crane, Hart, 343, 346, 507; *The Bridge*, 346, 507
Crane, Stephen, 207, 227, 236–39, 240, 341, 492; "The Blue Hotel," 238; "The Bride Comes to Yellow Sky," 237, 238; "Experiment in Misery," 239; "The Five White Mice," 237; *Maggie*, 238, 341; "One Dash—Horses," 237; "The Upturned Face," 238; "Why Did the Young Clerk Swear?" 227
Crapsey, Adelaide, 343, 344
Crawford, Cheryl: *One Naked Individual*, 392
Creeley, John, 366, 378
Crèvecoeur, Hector St. John de, 198; *Letters from an American Farmer*, 198; *Sketches*, 198
Croly, Herbert, 489
Cruse, Harold, 405, 412; *Crisis of the Negro Intellectual*, 412
Cummings, E. E., 343, 347, 348
Curtis, G. W., 53
Curtius, Ernst R., 377
Cushman, Charlotte, 403
Cuvier, Baron Georges, 39

Daly, Augustin: *Pique*, 390
Dalys, Carroll J., 483
Damon, S. Foster, 347, 348; *Tilted Moons*, 347
Danno, Yoko, 503
Dante Alighieri, 124, 125, 126, 130, 180, 181, 314; *Divine Comedy*, 180
Darwin, Charles, 60, 264
Davenport, John, 192
Davidson, Donald, 343, 352
Davies, Ossie, 487
Davis, Angela, 427
Davis, George, 427
Davis, Rebecca Harding: "Life in the Iron Mills," 33, 234
Davis, Richard B., 189, 194, 196
de Bono, Edward, 300
de Bry, Theodore, 194
Deeter, Jasper, 402
Defoe, Daniel, 12, 13, 508; *The Journal of the Plague Year*, 508; *Robinson Crusoe*, 12, 13
Delany, Samuel R., 132, 299, 340; *The Einstein Intersection*, 132, 340
Deleuze, Gilles, 461
DeLillo, Don, 307, 336; *End Zone*, 336
de L'Isle-Adam, Villiers, 177
De Man, Paul, 460
Demuth, Charles, 368, 369; "I Saw the Figure 5 in Gold," 369; "Tuberoses," 369
Derrida, Jacques, 43, 133, 380, 459, 460, 461, 497; *Of Grammatology*, 459, 460

DeVoto, Bernard, 90, 91, 333
DeVries, Peter, 303
Dewey, John, 343, 345
Dick, Philip K., 300
Dickey, James, 274, 306, 331; *Deliverance*, 331; "Madness," 331
Dickens, Charles: *Martin Chuzzlewit*, 155
Dickinson, Emily, 75, 76–85, 113, 205, 217, 233, 368, 395, 435, 466, 470, 476, 480; "Bereaved of all, I went Abroad," 81; *Bolts of Melody*, 76; "For every Bird a Nest," 82; "I Dwell in Possibility," 78; "I like to see it lap the Miles," 81; "I saw no Way—the Heavens were stitched," 81; "My Life had stood —a Loaded Gun," 80; "On this wondrous sea," 82; "A Route of Evanescence," 81; "There's a certain Slant of light," 78; "This was a Poet," 82
Dickinson, John, 199, 205
Dickinson, Lavinia, 78, 84, 395
Dickinson, Martha, 76
Dickinson, Susan G., 77
Disney, Walt, 338, 445
Disraeli, Benjamin, 234
D'Israeli, Issaac: *Curiosities of Literature*, 32
Dixon, Thomas: *The Clansman*, 288
Doctorow, E. L., 307, 338, 499; *Michael Kohlhaas*, 338; *Ragtime*, 338, 499
Dodson, Owen, 423
Dolmetsch, Arnold, 122
Donnelly, Ignatius, 480, 481; *Caesar's Column*, 481; *The Golden Bottle*, 481
Doolittle, Hilda, 205, 344, 371; "Helen in Egypt," 371; "Hermetic Definition," 371; "Oread," 344
Dos Passos, John, 168, 267–68, 348, 453, 499, 500; *Manhatten Transfer*, 267, 268; *U.S.A.*, 267, 268, 499
Dostoyevsky, Fedor, 39, 40, 146, 313, 491, 497; "Dcojnik," 491; "The Double," 40; *The Idiot*, 452; *Notes from the Underground*, 40
Douglas, Aaron: "Idyll of Deep South," 429
Drake, Joseph R.: *The Culprit Fay and Other Poems*, 47
Dreiser, Theodore, 94, 120, 226, 240, 243, 245, 246–50, 270, 500, 506; *An American Tragedy*, 245, 248, 250; *The Bulwark*, 248; *The Financier*, 248, 249, 250; *Free and Other Stories*, 250; *The 'Genius,'* 248, 249; *The Hand of the Potter*, 248; *Jennie Gerhardt*, 249; *Sister Carrie*, 243, 247, 249, 270; *The Titan*, 248; *A Traveller at Forty*, 249
Duberman, Martin: *In White America*, 400
DuBois, W. E. B., 406, 408, 427; *The Black Fire*, 427
Dufrenne, Mikel, 455
Dunbar, Paul Laurence, 426, 427, 430, 481; *Fanatics*, 427; *The Sport of the Gods*, 426
Duncan, Robert, 488
Dundes, Allen, 417
Dunlap, William, *André*, 478
Dunne, J. W., 104
Durand, Gilbert, 467, 468
Dürrenmatt, Friedrich, 103, 104; *The Pledge*, 104
Duyckinck, Evert A., 53, 61

Eastman, Max, 168, 489
Eble, Kenneth, 242
Edwards, Harry S.: *Eneas Africanus*, 160
Edwards, Jonathan, 196, 197, 205
Eickenmeyer, Rudolf, 228
Eiseley, Loren, 14
Eliot, George, 116
Eliot, T. S., 119, 122, 126–33, 153, 173, 179, 263, 347, 348, 356, 361, 363, 367, 414, 489, 490, 495, 496; *Ash Wednesday*, 133; *The Cocktail Party*, 133; "Dans le restaurant," 129; *Four Quartets*, 119, 128, 131, 132; "Gerontion," 132; "The Hollow Men," 132; *Murder in the Cathedral*, 132, 133; "Portrait of a Lady," 129, 179; "Prufrock," 128, 132; "Sweeney Erect," 130; *The Waste Land*, 119, 127, 128, 131, 132, 153, 173, 414, 455, 489

Eliot, Vivienne, 131
Elkin, Stanley, 341
Ellis, Edward, 236
Ellison, Ralph, 330, 414, 426, 427, 428, 429, 430, 431; *Invisible Man*, 414, 426, 428; *Shadow and Act*, 411, 414
Emerson, Ralph Waldo, 3, 4, 5, 6–9, 12, 70, 81, 82, 83, 95, 211, 257, 278, 289, 329, 354, 358, 359, 363, 422, 476, 479, 491; "The American Scholar," 8; *English Traits*, 5, 9; *Essays*, 7, 9; "Ode: Inscribed to W. H. Channing," 479; "The Poet," 81; "Self-Reliance," 81
Erickson, Erik, 10
Euripides, 352, 358; *Bacchae*, 358
Eveleth, George, 38
Everson, William (Brother Antoninus), 351, 381
Ezekiel, 132

Falkner, Col. William C., 136, 137, 222, 223; *The White Rose of Memphis*, 137, 222, 223
Falkner, John W. T., 136
Farley, Robert, 136
Farmer, Philip J., 340, 341
Farquhar, George: *The Beaux Stratagem*, 390
Farrell, James T., 279, 500; *Studs Lonigan*, 279
Fast, Howard, 464
Faulkner, William, 58, 135–61, 168, 246, 271, 288, 298, 323, 329, 444, 453, 463, 465, 466, 468, 469, 471, 473, 474, 483, 494, 500, 501, 502, 503; *Absalom, Absalom!*, 140, 147, 152, 156, 157, 158, 170, 288, 474; *As I Lay Dying*, 136, 153, 154, 155, 159, 468, 494; *The Bear*, 159, 160; "Dry September," 160; *A Fable*, 160; *Flags in the Dust*, 151, 468; *Go Down, Moses*, 136, 139, 141, 153, 158, 159; *The Hamlet*, 142, 158; *Light in August*, 147, 156; *The Mansion*, 160; *The Marionettes*, 136, 149; *Mayday*, 150; *Mosquitoes*, 151; *The Reivers*, 160; *Requiem for a Nun*, 141, 145, 156; "A Rose for Emily," 146; *Sanctuary*, 143, 145, 147, 156, 468; *Sartoris*, 145, 151, 468; *Soldier's Pay*, 151, 502; *The Sound and the Fury*, 146, 147, 150, 151, 152, 153, 468; *The Town*, 160; *The Wild Palms*, 158; *The Unvanquished*, 139, 158
Fenno, John, 202
Fiedler, Leslie, 225, 259, 298, 490; *Love and Death in the American Novel*, 259
Field, Andrew, 285–86
Fiske, John, 192, 478
Fitzgerald, F. Scott, 102, 163–78, 185–86, 220, 246, 258, 268, 274, 328, 495, 499, 501; "Bernice Bobs Her Hair," 177; "The Cruise of the Rolling Junk," 166; *The Great Gatsby*, 163, 168, 169, 170, 172, 173, 174, 175, 246, 447; *The Last Tycoon*, 163, 499; "May Day," 177; *Tender is the Night*, 102, 163, 175, 176, 177; *This Side of Paradise*, 164, 177; "Winter Dreams," 165
Fitzgerald, Zelda, 169, 220
Flaubert, Gustave, 116, 145, 453; *La Tentation*, 145; *Madame Bovary*, 116, 145
Fletcher, John G.: "The Skaters," 344
Foote, Shelby, 141, 470, 471; *Jordan Country*, 471; "A Marriage Portion," 471, 472; "Pillar of Fire," 471; Rain Down Home," 471
Forbes, Waldo Emerson, 4
Foreman, Richard, 398, 399; *Pandering to the Masses*, 399; *Particle Theory*, 399
Forest, Leon: *There Is a Tree More Ancient than Eden*, 429, 431
Fornes, Maria I., 398
Forrest, Edwin, 389
Fosdick, Charles A. (Harry Castlemon), 236
Foster, Hannah: *The Coquette*, 189, 202
Foucault, Michel, 460, 461; *Language, Counter-Memory*, 460; *The Archaeology of Knowledge*, 460; *The Order of Things*, 460
Fourier, Charles, 70
Fox, William P., 306, 331; *Ruby Red*, 332

Franklin, Benjamin, 12, 14, 196, 197, 440, 468; *Autobiography*, 196; "Dogood Papers," 203
Frederic, Harold, 211, 212, 239; "The Editor and the Schoolma'am," 239
Freeman, Mary W., 225
Freneau, Philip F., 189, 198, 200; "The Beauties of Santa Cruz," 200
Freud, Sigmund, 10, 90, 115, 149, 201, 257, 309, 341, 444; *The Interpretation of Dreams*, 309
Friend, Beverly, 299
Frost, Leslie, 348
Frost, Robert, 84, 343, 344, 355, 356–58, 359, 385, 466; "Birches," 358; *In the Clearing*, 358; "Kitty Hawk," 358; "Out, Out–," 357; "A Servant to Servants," 358; "The Subverted Flower," 357; "Wild Grapes," 358
Frye, Northrop, 316
Fuller, Henry Blake, 240, 241, 481; *With the Procession*, 481
Fuller, Margaret, 3, 5, 36, 436
Fullerton, Morton, 251

Gabriel, Ralph: *The Course of American Democratic Thought*, 434
Gaddis, William, 303, 340, 341, 473; *JR*, 473
Gaines, Ernest: *The Autobiography of Miss Jane Pittman*, 415, 427; *Catherine Carmier*, 415; *Of Love and Dust*, 415
Galdós, Pérez, 233
Gandhi, Mahatma, 11
Gardner, John, 306, 337
Gardner, Nathaniel, 203
Garland, Hamlin, 75, 226, 240, 241, 505; *The Goldseekers*, 241
Garson, Barbara, 487
Gaskell, Elizabeth Cleghorn, 234
Gass, William, 336, 473, 497; *Omensetter's Luck*, 497
Gaudier, Henri, 129
Gautier, Théophile: *Mademoiselle de Maupin*, 284
Gay, John: *The Beggar's Opera*, 389
Gayle, Addison, Jr., 424, 425; *The Way of the New World*, 424, 425; *Wayward Child*, 424
Gelber, Jack, 487, 505
Genette, Gérard, 469, 471
Gerhardt, Ranier M., 377
Gide, André: *The Counterfeiters*, 308
Gilder, R. W., 224
Gingrich, Arnold, 277
Ginsberg, Allen, 374, 378, 473, 488, 503; "Howl," 378, 379, 473; "Kaddish," 378
Giovanni, Nikki, 499
Glasgow, Ellen, 263–65; *Barren Ground*, 265; *The Descendant*, 265; "Jordan's End," 264; *The Romantic Comedians*, 265; *The Sheltered Life*, 265; *Vein of Iron*, 264; *Virginia*, 264
Godfrey, Thomas: *The Prince of Parthia*, 389
Godwin, Gail, 485
Goethe, Johann Wolfgang von, 252, 282, 314, 491; *Werther*, 282
Gold, Michael, 489
Goldsmith, Oliver, 210
Goodrich, Samuel G.: *The Outcast and Other Poems*, 21
Gordon, Caroline, 287, 288, 323
Gottfried, Martin, 401
Graham, Shiela, 512
Grant, Madison, 169
Grass, Gunter, 103
Graves, Robert, 315, 371; *The White Goddess*, 315
Green, Paul, 423
Griffith, David W., 177
Grimm, Herman, 4, 5
Grinevskii, Aleksandr, 287
Gris, Juan, 262
Griswold, Rufus, 36, 37
Gutman, Herbert, 426

Hakluyt, Richard: *Voiages*, 194
Haley, Alex: *Roots*, 499
Hall, Edward: *The Silent Language*, 183
Hamilton, Alexander, 205
Hammerstein, Oscar, II: *Show Boat*, 392; *The Sound of Music*, 392
Hammett, Dashiell, 448, 483
Hammon, Britton: *Narrative*, 429
Hansberry, Lorraine, 418, 423, 487; *The Drinking Gourd*, 418
Hariot, Thomas, 194, 477
Harris, Joel Chandler, 93, 223
Harris, Wilson, 53

Harrison, Constance C.: *The Anglomaniacs*, 235
Harrison, Harry, 300
Hassan, Ihab, 490
Havelock, Eric A., 122, 497; *Preface to Plato*, 122
Hawkes, John, 280, 303, 305, 325–26, 472, 505; *The Cannibal*, 325; *Death, Sleep and The Traveller*, 326; *Second Skin*, 325; *Travesty*, 326
Hawks, Howard, 142
Hawthorne, Julian, 21
Hawthorne, Nathaniel, 17–33, 55, 108, 111, 193, 208, 211, 214, 230, 231, 232, 310, 322, 327, 440, 441, 468, 479, 496, 497, 501; *The American Claimant Manuscripts*, 19; *American Notebooks*, 24; "The Artist of the Beautiful," 32, 496; "The Birthmark," 496; *The Blithedale Romance*, 28, 29, 479; "Chippings with a Chisel," 22; "The Custom House," 24; *The Elixir of Life Manuscripts*, 19; "Endicott and the Red Cross," 25, 32; *Fanshawe*, 27; "The Gentle Boy," 23, 30; "The Gray Champion," 23, 25; "The Great Stone Face," 22; "Dr. Heidegger's Experiment," 32; *The House of the Seven Gables*, 17, 28, 182, 230; "Howe's Masquerade," 25; "Little Annie's Ramble," 33; *The Marble Faun*, 33; "The May-Pole of Merry Mount," 25, 208; "My Kinsman, Major Molineux," 22, 25, 452; "The Old Manse," 23; "The Prophetic Pictures," 22; Rappaccini's Daughter," 23, 496; "A Rill from the Town-Pump," 21, 33; "Roger Malvin's Burial," 23, 30; *The Scarlet Letter*, 27, 28, 231, 232, 479; "Septimius Felton," 20; *The Snow Image*, 23; "Sunday at Home," 33; "Wakefield," 22, 31; "Young Goodman Brown," 31
Hawthorne, Sophia, 21, 22
Hay, John, 100, 234
Haycraft, Howard, 302
Hayden, Robert, 420, 421, 422; *Angle of Ascent*, 421, 422
Haydon, Benjamin R., 9
Hayes, Phillip, 423
Hazard, Roland C., 16
Hearn, Lafcadio, 224
Hegel, Georg Wilhelm Friedrich, 101, 442, 449, 460
Heidegger, Martin, 310, 325, 455
Heinlein, Robert A., 299, 300, 340
Heller, Joseph, 305, 336, 463, 499; *Catch-22*, 336, 499; *Something Happened*, 336
Hellman, Lillian: *Scoundrel Time*, 393
Hemingway, Ernest, 95, 129, 163–72, 178–86, 205, 262, 368, 465, 469, 474, 489, 499, 500, 501, 502; *Across the River and Into the Trees*, 170, 171, 180, 181, 184; "An Alpine Idyll," 185; "Big Two-Hearted River," 184; "Bimini," 181, 182; "A Clean, Well-Lighted Place," 185; "The Doctor and the Doctor's Wife," 182; "The Faithful Bull," 183; *A Farewell to Arms*, 163, 165, 170, 178, 179, 184; *For Whom the Bell Tolls*, 170, 171, 172, 180, 184; "The Gambler, the Nun, and the Radio," 184; "Garden of Eden," 166; "The Good Lion," 183; "Hills Like White Elephants," 183, 184; *In Our Time*, 170, 182, 184; *Islands in the Stream*, 171, 181, 182, 499; "The Killers," 185; "The Light of the World," 183; *Men Without Women*, 499; *The Nick Adams Stories*, 168, 182; *The Old Man and the Sea*, 168, 181, 182; "The Passing of Pickles McCarty," 166; "The Revolutionist," 185; "The Sea Change," 474; "The Short Happy Life of Francis Macomber," 183; "Soldier's Home," 185; *The Sun Also Rises*, 129, 169, 170, 179, 180; "The Three-Day Blow," 185; "Three Shots," 183; *Three Stories and Ten Poems*, 168; *To Have and Have Not*, 167; *Torrents of Spring*, 166, 169; *Winner Take Nothing*, 499
Hemingway, Mary, 168
Hemingway, Tyler, 168
Henderson, Alice C., 345
Henderson, Stephen, 421
Henry, O., 464

Henry, Patrick, 199
Herbert, George, 76
Herbst, Josephine, 292
Herder, Johann Gottfried von, 16
Herrick, Robert, 240, 241, 480, 481, 482; *The Memoirs of an American Citizen*, 481
Hersey, Harold, 120
Hesse, Herman, 315
Higginson, Thomas Wentworth, 83, 84, 230
Hill, Geoffrey, 367
Himes, Chester, 415, 429; *Lonely Crusade*, 415; *The Third Generation*, 415
Hirsch, E. D., 455
Hitchcock, Edward, 82
Hoffman, E. T. A., 42
Hogg, Thomas E., 222
Holls, F. W., 5
Holmes, Oliver Wendell, 11
Homer: *The Odyssey*, 125, 176
Hopkinson, Francis, 198
Horace, 196
Hosmer, Harriet, 21
Hosmer, Horace, 11
Houssaye, Sidonie de la, 223
Howard, Richard: *Fellow Feelings*, 386; *Findings*, 386; *Two-Part Inventions*, 386; *Untitled Subjects*, 386
Howe, E. W.: *The Story of a Country Town*, 234
Howe, Irving, 490
Howe, Julia W., 224
Howells, William Dean, 75, 90, 94, 117, 207, 225, 226, 227–34, 235, 237, 240, 436, 480, 481, 482, 505; "A Difficult Case," 231; *A Foregone Conclusion*, 230; *The Lady of the Aroostook*, 230; *Literary Friends and Acquaintance*, 228; *A Modern Instance*, 207, 227, 229, 232; *The Rise of Silas Lapham*, 270; *The Shadow of a Dream*, 232; "A Sleep and a Forgetting," 231; *Stops of Various Quills*, 233; *Suburban Sketches*, 228; *Their Wedding Journey*, 228, 229; *A Traveler from Altruria*, 481
Hubbard, William, 205
Hughes, Langston, 407, 409, 419, 423
Hughes, Ted, 367
Hugo, Victor, 262
Huizinga, Johan, 43
Hunter, Kermit: *Walk Toward the Sunset*, 400
Hurston, Zora N., 409, 410, 430; "John Redding Goes to Sea," 410; *Jonah's Gourd Vine*, 410; *Moses, Man of the Mountains*, 427; *Mules and Men*, 417; "Spunk," 410; "Sweat," 410; *Their Eyes Were Watching God*, 410
Husserl, Edmund, 455
Huxley, Aldous, 151, 171, 300; *Crome Yellow*, 151

Ibañez, Blasco, 233
Ibsen, Henryk, 261, 458; *A Doll House*, 458
Ibuse, Masuji: "Sanshouo," 502
Ignatius, Saint, 129
Ingarden, Roman, 455
Inge, William, 401, 487
Ingram, John H., 37, 38
Irving, Washington, 36, 203, 208, 209, 213, 214, 478; *The Adventures of Captain Bonneville*, 209; *Alhambra*, 36; *Astoria*, 210; *Bonneville*, 210; *Bracebridge Hall*, 209; *Letters of Jonathan Old Style, Gent.*, 209, 210; *Old Christmas*, 209; "Rip Van Winkle," 210; *Salmagundi*, 203, 209
Irwin, John T., 149
Ives, Charles, 8, 14

Jakobson, Roman, 123, 454, 473
James, Henry, 33, 45, 70, 99–118, 172, 176, 227, 230, 232, 252, 255, 258, 271, 436, 440, 441, 460, 466, 468, 469, 499, 501, 503; *The Ambassadors*, 45, 99, 104, 108, 111, 112, 113, 117, 182; *The American*, 101, 102, 104, 105, 176; *The American Scene*, 113; *Autobiography*, 105, 116, 118; *The Awkward Age*, 104, 110; "The Beast in the Jungle," 104, 107, 111; "The Bench of Desolation," 107; *The Bostonians*, 109; *Daisy Miller*, 102, 114, 176, 202; "The Figure in the Carpet," 105, 106, 114; *The Golden Bowl*, 113,

117, 503; "The Great Good Place," 116; *Hawthorne*, 33; *The Heiress*, 102; *The Innocents*, 103; *In the Cage*, 114, 505, 506; "Is There a Life After Death?" 106; "The Jolly Corner," 103, 104, 116; "The Lesson of the Master," 100, 105; "A Light Man," 100; *Madame de Mauves*, 499; "The Middle Years," 107, 114; *Notebooks*, 100, 112; *Partial Portraits*, 116; *The Portrait of a Lady*, 99, 101, 104, 105, 108, 172; *The Princess Casamassima*, 99, 104, 106, 108, 109, 451, 497; "The Private Life," 100; *Roderick Hudson*, 102, 104; *The Sacred Fount*, 105, 110, 112; *The Sense of the Past*, 104; "The Turn of the Screw," 99, 103, 104, 105, 106, 107, 114, 115, 505, 506; *Washington Square*, 102; *William Wetmore Story and His Friends*, 118
James, William, 220, 355, 358, 437
Janov, Arthur: *The Primal Scream*, 182
Jeffers, Robinson, 343, 350–52, 360; *Cawdor*, 352; *Dear Judas*, 351; *The Double Axe*, 351; *Medea*, 352; "Post Mortem," 351; *The Women at Point Sur*, 351
Jeffers, Una, 351
Jefferson, Thomas, 121, 193, 195, 198, 355; "Declaration of Independence," 193; *Notes on the State of Virginia*, 195
Jewett, Sarah Orne, 224, 225, 251; *The Country of the Pointed Firs*, 224, 225
Johnson, James W., 424, 426, 427; *The Autobiography of an Ex-Coloured Man*, 424, 426
Johnson, Uwe: *Mutmassungen über Jakob*, 179
Jones, Gayl: *Corregidora*, 428, 431
Jones, Hugh, 196
Jones, James, 273, 297, 299, 465; *From Here to Eternity*, 299; *Some Came Running*, 299; *The Thin Red Line*, 299
Jones, LeRoi (Imamu Amiri Baraka), 407, 422, 423, 487; *Dutchman*, 423, 424
Jones, Lucile, 431
Jones, Samuel Arthur, 11, 14, 51
Joyce, James, 102, 118, 123, 132, 285, 287, 296, 369, 416, 453; *Finnegans Wake*, 123, 285, 369; *The Portrait of the Artist as a Young Man*, 118; *Ulysses*, 123, 128, 132, 453, 455
Jung, Carl Gustav, 29, 31, 46, 80, 328, 445

Kafka, Franz, 321; *The Trial*, 452
Kahle, Hans, 166
Kalman, C. O., 167
Katz, Steve, 307, 336
Keats, John, 40, 172, 363, 369, 451; *Endymion*, 369
Kelley, William M., 429
Kennedy, Adrienne, 398, 423, 424, 487; *Funny House of a Negro*, 424
Kenner, Hugh, 8
Kent, Rockwell, 57
Kerouac, Jack, 303, 306, 341, 465; *The Dharma Bums*, 341
Kerr, Walter, 401
Kesey, Ken, 310, 332, 336–37, *One Flew Over the Cuckoo's Nest*, 337
Kierkegaard, Sören, 112, 326
Killens, John O., 431, 463
King, Clarence, 221
King, Martin Luther, 421
King, Grace, 224
Kingsley, Charles, 234
Kinnell, Galway, 385
Knight, Ethridge, 427
Knight, Sarah Kemble, 205
Knott, Bill, 386
Kopit, Arthur, 400, 487; *Indians*, 400
Kornbluth, Cyril, 300
Kosinski, Jerzy, 307, 473; *The Devil Tree*, 472
Kraitsir, Charles, 16
Krampf, Carl, 485
Kreymborg, Alfred, 345
Krutch, Joseph Wood, 389, 490

Lacan, Jacques, 43, 115, 469, 497
Laing, R. D., 308
Lambinet, Emile Charles, 105, 113
Landor, Walter Savage, 123
Lardner, Ring, 268–69; *Some Champions*, 268
Larkin, Philip, 367, 374

Larson, Nella, 101, 102; *Quicksand*, 101
Lawrence, D. H., 332
Lawrence, Lars, 465
Lawson, John Howard: *Roger Bloomer*, 393
Lear, Edward, 37, 287
Lee, Arthur, 195
Lee, Garland, 423
Lee, Leslie, 423
Le Guin, Ursula K., 300, 340; "Aberrant," 340; *The Left Hand of Darkness*, 340
Lesser, Simon O., 451, 452
Levertov, Denise, 383, 487, 488; "During the Eichmann Trial," 382; *Rehearsing the Alphabet*, 487; *Sorrow Dance*, 487; *To Stay Alive*, 487
Levin, Harry, 490
Lévy, Maurice, 44
Lewis, Oscar: *La Vida*, 442
Lewis, R. W. B.: *The American Adam*, 259
Lewis, Sinclair, 269, 349, 464, 500; *Arrowsmith*, 269; *Kingsblood Royal*, 269; *Main Street*, 269
Lindsay, Vachel, 343, 349
Lippmann, Walter, 438
Locke, Alain, 427
Locke, John, 15
Lodge, George Cabot, 269–70, 343, 347
Loftis, N. J.: *Black Anima*, 425
London, Eliza, 257
London, Jack, 257–59, 310, 464, 482; *Martin Eden*, 258; "The Red One," 259; "The Wife of a King," 259
Longfellow, Henry Wadsworth, 11, 43, 69, 208, 217, 218; *Hyperion*, 43; *Outre-Mer*, 217, 218
Loring, Betsy, 201
Lovecraft, H. P.: *Necronomicon*, 301
Lowell, Amy, 345
Lowell, James Russell: *The Bigelow Papers*, 217
Lowell, Robert, 21, 26, 208, 357, 374–75, 381, 382, 400, 488, 496; *Ariel*, 382; *The Dolphin*, 375; "Domesday Book," 375; "End of the Year," 375; "Fall Weekend at Milgate," 375; *Life Studies*, 366, 382; "Near the Ocean," 375; *The Old Glory*, 400; "The Quaker Graveyard at Nantucket," 375; *Selected Poems*, 374; "Waking Early Sunday Morning," 375; "Ulysses, Circe, Penelope," 385
Lowndes, Robert A., 300
Lowry, Malcolm, 177
Luhan, Mabel D., 351
Lukács, Georg, 498
Lurie, Allison, 305
Lyon, Isabel V., 91
Lytle, Andrew, 332

McCarthy, Cormac, 331; *Child of God*, 331; *The Orchard Keeper*, 331; *Outer Dark*, 331
McCarthy, Joseph, 393
McCarthy, Mary, 307
McCosh, James, 437
McCullers, Carson, 287, 299, 329, 401, 465; *The Heart Is a Lonely Hunter*, 290, 291
Macdonald, Ross, 302, 338
McKay, Claude, 409, 426; *Banjo*, 426
MacLeish, Archibald, 343, 401, 476, 483
McLuhan, Marshall, 446, 447, 452, 497
McMahon, Thomas, 103
McMurty, Larry, 334–35
Mailer, Norman, 259, 268, 283, 303, 304, 309–11, 324, 332, 339, 414, 440, 441, 463, 465, 467, 485, 500, 508; *An American Dream*, 309; *The Armies of the Night*, 306, 441, 485, 508; *Barbary Shore*, 310; *The Deer Park*, 309, 310; *The Naked and the Dead*, 309, 324; "The Time of Her Time," 310
Major, Clarence, 415, 416
Malamud, Bernard, 303, 319–21, 465, 485, 486, 500, 501; "Angel Levine," 321; *The Assistant*, 321; *The Loan*, 321; *The Natural*, 486; *A New Life*, 320; "Take Pity," 321; *The Tenants*, 321, 486
Malcolm X (Malcolm Little), 427, 494, 498
Mallarmé, Stéphane, 36, 359
Malthus, Thomas, 13
Mann, Thomas, 171, 252

Maran, René, *Batouala*, 426
March, William, 298, 299; *The Bad Seed*, 298
Marcuse, Herbert, 447
Marinetti, F. T.: *Futurist Manifest*, 482
Marlowe, Christopher: *Doctor Faustus*, 393; *The Jew of Malta*, 129, 179
Martin, Jay, 283
Marx, Karl, 13, 55, 94, 259, 267, 274, 281, 308, 309, 319, 422, 444, 445, 455, 456, 493, 494, 498, 508
Masters, Edgar Lee, 343, 349; *Spoon River Anthology*, 349
Mather, Cotton, 189, 193, 205, 440; *Magnalia*, 189, 193; *Wonders of the Invisible World*, 193
Mather, Increase, 14
Matthiessen, F. O.: *American Renaissance*, 434, 488
Mauron, Charles, 467
Meeter, Glen, 485
Melvill, Allan, 49, 58
Melvill, Thomas, 49, 50
Melville, Herman, 13, 18, 45, 49–63, 113, 172, 206, 319, 322, 436, 440, 441, 469, 476, 479, 480, 482, 488, 494, 500, 501; "The Apple-Tree Table," 60, 479, 480, 482; "Bartleby the Scrivener," 13, 53, 60, 61; *Battle-Pieces*, 53; "Benito Cereno," 54, 60, 469, 488, 489; *Billy Budd*, 52, 54, 62, 501; *Clarel*, 53, 54; *Confidence-Man*, 50, 59, 61, 479, 480; "Hawthorne and His Mosses," 26; *Israel Potter*, 54; *Moby Dick*, 45, 50, 51, 53, 55, 56, 57, 59, 172, 206, 319, 501; *The Piazza Tales and Other Prose Pieces*, 60; *Pierre*, 50, 55, 58, 59; "The Story of China Aster," 50, 61; *Typee*, 53, 55
Mencken, H. L., 120, 246, 438, 473
Merrill, James, 365, 385, 386; *The Book of Ephraim*, 385
Merrill, Judith, 300
Merwin, W. S., 365, 367, 384, 485
Michaels, Leonard, 308
Michel, John B., 300
Michener, James: *Centennial*, 388; *The Source*, 338
Mill, John Stuart, 13
Millay, Edna St. Vincent, 344, 371, 372
Miller, Arthur, 395, 397–98, 401, 487; *After the Fall*, 398; *The Crucible*, 397, 474; *Death of a Salesman*, 397
Miller, Henry, 282, 284, 310, 497, 499; *Gliding into the Everglades*, 283; *Tropic of Cancer*, 282
Miller, Perry: *The New England Mind*, 205
Miller, Ron, 487
Milton, John, 130, 132; *Paradise Lost*, 132; *Paradise Regained*, 130
Mines, Mabour: *The Red Horse*, 399
Mitchell, Margaret: *Gone With the Wind*, 140, 288, 297, 298, 447
Mitchell, S. Weir, 482
Momaday, N. Scott: *House Made of Dawn*, 334
Moncrieffe, Margaret, 201
Monet, Claude, 105
Monroe, Harriet, 120, 127, 343, 345
Montale, Eugenio, 495, 496
Moore, George: *Confessions of a Young Man*, 256
Moore, Marianne, 370–71, 373, 503
Morris, Wright, 259, 303, 332–33; *Ceremony in Lone Tree*, 333; *The Territory Ahead*, 259; *The Works of Love*, 332
Morrison, Toni, 416, 417, 431; *The Bluest Eye*, 416, 431; *Song of Solomon*, 417; *Sula*, 417, 431
Morton, Thomas, 25, 190, 191; *New English Canaan*, 191
Motley, John Lothrop, 25, 208; *Merry-Mount*, 208
Motley, Willard: *Knock on Any Door*, 410; *Let No Man Write My Epitaph*, 410
Mottram, R. H.: *The Spanish Farm Trilogy*, 178
Mounier, Emmanuel: *Personalism*, 322
Mourier, Maurice, 44
Muir, Edwin, 489
Muir, John, 221
Mulder, William, 169
Murray, Albert: *Train Whistle Guitar*, 429
Mussolini, Benito, 121

Nabokov, Vladimir, 28, 103, 104, 273, 282, 285–87, 313, 328, 340, 470, 485, 499; *Ada*, 104; *Bend Sinister*, 286; *Invitation to a Beheading*, 286; *Lolita*, 28, 104, 286, 287, 313, 499; *Pale Fire*, 287, 485
Namier, Sir Lewis, 201
Nash, Ogden, 302
Nashville Fugitives, 355; *I'll Take My Stand*, 288
Nathan, George Jean, 401
Neihardt, John G., 343
Nelson, Truman: *The Sin of the Prophet*, 341
Nelson, William, 195
Nicholson, Jack: *Five Easy Pieces*, 283
Nietzsche, Friedrich Wilhelm, 259, 270, 449, 460
Nin, Anaïs, 273, 282, 284; *A Spy in the House of Love*, 284
Nizan, Paul, 308
Norris, Frank, 169, 239, 240, 270; *McTeague*, 447; *Moran of the Lady Letty*, 239
Norwood, Henry, 194

Oates, Joyce Carol, 305, 327–28, 465, 485, 486; *Expensive People*, 328; *Them*, 328; *With Shuddering Fall*, 328
O'Conner, Flannery, 290, 303, 322–23, 329, 465; "The Artificial Nigger," 322; "Everything That Rises Must Converge," 323; "Parker's Back," 322; *The Violent Bear It Away*, 322, 323
O'Connor, William Douglas, 67, 73; *The Good Grey Poet*, 67, 68
Odets, Clifford, 393, 397, 401; *Awake and Sing*, 393; *Till the Day I Die*, 397; *Waiting for Lefty*, 393
O'Hara, Frank, 365, 383, 384, 436
O'Hara, John, 168
O'Horgan, Tom: *Hair*, 400; *Jesus Christ Superstar*, 400; *Lenny*, 400
Olson, Charles, 366, 377–78, 482, 488; *Maximus*, 377
Onetti, Juan C.: "La Novia Robada," 146
O'Neill, Eugene, 58, 84, 394–96, 423, 473, 487, 491, 505, 506, 507; *Ah, Wilderness!*, 394, 395; *Anna Christie*, 396; *Beyond the Horizon*, 394; *Desire Under the Elms*, 473; *The Hairy Ape*, 395; *Hughie*, 506; *Lazarus Laughed*, 395; *A Moon for the Misbegotten*, 395; *More Stately Mansions*, 506, 507; *Mourning Becomes Electra*, 58, 84, 395, 473; *Strange Interlude*, 473; *A Touch of the Poet*, 506, 507
Ong, Walter J., 497
Oppen, George, 483
Oppenheimer, George, 401
Osborne, John, *Inadmissable*, 398
Ovid, 196
Owens, Rochelle, 487

Paine, Albert B., 88, 96
Paine, Thomas, 195, 197, 198, 199; *Common Sense*, 198, 199
Paley, Grace, 470
Panofsky, Erwin, 429
Parker, Dorothy, 168
Parkman, Francis, 220, 221; *The Oregon Trail*, 220
Parrington, Vernon L., 434
Pascal, Blaise, 326
Paterson, W. C., 436
Paulson, A. B., 485
Payne, Ben I., 392
Peabody, Elizabeth, 3, 15, 16
Penn, Arthur, 334
Peppin, Horace: "Holy Mountain III," 429
Percy, Walker, 330–31; *Lancelot*, 330, 331; *The Moviegoer*, 330
Perelman, S. J., 470
Perkins, Maxwell, 268, 296
Perry, T. S., 228
Phelps, Elizabeth Stuart: *The Gates Ajar*, 83
Philostratus, Flavius: *Life of Apollonius of Tyana*, 124
Pierce, Charles S., 220
Piercy, Marge, 386, 387
Pinter, Harold: *The Homecoming*, 458
Piscator, Erwin, 393
Plath, Sylvia, 366, 381, 382, 491, 496, 504; "Daddy," 382
Plato, 36, 129; *Philebus*, 129
Plenzdorf, Ulrich: *Die neuen Leiden*, 282
Poe, Edgar Allan, 35–47, 69, 77, 113,

214, 278, 301, 322, 441, 449, 478, 491, 497, 501; "Al Aaraaf," 47; "Berenice," 41, 43; "The Black Cat," 40; "The Cask of Amontillado," 41, 43; "A Descent Into the Maelstrom," 41; "Doctor Tarr and Professor Fether," 40; "The Domain of Arnheim," 36; "Dreams," 46; "The Duc de l'Omelette," 40; *Eureka*, 44; "The Facts in the Case of M. Valdemar," 43; "Fairy-Land," 47; "The Fall of the House of Usher," 41, 42; "To Helen," 46; "The Imp of the Perverse," 40; "The Island of the Fay," 46, 47; "Ligeia," 43; "Loss of Breath," 497; "Morella," 43; "Ms. Found In A Bottle," 41, 497; "The Murders in the Rue Morgue," 36; *The Narrative of Arthur Gordon Pym.*, 44, 45, 113, 441; "The Oval Portrait," 41, 43; "The Raven," 36; "Song," 46; "Sonnet—To Science," 47; "The Tell-Tale Heart," 41; "William Wilson," 40, 322
Poe, Rosalie, 37
Poggioli, Renato, 454
Pohl, Frederik, 300
Pope, Alexander: *Dunciad*, 349
Porter, Katherine Anne, 287, 291–93; "Flowering Judas," 292; *Old Mortality*, 291; *The Old Order*, 291; *Pale Horse, Pale Rider*, 291; *Ship of Fools*, 292; "Theft," 292
Poulet, Georges, 17
Pound, Ezra, 119–26, 129, 130, 341, 345, 373, 455, 482, 488, 494, 495, 503; *The Cantos*, 119, 121, 123, 124, 125, 126, 494, 495; *Mauberley*, 122, 482; *The Pisan Cantos*, 121; *Women of Trachis*, 495
Powers, J. F., 323–24; "The Green Banana," 323; "Lions, Harts, Leaping Does," 324; *Morte D'Urban*, 323
Prime, Benjamin Y., 196
Proud, Robert, 199
Proust, Marcel, 102, 104, 118, 458; *De cote de chez Swann*, 118
Puccini, Giacomo: *Manon Lescaut*, 314
Purchas, Samuel, 194
Purdy, James, 473
Pushkin, Alexander, 407
Puzo, Mario: *The Godfather*, 170
Pynchon, Thomas, 113, 303, 305, 307, 314–17, 324, 339, 340, 453, 473, 505; *The Crying of Lot 49*, 315, 316; *Godgame*, 315; *Gravity's Rainbow*, 314, 316, 317, 324, 453; *V.*, 314, 315

Quesenbury, William, 222
Quiroga, Elena, 146

Rabelais, François: *The Second Book*, 92
Rand, Ayn: *The Fountainhead*, 298
Rank, Otto, 149
Ransom, John Crowe, 343, 352–54, 488, 489; *The New Criticism*, 353, 488; *The World's Body*, 353
Rawlings, Marjorie K., 298
Reddie, T. J., 427
Reed, Ishmael, 307, 415, 416, 428; *Mumbo Jumbo*, 428
Remarque, Eric, 171
Renoir, Pierre Auguste, 105
Rexroth, Kenneth, 488
Reznikoff, Charles, 483
Ricardo, David, 13
Ricardou, Jean, 44
Rich, Adrienne, 366, 382, 383
Richard, Claude, 44
Richmond, Annie, 37
Ricketson, Daniel, 14
Riddell, Joseph, 460
Rimbaud, Arthur: *Illuminations*, 367
Robbe-Grillet, Alain, 103, 469
Robinson, E. A., 347, 385; "Eros Turannos," 347
Robinson, John, 205
Roe, E. P., 235; *Barriers Burned Away*, 235; *Opening a Chestnut Burr*, 235
Roethke, Theodore, 374; *The Waking*, 374; *Words*, 374
Rooney, Mickey, 276
Rosenfeld, Isaac, 278, 279; *An Age of Enormity*, 278; *Alpha and Omega*, 279; *Passage from Home*, 279
Rossner, Judith, 305
Rostand, Edmond: *Cyrano*, 150
Roth, Henry, 278; *Call It Sleep*, 278
Roth, Philip, 308, 321–22, 499; *Good-*

bye, Columbus, 499; *Portnoy's Complaint*, 322
Rothenberg, Jerome, 367
Roumain, Jacques: *Masters of the Dew*, 426
Rowson, Susanna H., 205
Royce, Josiah, 220
Ruffin, Edmund, 222
Ruykeyser, Muriel, 382, 434
Rush, Rebecca: *Kelroy*, 202
Rusk, Ralph, 5
Russell, Ezekiel, 418

Sacks, John, 508
Said, Edward, 460
Salinger, J. D., 230, 281, 282, 304, 499, 500, 501, 502; "Bananafish," 502; *The Catcher in the Rye*, 281, 499, 502; *Nine Stories*, 499, 502
Salt, Henry, 11, 12
Sanborn, Frank, 3
Sandburg, Carl, 343, 349, 350, 466
Santayana, George, 220, 343, 348, 363, 438
Saroyan, William, 394, 463; *The Time of Your Life*, 394
Sartre, Jean Paul, 304, 341
Saussure, Ferdinand de, 380
Saxon, Lyle: *Children of Strangers*, 289
Sayers, Dorothy L., 302
Schopenhauer, Arthur, 101
Schumann, Peter, 400
Schwartz, Delmore, 372–73
Scott, Sir Walter, 8, 23, 42, 158, 442; *Redgauntlet*, 158
Scrugg, Charles: "All Dressed Up But No Place to Go," 427
Seale, Bobby, 427
Sedgwick, Catherine, 25, 208
Selby, Hugh: *Last Exit to Brooklyn*, 341, 486
Sewall, Ellen, 10
Sexton, Anne, 381, 382, 485
Seyersted, Per, 242
Shaffer, Peter: *Equus*, 398
Shakespeare, William, 8, 36, 52, 81, 116, 130, 152, 160, 223, 287, 297, 354, 359, 390, 391; *Hamlet*, 29, 41, 452; *King Lear*, 116; *Love's Labour's Lost*, 359; *Macbeth*, 152; *Measure for Measure*, 328; *Richard II*, 160
Shan, Han, 380
Shange, Ntozake, 423
Shattuck, Lemuel, 4
Shaw, G. B., 395
Shaw, Lemuel, 49, 50
Shelley, Mary: *Frankenstein*, 32, 453
Shelley, Percy Bysshe, 130, 458; *The Cenci*, 458; *Defense of Poetry*, 504; *Queen Mab*, 130; *Triumph of Life*, 130
Shepard, Sam, 398
Shepard, Thomas, 14
Shew, Marie L., 37
Shklovsky, Victor, 458
Short, Nicholas, 192
Simenon, Georges, 448
Simic, Charles, 386
Simms, William G., 213, 214, 223; "Oakatibbe," 214
Simon, Claude: *L'Herbe*, 145, 146
Sinclair, Upton, 271, 463, 491; *The Jungle*, 271; *Singing Jailbirds*, 491
Singer, I. B., 303, 341, 342; "The Captive," 342
Sirk, Douglas: *The Tarnished Angels*, 156
Smart, Christopher: "Song to David," 200
Smith, Adam, 13
Smith, Betty, 512
Smith, Elihu H., 202
Smith, John, 194, 442, 513; *Generall Historie of Virginia*, 442
Smith, Patti, 487
Smith, Seba, 224
Smith, Sydney, 209
Snodgrass, W. D., 488
Snyder, Gary, 379–80, 503, 505; *Cold Mountain Poems*, 380; *Riprap*, 379
Socrates, 270
Sohseki, Natsume, 37; *Meian*, 504
Sophocles: *Trachiniae*, 495
Spanos, William, 490
Sparks, William H., 222
Spenger, Oswald: *Decline of the West*, 124
Spencer, Herbert, 246, 264
Spender, Stephen, 489
Spenser, Edmund, 30, 58; *Faerie Queene*, 30

Spicer, Jack: *After Lorca*, 380; *Books of Magazine Verse*, 380; *Collected Books*, 380; *The Heads of the Town*, 380; *The Holy Grail*, 380
Spielberg, Peter: "Family Circle," 473
Spiller, Robert E., 434; *The Cycle of American Literature*, 434; *Literary History of the United States*, 434
Spinoza, Benedict de, 351
Spofford, Harriet P., 79
Stalin, Joseph, 394
Stanley, Charlotte, 201
Stapleton, Olaf: *Star Maker*, 299
Starobinski, Jean, 436
Stedman, Edmund C.: *The Nature and Elements of Poetry*, 236
Steele, Richard, 210
Steffens, Lincoln, 436
Stegner, Wallace, 220, 333–34; *Angle of Repose*, 333; *The Blue-Winged Teal*, 333; *The Spectator Bird*, 333; *Wolf Willow*, 333
Stein, Gertrude, 261–63, 298, 368, 436, 437, 458, 470, 494, 505; *The Autobiography of Alice B. Toklas*, 437; *A Book Concluding With As A Wife Has A Cow*, 262; *Everybody's Autobiography*, 437; "The Good Anna," 261; *Ida*, 262; *Lucy Church Amiably*, 262; *Paris France*, 262; *Q. E. D.*, 263; *Three Lives*, 262
Steinbeck, John, 95, 273, 274–77, 297, 298, 465, 501; *Cannery Row*, 95; *East of Eden*, 274, 275, 276; *The Grapes of Wrath*, 276, 297, 447; "How Edith McGillicuddy Met R. L. Stevenson," 276; *In Dubious Battle*, 275; "The Murderer," 276
Sterling, George, 259
Sterne, Laurence, 57, 287; *Tristram Shandy*, 57
Stevens, Holly, 348
Stevens, Wallace, 8, 9, 314, 343, 348, 349, 355, 359–64, 373; "Bantams in Pine-Woods," 359; *The Collected Poems*, 363; "The Comedian as the Letter C," 359; "Credences of Summer," 360; "Description without Place," 359; *The Necessary Angel*, 362; "Notes toward a Supreme Fiction," 360; "Not Ideas about the Thing but the Thing Itself," 363; *Opus Posthumous*, 362; "The Snow Man," 362; "Sunday Morning," 350, 359; "Tea at the Palaz of Hoon," 362; "Thirteen Ways of Looking at a Blackbird," 361
Stevenson, R. L.: "The Ebb Tide," 132
Stewart, T. D., 50
Stieglitz, Alfred, 228, 346, 507
Stoddard, Charles W., 68, 225
Stoddard, Elizabeth B., 21; *The Morgesons*, 21
Story, William W., 111
Stowe, Harriet Beecher, 11, 116, 215, 216, 442; *The Papers of Harriet Beecher Stowe*, 216; *Poganuc People*, 216; *Uncle Tom's Cabin*, 116, 215, 216, 442
Strand, Mark, 367
Strasberg, Lee, 393
Stribling, T. S., 289
Strindberg, August, 396, 508
Stuart, Jesse, 273, 277; *Foretaste of Glory*, 277
Stuckey, Elma, 422, 423; *The Big Gate*, 423
Styron, William, 298, 329–30, 427, 444, 498, 500; *Lie Down in Darkness*, 329; *Nat Turner*, 329, 330, 427, 443, 498; *Sophie's Choice*, 330
Sudermann, Hermann: *Es Lebe das Leben*, 252
Sukenick, Ronald, 307, 308, 336, 472, 473; *The Fortune Teller*, 473
Swift, Jonathan, 37
Symonds, John A., 68
Symons, Arthur, 150

Talmadge, Constance: *Breakfast at Sunrise*, 177
Tanizaki Junichiro, 36, 37
Tate, Allen, 274, 288, 332, 343, 352, 438, 444, 451, 488, 489; *The Fathers*, 288; "Ode to the Confederate Dead," 352
Taylor, Bayard, 61, 480; *Eldorado*, 480
Taylor, Edward, 189, 190, 476
Taylor, Harold, 423
Taylor, John, 300
Teasdale, Sara, 343, 345
Tennyson, Alfred Lord, 69, 131, 476; *In Memoriam*, 131

Terry, Megan, 398, 487
Thackeray, William Makepeace, 101, 175; *The Newcomes*, 101; *Vanity Fair*, 175
Thatcher, George, 4
Thayer, Scofield, 348
Thomas, Dylan, 76
Thompson, John W., 136
Thoreau, Henry David, 3, 4, 5, 6, 9–14, 15, 60, 70, 211, 262, 287, 479, 480, 489, 499, 512; *Cape Cod*, 11; *Reform Papers*, 5, 6; "Resistance to Civil Government," 11; *Walden*, 5, 10, 11, 13, 14, 15, 60, 436, 480; *A Week*, 6, 10, 14
Thoreau, John, 10
Thorpe, Thomas B.: "The Big Bear of Arkansas," 222
Thurman, Wallace: *Infants of Spring*, 427
Todorov, Tzvetan, 460, 461
Toffler, Alvin, 300
Toklas, Alice B., 263
Tolstoy, Leo, 232, 233
Tomioka, Taeko, 503
Toomer, Jean, 426, 483; *Cane*, 426; "Fern," 483
Torrence, Ridgely, 423
Toynbee, Arnold, 490
Traven, B., 266, 267; *Land das Frühlings*, 267; *The White Rose*, 267
Trilling, Lionel, 341, 440, 450; *The Middle of the Journey*, 341; "The Other Margaret," 451
Tucker, St. George, 195, 222; *A Century Hence*, 222
Turgenev, Ivan, 101
Turpin, Waters: *O Canaan!* 409; *The Rootless*, 409; *These Low Grounds*, 409
Tutuola, Amos: *Feather Woman of the Jungle*, 408
Twain, Mark, 8, 45, 87–97, 100, 117, 226, 310, 333, 436, 441, 442, 464, 480, 491, 494, 499, 501; *A Connecticut Yankee*, 91, 92, 95; "A Dog's Tale," 96; *Europe and Elsewhere*, 96; *Huckleberry Finn*, 45, 93, 94, 95, 97, 262, 276, 499; *The Innocents Abroad*, 93; Life *on the Mississippi*, 90, 442; "The Man That Corrupted Hadleyburg," 96; *Mysterious Stranger*, 92; "The £1,000,000 Bank Note," 96; "To the Person Sitting in Darkness," 96; *The Prince and the Pauper*, 97; *Pudd'nhead Wilson*, 95, 96; *Roughing It*, 93; *Sketches New and Old*, 93; *Tom Sawyer*, 94, 97
Tyler, Royall, 45, 441, 478; *The Algerine Captive*, 45, 441; *The Contrast*, 478

Underhill, John, 205
Updike, John, 168, 257, 304, 306, 326–27, 465, 491, 500, 501, 507, 508; "The Astronomer," 326; *The Centaur*, 327; *Couples*, 327; *Month of Sundays*, 327; "Pigeon Feathers," 326; *Rabbit, Run*, 257, 327, 501, 507, 508

Valdés, Armando P., 233
Valdez, Luis, 392
Valera, Juan, 233
Valéry, Paul, 36; "La Soirée Avec Monsieur Teste," 36
Van Dine, S. S., 302
Van Itallie, Jean-Claude, 398, 487, 491; *The Serpent*, 491
Vassa, Gustavus (Olaudah Equiano), 494
Veblen, Thorstein, 267, 481
Verdenal, Jean, 131
Verlaine, Paul, 149, 150
Virgil, 130, 196, 314; *Aeneid*, 314; *Georgics*, 130
Voegelin, Eric: *Order and History*, 330
Voltaire (Francois-Marie Arouet), 123
von Kotzebue, August, 203
Vonnegut, Kurt, Jr., 103, 104, 266, 299, 305, 307, 308, 311–14, 332, 463, 465, 486, 499; *Breakfast of Champions*, 313; *Cat's Cradle*, 104, 313; *Mother Night*, 311, 312, 313; *Piano Player*, 312; *The Sirens of Titan*, 311, 312, 499; *Slapstick*, 311; *Slaughterhouse-Five*, 311, 312, 313, 486

Waggoner, David, 367
Wakoski, Diane, 382
Walker, Alice, 417, 429; *In Love and Trouble*, 417; *Meridan*, 429; "The

Third Life of Grange Copeland," 417
Walker, Margaret: *Jubilee*, 417, 418, 426, 427
Ward, Douglas T., 487
Ward, Elizabeth S.: *The Gates Ajar*, 217
Warner, C. D., 224
Warren, Robert Penn, 287, 289, 290, 329, 332, 343, 352, 354–56, 358, 444, 465, 500; *All the King's Men*, 290; "The Ballad of Billie Potts," 355; *Brother to Dragons*, 355; *Night Rider*, 289; *Selected Poems*, 354; *You, Emperors*, 354
Washington, Booker T., 407
Wasson, Ben, 149
Watt, Douglas, 401
Watts, Richard, Jr., 401
Waugh, Evelyn, 168
Webster, Noah: *American Dictionary*, 76
Wecter, Dixon, 88
Welles, Orson, 177, 330, 393; *Citizen Kane*, 330
Welty, Eudora, 273, 287, 293, 294, 444, 471; "Acrobats in a Park," 471; "The Burning," 472; *Delta Wedding*, 294; "First Love," 294, 472; "Flowers for Marjorie," 472; "June Recital," 472; "Pageant of Birds," 294; "Powerhouse," 294; "Shower of Gold," 472; "A Still Moment," 294; "Why I Live at the P.O.," 294
Wentworth, Frances, 201
Wesley, Richard, 487
West, Mae, 470
West, Nathanael, 280; *Miss Lonely Hearts*, 280
Westcott, Glenway: *The Pilgrim Hawk*, 298
Wharton, Edith, 100, 102, 175, 245, 250–54, 512; *The Age of Innocence*, 102, 251; "Bunner Sisters," 253; *The Custom of the Country*, 102, 251; *Ethan Frome*, 251, 253; *The House of Mirth*, 251, 252, 253; *Madame de Treymes*, 102; *The Spark*, 175; *Summer*, 251, 252, 253
Wheatley, Hannah P., 189
Wheatley, Phillis, 200, 201, 205, 418, 428; "Deism," 200; *Poems*, 200, 418
White, Charles F.: *The Plea of the Negro Soldier*, 422
White, E. B., 14
White, Edgar, 423
White, John, 194
White, Walter, 427
Whitman, Martha M., 66
Whitman, Sarah H., 38
Whitman, Walt, 7, 46, 65–76, 233, 240, 270, 278, 289, 296, 310, 367, 369, 436, 465, 468, 476, 495, 504; "By Blue Ontario's Shore," 73; "Cavalry Crossing a Ford," 73; "Chanting the Square Deific," 46; "Crossing Brooklyn Ferry," 71, 72; "The Half-Breed," 68; "I Sing the Body Electric," 73; *Leaves of Grass*, 65, 69, 71; "Lilacs," 71, 72; "A March in the Ranks Hard-Prest," 73, 74; "Out of the Cradle," 71, 73; "Passage to India," 73; "A Riddle Song," 74; "Song of Myself," 71, 72
Whittier, John Greenleaf, 208, 218
Wiesel, Elie, 342
Wilbur, Richard, 488
Wilder, Thornton, 297, 491, 492
Wilkins, Sallie M., 137
Williams, Joan: *The Wintering*, 150
Williams, John A., 429
Williams, Roger, 191, 477
Williams, Talcott, 66
Williams, Tennessee, 256, 273, 287, 293, 329, 487, 491, 501; *The Glass Menagerie*, 396, 397; *Last of the Mobile Hot-Shots*, 396; *One Arm and Other Stories*, 293; *Orpheus Descending*, 397; *Suddenly Last Summer*, 397
Williams, William Carlos, 26, 281, 368–70, 378, 507; *A Dream of Love*, 369; "The Great Figure," 369; "The Hunters in the Snow," 369; *In the American Grain*, 494; *Kora in Hell*, 368; *Paterson*, 369; "The Pot of Flowers," 368
Wilson, Dale, 167
Wilson, Edmund, 163, 412, 437, 438, 488, 490; *To the Finland Station*, 412; *The Wound and the Bow*, 488

Wilson, Robert, 398, 487; *A Letter for Queen Victoria*, 399
Windham, Donald, 396
Winters, Yvor, 344, 350
Wister, Owen, 482
Wolfe, Thomas, 273, 287, 288, 295–97, 299, 323, 444, 467, 468, 473; "I Have a Thing to Tell You," 299; *Look Homeward, Angel*, 288, 297
Wolfe, Tom, 306, 307, 440, 441, 442, 485, 508; *The Electric Kool-Aid Acid Test*, 306, 441, 442, 485
Wollheim, Donald A., 300
Wood, William, *New England's Prospect*, 191
Woolf, Virginia, 168, 292, 293; *To the Lighthouse*, 293
Woolman, John, 198, 499; *Journal*, 499
Wordsworth, William, 52, 73, 101, 123, 128, 263, 331, 363, 379; *The Prelude*, 73
Wouk, Herman, 465
Wright, Charles, 416
Wright, Frank Lloyd, 75
Wright, James, 384, 385; "At the Executed Murderer's Grave," 385; *The Branch Will Not Break*, 384, 385; *The Green Wall*, 385; *St. Judas*, 385; *Two Citizens*, 385
Wright, Richard, 279, 288, 410–14, 426, 427, 430, 501; *American Hunger*, 411; "Big Boy Leaves Home," 429; *Black Boy*, 411, 413; *Lawd Today*, 413; *The Long Dream*, 413; "The Man Who Lived Underground," 413; *Native Son*, 279, 288, 410, 412, 413, 426; *The Outsider*, 413, 414, 426; *Savage Holiday*, 413
Wycherly, William: *The Country Wife*, 324
Wyeth, N. C., 14
Wylie, Elinor, 343, 345

Yeats, William Butler, 348, 367, 374; "Sailing to Byzantium," 452
Yerby, Frank, 422, 427; *The Foxes of Harrow*, 427
Yezierska, Anzia, 345

Zamiatin, Eugene: *We*, 316
Zenger, John Peter, 204
Zola, Emile, 508
Zukofsky, Louis, 483